Seeds Bearing Fruit

SEEDS
BEARING
FRUIT

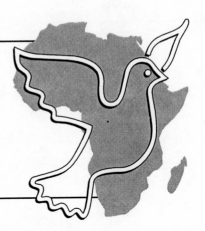

PAN-AFRICAN PEACE ACTION
FOR THE
TWENTY-FIRST CENTURY

edited by

Elavie Ndura-Ouédraogo,
Matt Meyer,
and Judith Atiri

Africa World Press, Inc.

P.O. Box 1892  P.O. Box 48

Trenton, NJ 08607   Asmara, ERITREA

Africa World Press, Inc.

P.O. Box 1892
Trenton, NJ 08607

P.O. Box 48
Asmara, ERITREA

Book and cover design: Saverance Publishing Services

Library of Congress Cataloging-in-Publication Data

Seeds bearing fruit : Pan African peace action for the 21st century / edited by Elavie Ndura-Ouedraogo, Matt Meyer, and Judith Atiri.
  p. cm.
Includes bibliographical references and index.
  ISBN 1-59221-781-8 (hard cover) -- ISBN 1-59221-782-6 (pbk.) 1. Peace-building--Africa. 2. Conflict management--Africa. 3. Pan-Africanism. 4. Africa--Politics and government--21st century. I. Ndura-Ouidraogo, Elavie II. Meyer, Matt. III. Atiri, Judith.
JZ5584.A35S43 2011
327.1'72096--dc22

                              2010034480

At the time of the liberation movements, there was a lot of hope, yet there were also the seeds of the troubles to come. Today, there are a lot of troubles, but in these presentations lie the seeds of new hope.

— *Bill Sutherland, Pan African elder, on the round table seminar at the 2004 Peace and Justice Studies Association (PJSA) conference*
— *1918-2010, Pan Africanist, Pacifist, and an Inspiration to us all*

Dedications

To all those who have refused to remain silent in the face of injustice and oppression, that your voices and wisdom may inspire current and future generations to struggle for peace and Africa's dignity.

— *Elavie Ndura-Ouédraogo*

We stand on the shoulders of those who have come before us, and peer out across the oceans with hope, towards future generations who will carry the struggle forward. This volume goes to press as the world mourns the loss of radical poet Dennis Brutus and I mourn the loss of a friend. May all our battles be led with the grace, determination, and lyricism that Dennis brought to all things. The young people in my own life, Michael Del and Molly Soo, remind me every day that the revolutionary task of naming our world and shaping it is an ongoing process. May all our campaigns be infused with the passion, curiosity, and innate sense of justice that Michael Del and Molly Soo bring to life.

— *Matt Meyer*

This book is dedicated to those who have given their lives in the active struggle for peace and to those who have abandoned their personal comforts in order to respond to the cries of all who are oppressed.

— *Judith Atiri*

TABLE OF CONTENTS

PART I
Tilling The Soil—
Grassroots Perspectives on War, Peace, and Alternatives

ACKNOWLEDGEMENTS

As I sit down to write these few words of gratitude on this very first day of the year 2010, I am especially mindful of the many people whose love and support have sustained me thus far. I am grateful for my parents Melchior Ndura and Angela Mudende who taught me how to stand tall and struggle for justice. My siblings Vincent, Adolphe, Auréa, and Sixte Vigny occupy a special place in my heart for always placing our family first. My children Star Shahuri and Queen Shahuri, and my step-daughters Azur, Cristal, Yasmine, and Perspective Ouédraogo will always be an inspiration for their strength and steadfastness. I am very grateful to my husband Boureima Ouédraogo for his unfailing love and support.

The contributors to this work deserve special recognition for the courage to raise critical questions and propose transformative actions that will help Africa to reclaim its independence and spirit of peaceful coexistence. My co-editor Matt Meyer did an extraordinary job recruiting and coordinating the contributors to create a volume filled with wisdom and hope critical to the transformation and progress of Africa in the 21st century and beyond. I am truly privileged to co-edit this second book with Matt Meyer.

I am indebted to Queen Shahuri and Svetlana Filiatreau for their assistance with the formatting of the book. They deserve special recognition for their outstanding skills and willingness to sacrifice their time during the holiday season to help get the work done on time. Queen Shahun's exceptional professional and skillful assistance with the editing and indexing processes made the timely publication of this volume possible. I am grateful for her unfailing support. Special thanks go to my George Mason University colleagues for helping to create the space and provide the support that such work requires. Africa World Press' staff Kassahun Checole, Damola Ifaturoti and Senait Kassahun deserve special thanks for their patience, persistence, and encouragement.

Finally, I will forever be indebted to my family for lending meaning and purpose to my life and my work, without them, such work would remain a mere academic exercise.

—Elavie Ndura-Ouédraogo, January, 2010

So much of this book, like many before it, is the work of more hearts and minds than we can count. At least this volume is graced with the names of three editors on the cover, and many contributors in the table of contents; one's sense of the collective nature of productive work—be it activist or academic—should be clear from the outset. I am not inclined to repeat those names already in print, save for one: without the camaraderie, friendship, fellowship, collaborative challenges, and consistent hard work of co-editor Elavie Ndura-Ouédraogo, this work would not now be in your hands.

Many writers included in this volume have been part of several networks of organizations worth mentioning. Though they bear no responsibility for the individual work contained herein, they remain stalwart examples of regional cooperation and solidarity. They are: War Resisters International, the Peace and Justice Studies Association and International Peace Research Association, the Child and Family Institute of New York's St. Lukes/Roosevelt Hospital, Human Rights Watch, TransAfrica, and the Committee for Academic Freedom in Africa. In addition, this editor is indebted to several gracious hosts throughout the continent, who shared their experiences, contacts, and lives with me during parts of the production of this book. They are: Ralph Sutherland and Esi Sutherland Addy, Mohamed Fofanah, James Roberts, Charlotte Mimi Kalonji, Grace Lula and Bony Ndeke, Dora Urujeni and Issa Higiro. Ramon Solhkhah is undoubtedly a gifted psychiatrist, but perhaps an even more astute fundraiser. His interest in, generosity for, and commitment to, this work deserves special mention. Casha Davis is more than an interpreter of words and languages; she is a bridge builder of enormous skill who has contributed to this and many related works in countless ways. My thanks for the friendship, advice, and support of Dinah Pokempner and Jo Becker.

Without the vision, support, and wisdom of Kassahun Checole, this work would not be possible. Without the careful eye, inquisitive and resourceful brain, and extra-large heart of Betsy Mickel, my work would be marked with bad spelling and poor grammar. Africa World Press' own Damola Ifaturoti and Senait Kassahun also warrant special mention. Finally, I must again thank my extended family, for putting up with me when I shift into "do not disturb" mode. I extend my heartfelt love and thanks to Bill Starr, Elspeth Meyer, Michael Del Meyer-Starr, and Molly Soo Meyer-Starr. As ever, my partner Meg Starr deserves the lion's share of my undying appreciation.

—Matt Meyer, December 2009

This year, 2009, has been an incredibly difficult one for me personally and for many all over the world. In the midst of the economic shaking, with people losing their homes and jobs, many have lost their center of gravity. I would like to acknowledge certain people who have helped to hold it together when it seemed that it would be easier to just give up and throw in the towel. It is with great pleasure that I acknowledge Matt Meyer and Elavie Ndura-Ouédraogo for not giving up on this project even through times when it seemed like there was no end in sight. I appreciate my friends and loved ones, Mum and dad, Margaret, Vivien, Peju, Tayo, Jackie and Dupsie, all of whom upheld me with words of encouragement. Finally to my maker, who through it all, stood by me and reminded me that He would never leave me nor forsake me. I hope that you all enjoy the discovery of the personal stories and heroic struggles of people just like you, who have managed to triumph in extremely difficult circumstances.

Aluta continua! (The struggle continues!)

—Judith Atiri, December 2009

Foreword

Nozizwe Madlala-
Routledge, M.P.
*Former National
Deputy Speaker,
South African
Parliament*

Reviewing the diverse essays of *Seeds Bearing Fruit: Pan African Peace Action for the 21ˢᵗ Century*, one cannot help but be struck by a common theme called out by authors and activists throughout our vast continent: small actions build upon one another to make for bigger changes—small ripples of hope that can combine to build a current so strong it can bring down the mightiest walls of resistance and oppression. An underlying common thread in the essays is the strong call for the re-conceptualization of conventional notions of security in a way that places people at the centre. Whether discussing the actions of a tiny, grassroots group, or a government working to shift its country away from the legacy of war, these stories chronicle people's consistent belief that we not only must work together for lasting, progressive change—but that our work, if stuck to, if united, if consistent, will indeed bear fruit.I cannot help but recall my own days as a student and as a grassroots activist, growing up in the KwaZulu-Natal region of South Africa under the racist apartheid regime. My mother believed in the power and importance of education, and was herself a teacher and primary school principal for over thirty-five years. The teachers at my high school believed in a non-racial future, and our motto was: "Shine where you are." But I also learned so much in discussions held at the nearby Phoenix Settlement, Gandhi's first Ashram. Some of those discussions were led by Steve Biko, who used to hold political summer schools at the Settlement, and who taught me to be comfortable and proud about my Black identity. Later, when I became a Quaker and joined the Religious Society of Friends, I became comfortable with the idea that we are all children of a loving God. And when I joined the underground movement against apartheid, ultimately becoming one of four South African Communist Party representatives to the Convention for a Democratic South Africa which negotiated the dismantling of apartheid, I became comfortable with speaking truth to power in a country where huge socio-economic inequalities remain. My work with the Natal Organization of Women and with the United Democratic Front taught me that mobilizing people could sometimes be an end in itself, building people's structures for power alongside of the decadent society we had to overthrow. My work in the Parliament of a Free South Africa, and as Deputy Minister of Defense, Deputy Minister of Health, and Deputy Speaker, has taught me about the complexities of making change in a world entangled with personal ambition and greed, with corporate controls and multinational machinations. Both experiences complement each other; without pressure from below and a clear and creative plan of action, we cannot hope for lasting change, justice, or peace. The lessons of these last tumultuous years hold significance for all advocates of peace with justice:

- We must rethink "security" and "defense" in ways that place people and their participation at the centre.

- Human security addresses socially differentiated experiences of insecurity and encompasses access to healthcare services as well as to the conditions that favor health as an absolute human right; and
- If the changes which we seek—equality, peace, and justice—are not felt concretely in the living conditions of the poorest among us, then we have failed in our respective duties as leaders, lawyers, activists, and citizens.

The logic of the country with the most powerful army in the world seems to be that peace can be made through war. Experience shows us the flaw in that logic. Experience in African wars shows that this logic leads to disaster. *Seeds Bearing Fruit* shows us that peacemaking is the way to peace.

The campaigns, initiatives, and ideas spotlighted in *Seeds Bearing Fruit* show that there is much good news and success to be celebrated. Good news can sometimes be in short supply. Too often in the humdrum of daily life, we forget to dream. But when we use our imagination, we can solve problems that may seem intractable. Often imaginative responses to demanding social issues can go unrecognized and unsung. I therefore congratulate the editors and authors of *Seeds Bearing Fruit*, for recognizing our collective reasons for hope. I urge all leaders, especially political leaders, to heed these voices. And I join with them in our collective struggle for an even better tomorrow.

INTRODUCTION
Seeds Bearing Fruit:
Dreaming, Hoping, and Struggling
for Peace in Africa

Matt Meyer
and
Elavie Ndura-
Ouédraogo

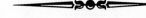

I am a WILD WOMAN
I am a PANTHER WOMAN...
A WARRIOR WOMAN...
A Warrior WILD for PEACE!

And
I will take you by the collar and come
up close to you...
and get up all in yo' face...
Make you drool and get wet 'round
the edges
for the taste of It...
(Peace)
The sweet of It...
(Peace)
The addiction-ness of It...
(Peace)

I am a WILD WOMAN!
I am a PANTHER WOMAN!
A WARRIOR WOMAN,
determined to make You want a piece
of this peace
That we must spread on to every slice
of humanity...
of family,
that we can reach with our sharp
weapon of peace.

Charlotte Hill O'Neal, Arusha, Tanzania,
excerpt from *Warrior Women of Peace* (2008)[1]

As passionate as a poem, as Pan African as an author raised in the U.S. living out her years in East Africa, this collection of essays, interviews, reports, and analyses seeks to grab your attention about the urgent tasks facing the continent today. But this book, the companion volume to *Seeds of New Hope: Pan African Peace Studies for the 21st Century* (Meyer and Ndura-Ouédraogo, eds., Africa World Press, 2009), is much more than simply a task list. It is a book about and in favor of action, with all the complexities and bias that it implies. As editors, we adhere to strict principles of academic integrity and honesty, seeking to give as full and detailed a picture as possible of any given situation referred to in these pages. Like many scholars around us, we are also proudly activists, believing that we cannot hope to understand the imperfect and unjust world in which we live unless we also struggle to change it. As Charlotte O'Neal suggests in the above poem, we define peace as a positive and active force, not one simply brought about by the absence of conflict. We embrace the apparent contradictions of a peace—filled with equality, democracy, freedom and justice— that must be *fought* for, one that is both a product of struggle but also a process by which to struggle. The essays in this volume are therefore from a decidedly activist and grassroots perspective, bringing the reader voices from every corner of the continent with news of contemporary work for peace.

Like *Seeds of New Hope*[2], the authors represented in this volume draw their inspiration from the elders that have gone before us and the youth who work in our midst. Mzee Bill Sutherland, a mentor to many of us (including poet O'Neal), noted years ago that there may be deep troubles and conflicts throughout the African continent. No matter how little one knows about Africa, we cannot help but hear of raging poverty and out-of-control wars. But, Sutherland reminded us, the seeds of the new society we hope for are embedded in our very current stories of small steps towards reconciliation. They are present in the seemingly minor, local acts of creative resistance. They will, undoubtedly, flower into new movements ready to right the wrongs of generations past. We are called upon to take careful notice of these signs.

Many contributors to this volume also come from the networks of academics and activists around the North American-based Peace and Justice Studies Association, the War Resisters International, and the International Peace Research Association. Our collaborations with Human Rights Watch, the Coalition to Stop the Use of Child Soldiers, and clinicians working in and around the Child and Family Institute of St. Lukes/Roosevelt Hospital in New York City also provided writers for this truly global effort. Most importantly, however, the majority of the authors contained herein are from the front lines of the struggles themselves, writing from first-hand experience about campaigns they themselves have been a part of. Those front lines suggest great conflict and injustice, but the truth is often hidden in more complex realities.

War Stories

The headlines roar of an Africa at war. Congolese groups in the east of that country are "rearming."[3] Anti-UN Protests in Central Africa "turn" violent.[4] In fact, one can learn, three UN officers were given little more than a slap on the wrist for gold trafficking. There is little denial of continued ivory smuggling, arms sales, and violence on the part of foreign troops towards the Africans they are supposedly protecting.[5] Congolese Archbishop Francois Maroy of the Archdiocese of Bukavu, speaking at an historic U.S.-based Congo Global Action conference, admitted that "Africa is like a revolver and the Congo is like its trigger."[6] Noting that the Congolese and Africans in general, are peace-loving people, the Archbishop quickly added that the Congo is used as a proxy for international conflicts and struggles, and that the current African wars are "wars of aggression imposed upon us."[7]

At the same conference, held in Washington D.C. in March 2008, Columbia University Professor Peter Rosenblum aptly noted that "so much of the story of the Congo is the story of the U.S."[8] Referring to the long history of corporate and quasi-governmental interests in the region, Rosenblum pointed to the fact that, with the global economy in a free fall, assumptions about who will benefit from the natural resources of the Congo or the continent are more difficult to make. One thing is certain, however. Even with democratically elected, relatively stable governments in a number of recently conflict-ridden areas, the multinational corporate contracts that govern the "wealth of nations" were signed and sealed long beforehand. The real issue regarding economic democracy and justice has as much to do with renegotiating those contracts as with dropping the so-called debt incurred by re-colonizing structural adjustment schemes.

It is therefore more than a minor issue in Pan African affairs that unionized Liberian rubber workers signed a "living wage" contract with Firestone in August 2008. Though it scarcely received any Western press, the agreement—culminating over eight decades of continuous struggle by the Firestone Agricultural Workers Union of Liberia—covers working conditions, housing, and educational assistance in addition to a substantial pay hike. United Steelworkers President Leo Gerard called it a "crucial victory in the global fight for worker's rights."[9] In a show of support almost as significant as the agreement itself, the United Steelworkers Solidarity Center (which generally only promotes the interests of Firestone employees in the U.S.) provided training and aid to their African counterparts. One can only wonder if similar people-to-people connections might enable justice campaigns to win victories on an even larger scale. A late August 2008 announcement by the Congo's Ministry of Mines suggested that a review of a quarter of the country's contracts were in a process of reappraisal, with the plan that the government—and not outside interests—would claim a 51% majority stake of the riches found on their land.[10] One wonders if global justice campaigns might develop enough strength that an even more equitable distribution of wealth could be initiated, with lasting peace and prosperity as the fruit of a process dedicated to the elimination of root causes of war.

This is a tall order at a time when increased military might appears to be the West's answer to most economic and political questions. The Bush administration's recognition of the "emerging strategic importance of Africa" led to the creation of the U.S. Africa Command (AFRICOM), an Armed Service force with the intent to police the nations vital to U.S. short-term oil needs. With U.S. oil imports from Africa increasing by over 65% from 2000 to 2007 alone, it is undeniable that AFRICOM's ultimate goal is to establish more U.S. bases on the continent, with a greater ongoing presence. Common concerns about this type of engagement, which has not significantly changed in the era of Obama, is that sustained U.S. military presence in Africa may cause, as it has in Iraq, increased "internal hostilities, regional instability, and anger at the United States."[11] Given the nature of sexualized violence in African conflict situations, the fact that misogyny, rape, and patriarchal attitudes are pervasive in the U.S. military[12] suggest an explosive scenario at best. Moreover, recent independent research on the U.S. civil-military imbalances in regards to operations in Africa suggest that, in order to effectively meet its own goals, the U.S. must focus more on development than on "defense" or diplomacy. "It is clear that the U.S. has not been very smart," writes Refugees International analyst Mark Malan, in "bolstering weak, fragile, failing or failed states. While the gains of targeted aid harnessed in pursuit of the fight against terrorism remain dubious at best, the U.S. has no coherent long-term foreign assistance strategy in the fight against global poverty."[13]

Just as AFRICOM was being announced to the world, a very different gathering was taking place, with heads of State and foreign ministers working to update the Cape Town principles on the protection of children. The 2007 Paris Commitments intensify previous efforts to call attention to, stop, and prevent the use of children under the age of eighteen in any aspect of military service. At the one year anniversary of the adoption of those commitments, Jo Becker, Children's Rights Advocacy Director of Human Rights Watch, became the first non-governmental representative to testify before the United Nations Security Council. "We are not here to celebrate," Becker proclaimed, as the Open Debate on Children and Armed Conflict began. Though the use of child soldiers decreased worldwide from 2004 to 2008, the UN focus must broaden beyond recruitment and use of children in war, Becker asserted, and must extend to "all situations" of conflict "where children's security and rights are violated." Suggesting that the Security Council's own credibility was on the line, Becker noted that the Congo was one of the few member states whose government forces were still utilizing child soldiers in some areas. Speaking on behalf of the large Watchlist on Children and Armed Conflicts, which brings together grassroots groups, non-governmental organizations, and the major international human rights agencies, Becker urged the UN to exercise its full power, stating that the "Security Council cannot expect to achieve accountability based on empty threats."[14]

The problems faced by seemingly intractable militarism and capital expansion are being countered by passionate movements committed to new global relationships. That the Congo Global Action conference was held at, and in cooperation with, the United States Holocaust Memorial Museum in Washington D.C. was no mere logistical venue choice. The cries of "Never Again" echoed in many speeches and even more memories, as participants recognized the parallels when one set of peoples are seen as expendable on the world stage. Rwandans, for example, deeply invested in ensuring that the "Never Again" they missed out on not be similarly disregarded in the future, have their own interpretation of what the phrase must now mean; they provide material support for the people of Darfur, Sudan. Bukavu's leading child rights advocate, Murhabazi Namegtabe of the Bureau pour le Voluntariat au Service de l'Enfance et de la Santé, put it this way: "Our kids don't ask for candy or toys, they ask for peace."[15]

Peace Stories

It is in this context that we turn to those voices not just calling, but working, for shifts in the basic paradigms defining our times. Some may interpret the need in substantially economic terms, as did Zanzibari radical A.M. Babu, whose push for "an economic strategy for the second liberation of Africa" is based on new democratic theories of "economic nationalisms" looking inward at state-specific initiatives.[16] Others reframe political and ideological debates, such as the activists of Nigeria's Human Rights,

Justice, and Peace Foundation (HRJPF), who call for acceptance of "Non-violent Mass Action as a Basic Human Right."[17] In viewing nonviolence as more than a mere tactic or even pacifistic philosophy, our colleagues at HRJPF challenge us to understand international treaties and natural laws as giving us not simply the right to justice and peace, but the basic right to resist and rebel. Even in military terms, as the people of Mauritius struggle to uphold the Pelindaba Treaty (which went into effect late in 2009), excitement built as Africa became the world's newest and largest Nuclear-Weapons-Free Zone. Only the tiny Indian Ocean island of Diego Garcia, used by the U.S. as a primary military base and training ground, stands in the way of making the Treaty a truly meaningful document.[18] There can be no irony lost in the fact that U.S. military maneuvers under a President of African descent prevent the African continent from taking a leadership role in actual disarmament. For the sake of this collection, we have tried to look beyond the "hopes" of mis-leading politicians, to people-based answers improving realities on the local level.

The first section of *Seeds Bearing Fruit* is titled "Tilling the Soil: Grassroots Perspectives on War, Peace, and Alternatives" because it brings together country-specific chapters which look at the effects of recent and ongoing conflicts on peace-building, conflict resolution, and nonviolent efforts. Editor Elavie Ndura-Ouédraogo writes poignantly about her native Burundi and the educational efforts for multiculturalism and peace there. Tchad Nonviolence organizer is interviewed by German solidarity activist Rudi Freidrich in an overview of the root causes of war in that Central African country. Writers Andrea Lari, Rob Kevlihan, Jan Van Criekinge, Emanuel Matondo and Rudi Freidrich all investigate differ-ent aspects of Angolan post-war society. Joseph Sebarenzi, the leader of Rwanda's Parliament in the years before the genocide, has gained much acclaim for his memoir *God Sleeps in Rwanda*[19]; his contribution here looks at the role of religion in healing his homeland after the horrors of 1994. Elaine Ognibene also looks at Rwandan recovery efforts; and music therapist Maria Gonsalves reviews work with young girls in post-civil war Sierra Leone. Picking up on that recurring theme of the power of women peacemakers, Roland Tuwea Clarke reports on reconstruction in contem-porary Liberia. Anneke Van Woudenberg's chapter on the wars in and around the Democratic Republic of the Congo opens a section on peace work in the midst of the worst conflict the world has ever seen. Editor Matt Meyer joined a team of psychiatrists and hospital-based educators, including Lindsay Feldman, Jennie Johanson, Ramon Solhkhah, Jennifer Bordo, and Kate Charles, to provide a series of pieces on youth rights and peace-building in the Congo, Rwanda, Sierra Leone, and Liberia. Taking a Pan Africanist perspective on the pressing questions of reparations and repatriation, elder Bill Sutherland's dialogue with Ghanaian-based former Black Panther Dhoruba bin Wahad is presented. Finally, the Pan African overview of the power of women—the hope of Africa—is recounted in short reports from Emira Woods, Lisa Veneklasen, Marianne Balle Moudoumbou, and Roxanne Lawson.

"Taking Root: Concrete Initiatives for Peace with Justice" frames the second half of Seeds. Opening with an interview co-editor Matt Meyer conducted with Ghanaian former Deputy Minister of Education Esi Sutherland Addy, this section spotlights peaceful solutions to country-, region-, and global issues. A multi-disciplinary look at building continent-wide cultures of peace is presented by the team of Nancy Erbe, Chinedu Bob Ezeh, Daniel Karanja, Neba Monifor, George Mubanga, and Ndi Richard Tanto. Nigerian activists Ifeoma Malo and Titus Oyeyemi document peacemaking initiatives in their West African country, while scholar Steve Sharra takes a Pan African look at biography and autobiography in peace-building. Nasri Adams and Gail Presby present features on Somalia, and Ousseina Alidou provides a challenging paper on nationalism in post-war Niger. The recent student crises in the Cameroon are discussed in a chapter by Molem Christopher Sama and Debora Johnson-Ross, and often-neglected histories of the Sudan are uncovered in pieces by Lou Marin and Light Wilson Aganwa. Nonviolent struggle, anti-militarism, and conscientious objection in Eritrea are reviewed in articles by Daniel Mekonnen, Yoel Alem, and Yohannes Kidane; an interview with Eritrean constitutionalist Paulos Tesfagiorgis looks at what still needs to be done to make peace a reality in the Horn of Africa. Activist/scholar Stephen Zunes showcases the work of Aminatou Haidar, and discusses the growing resistance in Western Sahara. The book concludes with an engaging dialogue between New York-based Afrikaleidoscope Radio host Elombe Brath of the Patrice Lumumba Coalition and Kenyan Nobel Peace Laureate Wangari Maathai.

Editor Judith Atiri commented recently on a current events class she was teaching to a group of European and Asian students. Like so many non-Africans, these students had barely a clue as to basic African geography (much less history), unable to distinguish between a town and a vast continent. "I'd like one day to travel to Paris," remains a common refrain," and to Africa too; what is the weather like there?!" Atiri showed her students a video adaptation about the genocide in Rwanda. In it, a dramatic clip of a private briefing led by the U.S. Deputy Assistant Secretary of State for African Affairs showed U.S. officials posing the same rudimentary questions so elusive to many in the West. "Who are the rebels?" "Who are the good guys?" Oversimplifications and false dichotomies may play a less causal role in warfare than the class issues of land ownership or corporate greed, but they surely do not help us in building for a just peace. As editors and activists, we have tried to avoid simplified stories and half-truths, while creating a readable text accessible to non-African scholars. We also recognize that, while attempting to present as balanced perspectives as possible (in a world where few are fully "good" or all "bad"), we are partisans—with our own bias about the nature of progressive struggle.

In bringing together a diversity of voices from throughout the African continent—for a broad audience of American, European, Asian/Pacific, and African students and scholars—we are therefore proud to present to the reader a cross-section of the "good guys." Most of them are women, many of them are considered rebels, and all of them are activists. None of them believe that the changes needed to build a peaceful and just Africa (or world) can be brought about solely through action in one community. All of them believe, and the editors concur, that we need Pan African and internationalist unity and struggle, to create a twenty-first century rich with the earth's abundant and sustainable resources, shared equitably by all. Let the planting begin!

Notes

1. Charlotte Hill O'Neal, Woman Warrior of Peace, Arusha, Lulu, 2008; see http://www.uaacc.habari.co.tz/

2. Matt Meyer, and Elavie Ndura-Ouédraogo, eds., *Seeds of New Hope: Pan African Peace Studies for the 21st Century,* Trenton: Africa World Press, 2009

3. Martin Plaut, Congo groups "rearming" in east, BBC Africa, August 4, 2008.

4. UN Integrated Regional Information Services, "Anti-MONUC Protest in Rutshuru Turns Violent, UNIRIN/AllAfrica Global Media, September 3, 2008.

5. See, for example, "UN Troops in Gold Warning," www.allAfrica.com, July 11, 2008.

6. Francois Maroy, speech at Congo Global Action conference, US Holocaust Memorial Museum, March 30, 2008.

7. Ibid.

8. Peter Rosenblum, speech at Congo Global Action conference, US Holocaust Memorial Museum, March 30, 2008.

9. James Parks, "Liberian Rubber Workers Sign Historic Labor Agreement," AFL-CIO Now blog, August 11, 2008.

10. Franz Wild, Congo Wants Majority Stake in Mine Contracts Without Studies, www.bloomberg.com, August 28, 2008.

11. Antonia Juhasz, Will the next war for oil be in Africa?, Foreign Policy in Focus Commentary, June 17, 2008.

12. See, for example, Helen Benedict, Why Soldiers Rape: Culture of misogyny, illegal occupation, fuel sexual violence in military, In These Times, August 13, 2008.

13. Mark Malan, U.S. Civil-Military Imbalance for Global Engagement: Lessons from the Operational Level in Africa, Refugees International, Washington DC, July 2008.

14. Jo Becker, Statement on behalf of the Watchlist on Children and Armed Conflict, Security Council Open Debate on Children and Armed Conflict, February 12, 2008.

15. Murhabazi Namegtabe, speech at Congo Global Action conference, US Holocaust Memorial Museum, March 30, 2008.

16. A. M. Baba, An Economic Strategy for the Second Liberation of Africa, Dar Es Salaam: Mkuki Na Nyota Publishers, Ltd., 1994

17. See <http://www.kabissa.org/civiorg/313>. Interestingly, in another largely unnoticed Pan African connection, life-long U.S. civil rights campaigner Bernard Lafayette, Jr. (a close friend of Dr. Martin Luther King) engaged in substantial nonviolence trainings throughout the Niger Delta in 2007 and 2008.

18. Peter Sands, "Diego Garcia: A Thorn in the Side of Africa's Nuclear-Weapon-Free Zone," Bulletin of Atomic Scientists, October 8, 2009

19. Joseph Sebarenzi, God Sleeps in Rwanda, New York: Simon and Schuster, 2009

PART I

TILLING THE SOIL—
GRASSROOTS PERSPECTIVES ON WAR,
PEACE, AND ALTERNATIVES

ONE

Building a Foundation for Sustainable Peace in Burundi: A Transformative Multicultural Education Approach

Elavie Ndura-Ouédraogo

Introduction

In a previous publication on peaceful conflict resolution in Burundi[1] I argue that education is a major avenue for social promotion and that the wider development of a civil society depends greatly on the education of the nation's youth. I later posit that the education received through family and academic institutions molds and in some ways determines our ways of thinking and our social, economic, and political attitudes, as well as our everyday actions.[2]

After more than forty years of ethnicized political and social turmoil that has caused massive casualties in Burundi, a small landlocked country in Central-Eastern Africa, the time has come to acknowledge the tragic failure of existing peace-building efforts and contemplate more promising possibilities. Havermans (1999) observes that a top-down process has so far characterized the peace process in Burundi. He posits that a bottom-up approach and the organization of grassroots support for the process as well as the promotion of local capacity building are necessary to create sustainable peace. He insists on the prime importance of education in the process by stating, "Most obvious in this regard is the necessity of a campaign for peace education on the value of democracy, national reconciliation and respect for human rights, from the primary schools upwards."[3] Similarly, Reyntjens (2000) calls for reforming the educational system as well as grassroots human rights education and awareness raising in order to support the peace process in Burundi.

In a French publication on the role of family and formal education in achieving sustainable peace in Burundi,[4] I outline the components of an academic program aimed at training agents of peace at all levels from kindergarten to higher education and even in professional and community development programs. Such a program would evolve in the following ten themes or stages: (1) exploration of history and of individual social and ethnic attitudes; (2) different perspectives on Burundian history; (3) a critical analysis of Burundian conflicts; (4) a comparative analysis of regional and international conflicts; (5) the consequences of social, economic, and political instability; (6) a critical analysis of armed solutions to social, economic, and political conflicts; (7) a critical analysis of peaceful conflict resolution approaches; (8) articulating individual and collective responsibilities in the reconstruction of Burundian and global society; (9) committing to labor for the peace process; and (10) program evaluation.

The purpose of this paper is to expand on the above program components by proposing a multicultural education framework that would lay a foundation for sustainable peace in Burundi. Four main points will guide the discussion. After exploring ways in which the Burundian educational system has served as the breeding ground for inequality and discord, I will discuss the consequences of the Hutu-Tutsi conflict. Then, I will define multicultural and peace education in the Burundian context and outline a transformative multicultural education framework for Burundian schools. A general conclusion will wrap up the discussion.

Burundi's Educational System: The Breeding Ground for Inequality and Discord

Formal education is the only path to state employment, which is the only alternative to peasant agriculture in the Burundian society and economy.[5] Consequently, as Reyntjens notes, inequality and exclusion begin with inequitable educational opportunity and access, which has promoted Tutsi hegemony in the civil service, the army, and the judiciary. The author also highlights discriminatory regional differences in the Burundian educational system: "six provinces, with about one-third of the population, have over half of the primary teachers. There are almost as many teachers in the province of Bururi as in the provinces of Cankuzo, Muyinga, Rutana and Ruyigi taken together. Net primary school attendance in 1996-1997 was 44.17 per cent in Bururi, compared to a mere 6.15

per cent in Bubanza. Bururi and Bujumbura account for 32 per cent of all secondary pupils, while these provinces represent only 11 per cent of the national population."[6] The only explanation for this disparity is that Bururi and Bujumbura are major Tutsi strongholds.

Therefore, Hutu citizens have been denied an adequate education because of inequitable distribution of schools and resources. Even the few Hutus who attempt to get an education become alienated and disenfranchised from the system because of discriminatory attitudes, policies, and practices. Some of the tactics used to force the Hutus out of the educational system vary from psychological and physical harassment and abuse by Tutsi classmates, teachers, and administrators to carefully orchestrated manipulation of secondary school and university admission and grade reporting policies and practices by Tutsi educators and policy makers[7]. As Lemarchand (1994) asserts, discrimination in the Burundian educational system has continually been the hallmark of the Second Republic. In fact, as Chrétien (1985) notes, earlier educational establishments and practices were discriminatory against the Hutus because they purposefully taught and reinforced the concept of Tutsi superiority over the Hutu and Twa populations.

Most damaging to the shaping of the Burundian ethnic landscape is the fact that these discriminatory policies and practices have been neither publicly exposed nor questioned. While they have occasionally surfaced in conversation among the limited educated Hutu circles, unschooled families and communities have rarely discussed them. Indeed, and this is one of the tragedies of oppression, they have often been accepted uncritically by uneducated Hutu populations as a confirmation of the Tutsi's intellectual superiority and the Hutu's lower intellect, thus reflecting the divisive stereotypes resulting from Western colonial philosophies and policies.

The Burundian educational system therefore is designed to empower and privilege the Tutsis while subjecting the Hutus into unquestioned oppression. It is not surprising, then, that when the few educated Hutus begin to question and challenge the Tutsis' unearned privileges and to demand the swift reform of the educational system and other national institutions, the Tutsi junta does not hesitate to deploy weapons in order to protect their political, economic, educational, and social monopolies. Ethnic discord becomes unavoidable. Pervasive inequality and injustice can only be tolerated for so long. At some point, the oppressed is bound to rise up against the oppressor and demand change. Capturing the urgency of the need for societal change in countries such as Burundi that are consumed by the tragic turmoil caused by ethnic discord requires an exploration and understanding of the consequences of the conflict. Thus, the following section discusses some of the major consequences of the Hutu-Tutsi conflict in Burundi.

The Consequences of the Hutu-Tutsi Conflict

In a previous publication on peaceful conflict resolution in Burundi,[8] I discuss five major consequences of the Hutu-Tutsi conflict in Burundi. One of the consequences of the unending ethnic conflict is the polarization of Burundian society along Hutu-Tutsi lines. As Eller (1999)[9] observes, the ethnic ceiling and the palpable obstacles to social mobility that the Hutus are confronted with every day has contributed to the coalescence of a sense of group identity and to an embitterment of the identity.

Another consequence of the Hutu-Tutsi discord is the unavoidable loss of mutual respect and trust, which often results in the development of extremely self-defensive attitudes and behaviors. This mistrust may provide a strong explanation for the continually failing peace negotiation efforts between the warring parties as the peace talks have become nothing but a series of unproductive charades that misuse national and international resources.

Additionally, the Burundian ethnic conflicts have created a social environment characterized by constant fear. People, mostly Hutus, are afraid of the recurrence of the painful past. They fear that nothing will ever stop the Tutsi junta from exerting their military power over the powerless Hutu population. And this fear has the potential of turning into rage. To borrow the words of Deutsch (1973), "both rage and fear are rooted in a sense of helplessness and powerlessness. They are emotions associated with a state of dependency."[10]

The next consequence of the Hutu-Tutsi discord may be considered the most dramatic yet. It is the destruction of the social fiber that held interethnic families and communities together in harmony and peaceful interdependence for centuries. This discord has turned members of interethnic families into undesirable and untrustworthy, albeit feared, elements among both Tutsi and Hutu communities. Looking at the current state of affairs, it is reasonable to argue that even when the prevailing conflicts are resolved, Burundi will emerge as a different society, with a delicate and fragile balance between the "ethnic good" and the "national good."[11]

Finally, the conflicts have caused irreparable damage to the national economy. From the burning of farms to the slaughter of cattle, to the destruction and looting of individual homes, schools, and churches, Burundi will forever bear the economic scars of interethnic discord. The

Burundian people from both sides will continually face the increasing fear of failing to afford the bare necessities to survive, which may increase ethnic tension and strife.

Looking at these tragic consequences of ethnic conflicts, it behooves both Tutsis and Hutus to summon the power of reason and examine possible strategies for achieving sustainable peace in Burundi. In the remainder of this paper, I will explore the applicability of multicultural and peace education to the Burundian context and outline a transformative, multicultural education framework for Burundian schools.

Multicultural and Peace Education in the Burundian Context

From the midst of seemingly irreconcilable ethnicized communities and warring factions, from the midst of confusing and discouraging failed peace talks, education emerges as a critical source of hope for sustainable peace in Burundi. However, in order for education to fulfill this mission, it must be transformed from the traditional colonial-based system that promoted Tutsi hegemony and Hutu oppression into one that aims at true liberation for all Burundians. Only education that is defined by multicultural and peace education principles and practices can help Burundian students from all ethnic groups develop the attitudes, dispositions, and skills necessary to positively contribute to the reconstruction of Burundian society.

I use multicultural education and peace education together to stress that they are interrelated and complementary transformative processes, which should not be dichotomized. The interrelated and complementary nature of multicultural and peace education is made apparent in the definitions and descriptions that scholars in the respective fields have developed. Nieto (2004) defines multicultural education in a sociopolitical context as follows:

> Multicultural education is a process of comprehensive school reform and basic education for all students. It challenges and rejects racism and other forms of discrimination in schools and society and accepts and affirms the pluralism (ethnic, racial, linguistic, religious, economic, and gender, among others) that students, their communities, and teachers reflect. Multicultural education permeates the schools' curriculum and instructional strategies, as well as the interactions among teachers, students, families, and the very way that schools conceptualize the nature

of teaching and learning. Because it uses critical pedagogy as its underlying philosophy and focuses on knowledge, reflection, and action (*praxis*) as the basis for social change, multicultural education promotes democratic principles of social justice.[12]

Therefore, the goals of multicultural education and of citizenship education overlap. According to Banks (2004), "an important goal of citizenship education in a democratic multicultural society is to help students acquire the knowledge, attitudes, and skills needed to make reflective decisions and to take actions to make their nation-state more democratic and just."[13]

The knowledge focus, transformative vision, and reflective practice that drive multicultural education are also major components of peace education. Salomon (2002) argues that peace education should yield four kinds of interconnected, dispositional outcomes: (1) accepting as legitimate the other's narrative and its specific implications; (2) being willing to critically examine one's own group's actions toward the other group; (3) being ready to experience and show empathy and trust toward the other; and (4) being disposed to engage in nonviolent activities.[14]

Within the Burundian context, therefore, the philosophy and foci of multicultural education and of peace education need to be combined in a symbiotic process that would transform students from all ethnic groups into informed, reflective, and committed agents of peace.

The following main goals would define multicultural and peace education within the Burundian context. It should enable students to research, discover, and appreciate their ethnic background, thus giving them the tools needed to understand the origins of their individual and collective narratives. Another goal of multicultural and peace education should be to develop students' understanding of, sensitivity to, and appreciation for people from different ethnic groups and their narratives. In addition, multicultural and peace education in the Burundian context should seek to enhance students' awareness of and appreciation for interethnic interdependence at both local and national levels. Finally multicultural and peace education should help students define and resolve to assume their individual and collective responsibilities in the quest for sustainable peace in Burundi.

Multicultural and peace education is to be conceived as a reform movement. As such, it emphasizes revising the structural, procedural, substantive, and evaluative components of the educational enterprise to reflect the social and ethnic diversity of the nation[15]. Effective multicultural education must yield agents of peace, and peace education must be multicultural in nature and scope. In the following section I outline a transformative multicultural education framework that should serve as the foundation for sustainable peace in Burundi.

A Transformative Multicultural Education Framework for Burundian Schools

Christine Sleeter (1996), one of the most renowned multicultural educators and scholars, argues that multicultural education is a form of resistance to oppressive social relationships. Using the metaphor of multicultural education as a social movement, she relates the power of multicultural education to yield educational equity and social justice. She clarifies that "movements aim to redistribute power and resources by confronting power relations in which a dominant collective has attained the power to define the society for the masses, to construct an ideology in which that definition makes sense, and to achieve hegemony".[16] She stresses that in a social movement, the goal is not simply to impact a specific policy change, "but more importantly to shift the power to control decisions, define situations, and allocate resources".[17]

Thus, effective multicultural education in the Burundian context should have three leading goals. First it should challenge Tutsi hegemony. Second, multicultural education should affirm the nation's ethnic diversity and yield equity and social justice for all Burundians. Third, it should lay the foundation for sustainable peace in the country, the region, the continent of Africa, and the world.

The transformative multicultural education framework that I am proposing has two complementary components. The first is a training program based on the ten thematic units outlined earlier. This multicultural education program may be shaped to match the age and educational level of the participants. This built-in flexibility makes it possible for the program to be added to the academic curriculum at any level from elementary school through college and to be used for professional and community development purposes. The second component is an application of the five dimensions of multicultural education developed by James Banks (2001)[18] to show how multicultural education can be infused in the school curriculum.

A Multicultural Education Program for Burundian Schools and Communities

Ten thematic units constitute the core of this program: (1) exploration of history and of individual social and ethnic attitudes; (2) different perspectives on Burundian history; (3) a critical analysis of Burundian conflicts; (4) a comparative analysis of regional and international conflicts; (5) the consequences of social, economic, and political instability; (6) a critical analysis of armed solutions to social, economic, political conflicts; (7) a critical analysis of peaceful conflict resolution approaches; (8) articulating individual and collective responsibilities in the reconstruction of Burundian and global society; (9) committing to labor for the peace process; and (10) program evaluation. For the purpose of this paper, I will discuss the desired outcomes for each one of the thematic units. A more detailed instructional plan will be provided in a training manual that will be developed at a later date.

Unit 1: Exploration of history and of individual social and ethnic attitudes. Using written texts and personal anecdotes, as well as traditional folktales and legends, this unit will engage the participants in a nonthreatening discovery process of the origins of their individual and collective ethnic-bound narratives. The participants will share their narratives, thus engaging in the legitimization process of the narratives of people from different ethnic groups. The participants will hence begin to engage in the reconstruction and reinterpretation of Burundian history and of their ethnic perspectives.

Unit 2: Different perspectives on Burundian history. In this unit, the participants will compare and contrast official and folk history. They will examine the biases that have shaped Burundian history, from colonial perspectives to ethnicized accounts of the Burundian people and their life experiences. They will critically analyze the impact of the differing perspectives on the development of their individual and collective narratives.

Unit 3: A critical analysis of Burundian conflicts. This unit will immerse the participants in intimate discussions of the causes and consequences of the Burundian conflicts. They will critically examine their own ethnic group's contribution to the conflicts as well as the part played by other ethnic groups in fueling the decades-long conflict. They will develop broader awareness of the effects of the conflicts on people from different groups and empathy for their suffering.

Unit 4: A comparative analysis of regional and international conflicts. In addition to developing the participants' awareness of the critical interdependence that defines the political and economic relations among the nations of the African Great Lakes region and the world, this unit will help the participants gain a better understanding of the devastating impact of war on human lives across ethnic and racial groups. The participants will develop a broader worldview by discussing and analyzing the causes and consequences of human conflicts outside their familiar Burundian context.

Unit 5: The consequences of social, economic, and political instability. In this unit, the participants will reconstruct the concept of victory. They will explore the multifaceted consequences of the Burundian conflicts and their devastating effects on people and communities of all ethnic groups. The participants will openly talk about how the ethnicized conflicts have impacted their lives. This intimate exchange will help them validate the narratives of other Burundians from different ethnic groups and develop empathy for their painful lived experiences.

Unit 6: A critical analysis of armed solutions to social, economic, and political conflicts. This unit will engage the participants in honest discussions of the role of the Burundian armed forces in the Burundian Hutu-Tutsi conflicts since independence. They will examine the consequences of discriminatory recruitment and retention practices that have consistently denied Hutus access to the Burundian military institution. The participants will also redefine the part that the Burundian military should play in the quest for sustainable peace in Burundi.

Unit 7: A critical analysis of peaceful conflict resolution approaches. This unit will bring to bear the failure of the destructive approaches used by the almost exclusively Tutsi army and of the blindfolded negotiations among the deeply divided groups of educated politicians to achieve peace in Burundi. The participants will explore "alternative dispute resolution principles" that "reflect the traditional African justice system's reliance on reconciliation of interests and relationships, primary use of nonviolent and nonadversarial methods of conflict resolution, lay participation, attention to both community and personal needs, and complementary disputing levels and modes".[19] They will compare and contrast violent and peaceful conflict resolution processes and their actual and predicted outcomes and define the characteristics or principles of the process that would be most effective in restoring sustainable peace in all Burundian communities.

Unit 8: Articulating individual and collective responsibilities in the reconstruction of Burundian and global society. In this unit, the participants will examine the complexity of the necessary social reconstruction process to yield sustainable peace in Burundi. They will explore and articulate the roles that must be played and the responsibilities that must be fulfilled at the individual, family, community, and national level in order to achieve needed social and political transformation. Such responsibilities include questioning, deconstructing, and beginning to unlearn the ethnic stereotypes that have weakened the fabric of Burundian society and the colonial misperceptions that have devalued African people and their mores and traditions. The participants will capture the prime importance of critical self-examination and individual transformation as a vital prerequisite for the group transformation and collaboration that social reconstruction requires.

Unit 9: Committing to labor for the peace process. The participants will compare and contrast their ways of life during times of peace and times of war and will thus gain greater appreciation for peaceful coexistence. They will reflect on their learning experiences from previous units and realize that in the same way that the Burundian conflict has impacted everyone's life, the peace process needs the positive contributions of every Burundian, Hutu, Tutsi, and Twa alike. They will understand that no international government or organization will hand-deliver peace to Burundi and that no one ethnic group or warring faction alone can achieve sustainable peace in Burundi. The participants will feel empowered to contribute constructively to the peace process. They will develop the dispositions and skills necessary to dedicate their time, talents, and resources to a collaborative process that transcends ethnicity and educational level, a process that will restore trust and hope, the only process with the potential to yield sustainable peace for the distressed Burundian people and their progeny.

Unit 10: Program evaluation. The effect of the program will best be assessed at the community level, in two complementary formats. One way would be gathering the participants who reside within the same community in biannual focus group interviews for at least five years. The interviews would yield data about how the program continues to impact the participants' interethnic relations as well as their attitudes and actions. Another way would be to observe interethnic interactions in both formal and informal settings, at regular intervals over a period of at least five years.

Applying Banks's Dimensions of Multicultural Education to the Burundian School Curriculum

Transformative multicultural education must be infused in the academic curriculum at all levels of schooling in order for the Burundian educational system to prepare students for reflective, critical, and peace-minded citizenship. Transformative multicultural education refers to educational policies and practices that are defined by the principles and goals of multicultural education (as defined by Nieto 2004) and peace education (as defined by Salomon 2002). In the Burundian context, transformative multicultural education refers to the comprehensive reform of the policies, practices, curricular, instructional materials and strategies that characterize the educational system. Transformative multicultural education empowers educators and students to become reflective agents of change who advocate for and labor to achieve equity, social justice, and peaceful coexistence in their interethnic communities and in the multicultural global community.

In this section, I discuss how James Banks's (2001) dimensions of multicultural education can be applied to the Burundian educational context in order to achieve the primary goals of transformative multicultural education. The five dimensions of multicultural education developed by Banks (2001) are (1) content integration, (2) the knowledge construction process, (3) prejudice reduction, (4) an equity pedagogy, and (5) an empowering school culture.[20] I will illustrate each dimension next.

Content integration. James Banks explains that "content integration deals with the extent to which teachers use examples and content from a variety of cultures and groups to illustrate key concepts, principles, generalizations, and theories in their subject area or discipline (ibid.). Content integration can be an important tool that helps Burundian educators and students affirm their ethnic and cultural identity as well as their political and social independence from their colonial past. For example, the language arts curriculum can include pastoral poetry, work song, folktales, and legends. The history curriculum can and should include both official and folk history in order to reflect different perspectives. Math and science curricula can include discussions of traditional farming practices, as well as native food and beer preparation and conservation.

The knowledge construction process. According to James Banks, this dimension "relates to the extent to which teachers help students to understand, investigate, and determine how the implicit cultural assumptions, frames of references, perspectives, and biases within a discipline influence ways in which knowledge is constructed" (ibid.). Burundian educators and students can analyze the knowledge construction process in all major curriculum areas by examining how the colonial perspective that pervades most subjects impacts their frames of references. They can evaluate instructional materials in order to uncover ethnic stereotypes and other forms of cultural biases and discuss how the biases have affected interethnic coexistence in Burundi. They can identify missing voices and perspectives in the curriculum and study how such omission impacts their knowledge construction process and their interethnic relations.

Prejudice reduction. This dimension "describes lessons and activities teachers use to help students develop positive attitudes toward different racial, ethnic, and cultural groups".[21] In a country like Burundi where society has been marked by decades of political turmoil and ethnic hostility, students are very likely to develop negative attitudes and misconceptions about different ethnic groups. This dimension engages all students in lessons and activities that challenge Tutsi hegemony and empower them all, Hutu, Tutsi, and Twa alike, to develop reflective appreciation for different ethnic groups. For once, the taboo cloud that has been hanging over ethnic membership must be lifted to allow students to openly discuss issues related to ethnicity in Burundi. Educators must involve all students in activities that stress cooperation and interdependence and reward them according to their individual merit rather than their ethnicity.

Equity pedagogy. James Banks explains that "an equity pedagogy exists when teachers modify their teaching in ways that will facilitate the academic achievement of students from diverse racial, cultural, gender, and social-class groups" (ibid.). In the Burundian context, an equity pedagogy includes using instructional materials that are relevant to and validate students' familiar world. In mathematics, for instance, teaching the concepts of speed, time, and distance using unfamiliar constructs like cars and aeroplanes in a countryside classroom further confuses the students. Such concepts would be most effectively taught using students' familiar knowledge, like traveling on foot or riding a bicycle. An equity pedagogy also includes being aware of and sensitive to students' individual life circumstances. For example, assigning homework to students who must walk over ten kilometers each way daily and arrive exhausted to a home that has no electricity is basically leading them to unavoidable academic failure.

An empowering school culture. As Banks indicates, "grouping and labeling practices, sports participation, disproportionality in achievement, disproportionality in enrollment in gifted and special education programs, and the interaction of the staff and the students across ethnic and racial lines must be examined to create a school culture that empowers students from diverse racial, ethnic, and gender groups" (ibid.). The Burundian educational system has consistently denied Hutu and Twa people access to an equitable education because of pervasive discriminatory and exclusionary policies and practices. An empowering school culture, therefore, requires that policy makers and educators reexamine the underrepresentation of the Hutus and Twas and the overrepresentation of the Tutsis in education, particularly in secondary schools and institutions of higher learning. This dimension requires that students be involved and engaged in interethnic discussions of issues of inequity in order to develop the skills they need to become reflective citizens who are concerned with the welfare of their fellow Burundians. This dimension also requires that educators build a comfortable learning environment by discouraging and confronting the pervasive Tutsi ethnocentrism and ethnicized harassment that invalidate and traumatize Hutu and Twa students and often force them out of the system.

Conclusion

Burundi and the other nations in the Great Lakes region of Africa are at an extremely critical juncture in the history of humankind. For many people and communities who have been engaged in the path of self-destruction for decades, the way back is clouded with fear and uncertainty and therefore as unsure as the way forward. But one must pause and wonder how much longer governments can annihilate the people that they are supposed to serve and how much longer neighbors can lash their machetes on the necks of their neighbors. One must wonder how long it will take the various power-hungry, warring factions to realize that darkness shall not set over one hill while the sun forever shines over the hill next door.

As a people, we must wonder whether hope and peace will ever return to inspire the unwritten songs and poetry of the African spirit and rock our African children into undisturbed sleep caressed by motherly lullabies. As African people, we must trust in our capacity to venerate human life and neighborly relations and our power to reclaim peace for the people of Burundi and of the Great Lakes region of Africa.

This paper exemplifies one way of reclaiming peace in order to start reconstructing the Burundian society that has been shattered by decades of ethnic discord. It advocates for the reform of the Burundian educational system in order for the Burundian people to take charge of their own redemption from the vestiges of ethnicized political turmoil. Any effective reform, however, must be inspired by an unshadowed willingness to confront the painful truths about inequity and social injustice. Thus, this paper begins with a discussion of the ways in which the Burundian educational system has served as the breeding ground for inequality and discord by sustaining discriminatory policies and practices that elevated the Tutsi to hegemonic status while subjecting the Hutus into annihilating oppression and the Twas into disempowering invisibility. The paper then analyzes the multifaceted consequences of the Hutu-Tutsi conflict, noting that the decades-long turmoil has affected all the spheres of human life and eroded the very fabric of Burundian society. Building on this deeper understanding of the Burundian situation, the paper defines the need for multicultural and peace education to be introduced into the Burundian educational system. It outlines a transformative multicultural education framework for Burundian schools and communities. This framework has two main components: (1) a stand-alone training program organized around ten thematic units, and (2) a school-bound cross-curricular and inclusive program based on Banks's (2001) dimensions of multicultural education.

In the foreword to Paulo Freire's (1993) acclaimed and liberatory book, *Pedagogy of the Oppressed*, Richard Shaull states,

> There is no such thing as a neutral educational process. Education either functions as an instrument that is used to facilitate the integration of the younger generation into the logic of the present system and bring about conformity to it, or it becomes the practice of freedom, the means by which men and women deal critically and creatively with reality and discover how to participate in the transformation of their world.[22]

This paper outlines ways in which Burundian policy makers and educators can join forces in order to create an inclusive educational system that will liberate all Burundian men and women, regardless of ethnicity, and empower them to actively participate in the transformation of their shared Burundian society. Liberatory education must be inclusive of all voices and talents. As Paulo Freire (1993) clarifies, "Education as the practice of freedom—as opposed to education as the practice of domination—denies that man is abstract, isolated, independent, and unattached to the world; it also denies that the world exists as a reality apart from people".[23]

There cannot be a Tutsi, a Hutu, and a Twa solution to the Burundian crisis. All Burundian people are forever bound in a destiny that only they can define. No outside government or organization will deliver a future of peaceful coexistence to Burundi. The power of social reconstruction lies in the hands of Burundians of all ethnic groups. Introducing a transformative multicultural education framework into the formal education and community development systems will help Burundians of all ages reclaim lost hope, regain interethnic trust, and lay the foundation for sustainable peace in their communities and the nation.

Epilogue

I have traveled to Burundi four times since this chapter was first drafted and presented at the 2004 PJSA conference. I have collected research data documenting perspectives on and practices in peacebuilding in Burundi schools and communities. My research data and personal interactions with Burundian people attest to a positive shift in the attitudes and relations in the country. There is a democratic consciousness that provides a needed foundation for people's voice and empowerment. The people of Burundi readily share their painful memories of interethnic conflict and war. Most importantly, they share their hard-learned lessons of destruction and suffering, and their hope for lasting peace. Nevertheless, there is still much work to be done. More schools have been built to increase equitable access, but many of them still lack quality teachers and instructional materials. A quick drive from Bujumbura reveals ever growing and worrisome economic disparity between urban and rural populations. Whether the country can further its quest for sustainable peace amidst such severe inequalities is a question that Burundian leaders should examine without much delay.

Notes

1. Elavie Ndura, "Peaceful conflict resolution: A prerequisite for social reconstruction in Burundi, Africa," in *Conflict resolution and peace education in Africa*, ed. Ernest. E. Uwazie (Lanham: Lexington Books, 2003), 151-60.

2. Elavie Ndura, « La contribution de l'éducation familiale et scolaire à la réalization d'une paix durable au Burundi, » *Tuj-i-Buntu* 40(2004): 4-7.

3. Elavie Ndura, 2003. Ibid.

4. Elavie Ndura, 2004. Ibid.

5. Filip Reyntjens. *Burundi: Prospects for peace.* London: Minority Rights Group International, 2000.

6. *Ibid.*, 25.

7. Elavie Ndura, 2003. Ibid.

8. *Ibid.*

9. Jack D. Eller. *From culture to ethnicity to conflict: An anthropological perspective on international ethnic conflict.* Ann Harbor: University of Michigan Press, 1999.

10. Morton Deutsch, "Conflicts: Productive and destructive," in *Conflict resolution through communication*. Ed. Fred E. Jandt (New York: Harper & Row, 1973), 190.

11. Elavie Ndura, 2003. Ibid. 154.

12. Sonia Nieto, 2004. *Affirming diversity: The sociopolitical context of multicultural education* (4th ed.). Boston: Pearson (2004), 346.

13. James A. Banks, "Democratic citizenship education in multicultural societies," in *Diversity and citizenship education: Global perspectives*, ed. James. A. Banks, (San Francisco: Jossey-Bass, 2004), 3-15.

14. Gavriel Salomon, "The nature of peace education: Not all programs are created equal," in *Peace education: The concept, principles, and practices around the world*, ed. Gavriel. Salomon and Baruch Nevo, (Mahwah, New Jersey: Lawrence Erlbaum Associates, 2002), 3-14.

15. Geneva Gay, "Curriculum theory and multicultural education," in *Handbook of research on multicultural education*, ed. James A. Banks and Cherry. A. McGee Banks (San Francisco: Jossey-Bass, 2001), 25-43.

16. Christine E. Sleeter. *Multicultural education as social activism*. Albany: State University of New York Press, 1996.

17. *Ibid.*, 224

18. James A. Banks, "Multicultural education: Characteristics and goals," in *Multicultural Education: Issues and Perspectives*, ed. James A. Banks and Cherry A. McGee Banks (4th ed.), (New York: Wiley, 2001), 3-30.

19. Ernest E. Uwazie, "Conflict resolution and peace education in Africa: An introduction," in *Conflict resolution and peace education in Africa*, ed. Ernest E. Uwazie, (Lanham: Lexington Books, 2003), 1-8.

20. James A. Banks, "Multicultural education: Characteristics and goals," in *Multicultural Education: Issues and Perspectives*, ed. James A. Banks and Cherry A. McGee Banks (4th ed.) (New York: Wiley, 2001), 3-30.

21. *Ibid.* 21.

22. Richard Shaull, Foreword to *Pedagogy of the oppressed*, by Paulo Freire (New York: Continuum, 1993), 16.

23. Paulo Freire, *Pedagogy of the oppressed* (New York: Continuum, 1993), 62.

Two

Chad: "Social Misery and Corruption Are the Main Causes of Violence" An Interview with Koussetogue Koude

Rudi Friedrich

The following interview with Koussetogue Koude of Chad took place in 2005. Koude, an academic and activist from Ndjamena, has been active with several Tcadian human rights associations, including Tchad Nonviolence. Interviewer Rudi Friedrich of Germany's Connection e.V. has published extensively on nonviolence in Africa. Both Koude and Friedrich are associates of the War Resisters International. This interview was translated by Florence Gomez of the Colorado College Romance Languages Department.

RUDI FRIEDRICH: What is the actual social and political situation in Chad?

KOUSSETOGUE KOUDE: First, the political situation in Chad: At the moment, it is marked by President Idriss Deby's determination to stay in office despite the 1996 constitution, which does not allow him to be in power for three electoral mandates in a row. Nevertheless, very determined to stay in power and thanks to the absolute devotion of the whole national assembly, President Deby proceeded to enact important constitutional changes that enabled him to remain president almost for life.

Second, the Darfur crisis has repercussions on the stability of Chad. For the majority, people who are victims of the persecutions of progovernment Sudanese militias (the unfortunately well-known

"Janjawids")—are from the Zaghawa ethnic group to whom President Deby himself belongs, as well as most of the higher ranked officers of the Chad army. More and more continuing rumors reveal serious discontent with the high army leadership supportive of the Darfur rebellion (led by people belonging to ethnic groups who live on the border of Chad and Sudan).

Finally, the social situation: poverty and misery are the daily lot of the majority of the country's population. Workers, and particularly those of public administration, are not spared. For instance, some have not been paid for several months, and in some remote regions, some have gone without a salary for up to ten months. This greatly promotes corruption, being the true national sport. Corruption is practiced in higher ranks of the state, despite the recent creation of an office of ethics that supervises the government. Also, the public administration of Chad, [which] has been the largest job provider, has not been hiring since 1990, with some exceptions. The rate of graduates without jobs keeps rising, and youth [are] idle. Many young people escape toward neighboring counties to study or find a job, while the well-off leave to more promising places. Our universities, schools, health centers, etc., only exist in name. This is because of the constant social dissatisfaction that paralyzes all sectors of activity....

RF: What organizations are the biggest hurdles for a nonviolent and democratic society?

KK: Social misery, poverty, generalized corruption (mainly in public administration where nothing is done unless you tip people), the good old boy system, etc., are the main causes of violence and the setback of the democratic process, which was engaged since the "sovereign" national conference of 1993. On top of this, you can add ideologies of hatred and exclusion of others that are easily conveyed throughout the country. All these elements form real obstacles to peace and democracy.

RF: What kinds of activities are led today by NGOs?

KK: Today there is in Chad a kind of generalized pessimism that took possession of the whole civil society after more than fifteen years of fighting for democratic change. People of Chad believe in fatalism and resignation. The civil society organizations that invested so much in peace and democracy still believe in those concepts even if it is with less enthusiasm than in the nineties.

Activities of the organizations of civil societies are essentially aimed at education and training, which is the token of a true, long-term change. In recent years, a particular stress is put on the Anti-Cleavage Youth Association (ACYA)/l'Association Jeunesse Anti-Clivage (AJAC) to emphasize the fight against some culturally rooted violence, as for example the specific case of the Bouvier children who were like slaves in the hands of their masters. Their parents entrust those children to nomadic cattle breeders, who use them in their countryside activities in exchange for a cow. It is a business in kind that is done on the backs of those poor kids who are regularly ill-treated, exploited, exposed to farmers' violence when the herds damaged the fields. For a few years now, the AJAC has worked to get those children back on track and socially reinsert them through internships to learn a career.

RF: What is the role of industrialized countries in the oil project?

KK: Many of the friendly countries as well as the international organizations interested in the Chad oil project really insisted that oil exploitation has positive consequences. Mainly for people who live in the regions where exploitation fields and pipe lines run. Those populations are victims of expropriation in the name of public utility. As I have already mentioned, people of Chad live in social misery and poverty. Populations who are victims of expropriation because of oil exploitation are not fairly compensated. And to top it all, a part of the money allocated to oil exploitation was spent to buy arms for the army of Chad. Only the future will tell us if the oil exploitation of Chad will make its population happy, unlike what is happening in other African countries with oil such as Angola, Congo-Brazzaville, or Nigeria.

According to the AJAC, oil income must be used to fight against misery and poverty, and all the population of this country, not only a few individuals, clans, or groups, close to power, must benefit from it.

RF: What is the proportion of exchanges between African NGOs on the topic of nonviolence and human rights?

KK: African countries find themselves confronted by similar situations. A tight cooperation between African NGOs and the regular exchange of experiences, at levels both national and regional, can only reinforce initiatives in favor of peace and democracy in our countries. Many networks already exist, even though they may not yet be operational.

RF: What is your experience of international and/or African conferences about nonviolence and human rights?

KK: For almost four years now, I have participated in an African teacher-training workshop in human rights and the fight against torture. This workshop—as its name indicates, aims at preparing a large number of local actors, human rights managers, in order to reinforce their capacity of action in their respective countries. Gathering every year about fifty participants from roughly twenty African countries, this workshop is also a place where experiences are exchanged and where action happens in concert and synergy. People who attend this workshop are going to teach the people in their turn and so on. They also have to write reports on a regular basis stating the activities organized and their impact, the difficulties they met, and improvements to consider, as well as the expectations. I must say that these kinds of initiatives are to be encouraged because they are promising for the future.

RF: How can European NGOs support both the work of nonviolence in Chad and other pacifist organizations?

KK: Beyond financial and material support, I think that a real partnership based on our respective experiences—NGOs of the North and the South—our successes or our failures in this or that domain, etc., is to be encouraged.

THREE

Power, Interests, and Human Rights: A Case Study of Angola

Andrea Lari
and Rob Kevlihan

This article was developed from an earlier draft prepared for delivery at the 2004 annual conference of the Peace and Justice Studies Association held in San Francisco, October 14-17, 2004, and a working paper published by the Institute of Strategic Studies in South Africa.

> In October 2001, one morning, when my wife was pregnant, they arrived and she could not flee quickly enough. I was able to flee with the four children, but she was caught by the soldiers and they shot her to death.
> –Testimony from an internally displaced person in Angola included in the Médicins Sans Frontières (MSF) report on Angola[1]

Angola's long war finally came to an end on April 4, 2002, with the signing of a Memorandum of Understanding between the Forcas Armadas Angolanos (FAA—the Angolan military) and the União Nacional para a Independência Total de Angola (UNITA). This historic agreement was greatly facilitated by the death of UNITA's leader, Jonas Savimbi, in February 2002. That a conflict that lasted so long (since Angolan independence in 1975) could suddenly end with the death of one of its major protagonists is startling. However, other factors, including military advances, the counterinsurgency strategy of the government, a changing geopolitical context (in particular the end of Cold War support to both sides and the pressure of international sanctions against UNITA) undoubtedly set the scene for this dramatic denouement.[2]

The history of the Angolan civil war in the 1990s is one of failed opportunities for peace. Initially, it seemed that the end of the Cold War offered the hope of a new beginning for Angola, with international agreements leading to the independence of Namibia from South Africa and the withdrawal of Cuban troops from Angola. However, elections organized under the Bicesse Accord (1991) for 1992 resulted in a defeat for UNITA leader Jonas Savimbi in the first round of the presidential election, in an electoral process deemed by international observers to have been essentially free and fair.[3] As a result of UNITA's refusal to accept this result, the UN Security Council imposed a first set of sanctions in September 1993 (under Resolution 864 of the UN Security Council).

UNITA's return to war in 1993 allowed it to take large swaths of the countryside, including the diamond-rich Cuango basin, virtually unopposed. Two years of heavy fighting ensued, which lasted until a new ceasefire came into place with the signing of the Lusaka Protocol by both parties in November 1994. The Lusaka protocol ended the fighting and obliged UNITA to accept the results of the 1992 election, demobilize, disarm, and hand over occupied territory to state administration. In return, UNITA agreed to participate in a government of national unity and reconciliation (known by its Portuguese acronym as GURN).

The process of implementation of the Lusaka Accord proceeded unevenly post- 1994, held up primarily by an apparent lack of trust between the two parties. Despite promises to fully demobilize and disarm, UNITA retained considerable military capacity. A spiraling political situation ultimately led to another return to war, with UNITA largely being blamed by the international community. By mid-1997, further UN sanctions were imposed on UNITA (Resolution 1127, August 1997, and Resolution 1135, November 1997) because of continued delays in the full implementation of the Lusaka Accord, including demobilization and handing over of UNITA-controlled areas to state administration. In June 1998, the UN imposed a further set of largely financial sanctions (Resolution 1173) on UNITA when it became clear that the Lusaka process had broken down and UNITA continued to delay handing over of territories. During the following months, UNITA went further and began occupying a number of districts previously handed over to the government. The Government of Angola (GoA) responded with an offensive in December 1998 that was strongly countered by UNITA. UNITA's capacity to field a well-equipped conventional force at this time highlighted the obvious failure of the UN-imposed sanctions. The Angolan government reacted by asking the UN to withdraw the MONUA observer mission in place. Renewed government offensives in 1999 and 2000 finally deprived UNITA of control of most of Angola's large towns, many key bases, and their capacity to wage conventional warfare. These offensives coincided with a tougher stance by the international community on the imposition of sanctions, led by the Canadian government that chaired the UN UNITA sanctions committee during this time.[4]

From 2000 onward, the Angolan government (which retained the title of GURN and continued to include elements of UNITA that had not gone back to war) began to implement a counterinsurgency strategy aimed at depriving UNITA of any possible sources of support in rural areas. This was primarily achieved through so-called *limpeza* (cleaning) activities by the FAA. *Limpeza* campaigns were used by FAA to clear areas of the countryside considered to harbor UNITA elements. Typically populations were forcibly moved from their lands to the nearest urban center, and crops were destroyed to ensure that UNITA had no access to food. This movement was accompanied by the use or threat of force and sometimes resulted in the immediate deaths of innocent civilians. It also put these civilians at a higher risk of death due to starvation and infectious diseases in the short to medium term, since FAA failed to provide them with basic food and health assistance in areas under military control. Simultaneously, UNITA stepped up its efforts to control civilian populations through inflicting protracted violence and targeting alleged government supporters or informers. UNITA also prevented civilians from leaving areas under their control. Entire villages were also forced to follow UNITA troops and provide support services.[5]

These were the principal motives for people leaving their homes from 2000 to early 2002, contributing to the dreadful humanitarian situation in the country, and were entirely the result of the manner in which both the Angolan government and UNITA decided to conduct the war.[6]

Domestic Political/Legal System and Protection

The first point of reference in a review of systems of protection for vulnerable people invariably must be the domestic systems of the state in which these people find themselves at risk. The Angolan state, while certainly a weak state under pressure during the war, could not be described as a failed state. Much of the literature on states in Africa focuses on the fragile nature of state institutions, the importance of patrimonialism in systems of governance, and the existence of shadow structures to facilitate this patrimonialism.[7]

Angola presents a mixed picture in this respect. Unlike many African governments at war, it retained significant coercive capacity (principally because it could finance its military using oil money) and systems of civil administration that functioned to some extent in certain parts of the country—particularly in the capital city, in southwestern areas, and along the coastal strip more generally. In the interior, where much of the fighting occurred, what civilian state governance structures that did exist were often confined to garrison towns and adjacent areas. As a consequence, large swathes of the countryside were essentially a no-man's-land.

UNITA, particularly from 2000 onward, saw a steady erosion in its own nonmilitary institutions (for example, its health care and education activities), largely because of the combined impact of military pressure and sanctions. Militarily, although UNITA continued to harry government positions and retained the capacity to engage in short hit-and-run attacks on supposedly secure government areas, it had lost the capacity to hold towns of any significance for any great length of time.

In the aftermath of the failed election, the ruling Movimento Popular para Libertação de Angola (MPLA) maintained control, despite the retention of elements of UNITA in GURN. However, while MPLA members occupied key positions within the government, power increasingly became concentrated under the presidency, with President José Eduardo Dos Santos maintaining tight control. Named after the location of his residence, Futungo, Dos Santos's regime centralized control of key elements of the state, including the armed forces and paramilitary police, and of oil revenues from the state oil company and foreign investors—with little requirement for transparency or accountability in how these revenues were utilized. Key political appointments, particularly provincial governors, also continued to be under the control of the president. As a result, Angola continued to be ruled by what was essentially a highly centralized, authoritarian regime, despite the veneer of democratic legitimacy provided by the victory of Dos Santos in the first round of the presidential election.

This is not to imply that the regime exhibited a highly organized structure at all times. The GoA was successful in maintaining a strong military and coercive capacity within its military, but still suffered from logistical problems that prevented it from adequately supplying all of its military all of the time, increasing the risk of military ill-discipline. In other sectors, rule by confusion or neglect was frequently the apparent modus operandi. This lack of institutional capacity or apparent interest of key government ministries such as the Ministries of Health, Education, and MINARS

(Ministry of Assistance and Social Reintegration), particularly in the war-affected zones of the interior, frequently made for frustrating and ineffective encounters between international actors, local civil society, and state institutions. Central ministries also exhibited little control over provincial locations, particularly over health and education activities in the provinces of the interior, where local provincial ministries came under the direct control of provincial governors.

Outside of Futungo, other central governing organs remained weak. The dismissal of the prime minister and lack of a new appointee by President Dos Santos between 1998 and 2002 are indicative of the weakness of the Angolan legislature. Other potential power bases within various ministries were undercut by the power of provincial governors—themselves directly appointed by the president. Direct appointment of governors also reduced the relative ability of MPLA cadres at the local level to influence even local government decisions.

The third pillar of governance, comprising the constitution (approved in September 1992) and the judicial system, proved even weaker. The Angolan constitution, while rhetorically quite a progressive document, has in practice had little impact on how the country is governed. The Angolan judicial system was in a state of collapse throughout the 1990s, with limited personnel and only 13 of 164 municipal courts functioning.[8] Minimal sums were set aside for judicial institutions by the GoA throughout the decade, a clear indication of just how little priority it accorded to this area.[9]

In the same period, the number of internally displaced steadily crowding the capital Luanda and provincial towns and filling formal settlements increased. At the peak of the humanitarian crises in early 2002, there were some 300 camps, hosting a confirmed number of 1.2 million people.[10] The government rarely provided humanitarian assistance to these camps, relying on the services of humanitarian actors that progressively became overstretched and unable to assist this high number of people. Because of declining security conditions, humanitarian organizations had to pull out of UNITA areas in 1998-1999 and, as a result, operated solely in government zones, providing de facto material support to the government as a result. Despite some attempts by humanitarian actors (principally a small number of NGOs) to work in UNITA zones from neighboring countries post-1999, UNITA proved either unable or unwilling to allow access to their zones of operation.

Internally displaced persons (IDPs) suffered frequent abuses at the hands of government forces, including harassment, extortion, property dispossession, and rape. Victims, as a result of the almost nonexistent judicial system, had little recourse to legal protection from their own government.

The only major legislative initiative by the Angolan government was designed to provide some protection for IDPs during resettlement or return processes—not during initial displacement or while they resided in displaced camps. These norms were required because of instances of forced return or resettlement of IDPs to sites that were either vulnerable to UNITA attacks (during the war), in mine-infested areas, or without proper access to basic resources and amenities (including adequate arable land, potable water, and other essential services).

The resettlement norms covered the conditions that were required for IDPs to be resettled either in their home areas or in alternative areas considered to be secure. The norms were developed in two documents, the Norms for the Resettlement of Displaced Populations (Normas sobre o Reassentamento das Populacões Deslocadas) and the implementing Regulations (Regulamento, published by the GoA on December 6, 2002, which served to operationalize the Normas). The Norms are based on the UN's Guiding Principles on Internal Displacement and on paper provided minimum standards for return and resettlement. However, the late date of approval of the Regulamento after one million IDPs had already returned home is indicative of the lack of relevance of the legislation to conditions on the ground. Despite being publicly acknowledged shortly afterward by the Minister for Social Assistance and Reintegration, João Baptista Kussumua, as an important government initiative to protect Angolans during the process of return,[11] government compliance with the norms remained poor. The UN's humanitarian coordinator, Erick De Mul,[12] estimated that only 30 percent of those returning did so in compliance with the Norms.[13] De Mul presented this as a good result given the prevailing conditions in Angola.

National NGOs and Networks

The emerging literature on transnational networks and human rights in the late 1990s pointed to the salience of advocacy networks transnationally and domestically. By building new links among actors in civil societies, states, and international organizations, they multiply the channels of access to the international system and make international resources available to new actors in domestic and political social struggles.[14] However, in the case of Angola, the extent of such transnational linkage was relatively low, with both national and international advocacy having little impact on the behavior of the Angolan government. The Angolan case would seem to support a more (classical) realist perspective on the effectiveness of human rights advocacy in the absence of a strong domestic reaction in powerful states to advocacy activities and when other interests of international states are involved.

Within Angola, the lack of space for effective civil society interaction with the Angolan government, along with difficulties in civil society organization and mobilization in areas with active MPLA party cadres, made for a difficult operating environment. Confronted with the increased level of violence that stranded the civilian population during the last phase of the war, national groups and organizations focused their actions and advocacy efforts on calling for the end to hostilities through negotiation and dialogue between the warring forces. Networks such as the Inter-Ecclesiastical Committee for Peace in Angola (COIEPA) and the Network for Peace (Rede da Paz), insisted that there was no military solution to the Angolan crisis and that other means should be found. When the war suddenly ended through what amounted to a government military victory, many of civil society's most prominent groups and leaders were unprepared to address the changed situation.[15] Other national networks, such as Fórum das Organisações Não-Governamentais Angolanas (FONGA), were relatively quiescent with respect to joint public initiatives, though they did raise human rights issues in private meetings with visiting dignitaries, particularly UN officials.

Throughout the period under review, several isolated initiatives on human rights were implemented by various Angolan groups in local settings. The main focus of their work was on human rights promotion, rather than protection activities per se, and included human rights awareness activities through training and sensitization on the Angolan Constitution and international human rights instruments. Only a few groups managed to apply a countrywide perspective, mainly as a result of associations with already existing and widely spread church networks. For instance, the Cultural Center Mozaico (run by members of the Dominican Order) carried out training in various provinces, often in collaboration with Justice and Peace Commissions created within the Catholic Dioceses. These training activities brought together representatives from different sectors of the community, in particular from the police and local administration, together with those who had suffered violations.[16]

More proactive national advocacy initiatives included the Ad Hoc Commission report on human rights violations in Cabinda (in December 2002), the establishment by the Catholic Church of Movimento Pro-Pace and a number of outspoken pastoral letters from the Catholic Bishops conference. These efforts coupled with other laudable but isolated initiatives did not lead to an organized system of monitoring, reporting, and advocacy on violations of human rights. While the stated philosophy of many national organizations was that confrontation was not the way to get things done, fear of a negative government response to public criticism also played a role, given the constricted space in which civil society was allowed to operate. In addition, the GoA proved itself to be adept at co-opting elements of civil society through direct financial support and/or through the use of quasi-governmental (and patrimonial) organizations such as the Fundação Eduardo Dos Santos (FESA).[17]

Donor Governments and International Human Rights Protection

In the absence of any serious efforts to provide protection at the national level, and, indeed, with the Angolan government (itself the main actor responsible for providing protection for its own citizens) being one of the main perpetrators of serious rights abuses through the use of *limpeza* activities, it seems appropriate to consider the efficacy of external actors in putting pressure on the Angolan government to protect their own people and live up to their commitments under domestic and international law.

Stokke states that the 1990s saw many Western governments taking an increasingly aggressive stance against countries where serious human rights violations were occurring, particularly in Africa. Political condition-ality became increasingly prominent among donor governments from the end of the Cold War. With Cold War rivalry removed from the equa-tion, Western governments felt freer to pursue basic political concerns vis à vis governments of the south. The establishment and strengthening of Western norms and interests—in particular, relating to human rights (especially civil and political rights) and governmental systems (democ-racy, rule of law)—assumed greater prominence in the foreign policies of Western governments toward the South.[18]

Despite this increased international prominence of political condition-ality toward governments of the South in particular, donors maintained a remarkably low profile in dealing with the Angolan government, perhaps best reflecting Chandler's analysis that despite the universality of human rights, the impact of action on human rights is highly selective, with realpo-litik continuing to play an extremely important role.[19] In realpolitik terms, the most striking aspect of Angola's situation is the lack of donor leverage. Unlike the vast majority of countries in sub-Saharan Africa, Angola effec-tively managed to insulate itself from pressure from foreign governments. While the GoA has a reputation for being extremely defensive toward international criticism and was unenthusiastic about international involve-ment after the failure of the Lusaka process, unilateralism in the absence of material power can only go so far. In the case of Angola, their independent approach was backed up by oil. Western states did impose conditionality on further International Financial Institution (IFI) lending, primarily with the objective of improved transparency in accounting for oil revenues. However, throughout the 1990s, the Angolan government succeeded in expanding revenues from its offshore oil reserves—either directly through bonus payments and royalties from oil companies or through oil-backed lending on the basis of future income. Income from oil was controlled by Futungo, with government transparency in the amount and use of these revenues abysmal.[20] This ability to rely on private resources and financing meant that the international donor community had little leverage over the Angolan government using the classic leverages of conditionality on IMF and World Bank loans and bilateral aid.

However, lack of effective leverage is only one part of the story. Angola's astuteness in setting countries off against each other in oil exploration and extraction also meant that the international community frequently remained fragmented and largely self-interested in its dealings with the country throughout these years, giving the Angolan government a relatively easy ride with respect to human rights concerns. The horrendous humanitarian situation in the country also meant that Angola continued to receive significant amounts of humanitarian aid, despite the government's failure to account for its oil revenues or invest significant resources in humanitarian aid itself.[21] Such humanitarian assistance was channeled primarily through the UN and NGOs and effectively substituted the Angolan government's task of caring for its own people—a classic catch-22 dilemma in international humanitarian action, given the chronic humanitarian situation in-country.

UN Protection Initiatives

This weak-donor position inevitably led to a weak UN political presence in-country and to weakened UN efforts at human rights protection, particularly after the failure of UN peacekeeping efforts. The UN human rights presence in Angola began in 1996 as a small unit attached to the United Nations Verification Mission in Angola (UNAVEM II). The mission expanded in 1997 under UNAVEM III, becoming in June of the same year the United Nations Observer Mission in Angola (MONUA). At this point the human rights unit was consolidated into the Human Rights Division (HRD). When MONUA's mandate was not renewed upon request of the GoA in February 1999, HRD was asked to continue its activities, though still confined to building the capacity of its institutions and implementing activities for raising human rights awareness.

As the country began to plunge into war again toward the end of 1998, HRD (already handicapped by a very limited mandate and in the hope that with time and more confidence, the GoA would accept its protection function, including human rights investigation and public reporting) maintained a very low profile. Activities included limited training of police and military officials and ad hoc programs with civil society. HRD did score some small successes during this time. One example was their support in the establishment of a human rights committee in IDP camps in Viana (on the fringes of Luanda) that was successful in addressing abuses in these camps. However, despite the fact that most of the egregious violations were happening around combat areas in the interior of the country, HRD never managed to expand to the central highlands and eastern provinces, limiting its action to the capital and the safest provinces in the coastal region. Even in Luanda, the remote location of its office at the edge of town impeded greater communication with partners and provision of public information regarding its activities.[22]

Only in August 2002 (after the signing of the April 2002 cease-fire), did the UN Security Council finally provide the new United Nations Mission in Angola (UNMA) with a six-month mandate including "the protection and promotion of human rights."[23] The real impact of having a stronger mandate was minimal. A planned expansion in the country through regional offices never took place, while the deployment of additional officers authorized by the UN resolution to increase the size of the mission was delayed for several months. One month before the end of the new mandate when the then UN commissioner for human rights, Sergio Vierra de Mello, visited Angola, the NGO network in Angola (Comité de Organizações Internacionais Não-Governamentais em Angola or CONGA), disappointed by the delay in implementing its mandate, produced a letter stressing how violations were still widespread and criticizing the UN response as seriously inadequate.[24]

In February 2003, HRD was merged into a Technical Unit supervised by the resident/humanitarian coordinator and was tasked with completing the residual tasks of UNMA, including social reintegration of demobilized soldiers, de-mining, and technical assistance in the preparation of elections.[25] The human rights component of the unit was restricted once more, this time confined to strengthening Angolan human rights institutions. The unit now reports directly to the UN high commissioner for human rights. With this significant dilution of the mandate, a short window of opportunity to boost protection activities at a crucial time in Angola's postwar transition by the UN was lost.

While HRD prevaricated and failed to take a lead role, the UN Office for the Coordination of Humanitarian Assistance (OCHA) and the UN High Commissioner for Refugees (UNHCR) initiated a process to devise a countrywide protection strategy based on creating provincial protection groups and, using the UN Guiding Principles on Forced Displacement, training of personnel, both from local authorities and humanitarian organizations. This move was made in the face of widespread human rights violations suffered mainly by displaced groups during the war. A decision was taken early on to include government officials in protection groups at all stages, including at the local level. The result was that too often this approach meant that nongovernmental participants were immobilized from effective action within these forums, because of fear of negative consequences and lack of confidence in the process.

OCHA took a strong lead role in these developments, attempting to fill an institutional vacuum within the UN system. Despite the structural weakness of the UN in pushing protection activities with the Angolan government, OCHA was successful in developing an information network that fed some information on human rights violations to the UN resident coordinator and more broadly within the UN system, allowing the resident coordinator some scope for advocacy on human rights issues. OCHA personnel in the field were also active in bringing some acute violations to the attention of local authorities, with varying success. The primary tasks of OCHA field officers included coordination of humanitarian activities, local liaison with government and NGO counterparts, needs assessments, and, frequently, security coordination. As a result, field officers, despite their (at times) strong personal commitments to human rights protection, were often overwhelmed by duties other than protection activities. In addition, field officers typically had a strong background in humanitarian rather than protection activities and, as a result, were often technically unprepared to carry out protection initiatives.[26]

UNHCR's operations were concentrated around the capital and in only two northern provinces, working both with returning refugees and the resettlement of IDPs. Protection activities focused on the creation of human rights committees to deal with human rights abuses and seek redress before local authorities. These had mixed results mainly due to high staff turnover and a consequent lack of consistency in approach. Due primarily to weak in-country capacity, funding difficulties, and an ambiguous commitment to IDP protection work countrywide, UNHCR did not play a greater role in human rights protection activities, despite recommendations by an internal UNHCR evaluation team that visited the country at the end of 2001 to strengthen their protection activities.[27]

Overall, UN activities in the field of protection suffered from the same structural weakness (i.e., lack of leverage/bargaining power) that led to a weak donor effort vis à vis Angola. In the absence of strong support from donor nations, the UN was placed in an institutionally weak position in Angola. This was exacerbated by an Angolan government perception that the UN had failed Angola in the previous peace process. As a result, protection activities suffered from recurrent subordination to UN concerns to maintain some political presence in-country, presumably in order to maintain a dialogue with the Angolan government and secure a possible UN role in any new peace process.

This weak institutional commitment to vigorous protection activities was exacerbated by a lack of clear ownership within UN agencies on protection activities. There was no effective "lead agency" for protection strategies and activities within the UN system. A chronic lack of funding by donors for protection programs, particularly mainstreamed in the UN's Consolidated Annual Appeal's process (which was itself based on a human rights approach), cannot have helped in this regard.

Advocacy Groups, Humanitarian Agencies, and Human Rights Protection

The most significant action highlighting (and denouncing the perpetrators of) the serious protection problems faced by the civilian population during the war in Angola was undertaken by international humanitarian and human rights advocacy organizations, most notably at an Arria Formula[28] meeting held with members of the UN Security Council in New York in March 2002. The agencies urged the GoA, the UN, and the international community to address the humanitarian crisis and pay more attention to the protection needs of the internally displaced. It was also stressed that lack of good governance, transparency, and accountability were impeding greater respect for human rights.[29] Three of the agencies that participated in the Arria Formula—Médicins Sans Frontières (MSF), Human Rights Watch (HRW), and Oxfam—also highlighted the lack of attention to large-scale human rights abuses committed during the war. However, the impact of their advocacy on members of the UN Security Council was minimal.

Outside of such "high politics," international humanitarian organizations also sought to raise public awareness of the human rights situation in Angola throughout this period. MSF took the strongest public role. MSF sections had a significant presence in Angola throughout the war, being collectively located in almost all Angolan provinces, employing around 150 international staff. Through assisting recently arrived displaced persons in therapeutic and other feeding and health centers, MSF collected hundreds of testimonies that documented a series of violations suffered by those trapped in conflict-affected areas. MSF published a series of reports on the situation in Angola, using these testimonies to highlight human rights abuses being perpetrated by both sides.[30]

These testimonies and other evidence highlighted that the lack of access of humanitarian agencies to isolated communities because of the conflict—mainly to those populations forced to remain under UNITA control—was a major concern. These concerns proved to be well founded after the April 2002 cease-fire when a so-called "hidden caseload" of 500,000 malnourished and debilitated people was "discovered." Despite urgent needs in camps where these populations gathered from April 2002 onward, a hiatus of almost five weeks in humanitarian response occurred— apparently due to a combination of GoA resistance and UN politicking, which effectively impeded the timely delivery of humanitarian assistance.[31]

International human rights organizations did not maintain a permanent presence in Angola, and as a result, their efforts were largely confined to mobilization of external actors on these issues. HRW took an active role in highlighting the abuses occurring, including (in July 2002) a critique of the insufficient protection efforts of the GoA, raising the complete lack of implementation of approved legislative measures guiding return and resettlement processes and the lack of clear ownership among UN agencies in implementing an interagency protection strategy that was developed between 2000 and 2001.[32] The established system and structures did not prevent, for example, cases of forced and disorganized return or settlement of populations to or in areas that were not secure, leaving these populations at risk from UNITA attacks (during the conflict) and/or at risk of death or serious injury from landmines and unexploded ordinance.

However, this lack of clear ownership on protection within the UN system became a moot point with the handover of protection activities to HRD in August 2002. This led to the effective discontinuation by OCHA and, to some extent, UNHCR of protection activities, in the wake of the (brief) expansion in HRD's mandate to include protection activities. Years of painstaking work, particularly on the part of OCHA, were effectively lost in this handover. The HRW report was criticized by some within the UN system for having contributed to this loss, though lack of capacity and/or willingness within the UN system to collaborate in ensuring a successful handover that built on existing achievements was a critical factor in this loss and subsequent failure to take advantage of the opening offered by the new mandate. In effect, HRD proved unwilling or incapable of accepting the responsibility that was assigned to it to take on this burden.

In addition to participation in UN-led human rights initiatives, humanitarian NGOs periodically organized other ad hoc initiatives with respect to Angola. The majority of these initiatives were not public—typically they targeted high-ranking UN officials visiting Angola or sometimes representatives of donor governments. In 2001, for example, Oxfam took a lead role in organizing a joint NGO letter to UN Ambassador Gambari, highlighting the human rights situation—particularly violations of human rights—in Angola. The letter was signed on to by twelve members of the steering committee of the international NGO network, CONGA.[33] CONGA representatives also frequently made joint verbal representations to visiting delegations.

Other more public forms of human rights advocacy included a report by the Irish Catholic NGO Trócaire (in cooperation with the Windhoek-based Group of Indigenous Minorities in Southern Africa [WIMSA] and the Angolan NGO Organização Cristã de Apoio ao Desenvolvimento Comunitario) on the plight of the minority San people,[34] and a statement condemning government tactics in eastern Moxico province by GOAL, another Irish NGO.[35] This statement coincided with the final government offensives against UNITA prior to the death of Savimbi, which resulted in very high rates of displacement.

In general, NGO protection efforts did not meet with any greater success than other protection efforts in Angola. Public advocacy also occurred very late in the conflict cycle—despite the availability of detailed information on human rights abuses committed by the warring parties. The first major reports were released in late 2001—despite the occurrence of widespread violations from mid-1998 onward.

Nonetheless, public initiatives did serve to highlight the tragic situation confronting ordinary Angolans and bring some pressure to bear on both the Angolan government and the international community to do more. The limits of the strength of the Angolan government are also evident in its relations with NGOs involved in public advocacy. Despite issuing a number of strong reports, MSF did not face significant sustained criticism from the Angolan government and was allowed to continue its humanitarian operations—perhaps indicating the relative importance of the MSF humanitarian operation to the country, and also their strong standing internationally, particularly after receiving a Nobel Peace Prize. Given this apparent strength, the lack of broader joint public initiatives by humanitarian NGOs working in Angola (through networks such as CONGA) is perhaps more indicative of weak inter-NGO coordination mechanisms (both in-country and outside), at least with respect to human rights initiatives, and a failure of these agencies to mobilize themselves for this type of collective action. It is also to be noted that the one NGO taking a lead in this area—MSF—did so largely by adopting a "go it alone" policy with respect to the development and release of these reports. The reluctance of some humanitarian NGOs to engage in human rights protection activities, because of mandate issues and/or service delivery imperatives, also played a role in inhibiting cooperation in this area. Ongoing uncertainty regarding NGO registration in-country may also have conditioned relatively passive behavior among international NGOs with regard to human rights.

However, it should also be noted that the humanitarian presence in government-controlled areas—with somewhere in the range of 100 international NGOs working in government garrison towns and secure areas throughout the country—also acted as a form of de facto accompaniment of the civilian population, providing some measure of protection in addition to material support.

Analysis of Protection Activities

Synthesizing this analysis of the various levels of protection activities presents a disappointing picture of its efficacy in Angola during the period under review. While the Angolan government cannot be blamed for rights violations carried out by UNITA, it can be held responsible for its failure to protect its own people from the negative impact of its own limpeza activities and for violations that were perpetrated by its armed forces.

Donor governments' response to these violations was muted in the extreme, with little concerted effort on the part of Western governments to put serious pressure on Futungo. Given the documented trend towards more robust human rights protection by Western governments in the South during this period, the relative lack of economic leverage these governments enjoyed over the Angolan government and economic interests—in particular oil—must have played a decisive role in this weak response.

It is a cliché often repeated by UN officials that the UN is only as strong as the member states will allow them to be. This was certainly the case with respect to many of the UN's human rights activities in Angola. A weak mandate after the pullout of MONUA left HRD isolated and hanging on by a shoestring as the only quasi-political UN presence in-country. However, the failure of the HRD to capitalize even modestly on its expanded mandate from 2002 onward is also indicative of a lack of boldness on the part of the one UN unit specifically tasked with human rights activities in Angola. The truth is that HRD rarely set foot outside of Luanda, was politically hamstrung from the beginning, and when it finally had the mandate to do something meaningful, failed to accept the challenge. In many respects, HRD represented a face-saving device for the perceived failure of the UN political presence in Angola's first peace process and, as such, was there primarily to maintain the fig leaf of a UN political presence.

On the humanitarian side, UN agencies, principally through OCHA and the activities of the humanitarian coordinator Erik de Mul, integrated some degree of protection activities—primarily limited to collection of information and analysis of patterns of violations—into their operations, with some limited success. However, limited political leverage and inter-mittent donor commitment to bringing pressure to bear meant that their activities could never match the scale of violations occurring through-out the country. UN protection activities were principally guided by the medium-term objective of strengthening the GoA's institutional capacity for protection and generally (with one or two exceptions) avoided more publicly confrontational approaches.

In addition, too often OCHA field staff tasked with protection responsibilities lacked sufficient training, capacity, and support to truly take on these tasks in a comprehensive way—the day-to-day imperatives of humanitarian activities frequently took precedence over protection activities.

Equally, international NGOs working in the humanitarian sector failed to present a consistent public message about what was occurring in Angola. While the quality of NGO coordination was inconsistent throughout the period, some private CONGA advocacy did take place. However, CONGA did not at any point publicly draw attention to the human rights situation in Angola. Individual humanitarian NGOs—most notably MSF—did publicize some aspects of the human rights situation, though to little effect. In the same vein, international human rights orga-nizations, most notably HRW, provided more comprehensive analysis of the human rights situation, but again to little effect in terms of changing the behavior of the Angolan government. Angola's low profile interna-tionally, despite its oil resources and chronic humanitarian crisis, cannot have helped in mobilizing interest. National human rights organizations remained weak throughout the war, with some limited advocacy activi-ties again having little effect, and are indicative of the generally weak and marginal status of civil society actors in Angola.

The New Postwar Situation

The ending of the armed conflict between UNITA and the GoA in April 2002 and the subsequent change toward a more stable situation throughout most of the country has fundamentally changed the human rights landscape of Angola. With the exception of the continued low-intensity conflict in Cabinda, the absence of war means that many of the issues of recent years, in particular, violations of international humanitarian law, will become less significant in the medium term. The absence of war also removes one of the major excuses for wholesale diversion of resources and tolerance of endemic corruption. Given Angola's vast natural wealth and the expanded potential for exploitation of this wealth in the context of peace, access to economic and social rights will now become even more pertinent than ever before. Nevertheless, where large-scale rights violations continue to occur in Angola—such as in the recent forced expulsions of nonnationals from diamond areas in northeast Angola or continued violations in the oil-rich Cabinda enclave—the international community continues to face the same weaknesses in pressuring the Angolan government.

However, the increased levels of debt that Angola accepted in order to win the war, and its current efforts to access IMF funds, may provide one notable leverage point—both with respect to human rights violations in places such as Cabinda and with respect to further reform of its administrative, financial control, and budgeting systems in order to ensure greater transparency in the use of government (particularly oil) revenues.

Equally, Angola's own desire to be perceived as a leading southern African country is evidenced by its recent tenure as a nonpermanent member of the UN Security Council (which ended at the end of 2004) and its equally recent chairmanship of Southern African Development Community (SADC). While these appointments have represented major foreign policy successes for the Angolan government and can be construed as external recognition, and indeed legitimation at regional and international levels, such leadership positions may also provide some scope for pressure to be brought to bear. Leadership involves duties in addition to benefits of prestige.

Lessons Learned and Future Challenges

What lessons can be drawn from this case study? The bottom line appears to be that when a repressive government has financial autonomy from international financial institutions controlled by Western governments, is not overly reliant on external bilateral aid, and is clever enough to play Western countries against each other in the allocation of natural resources (in this case oil), it can effectively isolate itself from significant pressure to reform.

That said, the Angolan government still borrowed from somewhere to finance its war—no serious attempt appears to have been made to focus attention on these alternative private sources of funds or to use other means for leverage to be brought to bear. In the same way, no effort seems to have been made by foreign governments with oil interests to present a united front on Angola. A troika of the U.S., Russia, and Portugal had taken a lead role in the Angola peace process, but did not act as a lead group in engaging with the Angolan government on issues related to human rights.

Beyond this glaring inability or unwillingness of the international community to exercise influence, lessons with respect to Angola itself include the need for continued development of Angola's own judicial system and strengthening of the rule of law; setting up the necessary mechanisms for achieving the redress of human rights violations; the need for support for genuine nascent civil society institutions, combined with an analysis of the hegemonic activities of the Angolan government with respect to civil-society organizations; and the development of strategies to cope with this. Such an approach must include an emphasis on state/society interaction and strengthening the rule of law and the need for greater discussion around the issue of impunity regarding the most egregious violations and crimes of war committed during the civil war. The substantial participation in this discussion of groups from Angolan civil society (including the churches, which represent possibly the strongest institutions outside of state control) may serve to ensure a proper reconciliation process. When and how such a sensitive process could take place should clearly be in the hands of the Angolans themselves, particularly Angolan civil society and those most affected by the war.

With respect to the UN system, it seems clear that there needs to be a clearer delineation of responsibilities within the UN humanitarian system for human rights protection activities, the implementation of effective models, and the proper resourcing and support for these activities.

As for humanitarian NGOs, greater coherency is required on possible joint mechanisms for protection activities. Joint frameworks developed outside of a particular country context may provide the necessary "cover" to allow humanitarian NGOs to engage in public initiatives on human rights violations in a coherent manner.

Conclusion

Angola stands at a crossroads. The country now has an opportunity for broad-based development that could benefit the whole population. Indeed, with extensive oil and diamond resources and a population of only around twelve million, Angola could be an economic powerhouse in the region. However, continued appropriation of community resources by elite groups for personal gain remains a major obstacle to national development. The war has ended, but issues of structural inequality, perceived ethnic bias, and lack of accountability of the governing class remain ever-present. Unresolved, these issues may provide the basis for an upsurge in a new phase of contention.

With the country currently going through a process of normalization in the postwar period, key human rights interventions now need to target how this normalization process takes place in order to protect human rights, including access to economic and social rights such as education and health, and should seek to influence this process so that the ultimate outcome of normalization is a more equitable society that benefits all Angolan citizens equally. One can only hope that Angola may soon realize the promise of its early idealism to the benefit of the Angolan people.

> Amanhã / entoaremos hinos à liberdade / quando comemorarmos / a data da abolição desta escravatura /
> Nós vamos em busca de luz / os teus filhos Mãe (...) / Vão em busca de vida.[37]

> Tomorrow / We'll sing songs of liberty / When we'll celebrate / The date of the abolition of this slavery / We are looking for the light / Your sons, Mother / Are looking for the life.

Notes

1. Médicins Sans Frontières, *Angola, Sacrifice of a People* (MSF, 2002), 15.
2. Rob Kevlihan, "Sanctions and Humanitarian Concerns: Ireland and Angola, 2001-2," *Irish Studies in International Relations* 14 (2003): 95.
3. Tony Hodges, *Angola from Afro-Stalinism to Petro-Diamond Capitalism* (Oxford: James Currey, 2001), 14.
4. This account is based on an unpublished document written by Allan Cain, country director of the Development Workshop, provided to one of the authors during his time in Angola from 2000 to 2002. Mr. Cain has been resident in Angola since the 1970s and was present when these events took

place. Any opinions, errors, or omissions are those of the authors and not of Mr. Cain.

5. Andrea Lari, *Returning Home to a Normal Life? The Plight of Displaced Angolans*, ISS Paper 85, Pretoria, February 2004, p. 2.

6. The existence of such activities and their impact on ordinary people is documented in much greater detailed MSF reports, including *Angola: Behind the Façade of "Normalization"—Manipulation, Violence and Abandoned Populations*, Médecins Sans Frontières (Luanda: 2000).

7. See for example, Jean Francois Bayart, *The State in Africa: The Politics of the Belly* (London and New York: Longman, 1993); Patrick Chabol and Jean Pascal Daloz, *Disorder as a Political Instrument* (Oxford: James Currey, 1999); Christopher Clapham, *Africa and the International System: The Politics of State Survival* (Cambridge: Cambridge University Press, 1996); Jeffrey Herbst, *States and Power in Africa: Comparative Lessons in Authority and Control* (Princeton: Princeton University Press, 2000); William Reno, *Warlord Politics and African States* (Boulder, CO: Lynne Rienner, 1998).

8. Comissão dos Direitos Umanos da Orden dos Advogados de Angola, Diagnóstico preliminar sobre o sistema da admnistração da justiça em Angola—Perspectiva Estático-Estrutural (Luanda, March 2001), 71.

9. Personal correspondence by the author with a human rights specialist who frequently visited the country in those years and produced two reports in March 1998 and April 2001.

10. Office for the Coordination of Humanitarian Affairs in Angola (OCHA), *Humanitarian Situation in Angola—Monthly Analysis* (Luanda: January 2002).

11. Per speech given by Kussumua at the launch of the UN's Consolidated Annual Appeal in Luanda on November 26, 2002.

12. De Mul is also the UN resident coordinator, deputy special representative of the UN secretary general, and, as such, acting officer in charge of the United Nations Mission in Angola (UNMA).

13. IRIN, 2002, "Interview with Erick De Mul, UN Humanitarian Co-ordinator, 13th Nov 2002," available at http://wwww.reliefweb.int/w/rwb.nsf/ByCountryByMonth/0003b86e61b3b6e085256b1f0075614c?OpenDocument&Start=6.22.37&Count=30&Expand=6.22 [August 28, 2004].

14. Margaret E. Keck and Kathryn Sikkink, *Activists Beyond Borders: Advocacy Networks in International Politics* (Ithaca, NY: Cornell University Press, 1996), 1.

15. For an analysis of the strengths and weaknesses of civil society actors, see N. Howen, *Peace Building and Civil Society in Angola: A Role for the International Community* (London: October 2001).

16. Other groups like the Action for Rural Development and Environment (ADRA) provided training to community representatives in various provinces. More localized interventions worth mentioning include Education for

Citizenship run in Huila province by Fr. Pio Wakussanga and the Human Rights Program led by the Development Workshop in Huambo province.

17. For more information about FESA, see C. Messiant, "La Fondation Eduardo dos Santos (FESA)," in *Politique Africaine* 73 (March 1999): 83.

18. Olav Stokke, "Aid and Political Conditionality: Core Issues and State of the Art," in *Aid and Political Conditionality*, ed. Olav Stokke (London: Frank Cass, 1995), 68.

19. David Chandler, *From Kosovo to Kabul, Human Rights and International Intervention* (London: Pluto Press, 2002), 86.

20. For further information on this aspect, see Human Rights Watch, *Some Transparency, No Accountability: The Use of Oil Revenue in Angola and Its Impact on Human Rights* (January 2004); Global Witness, *A Crude Awakening* (December 1999); and *All the Presidents' Men* (March 2002).

21. Common Country Assessment 2002, Angola. *The Post-war Challenges* (Luanda: 2002), chap. 4, pp. 84-94.

22. Personal correspondence by the author with a human rights specialist who frequently visited the country in those years and produced two reports in March 1998 and April 2001.

23. UN Security Council Resolution 1433 (2002).

24. Open letter from the CONGA NGO network, Angola, to the United Nations High Commissioner for Human Rights, Sergio Viera de Mello (Draft) (Luanda: February 2003), 2.

25. For details on the Unit's main activities, visit: http://www.ohchr.org/english/countries/field/angola.htm.

26. Human Rights Watch, *The War Is Over: The Crises of Angola's Internally Displaced Continues* (July 2002), 8.

27. Ibid., p. 9.

28. This is a mechanism that allows members of the Security Council to consult with nonstate actors.

29. Human Right Watch, *World Report 2003*, 2003, p.16.

30. Including, *Angola: Behind the Façade of "Normalization"—Manipulation, Violence and Abandoned Populations*, Médecins Sans Frontières (Luanda: 2000), and *Angola, Sacrifice of a People* (MSF, 2002).

31. Fabrice Weissman, ed., *In the Shadow of "Just Wars": Violence, Politics and Humanitarian Action* (Ithaca, NY: Cornell University Press, 2004), 109.

32. Andrea Lari was a researcher with HRW during this time and was involved in writing this report.

33. Known as the CONGA Liaison Group.

34. Trócaire, *Where the First Are Last: San Communities Fighting for Survival in Southern Angola, 2004.*

35. GOAL Press Release, Feb. 11, 2002; "Angolan Fears Raised," available at www.goal.ie/html/newsroom/angolian_fears_raised10202.htm [Sept. 26,

2002]. Rob Kevlihan was country director with GOAL in Angola when this statement was released.

36. From the poem "Adeus à hora da largada," by Agostinho Neto (1922-1979), first president of the Popular Republic of Angola.

FOUR

Angolan Society Devastated after Four Decades of War

Jan Van Criekinge

In February 2002, Jonas Savimbi, leader of the UNITA antigovernment army, was killed during fighting with government troops in eastern Moxico province. His death changed the face of Angola's political landscape dramatically: a cease-fire agreement has been in place since April 2002. The beginning of a better future? Belgium based coconvenor of the War Resisters International Africa Working Group Jan Van Criekinge visited Angola in June 2003 at the invitation of a very dynamic civil society. This is an excerpt of his report.

Angola is one of the countries in the world that have been most affected by war and violence over the past four decades. The country lies devastated, its infrastructure destroyed, its citizens brutalized by four centuries of slavery, colonialism, war, bloody political conflict, and corruption. The long guerrilla war (since 1961) against Portuguese colonialism under the Salazar dictatorship did not even stop with independence in 1975. Divided among three rival movements—MPLA, UNITA, and FNLA—that represented different ethnic and social groups, each supported by different international powers in the Cold War, the country became a major victim of the ideological power struggle in Southern Africa. Even the end of the Cold War and the collapse of the apartheid system in South Africa did not bring peace any closer. Different efforts to broker peace agreements between the MPLA-government and the "guerrilla rebels" of Savimbi's UNITA have failed over the last decade. The involvement of the United Nations resulted in a disastrous election campaign during 1992. Few recent wars have been as bitterly controversial, both inside and outside the country.

The conflict in Angola has also come at incredible cost. In this twenty-seven-year-long civil war, which pitted the originally Marxist MPLA government against the "rebels" of UNITA, more than one million people were killed, another four million displaced, and most of the country's rural and economic infrastructure—like bridges, roads, and railways—virtually destroyed. No one knows for sure how many landmines are still scattered across Angola, especially in the eastern provinces, but the country is believed to be one of the world's most heavily mined—a threat that will haunt its citizens for decades to come. Malnutrition and disease are widespread. The education system lies in ruins. At the end of 2003, the United Nations estimated that over half a million Angolans would confront starvation if not assisted immediately by international food supplies.

Economic Disparity

Participants at a recent international donor meeting for Angola in Geneva said donors would continue their support in key strategic areas, but international assistance would be dependent on increased efforts by the government of President Jose Eduardo Dos Santos, particularly towards greater transparency. There were also great fears that deepening economic disparity between the small number of extremely wealthy people and the poor majority of Angolans could lead to violent "ruptures" within society. John Rocha from the NGO Angola 2000 said that a recent survey conducted by his team had shown Angolans had high expectations of a "peace dividend" from the government with the end of the war. "It is no secret that a tiny elite [has] most of the wealth in the country. People are prepared to wait for some change in their daily lives but the government has to start delivering. If people do not see changes in the future, there really is no telling what their reaction may be," Rocha said.

On the other hand, a small but powerful elite around President Dos Santos has made big profits from the war: the oil industry in particular is growing. Today, Angola is the second greatest oil-exporting country in sub-Saharan Africa. According to *The Economist*, Angola is "one of the fastest growing countries in Africa and will receive US $3.5 billion of investments from international oil companies." However, this picture is misleading, as it gives the impression that the Angolan economy as a whole is prospering. In essence, all sectors are stagnant, except the oil and diamond businesses. But according to several reports by the Britain-based NGO Global Witness, "a lack of transparency has encouraged massive official corruption, impoverishing people and obstructing the peace initiatives." Additionally, there is "a major problem in the transparent use of growing oil revenues by the Angolan government, leaving a war-torn population with little benefit from massive expected foreign investments."

However, as the war formally ended on April 4, 2002, with the signing of the Memorandum of Understanding between the two opposing parties, peace and the process of reconciliation seems quite sustainable in Angola (with the exception of the oil-rich province of the Cabinda enclave, where the FLEC paramilitary group is still fighting for independence and the government forces have committed lots of violations of human rights and have threatened local peace activists). In this process, grassroots groups and churches played a very important role. For instance, a report by Alex Vines highlights the important role that NGOs will need to play within an atmosphere characterized by "elite domination, using the almost perpetual state of war as an excuse."

Development of Civil Society

Civil society as such did not really develop in Angola before the ruling MPLA party had renounced its monopoly on all social and political activity. Even today the civil society operates in an atmosphere where war has been used by the government to repress what it feels is against its interests.

For example, press freedom is guaranteed on paper, but the Angolan government has often been accused of censoring the independent media. Journalist Rafael Marques has been stopped from leaving the country several times and spent some time in prison after writing critical articles about the corruption of the presidency. The independent journalists that I met in Luanda (from Radio Ecclesia and the weekly papers *Folha 8* and *Angolense*) were all afraid of speaking very openly about the mismanagement and corruption at the higher levels of politics, military, and the international business community as they feared prosecution and even personal threats.

But the independent press has not been the only victim in civil society. The government's attempts to silence those it deems a threat to its interests have also led to a lot of tension between the state and the churches. This occurs especially in the southern provinces, where the question of land rights provokes sharp confrontations between former army generals (who have been able to illegally occupy large fazendas) and local farmers and nomadic pastoralists, and where the church is playing a great role in the struggle for social justice.

A local Catholic priest, Padre Jacinto Pio Wacussanga, president of the radical human rights association ALSSA, has taken a leading role in defending the rights of the landless laborers against the "new" military landlords. In 2003 he and his colleagues received repeated death threats. But they are convinced of the strength of nonviolence as a means of changing society.

The independent media, human rights organizations, and churches are helping to stabilize the peace so much desired by the great majority of the Angolan population. The consolidation of peace depends primarily on how the reconstruction process addresses the profound social divisions, political alienation from the one-party state and its institutionalized corruption on all levels, and the poverty that sustained the war for so many years. The reconstruction should, in the first place, meet the needs of the millions of desperately poor people living in rural communities who, completely isolated from large urban and economic centers and confronted with the deadly consequences of widespread land mines in their daily lives, have so far seen too few tangible benefits of peace.

The resettlement of some four million displaced persons and war refugees continues to be a cause of some concern. But major confrontations have been avoided so far, due to the mediation of churches and other grassroots initiatives.

Women and Children

One of the many initiatives taken by Angolan women is the peace group MPD (Mulheres, Paz e Desenvolvimento—Women, Peace and Development). In May 2000—even before the formal end of the war—the MPD launched an "Apelo de Mulheres para a Paz" (Women's Appeal for Peace) in which they asked all the parties involved in the war to immediately stop the brutal recruitment of soldiers. MPD's chair, Cesinanda de Kerlan Xavier, said that the appeal got lots of reaction in society at the time when the Dos Santos government was launching the "final total war for victory." "As women and mothers we no longer wanted our sons and husbands taken away for a war that was destroying us all. We expressed the great desire for peace and development among the Angolan women."

How many young girls were used by Angola's warring parties during its twenty-seven-year war is anyone's guess. Denial—by both sides—and fear of discrimination and stigma among former girl soldiers continue to stand in the way of any effort to come up with precise figures.

In the past, both the government and the former rebel group UNITA have denied recruiting child soldiers. However, Human Rights Watch

(HRW) has claimed that minors were widely used by both sides during the conflict. Conservative estimates put the number of children who bore arms for UNITA at 6,000. HRW has noted that the actual figure was probably much higher. The refusal to acknowledge the role played by child soldiers, especially girls, during Angola's hostilities has complicated efforts by aid groups to address the problem. Christian Children's Fund (CCF) in Angola is one of the few NGOs that has attempted to tackle the needs of children who participated in the war, but it says it has had to broaden the scope of its project to include all children, not only child soldiers.

What Does the Future Hold?

International donor organizations have criticized Angola's alleged lack of fiscal transparency and continuing human rights abuses. Human Rights Watch has claimed in a report from January 2004 that more than U.S. $4 billion in state oil revenue "disappeared" from Angolan government coffers between 1997 and 2002, an amount roughly equal to the entire sum the government spent on all social programs during the same period. According to HRW, "an estimated 900,000 Angolans are still internally displaced. Millions more have virtually no access to hospitals or schools, [and] according to United Nations estimates, almost half of Angola's 7.4 million children suffer from malnutrition."

International agencies have to help millions of Angolans to survive, although Angola could be one of the richest countries in Africa if its wealth were used in a better way. Observers have pledged support for the demobilization process and offered to help in further implementing the terms of the Lusaka Protocol, on which the peace agreement of April 2002 is based.

The large number of weapons which remain in private hands has also been noted as a threat to stability, with an estimated one third of the country's 14 million calling for Angola to undertake a process of national reconciliation in which general elections should be held in 2006. But it still has a long way to go.

Recommended Websites

Global Witness: http://www.globalwitness.org

Angola Human Rights Watch: http://www.hrw.org/wr2kr/Africa/Angola.html

IRIN (Integrated Regional Information Network of OCHA, United Nations Humanitarian Office): http://www.reliefweb.int/rw/dbc.nsf/doc104?OpenForm&rc=1&cc=ago

Angola Peace Monitor, monthly published by the British NGO Action for Southern Africa (ACTSA): http://www.actsa.org/page-1084-Angola%20 Peace%20Monitor.html

Nederlands Instituut voor Zuidelijk Afrika (Dutch NGO specialized in support for independent media in Southern Africa): http://www.niza.nl

Recommended Books on the Angolan Civil War and the Economic Impact of the Oil and Diamond Industries

Fernando Anreson Guimarães, *The Origins of the Angolan Civil War: Foreign Intervention and Domestic Political Conflict* (Macmillan, 1998)

Tony Hodges, *Angola from Afro-Stalinism to Petro-Diamond Capitalism* (African Issues series, Fridtjof Nansen Institute (Oslo), James Currey (Oxford), Indiana University Press (Bloomington), in association with the International African Institute, Oxford, 2001, 199 pp.

FIVE

Building Peace after Genocide in Rwanda: Religion, Spirituality, and Postconflict Reconciliation

Joseph Sebarenzi

Introduction

Religion possesses one of the most powerful traditions and tools, not to mention doctrines, for peace building and reconciliation.[1] Religion is pervasive in the life of Rwandans, whether in private encounters or in public arenas. Rwandans have a common saying, *Imana yirirwa ahandi ikarara i Rwanda* (God may spend the day elsewhere, but always spends the night in Rwanda). Such a cultural system of beliefs, with God always in the foreground, can be used as a basis for, and as a powerful tool in, the reconciliation efforts between the Hutu and Tutsi.

The conflict between the Hutu and Tutsi in Rwanda is deep-rooted and has escalated into violence over the last five decades. The climax of this ethnopolitical violence was the genocide against the minority Tutsi in 1994, during which time more than one million people were slaughtered in ninety days.

In the aftermath of the genocide and after the new regime came to power, the government embarked on a series of reconciliation programs. So far, however, reconciliation efforts have been limited to traditional peacebuilding activities, including power sharing between the two ethnic groups, the demobilization and integration of ex-combatants, a commission on unity and reconciliation, and the trials of genocide perpetrators. Not only are these activities poorly implemented, they also lack a spiritual dimension, thus overlooking the historical role of religious beliefs in the lives of Rwandans, as well as the spiritual revival that has been taking place since the end of the genocide.

In this chapter, I argue that effective reconciliation between the Hutu and the Tutsi requires going beyond the conventional framework; it must also entail the inclusion of a spiritual dimension as a basis for reconciliation. The effort should also include the involvement of religious institutions, whose followers make up 100 percent of the Rwandan population. This analysis is divided into four subheadings. Section one discusses the destructive nature of the conflict between the Hutu and Tutsi. Section two analyzes the attempts at reconciliation so far. Section three explains the need for a spiritual or religious dimension to supplement conventional reconciliation activities. And section four highlights the survival of religious beliefs despite the reprehensible behavior of some church leaders and some believers during the genocide.

The Destructive Nature of Violence in Rwanda

The cycles of violence for almost half a century between the Hutu and Tutsi have led to a huge loss of lives. It is beyond comprehension and is extremely paradoxical, since both groups speak the same language, share the same religion, live side by side, and have extensively intermarried.

The first incident of interethnic violence occurred in 1959 at the beginning of the struggle for independence. The struggle evolved into violent political competition by the two ethnic groups, reflecting the "divide-and-rule" policy implemented by the colonial power. The MDR-Parmehutu party won the elections in the early sixties, and Gregoire Kayibanda was Rwanda's first president. This victory took place in the midst of extreme violence that left a great number of Tutsi dead and drove many more into exile. From 1959 to 1967, some 20,000 Tutsi were killed, and 300,000 fled in terror to neighboring countries.[2] With such a catastrophe, coupled with a win-lose political situation, the relationship between the two ethnic groups deteriorated.

With the violent ethnic conflict and the unsatisfactory election process during the 1960s, the new government had a duty to initiate reconciliation between the two communities, reach out to the Tutsi, and make them feel safe, in order to maintain peace in the country. Instead, the government endlessly celebrated the Hutu political victory over the Tutsi, thereby encouraging the stereotypes against the already frightened Tutsi community.

The newly elected government eventually evolved into a dictatorship, escalating the tensions between Hutu from the north and those from the south. In 1973, another wave of violence occurred against the Tutsi. Many Tutsi were killed, and many more were forced to flee the country. As a young boy, I witnessed the house burnings and lootings. Shortly after the cessation of violence, President Kayibanda was ousted through a bloody coup d'état by Major General Juvenal Habyarimana, another Hutu.

In 1990, Tutsi refugees formed the Rwandan Patriotic Front (RPF) and attacked Rwanda from Uganda. This was the beginning of a four-year war that culminated in the genocide against the Tutsi. More than one million Tutsi were killed in ninety days from April 6 to July 4, 1994. The number of dead bodies in Rwanda accumulated at nearly three times the rate of Jewish dead during the Holocaust; it was the most efficient mass killing since the atomic bombings of Hiroshima and Nagasaki.[3] My parents and my six siblings were among the dead; my stepbrothers and sisters and many other relatives were also killed.

In July 1994, the RPF, led by Major General Paul Kagame, a Tutsi, seized power. Instead of upholding respect for human rights and abstaining from acts of vengeance, it "indiscriminately committed widespread and systematic killings of Hutu in a process of rough retribution for the genocide."[4] The RPF is actually alleged to have committed war crimes and crimes against humanity against the Hutu before, during, and after the genocide. The new government is accused of having been engaged in the massive slaughter of civilians whom it considered supporters of the enemy, both in Rwanda and in the Democratic Republic of the Congo.[5] In the Democratic Republic of the Congo, the "RPF soldiers committed massacres, other atrocities, and violations of international humanitarian law, especially in the Eastern provinces, including crimes against humanity."

These blameworthy acts impeded the chances for reconciliation between the two communities. Furthermore, like previous governments, Kagame's regime engaged in triumphalist celebrations accompanied by the implicit assimilation of all Hutu genocide perpetrators. Eventually, the new government developed into an oppressive regime and repressed whomever opposed any of its policies.

Under successive regimes, the consequences of violence have been catastrophic. Rwandans, regardless of ethnic background, carry scars of brutalities and dehumanization. Under the surface, the tensions between the Hutu and Tutsi remain strong, but rather than address these tensions, the government acts like everything is fine between the two groups. There have, however, been some attempts at reconciliation between the two communities since the new government came to power in July 1994.

Reconciliation Efforts

The new regime has declared reconciliation its utmost priority. It is self-designated a "government of national unity." Consequently, it has made some efforts to reconcile the Hutu and Tutsi and has indeed achieved some tangible results. However, the government has not really been able to provide healing for the consequences of violence (fear, anger, resentment, feelings of insecurity, and so on). These emotions need to be dealt with in order to lay the foundation for a lasting reconciliation. This remains a far-reaching goal.

The government was able to accomplish some conventional aspects of postconflict reconstruction, including refugee repatriation, the inclusion of former soldiers into the army and police, the inclusion of both Hutu and Tutsi in the government, the creation of a commission for unity and reconciliation, and the bringing of the perpetrators to justice. These achievements are remarkable, but more is needed. There are two specific components of reconciliation, power sharing and justice, that must still be incorporated into the government's agenda.

Power sharing in the aftermath of mass violence is obviously a prerequisite to reconciliation in divided societies. Unlike previous regimes in Rwanda, in which Hutus were excluded from power, the current Kagame regime comprises a significant number of Hutus at all levels of government. However, these Hutu have limited powers; one may even say that they are in positions of power but have no real power, which is a source of frustration. This is also a result of ethnic enginering. Some Tutsi have also been installed as "figureheads," as it were. When this is done to people from the opposite ethnic group, it would seem to arise from discrimination and favoritism. The Hutus in the executive branch of the government do not really represent their ethnic group; they are handpicked by the president, who uses them as long as they serve his purposes. This unpleasant situation has resulted into the resignation of President Pasteur Bizimungu and has led to the exile of other prominent Hutus, including two former prime ministers.

In deeply divided societies, the mere inclusion of members of the opposite group in the power structure/government is not enough. The former rival groups need to fairly share power, to partner, and to have some form of veto power on sensitive matters. Such a community of power is called consensus democracy. A well-designed model of consensus democracy can undoubtedly help Rwandans overcome the legacy of violence and put an end to destructive power struggles between the minority and majority groups. Consensus democracy has the advantage of encompassing the attributes of democracy and the win-win aspects of reconciliation. So far, the government has altogether rejected the idea of a consensus democracy, opting for a sham democracy and avoiding confronting the conflict.

Justice is the second pillar of reconciliation in postconflict reconstruction. In the face of a huge number of perpetrators, and the unrelenting cry for justice by victims, the government had a tough decision to make. On the one hand, the survivors demanded punitive justice, and on the other hand, the international community pressed for a more flexible justice—restorative justice. The government opted for a mix of both kinds of justice and classified the suspects into four categories.

The first category includes the masterminds behind the planning of the genocide and the perpetrators of particularly heinous murders or sexual torture. Suspects in this category are tried by ordinary courts, and are subject to the death penalty. The accused from the other three categories are handled by *Gacaca* jurisdictions and can receive reduced sentences if they fully confess to their roles in the genocide, plead guilty to the crimes committed, and apologize to the victims. These three categories are in descending order of crimes committed.

The second category includes those guilty of voluntary homicide, of having participated in or been complicit in voluntary homicide or acts against persons resulting in death; those having inflicted wounds with intent to kill; and those who committed other serious violent acts that did not result in death.

Those who committed violent acts without intent to kill constitute the third category.

In the fourth category are those who committed crimes against property.

Gacaca is a conciliatory type of justice, which was traditionally used to settle civil disputes between neighbors or families. The government defines *Gacaca* as a system of participative justice whereby the population is given the chance to speak out against the committed atrocities, and to judge and punish the authors, with the exception of those classified by the law in the first category, who will be judged and punished by the ordinary courts according to common law rules. The *Gacaca* system was initiated primarily because of the need to speed up the trials of more than 100,000 detainees on the charges of genocide. Some 26,000 judges were elected throughout the country to help try the cases.

Critics of the *Gacaca* system argue that genocide cannot be dealt with through a justice system designed for minor offenses. "Generally, the types of conflict dealt with by *Gacaca* are related to land use, land rights, cattle, marriage, inheritance rights, loans, and damages to properties caused by one of the parties or animals."[6] Another criticism relates to the unfairness of *Gacaca*, given the fact that it deals with genocide committed against the Tutsi but does not provide a hearing for crimes committed against the Hutu by the Tutsi.

After a pilot phase, the *Gacaca* courts were finally launched in March 2005. Unfortunately, they have not improved the relationship between the two communities, and complaints abound on each side. The Tutsi survivors complain that most suspects deny their part in the genocide, while others confess without showing any sign of remorse. Some of the suspects, on the other hand, claim innocence, and maintain that *Gacaca* is a political tool designed to discriminate against the Hutus and to silence voices crying out for political change. As a consequence, in 2006, more than 10,000 Hutu fled to neighboring Burundi and to Uganda. So far, the expected apology that the Tutsi survivors want has not been forthcoming, nor has forgiveness been given to the perpetrators. More seriously, the major parties to the conflicts, both the survivors and the suspects, do not trust the process. This is one huge hurdle that must be crossed before the system has any credibility. Only if people see the system as being credible will it be effective.

To overcome these obstacles, the government should create a truth and reconciliation commission, similar to that in South Africa, that would look into all the human rights violations committed by both sides. It would also help to initiate a debate on a model of restorative justice that would fit the complex Rwandan situation.

The process of reconciliation has definitely not been going well. The tensions between the two communities remain strong. Some of the Hutu perpetrators have failed to admit to their crimes, and some of the Tutsi have found the crimes difficult to forgive. The communities continue to live side by side, with a fear of future violence or revenge. Recently, Hutu refugees have made allegations on the BBC of preparations under way in Rwanda for widespread revenge against the Hutu. These allegations were categorically rejected by a government representative. In any case, this situation shows how ineffective the process of reconciliation has been so far. It also reflects the urgent need for alternatives to the current approach. The recourse to religious beliefs as a complement to conventional peacebuilding activities may help.

The Need for a Spiritual Dimension to Reconciliation

Spirituality or religious practices are ubiquitous in the lives of Rwandans. From daily greetings and exclamations to wedding and funeral ceremonies, the name of God is constantly invoked. Rwandans, both leaders and ordinary people, believe that nothing is impossible with God; they are convinced that what is impossible with men is possible with God. Those who are spiritually active maintain that the complex task of reconciliation between the Hutu and Tutsi will not be achieved unless Rwandans seek God's help and act in accordance with His will. If adequately utilized, such beliefs may constitute a potential tool for effective reconciliation.

The common greeting in Rwanda is "Praise Jesus!" and the response is "Forever!" Muslims use the word "salaam," which means "peace." The greeting used to be "Amashyo!" and the response was "Amashyongore!" These relate to the ownership of cows, but with the introduction of Christianity at the end of the nineteenth century, the most popular greeting became a reference to God or Jesus. The twentieth century saw a large number of Rwandans converted to Christianity.

Former King Rudahigwa was also a Christian convert. He was baptized Leon Charles, and became a strong advocate of the new spirituality, which was substantially similar to local spirituality in terms of values such as reverence to God, love, and justice. The king was so enthusiastic about Christianity that he "offered" Rwanda to Christ. This prompted the widespread conversion of Rwandans to Christianity, especially to Catholicism. Rudahigwa's successor, King Kigeli V, was also and remains a devout Christian. From his exile in the United States, he regularly calls Rwandans to reconciliation and to trust in God. He told me that the fear of God would constitute a strong foundation for the reconciliation of Rwandans.

In the aftermath of the 1994 genocide, some political leaders have sought wisdom and help from God in the process of reconciliation. On the eve of the year 2000, the president and other high-ranking officials joined Christians of all denominations for a special prayer service. This unique event took place in the major stadium located in the capital, Kigali. The prayer topic was reflective of the faith of Rwandan Christians: "If my people, who are called by my name, will humble themselves and pray and seek my face and turn from their wicked ways, then will I hear from heaven and will forgive their sins and heal their land."[7]

I participated in this gathering and spoke at it as a Christian and as the head of Parliament. In my address, I cited a biblical passage in reference to the role of God in postconflict reconstruction: "Unless the Lord builds the house, its builders labor in vain. Unless the Lord watches over the city, the watchmen stand guard in vain."[8]

The ultimate purpose of the prayer was to draw Rwandans to turn away from hatred, live by spiritual values, and allow God's blessings to flow on the nation. This was in line with the theology of reconciliation, whose cardinal point is that reconciliation is first and foremost the work of God, and we human beings are but agents of that reconciliation. For us to be faithful and effective agents of God's reconciliation, we must take care to maintain close contact with God.

In Rwanda, peace education—with an emphasis on spirituality—should be instituted to equip children with strong beliefs in peace and human rights. As Martha Minow argues, "If we can educate young people to respect others, to understand the cost of group hatreds, to avoid stereotypes, to develop tools for resolving disputes, to choose to stand up to demagogues, and to be peacemakers, we might hope to prevent future violence."[9]

In Rwanda, religious studies used to be one of the most important classes, and schoolchildren used to recite daily prayers, but these have significantly diminished. Such programs should be reinstated, and peace education as a whole should be part of the curriculum for reconciliation to be implemented and sustained.

In addition to its role in building peace, spirituality can be a powerful anchor in times of tragedies. It can help Rwandans recover from past traumatic events. When people ask me how I cope with the ordeals that I went through, I simply say: It is God's blessing! This is directly related to my upbringing in Christianity. Spirituality helps victims to accept without resistance whatever harms have already been inflicted on them and to trust God regardless of circumstances. I always say that there is nothing I can do to bring back my parents. I cannot undo what has already been done. What matters now is to focus on the future, to resist any temptation for revenge, and to recall that all of us as human beings remain accountable to God.

In his peacebuilding work in Ghana, Hizkias Assefa observed that people believe that they are accountable for their behavior to an entity greater than themselves and that even if they managed to deceive each other, there is an all-knowing, all-perceiving being who challenges them to be honest.[10] Such a belief is vital to reconciliation, and most Rwandans are sensitive to it. It would therefore be worthwhile for policymakers to incorporate it into all programs and activities pertaining to reconciliation.

If Rwandan policymakers endorse the use of spirituality in reconciliation, ordinary people will be open to the idea. Rwandans are generally obedient to authority as a result of ancient beliefs that kings represent God on earth. Rwandans tend to believe in and obey what political and religious leaders ask them to do. During successive tragedies, people did what they were asked to do by Rwanda's leaders. The thinking is that if they do evil when asked by their leaders to do so, they will also do good if encouraged by leaders. This was the root of my proposal for a spirituality-based ritual in the truth and reconciliation commission. I suggested the following ritual:

> The ritual ceremonies would take the form of gathering around drinks, dances, speeches, and prayers. Each offender would

swear in the name of God that s/he will never again commit a crime against the other community. Victims would also swear to never take revenge. The gathering will pray for the offenders, the victims, and their families. The elderly, family members, and community representatives as well as church and political leaders would congratulate the offenders and the victims, and then they would also pledge to spare no efforts in promoting reconciliation between Hutu and Tutsi.

Such a ritual, chaired by church and political leaders, and invoking God as a witness would seriously compel Rwandans to keep their reconciliation commitment.

Spiritual beliefs are not an exclusive attribute of Rwandans. Other cultures also seek guidance and strength from God, especially in times of challenges. President Anwar Sadat of Egypt and Prime Minister Menachem Begin of Israel at Camp David in 1978 called upon God's help for peace in the Middle East. The two leaders, along with then-president of the U.S. Jimmy Carter, issued the following statement:

After four wars, despite vast human efforts, the Holy Land does not yet enjoy the blessings of peace. Conscious of the grave issues that face us, we place our trust in the God above of our fathers, from whom we seek wisdom and guidance. As we meet here at Camp David, we ask people of all faiths to pray with us that peace and justice may result from these deliberations.

Religion or faith is definitely essential for reconciliation. Reconciliation rooted in religious beliefs has the likelihood of being sustained. Some leaders use religion as a political tool, without acting accordingly, which is truly unfortunate! I believe that in Rwanda, reconciliation is likely to occur if the Hutu and Tutsi embrace spirituality, engage in genuine repentance and forgiveness, and consider themselves first and foremost sons and daughters of the same God. However, repentance and forgiveness are difficult unless one is equipped with strong spiritual values.

The Survival of Religious Beliefs:
True Repentance, Apology, and Forgiveness

True repentance, apology, and forgiveness are essentially spiritual values. These values compel people of faith to humble themselves and to apologize and forgive; their beliefs compel them to do so. "For if you forgive men when they sin against you, your heavenly Father will also forgive you;

but if you do not forgive men their sins, your Father will not forgive your sins[11]." (Matthew 5:14-15). Not only is forgiveness a religious and moral responsibility, it is also transformative for both victims and perpetrators.

In Rwanda, perpetrators are encouraged to apologize in order to take advantage of the provisions of the law. Victims are asked to forgive for reconciliation to take place. However, no mention is made of apology and forgiveness being the right thing to do according to religious principles. This would have helped Rwandans find meaning in such a difficult process and subsequently to engage in it.

Lederach informs us that in Nicaragua, religious beliefs were used in the process of reconciliation. At the opening of each village meeting, the Nicaraguan conciliators read, "Truth and mercy have met together; peace and justice have kissed".[12] In this context, mercy includes acceptance, forgiveness, support, compassion, and healing. For the Nicaraguan participants, without compassion and forgiveness, healing and restoration would have been out of the question.[13] This seems to have helped the country move toward peaceful coexistence.

However, as Madikizela remarks, the subject of forgiveness creates a lot of skepticism among some people, who find it hard to imagine how perpetrators can genuinely and meaningfully apologize other than in self-interest, and how victims can forgive in the face of tragedy.[14] It is true that repentance and forgiveness are difficult to imagine in the wake of mass violence. But it is exactly for that reason that spiritual beliefs become essential in reconciliation.

Spiritually-minded people embrace repentance or forgiveness with the belief that they are the proper things to do. They do so with the conviction that God wants them to adopt that lifestyle, with the belief that heaven belongs to the humble and the forgiving. This may sound naive or even irrational. But as one anthropologist noted, irrational beliefs can serve the purpose of stability far better than rational ones. Whether repentance and forgiveness can be scientifically proven does not matter very much; what counts is that they can be effective. They can transform the hearts of the victims and the perpetrators, and they can help break the cycle of violence between the Hutu and Tutsi.

Confession and apology are not only spiritual responsibilities, they are also liberating. Perpetrators can never enjoy inner peace unless they lay down their burden of wrongdoing. Genocide perpetrators remain haunted by fear, guilt, and other trauma associated with their crimes until they take the opportunity to safely confess and, ideally, receive pardon. The Bible confirms the healing power of confession: "Therefore, confess your sins to one another, and pray for one another so that you may be healed".[15]

Making apology also contributes to the healing of the victim, because it is a sign that the perpetrator acknowledges the suffering of his/her victim and makes a commitment to not repeat the offense in the future. It is difficult for both parties, but very important to the reconciliation process.

As mentioned earlier, victims are encouraged to forgive and not to engage in revenge. The Bible prohibits revenge: "Do not seek revenge or bear a grudge against one of your people, but love your neighbor as yourself".[16] Jesus categorically rejects the culture of revenge found in the Old Testament, telling his disciples: "You have heard that it was said, 'an eye for an eye and a tooth for a tooth.' But I tell you, do not resist evil by evil".[17]

In addition, forgiveness relieves victims of burdensome emotions that may otherwise be manifested through resentment and vengeful acts. Olga Botcharova notes that forgiveness is the culmination of healing, the most vital need of a victim and a way to freedom from victimhood[18] (Botcharova, 290). Forgiveness is not weakness, but strength, and it is a move toward self-healing and toward the healing of the offender. It corresponds to both spiritual values and pragmatism. However, forgiveness should never be confused with giving up on justice or condoning injustice. The Bible recommends maintaining justice in courts[19] and upholds the combination of true justice with mercy and compassion.[20] This is typically a restorative justice; it has the advantage of focusing on restoration of broken relationships, not on the punishment of the offender. Such justice is the one preferred by Rwandan believers, because punitive justice would inevitably perpetuate hatred between the Hutu and Tutsi.

Conclusion: Spiritual Values Are beyond Religions and Religious Individuals

Spiritual values and faith go beyond mere declarations of spirituality; they do not depend on how religious institutions or religious individuals act. Spiritual values are profound and are deeply anchored in religious faith. Rwandans did not give up their core beliefs following the involvement of some "believers" in the perpetration of genocide. Many Rwandan genocide victims remained committed to their core spiritual beliefs even though some pastors, priests, and nuns took part in the genocide. The comforting factor may have been the courage of some believers who resisted evil and protected those at risk of extermination.

My family has experienced firsthand the ambivalent behavior of believers. On the one hand, my sister Edith Yehofayire was among the people killed in a Christian church during the genocide. She was killed along with her three daughters and many other relatives. On the other hand, my stepsister, Brigitte Mukarugambwa, her husband, and their four children were protected by two Hutu Christian women. These brave women, thanks to their spiritual beliefs, took great risks protecting those who were being hunted down, at the cost of their own lives.

Most Hutu Muslims did not participate in the genocide, and some took the risk of hiding Tutsi. They resisted the strong and forceful campaign by the government machinery.

One of the notorious killers was Ngeze Hassan, now serving a life sentence at the UN court tribunal in Tanzania. Strangely, however, he protected a number of Tutsi. I assume that he was torn between allegiance to Muslim beliefs, which recommend love, and evil ideas of hatred. He acted against Islam and against spiritual beliefs, and as such he, not his religion, is responsible for his crimes.

Some religious dignitaries collaborated with political leaders at the expense of the teachings of their religions. For a few years, Catholic archbishop Vincent Nsengiyumva was a member of the central committee of MRND, the ruling party at the time of the genocide. Fellow Christians and non-Christians raised questions about the incompatibility between religion and partisan politics. The archbishop eventually quit the political party, but remained close to political leaders and failed to denounce the genocide. His involvement in politics may have motivated his murder by Tutsi rebels during the genocide. Many other church leaders failed to resist the system and took part in the genocide. Some were arrested and are presently being held at the UN tribunal in Tanzania.

The appalling behavior of church leaders in the genocide caused some Rwandans to wonder why God allowed such evil to happen. They have become disillusioned and disappointed with their churches and clergy. Some believers have not yet recovered from the disappointment. But most believers swiftly shifted the blame from God and church institutions to individual wrongdoers. Pope Jean Paul II declared that the members who went against their religion's teachings are to answer for this and that the Church cannot be held accountable for them. In Rwanda, however, the number of Catholics has decreased, as many Catholics felt betrayed by their religion.

The astonishing fact is that Rwandans have, on the whole, been experiencing a spiritual revival since the end of the genocide. A similar revival occurred during the first half of the twentieth century. Peter Hammond wrote in *Holocaust in Rwanda* that from the 1930s through the 1950s, Rwanda and Burundi were swept by a remarkable spiritual revival.

In the last ten years, more than thirty new Christian denominations have been created, and they all have an impressive and growing number of members. People have embraced new churches as a rejection of traditional denominations, whose members and leaders were directly or indirectly associated with the genocide and other tragedies. A significant number of believers have joined new churches as a quest for peace and reconciliation, which they believe is the work of God through humans. For Christians in Rwanda, real reconciliation is literally the work of God, as he makes a breakthrough in what is, humanly speaking, an impossible situation[21] (Carr, 9).

The government, however, has so far not taken advantage of this unique opportunity. The role of religion in the past and the current spiritual revival have been overlooked by the government. It has not encouraged churches to engage in topics relevant to reconciliation. And so far, churches have generally avoided discussions of peace, justice, and reconciliation for fear of being accused of getting involved in politics.

Reconciliation is by nature a long-term and demanding process; the process is even more complicated when dealing with genocide, war crimes, and other gross human rights violations. The conflict between the Hutu and Tutsi falls into this category. Reconciliation between the two communities requires more than conventional peacebuilding activities, more than having both communities in government institutions, more than the mere repatriation of refugees, and more than simply punishing the culprits.

Reconciliation in Rwanda may not be sustainable with just the efforts of the truth and reconciliation commission, the implementation of consensus democracy, and the implementation of restorative justice, which are ordinarily effective ingredients for addressing the consequences of mass violence in divided societies. A lasting reconciliation requires utilizing people's beliefs, faith, and religion to better access empathy, genuine repentance/apology, and forgiveness, which are generally spiritual values. Rwandans of all ethnic and religious backgrounds strongly believe in God's omnipotence and omnipresence. Their strong belief system should be tapped into and used in the reconciliation process. If the government does not take advantage of Rwanda's historical attachment to religion and the current spiritual revival, it will have missed a great opportunity. If the issue of reconciliation is not handled properly, with structures set in place to forge lasting trust and build community between the two groups, the present situation of submerged ethnic tensions may very well lead to a reerruption of violence.

Notes

1. Olga Botcharova, "Implementation of track two diplomacy: Developing a model of forgiveness," in *Forgiveness and reconciliation: Religion, public policy, and conflict transformation,* ed. Raymond G. Helmick, SJ, and Rodney L. Petersen (West Conshohocken, PA: Templeton Foundation Press, 2001), 269-94.

2. African Union. *Rwanda: The preventable genocide.* The Report of the International Panel of Eminent Personalites to Investigate the 1994 Genocide in Rwanda and the Surrounding Events, 2000, vi

3. Philip Gourevitch, We wish to inform you that tomorrow we will be killed with our families (New York: Picador,1998), 4.

4. African Union, *Ibid.*, 254

5. Alison Des Forges, Leave none to tell the story: Genocide in Rwanda (New York: Human Rights Watch, 1999), 27.

6. Luc Reychler and Thania Paffenholz, *Peacebuilding: A field guide.* (Boulder, CO: Lynne Rienner, 2001), 129.

7. 2 Chronicles 7:14.

8. Psalms 127:1.

9. Martha Minow, "Education for Coexistence," in *Imagine Coexistence: Restoring Humanity After Violent Ethnic Conflict,.* ed. Antonia Chayes and Martha Minow. San Francisco: Jossey Bass, 2003), 214. See also Martha Minow, *Between Vengeance and Forgiveness.* Boston: Beacon Press, 1998.

10. Hizkias Assefa, "Coexistence and reconciliation in the northern region of Ghana," in *Reconciliation, justice, and coexistence: Theory and practice,* ed. M. Abu-Nimer (Lanham, MD: Lexington Books, 2001), 165-85.

11. Matthew 5:14-15.

12. Psalms: 85-10.

13 John Paul Lederach, *Building peace: Sustainable reconciliation in divided societies.* (Washington, DC: United Institute of Peace, 1999), 28.

14. Pulma Gobodo-Madikizela, Pumla. 2002. Remorse, forgiveness, and dehumanization: Stories from South Africa. *Journal of Humanistic Psychology* 42(1), Winter 2002, 12.

15. James 5:16.

16. Leviticus 18:19.

17. Matthew 5:38.

18. Olga Botcharova, *Ibid.*, 290

19. Amos 5:15.

20. Zechariah 6:9.

21. Lucy Carr, Understanding and responding to genocide in Rwanda: Approaches of Christianity and African religions (p. 9). Presented in November 1994. Available at http://www.grandslacs.net/doc/0007.pdf

Six

"We Wish to Inform You..." Gil Courtemanche's *A Sunday by the Pool In Kigali*

The mobilization for the final termination campaign swung into full gear only when Hutu Power was confronted by the threat of peace.

—Philip Gourevitch

The irony of the words above demands serious examination. How exactly can peace generate war and, in Rwanda, genocide? What stories that we read are true? How can we tell? Articles in journals, magazines, and newspapers echo each other. Wars, violence, terrorism, and genocide compete with lies, deception, and hypocrisy for lead stories in the daily news. Iraq, Haiti, Somalia, Kosovo, Rwanda, Israel, Palestine, Nigeria, Congo, Cuba, Sudan; the list seems endless as it grows. Although many write about international conflict and its consequences, several authors believe that fiction speaks truth in ways that news bullets cannot offer. In his new book about humans' "terrible love of war," psychologist James Hillman states, "War's inhumanity is captured best by poets and novelists, for their imaginations reach into the afflicted soul beyond reporting of the facts."[1] Novelist John Le Carré agrees, because "lies that have been distributed are now so many and so persistent that arguably fiction is the only way to tell the truth" about war.[2] Writing about Rwanda's genocide in *A Sunday at the Pool in Kigali*, Gil Courtemanche offers readers a fictional counterpoint to Philip Gourevitch's history of the background to the genocide and an account of its aftermath. In an interdisciplinary and multicultural narrative, Canadian journalist Courtemanche reaches into his own "afflicted soul" and reports far beyond the facts.

When interviewed on CBC, Gil Courtemanche was asked why his novel was so "relentlessly graphic." He stated, "I tried to write a sweet book about genocide. But it wasn't possible."[3] His satiric response suggests the tone of the novel. This article examines *A Sunday at the Pool...*, explaining the fictional style and factual, political content of a story in which the activity at the pool at Hôtel des Mille Collines becomes a microcosm of life in Rwanda in the early 1990s. Revealing the competition among diverse facets of society, including the Belgians, Canadians, and United Nations peacekeepers, Courtemanche uncovers the desire for power, influence, and wealth; he also illustrates the growing resentments and fears that tear apart ordinary lives. His satiric, sometimes poetic, and often ironic writing about social disorder, religious hypocrisy, artificial decolonization, rhetorical "development," and AIDS sets the stage for deconstructing the "collateral language" that governments and media often use to deceive the public.[4]

In this complex novel, journalist Bernard Valcourt is sent by the Canadian International Development Agency to Kigali, five years after the death of his wife and departure of his latest lover, to be codirector of a TV station in Rwanda for education about health and AIDS. Because the government "found reasons" not to launch the TV show, a disillusioned Valcourt pretends to be writing a book. Lethargic, he is not writing a book; he is "waiting for a scrap of life to excite him and make him unfold his wings."[5] That "scrap of life" appears in Gentille, a beautiful young Tutsi who thinks that she is Hutu and with whom he falls in love. The love story is neither a subtext nor a parallel plot but an integrated part of a narrative about the love in and of a country in which civil anarchy reigns. Another "scrap of life" appears in Valcourt's documentary about AIDS, especially his focus on Cyprien and Methode, Rwandans who understand better than most the cause of the conditions in their country and who try "to teach [Valcourt] how to live while waiting to die."[6] With increased understanding of Rwandans' philosophy about life and death, along with escalating horror about both the massacres and the one-third of Kigali adults who are dying of AIDS, Valcourt shifts from indifference to action; although he cannot save the people he loves from genocide or AIDS, he can tell their story. Courtemanche uses that story to track the catastrophe, to show that individual lives are the history that matters, and to prevent the readers' amnesia about such events.

Close to the end of the novel, Courtemanche writes about the ten Belgian Blue Berets who were taken prisoner, beaten, and murdered by members of the presidential guard. He notes, "The UN forces made no attempts to free them. The Belgian contingent was recalled by its government. Before leaving, several Belgian soldiers tore up their United Nations badges and spat on the floor."[7] The day is the day before Bernard Valcourt and Gentille's wedding day on April 9, 1994. That day, "CNN spends twenty seconds on the recurrence of ethnic problems in Rwanda, giving assurances, however, that foreign nationals were safe." BBC said little more. "Radio-France Internationale talked about recurrent confrontations and ancestral tribalism, wondering if Africans would ever rid themselves of their ancient demons."[8] During the first nine and one-half months "of fighting exactly one dispatch on the subject report from Rwanda appeared in *The New York Times* and *Washington Post*."[9] Skeptical about "the viability of UN deployments, Richard Clarke, who oversaw peacekeeping policy, believed that another UN failure could doom relations between Congress and the United Nations; he sent a memorandum about "the safety and security of Rwandans" that suggested that the United States was leading efforts "to ensure…the Rwandans were not abandoned." But, as Samantha Power states, "The opposite was true,"[10] *A Sunday at the Pool..*, reveals how the opposite was true, how humanitarian efforts failed, and how the rhetoric of moral concern, to most, was a lie. Courtemanche captures that rhetoric, exposing the language used to brainwash or mislead the local and global population. In their collection *Collateral Language*, John Collins and Ross Glover maintain that the "more control the state has over the language a population hears and the images it sees, the easier it is to develop 'democratic consent.'"[11] In his novel, Courtemanche repeatedly shows how language control promoted and/or allowed genocide. In addition, his blunt narrative and uncompromising clarity about the abuses, rapes, and genocide place him with a distinct group of writers "linked by their willingness to bear witness." These writers have developed what Nicolaus Mills terms a "language of slaughter" that portrays the suffering it describes "unblinkingly while simultaneously making the point that the governments and individuals have the power—if they will only use it to stop this mass suffering."[12]

The novel begins with a protagonist who is an astute observer but a distant man; "paralyzed by the fear of re-entering life fully," middle-aged Bernard Valcourt, a French-Canadian journalist and alter ego to the author, watches, analyzes, and comments, but he feels little and does not act.[13] Still grieving over his wife's death and his partner's departure, he tries to "void love" but awakens to a love of erotic fervor with Gentille. The author uncovers Rwanda's dual obsessions with race and sex, as well as the official refusal to acknowledge the AIDS epidemic. Calling his novel "a chronicle and eye-witness report," he uses real names for characters who actually existed and the "liberty of invention" to convey the true horror of those who planned and executed the genocide. Like the author, Valcourt has no illusions of being drawn to Rwanda on a moral mission. Instead, he sees himself as part of the group of international experts and aid workers, middle-class Rwandans and prostitutes, or melancholy expatriates of various origins who hang out at the pool. To Valcourt, those at the pool participate in a surrealistic drama that they repeat each day: French paratroopers put on "Rambo airs," the "vacuous" whites stress their own importance, the noisy Germans descend like "a battalion of moralizing accountants," and the Quebecois and Belgian aid workers "vie in loud laughter" as they work on "development," that "magic word which dresses up the best and most irrelevant of intentions."[14]

That "magic word" offers an example of the collateral language used to deceive and keep control. The narrator suggests that the "obligatory symbols of decolonization: Constitution Square, Development Avenue, Boulevard of the Republic, Justice Avenue," are the ironic names symbolizing a democracy that does not exist and contradicting conditions in the underbelly of the city, where the poor are sick and dying in mud houses. Deliberate silence appears as a different type of deception. When a Belgian embassy counsellor stops by the pool, he affects "an air of discretion" to avoid speaking about the peace accord and transfer of power that President Habyarimana accepts every six months but never signs, "claiming it's the rainy season, or…his secretary's husband is sick."[15] In a place where "rumors kill" and are "checked out afterward," Rwandans "handle concealment and ambiguity with awesome skill."[16] Valcourt is tired of both the concealment and "pretentious…language" of those who engage in a contest for power.

Lisette, the Canadian consul, in despair over having her golf bag stolen, is but one minor contestant. Golf is her only pleasure, her only "civilized activity." She "abhors" Rwanda, but because she "doesn't know anything but the art of lying politely," she feels "better off" in Kigali than "answering the phone in departmental offices in Ottawa." As Courtemanche satirically notes, Lisette suffers in luxury.[17]

Canada's commander of UN troops does not compete in the lying game like Lisette; he is a "miracle of mimesis…apprehensive, ineloquent and naïve, like Canada."[18] His role, Courtemanche states, is to lead the UN Assistance Mission for Rwanda; UNAMIR's role is to ensure terms of the Arusha peace accord.[19] The major general, a man of duty, is startled, however, when a grenade explodes: "He is not yet used to this peace that kills on a daily basis."[20] Over the days that follow, the general "listens politely to what he already knows." Disturbed by what he sees, he asks for permission to intervene and seize the deposits of arms, but his request is denied. Later, when Valcourt asks him why he does not act when a Rwandan friend, Cyprien, is murdered, the general responds: "I would like to protect civilians, but I do not want to risk…without written authorization. I am not here to save Rwandans, I am here to ensure respect of the Arusha accord."[21] Moreover, he states that the police chief, Colonel Theoneste, swears that he punishes misconduct.[22] The narrator comments, "In UN eyes, the massacre of Cyprien and his wife and children was mere 'misconduct.'"[23] The absurd language of reduction and the reversal of expectations inundate the novel.

Soon after a background history about the "two beginnings" that led to the division of Hutus and Tutsis, Courtemanche offers an example of abuse, fraudulent language, and inaction. When Gentille sees "the body of Melissa," a hotel prostitute and friend, on the metal awning over the pool bar and a "fat, naked Belgian" waving his arms and shouting "The disgusting whore!" she screams, "He tried to kill her! Call the police!"[24] However Gentille might yell, the "hotel management never called the police." The head of security at the Belgian embassy explains to Valcourt and Gentille that "a cheap little prostitute" tried to rob the Belgian, who had only defended himself. At the hospital emergency room, Valcourt and Gentille discover that no Melissa "had been admitted." Unable to find Melissa's body, they go to "the public prosecutor's office to lodge a complaint. The assistant chief prosecutor receives them out of "respect for Valcourt, the citizen of a donor country and above all a neutral country that asked no questions and gave with its eyes-closed…"[25] When Valcourt questions the republic's representative about the murder, however, the man insists that his people are "seeking the path to greater democracy…in our own ways that may surprise others… but must be respected."[26] Besides his hypocritical response, he issues a thinly veiled threat: attributing Valcourt's behavior to "vicissitude of loneliness," he asks, "Monsieur Valcourt, your television contract is still in force, is it not?"[27] The irony of Courtemanche's message is clear: Valcourt, accused of an "error of judgment," is threatened for questioning those in power, while the murderer goes free. Over the course of the novel, Courtemanche connects what appears to be an "ordinary" sex-related crime to the broader behavior of Hutu militiamen, local participants in the genocide, and the blindness of foreign visitors. There is, Courtemanche argues throughout, a direct parallel between men who sow hate with their words and hate with their sperm.

The duplicitous language used to encourage participation in the massacre is identified by both Courtemanche in the novel and many journalists who write about the role of the media in Rwanda. Radio-TV Libre des Mille Collines is the primary station where "broadcasts were a background score to the killings."[28] During a poignant fifth chapter, Valcourt engages in dialogue with Cyprien, a married man who loved his wife and children, sold tobacco, enjoyed random sex, was HIV-positive, and wanted to live long enough to be part of his friend's film. It is, however, in the slaughter of Cyprien, his wife Georgina, and their children that Courtemanche demonstrates the power of the language of Hutu proselytizing and media manipulation.

While visiting Cyprien at home, Valcourt learns about the train-ing of fanatics, the militiamen arriving in Kigali, and the lists of Tutsi names identified for execution. Cyprien also tells him what his cousin, a member of the president's party and a guard in the prisons, said about "the important work for the survival of Rwanda, which is threatened by the cockroaches [slang for Tutsis]. We're eliminating them, he said, "as soon as they arrive."[29] Cyprien knew much more about the massacres that would occur, about his country that had "gorged so greedily on lies and false prophecies."[30] Although as a Tutsi he knows he is at risk, as a friend he wants to help Valcourt and Gentille, so he insists on going to the hotel with them when they leave, despite the deadly roadblocks. Walking back home, Cyprien confronts militiamen who shout the superiority of the Hutus to the cockroaches and sing a popular refrain about work: "We're starting the work, and the work's going to be done right." "Work" was the term always used in the propaganda. It referred to the *corvée* collec-tive and annual community service when the residents of each commune were supposed to participate in cutting down weeds and cleaning up the roads.[31] Courtemanche writes, "No one nowadays understood the word to mean overgrown weeds. But as long as the calls to violence remained in the realm of parable or poetic hyperbole," friendly countries did not have to worry about inhumanity. France, for example, saw Rwandans as "negligible weight," as outside the circle of real humanity, and were ready "to sacrifice to preserve France's civilizing presence in Africa" by condoning the behav-ior and feeding the military with its arms and advisers.[32] Like the Belgians, the French practiced arrogance and blindness; they reinterpreted actions with words constructed to meet their own needs.

Writing about the history of this linguistic violence, Darryl Li asserts that the Rwandan radio station fostered a "culture of obedience." In the ideological universe of Radio-TV Libre des Mille Collines, "one never spoke of killing, but only of 'work' or 'clearing the brush' (courtesy of 'tools,' rather than machetes or clubs…). Hutus rarely used the word "Tutsi"; instead, they used *inyezi* (cockroaches) or *inkotanyi* (the self-given name of RPF fighters).[33] They ruled the behavior of the masses by a language of indirection. Scholars agree that RTLM was a "hate radio" station linked to an elite circle of Hutu hard-liners[34] and that through radio "the genocide unfolded in thousands of locales," bringing ordinary Rwandans into the massacres "in ways at once both terrifying and mundane."[35] Cyprien had tried to explain this phenomenon to Valcourt.

When Valcourt goes to claim Cyprien and Georgina's bodies, the police lie, as the Belgian representative did about Melissa. They tell Valcourt that Cyprien had fallen "blind drunk" in front of a car, as had his wife. Courtemanche uses "the language of slaughter" to tell the grim and barely readable true story: As Cyprien returned home, militiamen shouted, "Come party with us, Cyprien...." Just beyond, "his wife was lying with her skirt pulled up onto her belly. Two young militiamen, laughing hilariously, were holding her legs apart and a third was holding her hand still. A breast was hanging out of her torn, bloodstained T-shirt. The roadblock commander held a revolver to Cyprien's temple," stating: "We've tried everything but nothing works...She can't be normal. We've had her two at a time, one by the front, the other by the back door. And we did it hard...then we used a stick...you know all the secrets...so you're going to show us, Cyprien... what a man's got to do to make your wife come." As the shock begins to fade, Cyprien mounts his wife delicately, as the militiamen howl their impatience and one savagely slashes him "across the back with his machete."[36] Offering a microcosm of the type and tone of the slaughter that appears act after malicious act, Courtemanche allows readers to grasp both the horror and the numbing regularity with which the genocide occurred.

The belching sergeant, however, ignores Valcourt's questions about what really happened and continues "to lie with an assurance and contempt for veracity," stating that Cyprien's children were with relatives. Valcourt later discovers the bodies of the two boys in a huge pool of blood. Seeking Cyprien's girls at the orphanage run by Belgian nuns and sponsored by the president's wife, Valcourt and Gentille were not welcome. The mother superior's words were self-protective: she informed them about the "excellent reputation" of her establishment and how parents, "good, charitable people," invested "a great deal of money" to adopt children that "were sound in body and mind." Valcourt does not raise his voice, but he does contradict her: "You are trying to reduce Rwanda's trade deficit by selling babies," by exporting "fresh young flesh."[37] When Valcourt returns to the pool, his friend Raphael tries to explain: "We're all Rwandans, all prisoners of the same twisted history...I was born filled with hate and prejudice." In each of Cyprien and his wife's wounds, "in the killing of the boys, in the way it was done and the weapons used, there are messages. Each atrocity is a symbol and an example" of what is to come. You've seen a "small rehearsal for a genocide."[38] Focusing on the fallacious language of murder and marketing children, Courtemanche establishes the nature of a place where truth disappears.

The fraudulent use of language appears everywhere in Courtemanche's novel because it was used everywhere in Rwanda, as well as in language about Rwanda by European countries, the United Nations, and the United States. Close to the conclusion, as people began to worry about the massacres, they are assured by authorities that there "was no reason to panic... The Rwandan army with excellent support from its French advisers, who were very active, was in control of the situation."[39] Those words from the novel sound perilously close to Richard Clarke's rhetorical lies at the beginning of this essay about safety and the U.S. ensuring support. They are, in fact, an invitation by the author to see through such political hypocrisy.

Another example of language control appeared in the omission of, or, according to Samantha Power, substitution for, the "g-word." The United Nations, Belgium, France, and the United States refused to say the g-word because that word would demand action. Even General Dallaire, the French-Canadian in charge of UNIMAR, aware of the need to act, was "self-conscious" about calling the killings "genocidal." He had to leaf through the Geneva and Genocide Conventions to look up the relevant definition, and even then he settled on the phrase "acts of genocide." On April 30, 1994, however, Dallaire is cited using the word in a warning that unless the community acts, it "is unable to defend itself against accusations of doing nothing to stop genocide."[40] After the reality of genocide had become "irrefutable," when "bodies choking in the Kagera River" appeared on America's nightly news, "the brute fact of the slaughter failed to influence U.S. policy except in a negative way." The Clinton administration opposed use of the term. Christine Shelly, the State Department spokesperson, began a two-month dance to avoid the "" Instead, phrases such as "acts of genocide" or "ethnic cleansing" served public statements. The UN Security Council was becoming divided over whether to use the word, and on American (and British) insistence, the word "genocide" was excluded from the Security Council statement. Power concludes her comments about the lack of response noting that Rwanda generated no sense of urgency and could safely be avoided by Clinton at no political cost. When General Romeo Dallaire appealed for reinforcements from the UN, not only did he not get more troops but his numbers were cut from 5,000 to 270 on a recommendation to the UN Security Council by Madeleine Albright.[41] Kofi Annan ordered Dalliaire not "to compromise" his impartiality and to avoid combat "except for non-Rwandans." Rwandans pleaded for help but "UN soldiers shooed them away. When peacekeepers had departed," 20,000 Rwandans were killed in three days. Abroad, the "ethnic bloodshed" was thought to be "regrettable but not particularly unusual."[42]

"At the Hôtel des Mille Collines," Power writes, ten peacekeepers and four UN military observers helped to protect the several hundred civilians sheltered there for the duration of the crisis."[43] Those "civilians" are the "almost one thousand" people gathered around the pool in Courtemanche's novel. A few of those characters' comments capture the awareness of and guilt about the escalating brutality. For example, Father Louis, administrator of the World Food Program in Rwanda, after too many years of silence recognizes that his language of "tolerance and moderation" was a way to escape responsibility and consort with bandits and murderers. After an excess of alcohol, he tells Valcourt the truth about the irony of reason and what "reasonable people have accomplished." Holding "good, reasonable, Christian" people accountable for promoting wars, he maintains that when circumstances don't lead "reasonable people to war they close their eyes to injustice—no, they organize injustice. And when they don't organize it, they tolerate it, encourage it, abet and finance it." Stating "I can't keep quiet any longer," Father Louis holds humanitarian organizations that would rather collaborate with a dictator than denounce him and churches, including his Catholic Church and its "blind followers," responsible. Through magnificent "preaching which is empty of meaning...we have been condoning the worst imaginable crimes, in the name of...an abstract eternity," he says.[44]

Father Louis's bold comments about the danger of silence and apathy come close to the words of Methode, Valcourt's friend who dies of AIDS and offers another view-from-the-inside argument. Methode never pretended that he did not know, nor was he silent. The few words that he can speak state the truth in a direct way that others avoid. Stylistically, Courtemanche structures his friend's dying ceremony as a "funerary feast," which Methode terms "the Last Supper," while assuring his friends that he did not take himself for "Jesus Christ." This "feast" is both a contradiction of and an example of what will occur. Although the last days before Methode's death are a celebration of life, his death is prophetic of two different kinds of massacres. The author (and Valcourt) uses the tape of Methode's last stand as an educational history lesson about Tutsi-Hutu relations and AIDS, and about love and hate, as well as a mirror of life in Rwanda.

With only a few days left, Methode desired a "triumphant end" for his life; he wanted to die "clean, drunk, stuffed with food and in front of the television at the hotel.[45] In fact he states that he would "rather die of AIDS than be hacked up by a machete...the fate waiting for all Tutsis."[46] Since the sickness had been keeping him in bed, "Methode had been reading everything he could find about the Jews." Because he was a Tutsi, he felt that he was sharing a similar fate. The Holocaust was a "monstrosity of Western civilization. The original sin of Whites. Here, it would be the barbarian Holocaust, the cataclysm of the poor, the triumph of machete and club."[47] Methode knew that soon there would be "lots of severed arms and legs, women with bellies ripped, children with feet cut off" so that the "Tutsi cockroaches" would be unable to fight.[48] Considering what was to come, Methode wanted to tell his story to Valcourt. Pushing out his words one at a time, Methode says, before we pretended, but today we say "he's Tutsi, Hutu, he's got AIDS…We're often wrong, but it doesn't matter. We live so much with fear it makes us feel better to finger the enemy, and if we can't guess who he is, we invent him."[49]

A short while after Methode dies, about 100 people gather in the hotel conference hall to view Valcourt's film. Methode appears to tell his story and begins with self-description: he is a disc jockey, someone who works at the People's Bank, a man whose favorite music is country and who loves songs, a Tutsi, but "above all" a Rwandan. "I am going to die of AIDS," a sickness the government said did not exist, he says, explaining that he is talking about AIDS because most refuse to talk and "staying silent kills." Prophetically, he announces that "millions" will die of AIDS and malaria, "but most of all from a worse sickness for which there's no condom or vaccine. This sickness is hate. In this country there are people who sow hate the way ignorant men sow death with their sperm in the bellies of women who carry it away…to the children they conceive." Methode closes with his family history and his final words: "So here I am, a Hutu-Tutsi and victim of AIDS, possessor of all the sicknesses that are going to destroy us. Look at me. I'm your mirror, your double who's rotting from inside. I'm dying a bit earlier than you, that's all."[50] The power of his words resonate. Courtemanche builds the bridge between Hutus and Tutsis, Rwandans and foreigners, as atrocity gains human face and takes on true meaning. At the cemetery the next day, Valcourt listens as Radio Libre des Mille Collines broadcasts the news that "a terrorist named Methode had died the night before and the local militia would consider anyone seen at his burial as an accomplice to be eliminated."[51] The same night, Raphael's house is burned down, and, soon after, Raphael is slaughtered. Those acts indicate the veracity of Methode's words.

The stories above symbolize the heart of the novel and offer a few examples of the language that Courtemanche exposes and the literary techniques that he uses. This essay, however, illuminates only a few crucial parts of the story. Missing pieces include the depth of Valcourt and Gentille's relationship: their marriage, Gentille's capture, disappearance, brutal abuse, and death recorded in her diary. Another missing piece is an analysis of the sexuality that Courtemanche celebrates and the sexual abuse of women that he condemns. Both are linked to each other and to the other stories that resist any single or definite conclusion. Instead, Courtemanche challenges readers, leaving them in a chaos of knowledge without one right answer, only a possibility of multiple "right" choices. The novel itself ends shortly after the assassination of the president on April 6, 1994, the wedding on April 9, and the maniacal genocide that began long before but erupts uncontrolled in the following days. Abducted, in a sense, when Gentille was kidnapped, Valcourt returns to Kigali after the official war is over to discover the truth about what happened to his wife. His search and decision to stay in Rwanda close the novel.

Upon his return, Valcourt makes it clear that he does not seek revenge. When asked, he states, "Get even with who?...With Belgian priests who sowed the seeds of a kind of tropical Nazism here, with France, with Canada, with the United Nations who stood by and let negroes kill other negroes? They're the real murderers, but they're out of my reach."[52] All Valcourt (and Courtemanche) wants to do is to know the truth about what happened and tell the story. What he does discover ironically reveals how little has changed. Valcourt does find and question Modeste, the man who abused Gentille. Modeste is rooted with the Hutu rebels at the refugee camp in Goma, "an immense depository" of suffering humanity. Upon his arrival, Valcourt finds out that the Hutu soldiers and militiamen "were reigning over a new republic of cholera and tuberculosis." Already having re-created their former world, they "were fleecing the humanitarian organizations, extorting, raping, killing. The power they had lost in their country, they were now exerting over these hundreds of thousands of refugees..."[53] Valcourt sees that propaganda is still "as powerful as heroin," dissolving all capacity to think.[54] When questioned, Modeste lies without shame. Even after Valcourt reads him the words from Gentille's diary the way a court clerk would read "in a voice devoid of emotion the particulars of an indictment for an especially gruesome crime," Modeste thanks the Hutus for eliminating "a whore." Returning to the hotel, Valcourt finds "a new martial, arbitrary order being set in place" all over again by the Tutsis. The cycle continues, as Courtemanche uses the story of the individual's destiny as an allegory of sorts for what Fredric Johnson calls "the embattled situation of the ...society."[55]

Despite what he knows, Valcourt chooses to stay and work against the odds. With a new mate, a Swedish doctor, he adopts a little Hutu girl whose parents have been condemned to death and works with a group that defends the rights of people like the parents accused of genocide.[56] Courtemanche makes Valcourt's transition clear; he also leaves readers with an understanding that if we accept the killing of others as a regrettable cost of civil war, we abandon our moral center. We become like the enemy. Valcourt rejects hate; he chooses instead what some might consider a contradictory but peaceful response.

Courtemanche's narrative about collateral language is especially important to readers in a time when massacres and the truth about such events "are not permitted to impose themselves" on the government, especially one continuing "the standard recitation of distortions" about political events.[57] Decoding the distorted language and reading the "language of slaughter" in the novel reveals more than the exposed surface of a civil war; it offers an acute awareness of the war that continues in the physical and psychological wounds of survivors. Those wounds, as Chris Hedges writes, are "unseen" and "lifelong crucibles."[58] Ten years after the genocide, journalists offer facts to support that truth; they write about the emotional wounds that remain, the "second genocide: rape and AIDS" that Rwanda faces,[59] the extended grief that exists and survival strategies that vary,[60] the war crimes that have not yet been addressed and the *genocidaires* who have not yet been tried,[61] the continuing massacres of Congolese Tutsis,[62] the not-yet-successful efforts at participatory justice,[63] and the people "pretending" to forgive because it is law. [64]

Courtemanche's message is not just about the numbers of people who were slaughtered, but about the rest of a world community that could have prevented it and chose not to. That fact alone raises questions that we need to answer. Why did the peacekeeping efforts fail? What exactly are the moral criteria for humanitarian intervention? As several scholars state, "No longer can human-rights abuses, much less genocide, be considered excusable in some places but not in other, depending on political expediency"; the international community needs to adopt a collective approach.[65] Why, Mark Raper asks, "did powerful nations not act?"[66] "How should the international community act when governments massacre their own people? When," questions Mills, "do human rights supersede those of sovereignty and how do we move from a general compassion for the victims to concrete action that saves lives?"[67] Samantha Power suggests that what the U.S. could have done was make UNAMIR a force to contend with instead of promoting fallacious notions of the "greater good." Ironically, the U.S. argued instead against intervention from the standpoint of people committed to protecting life, and "the willful delusion" about what was happening created no moral imperatives.[68] Raising such questions and exposing delusions in an understated prose, Courtemanche simultaneously shows how difficult it is to get people to respond to such horrors.

Finally, reading about an atrocity that could have been prevented challenges us in a world where human rights abuses continue and appear daily in the news, as well as in some brave new novels such as Anthonia Kalu's *Broken Lives and Other Stories* about the horrors of the Nigeria-Biafra War or in Nuruddin Farah's *Links,* a novel about Somalia where "the civil war then was the language."[69] James Traub's article about what "happens when the shooting stops" and efforts at peacekeeping in Haiti and Kosovo, and numerous articles about the Sudan report events similar to what happened in Rwanda. In the Sudan, the UN has "suppressed" its report on a "reign of terror" as well as evidence of "human rights abuses, war crimes, and crimes against humanity." As Eric Reeves notes, "So far, the world has [again] failed to respond."[70] Alexandra Zavis agrees, stressing the unwillingness of aid organizations to label this crisis a "genocide."[71] Roger Smith corroborates Zavis's view identifying the State Department's current discussion about whether the mass killings in Darfur constitute genocide as nothing more than a "symbolic" act with no real impact. "To enlist others in the effort to prevent genocide," he writes, "moral authority is required," something America seems to lack.[72] Ed Johnson notes that this crisis remains "bleak" as the Sudanese military continues to bomb villagers,[73] and an Associated Press story stresses again the limited view as diplomats focus on Darfur but ignore two other major areas of both Uganda and the Sudan. As UN official Dennis McNamara states, "We can't be politically selective if we want...a solution when the causes are linked...If we stabilize one part, and not the other," there is little change.[74] In fact, almost every article on the massive slaughters and violent gang rapes of girls and women in Darfur, Goma, and Bukavu compares or associates what is happening in the Sudan, Congo, and Uganda to remembrances of Rwanda.[75] Although Secretary of State Colin Powell finally declared that the United States views the killings in Darfur as genocide and called on the United Nations Security Council to recognize the urgency of the situation, recent news stories report inaction and criticism. There are, for example, signs of trouble for a draft Security Council resolution, and, as Jesse Jackson states, the Darfur situation offers "another example of the excessive U.S. patience in the face of a crisis involving Africans."[76]

At the close of *A Sunday at the Pool...,* Victor, the man who runs the hotel, wants Valcourt to "gather survivors' first-hand stories" and make them public so that the genocide would not be forgotten."[77] Ten years later, a nineteen-year-old survivor of the Rwandan genocide, Jaqueline Murekatete, perhaps best explains that need for story. She feels that it is her "responsibility" to her family and the people who died to let the world know what happened. Because the behaviors continue, Murekatete's goal is to tell people her story "in the hope of preventing similar atrocities."[78] Exposing the soul of Rwanda's history in his novel, Courtemanche captures "war's inhumanity" and draws readers into the lived reality of the Rwandan genocide. *A Sunday in the Pool...* takes us beyond journalistic facts into the heart of darkness, revealing the horror of what reasonable people can do to each other when prodded and filled with fear. Uncovering the space between words and deeds, it also invites readers to make political and moral judgments that would promote action and prevent "similar atrocities."

Notes

1. James Hillman, *A Terrible Love of War* (New York: The Penguin Press. 2004), p. 48.

2. Mel Gussow, "Interview with John Le Carre," *The New York Times,* January 11, 2004, p. A5.

3. Waters2 [MATT: I don't understand what work this refers to.]

4. Collins, John and Ross Glover, eds. *Collateral Language: a User's Guide to America's New War* (New York and London: New York University Press, 2002).

5. Gil Courtemanche, *A Sunday at the Pool in Kigali,* tr. Patricia Claxton (New York: Alfred A Knopf, 2003), p. 6.

6. Ibid., p. 88.

7. Ibid., p. 224.

8. Ibid., pp. 228-229.

9. Philip Gourevitch, "*We Wish to Inform You that Tomorrow We Will Be Killed With Our Families*": Stories from Rwanda (New York: Farrar Straus and Giroux: 1998), p. 296.

10. Samantha Power, "*A Problem From Hell*": America and the Age of Genocide (New York: Basic Books, 2002), pp. 364, 369.

11. Collins and Glover, *Collateral Language* (see n. 4), pp. 3, 12.

12. Nicolaus Mills, "The Language of Slaughter," in Nicolaus Mills and Kira Brunner, eds., *The New Killing Fields: Massacre and the Politics of Intervention* (New York: Basic Books, 2002), pp. 6-7. Mills attributes Joseph Conrad's *The Heart of Darkness* with laying "the foundations for this language of slaughter," and he includes writers such as Thomas Hardy, Siegfried Sassoon and Primo Levi as finding the right words for the horror they report (pp. 8-15). Courtemanche too dismisses the language of war as "deceptive" and offers concrete information to allow readers to grasp the horrors that occur.

13. Courtemanche, *A Sunday at the Pool in Kigali* (see n. 5), p. 70.

14. Ibid., pp. 4-6.

15. Ibid., pp. 9-10.

16. Ibid., p. 12.

17. Ibid., p. 13.

18. Ibid., p. 14.

19. On August 4, 1993, with support of Western powers, the Arusha Accords, a power-sharing agreement, emerged. "Under its terms the Rwandan government agreed to govern with Hutu opposition parties and the Tutsi minority." UN peacekeepers would assist in demilitarization and help provide a "secure environment."

    Power, *"A Problem From Hell"* (see n. 10), p. 336 Gourevitch maintains that this peace agreement established a blueprint for a transitional government, as well as a peacekeeping force, but he sees the Accords as a "political suicide note." *"We Wish to Inform You"* (see n. 9), p. 99.

20. Courtemanche, *A Sunday at the Pool in Kigali* (see n. 5), p. 70.

21. Ibid., p. 115.

22. Colonel Theoneste Bagasora, an intimate of Madame Habyarimana and a charter member of the *akazu* and its death squads, ... had said in January of 1993 that he was preparing the apocalypse." Gourevitch, *"We Wish to Inform You"* (see n. 9), p. 113. After he returned to Africa to testify at the International Criminal Tribunal, General Romeo Dallaire published an account titled *Shake Hands With the Devil: The Failure of Humanity in Rwanda* in which he states, "One of the devils was Bagosora." Guy Lawson, "The Rwanda Witness," *The New York Times Magazine*, April 4, 2004, , p. 18.

23. Courtemanche, *A Sunday at the Pool in Kigali* (see n. 5), p. 115.

24. Ibid., p. 74.

25. Ibid., p. 75.

26. Ibid., p. 76.

27. Ibid., p. 79.

28. Darryl Li, "Echoes of Violence," in Mills and Brunner, *The New Killing Fields* (see n. 12), p. 118.

29. Courtemanche, *A Sunday at the Pool in Kigali* (see n. 5), p. 86.

30. Ibid., p. 93.

31. See Li, "Echoes of Violence," in Mills and Brunner, *The New Killing Fields* (see n. 12), p. 120, on *umuganda*, a weekly ritual of communal labor. See Gourevitch, *"We Wish to Inform You"* (see n. 9), p. 95, on community building.

32. Courtemanche, *A Sunday at the Pool in Kigali* (see n. 5), p. 96. See also Gourevitch, *"We Wish to Inform You"* (see n. 9), pp. 75, 93; and Power, *"A Problem From Hell"* (see n. 10), p. 382.

33. The Rwanda Patriotic Front consisted of armed Tutsi exiles situated at Uganda's border. Power, *"A Problem From Hell"* (see n. 10), p. 336.

34. Li, "Echoes of Violence" (see n. 12), p. 117.

35. Ibid., p. 119. See also Gourevitch, *"We Wish to Inform You"* (see n. 9), pp. 94-98; Bill Berkeley, "Road to a Genocide," in Mills and Brunner (see n.

12), p. 111; Robert Gellately and Ben Kiernan, eds., *The Specter of Genocide: Mass Murder in Historical Perspective,* (Cambridge: Cambridge University Press, 2003), p. 334. Another media source was the Hutu paper *Kangura* ("Wake up!") that published a list of its "Ten Commandments of the Hutu." Power writes, "Like Hitler's Nuremberg laws…these ten commandments articulated the rules of the game the radicals hoped to see imposed on the minority…" (Gellately, pp. 338-9); Gourevitch sees these commandments as a revised way to reconcile "the Hamatic myth and the rhetoric of the Hutu Revolution…" (pp. 85-88).

36. Courtemanche, *A Sunday at the Pool in Kigali* (see n. 5), pp. 97-98.

37. Ibid., p. 108.

38. Ibid., p. 109.

39. Ibid., p. 172.

40. Power, *"A Problem From Hell"* (see n. 10), p. 358.

41. "Months before the killing began, Dallaire had contacted his United Nations superiors…requesting permission to undertake deterrent operations; seven times he asked, and seven times he was turned down." His forces were cut twice; first to 450 and then to 270. Lawson, "The Rwanda Witness" (see n. 22), p. 20. Information in The National Security Archive documents both the knowledge that the U.S. possessed and the step-by-step refusal of the U.S. to respond. A memo on April 28, 1994 reveals Albright's refusal to respond to a UN willingness to contribute "a special peacekeeping fund" for Rwanda: "Albright deferred to await instructions from Washington." William Ferroggiaro, "The U.S. and the Genocide in Rwanda 1994: Information, Intelligence and the U.S. Response," *The National Security Archive,* http://www.gwu.edu/~nsarchiv/NSAEBB/NSAEBB117/ 1-21, pp. 3, 7.

42. Power, *"A Problem From Hell"* (see n. 10), pp. 351-353, 365.

43. Ibid., p. 368.

44. Courtemanche, *A Sunday at the Pool in Kigali* (see n. 5), pp. 162-64. See also Gourevitch, *"We Wish to Inform You"* (see n. 9), pp. 57-58, 81.

45. Courtemanche, *A Sunday at the Pool in Kigali* (see n. 5), pp. 41-43.

46. Ibid., p. 43.

47. Ibid. Writing about the genocide that still haunts Rwanda a decade later, Craig Nelson notes that the Hutu murdered the Tutsis "at a rate five times that the Nazis used to exterminate the Jews in World War II" "Genocide Haunts a Tormented Land," *Times Union,* April 4, 2004, p. 8.

Numerous writers associate the Jews and Holocaust with what occurred in Rwanda. Even in 1964, for example, Sir Bertrand Russell stated that Rwanda was "the most horrible and systematic massacre…since the extermination of the Jews by the Nazis." Gourevitch, *"We Wish to Inform You"* (see n. 9), p. 65. In 2004, Howard French argues that "emotionally overpowering but deeply flawed analogies" with "European Jewry" and the Holocaust drove Washington's policy in Africa. *A Continent for the Taking: The Tragedy and Hope of Africa* (New York: Alfred A. Knopf, 2004), pp.142-3.

48. Courtemanche, *A Sunday at the Pool in Kigali* (see n. 5), p. 44.

49. Ibid.

50. Ibid., p. 61.

51. Ibid., pp. 66-67.

52. Ibid., pp. 253-54.

53. Ibid., p. 254.

54. Ibid., p. 255.

55. Ibid., p. 69.

56. Ibid., pp. 259-60.

57. Richard Cohen, "Convention's Message vs. Reality," *The Daily Gazette,* September 4, 2004, p. A7.

58. Chris Hedges, *What Every Person Should Know About WAR* (New York: Free Press, 2003), p. xii.

59. Craig Nelson, "Genocide Haunts a Tormented Land" (see n. 47), p. 8.

60. Mark Raper, "Remembering Rwanda 1994-2004," *America,* April 19-26, 2004, p. 17; Catherine Wagner Minnery, "Remembering Rwanda...: 10 years After the 1994 Genocide," Art Exhibit and Essays, April 7, 2004.

61. Mark Raper, Ibid.; Guy Lawson, "The Rwanda Witness," *The New York Times Magazine,* April 4, 2004, p. 18.

62. Aloys Niyoyita, "Anguished Survivors Bury Victims of Massacre." *Times Union,* August 17, 2004, Nation/World, p. A5; "180 Refugees Killed in Camp in Burundi," *Democrat and Chronicle,* August 15, 2004, p. 14A; "Besides Darfur, Sudan is Tied to 2 Other Conflicts," *The Daily Gazette,* September 4, 2004, p. A5.

63. George Parker, "Justice on a Hill," in Mills and Brunner (see n. 12), p. 131.

64. Raper, "Remembering Rwanda" (see n. 60), p. 16; Kathleen Hage, "Rwanda's Long Road to Reconciliation," *National Catholic Reporter,* April 23, 2004, p. 4; Parker, "Justice on a Hill" (see n. 63), p. 151. A current report by Swedish and Canadian non-governmental groups tracking armed conflict maintains a decline in the number of global conflicts, but the information above and below contradicts what appears to be an overgeneralized study. Charles J. Hanley, "Report: Bloodshed Declining Globally," *The Daily Gazette,* August 30, 2004, pp. A1, A4.

65. Raper, "Remembering Rwanda" (see n. 60), p. 3. [MATT: Not sure if this is right – the only note in text read "*(America, 3)*"—so I surmised it was this article.]

66. Ibid, p. 16.

67. Mills, "The Language of Slaughter" (see n. 12), p. 5.

68. Power, "*A Problem From Hell*" (see n. 10), pp. 382-5.

69. Nuruddin Farah, *Links* (New York: Riverhead Books, 2004), p. 119.

70. Eric Reeves, "Sudan's Reign of Terror," *amnesty now* (Summer 2004), p. 16.

71. Alexandra Zavis, "Hotel Rwanda Film Reflects the Horror of Genocide," *Times Union,* March 4, 2004, p. A4; "Fleeing Sudanese Unable to Bury Dead," *The Daily Gazette,* July 7, 2004, p. D10; "Sudan's Darfur Refugees Tell of Attacks, Rape," *The Daily Gazette.*July 2, 2004, p. A4; "Trees in Chad Shelter Refugees," *The Daily Gazette,* July 8, 2004, p. C10. Catherine Wagner Minnery reveals the consequences of the "delusion," the failure to respond, in her art and the comments that accompany drawings, paintings, and collages in her exhibits "Called to Witness" and "Remembering Rwanda…10 years after the 1994 genocide." She also wonders why the United States failed "to care enough to find a way to respond" (Personal interview and Karen Bjornland, "Exhibit a Haunting Reminder of Rwanda Genocide," *The Daily Gazette,* May 12, 2004, p. C7.

72. Roger Smith, "American Self-Interest and the Response to Genocide," *The Chronicle of Higher Education,* July 30, 2004, p. B9.

73. Ed Johnson, "Darfur Refugees Still Wait as U.N. Deadline Runs Out." *The Daily Gazette,* August 31, 2004, p. D10.

74. Aloys Niyoyita, "Anguished Survivors Bury Victims of Massacre" (see n. 62), p. A5.

75. Jan Goodwin, "Silence=Rape," *The Nation,* March 8, 2004, pp. 18-22; Steven R. Weisman, "Powell Says Rapes and Killings in Sudan Are Genocide," http://www.nytimes.com/2004/9/10/politics/10sudan.html, p. 2.

76. Weisman, "Powell Says…" (see n. 75), p. 1; "Powell Finds Genocide in Darfur Region," http://www.msnbc.msn.com/id/5926635/, p. 5.

77. Courtemanche, *A Sunday at the Pool in Kigali* (see n. 5), p. 253.

78. Frank Eltman, "Survivor Tells of Rwandan Genocide," *The Sunday Gazette,* March 21, 2004, p. B4.

Bibliography

Berkeley, Bill. "Road to a Genocide." In *The New Killing Fields: Massacre and the Politics of Intervention,* ed. Nicolaus Mills and Kira Brunner. New York: Basic Books, 2002: 103-16.

"Besides Darfur, Sudan Is Tied to 2 Other Conflicts." *The Daily Gazette,* September 4, 2004: A5.

Bjornland, Karen. "Exhibit a Haunting Reminder of Rwanda Genocide." *The Daily Gazette,* May 12, 2004: C7.

Cohen, Richard. "Convention's Message vs. Reality." *The Daily Gazette,* September 4, 2004: A7.

Collins, John, and Ross Glover, eds. *Collateral Language: A User's Guide to America's New War.* New York and London: New York University Press, 2002.

"Congo: Troops Won't Invade Rwanda." *The Daily Gazette,* June 22, 2004: A3.

Cose, Ellis. "Learning to Heal." *Newsweek,* April 12, 2004: 54-55.

Courtemanche, Gil. *A Sunday at the Pool in Kigali.* Tr. Patricia Claxton. New York: Knopf, 2003.

Eltman, Frank. "Survivor Tells of Rwandan Genocide." *The Sunday Gazette,* March 21, 2004: B4.

Farah, Nuruddin. *Links.* New York: Riverhead Books, 2004.

Ferroggiaro, William. "The U.S. and the Genocide in Rwanda 1994: Information, Intelligence and the U.S. Response." *The National Security Archive.* http://www.gwu.edu/~nsarchiv/NSAEBB/NSAEBB117/ : 1-21.

French, Howard W. *A Continent for the Taking: The Tragedy and Hope of Africa.* New York: Knopf, 2004.

Gellately, Robert, and Ben Kiernan, eds. *The Specter of Genocide: Mass Murder in Historical Perspective.* Cambridge: Cambridge University Press, 2003.

Goodwin, Jan. "Silence=Rape." *The Nation,* March 8, 2004: 18-22.

Gourevitch, Philip. *"We Wish to Inform You that Tomorrow We Will Be Killed With Our Families": Stories from Rwanda.* New York: Farrar Straus and Giroux: 1998.

Gussow, Mel. "Interview with John Le Carre." *New York Times* (January 11, 2004): A5.

Hage, Kathleen. "Rwanda's Long Road to Reconciliation." *National Catholic Reporter,* April 23, 2004: 3-4.

Hanley, Charles J. "Report: Bloodshed Declining Globally." *The Daily Gazette,* August 30, 2004: A1, A4.

Hedges, Chris. *What Every Person Should Know About WAR.* New York: Free Press, 2003.

"Hutus Blamed for Massacre." *The Daily Gazette,* September 4, 2004: A5.

Hillman, James. *A Terrible Love of War.* New York: The Penguin Press. 2004.

Jameson, Fredric. "Third-World Literature in the Era of Multinational Capitalism." *Social Text* 15 (Autumn 1986): 65-88.

Johnson, Ed. "Darfur Refugees Still Wait as U.N. Deadline Runs Out." *The Daily Gazette,* August 31, 2004: D10.

_____. "Red Cross Launches Huge Aid Effort in Sudan." *The Daily Gazette,* August 28, 2004: A4.

Kalu, Anthonia C. *Broken Lives and Other Stories.* Athens, OH: Ohio University Press, 2003.

Lawson, Guy. "The Rwanda Witness." *New York Times Magazine,* April 4, 2004: 18-20.

Li, Darryl. "Echoes of Violence." In *The New Killing Fields: Massacre and the Politics of Intervention,* ed. Nicolaus Mills and Kira Brunner. New York: Basic Books, 2002: 117-28.

Melson, Robert. "Modern Genocide in Rwanda: Ideology, Revolution, War, and Mass Murder in an African State." In *The Specter of Genocide: Mass Murder in Historical Perspective*, ed. Robert Gellately and Ben Kiernan. Cambridge: Cambridge University Press, 2003: 325-338.

Mills, Nicolaus, and Kira Brunner, eds. *The New Killing Fields: Massacre and the Politics of Intervention.* New York: Basic Books, 2002.

Mills, Nicolaus. "The Language of Slaughter." In *The New Killing Fields: Massacre and the Politics of Intervention,* ed. Nicolaus Mills and Kira Brunner. New York: Basic Books, 2002: 3-15.

Minnery, Catherine Wagner. "Remembering Rwanda...: 10 Years After the 1994 Genocide." Art Exhibit and Essays. April 7, 2004: 1-9.

Minnery, Catherine Wagner. Personal interview. April 14, 2004.

Nelson, Craig. "Genocide Haunts a Tormented Land." *Times Union,* April 4, 2004: A1, 8.

Niyoyita, Aloys. "Anguished Survivors Bury Victims of Massacre." *Times Union.* August 17, 2004: Nation/World A5.

"180 Refugees Killed in Camp in Burundi." *Democrat and Chronicle,* August 15, 2004: 14A.

Parker, George. "Justice on a Hill." Mills and Brunner. 129-53.

"Powell Finds Genocide in Darfur Region." http://www.msnbc.msn.com/id/5926635:1-6.

Power, Samantha. *"A Problem from Hell": America and the Age of Genocide.* New York: Basic Books, 2002.

Raper, Mark. "Remembering Rwanda 1994-2004." *America,* April 19-26, 2004: 14-17.

Reeves, Eric. "Sudan's Reign of Terror." *amnesty now* (Summer 2004): 16-19.

Rossouw, Henk. "Rwanda's Search for Justice." *The Chronicle of Higher Education,* August 9, 2002: 1-43.

Smith, Roger W. "American Self-Interest and the Response to Genocide." *The Chronicle of Higher Education,* July 30, 2004: B6-9.

"Sudan's Grim Lessons." *The Daily Gazette,* July 2, 2004: A7.

Traub, James. "Nation Building." *The New York Times Magazine,* April 11, 2004: Section 4: 1, 4.

Walzer, Michael. "Arguing for Humanitarian Intervention." In *The New Killing Fields: Massacre and the Politics of Intervention,* ed. Nicolaus Mills and Kira Brunner. New York: Basic Books, 2002: 19-35.

Weisman, Steven R. "Powell Says Rapes and Killings in Sudan Are Genocide."http://www.nytimes.com/2004/9/10/politics/10sudan.html/ : 1-3.

Zavis, Alexandra. "Hotel Rwanda Film Reflects the Horror of Genocide." *Times Union,* March 4, 2004: 34.

_____. "Fleeing Sudanese Unable to Bury Dead." *The Daily Gazette,* July 7, 2004: D10.

_____. "Sudan's Darfur Refugees Tell of Attacks, Rape." *The Daily Gazette.* July 2, 2004: A4.

_____."Trees in Chad Shelter Refugees." *The Daily Gazette,* July 8, 2004: C10.

SEVEN

Music Therapy and Peaceful Hearts for Girls at War: Assessing Psychosocial Needs through Song in Sierra Leone

Maria Gonsalves

Creativity in the lives of those who have endured trauma and lived through violence can be understood as resistance to oppression. It can embody "the refusal of victimhood and helplessness. . . . Creating something new is an act of defiance in the face of destruction."[1] The music that grows out of music therapy sessions is enlightening, enlivening, and empowering and restores humanity.

In June 2002, I served as a research assistant to Dr. Susan McKay, a nurse, psychologist, and professor of women's studies at the University of Wyoming. We spent three weeks talking with and learning about girls in Sierra Leone, a nation that endured a ten-year civil war that began in 1991 with a rebellion against the Freetown government by the Revolutionary United Front (RUF). This was part of a larger study led by principal investigators McKay and Dr. Dyan Mazurana that focused on girls in militaries, paramilitaries, and armed opposition forces. The study was funded by the Canadian International Development Agency and the International Center for Human Rights and Democracy. "An eighteen-month study of girls in paramilitaries, militaries, and armed opposition groups in three African countries . . . was conducted for the purpose of uncovering . . . girls' presence and roles within fighting forces and in demilitarization, demobilization, and reintegration (DDR) processes."[2]

Healthy reintegration of children (defined as people under the age of 18 by the UN Convention on the Rights of a Child[3] [UNICEF n.d.]) who have been used in armed conflicts into their communities is of major international concern. The future well-being of communities is largely dependent on a physically and psychologically healthy youth population. Yet evidence indicates that children returning to their communities after military service suffer from physical and psychosocial war trauma and lessened life opportunities. While boys involved in fighting forces typically undergo a formal demobilization and have been the focus of most research, girls are far more widely associated with fighting forces than is reported. Their experiences and roles in these forces are complex, vary by context, and are worsened by sexism and misogyny.

"Few studies have focused specifically on girls and their experiences due to and often contributing to their often informal status and perceived 'invisibility'."[4] Girls' presence in fighting forces has been "hidden" by local groups, governments, and international bodies that keep secret, overlook, or are unwilling to recognize, during the crucial postconflict reintegration period, girls' involvement and needs such as skills training, education, and community sensitization.[5] However, recent research has analyzed their roles in fighting forces and their demobilization and reintegration experiences.

The research McKay and I conducted in Sierra Leone highlighted the fact that these needs are inadequately addressed on multiple levels. In particular, girls who return from fighting forces with babies born from rape or rebel owner-"husbands" are at high risk for further trauma and mental health problems. After the fighting stops or when girls leave fighting forces, they face onerous challenges. For girls who return directly to their communities, social reintegration can be difficult because of stigma and associated shame that results from the experiences they have had, especially gender-based violence.[6]

As a follow-up to this research, I contributed to a pilot community-based assessment of the process of girls' reintegration into their community, and the community's response to their return, headed by McKay and Dr. Mary Burman of the University of Wyoming. The key research concerned psychosocial reintegration of young mothers and their children and factors facilitating successful reintegration. Local music and dance traditions were used in this study to elicit girls' stories and feelings as well as those of women elders in the community. Music not only served as an important method of healing and acceptance, but was also the most effective tool with which to conduct a needs assessment. Specifically, song served as the primary way that these young mothers could express their psychosocial needs.

Trauma

"To study psychological trauma is to come face-to-face with both human vulnerability in the natural world and the capacity for evil in human nature."[7]

The Diagnostic and Statistical Manual (DSM-IV-TR 2000) describes "extreme traumatic stressors" as they relate to post-traumatic stress disorder (PTSD), namely,

> direct personal experience of an event that involves actual or threatened death or serious injury, or other threat to one's physical integrity; or witnessing an event that involves death, injury, or a threat to the physical integrity of another person; or learning about unexpected or violent death, serious harm, or threat of death or injury experienced by a family member or other close associate (Criterion A1).[8]

The above definition is a clinical guideline that tries to quantify symptoms and criteria for diagnosis. But in actuality, "what constitutes a traumatic event is, after all, difficult to delineate, even for professionals."[9] Traumatic experiences take many forms. According to the literature, developmental traumas include natural disasters; adverse circumstances such as living without a parent, poverty, displacement, or separation from a loved one;[10] sexual, physical, and emotional abuse; automobile accidents; serious illness; invasive medical procedures;[11] assault; experiencing or witnessing violence; and war.

"Shock trauma," on the other hand, "occurs when we experience potentially life-threatening events that overwhelm our capacities to respond effectively."[12] These include many of the other experiences listed above, such as natural disasters, automobile accidents, and serious illness. The focus of my work and of this article has been with victims of repeated exposure to violence, including sexual abuse.

Although I differentiate between these two perceived distinct forms of traumatic experiences, I do not consider them mutually exclusive or representative of different symptomology or to require qualitatively different forms of therapy. The categorization of traumatic experiences is not as simple as the above differentiation implies. Moreover, the interrelationships among different traumatic experiences are extensive and often convoluted. For instance, Pavlicevic[13] discusses individual violence as opposed to collective violence, implying, as I understand it, a categorization of developmental traumas such as familial physical and sexual abuse with single-event shock traumas such as a rape or assault—an array of traumatic experiences that Levine, for example, does not group together. Essentially, all potentially traumatic experiences are "experiences of real or perceived threat to survival,"[14] regardless of their source or category.

Developmental Traumas

It is not surprising that many trauma researchers refer to Bowlby's attachment theory when describing developmental trauma.[15] Frank-Schwebel[16] attributes the occurrence of developmental trauma to the recurrence of disruptions in the area of early mother-child interaction or attachment bond. From this perspective, children without warm, empathetic primary attachments or adequate nurturing are at risk for trauma responses.[17] "Not only does the child need the mother for protection, [the child] also needs her to develop a sense of self in relation to other. Thus, implicit in 'attachment' are the roots of empathy and relationship."[18]

Austin states that the healthy, individuating self can "become impaired early in childhood when threatened with abandonment by the mother."[19] Developmental trauma, therefore, can be considered a preverbal wound to the self, as the provoking experiences occur before verbal skills are developed. As a precursor to the discussion of music within this context, I note that because developmental traumas often occur before verbal skills are developed, voice and sound can serve as transitional objects in music therapy work with trauma victims who did not develop a secure attachment as infants.[20] Often, chronic physical, sexual, and/or emotional abuse begin at an early age, during critical developmental periods, and are either the result of or result in disruptions in early attachment relationships.

> As infants we depend on our primary caregivers for our physical and emotional safety, and these first relationships color all subsequent relationships. The impact of these early experiences of threat to survival—or loss of safety—have [sic] been another important perspective from which to think about trauma.[21]

This kind of "personal violence," however, is not always distinct from collective violence. Children growing up in a pervasively unstable environment, in a culture and community of violence, may "experience the external world as threatening and unsafe," denoting the interruption in development and the potential for experiences of trauma. "The experience of feeling unsafe can impact upon the child's emotional and psychological development."[22] Bowlby's theory of attachment, which focuses on early socioemotional relations, has taught us that a loss of safe attachments results in a loss of safety. This loss of safety produces deficits in the feeling of empathy, in the formation of lasting relationships, and in denial of feelings.[23] There are numerous paths to this loss of safe attachments.

Personal developmental trauma can also be the cause of collective, institutionalized, or intergenerational violations of human security or threats of violence. Psychiatrist Daniel Stern, author of *The First Relationship*,[24] has studied in detail the complexities of mother-infant interaction. "Stern (1977) considered how the mother would bring her own life experiences into the interaction with the infant, and how experiences of loss and patterns of response can be passed through generations."[25] This can be representative of sociologically based patterns of relating and establishing emotional harmony or incongruity, which, in many cases, can serve to predict trauma responses.

Shock/Single-Event Trauma

Shock traumas, as quoted by Levine,[26] can involve single-event traumas such as automobile accidents or terrorist attacks such as those of September 11, 2001, in the U.S. Rape or other assault, natural disaster, or the death of a loved one could also be considered single-event, potentially traumatic experiences. In the same way that personal violence is often enmeshed within the context of collective violence, shock traumas are commonly part of a larger, contextually significant landscape of everyday violence.

Sutton[27] reminds us that all of these experiences require understanding of their contextual significance. Although a woman may experience being raped on one occasion, the community in which she lives may be one that induces fear in her on a regular basis, causing her to perceive herself as consistently vulnerable[28] and transforming what could have been labeled a single-event, personal trauma into a chronic, societal trauma. Similarly, rape is often used as a psychological tactic during war to strain communities and induce cultural disintegration. Certainly this type of trauma is one part of a larger societal trauma that is experienced during wartime. Such was the case during the civil war in Sierra Leone, described in a series of vignettes later in this chapter. Similarly, while the death of a loved one in and of itself may appear to be a single event, witnessing the violent death[29] of a loved one within a community of violence or during wartime could also make the label "single-event trauma" inadequate and inappropriate.

The differentiation between single-event traumas and chronic shock traumas is also confusing. Although it may appear that chronic traumas refer directly to developmental traumas occurring over extended periods of time at a crucial period in one's development, e.g., sexual abuse in childhood, this isn't exclusively the case. For instance, serious or terminal illness, the onset of which might be in adulthood, can be chronically traumatizing. "The impact of a sudden onset or diagnosis of a chronic disease" can produce posttraumatic stress, and the "devastating losses that accompany the progressive stages of a terminal illness"[30] may result in chronic shock trauma.

My work in Sierra Leone as a research assistant and my work as a music therapy intern at a state psychiatric facility in New York City have brought me into the lives of people who have experienced developmental traumas at early ages, stemming from poor caretaking and poor early attachments, as well as repeated single-event traumas. However, single-event traumas, which include physical and sexual assault, rape, robbery, and displacement, are, for most of the people with whom I've worked, the results of a collective, institutionalized culture of violence.

From my perspective, collective violence is transformed into a personal trauma that must be endured on an individual level. Typically, as clinicians, we treat it as such. A couple of the vignettes included in this article demonstrate this form of treatment. But does music therapy allow for a collective perspective when working with trauma? My experiences have taught me that it does, and this is my perspective when working with trauma victims.

Collective Violence

Pervasive violence within communities undermines basic human security. Pavlicevic writes,

> violence is not always explicit or sudden with bullets, knives, [or] pangas, and need not result in overt injury, death, or [the] disappearance of family or friends. As a collective, institutionalized phenomenon, there is a violence that is low-key, highly institutionalized, 'acceptable,' and deadly. This may manifest as slow eroding of 'life': a paucity of material well-being, the absence of a sense of security, the absence of a supportive social network, and fragile life relationships.[31]

This violence can be understood as a lack of basic human security.

Pavlicevic refers to the above-mentioned institutionalized violence in a case example in which she discusses her music therapy work with a South African girl[32]. Issues of economic violence, sociopolitical violence, medical violence, and educational violence all contributed to the trauma that this particular client endured. This violence cannot be classified according to the strict interpretation of developmental or shock traumas discussed above. It is part of a larger framework of violence that denies and destroys individuals' humanity.

This kind of systemic, sociological trauma can be seen in all aspects of daily life for those living in communities with low socioeconomic status, political violence or terror, and war. Murray[33] references this systemic level of trauma in the lives of children affected by the "troubles" in Northern Ireland. Housing, education, employment, and family life display the evidence of the enduring violence and fear. This creates an unstable environment that renders children (and others) helpless and powerless.

Dr. Martha Bragin, a trauma clinician who works on psychosocial programming to mitigate the effects of war, state, and community violence on children and adolescents, refers to sequential traumatization as a form of collective trauma. Sequential traumatization affects development and refers, for example, to those who have endured war and are exposed to every aspect of the postwar process.[34] Once again, the girls with whom I worked in Sierra Leone are prime examples of victims of sequential traumatization. Additionally, I believe that sequential traumatization overlaps with developmental trauma. My later clinical vignette about my work with Tischa, a victim of sexual abuse and abandonment, exemplifies this.

Trauma Therapy and Treatment

> Traumatic experiences present victims with the inescapable truth that reality can damage their sense of safety and trust. To sustain a sense of hope in the face of such an external onslaught, a person must have a sufficiently enduring sense of identity and interpersonal connectedness. The ability to tolerate the traumatic experience involves a capacity to bear pain in the presence of another human being; this constitutes the core of mature intimacy.[35]

The specialized area of trauma therapy is nearly as vast and diverse as trauma symptoms. How and why therapy can be effective in helping those who have been traumatized are complex questions that I have sought to answer in my own research as I have gained experience with trauma victims and collected their responses to my therapeutic stances and interventions in both verbal and music therapy groups. In the following pages, I make only brief reference to those treatment models and approaches that I have explored before sharing my own work within music therapy vignettes, which draws on the worldviews of others with regard to trauma.

The prevailing approach to trauma treatment endorses the cathartic expression of the trauma. This has historically involved the uncovering and retelling of the traumatic experience with the intent of integrating the traumatic experience and the various splits of self into the survivor's understanding of who she is. "Because the symptoms and emotions associated with trauma can be extreme, most of us . . . will recoil and attempt to repress these intense reactions."[36] This suppression sometimes involves denial, memory repression, or verbal avoidance of the traumatic experience. "Unfortunately, this denial can prevent us from healing."[37] In this model of treatment, the therapist bears witness to the survivor's trauma as she remembers and retells the experience. Drawing from a Gestalt perspective, the process of "integration" strives to make a whole out of the fragments of self that trauma survivors often experience.[38] The fragmentation that trauma causes can lead to a split self that sometimes becomes a literal dissociation, a now-more-commonly acknowledged symptom of trauma.[39] According to Austin,[40] who developed and codified a series of techniques that she describes as "vocal holding techniques," when unconscious experiences are "contacted and communicated with, these younger parts can be reunited with the ego . . . the vital energy they contain can be made available to the present-day personality. Developmental arrests can be repaired, and a more complete sense of self can be attained."[41]

It can be argued, however, that this cathartic retelling of a traumatic experience or history is a form of reexperiencing that may not be appropriate in every context. Some argue that therapists can become seduced into evoking discussion of the trauma and must continually evaluate and reevaluate the motivation for and relevance of bearing witness to the client's traumatic experience.[42] Additionally, "some of the effects of trauma may mitigate against the use of therapy."[43] Some argue that the painful reliving of memories is not necessary in order to heal trauma.[44] In any form of therapy, music therapy being no exception, clinicians run the risk of retraumatizing victims. Montello mentions that this is even possible through "spontaneous musical involvement."[45]

Certainly the model of treatment should be carefully chosen on the basis of the needs of the client. In much of Western society, which is commonly described as individualistic in comparison to non-Western cultures, work with the individual victim at the level of the microsystem is often valid and appropriate. In many non-Western cultures as well as some Western communities or subcultures, however, work on the levels of larger systems is important, and individual-level work can even be contraindicated. While trauma has been perceived by many as belonging to the domain of individual experience, it must be acknowledged as being related to broader structures including family, communities, nations, and international communities.[46] Bronfenbrenner[47] uses the concepts of the mesosystem, exosystem, and macrosystem to put culturally sensitive or culture-centered trauma work into a different framework. Relations among home, school, neighborhood, peer groups, government agencies, local councils, and school administrations as well as the subculture or culture as a whole are important and may need to be given great consideration when working with trauma survivors.[48] From this perspective, integration of the trauma at the individual level alone will provide an opportunity for only partial healing.

Turner, McFarlane, and van der Kolk make reference to conventional treatments as well as methods based "either on common sense or on novel ways of approaching the process of treatment."[49] Many trauma therapy models emphasize the recovery of feelings of efficacy and power.[50] Increasing feelings of self-worth, safety, and invulnerability are valuable goals that are achieved through stabilization, the processing of the experience on sensory/emotive levels, and reengaging and reconnecting with others.[51] Restoring connections with other individuals, within the family, and within the community is, from my perspective, the single most important aspect of trauma therapy treatment.

One of the novel ways of approaching the process of treatment is based on Peter Levine's concept of the somatic, physiological processes that are engaged when one encounters a traumatic experience[52]. His treatment philosophy is based on the premise that the mind and body work together as a unit and must be treated as a unit for healing to occur. From this perspective, resolving traumatic symptoms through the traditional study of its effects solely on the mind is inadequate. This approach to healing trauma is rooted in individual, one-to-one work. "At the moment, the work of transforming trauma within groups of people is still in its infancy."[53] However, exploration of psychosomatic philosophies (as I refer to them) and the methods that grow out of them are part of the process of discovery—the discovery of trauma treatment models for various survivors in various contexts.

Levine[54] states that the body has a profound reaction to trauma as the mind alters its state as a protective reaction. After the event, the mind often returns to normal. At this point, the body's response is also meant to normalize. "When the restorative process is thwarted, the effects of trauma become fixated, and the person becomes traumatized."[55] Therefore, treating the victim solely through the process of verbal therapy is inadequate. Creative methods of treatment that engage the body, inclusive of the creative arts therapies, are better able to access the trauma that is "trapped in the body" rather than solely exploring the trauma that rests at the level of the psyche. As van der Kolk, Turner, and McFarlane suggest, the experiences are processed on the sensory/emotive levels[56]. Protomusicality, as the "shared capacity for engaging in communication through sound and movement,"[57] allows us to process on these levels, as we engage with the world on a sensory level. Clinical vignettes later in the paper exemplify this principle.

Levine[58] references the freeze response of mammals when in danger. This altered state of consciousness is shared by all mammals, and occurs when death appears imminent. This immobility response is, first, an attempt at "playing possum" and, second, an "altered state in which no pain is experienced."[59] This instinctive surrender has often been misjudged as cowardice or weakness. However, movement into and out of this state of immobility is an adaptive response that is key to avoiding the debilitating effects of trauma.[60]

However, becoming psychologically stuck in the immobility response even after the danger has passed does not allow the release of the residual energy. Consequently, the victim is left in the traumatic maze with the experience of continual distress—trauma symptoms[61] (or, as Austin puts it, being stuck in the trauma vortex. Similarly, the first chapter of van der Kolk, McFarlane, and Weisaeth's book *Traumatic Stress*[62] is titled "The Black Hole of Trauma." The frozen residue of energy that has not been resolved and discharged remains "trapped in the nervous system, where it can wreak havoc on our bodies and spirits."[63]

The treatment of trauma symptoms understood to be the result of the above processes demands a focus on health rather than pathology. "What we need to do to be freed from our symptoms and fears is to arouse our deep physiological resources and consciously utilize them."[64] Tapping into these deep physiological resources invites us to restore a sense of hope where insecurity, a sense of helplessness, and a lack of regularity have divorced us from such a sense of hope. And this demands that we replace the focus on pathology with the focus on our inner resources.

Levine writes, "While trauma can be hell on earth, trauma resolved is a gift of the gods—a heroic journey that belongs to each of us[65]." We can all claim ownership precisely because we all have the innate capacity to heal our traumas.[66] A discussion about what constitutes the potentially ambiguous concept of healing or resolution of a trauma might be fruitful. We can, however, imagine that it implies reduction of symptoms, reduction of distress, and/or reduction of impairment in social, occupational, and other important areas of functioning.[67] Ultimately, this resolution is an increase in survival skills and, most important, the reexperiencing of intimate connections to others, which is difficult to endure following traumatic experiences.

"The healing of trauma is a natural process that can be accessed through an inner awareness of the body."[68] This is especially important because traumatic experiences as acts of violence disturb our senses of "bodily connectedness."[69] Treatment, therefore, requires the restoration of wholeness to an organism that has been fragmented by trauma.[70] "Music offers experiences of ourselves as embodied in sound and silence. . . . It follows that music therapy can be of use to those vulnerable to the effects of trauma because of these qualities of musical embodiment."[71] Moving through trauma requires "quietness, safety, and protection."[72]

> Internally resonating vibrations break up and release block-ages of energy, allowing a natural flow of vitality and a state of equilibrium to return to the body. These benefits are particularly relevant to traumatised clients who have frozen, numbed-off areas in the body that hold traumatic experience.[73]

Additionally, music is a multidimensional alternative route to inner awareness. The use of music in music therapy may ask that the client take notice of his or her body as it relates to his or her emotions, memories, and present sensory experiences and use this information as a tool for healing.

In comparison to the traditional cathartic approach of retelling and reexperiencing, Levine's approach suggests that confronting the trauma head-on will allow for the continuation of that trauma that provoked the original response. It will "immobilize us in fear" when, instead, "the solution to vanquishing trauma comes not through confronting it directly, but by working with its reflection, mirrored in our instinctual responses."[74] I believe this reflection and these instinctual responses are available in the making of music.

"Recovery after warfare requires change at multiple levels: political, national, community, family, and individual levels."[75]

As mentioned earlier in this chapter, "trauma has been discussed extensively as a topic belonging to the domain of the individual experience."[76] But the multilevel impact of trauma that can affect the collective in the familial, generational, communal, social, national, and political domains was highlighted for me when I worked as a research assistant in human security and girl soldiers in Sierra Leone, West Africa.

Sierra Leone is a West African nation that endured a ten-year civil war that began in 1991 with a rebellion against the national government by the Revolutionary United Front (RUF) or "rebel army." Fifty thousand people were killed, three million were wounded, and 50 percent of the country's population fled to the capital city of Freetown, where they lived in camps set up for the internally displaced. Additionally, thousands of limbs were amputated. The use of child soldiers, often abducted from communities, was widespread, including girls, who fought and served as spies, camp followers, and wives. The experiences of girls are especially significant, because they were more widely associated with the fighting forces than reported and because most did not undergo formal demobilization processes but were "spontaneously reintegrated" into their communities when possible. Consequently, they did not receive the government benefits for which many male child soldiers were eligible.

The fact that the violence experienced during wartime is human-induced and, in the case of civil war, perpetrated against one's own community is especially significant because it undermines personal integrity and destroys loyalties to families and communities. This is a process of dehumanization. Merle Friedman, a psychologist working in South Africa, lectured as part of a plenary session entitled "Warfare, Human Rights, and Recovery" at the International Society for Traumatic Stress Studies 20th Annual Meeting in November 2004. Friedman spoke about this process of dehumanization, stating that nearly every human being has a deep resistance to killing and that nearly everyone hesitates before doing so. Therefore, the need to create a feeling of hatred and to dehumanize the enemy is essential for warfare. Additionally, self-directed dehumanization is necessary to distance oneself from the atrocities that one is committing. The results are negative resilience and/or denial and dissociation.[77]

A war creating hatred, violence, and, according to Friedman, denial and dissociation is the result of complex political, economic, and sociocultural processes. For this reason, I do not herein explore the causes of the war in Sierra Leone. Instead, I discuss the girls with whom I and my research team worked. We tried to learn about their needs from a community-based perspective, opening ourselves to an understanding of the multilevel impacts of the violence in Sierra Leone. However, we learned that complex causes warrant complex resolutions on multiple levels.

In June 2002, I assisted Dr. Susan McKay in researching girls associated with the fighting forces in Sierra Leone. That study highlighted the vulnerability of girls returning from the fighting forces with babies born from rape or rebel or owner-"husbands." Young mothers, in a society suffering from collective societal trauma, were identified as among the most marginalized, neglected, and underserved of all the girls returning to communities. The violation of community norms by these girls and their inability to care for their children economically led to further despair and hardship, including an increase in health risks.

It must be emphasized that the chronic inattention and underfunding that these young mothers received was in the context of a mass communal trauma. No Sierra Leonean was unaffected by the war. As Pavlicevic[78] stated in regard to South Africa, "To live in South Africa is to live in a violent society. I would suggest that violence, here, is not a single phenomenon, but complex and multifaceted, impacting on all who live there."[79]

The same can be said for Sierra Leone. The massive upheaval in Sierra Leonean society created social disruption and the loss of its ability to function. Social systems failed, and communities experienced physical depletion and a fatigued population, resulting in a severely strained infrastructure. "When culture loses important aspects of its ability to function and becomes incapable of guiding grief reactions or provid[ing] support, individuals are left unprotected and left to their own devices."[80] This was the political, social, and psychological situation in which these young mothers were struggling to survive.

Our second trip (October 2003) was a pilot study of a community-based psychosocial needs assessment of these young mothers. We studied the process of the girls' reintegration and community responses to their return. Our team of four conducted the research in the village of Mambolo, Kambia District, western Sierra Leone. We stayed in the chief's compound and were introduced to the community by the chief of police. Both of these local men had important roles in the sensitization of the community regarding the return of the girls.

We also worked with local child protection officers; teachers; traditional healers; leaders of the women's secret society; traditional birth attendants; other elders; families; guardians; and the girls themselves. We met with girls and their mothers; girls and their babies; girls without family; girls who had reintegrated into new communities; girls working in the commercial sex trade; and girls in skills-training programs. Our translator, Mamuna, was a local teacher born and raised in the community. She and a local male teacher traveled throughout the village and the surrounding area to find the young mothers currently living in the area.

We were aware of the indigenous use of music, dance, and drama and that these were important methods for healing and acceptance, accompanying cleansing rituals, initiation rituals, and other ceremonies. It became very clear that song specifically was a culturally relevant and accepted way of communicating. Many community members greeted us in song. Although this is discussed in more detail later, note that the women elders communicated with us almost exclusively through song.

The Young Mothers: Their Songs

Song 1: "Immunizing Our Children"

As I was asking Mamuna why the girls had been using our names in the song that had just been sung, another girl began singing. The tempo was quicker than many of the songs had been, and all the girls, including Mamuna, obviously knew the song. They clapped along, just on top of the beat, pushing them to keep the quick tempo. The affect of the girls brightened overall, and I felt a sense of relief as they sang. I hummed along the second time through the song, an octave higher, feeling the bright energy of the tune.

"So, she is singing about immunization—the hospital. She is advising the suckling [breastfeeding] mothers to take their children for maculate [immunization]. You get it? Advising the suckling mothers to take their children for maculate. That's very important," Mamuna translated.

I suddenly realized why the song had such a different quality. It wasn't necessarily about the war. The link to the rebels was the fact that the children who needed immunization were products of the war.

"Yes," I responded. "Is that a song you improvised?" At that point, I was desperately trying to discover something that would help me distinguish between composed and improvised songs.

"Not improvised. She heard it somewhere else. She heard it from us at the hospital. That is the song we normally sing to the mothers," Mamuna clarified very easily.

"So this is a common song sung in the hospital?" I asked.

"Yes, we have a lot of them."

"Why do you like this song?" I asked the girl directly, expecting Mamuna to translate. I was curious why she chose this song. Mamuna and the girl spent a moment in discussion.

"Okay. She is saying that it is an educating song. It reminds her always to carry her child to the hospital for immunization," Mamuna finally replied.

Discussion of "Immunizing Our Children"

This song not only represents the multidimensional nature of music in the lives of these girls but also reminds us of its cultural and contextual relevance. Music is woven into the very fabric of Sierra Leoneans' lives.

As Mamuna clearly stated, music is used even in clinics (hospitals) as an educational tool to remind women to immunize their children. In her discussion of African clients, Pavlicevic[81] says that "music in music therapy can have a social emphasis and a political role in building social cohesion and community."

While some girls report feeling love and compassion for their babies, others report ambivalence. Returning to communities without an education or skills and with an extra mouth to feed, the mouth of a baby who was born of a rebel husband outside of the context of culturally authorized marriage, can make survival extremely difficult. Some girls have reported feeling resentful of their children. McKay, the principal investigator of the research, asserts that poor attachment in some of the relationships further distances girls from their babies and enhances the vulnerability of the children.

Despite this possibility, the girls have learned and internalized the community's song, assisting them in the care of their children. This is one more reason the girl's choice to sing that song at that moment—during an emotional discussion of songs related to the war—was significant.

As noted, African clients have a powerful relationship with music: direct experiences of specific musical genres to invoke healing spirits, as well as music to generate group healing trances.[82]

Consequently, we used music to conduct our needs assessment and to gain psychosocial insight. While this song gave us insight into the basic need for immunizations so that children might survive, we learned that the strength of this song was felt by all mothers, regardless of whether they had been in the bush with the rebels. Before long, however, girls began singing songs pertinent to their experiences with the fighting forces.

Song 2: "Escaping the Rebels"

"Did the woman with the baby have to go? The one who was here— did she have to go?" McKay asked. She was trying to figure out why one of the girls had left our meeting in the open-air roundhouse in the chief's compound, the space that became our mosquito net–covered sleeping area at night.

In the midst of McKay's inquiry, one girl began singing in her local dialect, and before long all eight girls had joined in. "Susan, they are singing your name!" McKay's attention was pulled in a new direction, and she began clapping in unison with the girls, who were keeping their rhythm with their hands as they sang. A drum hung over the entrance of the roundhouse, but we were told that it was for use in special ceremonies only and was unavailable to us or the girls with whom we worked.

The song continued for only two and a half minutes. The girls reduced the volume of their singing as they came to a cadence at the end of one of the phrases. All eight girls ended the song simultaneously.

"Yeah, that is their song," Mamuna, our translator verified.

"What is the name? What is the song?" I asked, seeking clarification. The girls talked among themselves as we tried to get a translation before they spontaneously began another song, which we learned was possible at any moment, often without request or prompting.

"She is saying that she wants to join a motorcar. She wants to join a vehicle to escape from the war. But the vehicle left before she came. So that makes her to walk by foot. She strains a lot because she has missed the vehicle," Mamuna translated, struggling to find the right method of conveying the sentiments in English.

"Is it improvised?" I asked. I pressed further, trying once again to make the distinction between composed and improvised song.

"Improvised, yeah," Mamuna repeated, appearing unsure.

"But how come you know all the words?" I asked, nearly certain that Mamuna and other girls appeared to know the song.

"Well, you know, when someone improvises a song, everyone would like to sing it. Especially when she get out [of the war]. Some people, whenever she sings, and we sing after her. The song expose to everyone," Mamuna clarified in her best English.

"Oh, so she sings once and you all hear it and then you respond." I thought she was saying that a call-and-response style of singing was being used within the improvised song at that moment in the roundhouse.

"Respond to the song," she echoes. "It's all over the town."

"Aha," I thought.

"Because it has taken a long time when practicing the song. We have come used of the song now. It is very familiar to us now." Mamuna explained that the town heard the song sung by this girl so frequently that it became familiar—and now the local people knew the song.

"But it is her song. She made it up and now the village knows it?" I asked.

"Yes, because you know when the disarmament come, everyone was allowed to sing, and she sung the song," Mamuna told me.

Discussion of "Escaping the Rebels"

The girl Mamuna was speaking about above is the girl who began that particular song in the roundhouse that day. Mamuna implied, at the close of the vignette, that girls were not able to sing before the war was over and/or when they were with the rebels. This is an example of the kind of cultural disintegration that accompanied the violent lives of those affiliated with the fighting forces. Music builds social cohesion and is part of ritualistic society. It is possible, then, that these girls experienced significant gaps in their musical, and therefore, their cultural histories. While it is unclear whether song was forbidden in the rebel army, it is clear that songs came easily to the girls following disarmament.

The history of this song, which came to be known by the entire village, is evidence that music can facilitate the expression of difficult emotions and help break the silence of isolation.[83] While this girl's experience of isolation may have changed as a result, her inability to access resources and reintegrate into the community perpetuates her vulnerability. "Under a variety of conditions, therefore, culture may be inadequate to maintain individual support and social resources. Individual or group self-help strategies may then be required."[84] Music, in this context, served as a group self-help strategy in both its use throughout the community and its use during our meeting.

Also significant is the message conveyed in the song, which speaks to the political aspect of the girls' affiliation with the fighting forces. While every girl with whom we worked in Mambolo had been abducted, there are girls in many fighting forces who enlisted or volunteered for any number of reasons—often out of a desperate need for safety. Regardless of the method by which children came to be part of the rebel army, however, child soldiers are perceived to be aggressive and violent and are often blamed for the atrocities that they may have committed against their own communities. This social perception and the fear and anger that accompany it do not make for the children's successful reintegration into the community.

Stige[85] clearly takes this position in his own work, emphasizing that one cannot work with a client (or trauma survivor) as an isolated individual, but must see the client as a cultural component of the community. He states:

> While working directly with the individual and/or group, crucial interventions in the process may also be directed toward the community itself . . . in order to work with attitudes and traditions that create barriers in the community. Very often also lack of economic priorities given by the municipality or other funding agents limit[s] the clients' possibilities for growth and

development. The work of the music therapists therefore also has a political dimension to it; they cannot be indifferent about the political discussion of education, health, and culture.[86]

For these reasons, community sensitization programs were designed to help communities welcome children back into villages as opposed to rejecting and stigmatizing them. In Mambolo, the chief ordered the town crier to announce that community members must accept the girls specifically and their babies. Many community members, including the girls themselves, reported that the verbal abuse subsided. Increased tolerance in the community meant increased access to food, health care, education, and social networks for the girls.

Although she did not hire the town crier, the girl who wrote the song in the above vignette made a personal and political statement regarding her innocence. The vehicle by which she nearly escaped represented her attempted salvation. Once she missed the vehicle, she made the decision to escape by foot, regardless of the cost to her physical body. This song tells her community as well as the two white visitors asking about her life that she was with the rebels against her will and risked her life to escape them.

Song 3: "Should I Cry?"

"So she is telling us about her—the missing—when she was playing and she was inside the room and the music she was playing (singing) .... The rebels came and moved her mother and her father, and they killed both of them. And she was carried by the rebels and she was playing music," Mamuna explained, translating a story that one of the girls told. This girl sang through her abduction after experiencing the violent death of her parents.

"Playing music while carried by the rebels? What is your favorite song to sing about your life now?" I asked. Girls had seemed resistant to singing specifically about their experiences with their rebel captors. Consequently, I changed the subject and opened the floor to possible songs about their current lives and experiences. We were, after all, interested in their processes of reintegration.

The girl began singing a melody by herself. She sang only half a phrase before her song turned into a sob. She buried her head in her hands and cried. In the silence that surrounded her, I intuitively moved my metal chair closer to her, cringing as the metal chair scraped against the cement floor of the roundhouse. No one spoke for a few minutes, and I realized that I was silent because no Sierra Leonean girl had ever cried in my presence. I didn't take my eyes off her but lightly touched her right arm.

Finally, I asked, "What are you feeling?" When I realized that I might need to speak directly to our translator to retrieve the answer, I turned to Mamuna. "What is she feeling?"

Without translating my question, Mamuna replied, "She is feeling very discouraged because she has lost her parents."

I felt frustrated that the girl was not able to answer for herself. "Can we sing a song about it? Would it be helpful?" My remedy: more song. This seemed like a natural solution.

Mamuna stopped me before I could go any further. "She tried to sing but as soon as she started singing, the feeling came out. So let us don't encourage her to sing that song again," Mamuna answered.

"Can I play her a song on my flute?" I asked, still pushing for more music.

"Let me ask her." Mamuna translated my question this time. Other girls responded as well, and a dialogue ensued. "They said 'yes.'"

"Would it be helpful?" I was cautious.

"Yeah. They are telling you that since the lady is crying they too are thinking the same thing that happened like that. So if you sing the song with the flute it might help them," Mamuna told me, referring to an emotion that all the girls in the group shared, an emotion that Mamuna would like to avoid stimulating.

I decided that this was the affirmation that I needed in order to play, and I stood up to face all the girls and began.

The maritime Canadian waltz that I played felt like a lullaby in the roundhouse on that day. I watched the girls closely as my fingers slid on and off of the keys in patterns they easily recognized, and I didn't think about the music much as I played through the A section twice. All of my energy was focused on the faces of the girls, our translator, and McKay. I began the B section in the higher register, and felt my eyes close as I felt my heart travel into the wooden flute, riding on my airstream. The last time through the B section, I began slowing down and opened my eyes just before the final note to find the girls looking up at me and smiling.

Discussion of "Should I Cry?"

Immediately following my song, the girls stated that they had to leave—all of them, simultaneously. The emotional experience of this group meeting had had a powerful effect on us all. While I understood very clearly that Mamuna did not want to encourage the girls' tears, it wasn't until McKay and I met with the women elders in the community that we learned the cultural protocol with regard to the expression of sadness and despair. It must be avoided at all costs.

Médecins Sans Frontières (MSF), an international nongovernmental organization (NGO) also known as Doctors Without Borders, was working in Sierra Leone when we were conducting our research. In brief, MSF "delivers emergency medical aid to victims of armed conflict, epidemics, and natural or man-made disasters, and to others who lack essential health care due to geographical isolation or discrimination."[87] Additionally, "MSF unites direct medical care with a commitment to bear witness and speak out against the underlying causes of suffering."[88] While "bearing witness" carries one connotation in Western society, namely the retelling of traumatic experiences in the presence of another, we learned that "speaking out against the underlying causes of suffering"—and the violence to which we refer as trauma-inducing—requires another perspective in Sierra Leone.

It wasn't until a year after this trip that I was introduced to a film made by MSF entitled "Should I Cry?" at the International Society for Traumatic Stress Studies international conference called "War As a Universal Trauma." This film documented the ways grief and loss are processed in Sierra Leone. It clarified for me the confusion connected to the experience of never previously having seen a Sierra Leonean girl cry, despite the fact that I had worked with more than 100 Sierra Leonean girls. "Crying is not the Sierra Leonean way to react to loss," one Sierra Leonean man in the film states. But the wounds are present. "I don't like to reflect my mind on it," explains another Sierra Leonean. And this explains why Mamuna not only answered for the girl when I asked her questions but also requested that I "process" her emotion in song. As one audience member pointed out in a presentation I once gave at a trauma conference in a state psychiatric facility, music, and specifically song, may have been quite connected to the trauma this girl experienced, as she clearly recollects singing during her abduction. I trust that Mamuna knew, better than I, what song meant for this girl, and the processes that would allow her to tap into her inner resource, allowing her, as MSF states in the film, to notice her own capacity for healing.

The Women Elders: Their Song

Song 4: "Let Us Forget What Has Passed"

"Okay, what would they like to learn? What would help them assist these girls more?" McKay asked Mamuna, working hard to figure out how the women elders could be trained to better assist the young mothers.

There was some discussion among the elders and Mamuna. Mamuna looked at McKay, confused, and turned to me for further clarification.

I wasn't sure how to clarify any further. "What do they need to learn? What are their weaknesses in dealing with these children?" I asked.

"Let me ask them," Mamuna responded and quickly turned to the women elders to explain the question.

"Some of them said since they are TBAs (traditional birth attendants), they are going to teach them to do deliveries. Some of them are going to teach them how to cure using native medicine, by showing them different types of leaves that would cure the sick person," Mamuna translated.

"So, teach them how to make money," McKay said, sighing. I knew she desperately wanted information about the psychosocial needs of the girls.

"Is being a traditional healer with native medicine or a TBA, does that earn them enough money to be self-sufficient or do they also need a husband?" I asked, trying a different route.

"They also need to have a husband," Mamuna responded automatically, stating an obvious cultural fact.

"So, will these girls survive if they can never get husbands?" I asked. Many community members had told us that boys don't want to marry girls who had been with the rebels because the girls know how to kill, and the boys are afraid of them.

"They can too get married," Mamuna said. She didn't seem to think that there would be a problem. "When they are doing this skill . . . man will come for the person, will come to her and say, 'I would like to marry you.'"

"So she'll be more desirable if she has a skill?" I asked.

"Yeah. A skill. As long as you are trying to get benefit in your future, a man will marry you," Mamuna explained. It seemed quite simple to her and contradicted other stories we had heard.

I responded, "Even if you come from the bush, you are associated with the rebels, you have children without a father around, if you have a skill, a man will be more likely to marry you?" I wanted to be sure that I had understood her right.

"Yeah, that's what they mean," Mamuna said.

McKay decided to get right to the point. "If there was a program that would teach them how to talk to young mothers to help them get over their trauma and maybe visit them often to see how they're doing, that kind of thing—it's a little different than teaching a trade—to actually become a mother to these girls to help them through their difficulty . . . is that the kind of thing these women would be willing to do?"

Immediately all forty women began clapping. Mamuna then began translating McKay's request, and after two full minutes, the women burst into song. They stood up from the cement seats along the periphery of the roundhouse walls and sang together in call-and-response style. They clapped as they sang and remained very rhythmic. At the close of the song, they cheered together, "A porto, oh, yea! A porto, oh yea!" I realized they were referring to us—the *portos*—using the generic term for "white person."

Mamuna smiled brightly. "They have a nice song! They are having nice songs! Yea … let me tell you first the answer before giving you the meaning of the song." Mamuna then addressed the women to clarify their answer to McKay's question. "So, the answer they gave, they said beside learning the skill, they encourage them by singing, singing nice songs to them so that they will forget what has passed to them by not thinking all the time what was passed. So that is why they [would call them] together, [to sing] some songs, by learning some songs. So that is the example they have made," Mamuna said, explaining that the song the elders had just sung was an example of a song that they would sing with the girls in the role that McKay had suggested.

"So the meaning of the song," Mamuna continues, "is let us forget what has passed. Just don't keep on thinking about what has passed. So please, please, let us forget what has passed."

Discussion of "Let Us Forget What Has Passed"

In Sierra Leone, it is understood that memories intensify trauma by opening wounds. McKay had asked whether the elders would be willing to be trained to work with girls' psychosocial needs. The song with which the elders spontaneously responded reflected the local understanding of the route to health and healing. This is in keeping with Mamuna's response to the tears of the girl who had shared the story about the role of song for her following her parents' deaths and during her abduction. In a discussion of the impact of the Troubles in Northern Ireland, Smyth[89] describes a culture of "denial and silence which prevailed" in the country at one point. She quotes Turner, McFarlane, and van der Kolk,[90] who point out that "traumatisation may lead to problems in tolerating intimacy, the impulse to avoid the suffering caused by the traumatic situation, and shame and guilt, all of which are factors that may impede therapeutic engagement."[91]

Certainly the women in Sierra Leone were communicating that avoiding the suffering was important, and this discussion of Northern Ireland reminds us that it is a common response to trauma. Smyth goes on to offer nonverbal methods, including music therapy, as potentially capable of offering a "diversity of paths to integration and potential resolution to those who have been traumatized."[92] It appears that song, in Sierra Leone, can simultaneously demand tolerance for intimacy and "provide a vehicle for exploring the traumatic experience without requiring a tolerance for intimacy,"[93] depending on the context of the song and the individual experiences. Either way, however, song is the modality through which Sierra Leoneans actively process. Intimate or not, it can remind one of traumatic experiences or plead with one to forget them.

The Young Mothers: Their Songs

Songs 5-7: "Men of Today"

"I wonder if anyone is loving anyone right now (in a relationship)—if any of you have husbands or boyfriends," I asked following an extensive discussion about skills training from which I couldn't manage to steer us away.

Mamuna became momentarily distracted, shooing away a boy who approached the roundhouse, intrigued by the meeting. "I said, 'When you come here, do you see any man here? No, so go!!'" she explains.

Mamuna asked me to repeat my question, and she then translated to the group of girls. "That one explains about herself. Since she was still healing trauma—traumatized—she doesn't need any man by this time."

"Anyone else?" I asked, wondering if a local word exists for "trauma" and how the girl might have explained this.

"After learning the skills, she'll have a man," Mamuna translated for another girl.

"Is there a man now or are you hoping to meet a man?" I inquired further.

"After the skills [training]," Mamuna explained for the group.

Girls began speaking simultaneously, and Mamuna had to call on them one at a time to clarify their individual responses.

"Me, I don't get man," one girl offered in English. I was surprised.

"She don't have any man," Mamuna translated.

"No?" I asked, hoping to elicit more information.

"No. The rebel impregnated her, when she had that child. But not now. She doesn't need no child, no other child yet, until she chooses the right man," Mamuna translated.

"Yes?" Mamuna called on another girl. "Since when she was from the bush, when she was impregnated by that RUF man, he lost, he disappeared. And now she's presently living with her mother and she hasn't got any man yet," Mamuna translated for yet another girl.

"Yes?" Mamuna called on a third girl. "Oh. She said when in the bush she had two children. So, when she came here, she doesn't meet her parents. They were killed. And now she's always thinking over that. How can she take care of these children? And if she should have been fortunate to join this program [a skills training program], she'd be happier. So, she'd like to learn a skill and after learning a skill she will be able to provide for her children in the end," Mamuna said.

The girls continued to talk about their need for skills training. It was interesting that the answers to my questions about boyfriends and husbands were focused on skills training. The girls were hoping that we would clearly hear their desire for opportunities to be economically self-sufficient, to provide for themselves and their children, and ultimately to survive. Despite our consistent reiteration that we were simply doing research that would benefit girls in their positions in the future and that we could not offer them direct material assistance, these girls would have been doing themselves a disservice if they didn't appeal to visiting foreigners for support. So I attempted to redirect the meeting, asking the girls to share intangible feelings and emotions in song.

"She is saying the same thing as they said about not marrying now. She would like to learn a skill," Mamuna reiterated for the fourth time.

"I wonder," and I paused, trying to decide on a tactic. "This is so important, and I wonder if we could maybe sing a song about how you feel about men right now—about, perhaps, how this issue is important or about good or bad feelings toward men," I blurted.

Immediately after Mamuna's translation, a girl began singing a slow song. The other girls began clapping, and one by one joined in the melody. The second time through the same phrase, the entire group, including Mamuna, joined in.

"Ah . . . oh . . . marvelous song!" Mamuna exclaimed.

The girl who began the song sang the next phrase solo, then the rest of the group repeated it in unison. The song ended after the original verse was sung one more time through.

"Oooo, marvelous song!" Mamuna exclaimed again at the song's close. Then she began translating the lyrics. "These men today, they like to disappoint women. They are telling you sweet words but they are not going to benefit you in the end. And later on they disappear from you. After having contact with you, they will leave you and go somewhere else. So men of today, they are bad."

"Maybe another song about men?" McKay asked.

Mamuna laughed with the girls as she told them in Krio, "A one again for men [another song about men]. This is the first time of hearing this song. I don't ever come across it. I don't know it." Mamuna explained that the song just sung was new to her.

"But did anyone else know it?" I asked, curious about how often these girls were able to spontaneously improvise songs about their emotional states.

"Yeah, you can hear them when they are answering the song," Mamuna responded, referring to the call-and-response style. "It seems as though they are familiar with the song."

Before I could respond, another girl spontaneously began singing. She sang an entire eight-measure phrase by herself as the others began clapping.

"Okay, I know this one," Mamuna said as the singing continued. The entire group, including Mamuna, repeated the eight phrases. All sixteen measures were repeated one more time in the same form, and then the group ended together.

"Whatever they have done to us, the men, whatever they have done to us, if they are doing bad to us, God will fight them in a bad way. But if they are doing good to us, God will help them in a good way. Yes . . . the good will follow them and if it is bad, the bad will follow them too," Mamuna translated.

The girls began talking freely among themselves while Mamuna translated. Then one girl sang a four-beat phrase and the others responded with a different four-beat phrase. This song was sung in a much lower register than the others, and this trading of phrases continued throughout the song.

"It normally goes, this song, it goes to the disappointing men. Whatever they have promised the ladies—to marry them, and have one child—then they disappear. So it's asking 'if they do that one to you, are you going to be happy?' That's the meaning of the song. 'If I do that one to you, will you be happy or not?' " Mamuna explained that the song was asking the men to reflect on their behavior and to imagine what they might feel had they been treated as they have treated women and girls in their communities.

"They are singing to the men," I responded.

The girls began talking softly and appeared to be trying to remember another song. But Mamuna still appeared to be invested in the last song and nodded her head. Finally, she said, "If I do that to you, how will you feel? Will you be happy or not? I will not be happy. I will not be happy. I will not."

Discussion of "Men of Today"

In traditional verbal interview style, most of the girls were able to share with us that they did not have a desire to be married. But when we attempted to· ask the girls why, the answers we received were related to skills training. Outside the context of song, there appeared to be an inability to share feelings or emotions, and intangible needs.

For example, McKay and I had tried numerous times, during the course of both fieldwork trips, to ask the girls directly about their psychosocial needs. I literally asked, "What does your heart feel?" "How is your mind?" "What hurts and what feels good?" But the girls always responded with tangible needs. Girls told us that their hearts needed sewing machines to practice their skills, medicine to get well, and food for their babies. I was astonished when I realized that their feelings toward men, following the extreme sexual violence they had experienced during the war, were accessible in song.

To some extent, the girls attempted to convey, in spoken conversation, the sentiments the songs expressed. These expressions, however, required the listener to make assumptions about what the girl was implying. The responses were not direct, perhaps because the possibility of vulnerability was too great. When conveyed through the structure of a song, however—with rhythm, groove, and a tune—a clear frame can be placed around the emotions and, in this way, they are contained.

Lakoff's model of cross-domain mapping[94] discussed earlier, is applicable here. Music, as a metaphorical indicator, can provide insight into psychological and emotional states. This last vignette, including songs five through seven, are lower in pitch and slower in tempo than the other three songs discussed in this article. Additionally, the basic beat of songs five through seven has a larger time value so that the basic beat felt slower (girls were clapping the half note as opposed to the quarter note). We can attribute the conceptualization of feeling states to spatial orientations and then link them to the musical realm. While not celebratory in nature, as other songs felt, these songs about the girls' anger toward men were much lower and slower than the songs that preceded them. The previous songs had been upbeat, high, and fast. These music states correspond with down, low, or even slow mental states. Although the songs' lyrics, translated by Mamuna, appeared to express anger and resentment, the musical elements of the songs clarified that many experiences of sadness (and tears) lie beneath the Sierra Leonean exterior.

The ramifications of this self-described anger reach more widely than the circumference of the lives of these young mothers. While we do not know how many total young mothers are reintegrating from the fighting forces, it seemed clear while we were in Kambia that at least a hundred young mothers could have been identified had we spent more time in the single village.

It is clear that traditional gender roles and relations are shifting as girls emerge from the fighting forces unwilling to marry. Social roles and values are radically different for these girls than they were for any previous generation. How will this change Sierra Leonean culture? How is this reality affecting the perceptions of these young mothers? Is it limiting their possibility for growth, development, and inclusion in society?

> Provided that the individual does not interfere with the group's capacity to reproduce or remain viable in its niche, cultural social roles, shared values, and historical continuity will act as key stress manager[s]. If the individual does not fit, social extrusion and stigmatization may result as a cultural defense reaction to the unwanted information or behavior.[95]

And so the struggle continues, with no evident end in sight.

Conclusion: Restoring Connection and Personal Capacities for Healing

The Sierra Leonean girls discussed here presented unwanted information and/or behaviors to their communities. The key stress managers of sociocultural roles, shared values, and historical continuity were not available to provide assistance in the construction of relationships in the lives of these individuals. Additionally, trauma victims already experience disruptions in their interpersonal relationships and struggle to sustain those that are emotionally and psychologically healthy. Therefore, the restoration of connection and building of social cohesion are essential components in the healing process of trauma survivors.

In the case vignettes described above, music exposed its capacity for "stimulating and cementing social integration and personal relationships."[96] Being invested in shared music-making requires that two people are engaged in relationship. As Pavlicevic[97] writes of South African children, ". . . the act of shared music-making in music therapy offers the opportunity and confidence to rebuild relationships with themselves, with one another, and ultimately, hopefully, within their communities."[98]

Reinvesting in oneself following exposure to profound violence is crucial, as every individual must learn how to access his/her personal capacity for healing.

> Music created through a process of interaction between people can take on a life of its own, and in turn transform those who create it. The transformation is temporary, but the experience of having been transformed, and the discovery of new possibilities, are more permanent.[99]

The young mothers with whom we worked in Sierra Leone taught us that they had discovered their personal capacity for healing through song long before we arrived. Songs that these girls had spontaneously sung weeks, months, and/or years earlier were now readily known and sung within the community.

A "sense of self, other, and relationship is a central part of musical engagement, and has important implications for a more general notion of human rights."[100] Rebuilding relationships with one another was also crucial for the survival of the young mothers. Many of them did not want to publicly announce their histories, and did not know who to trust. In the roundhouse during our meetings, girls came to know one another and share with one another and thereby further enable their own personal capacities for healing. Most of these exchanges appeared to occur through song.

The potential for intimacy is "primarily an ability to tolerate one's inner world and the contradictions it presents. Withdrawal from intimacy in personal relationships is one of the most enduring effects of trauma. This makes it particularly important to understand the role of intimacy in the therapeutic relationship."[101] Tischa and Ed both restored connections through an intimacy generated in their active music-making. Because Ed was in a music therapy group, he had the opportunity to explore these kinds of connections with a number of people simultaneously. Alternatively, Tischa, working in the context of individual therapy, developed a single strong attachment to me, her therapist.

In Sierra Leone, where access to social systems at many levels of society appeared possible, it became clear that social cohesion was crucial for the survival of the young mothers and their babies. The women elders confirmed that song was the path they would take if asked to assist the girls. Women elders sang songs reminding us of the importance of the sociocultural context of which the girls are a part.

Dixon,[102] in his discussion of music therapy and international trauma, states that "the way music-making reaches and draws out the essential humanity of the most unreachable people places it in direct opposition to political violence, which denies the humanity and individuality of its victims."[103] Musical interaction simultaneously reveals our uniqueness as individuals as well as the connections between us, constituting our common humanity.[104] Therefore, music in music therapy can assist individuals in revealing personal capacities for healing and in restoring reengagement and connection with others. As many of the case vignettes demonstrate, creativity following exposure to profound violence has the capacity to enable the building of social cohesion and community that rejects oppression and abuse and, instead, embraces human security and peace.

Notes

1. Marie Smyth, "The Role of Creativity in Healing and Recovering One's Power After Victimization," in *Music, Music Therapy, and Trauma: International Perspectives*, ed. J.P. Sutton, 76 (London: Jessica Kingsley Publishers, 2002).

2. D. Mazurana, S. McKay, K. Carlson and J. Kasper, "Girls in Fighting Forces and Groups: Their Recruitment, Participation, Demobilization, and Reintegration," *Peace and Conflict, Journal of Peace Psychology* 8, 2 (2002): 97-123.

3. UNICEF, "Convention on the Rights of the Child", UNICEF, http://www.unicef.org/crc/crc.htm.

4. Maria Gonsalves, *Human Security and Girls in Fighting Forces* (Unpublished manuscript, University of Wyoming, Laramie, 2002).

5. Dyan Mazurana and Susan McKay, *Where Are the Girls? Girls in Fighting Forces in Northern Uganda, Sierra Leone, and Mozambique: Their Lives During and After War* (Montreal: Rights and Democracy, International Centre for Human Rights and Democratic Development, 2003).

6. Ibid.

7. Judith Herman, *Trauma and Recovery: The Aftermath of Violence from Domestic Abuse to Political Terror* (New York: Basic Books, 1992), 7.

8. American Psychiatric Association, *Diagnostic and Statistic Manual of Mental Disorders (DSM-IV-TR)* (Washington, DC: American Psychiatric Association, 2000), 463.

9. Eve Carlson, *Trauma Assessments: A Clinician's Guide (*New York: Guilford Press, 1997), 109.

10. N. Djapo, R. Katalinski, H. Pasalic, et al., "Long-term Postwar Adjustment of War-exposed Bosnian Adolescents" in R. Stuvland and M. Black, Chairs, *UNICEF Psychosocial Projects in Bosnia and Herzegovina 1993-1999* (Symposium conducted at the "Psychosocial Consequences of War: Results of

Empirical Research from the Territory of Former Yugoslavia" Conference, Sarajevo, Bosnia, July 2000), 287.

11. Peter Levine, *Waking the Tiger: Healing Trauma* (Berkeley, CA: North Atlantic Books, 1997), 1.

12. Ibid., 10.

13. Mercedes Pavlicevic, "Between Chaos and Creativity: Music Therapy with Traumatised Children in South Africa" in *Music, Music Therapy, and Trauma: International Perspectives,* ed. Julie Sutton, 97-118 (London: Jessica Kingsley Publishers, 2002), 102.

14. Julie Sutton, "Trauma in Context" in *Music, Music Therapy, and Trauma: International Perspectives,* ed. J. P. Sutton, 21-40 (London: Jessica Kingsley Publishers, 2002), 25.

15. N. Murray, "The Therapeutic Use of Music with Children Affected by the Troubles in Northern Ireland and the Challenges Faced by the Therapist" in *Working with Children and Young People in Violently Divided Societies: Papers from South Africa and Northern Ireland,* ed. M. Smyth and K. Thomson, (n.p.) (Derry, Londonderry: INCORE/UN University: University of Ulster, 2000), 2.

16. Adva Frank-Schwebel and David Yellin, "Trauma and Its Relation to Sound and Music" in *Music, Music Therapy, and Trauma: International Perspectives,* ed. J. P. Sutton, 193-207 (London: Jessica Kingsley Publishers, 2002).

17. Diane Austin, "In Search of the Self: The Use of Vocal Holding Techniques with Adults Traumatized as Children," *Music Therapy Perspectives* 19, 1 (2001): 22-30.

18. Pavlicevic "Between Chaos and Creativity," 102.

19. Austin, "In Search of the Self," 231.

20. Austin, "In Search of the Self," Frank-Schwebel and Yellin, "Trauma and Its Relation to Sound and Music."

21. Sutton, "Trauma in Context," 25.

22. Murray, "The Therapeutic Use of Music with Children."

23. Ibid.

24. Daniel Stern, *The First Relationship* (Cambridge: Harvard University Press, 2002).

25. Murray, "The Therapeutic Use of Music with Children," 2.

26. Levine, *Waking the Tiger: Healing Trauma.*

27. Sutton, "Trauma in Context."

28. Pavlicevic, "Between Chaos and Creativity".

29. Alan Turry, "Don't Let the Fear Prevent the Grief: Working with Traumatic Reactions Through Improvisation" in *Caring for the Caregiver: The Use of Music and Music Therapy in Grief and Trauma,* ed. Joanne Loewy and Andrea Hara, 44-53 (Silver Spring, MD: American Music Therapy Association, 2002).

30. Joanne Loewy, "Caring for the Caregiver: Training and Development." In *Caring for the Caregiver: The Use of Music and Music Therapy in Grief and Trauma*, ed. J. V. Loewy, and A. F. Hara, 1-8 (Silver Spring, MD: American Music Therapy Association, 2002), 25.

31. Pavlicevic "Between Chaos and Creativity," 99.

32. Pavlicevic "Between Chaos and Creativity."

33. Murray, "The Therapeutic Use of Music with Children."

34. Martha Bragin, "Can Anybody Know Who I Am? Reflections on Working with Refugee and Immigrant Children and Families" in M. Bragin, *Refugee and Immigrant Families and Children Project*, (Presentation conducted at the White Institute Child and Adolescent Psychotherapy Training Program New York, NY, December 2004).

35. Stuart W. Turner, Alexander C. McFarlane, and Bessel A. van der Kolk, "The Therapeutic Environment and New Explorations in the Treatment of Post-traumatic Stress Disorder" in *Traumatic Stress: The Effects of Overwhelming Experience on Mind, Body, and Society*, ed. B. A. van der Kolk, A. C. McFarlane, and L. Weisaeth (New York: Guilford Press, 1996), 538.

36. Levine, *Waking the Tiger: Healing Trauma*, 48.

37. Ibid., 48.

38. I. Powch, R. Scurfield, L. Daniels, et al., "Gestalt and Emotion-focused Approaches to Posttrauma Therapy" in J. Ruzek and P. Watson, Chairs, "War as a Universal Trauma," (Symposium conducted at the meeting of the International Society for Traumatic Stress Studies, New Orleans, LA, November 2004).

39. Powch, Scurfield, Daniels, et al., 2004.

40. Austin, "In Search of the Self."

41. Ibid., 236.

42. Neil Boothby and Jennifer Crawford, "Former Child Soldiers in Mozambique: A Life Outcome Study" in J. Ruzek and P. Watson, Chairs, "War as a Universal Trauma," (Symposium conducted at the meeting of the International Society for Traumatic Stress Studies, New Orleans, LA. November 2004).

43. Smyth, "The Role of Creativity in Healing," 77.

44. Levine, *Waking the Tiger: Healing Trauma*, 39.

45. Turry, "Don't Let the Fear Prevent the Grief," 48.

46. Spei, personal communication, November 17, 2004.

47. As cited in Brynjulf Stige, *Culture-centered Music Therapy* (Gilsum, NH: Barcelona Publishers, 2002), 129-131.

48. Stige, *Culture-centered Music Therapy*, 129-31.

49. Turner, McFarlane, and van der Kolk, "The Therapeutic Environment and New Explorations," 538.

50. Turry, "Don't Let the Fear Prevent the Grief."

51. Turner, McFarlane, and van der Kolk, "The Therapeutic Environment and New Explorations;" Turry, "Don't Let the Fear Prevent the Grief."

52. Levine, *Waking the Tiger: Healing Trauma*, 6.

53. Ibid., 7.

54. Ibid.

55. Ibid., 6.

56. Turner, McFarlane, and van der Kolk, "The Therapeutic Environment and New Explorations," 538.

57. Stige, *Culture-centered Music Therapy*, 87.

58. Levine, *Waking the Tiger: Healing Trauma*.

59. Ibid., 16.

60. Ibid., 17.

61. Ibid., 21.

62. [62] B. van der Kolk, S. Turner, and A. McFarlane, eds., *Traumatic Stress: The Effects of Overwhelming Experience on Mind, Body, and Society*. New York: Guilford Press, 1996.

63. Levine, *Waking the Tiger: Healing Trauma*, 19.

64. Ibid., 31.

65. Ibid., 12.

66. Ibid., 32.

67. American Psychiatric Association. *Diagnostic and Statistic Manual of Mental Disorders*.

68. Levine, *Waking the Tiger: Healing Trauma*, 34.

69. Sutton, "Trauma in Context," 35.

70. Marie Smyth, Ibid., 60.

71. Levine, *Waking the Tiger: Healing Trauma*, 35.

72. Ibid., 35-36.

73. Austin, "In Search of the Self," 235.

74. Levine, *Waking the Tiger: Healing Trauma*, 65.

75. S. Turner, M. Friedman, and S. Bloom, "Warfare, Human Rights, and Recovery" in J. Ruzek and P. Watson, Chairs, *War as a Universal Trauma*, (Symposium conducted at the meeting of the International Society for Traumatic Stress Studies, New Orleans, LA, November 2004).

76. Spei, personal communication with the author, November 17, 2004.

77. Turner, Friedman and Bloom, "Warfare, Human Rights, and Recovery."

78. Pavlicevic "Between Chaos and Creativity."

79. Pavlicevic "Between Chaos and Creativity," 99.

80. M. DeVries, "Trauma in Cultural Perspective" in *Traumatic Stress: The Effects of Overwhelming Experience on Mind, Body, and Society*, ed. B. van der Kolk, A. C. McFarlane, and L. Weisaeth (New York: Guilford Press, 1996).

81. Pavlicevic "Between Chaos and Creativity."

82. Pavlicevic "Between Chaos and Creativity."
83. Smyth, "The Role of Creativity in Healing."
84. M. DeVries,1996, 408 (2nd time)
85. Stige, *Culture-centered Music Therapy*.
86. Ibid., 118.
87. Médicins Sans Frontières, *U.S. Annual Report 2003: MSF 2003* [Brochure] (New York: Médicins Sans Frontières, 2003).
88. Ibid.
89. Smyth, "The Role of Creativity in Healing."
90. S. Turner, A. C. McFarlane, and B. A. van der Kolk (1996)
91. Smyth, "The Role of Creativity in Healing, 77.
92. Ibid., 77.
93. Ibid., 77.
94 Kenneth Aigen,, *Music-centered music therapy*, Gilsum, NH: Barcelona Publishers, 2005
95. M. DeVries, 1996
96. Michael Swallow, "The Brain – Its Music and Its Emotion: The Neurology of Trauma" in *Music, Music Therapy, and Trauma: International Perspectives*, ed. Julie Sutton, 41-56 (London: Jessica Kingsley Publishers, 2002), 42.
97. Pavlicevic "Between Chaos and Creativity."
98. Pavlicevic "Between Chaos and Creativity," 116.
99. Matthew Dixon, "Music and Human Rights" in *Music, Music Therapy, and Trauma: International Perspectives*, ed. Julie Sutton, 119-32 (London: Jessica Kingsley Publishers, 2002), 128.
100. Ibid., 130.
101. S. Turner, A. C. McFarlane, and B. A. van der Kolk, 1996, 538
102. Dixon, "Music and Human Rights".
103. Ibid., 131.
104. Ibid., 131.

EIGHT

The Role of Traditional Women in Postwar Reconstruction in Liberia

Roland Tuwea
Clarke

This article explores the issue of traditional women's roles in postwar reconstruction in Liberia, social and political reconstruction, and peacebuilding programs.

The article looks at and elaborates on the currently increasing power of non-traditional women in the economic, political, and social structures of Liberian society. In doing so, it identifies the gap that exists between traditional and nontraditional women and creates an inclusive framework in order to close the gap and build capacity for power balance and social equality along gender lines. This framework also creates opportunities for participation of traditional women in postwar reconstruction programs from grassroots to national levels.

The framework suggested in this article contrasts greatly with the current framework in that it has to do with undermining the many decades of traditional practices that clearly defined gender roles that give men more power. This means exposing a system that has been accustomed to male domination for many decades and eliminating the mentality that essentialized traditional women and viewed them as subordinate to men. Unfortunately, recognizing traditional women's roles inevitably has the potential to create conflict between men and women regarding roles and power differences, especially in a male-dominated culture like Liberia.

Despite these realities, I am hopeful that the article will offer substantial opportunity to Liberians to see the need and importance of increasing women's participation in social and political reconstruction.

In order to minimize and mitigate these risks, this article offers educational opportunity and awareness to Liberians by creating an understanding and increasing awareness of the importance of creating an inclusive framework in national postwar reconstruction. It encourages traditional women to participate in social and political reconstruction and in decision making. In doing so, these women can become significant factors in sustaining social justice, democracy, and peacebuilding. It intends to offer more educational opportunities in rural communities to further create explicit understanding of the issue it tries to address. Most importantly, it provides traditional leaders with intensive educational awareness programs to address and heal their concerns.

The desired impact is to challenge a broken Liberian society to engage in reconstruction processes that redefine and reconstruct the roles of women, especially traditional women, in society.

In order to address this issue, it is necessary to consider several questions: Is Liberian society willing to accept the responsibility of recognizing traditional women in a reconstruction process? If the society desires true reconstruction, reconciliation, and democracy, it must accept and recognize the role of traditional women as a key factor for reconstructing a peaceful and stable society. How would the impact of women's involvement be significant to Liberian society? Will contemporary men in Liberia see the revival of traditional women's roles as a huge contribution to the present cultural, religious, and political shift in Liberia? Will traditional Liberian men shift their cultural values and identities to increase their acceptance of the changing role of traditional women in society? These questions illustrate the seriousness of this study and suggest my commitment to engage in this research.

In order to unveil this subject, two theoretical perspectives must be considered. The first perspective to consider is feminism, which is the most popular approach to the study of women. On the other hand, the religious perspective (Islam and Christianity)—the practice of religion is crucial to and dominates Liberian society—is the contrasting theory to feminist theory. These theoretical perspectives will be part of the literature of this article.

The thrust of this work is to collaborate with other studies of women's roles in Liberia that continue to break ground for power balancing and equality. It will contribute to creating a framework of awareness and understanding of what power is and how Liberian society can provide constructive opportunities for more women's participation in the ongoing democratic and political reconstruction process. In addition, it creates awareness for traditional women to see their vulnerability and the social injustice and aggression against them; more importantly, it creates opportunities and a better future for traditional women in Liberia.

A Brief History of Liberia

Liberia, which translates as the "Land of Freedom," was founded by a group of freed slaves from the U.S. during the period of 1818 to 1822 by an organization known as the America Colonization Society (ACS). The ACS was heavily supported by the United States government. This new group created another ethic group known as the Americo-Liberians and became part of the sixteen main ethnic tribes in Liberia. The ACS dominated the political, religious, health, and educational systems in Liberia until the first indigenous president was elected in the mid-1900s.[1] As of 2004, the population of Liberia was over three million, and Americo-Liberians made up 15 percent of that number.[2] Half of the 15 percent is made up of freed slaves from the U.S., and the other half from the Caribbean.

Indigenous Liberia

When the settlers arrived on the coast of Liberia, whether it was a free land and there were no occupants is debatable. In fact, Africa during this era was viewed as a dark continent by the settlers. Gilbert and Reynolds[3] state that Liberia was declared as the lone star of Africa, signifying the first independent country on the continent. However, other studies have shown that the region of Liberia was inhabited as far back as the twelfth century. The Mende, Bassa, Deys, Kru, Gissi, and Gola were the first to arrive on the land. The influx of these early tribes started when the Western Sudanic Mali Empire declined in 1375 and 1591. When these tribal groups migrated, they brought with them skills like cotton spinning, cloth weaving, iron smelting, and the cultivation of rice and other crops. In addition, these tribal groups also instituted forms of government adopted from the Mali and Songhay Empires. Since this era, more tribes began to grow as a result of migration. Keep in mind that there was much opposition to and violence toward the new tribes that were migrating, especially the Vai and the Grebo tribes. However, the indigenous tribal groups make up 80 percent of the population of Liberia and total sixteen ethic groups since 1821.

This historical perspective of Liberia suggests that the creation and formation of the nation of Liberia was chaotic and problematic. It also created grounds for disunity and discrimination among occupants in the land. Occupants of the land came from different parts of the world, speaking different languages, held different forms of leadership styles and different traditional practices; most importantly, the government of freed slaves from the U.S., which dominated for many decades, was not inclusive at all. Therefore, there is no doubt that the formation of the nation set the grounds for civil uprising and violence in the land. Let us shift our attention to the most recent era.

According to Dunn-Marcos, Kollehlon, and Ngovo,[4] Liberians have recently witnessed two faces of war over a decade and a half. Since 1989, Liberia's two civil wars, between 1989-1996 and 1999-2003, devastated and displaced hundreds of thousand of Liberians and other nationals. These two wars paralyzed the political, educational, social, and economic systems in Liberia.

Figure 1: Population of Liberia

In addition, Steven Radelet[5] of the Center for Global Development in an article entitled "Reviving Economic Growth in Liberia" points out that Liberian civil turmoil and decimation can be traced back to twenty-five years of gross economic mismanagement and fourteen years of brutal civil war that destroyed more than 270,000 lives, made over 500,000 citizens refugees, and resulted in a complete destruction of the social, political, economic, and governance systems. Liberia's nightmare finally came to an end when a democratically elected government was inaugurated in January 2006. This new government now faces the challenge of reconstructing new policies, reconciliation and peace, and strong systems of government through postwar election as mandated.

Article XVII and IX of the Comprehensive Peace Agreement in Ghana[6] outlines the formation and organization of the postwar democratic election. Parties to the peace accord emphatically agreed to an October 2005 deadline for postwar election in Liberia that will be inclusive and transparent with the international community involvement.

Nicolas Cook,[7] a specialist in African affairs at the Foreign Affairs, Defense, and Trade Division, describes the postwar reconstruction election in Liberia in October 2005, with a presidential run-off in November as groundbreaking for democracy and reconstruction. The election fulfilled a key goal of an August 2003 peace accord in Ghana, which ended the civil war and created the framework for postwar reconstruction, peace, and democracy building. On November 15, 2005, the National Elections Commission[8] (NEC) of Liberia declared Ellen Johnson-Sirleaf the winner of the presidential race, making her the first-ever female president in Africa.

Ellen Johnson Sirleaf and Steven Radelet[9] in an essay state that Liberia's new postwar government faces a huge challenge of rebuilding a country from the ashes of war. They point out that for success to be achieved, the new government needs to implement and reconstruct polices aimed at political and economic stability; it would have to rebuild institutions that promote human capacity for all and create political and economic opportunities for all and not for a small elite. In addition, these opportunities must be inclusive and equitable for all Liberians, especially along gender lines.

Liberian Women's First Recognition

> It takes a village to raise a child,
> but if a woman does not bring forth a child,
> the village would not have a child to raise,
> the village would not have a
> King to lead and an Ancestor to worship.
>
> – Roland Clarke

In 1910, women in Liberia became organized and recognized for the first time because of their talent in arts and quilting. Liberian women were traditionally recognized for their hospitable, cultural, arts, and craft skills. In 1857 and 1858, Liberia hosted national fairs where for the first time, women exhibited their skills in various needle arts and where many prizes were awarded.[10] This organization did not represent every woman. It was made up of women descendents of freed slaves who brought these skills with them from the U.S. There is also evidence that traditional women were skillful enough to participate in national programs. They could demonstrate traditional arts like singing and dancing, storytelling, and traditional crafts. However, women collectively continue to be filtered through the lens of these stereotypes and myths for participation in political, social, educational, and. economical development in Liberia. I must emphasize that this new women's organization only represented women with formal education, mostly from the Americo-Liberian descent, and women whose husbands were leaders in the Liberian government during that period. Therefore, the above information offers us a clear picture of the gap that exists between traditional women and nontraditional women.

On a practical note, traditional women's first recognition came when Samuel Doe took over in 1980. This was a revolution for all, regardless of the challenges and failures the government had. This was the very first time indigenous and traditional women took to the chanting for freedom and singing freedom songs, like, "Native woman born soldier." This gave birth to more involvement of women in the government, an eye-opening time for traditional women in Liberia. Since then, women from every background began to speak out and demand women's rights and freedom, including the current president, Dr. Ellen Johnson Sirleaf.

> Women are more concerned about people....
> They are in the homes carrying the burden
> of the home and the family. [From that experience,]
> women bring a sensibility, a sensitivity,
> to those things which bring peace.
> > – President Ellen Johnson Sirleaf

> Women have played a leadership role in
> the cause of peace. But their efforts have
> not been recognized, supported or rewarded.
> > – UNIFEM Executive Director Noeleen Heyzer

> What women want, God wants. Congolese mothers want peace.
> – Banner carried by women in the Democratic Republic of Congo

Analysis of the Election

In order for me to design and analyze the election graphs, I had to view the data of the National Election Commission of Liberia through their website. Part of my limitation is that the data reviewed only reflects information of 2005 election results. From my understanding, there were follow-up elections, but those data were not available. However, from the data review, I was able to produce the graphs shown below. These graphs illustrate results and statistics of the 2005 election that point out the huge gender gap in decision making and in the Liberian legislators.

Figure 2: 2005 Total Voters Registered

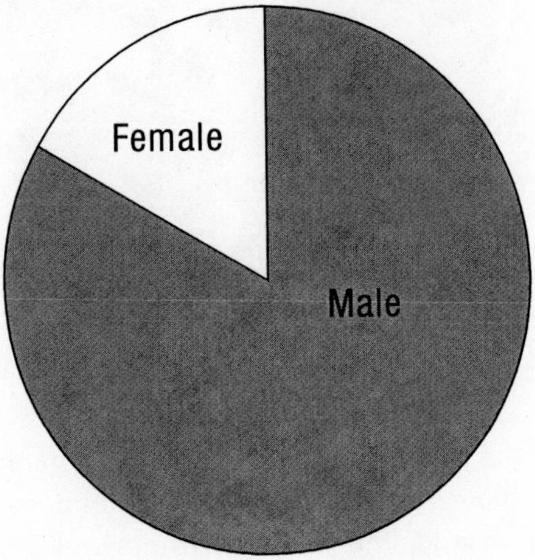

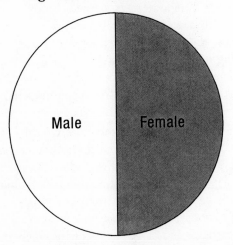

25 men and only 5 females were registered to vote

Figure 3: Elected to the Senate

50% male and 50% female elected to the senate

Figure 4: Elected to the House of Representatives

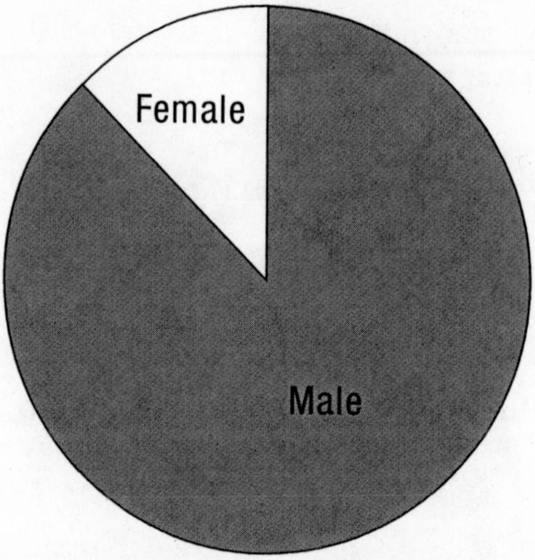

56 men were elected as compared to 8 women

It is clear that the three graphs above show another limitation. There is no data that show the gap between traditional and nontraditional women. However, the election guidelines and constitution of Liberia clearly exclude traditional women and limit their chances of becoming elected into officers and in decision making. The economic and educational requirements are the walls that prevent traditional participation in postwar reconstruction.

In addition to these challenges, women are disadvantaged and the proportion of elected legislators is overwhelming unequal. From this backdrop, it is fair to deduce that traditional women in Liberia continue to struggle to cross the trace holes and gaps that deny and exclude them from participating in postwar reconstruction. This is not only a Liberian problem, it occurs in other African countries that are undergoing postwar reconstruction as well. Some East African countries have made improvements in closing gender gaps, yet for Liberia, more work needs to be done.

In an article entitled "Women and Post-Conflict Reconstruction in Africa,"[11] Harriette Williams points out that women experience and suffer disproportionately from the effects of war and violence. While they advocate for peace and stability, they often find themselves unjustifiably marginalized and essentialized in the reconstruction and peace building process. Williams points to research in some eastern African countries concerning women's equal participation in government in which she identifies that, in 2003, Rwanda accounted for 48.8 percent of women participating in decision making; in Mozambique, the number was 34.8 percent; in South Africa, 32.8 percent, and in Burundi, 30.5 percent. Williams agrees that there has been significant progress in closing the gap of gender equality since 1995, but some countries like Liberia, Sierra Leone, and Ghana need to work harder to increase women's participation in government.

Creating Inclusive Framework

A leader is only born from a woman....
If you educate a woman, you have educated the society....
— Roland Clarke

Fig 5: New Construction

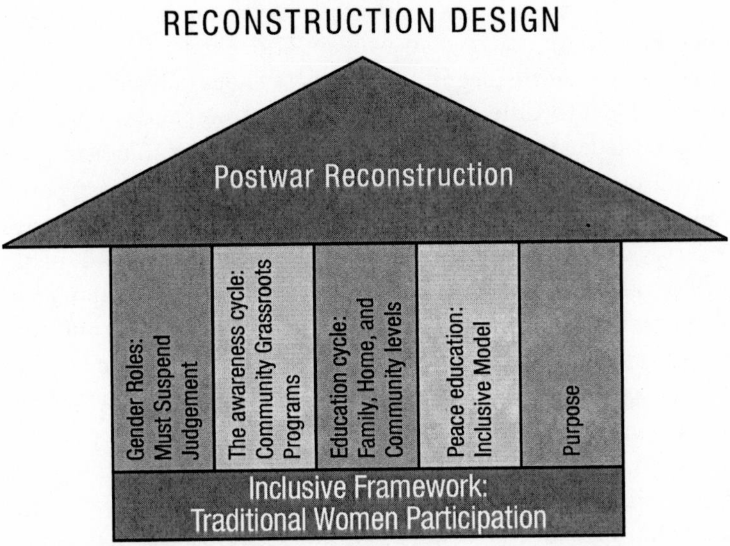

RECONSTRUCTION DESIGN

Postwar Reconstruction

Gender Roles: Must Suspend Judgement

The awareness cycle: Community Grassroots Programs

Education cycle: Family, Home, and Community levels

Peace education: Inclusive Model

Purpose

Inclusive Framework: Traditional Women Participation

In order to close the gender gaps at all levels, between male and female and between traditional women and nontraditional women, postwar reconstruction must be inclusive, especially from the grassroots level. It must cement concrete pillars in reconstructing a sustainable Liberian society. Gender roles must be redefined and gender differences must be subordinated. The Liberian society must elevate gender similarities in the areas of education, leadership capacity, and peacebuilding. The danger of gender difference is that it undermines and undercuts the creation of inclusive programs that encourage traditional women to participate in reconstruction as embedded in feminist theory. It is important that we have an understanding of these concepts from the feminist perspective to create awareness of the importance of women's participation in national reconstruction.

Feminist writers often note that the issue of gender difference is not as important to society as is that of gender similarity. Feminist studies continue to argue the danger of gender difference; these studies hold that gender differences break grounds for gender inequalities and power imbalances toward women.

Kimball[12] wants us to ask these real questions: Are men and women more similar than they are different? In fact, why do people in society continue to ask about and search out the differences and similarities between men and women? In any case, she believes that gender differences exist on several levels: individual, interpersonal, institutional, symbolical, and discursive. At each of these levels, gender differences interact with power such that men have more power than women; also, gender differences essentialize women. Kimball suggests that society should change not only the knowledge of gender differences as it relates to power and women, but also the way knowledge is constructed in society and in the minds of people.

In addition to Kimball, Mary Crawfod, a feminist theorist, points out that language has a huge impact on the study of gender differences. Language serves as an agent of change as it shapes social reality. Language is a source of power and has an influence over society's perception of how it views things. For her, focusing on gender-related differences and similarities can help weaken the negative images held about women. Such negativity leads to real dangers, such as making the value judgment that men and women are socially unequal.

Furthermore, Martha Thompson's article "Women, Gender, and Conflict" points out the importance of making the roles of women visible in society in order to have some clear understandings of how these roles play out in civil conflict. The author believes that if society does not have an understanding of the specific roles, capacities, and vulnerabilities of women in war and conflict, society will continue to construct strategies and responses that do not address gender differences and that women will become disadvantaged and marginalized.

Feminist researchers maintain that the study of gender-related differences and similarities have the ability to dispel myths and stereotypes about women. The negativity of focusing on differences breaks ground for making value judgments and suggests that men and women are unequal. In addition, our interaction with stereotypes, dichotomies, social hierarchies, masculinism, and androcentrism powerfully filters our understanding of our social reality. It constructs our understanding of how women should be included in the reconstruction process of any society.

Contrasted to feminism, religious theory has influenced many societies and cultural perspectives of women's roles, especially in Liberia. Religion is part of human nature, and we humans subscribe to religious teachings and practices. Religion has been controversial and conflict-generating because of differing human cultures and traditional beliefs; however, if one theorizes any religion as it relates to gender roles, those roles generally favor men by giving men more power. One important phenomenon for consideration is that, cross-culturally or universally, religion as a perennial and perhaps inevitable factor is a powerful constituent of cultural norms and values, and because it addresses the most profound existential issues of human life (e.g. freedom and inevitability, fear and faith, security and insecurity, right and wrong, sacred and profane), religion is deeply implicated in individual and societal conceptions of peace, justice, democracy, and equality.

In addition, the German-born psychoanalyst and social thinker Erich Fromm claims that all societies, cultures, and human beings in general are religious in that they develop a general framework for understanding the fundamental problems and issues that confront humanity.

Islam and Christianity have been very active in the reconstruction process of the Liberian political and democratic process. These religions' teachings of power and the roles of women in society clearly favor men. Interestingly, in Liberian society, Islam and Christianity continue to work together to influence the educational, political, and social institutions. In contrast to the increased aggression that occur between Christians and Muslims in other countries, in Liberia, these groups enjoy some degree of collaborative effort as they work together, overcoming their religious differences, to advocate for and sustain peace and democracy in the country.

These theoretical perspectives give us two separate lenses in defining gender roles in society. Before making any kind of judgment, one must understand that feminist theory is highly influenced by Western individualist culture. On the other hand, the religious theory described above is influenced by African collectivist culture.

Therefore, this work is not attempting to make any judgment of right or wrong, rather it seeks to draw attention to the structure of postwar reconstruction that is inclusive of every individual and that eliminates the alienation of traditional women. In order to address this idea, we must draw from others who have worked and researched this area.

In a 2007 article entitled "Understanding the Impact of Women Members of Parliament on Peace, Security, and Decision-Making, " Nathalie Lasslop, the project researcher for the Association of European Parliamentarians for Africa (AWEPA), supported by the Danish Ministry of Foreign Affairs, points out that women's participation in society is not only a question of women's representation in democratic process and leadership. She explores the issue of how women can contribute to a new dimension of politics.

Drawing from the Fourth World Conference on Women held in Beijing in 1995, the resolution called the Platform of Action calls for institutions and governments around the world to embark on positive steps to increase women's participation in higher positions. The writer points out two challenges that are paramount in the process of bridging the gender gap: The first has to do with the massive increase of female representatives needed to better reflect the demographic percentages in society; the second involves gender inclusion awareness by men that allows women into the decision-making process.

Also, Sanam Naraghi Anderlini in an article entitled "The Untapped Resource: Women in Peace Negotiations," states that women in Africa continue to be excluded from many peace tables and societal reconstruction processes. She believes that this is the result of a belief that participants at peace and reconstruction tables must be those having power to implement an agreement; women, it is argued by many societies, rarely have such power. In addition, gender inequality is embedded in the cultural and traditional practices that socially construct women's exclusion from societal reconstruction processes.

Naraghi Anderlini is not the only writer who identifies the exclusion of women's participation in African society; in "Women and Elections in African Politics," Kemi Ogunsanya exposes us to the fact that African women seeking leadership roles come up against cultural biases and stereotypes in their societies. Ogunsanya alluded to the many obstacles and challenges African women are faced with, ranging from oppressive cultural traditions, illiteracy, and domestic violence to religious structures that stand in the way of women's inclusion in the reconstruction processes in their societies.

However, Khadiagala and Lyons (2006) point out that postconflict reconstruction furnishes many possibilities for redefining gender roles, redrawing the rules that underpin women's rights, and propelling women into leadership positions across society.

Khadiagala and Lyons argue that postconflict reconstruction must encourage inclusion policies that address gender disparities in the right to education, power, and resources. They claim that the process from war to peace must allow for greater involvement of women in the rebuilding and reconstruction of society.

Summary

Power can be a phenomenon of positive change in the lives of people and communities in any society; on the other hand, power can produce some negative elements when it becomes unbalanced and unequal.

Power is generally defined as the capacity to bring about change; it takes many forms, comes from many places, and is measured in many ways; to understand power it is essential to understand who has it, who does not, and how those who do not have it can get it.

The hierarchical structure of power according to the above figure clearly favors men and places nontraditional women at the other end of the continuum. Traditional stereotypes, myths, and perceptions have been the filters to define traditional women's roles in society. These factors have disadvantaged and alienated traditional women for many decades. According to the graph above, women who are included in the social and political development are those with Western education as reflected and illustrated in the continuum and graph below.

Fortunately, the 2005 postwar reconstruction election has produced a nontraditional woman head of state, and it is clear that a huge number of nontraditional women are driving on the express highway of freedom and democracy; therefore, the Liberian reconstruction process must equally distribute power among genders according to the true concept of power. Liberian society must learn that inequality and power imbalance is the result of prejudice and social injustice in any society. Furthermore, distribution of power is not only unequal, it is unfair and unjust. While it is true that some nontraditional women are participating in the reconstruction process, traditional women are struggling tremendously to cross the bridges that essentialize them and favor men with more power.

As stated above, I believe power can be an effective phenomenon to bring about cultural change and stability in a new era. Therefore, society must find ways to reconstruct power along gender lines; when this happens, negotiation and collaboration become possible.

On a positive note, the Liberian reconstruction process is developing a system of social equality among genders. The society is coming to recognize and believe in the power of women as a potent tool in sustaining peace and stability. Any society that believes in and commits to this concept of women's inclusion in reconstruction and recognizes women as powerful contributors to a peaceful society is on its way to recovery from gender inequality and power imbalance. In addition, in a system of reconstruction in which the outcomes are unknown but the fundamental rules of the game provide a safe arena in which both genders in the society are able to compete, all major parties are allowed to retain at least some of their power: democracy and social justice are sustained. The question for Liberia is whether traditional women are included in the reconstruction process. If not, let me suggest that the process must be reconstructed.

Finally, I want to suggest that conflict resolvers can be a resource and encouragement to Liberian society as it reconstructs the framework of gender equality, power balance, and recognition of traditional women's roles. Professionals in the field can provide support in developing a system for the inclusion of traditional women in Liberia. In doing this, we must consider the cultural context and identity of Liberian society.

In addition, there is a need for continued research to conduct and analyze the statistics of nontraditional women's inclusion in the current Liberia National Legislature (the House of Representatives and Senate) and also to address the issue of how nontraditional women can empower more traditional women so that their roles can be recognized and become acceptable to Liberian society.

Notes

1. R. Dunn-Marcos, K. T. Kollehlon, and B. Ngovo, *Liberians: An Introduction to Their History and Culture* (Center for Applied Linguistics, Washington, DC, 2005), http://www.cal.org/co/liberians/liberian_1.pdf.

2. E. Gilbert and J. T. Reynolds, *Africa in History: From Prehistory to the Present* (Canada: Pearson Education Canada Ltd., 2004).

3. Ibid.

4. Dunn-Marcos, Kollehlon, and Ngovo, *Liberians: An introduction to their History and Culture.*

5. Steven Radelet , *Reviving Economic Growth in Liberia (*Center for Global Development, Washington, DC, 2007), http://www.cgdev.org/files/14912_file_Liberia_Growth.pdf .

6. Comprehensive Peace Agreement Between the Government of Liberia and LURD and MODEL and Political Parties of Liberia, (Accra, Ghana, 2003).

7. Nicolas Cook (2005 Cook, N. 2005. Liberia's postwar recovery: Key issues and development. CRS Report for Congress, CRS Web, and code 33185. Congressional Research Service. The Library of Congress.

8. The National Election Commission of Liberia. 2005. htt://www.necliberia.org/result.

9. Ellen Johnson Sirleaf and Steven Radelet (2008 Sirleaf, E. J., and S. Radelet. 2005. The good news out of Africa: Democracy, stability, and the renewal of growth and development. http://www.cgdev.org/content/publications/detail/15416.

10. Dunn-Marcos, Kollehlon, and Ngovo, *Liberians: An introduction to their History and Culture*

11. Harriette Williams,"Women in post-conflict reconstruction in Africa," *Conflict Trends (2006)*, http://www.accord.org.za/ct/2006-1/ct1_2006_pg30-34.pdf.

12. Meredith Kimball, *Gender similarities and differences as feminist contradictions* (New York: John Wiley and Sons, 2001).

13 Mary Crawford, *Gender and Language* (New York: John Wiley, 2001).

14. Martha Thompson, "Women, gender, and conflict: Making the connection," *Development in Practice* 16, 3-4 (2006): 342-353.

15. Natalie Lasslop, "Understanding the Impact of Women Members of Parliament on Peace, Security, and Decision-Making". *Conflict Trends* (2007), http://www.accord.org.za/ct/2007-1/CT1_2007_pg32-39.pdf.

16. Sanam Naraghi Anderlini, "The Untapped Resource: Women in Peace Negotiations," *Conflict Trends (2003)*, http://www.accord.org.za/ct/2003-3/pg18-22.pdf.

17. Kemi Ogunsanya, "Women and Elections in African politics," *Conflict Trends (2006)*, http://www.accord.org.za/ct/2006-2/CT2_2006_pg14-18.pdf.

NINE

A New Era for the Congo?

Anneke van
Woudenberg

At the old Catholic mission on a steep hill just outside the gold mining town of Kilo in eastern Democratic Republic of Congo, thousands gathered at the doors of the crumbling school, built by Belgian missionaries at the end of the nineteenth century. Huddled in groups, the people waited patiently. The church bells rang, and the early morning sun lit up the distinctively Belgian buildings, set amidst the huge rainforest. The priest, Abbé Jean Pierre, stood at the top of the church steps smiling broadly. "This is an historic day for Congo," he said. "This is the day we vote for peace."

The hope for peace was especially poignant for the residents of Kilo on that steamy morning. They stood in the shadow of a mass grave on the crest of the hill, barely a hundred yards from the polling station. Three years ago, dozens of people were killed in a single day. The victims, mostly civilians, were stripped naked, placed face down on the ground and killed with spears. There are countless such mass graves all over the country.

Unsurprisingly, the hopes for peace are shared by millions of the priest's compatriots in this vast country, nearly the size of western Europe. This summer's first round of elections and the runoff to be held later this month mark Congo's first democratic elections for more than forty years. Voter turnout was a remarkable 70 percent. Many voters walked for miles to reach polling stations.

Some came the night before, sleeping outside in order to be sure of being able to vote the following day. An elderly blind man at a polling station just south of Kilo said he walked for thirty miles through the forest to vote, led by his young granddaughter. He told me: "I am tired of war."

Late that night, after traveling through dozens of villages to observe the voting, I stood outside a polling station on the outskirts of Bunia, scene of fierce fighting in recent years, with Marie, an election worker. She, too, hoped that the elections would be a turning point for Congo. After five hours of ballot counting by candlelight, she said softly, "I am so proud to be part of this process. I will remember this day forever."

That these elections are happening at all can be seen as a small miracle. For five years between 1998 and 2003, Congo was wracked by a deadly war in which millions died. Armies from six African nations fought here, backing a host of local rebel groups who vied for power in this country, whose citizens are desperately poor despite its extraordinary mineral wealth. The war became known as Africa's first "world war." When the foreign armies withdrew, a transitional government was installed in the capital, Kinshasa. In this vast country with few roads and almost no electricity, elections were to be organized within just three years. The challenge was immense. The fractious government of former enemies spent much of their time squabbling as local warlords continued to devastate eastern Congo. After much arm-twisting by the international diplomats and their government's investment of more than £200 million, the first round of elections finally took place in July. The runoff will be held on October 29.

Even now, however, the omens are mixed, at best. Three weeks after election day, on the night that first-round results were to be announced, gun battles broke out in Kinshasa between the Republican Guard of candidate and current president Joseph Kabila and the armed troops of his main challenger, vice president Jean-Pierre Bemba.

Huddled around radio sets, millions of Congolese waited for news. As the appointed hour for the announcement of election results came and went, only dance music—the irrepressible beats of Congolese *soukous*, which has made the country's music renowned worldwide—distracted the expectant and worried listeners.

There was good reason to be worried. United Nations peacekeeping troops had to evacuate the president of the Independent Electoral Commission when fighting came too close to his office. He had to make the delayed announcement of election results in a hastily prepared alternative location. Kabila emerged as the frontrunner out of a field of thirty-three candidates, though without an absolute majority. A runoff vote between Kabila and his nearest challenger, Bemba, was announced for this month.

Two days of street battles followed. At one point, fourteen ambassadors were trapped in Bemba's residence, where they had gone to urge calm. Presidential guards exchanged fire with Bemba's troops on the streets outside. UN peacekeepers, supported by a small European force, eventually freed the ambassadors and defused the crisis. During those days, dozens died. It was an ominous start to the new political era that the Congolese people hoped for.

———⟫●⟪———

The focus on elections was understandable given that decades had elapsed since the last democratic polls, but in truth Congo's problems are not going to be fixed by elections alone. The armed rebel groups, rampant corruption, greed for the country's mineral wealth, and a national army that commits rape and murder, all combined with a pervasive culture of impunity, require a transformation of the country itself.

Instead, those who gained power through the barrel of a gun, and have therefore gained the most important positions in Congo's transitional government, simply legitimated their seizure of power by becoming electoral front-runners. Kabila and Bemba, together with another vice president and former leader of a Rwandan-backed rebel group, were the only three candidates who—through their access to government funds and their control of private armed forces—were able to conduct a national election campaign. Bemba and Kabila control their own media and have their own planes, a luxury others lacked. This race provided few opportunities for new political actors to succeed.

As so often happens, international efforts did little to improve the situation. Ambassadors of fifteen governments—including Britain, France, South Afric, and the United States—established a structure to help guide Congo's transition to democracy. But they preferred to look the other way on tough matters that could affect the elections. Diplomats dismissed concerns about corruption or the need to disarm private militias and integrate them into the national army, saying it would be unproductive to push too hard at such a delicate time. It was important, they said, "not to rock the boat."

This was shortsighted at best. Congo's only well-established political opposition party was left outside the electoral process. Based on principles of nonviolence, Etienne Tshisekedi's Union for Democracy and Social Progress refrained from any role in Congo's war—putting him and his party at a disadvantage when spoils were divided among the belligerents. Because they were not signatories to the final peace accords, they were excluded from ministerial positions in the carve-up that followed and thus lacked the access to governmental resources that allowed other contenders to influence the election process. Efforts by the international community to bring them into the process came too late. By then, the party had already made the fatal decision to urge their supporters not to register for the polls.

Lessons could have been learned from failed policies elsewhere, such as Afghanistan—a country with a similar history of criminal enterprise, pervasive conflict, and warlords—where international donors pushed elections as the answer to complex and deeply rooted problems and instead got renewed violence, aggravated divisions (both old and new), and the legitimization of warlords. The cost of that policy can be seen in the instability of Afghanistan today. Elections are important, but when held in the absence of fundamental reforms, they can result in new problems.

The failures of both Congolese politicians and international actors leave the Congolese people with unenviable choices. The day after the first-round results were announced, while street battles still raged in Kinshasa, I had lunch with a Congolese professor in Goma, near the Rwandan border in the east. He held his head in his hands. "We need new leaders in Congo," he said, "not the same ones who have been killing us."

Congo carries the tragic label of the deadliest war in the world today. An estimated four million people have died since 1998. Civilians continue to die at a rate of 1,200 every day, some directly from the violence, many others due to hunger and the lack of medical care. But this story of tragedy is not new. Congo has suffered horribly throughout its history—and powerful outside interests have often been directly to blame. This is a story of continuously missed opportunities and of criminal enterprise. The victims are always the same: ordinary Congolese. In 1885, Belgium's King Leopold II set up his private colony, the Congo Free State, the only colony in the world ever claimed by one man. Though King Leopold never set foot in his private fiefdom, he ruthlessly built up a business enterprise with slave labor that made him vast wealth from the exploitation of rubber and ivory. Up to ten million people died, mostly in the two decades before the First World War, when the international demand for rubber was at its height. In the words of Adam Hochschild, author of *King Leopold's Ghost,* the monarch was "a man as filled with greed and cunning, duplicity and charm, as any of the more complex villains of Shakespeare."

Courageous activists of the day reported on the atrocities—severed heads and hands and entire villages massacred—at the hands of the colonial masters. The British journalist Edmund Morel campaigned on the issue, giving birth to the first great human rights movement of the twentieth century. Mark Twain wrote "King Leopold's Soliloquy," an imaginary monologue by King Leopold in which he delivers an ineffective defense of colonization and rages about the media campaign against him. "Blister the meddlesome missionaries!" the king exclaims. "They write tons of these things. They seem to be always around, always spying, always eyewitnessing the happenings; and everything they see they commit to paper!"

Eventually—not least because of Morel and others witnessing the happenings, committing it to paper, and bringing it to the attention of the world—King Leopold was obliged to cede his colony to the government of Belgium, which ruled it for half a century. In 1960, Congo gained its independence from Belgium and held democratic elections, which brought to power a fiery young orator by the name of Patrice Lumumba. Standing against colonialist ideals, Lumumba is still revered by the Congolese, but his connections with the eastern bloc at the height of the cold war and support for African nationalism sealed his fate. With the complicity of the American government, Belgian agents organized his arrest and brutal execution. Thus came to an end the three-month rule of Congo's first and, so far, only democratically elected leader.

Lumumba's assassination was a devastating blow to Congolese and other African nations struggling for an end to colonial rule. Congo entered a new phase of dictatorship where greed remained a constant. Mobutu Sese Seko, Lumumba's former secretary, took power through a military coup and renamed the country Zaire. His thirty-two years of dictatorship were characterized by corruption on such a massive scale that it led to the popular coining of the term "kleptocrat," defined by the *Oxford English Dictionary* as "a ruler who uses [his] power to steal [his] country's resources." The president and his political elite plundered mercilessly, sending the country into a long, slow economic decline. Under Mobutu, the country's citizens perfected lessons of survival akin to those learned under Leopold and ones they would continue to use during Congo's years of war. Michela Wrong's account of the Mobutu years, *In the Footsteps of Mr. Kurtz*, accurately sums up the mentality that pervaded those years: "Keep your head down, think small and look after yourself."

Despite President Mobutu's excesses, his end came about not as a result of changes inside the country, but because of events in neighboring Rwanda. The 1994 genocide of Rwandan Tutsi and the slaughter of Hutu opposed to the regime had a cataclysmic effect on the politics of the entire region. Regional power dynamics changed as the governments of Rwanda and Congo toppled and western nations, driven by guilt for failing to stop the mass slaughter, skewed their policies in favor of the new Tutsi-dominated government in Rwanda. One diplomat said to me years after the genocide, "You must realize that the guilt factor now drives our foreign policy toward the region."

For Congo, the first impact of the genocide was the arrival of more than a million Rwandan Hutu refugees into the eastern border region in June 1994. The refugees were accompanied by the perpetrators of the genocide—the Interahamwe militia and other Hutu army extremists—who soon established their control over the refugee camps set up by the international aid community. Hutu forces prepared to renew attacks on Rwanda and carried their ethnic hatred of the Tutsi to those living in Zaire. The Rwandan government, in turn—backed by Uganda—invaded, launching a war that lasted from 1996 to 1997.

Rwandan army troops smashed the refugee camps, forcing the return to Rwanda of many of the Hutu refugees. Others, including large numbers who had been uninvolved with the genocide, fled deep into the forests of Zaire, where pursuing Rwandan troops massacred tens of thousands. Backing a hastily mounted rebel alliance of local groups, the Rwandan army marched on Kinshasa and ousted Mobutu, who had provided support to Rwanda's genocidal leaders in 1994. Laurent Kabila, the leader of this rebel alliance, was installed as president as hopes rose for a new era. Kabila ended the use of "Zaire" and established the Democratic Republic of Congo, now in name at least a democratic country.

In reality the new regime differed little from the old. Kabila quickly adopted the practices that Mobutu, building on Leopold's legacy, had perfected: corruption, economic mismanagement, and favoritism toward the family clan. Seeking to free himself from the Rwandan support that had helped him to victory, Kabila launched new campaigns of ethnic hatred against anyone linked to Rwanda, including the Congolese Tutsi who shared some cultural characteristics with those across the border in Rwanda. Hundreds of Congolese Tutsi were killed in cities across the country.

Unwilling to lose their new influence in the mineral-rich Congo, and concerned about the targeting of Congolese Tutsi, Rwanda and Uganda launched a new Congo war in 1998, which eventually drew in other African countries, including Zimbabwe, Angola, Namibia—on Kabila's side—and Burundi alongside the Rwandans and Ugandans. The war spawned a host of rebel groups and local militias who sought to gain power and influence through armed force, often using ethnicity as their rallying cry.

In January 2001, Kabila was assassinated by one of his bodyguards in the presidential palace in Kinshasa, thus bringing a violent end to another of Congo's leaders. His 29-year-old son, Joseph, succeeded him as president. The change in leadership from father to son opened up new opportunities for diplomacy. Joseph Kabila and the main rebel leaders signed a power-sharing agreement in Sun City, South Africa, in 2002, which led to the establishment of a transitional government the following year. The government included four vice presidents, each from one of the main rebel groups who had fought in the war.

<hr />

Actors in Congo's sad history have been motivated by the desire to control the country's rich natural resources. In Leopold's day, this was primarily rubber and ivory. Today, competition focuses on control of gold, diamonds, copper, cobalt, and coltan (columbite-tantalite, used in laptop computers and mobile phones). Politicians and foreign armies have struck deals that enriched themselves and contributed to the financing of the war and the purchase of weapons, but provided few or no benefits to the Congolese people. In the memorable phrase of one miner in eastern Congo who labored in the gold mines: "We are cursed because of our gold. All we do is suffer."

A myriad of reports has documented the link between the war and the illegal exploitation of Congo's natural resources. Yet little or nothing has been done to address the issue. In a series of reports published between 2001 and 2003, a UN panel concluded that mineral exploitation was funding Congo's warring factions. According to the panel, Rwandan, Ugandan, and Zimbabwean army officers as well as the Congolese elite were growing rich from the war, killing and abusing Congolese citizens in the process. A range of other organizations including Human Rights Watch, Amnesty International, and Global Witness, also documented how the battles to control Congo's mineral wealth, such as its gold and diamonds, resulted in massacres and rape. The International Court of Justice issued a landmark judgment in 2005 that concluded that the occupying Ugandan army had killed and tortured Congolese civilians, had supported abusive local armed groups, and had looted, plundered, and exploited Congo's natural resources, all in violation of international law. The court recommended that the Ugandan government make reparations for injuries caused. (Trade statistics obtained by Human Rights Watch show that Uganda exported $60 million worth of gold in 2002, less than 1 percent of which was produced domestically. The rest was smuggled in from Congo. Rwanda also profited from the re-export of mineral resources originating in Congo.)

Since Congo's minerals are predominately destined for multinational corporations based in Europe and North America, accusations have also been leveled at these businesses for their role in contributing to Congo's ills. The UN panel found that dozens of European and North American corporations had breached international business norms in their operations in Congo. The panel's findings sat uncomfortably with UN Security Council members, who were reluctant to punish or even seriously investigate corporations based in their own countries. Thus far no such corporation has been sanctioned, although several have reformed their practices following publicity of their role in Congo.

A special Congolese parliamentary commission established that dozens of contracts signed during the war years were either illegal or of limited value for the Congolese people. It recommended their termination or renegotiation. The report's findings, which named senior Congolese politicians, were never debated. Hundreds of copies of the report destined for members of Parliament disappeared. Commission members received death threats. Some diplomats urged that the report's findings not be discussed before elections, claiming that such a debate might "trouble the electoral process."

The questionable exploitation of Congolese resources has not ended but rather apparently accelerated with the end of war and the establishment of the transitional government. World Bank officials say privately that the number of grants for exploration rights to important mineral-rich areas increased fourfold in 2005. Many of the deals involved dubious provisions that would do little for the development of the country.

On the ground as well, particularly in the mineral-rich eastern part of the country, ongoing conflict during the past three years of transition has been linked to competition for resources. Last year, government soldiers used villagers as slave labor, forcing them to dig for gold in the mines of Bavi, in northeastern Congo. The soldiers threatened to kill the local people if they refused to comply. They arrested one of the local chiefs, beat him, and put him in a hole used as an underground prison. He told me: "I had tried to stop what they were doing, to defend the people. They tied me up and hit me. We were powerless against them." For twelve hours a day, hundreds of local men and boys scrambled in the dirt for gold that would only line the pockets of the military.

The international community acknowledges that natural resource exploitation has played a central role in exacerbating conflict in Congo. And yet, almost nothing has been done to control it. If there is no progress on this crucial issue, military conflict is likely to continue.

Local rebel groups continue to rape and kill, as do foreign armed groups from Rwanda and Uganda. But one of the largest threats to Congolese civilians is now the new Congolese army itself, a mixture of soldiers from the disbanded rebel groups and from the old national army.

Ten days after the elections, I happened to see two soldiers marching a small group of civilians along the road from Gethy, a town in northeastern Congo. The six, members of a single family, carried chairs, benches, and corrugated metal roofing on their heads. Forced labor, looting, and rape of civilians by soldiers are commonplace here, so my companion, a Congolese human rights activist, and I stopped to ask questions. One of the women, carrying a child on her back and a church bench on her head, said nothing as she looked beseechingly at us. Her hands trembled. "There is no problem," laughed one of the soldiers. "We are escorting these people for their own safety."

The family members told a different story. They had been forced to flee their home two months before when soldiers had burned their village to the ground, killing their grandmother who was unable to flee. That morning, they had been searching for food in the fields when the soldiers had taken them at gunpoint to the church. They made the men remove the metal sheeting from the roof and ordered the women to carry the chairs and benches. The soldiers threatened to kill them all if they failed to obey. My companion gently but firmly pointed out that the soldiers' actions were illegal and that the people must be released immediately. On this occasion at least, the soldiers backed down. "An army of bandits," my companion said, as the family piled into our car and we brought them to a place of temporary safety.

Congolese civilians fear the new national army, just as they feared King Leopold's Force Publique—which had a policy of severing the hands of those who refused to collect rubber—and just as they feared Mobutu's security forces, known for their wide-scale looting and violence. Mobutu's forces twice pillaged the capital, in 1991 and 1993.

More recently, Congolese soldiers murdered and raped, as part of military operations to tackle insurgency groups opposed to the transitional government. Earlier this year, for example, a group of around twenty people hoped they had found safety when they gathered in a church in the village of Nyata, an hour's drive south of Bunia, after fleeing a battle between the army and a rebel militia. They were wrong. Dozens of soldiers opened fire from the door and through the windows of the church, despite the shouts from those inside that they were civilians. Seven people were killed, including two babies. When the firing stopped, a local leader tried to help two elderly injured women. He asked the soldiers why they had killed people inside the church. "This is not our problem. It's your problem," the soldiers replied.

In the southern province of Katanga, a similar deadly military operation was launched against another insurgent group there. As part of the operation, soldiers attacked the village of Kyobo and detained two dozen men, women, and children. They tied up the detainees with rubber cords and beat and burned them with red-hot iron rods. Through the walls, the detainees heard the screams of the others as they were being tortured. A few days later, soldiers executed six of the men and threw two of the bodies off a nearby bridge in an attempt to hide the evidence.

The Congolese army is riddled with corruption. Every month the top brass steal an estimated £1.5 million from funds set aside for soldiers' salaries. They inflate the numbers of soldiers in the ranks—a phenomenon known as ghost soldiers—in order to pocket more money. International donors attempting to reform the army have taken to babysitting the cash as it makes its way down to the lowest foot soldier. This has had some initial success, but even those privates who receive their full salary of £13 per month have barely enough to live on, and the incentive to loot and extort remains strong.

Another important constraint to reforming the military is that some former belligerents have been reluctant to commit their troops to an integrated national army. Instead they have preferred to retain their own military forces until they know how the elections will turn out. The largest such force is President Kabila's own 15,000-strong presidential guard, largely made up of men from his own ethnic group.

Vice President Bemba, too, has important numbers of private forces at his command. One of the diplomats who was trapped in Bemba's house while Kabila's and Bemba's forces battled together outside, admits that the international community has ignored the problem of these private militias, especially the presidential guard, for too long. Perhaps eager to find the glass to be half full, he says: "At least the problem has been recognized. It's just that nobody knows what to do about it."

While the diplomats ponder the problem, both Kabila and Bemba are widely reported to be obtaining more weapons for their militias.

———————➤●◄———————

Congolese agree that overcoming their country's problems requires justice. Yet there has been little appetite for this from their rulers, many of whom have hands soaked in blood. In the past two years, dozens of warlords accused of murder, torture, and rape have been appointed as generals or colonels in the Congolese army. Some members of the government claim that these appointments are a necessary evil to move the country away from violent conflict. Yet these attempts at inclusion have had the opposite effect, facilitating the emergence of yet more warlords, who see armed violence as the best way to achieve positions of power. Diplomats and politicians argue that there are times when justice must wait in order to establish conditions conducive to peace, but experience shows that such peace rarely lasts if accountability for major crimes does not follow.

The new International Criminal Court, in existence since 2002, is seen by many Congolese as offering the hope of justice for Congo's victims and the prospect of deterring future crimes. Two years ago, the court announced its first-ever investigation, focusing on crimes committed in eastern Congo. In March of this year, the court made its first arrest and initiated proceedings against Thomas Lubanga, a Congolese warlord responsible for torture, rape, and ethnic massacres, in Ituri district, in the northeast. The results were immediate: fear of arrest spread among others responsible for war crimes. One such person whom I met earlier this year in a remote part of Katanga, in southern Congo, expressed concern when I pointed out that it was a war crime to arrest and execute one's rivals. "I don't want to end up like Lubanga," he cried out.

Even here, however, hopes are disappointed. The prosecutor of the court has charged Lubanga with recruitment of child soldiers, a serious crime. But to date no action has been taken against other militia groups, individuals in Kinshasa, or soldiers from the Rwandan and Ugandan armies, even though they contributed to the deaths of over 60,000 people in Ituri.

The victims who suffered at the hands of more than a dozen warlords in this corner of Congo want to know why others are not being tried. "This is selective justice," one community leader said to me in Bunia, commenting on the single arrest. "It will not help us in revealing the truth of what happened and why we have suffered so much." A new and stable Congo is unlikely to emerge until perpetrators on all sides are held to account.

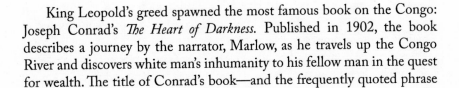

King Leopold's greed spawned the most famous book on the Congo: Joseph Conrad's *The Heart of Darkness*. Published in 1902, the book describes a journey by the narrator, Marlow, as he travels up the Congo River and discovers white man's inhumanity to his fellow man in the quest for wealth. The title of Conrad's book—and the frequently quoted phrase of its main character, Mr. Kurtz, who gasps "the horror, the horror" as he dies on a steamboat sailing down the Congo River—has often been used to refer to Congo's plight today, as if the country is somehow predisposed to dark atrocities and violence. But Conrad's real message is not Congolese barbarism but rather the greed of outsiders. He found in Congo "the vilest scramble for loot that ever disfigured the history of human conscience." A situation little changed a century later.

Powerful governments turn away from uncomfortable truths about the role played by the illegal exploitation of natural resources and multinational companies in fuelling violence in the Congo. They ignore wide-scale corruption and the horrific abuses carried out by the country leaders, as they did with Leopold and Mobutu. It is easy, and justified in part, to blame Congo's troubles on its leaders, but multinational corporations and leaders of neighboring governments must also be held accountable for the roles they have played in perpetuating massive violence that is largely unreported in the international press.

With the new elections about to take place, Congo again stands at an important crossroad in its history. Regardless of the outcome at the polls, political leaders will have to tackle head-on the underlying issues that destabilize the country. They must stop illegal exploitation of Congo's mineral wealth, hold to account individuals responsible for war crimes, and restructure the army so it protects Congo's citizens rather than preying on them. Perhaps most important, they must guarantee those civil and political rights that will permit new political actors to emerge so that Congo's next elections may provide a better choice for its people. The international community is all too eager to wash its hands of the troublesome and expensive process and move on. American and European diplomats grumble about the cost of UN peacekeeping in Congo. They would like to reduce the number of blue helmets soon after the elections and declare Congo's transition successful. While concerns about costs are understandable, reducing the number of peacekeepers too quickly will hinder the establishment of an effective new civilian administration and risks repeating the mistakes of the past. In the words of one senior UN official referring to the role of UN peacekeepers in the Congo in the 1960s, "We were here when it was a mess forty years ago, and if we don't help to fix it now we will be here again in forty years time."

For Congolese voters, the expectations are as simple as they are ambitious. In Congo's third largest city, Kisangani, which has been ravaged in recent years by battles between the occupying and opposing armies of Uganda and Rwanda, a mother of four children said she had one wish for her country. "We are tired of crying. We just want peace and to be able to see our children grow up. I hope the politicians understand that."

TEN

Research on the Effects of African Child Trauma (REACT): Child Soldiers and Treatment in Sierra Leone, Liberia, The Democratic Republic of the Congo, and Rwanda

Lindsay Feldman
Jennie Johanson
Jenny Bordo
Matt Meyer
Ramon Solhkhah
and
Kate Charles

Over the past several decades, the world has experienced an epidemic in the participation of youth under the age of eighteen on the battlefield. The Global Report on Child Soldiers (Coalition to Stop the Use of Child Soldiers, 2008) reports that more than 250,000 children are currently fighting in armed conflicts in more than thirty countries. Despite this, there is a paucity of research on the psychological effects of soldiering on children and how war and the trauma that accompanies it affect children's development, both emotionally and educationally. This is especially true when examining the impact of reintegration of child soldiers back into their communities.

To this end, St. Luke's and Roosevelt Hospital's Child and Family Institute (CFI) sent a pilot research team on a three week mission to four Sub-Saharan African countries at various stages of recovery from complex civil wars that had all utilized child combatants—Sierra Leone, Liberia, Democratic Republic of the Congo, and Rwanda. This team, composed of a child and adolescent psychiatrist, an educator and author of contemporary African studies, an international health policy expert, an international education consultant, an applied developmental psychology doctoral student, and a research assistant, sought to collect preliminary information on ways in which U.S.-based programs could appropriately support their

African-based colleagues. While in each country, the CFI REACT team interviewed the following four groups of people: medical and mental health professionals (including psychiatrists, other physicians, psychologists, and social workers), educational professionals (including teachers and other school personnel), government officials and policymakers, and, most importantly, African children impacted by trauma, including former child combatants. We conducted our interviews by administering a set of semi-structured questions (with video/audiotaping of the interview sessions with the permission of the participants).

The aim of this article is to give a brief history of each country visited and its current status, provide a general background of child soldiering, discuss similarities and differences between the countries, and offer opinions on what follow-up activities might best further the interests of former children of war. Specifically, we attempted to ascertain the similarities and differences in mental health and educational impacts of the traumatic experiences on, and the extent to which there exist rehabilitation programs for, former child soldiers.

The Child and Family Institute

New York's Child and Family Institute (CFI) provides diagnostic and therapeutic services for children by multidisciplinary mental health professionals. Children, adolescents, and their families are treated for issues from mild behavioral difficulties to severe psychiatric illness. In addition, the St. Luke's and Roosevelt Hospital's Division of Child and Adolescent Psychiatry, in conjunction with Columbia University, provides training for mental health professionals, and these program combine clinical and research training.[1]

The mission of the division is to provide comprehensive, accessible, coordinated, and clinically sophisticated child and adolescent care. Comprehensive care includes outpatient services, school-based day programs, home- and community-based services, and blended case management services, as well as crisis and emergency intervention. A school-based day program, the Comprehensive Adolescent Rehabilitation and Educational Service (CARES), provides a safe and therapeutic educational environment for New York City public high school students with emotional and behavioral difficulties. CARES provides both education and therapy, including substance abuse treatment for students who use drugs or alcohol. CARES teachers and clinical staff work to provide each adolescent with the education, life-skills training, and individual therapy needed in order to reach each one's goals. This program is run in collaboration with the New York City Department of Education.

CARES students are on one of two tracks within the program. The first track, the Adolescent Alternative Day Program, is a therapeutic day school for emotionally disturbed and truant adolescents (ages 14-18). The second track, the Comprehensive Addiction Program for Adolescents (CAPA), serves adolescents (ages 14-19) who are currently interested in stopping use of drugs or alcohol or are recovering substances users. In both programs, treatment integrates multidisciplinary therapeutic and educational components. CFI's experience with CARES helped frame our investigations in Africa. What similarities and differences, we pondered, are faced in the traumatic effects of direct wartime activities of child soldiers and the intense violence of urban gang life and poverty? How can educational and treatment protocols in one situation help inform positive work in the other?

Sierra Leone

The Republic of Sierra Leone was involved in a protracted and pugnacious civil war between March 1991 and February 2002. During this time, tens of thousands of people were killed, even more were injured, and, in a country of four million people, half the population was displaced (Zack-Williams, 2006). Thousands of children were recruited and drawn into the conflict, many by the force of the government (including the pro-government Civil Defense Forces; CDF), paramilitaries, the Rebel United Front (RUF), and the Armed Forces Revolutionary Council (AFRC) (Denov and McClure, 2007; Abraham, 2001). Children were often forcibly recruited, given drugs, and made to commit atrocities. Thousands of girls were also recruited as soldiers and often subjected to sexual exploitation. Many of the children were survivors of village attacks, while others were found abandoned. They were used for patrol purposes, attacking villages, and guarding workers in the diamond fields (Coalition to Stop the Use of Child Soldiers, 2008). Approximately 80 percent of children in armed groups were between the ages of seven and fourteen (7-14) (Women's Commission for Refugee Women and Children, 1997). Nearly 10,000 children in total were combatants in Sierra Leone.

In early 2002, government and international forces combined to defeat the RUF, and the government began a process of demobilization and demilitarization. The United Nations (UN) entered the country to ensure the security and stability of Sierra Leone, a task that has since been taken over by the Sierra Leonean government following the departure of UN forces in 2005. Recently, security has been reestablished, as evidenced by the completion of the first local government elections in thirty-two years in May 2004 (World Bank, 2008).

In June 2007, the Special Court for Sierra Leone found three accused men from the rebel Armed Forces Revolutionary Council (AFRC) guilty of war crimes, crimes against humanity, and other serious violations of international humanitarian law, including the recruitment of children under the age of fifteen years into the armed forces. With this, the Special Court became the first-ever UN-backed tribunal to deliver a guilty verdict for the military conscription of children (Human Rights Watch, 2007).

Liberia

The Republic of Liberia was involved in a fourteen-year civil war between 1989 and 2003 (U.S. Department of State, 2008), with a period of relative peace between 1997 and 2000. The war destroyed Liberia's economy and caused a decline in the standard of living for a majority of the population. More than 200,000 people died during the war, and over a million were displaced. As many as 20,000 children, some as young as seven or eight, were recruited by both the government and rebel forces. In Liberia, estimates are that nearly 70 percent of soldiers (in all factions, including governmental) were children. As many as 11,000 were girls (only 2,500 of whom went through the Disarmament, Demobilization, and Reintegration (DDR) process (UN DDR Resource Centre, 2008).

A peace agreement in August 2003 ended the war, and after two years of a transitional government, in late 2005, President Ellen Johnson Sirleaf (Africa's first democratically elected female president) was elected to power. While the country is in a more stable position currently and President Sirleaf has made incredible progress in restoring peace, the rebuilding process is slow and fragile. A peacekeeping force, The UN Mission in Liberia (UNMIL), is still present and helps to maintain security and structure. However, Liberia is still one of the poorest countries in the world.

Democratic Republic of the Congo

The Democratic Republic of the Congo (DRC) has a long history of civil war. The most recent war (also known as the Second Congo War or the African World War) between 1998 and 2002 was between government forces, supported by Angola, Namibia, and Zimbabwe, and rebels, supported by Uganda and Rwanda (ISS, 2001). This conflict brought extreme violence, massive population displacement, widespread rape, and the collapse of public health services. During the conflict, as many as three million people died and even more were displaced. Many children were recruited as combatants. Since the conflict began, as many as two million people have died as a result of malaria, diarrhea, pneumonia, and malnutrition, making this conflict and its aftermath the world's deadliest since World War II (IRC, 2003). In December 2002, a formal peace agreement was signed, and a transitional government was created in 2003. In 2005, a new constitution was approved, and in July 2006, a first round of presidential elections and parliamentary elections took place. In October 2006, there was a second round of presidential elections and local elections. At that time, Joseph Kabila was elected president, and a new government was formed. Still, the fact of ongoing fighting remains.

Rwanda

In early 1994, Hutu extremists who wanted to control Rwanda began a massacre of Tutsis, a minority ethnic group that made up about 15 percent of the population (7.2 million) at the time. The precipitating event that brought on the tragedy of the genocide was the assassination of President Juvenal Habyarimana when his plane was shot down. Within hours the killings began (BBC, 2004). Between April 6 and early July 1994, close to one million people were slaughtered. Many of the "genocidaires" were children. The Rwandan Patriotic Front (RPF), made up largely of Tutsis, ended the massacres by defeating the government responsible for the campaign of genocide. Many Rwandans fled to the eastern provinces of the DRC, but thousands died of starvation, disease, and lack of water. Paul Kagame, the former RPF commander, Rwanda's current president, and the first democratically elected president since the genocide, has done much to reconcile the country and secure its stability. For example, community-based Gacaca courts have been established to try many of the genocide-related cases. Approximately 818,000 perpetrators are to be tried by the Gacaca courts (Human Rights Watch, 2007).

It is important to note that children were not only partly responsible for the killing of Tutsis and moderate Hutus in Rwanda, they were also recruited from refugee camps to fight in eastern DRC.

Universal Responses to Trauma

A normal response to stress is "fight or flight." During this physiological response, adaptive hyperarousal occurs. In trauma victims, hyperarousal is reactivated in response to reminders of the threat and to new threats. Therefore, a traumatized child may become hypersensitive to threats. A traumatized child may develop anxiety, hyperactivity, impulsiveness, sleep disturbance, tachycardia, or hypertension. Essentially, a response that was adaptive becomes maladaptive[2]. This maladaptive response can manifest as mental illness in a myriad of ways. For example, the immediate and long-term effects of sexual abuse include anxiety disorders and posttraumatic stress disorder (PTSD), dissociative disorders, depression, low self-esteem, aggressive and impulsive behavior, interpersonal difficulties, and disturbed sexual behavior. PTSD, generalized anxiety disorder, and major depressive disorder are some of the most common sequelae to trauma[3].

Another normal response to stress is anxiety, which allows one to cope with stressful situations. However, when this anxiety becomes excessive or irrational, it can turn pathological and disrupt daily functioning. Specific anxiety disorders include generalized anxiety disorder, obsessive compulsive disorder, panic disorder, posttraumatic stress disorder, and social phobia. Each of these disorders has specific symptoms associated with it, but all of the symptoms include excessive, irrational fear, dread, and uncertainty[4].

PTSD is characterized by the Diagnostic and Statistical Manual of Mental Disorders, 4th edition (DSM-IV)[5], as an anxiety disorder that arises after exposure to an event that is outside the range of normal human experience and includes intense feelings of fear, terror, and helplessness. Symptoms include reexperiencing symptoms, avoidance of stimuli associated with the trauma, hypervigilance, and exaggerated startle response. Persistent symptoms of increased arousal must be present for at least one month, and the symptoms must cause clinically significant distress or impairment in social, occupational, or other important areas of functioning in order to receive a diagnosis of PTSD.

While many people who experience trauma feel distressed after the incident, posttraumatic stress becomes chronic only in a subsample of trauma survivors. The best way to predict the likelihood that one will develop PTSD is to examine the nature of the events. The highest rates of PTSD are associated with human-made trauma (e.g., torture or victimization), and the lowest rates are associated with natural disasters[6].

PTSD is one possible outcome of trauma, but is no more probable than any other mental illness and, in fact, is less common than depression and also than co-morbid depression and anxiety.

Major depressive disorder, or major depression, is characterized by DSM-IV[7] by symptoms that include persistent feelings of sadness, emptiness, hopelessness or pessimism, irritability, restlessness, loss of interest in activities that were once enjoyed, fatigue and decreased energy, difficulty concentrating or making decisions, overeating or loss of appetite, thoughts of suicide or suicide attempts, persistent aches and pains or headaches, and insomnia. Major depression interferes with a person's ability to work, sleep, study, and eat and prevents a person from functioning normally. Sometimes, an episode of major depression occurs only once in a person's lifetime, but more usually, it occurs repeatedly throughout a person's life.

Young children with depression often feign illness, refuse to attend school, cling to a parent, or worry that their parents may die. Older children may sulk, misbehave at school, act negative and irritable, and may feel misunderstood. Many of these symptoms of depression are normal characteristics of adolescence, and thus, depression in adolescents is often difficult to detect and diagnose. Depression in adolescents is often co-morbid with anxiety, disruptive behavior, eating, or substance abuse disorders[8].

Much research suggests the connection between trauma and subsequent mental illness, such as posttraumatic stress disorder, depression, and generalized anxiety disorder[9]. Little research has been conducted with regard to the mental health status of child soldiers in particular. There are some exceptions, however (for example, Bayer, Klasen, et al., 2007, and Derluyn, Broekaert, et al., 2004)[10].

Exposure to war is certainly an extreme form of trauma. Trauma is often doubly terrible for child soldiers, who not only witness and perpetrate violence but are also blamed or stigmatized for their role in conflict. Thus, their recovery and reintegration is made more difficult than if they were seamlessly reaccepted into society. The following study highlights the importance of social capital in the recovery of child soldiers and wartime nurses.

Communities and individuals respond differently to disasters. So-called "resilient" children possess various characteristics that foster positive development in the face of unfortunate circumstances (e.g., war, abuse, poverty) such as good social skills, a sense of future, a sense of humor, cognitive and self-regulation skills, positive views of self, and motivation to be effective in poor environments[11].

Child Combatants

As defined by the Paris Principles (UNICEF, 2007), the term "child combatant" refers to "any person below 18 years of age who is or who has been recruited or used by an armed force or armed group in any capacity, including but not limited to children, boys, and girls used as fighters, cooks, porters, messengers, spies, or for sexual purposes. It does not only refer to a child who is taking or has taken a direct part in hostilities." In many countries the world over, children are recruited by both government military and rebel forces for the aforementioned purposes (Coalition to Stop the Use of Child Soldiers, 2004). These children face great obstacles to positive development. Many are deprived of the most basic needs—food, water, security, and love—and are forced to commit violent acts. In addition, the education of child combatants is interrupted during their participation in conflict (Kline and Mone, 2003).

Both government and rebel forces use child combatants. The vast majority is male, but females are conscripted, too, often as sex slaves. Many children are kidnapped and forced into participating. Others voluntarily join the armed forces because they see it as a means to survival, for revenge, or to increase self-esteem (Mendelsohn and Straker, 1998). They are threatened with injury or death if they do not comply with orders.

Treatment

There are various forms of treatment that are available after trauma; however, little is known about which treatments are most effective. Even though research is still being conducted and is in the initial stages, we cannot afford to wait to make treatment recommendations for children.

Individual therapy includes art, play, cognitive behavioral flooding desensitization, and psychopharmacological therapy[12]. Art and writing therapy are effective forms because they serve as a creative outlet for the children to deal with their experiences, which facilitates verbal expression of feelings.

Group therapy has the potential to be very effective because it lets children know that they are not alone and that other individuals their own age are experiencing similar emotions. "Mini marathon" sessions are one form of group therapy that has proven effective. This method of frequent sessions should occur shortly after the traumatic experience and with children who have all endured a similar experience. However, the effectiveness of group therapy depends on the child's expressiveness. Children who do not speak up to share their experiences will likely become bored or daydream. Children should be encouraged and given equal opportunities to speak, and the groups should be run by a developmentally knowledgeable leader[13]. Another advantage to group therapies is a practical one; more people can be reached and treated using this method than could be treated individually, especially in rural areas.

Another type of therapy that has proven effective is dance/movement therapy. Adolescent boy soldiers in Sierra Leone who had undergone psychosocial intervention that was previously unsuccessful took part in this dance group, which fused longstanding ritual dance with connection with others for a greater purpose. This type of therapy allowed them to overcome their violent tendencies, reflect on their involvement in conflict, and foster empathy. This method was effective in helping youth overcome violent impulses and rediscover pleasure when other methods had not worked in the past.

No matter what type of treatment child soldiers receive, Mendelsohn and Straker (1998) suggest that children be demobilized and reintegrated with their families and communities as quickly as is possible after combat. They point out the need for rehabilitation, particularly because these children were not only the perpetrators, but also the victims of violence, and thus their mental health issues may be varied and profound. It is also suggested that rather than punishing child perpetrators of war crimes, these children should be rehabilitated.

Trauma and Treatment for Former Child Soldiers in Sierra Leone, Liberia, The DRC, and Rwanda

After conducting a comprehensive analysis of our interviews, we have synthesized the data and have summarized our findings as follows:

In Sierra Leone, we were told that the main issues affecting children are difficulty completing education, finding employment, earning money, and saving money; an increase in street children as a result of poverty; the occurrences of child trafficking, female genital mutilation, and sexual violence; widespread disease; overcrowding of homes; inflation; the lack of government commitment to children; mental health problems and drug use; few mental health practitioners; and human rights violations against children.

In DRC, the major issues include completing education and finding employment; the vast number of orphans; feelings of isolation, loneliness, and hopelessness among children, and particularly former child soldiers; lack of government commitment to human rights; the recent phenomenon of children being labeled as sorcerers and sent to the streets; sexual exploitation of and violence against women; young children working on the streets; economic stress, hardship, and poverty; and few competently trained mental health professionals were the main issues that we heard about during our interviews.

In Rwanda, we were told that of the following key issues facing Rwandans and Rwandan children today, in the aftermath of the genocide, are difficulty finding employment; difficulty identifying family members of orphans, displaced children, and former child combatants; people who currently maintain a genocidal ideology; few mental health professionals in general and, of them, there are very few with child training; and, finally, illiteracy among children.

As our research was initially construed, we planned to visit and learn about rehabilitation programs for children. However, there are few rehabilitation programs, per se, in the countries we visited. One of the exceptions is a program that we had the opportunity to visit and to learn extensively from—the Child Ex-Combatants Rehabilitation Center at Muhazi in Rwanda.

Rwanda's Child Ex-Combatants Rehabilitation Center at Muhazi

The camp operates under the auspices of the Rwanda Demobilisation and Reintegration Commission (RDRC). The director of the camp described the government's program to us.

The camp functions as a residential program for boys who have acted as soldiers, as cooks, porters, and spies and girls who have acted as sex slaves. (However, no females have come to the camp; we were told that it is much more difficult for girls to escape because they are constantly being watched.) The program is comprehensive in that children receive social support, psychosocial counseling, medical care, literacy training and formal education, family mediation if parents or relatives are located, reunification counseling, and they receive a kit of essentials to take with them when they leave. After they have been reunified with their family or a foster family, a member of the camp staff makes a follow-up visit to the child's new residence.

The camp opened in 2004 and is staffed by a single teacher, two social workers, a director to oversee the camp's activities, and a nurse to provide medical care. Children ages eight to eighteen have been at the camp, and six hundred children have been served so far. The camp can accommodate up to two thousand children; there were thirty-seven boys at the camp when we visited, ten of whom were to be reunited with their families at the end of June 2008. Nearly all of the returning children are illiterate, and formal education and vocational training are offered and encouraged. In addition, income-generating activities, such as farming and raising livestock, are taught.

Most of the children had been fighting or assisting in armed groups in DRC, but have Rwandan heritage; they are considered Rwandan citizens. Some had lived in DRC their entire lives. Thus, the children have not been raised in Rwanda and are not familiar with Rwandan culture. The camp teaches them traditional Rwandan song and dance as well as cultural norms.

The range in time participating in an armed group is three months to eight years. Most of the children escaped on their own; when they desert the armed groups, they report to MONUC (United Nations Mission in the Democratic Republic of Congo), and after disarming them, MONUC returns them to the Rwandan government and they are taken to the camp for rehabilitation services. Minimally, the children reside at the camp for three months; however, some children stay longer. Some reasons that children may stay at the camp longer include the family not welcoming the child back, the camp staff not being able to trace the child's family, or the child continues to behave in antisocial ways. We were told that some of the boys there now have been at the camp since 2004 because their families cannot be found. When the traditional family-tracing technique fails, they have other methods for trying to find the family. First, social workers map out the information that the child has provided about his home village, family, neighbors, and friends, and then the social worker travels to that location to collect information about and to trace the family. If that method is unsuccessful, social workers accompany the child to his home village and "let him see what he can remember" in order to trace the family. This physical tracing has been conducted with three children and was successful in finding one family.

A typical weekday consists of exercise, shower, breakfast, class, break, another class, lunch, a third class, a sporting activity, another shower, dinner, film-watching or a discussion about Rwandan traditions. At 9 p.m., the children go to bed. The boys sleep together in a cabin-style dormitory. On Saturdays, the boys do their own laundry, and on Sundays, they attend church and then have free time until dinner. Each child meets with a social worker for one hour per week.

One reason that so few children have come through the camp is that they are fearful to leave DRC to return home to Rwanda. The camp manager told us of the former combatants, "When they come here [Rehabilitation Center at Muhazi], there is some kind of fear. They are taught in the Congo, if you come here [to Rwanda], you will be killed."

Similarities and Differences

Although each country is dealing with unique issues, they all face many difficulties concerning children. Some of the major similarities are poverty, difficulties finding employment, the need for trained mental health professionals, and children being sent or choosing to live on the streets. Most of the interviewees endorsed not being able to address the mental health needs of children unless the more fundamental needs are taken care of, needs such as food, clean water, shelter, and clothing.

In each country, we were told of street children—children being sent to or voluntarily choosing to live on the streets. Often, when this happens, the child leaves home and takes to the streets, which causes extreme trauma. Numerous interviews documented this phenomenon, which was a particular problem in DRC, where many of the children were being labeled as sorcerers, which causes great stigmatization, results in isolation, and makes the child feel like a pariah. In DRC, we were told that churches were complicit in the labeling of children as sorcerers and went as far as to try to beat the witchcraft out of the children. We were told this may have been because the churches, like the families, could not afford to meet the basic needs of the children.

Conclusions

Despite some differences in political and geographic issues, the people and organizations we met with in each country share concern for their country's children and many of the key issues affecting children in each country overlap. However, before they can manage the mental health needs of children in their respective countries, broader public health issues, such as poverty, nutrition, housing, and employment, must be addressed. Despite this, the people we spoke to in each country recognized and were addressing the mental health needs of children in some way. We were told about the dearth of mental health professionals for children and were repeatedly asked to provide training and education for practitioners there.

We plan to continue our communication with these African agencies and conduct further research and evaluation of programs for all children, but particularly former combatants and street youth. In the meantime, we continue to work with human rights organizations in our own community to provide vital information about the situation in the countries we visited. As we network and join with others doing similar work in the United States and the Global North, we urge all clinical and educational professionals, colleagues, and students to take up the mantel of social responsibility in teaching and medicine. Only by sharing what we know, and opening ourselves up to learn from others, can we hope to make a difference in the lives of young people.

Notes

1. Betty Pfefferbaum and J. R. Allen, "Stress in children exposed to violence: Reenactment and rage," *Child and Adolescent Psychiatric Clinics of North America* 7 (1), 1998.

2. DeMond M. Grant et al.,, The structure of distress following trauma: Post-traumatic stress disorder, major depressive disorder, and generalized anxiety disorder. *Journal of Abnormal Psychology* 117 (3): 662-72, 2008.

3. American Psychiatric Association, *Diagnostic and Statistical Manual of Mental Disorders* (4th ed.) (DSM-IV). Washington, DC: American Psychiatric Association, 1994..

4. Ibid.

5. Rachel Yehuda et al., "Predicting the development of posttraumatic stress disorder from the acute response to a traumatic event," *Biological Psychiatry* 44 (12):1305-13., 1998.

6. American Psychiatric Association, Ibid.

7. John March et al., " Fluoxetine, cognitive-behavioral therapy, and their combination for adolescents with depression: Treatment for Adolescents with Depression Study (TADS) randomized controlled trial," *Journal of the American Medical Association* 292 (7), 2004: 807-20.

8. Lenore C. Terr, "Children of Chowchilla: A study of psychic trauma," *The Psychoanalytic Study of the Child* 34:547-623, 1979.

   Richard Famularo, et al., "Psychiatric diagnoses of maltreated children: Preliminary findings," *Journal of the American Academy of Child & Adolescent Psychiatry* 31 (5): 863-67,1992.

   Laurhl Kiser, et al., " Physical and sexual abuse in childhood: Relationship with post-traumatic stress disorder," *Journal of the American Academy of Child & Adolescent Psychiatry* 30 (5): 776-83, 1991.

   David Pelcovitz et al., " Post-traumatic stress disorder in physically abused adolescents," *Journal of the American Academy of Child & Adolescent Psychiatry* 33 (3): 305-12, 1994.

   Esther Deblinger et al., " Post-traumatic stress in sexually abused, physically abused, and nonabused children," *Child Abuse & Neglect* 13 (3): 403-8 , 1989.

9. Ilse Derluyn et al., "Post-traumatic stress in former Ugandan child soldiers," *Lancet* 363 (9412): 861-63, 2004.

   Christophe Pierre Bayer,, Fionna. Klasen, and Hubertus Adam, " Association of trauma and PTSD symptoms with openness to reconciliation and feelings of revenge among former Ugandan and Congolese child soldiers," *JAMA: Journal of the American Medical Association* 298 (5): 555-59, 2007.

10. Liliana Cortes and Marla Jean Buchanan, "The experience of Colombian child soldiers from a resilience perspective," *International Journal for the Advancement of Counseling* 29 (1): 43-55, 2007.

11. Lenore C. Terr, "Children of Chowchilla: A study of psychic trauma," *The Psychoanalytic Study of the Child* 34:547-623, 1979.

12. Ibid.

13. David Alan Harris, "Pathways to embodied empathy and reconciliation after atrocity: Former boy soldiers in a dance/movement therapy group in Sierra Leone," *Intervention: International Journal of Mental Health, Psychosocial Work & Counseling in Areas of Armed Conflict* 5:203-31, 2007.

ELEVEN

We All Experienced Politics: An Interview With Urbain Kioni, Omari Mwisha, and Amuli Lutula, Former Child Combatants from the Association Des Enfants Soldats Démobilisés, Democratic Republic of the Congo

—————➤●◆◄—————

Jenny Bordo
Kate Charles
Lindsay Feldman
Jennie Johanson
Matt Meyer
and
Ramon Solhkhah

Translation:
Bony Ndeke,
Ligue Des Femmes
Pour Le Développe-
ment Et L'Education
À La Démocratie
(Lifded),
June 2, 2008

Child and Family Institute's Project REACT conducted a series of interviews with former child soldiers throughout West Africa and the Great Lakes region. The following interview, held in Kinshasa with members of the Congolese Association of Demobilized Child Soldiers, is representative of the issues faced by so many young Africans who have survived war and violent conflict.

Urbain Kioni, President of the Association, on the Demobilization Process and the Formation of the Group

The Democratic Republic of the Congo (DRC) has undergone very troublesome moments. We, ex-child combatants, were still young, and we didn't know about politics—but we all experienced politics... [and the] misery of poverty. In 1996, the late President Laurent Kabila was in need of [more recruits for] the army, so the army resorted to recruiting young people. We had a spirit of vengeance and we were still young, so we became involved in the armed forces. "Kadogo" is the word for child soldiers, a practice which [we now know] is in violation of human rights laws regarding children.

UNICEF started making advocacy to denounce these actions. They condemned the use of children as soldiers and said we should demobilize. At the end of seven months of war, on May 17, 1997, when [most of us] came to Kinshasa, the UN and the DRC government were already starting the demobilization of child soldiers. The government, however, being young, had little or no money, and it was impossible for them to continue this kind of program. And in 1998, there was a second war in which we were again involved. The government was counting on our patriotism as fighters to defend our country.

In December 1998, thanks to UNICEF and the African Union, there was another decree for demobilization, [but] there was a delay in implementation. With the coming of Kabila the younger, he started by taking a loan to try to organize the demobilization of child soldiers. After three years, the demobilization process entered a pilot phase. In that symbolic phase, Omari, Amuli, and I were all part of the first group of 207 to be processed. The goal of that action was to take all children out of the army, to disarm us, and to take us back to the communities. Because many of the children were coming from the eastern part of the country, but had reached Kinshasa by the late 1990s, there was no way to send us back, since the east of the country was still in rebellion. That is why the government established the National Bureau for Child Soldiers,* a program based on a three-month process, with welcoming families here in Kinshasa.

Most children, however, did not find a family—neither their biological family nor a host family. We went through vocational training, and some of us continue to go to school. But at the end of that training, the situation of many children was still not at all good. I, for example, learned driving for three months. Despite my new life, I couldn't find any job. I now am studying finance management, but some have gone on living in very bad conditions, very poor and alone. Due to this situation, [we] came up with the idea of gathering, forming an association of former child soldiers who had been demobilized. [We aim to] raise awareness of ourselves, for self-help. As the provisional demobilization opportunities don't last for long, we came to feel abandoned…to struggle for our own fate. Each of us is struggling for our life in our own way.

Please know that what we are telling you comes straight from our hearts. I myself was born in 1984, and war broke out when I was already in boarding school. From then till now, I have not seen any member of my family again. I had been in the army from early in my thirteenth year till the time I was eighteen, when I finished the demobilization process. So one can only imagine….

Omari Mwisha's Story

I was born in Goma province in 1984. I was enrolled in the army by force, not willingly. In Goma city, I was in an area with ten other people. A vehicle came and captured us and brought us to a military camp. We were submitted to intense training; I was just fourteen years old.

After the training, we were brought to Rwanda, and once there we went on foot all the way back to Katanga. It has now been eleven years since I have last seen my family, and I have no news of them at all.

We underwent so many troubles at demobilization, spending ten months at the demobilization center. We were given $2,000 to resume the civil life, and thanks to that money, I bought a pig. I sold it to pay for university, but have learned about pig breeding and taking care of animals. I am still at university today, in the third year of undergraduate studies.

As far as our association, our partnership with LIFDED has given us trainings and given me great confidence. We were trained in pacifist resolution of conflicts and in nonviolent programs which helped to give me new hope. This training helped because I had lost hope in my life. Much of the time I was tempted to rejoin the army, to go back to the front. Thanks to LIFDED and the nonviolence trainings, my awareness has been raised about the importance of resuming and continuing my civilian life.

Amuli Lutula's Story

Actually, I'm not interested in talking about my life in the armed forces, but I'll give you some hints. After the death of my parents, I was enrolled in the army—in 1996 in Kivu. We went to Rwanda for training, then back to Bukavu. We attended a meeting with the late President Kabila, who tried to enroll us in the goal of liberating our country. We were sent to the front, and I was later in a famous refugee camp. It was very hard for me to talk about my life of those days, because when I went in the army I did many unbearable things… a lot of horror.

I saw how people were murdered. I saw most of my friends of my age group die. I'm really very pained to talk about it. If at any time I talk about it, I feel as if I'm living it again.

I was among the young people who were in the capital, Kinshasa, for the liberation. After liberating the capital, the new Kabila government made a lot of promises: to give us gifts, to get cash, to have cars to drive. Later on, we realized that these were lies and that we had been victims of exploitation as children. It is only now that I can understand that these leaders had political reasons. Even though it was for the liberation of our country, there was some hidden agenda. When the leaders of the rebellion came in Kinshasa, they started fighting amongst each other and not taking care of us.

I was one of the bodyguards of President Kabila. I was still young, with the intention of resuming my studies. I tried to enroll in school, but when the military saw me in a school uniform, they came to arrest me and put me in custody.

Then came the second war again, and we were asked to go back to the front. I was lucky: thanks to a friend, also a member of the presidential bodyguard, I succeeded in running away. When I was escaping, I found a lady who knew my parents and who recognized me. She told me it was time to run away from the army. I had my youth, but it was hard for me to cope with a new life as a student. I had been a soldier; how could I be with these students who were younger than me? The lady convinced me to cope with civilian life.

While I was studying, some soldiers recognized me. They said that I was betraying the country, and I was very frightened. Another friend of mine told me we could go and meet the general. We told him: "After being in the army, you promised we could resume our school and civilian life. You are a father, and you know that at this age we should not be in the army. Just release us and let us go back to our studies." He gave us the authorization and ordered us: "Please resort to humility in the school." Thanks to UNICEF, I am now an engineering student.

Concluding Remarks from the Association

If the government wants to succeed, they must listen to, hear, and focus on listening to children. They must listen to the children's concerns. They should not make any decisions on projects for children, but ask children what projects they need. They should look with value to those programs that have succeeded, to use as role models for the future.

For us, we can say frankly that we have already lost hope for our future. We didn't have any chance or opportunity to talk or speak, even in the media, about our problems and concerns. We have no hope because we have seen so many violations of the rights of children and human rights in general. In the eastern provinces, we are still hearing about the rape of women, the formation of child soldier units, and more. This country is still not concerned with human rights.

* The Official title of the 2001 DRC government initiative was the National Bureau for Demobilization and Reintegration.

PART II

TAKING ROOT— CONCRETE INITIATIVES FOR PEACE WITH JUSTICE

TWELVE

Youth Rights and Rites: Taking the Lead from African Child Ex-Combatants

———————⟫●⟪———————

Matt Meyer
Lindsay Feldman
Jennie Johanson
Ramon Solhkhah
Jenny Bordo
and
Kate Charles

For the better part of the last century, peace and nonviolence movements of the Global North have designed most of their youth programs around conscientious objection and moral resistance to war. Conscientious Objector (C.O.) rights, whether formally established through a nation's legal system or informally accepted, have been taken up internationally as asserting a young person's "right to refuse to kill."[1] Advocacy efforts have helped establish standards for alternative service, so that those who opt out of national military duty may find appropriate nonmilitary means of supporting their country. These alternatives, however, rarely satisfy the diversity of peoples wishing to resist the assorted nationalisms, imperialisms, militarisms, and religious doctrines currently contributing to modern warfare.[2] Furthermore, despite an increase in global recognition of the significance of the rights to conscientious objection, the fact of youth and child soldiering—of forced recruitment of young people into militaries and militias—has increased at an alarming rate. Over the past decade, special campaigns and coalitions have developed within the human rights community to address the issue of forced youth soldiering.[3]

This report, spotlighting activists and academics engaged in youth advocacy work in four African nations that experienced widespread use of child soldiers, begins with the recognition that these human rights efforts have made a difference; the use of child soldiers internationally has decreased over the past several years. In reviewing the literature and the experiences of former child soldiers, mental health clinicians, and educators in Sierra Leone, Liberia, the Democratic Republic of the Congo, and Rwanda, it is clear that a detailed and comprehensive exploration of the long-term psychosocial effects of extreme militarism on child ex-combatants has yet to be done.[4] Alternative modes of psycho-educational treatment, rehabilitation, and reconstruction need to be developed. Nevertheless, inspiring and instructive efforts by and for former child soldiers have developed in some of the worst civil conflict areas of contemporary Africa. Much more than a simplistic Western exportation of the call for C.O. rights to the southern hemisphere, a truly international, youth-centered peace movement will only be possible if we all take in and learn from these African voices, south to north. It is our assertion that these efforts must be better understood and supported—by a broad range of global groups, both grassroots and intergovernmental—if global youth rights are truly to be recognized and respected. The snapshots contained herein, of individuals and organizations working to better their local and regional conditions, provide a beginning of one attempt to build bridges for mutual solidarity.

The Battlefields of West Africa

Sierra Leone

In the midst of a civil war known for the intensity of its atrocities, it was easy for European and U.S. theorists to suggest that Sierra Leone was a perfect example of the "coming anarchy" in store for Sub-Saharan Africa and the least developed countries of the global south.[5] With descriptors such as "the new barbarism" used to pepper the essays of popular magazine articles describing genuinely horrific war crimes, it may be little wonder that many still view Africa as a continent full of darkness and woe. These views have recently been refuted, though, as a "contemporary echo" of colonial thinking: that Africa is essentially a blank slate, devoid of civil societies strong enough to combat corruption and chaos.[6] A more correct and nuanced view of contemporary Sierra Leone should understand the conflict as both brutal and misunderstood. With a relatively small population inhabiting an arable land mass filled with substantial quantities of diamonds, iron, and gold, postwar Sierra Leone should more logically be thought of as a potential regional economic powerhouse.

The conflict in Sierra Leone (1991-2002) has been summarized by some as a war rooted in weak patrimonial leadership, in a country keenly aware of the extent to which wealth and power are the products of personal relationships passed down from one generation to the next.[7] The fact, therefore, that children have been central to military campaigns should not be surprising, especially, also, given the youthful median age of the population. Child soldiers almost always come from families already disrupted by conflict and war and at least from communities with desperate economic conditions. Sierra Leonean psychiatrist Edward Nahim, long active with work helping to reintegrate former child soldiers into the postwar population and currently a consultant with the Ministry of Health, noted, "Boy soldiers are ideal. They are good at taking orders, they do not have many outside responsibilities, and for many of them war becomes a game they enjoy."[8] Once forced into fighting units, these children are also often introduced to addictive drug use. As one seventeen-year-old Leonean ex-combatant noted, "Drugs made me feel like I was not afraid of anything."[9]

Leonean scholars Kingsley Banya and Juliet Elu, in their pioneering work on child soldiering in Africa, suggest that the tactics of modern war are particularly devastating to women and girls, youth increased gender-based violence and attacks targeting family and community survival and development.[10] In this view, the impact of these conflicts extends far beyond those youth directly recruited to fight in the war, to the "millions more [who] die from the indirect consequences." Disruption of food supplies and health care services and increases in disease due to the destruction of sanitary water or refuse removal systems, all cause untold harm. One fourteen-year-old girl abducted by Sierra Leone's "rebel" antigovernment Revolutionizing United Front (RUF) as a "war wife" spoke eloquently about her physical and emotional anguish: "So many times I just cried inside my heart because I didn't dare cry out loud."[11]

The reintegration of ex-combatants, especially children, can be vital to the success of a lasting cease-fire and is certainly a necessary prerequisite to the building of a productive society. The now commonplace use of Truth and Reconciliation Commissions (TRCs), Special Courts, and International Tribunals have established international guidelines for disarmament and development. The South African-founded International Center for Transitional Justice (ICTJ) noted that ex-combatants and the various civil "accountability institutions" were of vital importance to one another. In the case of Sierra Leone, the ICTJ partnered with the local, grassroots Post-conflict Reintegration Initiative for Development and Empowerment (PRIDE) and assessed that former combatants were both "willing and eager" to participate in their country's TRC, believing that the TRC would help them get back to their civilian lives in their former communities.[12] It is noteworthy that, with close to 80 percent of former soldiers believing that Truth and Reconciliation Commissions would be good for the country, only 15 percent thought that they themselves had done anything wrong, and less than 4 percent thought they should be held directly responsible for legal or fiscal redress. Over 70 percent of ex-RUF soldiers stated that they had been forcibly recruited to fight.[13]

Despite studies that have indicated that more than 90 percent of the population of Sierra Leone has experienced significant exposure to traumatic events, the current assessment of mental health needs is within a normal range for West African societies.[14] This may be attributable, in part, to a number of successful nongovernmental-initiated interventions, including in the areas of cultural empowerment—utilizing forms of music, art, and dance therapy.[15] International relief and aid agencies have assisted Leonean efforts at rehabilitation, taking a practical approach to physical and emotional well-being. The large constituency of amputees, for example, has been given occupational training and therapy, as well as psychological support.[16] Greatest Goal Ministries is one such Leonean nongovernmental organization (NGO) working to increase the well-being of former child soldiers by helping to set up six teams of all-amputee football players who form part of an international league.[17]

Not only do NGOs work toward cultural empowerment and emotional healing, they also partner with government ministries to provide practical opportunities for youth whose schooling was cut short during the war. "Many young people obviously look to education," noted World Health Organization advisor Soeren Buus Jensen, "as their coping tool and hope for the future."[18] And while return to school can be used as one method of normalization, community-based healers also have restorative functions. As indicated by a recent conversation with Dr. Nahim, Sierra Leone's extended family system and social structures have served as strong healing forces. Though Nahim is the nation's only classically trained medical psychiatrist, there are many "cultural" therapists, with over 90 percent of postwar Leonean mental disorders "treated by the culture."[19]

On a governmental level, the disarmament, demobilization, and reintegration (DDR) process in Sierra Leone included special care for close to seven thousand child soldiers.[20] Though it seems clear that holistic psychosocial support for those children severely affected by the war, especially girls, is still needed,[21] many young people have successfully put the war behind them. Through normalizing activities in education and vocational programs, Sierra Leone's young adults focus their attentions on rebuilding a country still crippled by poverty and a dilapidated infrastructure. Governmental groups, such as the National Commission for War-Affected Children, work to unify services for young people from different circumstances, under the broad banner that all children need "love, peace, empowerment, and protection." Specific service work addressing postwar issues, however, appears to be mostly managed by private, grassroots groups. The plight of street children is one such prevalent postwar-based crisis that is managed primarily by creative NGOs.

The Leonet Street Children Project was founded in 1999 to help educate homeless youth about the opportunities available to them, and provide services—including housing—to help with immediate needs. Funded primarily by Leoneans living and working abroad, the project is directed by Mohamed Fofanah, a former street child himself. "Problems today," Fofanah noted, "stem from the lack of support for kids within a given family." Though most issues can be traced back to the losses suffered during the war, Fofanah also asserted that there is still a "lack of support" from the government in terms of the needs of children. "They say that primary school is free, but it is not—there are lots of hidden costs." When enrollment is high and includes children who might otherwise be fending for themselves on the street, then teachers just get "extra students and less support." Fofanah suggested that while there is a general desire to solve these issues, there is much difficulty in implementing large-scale plans.[22]

The Freetown-based Don Bosco School and Training Center provides similar evidence regarding the scope and source of current problems. "Sierra Leoneans are a very joyful people," remarked Don Bosco director Father Jose Ubaldino Andrade Hernandez. "They don't have depression: they have hunger!" With over two thousand street children in Freetown alone, the Don Bosco School, a private enterprise also funded internationally, can barely assist 10 percent of the current need. For nine months, they house, feed, and teach children, who are then involved in an intensive skills training and placement program. Fourteen social workers help get the displaced youth back into their original communities and working a trade. Since there are practically no jobs available, Don Bosco has set up partnerships with the owners of small shops, so that the young workers can begin as apprentices, with the hope of eventually working into paying positions. "There are many things we lost during the war that we have not been able to get back," stated Hernandez, speaking about the lack of opportunities, economically and otherwise. "The war was very long, but the process of peace has come very fast."[23]

According to the youth trainers at Talking Drum (TD) studios, a radio station that teaches students to voice their concerns on the airwaves, the issues during war time were all about moving away from the conflicts. "Now we are dealing with issues of human rights content, cultural content, and education," stated public information coordinator Abdul Rashid. "Some virtually lost their childhood during the war . . . but we cannot go back."TD is a project of Search for Common Ground, and—together with other NGOs—they campaigned for the passage of a Children's Act, which became law in 2008. Based on the principles set forth in the UN Convention of the Rights of the Child, this law includes basic mandates against child recruitment, military service, and child trafficking. With some hopes that the new Leonean government will make good on their stated commitments, the NGOs continue to apply pressure for greater accountability and resources. The young people at Talking Drum regularly air interviews with government ministers, challenging them about what can be done regarding continuing inequities. By enabling youth to find their voice and speak out, Talking Drum models a dynamic of empowerment. TD trainer Princess Coker summarized it in the following way: "We should allow children to make decisions for themselves."[24]

Liberia

Though civil wars with regional ramifications can too easily be blamed on neighboring countries, especially in modern-day Africa whose countries' borders were drawn by foreigners, it seems reasonable to assess that the conflict in Sierra Leone was at least exacerbated by the presence of Liberian President Charles Taylor. It is clear that Taylor helped finance both the Liberian war and the rebel RUF through the use of Leonean "blood diamonds" and the widespread recruitment of child soldiers. In Liberia, an estimated twenty-one thousand children were demobilized at the end of the war, in late 2003; an additional significant number had been abducted into sexual slavery.[25] In 2005, the widely acclaimed Ellen Johnson-Sirleaf was elected president of Liberia, the first woman in the history of the continent to rise to such a position. Though military and policing duties are still in the hands of the United Nations Mission in Liberia, there is a significant sense of optimism in the country. As people link the brutality of militarism with the masculine paternalisms of recent regimes, an excitement remains about Liberia's new leadership.

During Liberia's two major civil conflicts (1989-1996 and 1999-2003), girls played a role in the military forces. A Human Rights Watch (HRW) study produced immediately after the end of the war indicated special concern regarding the inclusion of girls in the demobilization process.[26] Very few girls participated in demobilization following 1996, and thus serious attempts have been made to understand and remedy the issues causing this lack of involvement in the current context.[27]

In addition to special services being offered to young mothers, the general responsibility of the state to provide meaningful educational opportunities for all former child soldiers has been cited as vital to reconstruction efforts.[28] The high rate of domestic, gendered, and sexual violence during and immediately following the war has been noted in other studies, supporting the general HRW conclusions on the need for greater postconflict support of girls. An unusually high rate of suicide is also present in the Liberian case, with between 25 to 50 percent of former child combatants having contemplated or attempted to take their own (and sometimes their babies') lives.[29] Local NGOs have partnered with long-standing international groups such as the Center for Victims of Torture to provide intensive therapeutic services for the most affected of these constituencies.[30]

In addition to receiving treatment for domestic, gendered, and sexual violence, postconflict, community-based children's organizations have helped diminish the ostracism these ex-combatants faced, enabling young people to meet new friends.[31] In addition, traumatized youth have been encouraged and trained to help care for younger children as "junior facilitators." They therapeutically share their own war experiences, while engaging in routine activities such as food preparation, laundry, gardening, and traveling together to school. This sense of normalcy has been key, much more than specialized and temporary aid programs, in establishing healthy new communities and lives. "Restoring spiritual harmony through traditional healing," as one example of cultural and social sensitivity cited by Banya and Elu, "is an essential first step in helping child soldiers demobilize and integrate into their communities."[32]

It is heartening that the Liberian government of Johnson-Sirleaf seems committed to vigorously supporting the rights of youth, including the special needs of young girls and former children of war. The country's sole psychiatrist, Edward McClain, also serves as minister of presidential affairs, a position akin to the United States Secretary of State. His encouragement of multiple forms of therapeutic and reintegrative approaches—from cottage centers where ex-combatants learn animal husbandry, to quasi-religious efforts under the leadership of former opposition fighter "Prophet" Joseph Bly, to more traditional Rehabilitation Camps—is indicative of a policy looking to utilize all potentially productive means of achieving lasting peace.[33] The Ministries of Education and of Health and Social Welfare have been particularly open to innovative initiatives.[34]

Nationwide workshops were held early in 2008 to assess how the government could assist the most vulnerable groups of the population, to contribute to Liberia's social work policy, which is currently in the process of being drafted. Based on the participants' comments during the workshops,

Joseph Greebro, deputy minster of social work, noted, "We might have lost two generations" to the war. "But I believe," Greebro suggests, "that we are now on the right track. There's a bright future."

This bright future is exemplified by the new plan to train and hire over one thousand social workers, making the prospect for collaboration between teachers and therapists enormous. As education policy is also being formulated, Greebro—himself a trained social worker—expects to place one counselor in every high school. In addition, though health centers and midwifery schools exist across the country, plans are in place to rebuild the formal hospital and education systems.[35] "Our needs are enormous," summarized Joseph Korto, minster of education, "but we are prepared to cooperate" with anyone interested in working for a progressive Liberian future.[36]

The Great Lakes Region and Africa's World War in the Congo

The Congo wars, claiming millions of lives between 1996 and 2003 alone, have earned the dubious distinction of being called Africa's "first world war." With the involvement of six African national armies, countless foreign ambassadors, and the first deployment of European Union troops, the Congo conflict has been viewed as a trial balloon for the recolonization of the continent. And though the current war may well be rooted in historic misadventures, the popular notion that the causes lie in long-standing tribal, ethnic, or regional rivalries is, at best, a significant oversimplification. A nation-state the size of Western Europe, with a far greater number of mineral resources than any other similarly sized single patch of land on the planet, has been the envy of every greedy businessman for over a century.

During that time, what is now the Democratic Republic of the Congo (DRC) served as the personal cash cow for the brutal dictatorships of Belgium's King Leopold II, and of Mobutu Sese Seko. Leopold and Belgium were the colonial rulers of the Congo from 1885 till 1960; Mobutu was head of state from 1960 through the 1990s. Mobutu, Africa's most notorious neocolonial master, was backed by the U.S. since his part in the 1960 CIA-coordinated assassination of democratically elected Pan African socialist Patrice Lumumba, who was only in power for little more than three months. Subsequently, the Congo's second elected president, Laurent Kabila (an associate of Lumumba), was assassinated in 2001 after only a few years at the helm.[37] Survival mechanisms for the common Congolese citizen during the years of kleptocracy became something of an art form. Now, instead of being known as the richest and most creative country on the planet, the DRC is still associated with the century-old "heart of darkness" literary refrain.[38]

The "small miracle" of the 2006 presidential elections, which resulted in Joseph (the son of Laurent) Kabila's consolidation of power, resulted in a fragile peace at best.[39] The January 2008 Goma peace accord, signed by the DRC government and some twenty-two armed groups, was supposed to institute a cease-fire throughout the war-torn eastern region of the country. According to Human Rights Watch senior Africa researcher Anneke Van Woudenberg, however, "six months after the peace agreement was signed there has been no improvement in the human rights situation, and in some areas it has actually deteriorated."[40] United Nations officials have documented over two hundred violations of the cease-fire in the January through July 2008 period, resulting in deaths of more than two hundred civilians and the rape of hundreds of women and girls. With the continued use of child soldiers and other significant violations of international law, the conflict continues as small groups vie for turf and influence. As a number of these groups also represent a carry-over of the Rwandan genocide of 1994—with several thousand leaders of the genocide making up the Congo-based Democratic Forces for the Liberation of Rwanda (FDLR)—the questions of border security and the basic right to survival are also raised. Without addressing the question of Congo-Rwanda relations and what to do about the "genocidaires," there can be little hope for disarmament and demobilization. As Friends of Law in the Congo president Eugene Bakama Bope points out, "There is no military solution to the FDLR problem." Political dialogue, and the active support of the international human rights and peace communities, is necessary.[41]

It seems clear that lasting peace cannot be built on a society or region still so full of structural injustice. The U.S.-based Friends of the Congo has suggested that the peace process was in danger before it even got started, as fundamental issues of social change and international reconciliation were not being addressed. "Impunity has reigned throughout the Congo for far too long," they noted, and justice—both judicial and economic—must be present for peace to exist.[42] Civil society is faced, more than ever, with the question of how to build at least temporary outposts of calm, as the struggle continues for an equitable distribution of the Congo's enormous wealth.

That being said, some international agencies have partnered with Congolese civil society to address some issues of immediate need. The Paris-based International Federation for Human Rights (FIDH), for example, helped assemble together six Congolese grassroots activists and brought their message of the possibilities for lasting peace to a wide, global audience. The Netherlands-based War Trauma Foundation has helped create

Project Colombe, an initiative of local groups from the DRC, Burundi, and Tanzania that works to sensitize and assist people who are dealing with traumatic stress in the eastern Congo and throughout the Great Lakes region. Their associated Mbila Centre in Kinshasa has trained fifty local aid workers in the treatment of trauma. And while data suggests that there is hope to be found in the relative successes of these initiatives, there is clearly still much to be done.[43] When local officers of an international grouping like the United Nations, which is supposed to be nonpartisan, are accused of supplying arms to one of the belligerent rebel factions, it is hard to believe that the outside world is taking the cause of peace and justice in the Congo seriously.[44]

More and more, local Congolese NGOs understand the need to work on their own and heed the pleas of the young people who have been most affected by the wars. The Kinshasa-based Ligue des Femmes pour le Développement et l'Education à la Démocratie (LIFDED) is one such group, and their executive director, Grace Lula, was one of the activists leading the FIDH work.[45] As an affiliate of Pax Christi International, LIFDED understands the need to work cooperatively and get information out to the global community. LIFDED places emphasis on independent work from a Congolese-centered perspective, training women and youth from grassroots communities across the country. LIFDED's seminars on nonviolence, conflict resolution, human rights, and empowerment have put them in direct support of organizations formed to network and assist former child soldiers, such as the Association des Enfants Soldats Démobilisés.[46] "Our main thought is that a child is wealth," stated LIFDED affiliate Floribert Kabeya of the International Catholic Bureau for Children (BICE). "At the root of all things comes this matter of poverty . . . and children have become not an object of law but a subject of law."[47]

The Reverend Biasima Rose Lala, leader of the Great Lakes Ecumenical Forum and coordinator of a children's aid project that serves both Kinshasa and Goma, reiterated these perspectives and helped change the legal framework for children affected by war. "The country is not poor," she noted, "but we have had bad management of resources that have not been well shared. People are frustrated and we go to war; parents are killed, children become poorer, and the vicious cycle continues." Lala became a member of the DRC Parliament in order to help monitor the policies created and resources allocated. "On June 3, 2008, the legislature voted in a bill for the Protection of Children," she noted. "The government is in the best position to deal with children's issues, but we have to put the resources into education and child protection. We must fight against corruption in government, and create local projects that keep in place the long and rich tradition of

African solidarity with one another. We must make people aware of being a nation and as a nation must protect what we have. Power is not a way of taking for individuals; power is a way of serving others. I am hopeful about the future...but it is not easy or quick to change people's mentality."[48]

"It is up to the new generation to inculcate another mentality," noted Charlotte Mivilu Kalonji, another associate of LIFDED and the secretary general of the political group Rassemblement pour une Nouvelle Société (RNS). Kalonji asserts that, for peace to be long lasting, young girls must take more of a lead, and women must "fight to impose their ideology."[49] The Voice of the Voiceless (VSV) organization similarly suggests the need for new mentality and training and makes the connections between war, violence, gender, and the economy. "We are making a plea for a governmental audit," stated VSV president Floribert Chebeya, "because there was a large amount of money put at the government's disposal for demobilization of child soldiers, but it didn't have much emphasis or effect."

Though VSV's primary work has been calling attention to human rights abuses—from the time of Mobutu to the present—they also play a role in speaking out against all governmental misconduct. "In Kinshasa, many youth gangs using drugs and causing violence are coming from the former armed forces," Chebeya continued. "When children were in the army, they were trained to kill and rape ... and some are still keeping these same behaviors. The leaders in towns across the country who are committing human rights abuses are almost all former child combatants. And economic changes are at the root of these behaviors."[50]

The psychologists and counselors at the League for the Defense of Children, Students, Women and Youth (LIZZADEL) take this analysis into account as they provide grassroots psychosocial services in several communities. "Our motto and our strategy," noted Dr. Mathieu Mukenge, "is to make confidential all information, and to add confidence to all the victims." Believing that positive self-esteem plays an important role in helping those with posttraumatic stress, With many of LIZZADEL's clients treated as outcasts in their own families and villages, LIZZADEL's counselors work hard on improving their client's self esteem. "We work as mediators between victims and their families," stated Mukenge "We use comparisons as a method of therapy, so that people know that they are not the only ones who have faced what they have gone through. We provide what we call holistic support—judicial, health, psychosocial, and economic—and try to put the focus on the expectations of the victims."[51]

Psychosocial support for those who have survived sexual violence is one type of service that LIZZADEL provides. In fact, one of LIZZA-DEL's most important partners is a special unit for survivors of sexual violence at Kinshasa's Hospital St. Joseph. "We need to make an outreach campaign around the whole country to let people know that we have free care," stated Dr. Valery Empamposa, coordinator of the St. Joseph's unit. With close to four hundred survivors treated as patients at the unit from 2007 to mid-2008 alone, the need for services is clearly not diminishing. "There is obviously a link between the war and rape," continued Dr. Empamposa. "In the Kivu region, all sexual violence has been linked to war. But in Kinshasa," she continued, "it's more linked to social structures: poverty, too many people living in one house, and undisciplined soldiers."[52]

Dealing with some of the roots of militarism, from the behaviors of former combatants to society's lack of support for girls and young people in general, has been a major concern of the Congo's traditional Protestant peace churches. Pascal Tsisola Kulungu, a leader of the Congolese Mennonite community and founder of the Center for Leadership Development, Peacebuilding and Good Governance, summarized his country's complex issues this way: "We have to find out how to build the future with the past. Our goal is to help people readjust and be considered useful people to rebuild the country." The small but active peace churches have provided significant support for building a Congolese Truth and Reconciliation Commission (TRC). Beatrice Dive, a TRC advocate from Ituri, has seen the government go back and forth in its commitment to a reconciliation process, including appointing as TRC commissioners some of those responsible for some of the atrocities. "There wasn't a sense," Dive noted, "of how deep and difficult the process would be." "In the east, where there has been so much suffering for so long, there is a tremendous rejection of those who were traumatized," added Laite Antoine Katembo, chair of the Commission for Justice, Peace, and Careful Creation. "That is not the natural African way here; that is the result of this long war." Georgette Nyembo, a church activist who prepared election observers for the Ministry of Reconstruction, noted that the first step in rebuilding the Congo is, as it has ever been, making it clear to every child that "there is a choice between the gun he's had and the other, nonviolent, lives he could lead."[53]

The complexities of the Congo's multinational war, with a myriad of interlocking financial, military, patriarchal, and historic factors, can no longer be used as an excuse for the continuation of conflict. With a vibrant civil society working collaboratively toward social change in several diverse communities, utilizing thoughtful, often indigenous techniques, it is time that the international community provides the type of attention and solidarity that would strengthen these grassroots groups in their efforts for democracy and peace. It has been too easy for human rights groups around the world not specifically focused on Africa or the Congo to incorrectly characterize or dismiss the Congolese movements as disorganized because of their great number and the diversity of tactics and ideologies they employ. Indeed, understanding both the complexities of the fighting and of the diverse regional movements for justice should be a starting point for designing a multifaceted approach for lasting peace. It is time to recommit the energies of global humanitarians, both to help the Congolese and their neighbors to end the Congo wars and to allow for the kind of Congolese self-determination that would diminish the causes of war as well.

Rebuilding after Genocide in Rwanda

Not unlike in the Congo, the multinational causes of the Rwandan civil war and subsequent genocide of 1994 continues to be debated. The Rwandan government's August 2008 Commission of Inquiry report accusing the government of France with direct complicity in the killings (while carefully omitting any responsibility for Rwanda's allies—the U.S. and Britain) has further enflamed commentators throughout Europe and North America. Given its relative stability, it is easy—from a distance—to castigate Rwandan president Paul Kagame as a "strongman," dictator, or petty puppet of U.S. interests or at least of the machinations of Ugandan president Yoweri Museveni.[54] The situation on the ground in the small, central African country, however, suggests a different picture, fourteen years after nearly one million people were killed in a few months' time.

The fact of the mass murders, though still denied by some perpetrators facing the indigenous, community-centered Gacaca courts,[55] cannot be credibly denied.

Rwandans have done careful documentation and commemoration of their dead. A room of photo snapshots of young people long dead grace one side of the Kigali Memorial Centre. The phrase "Bana bacu mwari kuzaba intwari z'igihugu" heads the entrance and summarizes mass sentiment: Children, you might have been our national heroes. Rwandans are quick to point out that their national language, Kinyarwanda, has always been spoken by all of the people of the country—Hutu, Tutsi, and Twa alike. More recently, emphasis is placed on the idea that the correct answer to any query about one's ethnicity is "We are all Rwandans."[56]

The Rwandan Union of Youth Affected by Armed Conflict (RUY-AAC-Kadogo) is one organization that takes that principle into its daily work. Made up of young people from all sides of the conflict, including some recently demobilized children returning from fighting in eastern Congo, the association promotes "a culture of nonviolence, human rights, unity and reconciliation" through trainings in trauma healing, entrepreneurship, HIV/AIDS prevention, and conflict mediation. "We try to teach the pre- and postcolonial history of Rwanda," noted RUYAAC secretary Umulise Naila, "so that people will understand the roots of the conflict."[57] Like their partners at the Maison de Jeunes, the regional youth center at Kimisagara, outside of Kigali, RUYAAC gets support from the Ministry of Youth, Culture, and Sports but serves as an independent body working for youth empowerment and critical thinking. Utilizing enormous facilities—including football fields, computer labs, auditoriums, offices, and classrooms—these groups help make consciousness about youth rights a reality for thousands of young people annually.[58]

Learning from history, and using historically based materials and tools for youth empowerment, is a special focus of the Rwandan NGO, MEMOS, led by Dora Urujeni, a member of Parliament and a women's rights activist. Urujeni, who joined Parliament in 2007 to represent women from Rwanda's northern province, is also a part of the Commission for Unity, Reconciliation, Human Rights, and Fighting Genocide and believes that education and economic development are the keys to reconciliation. "Not everything can or should be solved by governments," Urujeni noted. It is the job of citizens to "collectively learn from the negative historical aspects that helped destroy Rwandan society," and to use that knowledge to "overcome the past and reconstruct the future as desired by the young generation."[59] MEMOS has done extensive work promoting the activities of those who served as rescuers during the genocide. They are also working with the Peacemakers Institute's Bearing Witness program, which has organized international retreats at Auschwitz and is planning a major 2010 initiative in Rwanda.[60]

On an official and formal level, working with groups like Rwanda's Demobilization and Reintegration Commission or National Unity and Reconciliation Commission seems to yield positive and productive results, as these groups maintain deep connections to the communities and provinces they serve and hold deeply to their stated goals. Demobilization Commission chair Jean Sayinzoga has cooperated with all international and local human rights associations and tribunals and continues to monitor the conflict situations in the region, despite the fact that there are no longer children serving in the Rwandan Armed Forces. With sixty thousand youth having gone through the Commission's programs, and three thousand currently still receiving some form of treatment or training, Sayinzoga nonetheless noted concern over the fact that there are probably twenty thousand Rwandans still out of the country, probably in a neighboring militia—by choice or by forced recruitment.[61] Ally Mugema, manager of the Child Ex-Combatants Rehabilitation Centre at Muhazi—one of the commission's programs that provides services for Rwandan children coming from the Congolese front—agreed with this assessment of the work still needing to be done and noted that "even after the guns are silent, children still feel the effects of war in a spectacular way."[62]

Unity and Reconciliation Commission Executive Secretary Fatuma Ndangiza has focused her concerns over the past ten years on how to deal with these effects, managing day-to-day issues of justice and reconciliation after one neighbor kills another or one brother kills the rest of his family. "We believe," Ndangiza explained, "that no one is born evil; it is society that creates evil. We believe that the future of Rwanda is in the young people and that with education we can learn new ways of living."[63] With perpetrators and survivors living side by side in towns that came close to being destroyed just one generation ago (but are now flourishing), the government has many examples of hope to point to.

Rediscovering indigenous African cultural values and practices has been the key to Rwandan reconciliation. From the idea of basing society on moral principles (Itorero) to community-based peace building initiatives (Ingando), from using respected local mediators (Abunzi) to African volunteerism and solidarity (Ubudette), precolonial problem solving has been a hallmark of postgenocide Rwanda. "There is a lot of potential," Ndangiza proclaimed, "in our culture and in our country."[64] Reconciliation efforts have also been developed by religious groups, such as the extensive Rwandan Community of Friends (Quakers). They have, for example, joined with colleagues in Burundi to create model workshops on Healing and Building Our Communities (HROC). The models bring to the surface the fact that "hatred lingers and old wounds are raw as poverty and loneliness serve as a constant reminder of whom and what was lost." Overwhelming grief, in their view, plays a role in many daily activities, and the workshops—like their basic philosophy—draw from the principle that healing from trauma and building lasting peace, on the individual and communal levels, are inextricably connected. A Friends Peace House was built postgenocide as a safe space for conflict resolution, and staffers such as HROC coordinator Theoneste Bizimana continue to gather and disseminate information on specialized healing initiatives.[65]

Perhaps it should be no surprise that the chief work of one of Rwanda's few clinical psychiatrists, Dr. Nasson Munyandamutsa, also involves the connections between personal healing, culture, and lasting regional peace. Munyandamutsa is a consultant at the Institute of Research and Dialogue for Peace (IRDP), an NGO involved in research and practice on the causes of war from a grassroots Rwandan perspective. Describing himself as "allergic" to the issue of reconciliation immediately following the genocide, when "it was the fashion" for government and the international community to talk about unity, Munyandamutsa began to help IRDP look at how common people affected by the genocide could gain credibility in their own communities to speak out about their grief, anger, and hopes. One cannot begin to work for forgiveness if people are not being direct and honest about who is to blame. "You can't even think," he added, "unless you have security and feel safe." Taking oral histories in the form of videotaping and the written word, IRDP has produced popular DVDs and books (in several languages), aimed at spotlighting the "voice of the people."[66] According to Munyandamutsa, the Rwandan government has cooperated in these efforts and has helped to create the safe space needed for lasting reconciliation and progress. But IRDP continues to operate independently, to look toward an even brighter future.[67]

MEMOS executive secretary Faustin Bismark Murangwa reiterated this approach in discussing the struggle to understand how so much killing could take place in their country in just one hundred days. "In looking for the causes of the genocide," Murangwa explained, "we look for strategies for dealing with young people today, looking to the future." New MEMOS trainings focus on good leadership development, with unique use of forum theater techniques and role play. Going beyond the popular human rights conceptions of work against "crimes against humanity," MEMOS is working to raise consciousness about the more common crimes of war, sometimes seen as mundane after the horror of mass annihilation.[68]

The optimistic spirit consistently present among Rwandan grassroots activists and young people belies a nagging fear that violence, like the ideology of genocide, could return at any time. If the many official and alternative cultural, educational, historical, and psychosocial programs continue to be strengthened, however, Rwanda stands a better chance than many nations (including those of the global north) at achieving true reconciliation, healing, and peace. The challenges faced by the organizations and individuals cited here are more manageable, in many respects, than the challenges that they project to the world outside of Rwanda: to recognize that war itself can be a crime against humanity and that the prevention of modern genocide is the responsibility of all of us.

Notes

1.   See War Resisters International <wri-irg.org>, CONCUDOC; see also Devi Presad, *Conscription: A World Survey*, London: WRI, 1971.

2   Scott Bennett, *Radical Pacifism,* ; See also Central Committee on Conscientious Objection, and international Jehovah's Witness campaigns, as well as WRL pre- and post-WWII materials <warrresisters.org>..

3   See assorted statistics from the Coalition to Stop the use of Child Soldiers, www.child-soldiers.org.

4.   See the Coalition's psychosocial web page, *<www.child-soldiers.org/psycho-social>.*

5.   R. Kaplan, "The Coming Anarchy: How Scarcity, Crime, Overpopulation, and Disease Are Rapidly Destroying the Social Fabric of Our Planet," *Atlantic Monthly* (February 1994): 30-76.

6.   Kingsley Banya and Juliet Elu, "The Dilemma of Child Soldiering in Sub-Saharan Africa," in *Advances in Education in Diverse Communities: Research, Policy, and Praxis,* ed. Carol Camp Yeakey, Jeanita Richardson, and Judith Brooks Buck, vol. 4 (2004): 177-205.

7.   Ibid., p. 182.

8.   Ibid., p. 184, and from an interview conducted by Banya and Elu on July 8, 1999.

9.   Ibid, p. 189.

10. Ibid., p. 197.

11. Ibid., p. 199, excerpted from the 2001 report of the Coalition to Stop the Use of Child Soldiers

12. PRIDE, "Ex-Combatant Views of the Truth and Reconciliation Commission and the Special Court in Sierra Leone" (Freetown: PRIDE, in conjunction with ICTJ, 2002), 5.

13. Ibid., p. 8

14. Author's interview with Dr. E. A. Nahim, Freetown, May 24, 2008.

15. See Maria Gonslaves, "Music Therapy and Peaceful Hearts for Girls at War: Assessing Psychosocial Needs Through Song in Sierra Leone," in this volume; see also D. A. Harris, "Pathways to Embodied Empathy and Reconciliation After Atrocity: Former Boy-Soldiers in a Dance/Movement Group in Sierra Leone," *Intervention: International Journal of Mental Health, Psychosocial Work and Counseling in Areas of Armed Conflict* 5, 3 (Amstelveen: Intervention Foundation, 2008): 203-31; see also www.interventionaljournal.com.

16. The work of Handicap International in Sierra Leone has been documented on the CSUCS psychosocial web page, edited by Linda Dowdney. See especially Nick Heeren, "Sierra Leone and Civil War: Neglected Trauma and Forgotton Children." See also Victor Gbegba and Hassan Koroma, "The Psychological Impact of Civil War in Sierra Leone." Both are from CSUCS, 2006.

17. Author's interview with Greatest Goal Ministries-SL national program coordinator Mambud K. Samai, May 24, 2008.

18. Soeren Buus Jensen, *Mental Health and Substance Abuse in Post-Conflict Sierra Leone* (Freetown: WHO Sierra Leone, 2002), 45.

19. Author's interview with Dr. E. A. Nahim, Freetown, May 24, 2008.

20. Guillaume Landry, *Child Soldiers and Disarmament, Demobilization, Rehabilitation, and Reintegration in West Africa* (London: Coalition to Stop the Use of Child Soldiers, 2006), 12; from meetings in Freetown with UNICEF, September 15, 2005.

21. Alice Behrendt, Psychological Needs of Children Without Parental Support in a Post-Conflict Area: A Cross-Section Study in the District of Kalihun in Sierra Leone, Dakar: Plan Sierra Leone, May 2008, 68.

22. Author's interview with Mohamed Fofanah, Freetown, May 24-25, 2008.

23. Author's interview with Father Jose U.A. Hernandez, Freetown, May 24, 2008.

24. Author's interview with Abdul Rashid and Princes Coker, Freetown, May 25, 2008.

25. Landry, Child Soldiers, 7; from the CUCS Child Soldiers Global Report 2004, 76.

26. Human Rights Watch, How to Fight, How to Kill: Child Soldiers in Liberia, New York: Human Rights Watch, Vol. 16, No. 2 (A), 2004, 39.

27. Ibid., 40.

28. Ibid., 38

29. Alice Behrendt, *Mental Health of Children Formally Associated with the Fighting Forces in Liberia: A Cross-Section Study in Lofa County* (Dakar: Plan Sierra Leone and Plan Liberia, May 2008), 44, 71.

30. See CVT web site.

31. Susan McKay, Malia Robinson, Maria Gonsalves, and Miranda Worthen, "Girls Formerally Associated with Fighting Forces and their Children: Returned and Neglected," London: CSUCS Psycho-Social web page, 2006, 3.

32. Banya and Elu, "The Dilemma of Child Soldiering," 200.

33. Author's interview with Minster McClain, Monrovia, May 29, 2008.

34. From conversations with Deputy Minister of Education James Roberts, New York City, March 22, 2008, and Monrovia, May 29, 2008, and from his presentations at the 2008 Comparative International Education Society Conference, Columbia University Teachers College, New York, March 18, 2008.

35. Author's interview with Deputy Minster Joseph Greebro, Monrovia, May 29, 2008.

36. Author's interview with Minster Zorbo, Monrovia, May 29, 2008.

37. See Gérard Prunier, Africa's World War: Congo, the Rwandan Genocide, and the Making of a Continental Catastrophe, London: Oxford University Press, 2008; and Thomas Turner, The Congo Wars: Conflict, Myth and Reality, London: Zed Press, 2007; and Mahmood Mamdani, Saviors and Survivors: Darfur, Politics, and the War on Terror, New York: Pantheon, 2009

38. Joseph Conrad's *Heart of Darkness,* needless to say, was not a reference to "the horror, the horror" of the Dark Continent, but to the darkness in the hearts of the European colonizers.

39. See Anneke Van Woudenberg, "A New Era for Congo?" *London Review of Books* (October 19, 2006); see also Van Woudenberg's writings at Human Rights Watch, www.hrw.org.

40. Human Rights Watch, "DR Congo: Peace Accord Fails to End Killing of Civilians: Murder, Rape, Looting Continues Six Months After Goma Agreement," Brussels: Human Rights Watch, July 21, 2008.

41. Eugene Bakama Bope, "DRC Comment: Countering the FDLR," London: Institute for War and Peace Reporting, April 8, 2008; see www.iwpr.net.

42. See, for example, Friends of the Congo, "The Devil Is in the Details," Washington, DC: Friends of the Congo, January 25, 2008; www.friendsofthe-congo.org.

43. Petra Joosse, "Sensitization Around Psychological Trauma: The Results of a Campaign in a District of the DRC," *Intervention: International Journal of Mental Health, Psychosocial Work and Counseling in Areas of Armed Conflict* 5, 2 (Amstelveen: Intervention Foundation, July 2007): 144-49; see also Emmanuel Ntakarutimana, "The Challenge of Recovering from War Trauma in the Great Lakes Region" 6, 2 (July 2008), both found at www.interventionaljournal.com.

44. See, for example, Columbus Tusiime and Henry Mukasa, "Uganda: MONUC to Probe Officers Over ADF Rebels" (Kampala: New Vision, May 9, 2008), www.allafrica.com.

45. Author's interview with Grace Lula, Kinshasa, June 4, 2008; see also chapter in this volume.

46. See Bordo, Charles, Feldman, Johanson, Meyer, and Solhkhah, "We All Experienced Politics: An Interview with Former Child Combatants from the Democratic Republic of the Congo," in this volume!

47. Author's interview with Floribert Kabeya, Kinshasa, June 3, 2008.

48. Author's interview with Rev. Biasima Rose Lala, Nairobi, June 5, 2008.

49. Esperance Tshibuabua, "Charlotte Mivilu Kalonji: Les femmes doivent se batter et imposer leur ideologie," *Potentiel*, Kinshasa: Le Potentiel Edition 4053 (June 20, 2007); also from author's discussions with Mimi Kalonji, Kinshasa, June 2-5, 2008.

50. Author's interview with Floribert Chebeya, Kinshasa, June 3, 2008.

51. Author's interview with Drs. Gode Kayembe and Mathieu Mukenge and the staff of LIZZADEL/Masina, Kinshasa, June 3, 2008.

52. Author's interview with Dr. Valery Empamposa, Kinshasa, June 4, 2008.

53. Author's discussions with Kulungu, Dive, Katembo, and Nyembo, Kinshasa, June 4, 2008.

54. See, for example, Barrie Collins, "Rwanda: Obscuring the Truth About the Genocide," www.spiked-online.com.

55. See Simon Gabisirege and Stella Babalola, "Perceptions About the Gacaca Law in Rwanda: Evidence from a Mutli-Method Study," Special Publication No. 19 (Kigali: Rwandan Ministry of Justice in conjunction with the

Center for Conflict Management of the National University of Rwanda, and Baltimore: John Hopkins University School of Public Health Center for Communication Programs, April 2001).

56. As aptly and dramatically demonstrated in Ayuub Kasasa Mago and Debs Gardner-Paterson's film, *We Are All Rwandans,* Kigali: Catsiye Productions, Rwanda Cinema Centre, 2007, www.WeAreAllRwandans.com.

57. Author's interview with Umalise Naila, Kigali, June 6, 2008.

58. Author's interviews with Maison de Jeunes director Aime Kibuyei and finance Administrator Marie Jean Mukankuranga, along with MEMOS staff person Issa Higiro, Kimisagara, June 9, 2008.

59. Author's interview with Dora Urujeni, Kigali, June 12, 2008.

60. See www.peacemakerinstitute.org/BW_Retreats.html.

61. Author's interview with Jean Sayinzoga , Kigali, June 9, 2008.

62. Author's interview with Ally Mugema, Muhazi, June 11, 2008.

63. Author's interview with Fatuma Ndangiza, Kigali, June 10, 2008.

64. Author's interview with Fatuma Ndangiza, Kigali, June 10, 2008.

65. See Friends Peace House-Rwanda, HROC-Burundi, and African Great Lakes Initiative of the Friends Peace Teams-USA, Healing and Rebuilding Our Communities-Manual for Basic Workshop, Kigali: Friends Peace House, 2003, 6; see also www.quaker.org/fpt/agli/friends.htm.

66. See note 73 below, interview with the doctor.

67. Institute of Research and Dialogue for Peace, *Building Lasting Peace in Rwanda: Voices of the People,* (Kigali: Pallotti Presse).

68. Author's interview with Faustin Bismark Murangwa, Kigali, June 9, 2008.

THIRTEEN

Resistance, Reparations, and Repatriation: A Radical Agenda for Pan-African Justice
An Interview With Dhoruba Bin Wahad

⭐

Bill Sutherland

Dhoruba bin Wahad was a leader of the Black Panther Party based in New York City and was framed by the illegal U.S. Counterintelligence Program; he spent nineteen years in prison for crimes he did not commit. After successfully proving his innocence, he became a tireless advocate for the rights of U.S. political prisoners, introducing fellow former prisoner Nelson Mandela to the welcoming crowds of Harlem. He won a civil case charging the New York State Department of Corrections with discriminatory actions and subsequently relocated to West Africa in the mid-1990s. In July 2006, he spoke with Pan-Africanist elder Bill Sutherland in Accra, Ghana, where Sutherland had taken up residence some fifty-three years earlier.

BILL SUTHERLAND: I understand that there is going to be an international conference on reparations, here in Ghana, in July 2006. Are you involved in that work?

DHORUBA BIN WAHAD: Initially, I was reluctant to get involved, but when the issue of political prisoners arose, the legal status of political prisoners under a future dual citizenship law, it gave me some concerns. I think what's really needed is an endorsement, a manifesto of one document that the entire Pan-African movement can endorse, that relates to political prisoners in the Diaspora, and that's what my objective would be if I got involved.

I do know one of the coconveners here, Nana Gyepi. He's a young man, full of ideas. Gyepi is a minor chief. And he's been involved off and on with various people from the Diaspora for the past twelve or so years. There are also Ghanaian government officials who have endorsed the conference. The Ministry of Tourism and Capital Modernization has endorsed aspects of this conference. There's a split in the conference, between forces who feel that some of the activist organizations haven't been diplomatic enough in terms of bringing the issue in front of the legal tribunals, international tribunals. Another part feels that the ideology of Pan-Africanism and reparations is something who's time has arrived and it's time for us to push this, regardless of governmental endorsement or not. Those two camps have divided themselves into two different conferences.

BS: You were talking earlier, not on tape, about the whole question of reparations, repatriation, and Pan-Africanism as a whole and looking at this repatriation question in a broader and more radical political context, and many folks are talking about it today. Maybe say a little more about that and a little more about some of the ideas you've had: NGO and Pan-Africanist and how to move that forward.

DBW: Well, my senior brother Bill, you've been on this continent and been involved in the Pan-African movement and with African leaders for the better half of a century. And I'm sure your experience, and the history that you bring, can help us to understand why what we're doing now could be a mistake.

The first thing, when we talk about reparations, there's no question that reparations should be addressed, will have to be addressed. But I think that reparations have to be addressed in the context of Africa reclaiming its own history. You know, Amilcar Cabral once said that the process of African liberation is a process of Africans reclaiming their own history, their own historical personality. What Cabral meant was that when the Europeans came to Africa, they interrupted the African historical continuum. Africans were, at that point before Europe and even before the Arab invasions, operating from their own historical impetus.

It was African history, pure and simple. Good and bad, it was African history. But when the Europeans came and began their gradual conquest of the continent, at some point African history became a footnote to European history; it became the index. From that point on, Africa has been described as an adjunct to European history. Economically, we have operated as a adjunct to European economic development. Politically, our institutions, our cultural institutions, were weakened, undermined, and supplanted by values and institutions from the colonial powers. The chieftaincies were depoliticized and marginalized because of some chieftaincies resistance to European penetration.

All of these things happened in a process, and then Africans had to undergo a liberation process to undo this, to bring themselves back to who they were, to where they wanted to go. And that historical period roughly corresponded with the final stage of industrialization in the West, with the final development of what Nkrumah called the higher stage of imperialism, or neocolonialism. A lot of the African nations, Ghana being the first, became independent. But that independence was not genuine independence. It didn't encompass economic and political disengagement from the former imperialist systems.

And so it presented Africa with a dilemma. Africa was half in its history and half out of its history. The cold war, in my view, contextualized the liberation process of Africa and in many ways sidetracked it. With the end of the cold war, without the auspices and the sponsorship of one of the superpowers, Africa has spiraled out of control in this age of globalization. Africa has spiraled toward finance capitalism, foreign investments, the complete opposite of what used to happen when Europeans first came to this continent when we were talking about social planning, about building institutions to empower people, and about working people benefiting from their work. All of those ideals and principles that were valid ideals and valid principles are now thrown out. If you look at Ghana, and God knows, if anybody knows, you know, if you look at Ghana, all of the major infrastructural developments in this country came under improvement. None of the succeeding post-Nkrumah governments, all of which lacked a Pan-African perspective, have produced anything for the benefit of the masses of people here in Ghana.

BS: Well, is there still a Pan-African consciousness that is present amongst some elements in the society?

DBW: Today what we're confronted with is fifty-three nation states, and not one of them is a genuine African nation! There's not one genuine African nation on the African continent. They're all European clones; they're all imitations of European nation state models. None of them is genuine, and globalization, which is a product of international finance capitalism, globalization is unique. It's not like old-style imperialism. It's not like old-style neocolonialism. It's not the same anymore.

Elites now, in this global world, are cooperating with each other to exploit their people. They are no longer competing with each other to seize resources and exploit their people. There's a fundamental difference here, because historically capitalism relied on war for profit. Now, capitalism no longer relies on war per se; in fact, war is unprofitable in the long run. It might be short-term profitable for certain small corporations, arms corporations, that have a contract with the nation-state. We know about the private contractors in Iraq, making billions and billions of dollars off of that, off of that situation.

We also know that poverty on the African continent is a multibillion-dollar-a-year business. Just poverty, people starving in Africa, is a multibillion-dollar-a-year industry. Just as prisons are a multibillion-dollar-a-year industry in the United States. So when we see that these negative forces are reliant on a nation-state apparatus, we have to ask ourselves, "Well, what is that instrument? What is it called? What is it?" And I have always said that our formal enemy is the national security state. I've always maintained that the national security state is the end result of an evolutionary process.

It didn't just pop up; George Bush didn't just come out of nowhere. He's the end result of a process that began with emptying prisons in England to send settlers to Australia, or to the New World. That was the beginning of this process that we're seeing now. Now we have a situation where every major segment or region in the world has coalesced into an economic, political, and military block. There's the European Union, there's the Asian block of nations, there's the Pacific Alliance of nations, and now Africa is talking about an African Union.

But they're talking about an African union only on the barest political terms imaginable. When we look at the regional alliances, whether it's ECOWAS [Economic Community of West African States], or SADC [Southern Africa Development Community], we look at all these regional alliances and we realize that these regional alliances, instead of being conducive for unity, are obstacles to Pan-African unity. Why do I say that? Look at ECOWAS. ECOWAS has been the unfortunate observer of three major civil wars that have lasted seventeen and twenty years: Liberia, Sierra Leone, and now Ivory Coast.

These civil wars have torn this region apart. They have empowered criminal elements in this region and created the culture of armed conflict and thuggery that's going to take generations to eliminate. The trial of former Liberian president Charles Taylor is going to be the most important trial of an African leader in this century, so far, because everyone in this region was involved with the murder and mayhem in Liberia and profited from it. The leaders in this region profited from importation of small arms and guns and illicit diamonds and gold. They profited from trading relationships with the major arms dealers and the major powers. Charles Taylor launched his campaign from Ivory Coast. When the embargo was implemented on Liberia, he used Ivory Coast to smuggle out timber and to smuggle in arms. There's not an airport in West Africa where a plane lands, that the authorities in those countries do not know what that plane contains and where it's going.

So for arms to reach Liberia throughout Ivory Coast, through Burkina Faso, through Guinea, that means people were paid, money was transacted, and arrangements were made. And Charles Taylor knows those arrangements, knows those people that were involved, and Charles Taylor is the type of person, in my view, that is not going to take this weight alone. That's why that trial is important for us: to show us how the forces of imperialism have arrayed themselves under globalization, to destabilize Africa, to permit people like Taylor to come into power and stay in power and do what they do.

Look at the Eastern Congo, the same thing. The Eastern Congo is a *tsunami* every six months, is the equivalent of a *tsunami* in terms of death and carnage and human suffering. Imagine if that was in Eastern Europe, if hundreds of thousands of people were dying every other month in Eastern Europe! It would be in the Security Council. It would be a global crisis. I mean, for God's sake, the Koreans launch a missile, and it's a global crisis. They didn't even kill nobody! They just launched the missiles.

What I'm trying to say here is, the attention that the African continent gets internationally is completely dependent upon the relationships of Africa's elites to the elites of Europe and the elites of the United States. Finance capitalism has created a global process that imposes on Africa the necessity to create a Pan-African Union. There has to be an African Union. There has to be a union of African states that are just more than pieces of paper and alliances, and subregional alliances, that nobody follows. We have to have a union that has its own currency, which is used exclusively on the African continent and within the purview of that union. It must have its own minerals and trade market. In other words, how could we allow the Europeans to buy bauxite in Guinea? Set the price for bauxite? Determine the political climate in Guinea for the extraction of bauxite. We have bauxite in other places in Africa. Why isn't there an African commodities market, where if you buy bauxite in Africa, you have to buy it from the market? This way, you couldn't pit the elites in Conakry against the elites in Namibia. "Oh, I can get it cheaper in Namibia. You gonna have to give me a better deal." The mining companies couldn't do what they're doing in Angola and the Congo if there is such a thing as a trading consortium, and Africa has its own trading zone. The failure to move toward that is the indication of just how bogus African states are, because every African state would have an automatic interest in this.

Just imagine. When we look at how the Europeans and the West created their wealth, they created it out of nothing. Literally. They printed money as a means, as an IOU, more or less, to wage war. That currency now is the British pound, it's the American dollar, it's whatever. But it was all based on one thing: gold. Supposedly it was based on one thing. We can do the same thing. If today, in this day and age, we know exactly where the oil is, how much oil is there; I mean, we have all of these satellite photos and everything. We can determine where oil is, we can determine where gold is in the ground, we can make all these determinations. It's estimated that Nigeria, for instance, has over 160 billion barrels of oil. That can be translated into dollars, into "Afros," into an all-African currency, because currency is based on concrete material, whether it's gold, silver, or whatever standard. If we built a currency in Africa based on the minerals that are available in Africa, and that's the basis of our currency, and no one can trade inside Africa unless they use our currency, we've changed the whole paradigm of Africa's relationship to the rest of the world. The whole paradigm has changed.

And that's what I meant earlier when I said, "Africa's elites are not even really elites." They don't even look out for their own interests. They look out for the interests of everybody but themselves. They think that they have an interest in facilitating a mining company coming in and destroying the environment and extracting gold. Okay? But when the rains come and the erosion happens, and the floods go on, it's their people, it's our people, that suffer, that are the victims of the floods, are the victims of the famine. Whereas, we could have that same arrangement where the people benefited from that type of trade agreement. The people of Africa are not benefiting from its resources, because the people of Africa have no Pan-African government. They have no means of ensuring that their interests are protected. So when we talk about reparations, we have to talk about it in the context of globalization and what that really means.

When we talk about repatriation, it's the same thing. When we talk about our ability to come back to this continent that we were taken from, we are confronted with a historical backlog of legality that prevents us from doing this. When we were taken from here, for instance, we didn't need a visa. We didn't need, we didn't need to fill out documents and take them to anyone in order to be taken out of here. But now we have to do all of these things. Repatriation implies that people who lived in a certain place are being returned to that place, or permitted to return to that place.

So now that Africans are claiming their responsibility in the slave trade, we have to establish that we are in fact Africans with African ancestry and African families, because only as an African family, as an African citizen, can we file a petition in the international court, claiming our rights. We can't claim our rights in international courts and say, "I was kidnapped, my family was kidnapped, my relatives were kidnapped, from the Gambia, you know, 465 years ago, and I'm filing this suit now because I feel that my rights have been violated." They're going to tell me in the U.S., "Well, the Thirteenth Amendment of the U.S. Constitution says that you're a U.S. citizen, and that you have been given this U.S. citizenship. You were born in the United States, your family was born in the United States." At least, in the days of Nkrumah there was a certain ambient pan-African consciousness, a certain expectation that as Africans we were going to move forward together. That whatever our differences, whatever our drawbacks were, as Africans it was a new day, and we were going to move forward at that time. There's not that expectation now. The expectation today is that Africans basically can't do anything, and that unless they travel abroad, unless they come from abroad with expertise, then they're not going to achieve anything. And that type of attitude is a nonstarter. If you don't believe in yourself, you can't go nowhere.

First of all, you have to believe in yourself, and one of the things that Nkrumah's generation and your generation believed in was African people. You believed in yourself. Above all, we believed that we could achieve, we believed that we could move. We believed that we could liberate ourselves. And because we were fighting a foe—physically, ideologically, and spiritually—because we were fighting a very concrete European imperialism, it was relatively easy to identify with other Africans who were also fighting that same foe.

Today, we're told that corruption is the major malaise in Africa, that because of corruption, Africans can't progress. Of course, that's not true, because capitalism was based on corruption. It's legal corruption; it's legalized corruption. Corruption in and of itself is not the basis for Africa being backwards; the basis for Africa being backward is its elites who have availed themselves of other elites' power in order to stay in power themselves. And they are robbing and raping and pillaging this planet, this continent.

That's why repatriation cannot occur on this continent without class consciousness—because right now, as we speak, there are people looking for the gun of Nelson Mandela that he buried when he first got arrested. You know, when Nelson Mandela was underground in the ANC, early on, before he got arrested, he used to carry a pistol with him. And he was met at these various safe houses that the ANC and the Communist

Party in South Africa had. Before he was arrested, he had buried his gun at one of these safe houses, which is now a historical monument. And they are carrying out, right now as we speak, a search for this buried gun, because it's part of South Africa's history of resistance to apartheid. Now remember, when the ANC embarked on armed struggle, everyone was talking about how it was terrorism and armed struggle wasn't the way. Now a gun is an icon of that struggle! My point is, is that we have not created and maintained a proper respect for our history and struggle on this continent. Therefore, other people have been able to come along and co-opt that history, and co-opt that struggle. And it's these people that have come along that find ready identification on this continent with other people who are only interested in gaining wealth, influence, and power. So repatriation has become a class issue. It's become an issue similar to what we have with our bourgeoisie clergy in the United States who refuse to deal with political prisoners. Or who refuse to deal with the issues, like the Rockefeller drug laws in New York, which is imprisoning and criminal-izing generations of African youth.

We're dealing with a class of people in our community, and a class of people in Africa, who have a similar viewpoint, who have a similar relationship to power, and who have similar objectives. And these are the people who are defining Pan-Africanism and repatriation today. On the other side are the people who have been in the trenches, like yourself, who have been fighting at the barricades for revolutionary Pan-Africanism, for understanding of the African family as a whole, and its revolutionary potential—not just to change Africa but to change the world. I don't see myself as an African just devoted to changing Africa. I think that if we change Africa, we'll change the world. I think that if we could effectively build institutions to eradicate poverty, want, and hunger and disease on this continent, we could effectively build a world community to do the exact same. We could change the paradigm between rich and poor. I think that Africa being backwards, and Africa being the least developed region on the planet, in itself is a historical metaphor.

In terms of the institutions we're facing, I think that the African Union, unlike the OAU [Organization of African Unity], has the potential to become the basis for a united Africa. Having said that, I think that the obstacles in the way of that are daunting. There are serious obstacles to achieving that. But I think that African leaders on this continent as a whole realize that unless Africa can get itself together, as a region, as a continent, it will not enjoy any type of prosperity in the twenty-first century. The European Union has evolved from the European Common Market to an almost national super-state, almost a European super-state. It has its own military force, NATO, that no longer has a military and political mission in Europe. NATO's in Afghanistan, NATO's in the Congo. NATO's all over the place. And if we look at it, what's NATO stand for: North Atlantic Treaty Organization. They should change the name to European Police Organization of the World, because that's what it's become.

I remember years and years ago, when I said that NATO would deploy forces outside of Europe, everybody used to tell me that wasn't gonna happen. Now, NATO has deployed forces in Afghanistan; it's taken up the role of the U.S. government and the U.S. policies in Afghanistan, in Iraq. The only place that NATO hasn't deployed, in fact, is in Iraq. But it has deployed in other trouble spots, whether it's Bosnia-Herzegovina, Western Morocco, elsewhere. And these NATO forces are comprised of the former imperialist nations. These are some military of the former imperialist nations.

The major force that's deployed in the Eastern Congo today are the French, besides the United Nations. The French, of all people! Why don't you just deploy the Belgians!? I mean, if we have problems here in Ghana, why not bring back the British!? They know how to straighten, sort things out, they got this experience!!

What we're looking at with globalization is a new age of imperialism. You know, with the incense and suggestions that "I'm feeling you and you're feeling me,"—New Age imperialism. It's not the old-age imperialism with armies and storm troopers and occupying territories and setting up despots; it's new age imperialism. You have the [Ghanaian president] Kufuors in the pinstripe suits, talking about economic development, and partner-sharing with America, and investment. That's the economic aspect of imperial domination. Meanwhile, they sell the Ghana telecom to private corporations, selling water to private corporations. Privatizing everything: prison, water, everything.

In terms of the dual citizenship and the right of abode, here in Ghana they have passed a law indicating that Africans from the Diaspora have a right of abode. All that simply means is you can get an extended residence permit for about $200, instead of a thirty- or sixty-day visa. The right of abode, however, has clauses in it, and one of the clauses is that an individual from the Diaspora who has been convicted of a crime, or who has spent a year or so in prison, is not eligible for the right of abode as an African in the Diaspora. Of course, we know that any type of regulation like that just flies in the face of the reality of African American history. I mean, you, Bill, wouldn't be eligible; Martin Luther King would not have been eligible to be a citizen. None of us would be eligible.

This is what I mean about the class nature of the elites on the African continent. They got that idea about a law from consulting with the U.S. State Department, with the British High Commission, and they said, "Well, if a dual citizenship is to be valid, we can't have any criminals coming in here." So that clause is in there, forgetting the fact that the movement for liberation by people in the Diaspora was always criminalized. There was always law enforcement used to repress legitimate dissent.

Now we must ask: "Are you prepared in your application to make an exception in this clause to those who were incarcerated for political reasons?" What we're talking about is the fundamental understanding that the African experience has to be incorporated in any type of protocols and laws that you make. You can't make a law that flies in the face of the reality of the people you're making the laws for. And the reality of our situation is that we suffered political and racial repression under the guise of law enforcement. That's the reality. And if we could, and if this was a genuine effort to fashion a bill that would fit the Diaspora, they would have come to us and said, "You know, we're thinking about putting this clause in." But when it was our time to address this issue in Ghana, we marched down to the Parliament to present our views. Those views were basically dismissed because they were not thinking about the African Diaspora as us, they were thinking about the African Diaspora as investment. They were thinking about Africans coming here who had money. Africans coming here who have a certain class level and certain level of privilege.

This obviously is important for the political prisoners. Because I do not believe that individual states in Africa should bear the responsibility of passing a universal right of return, or a right of return bill, for the African Diaspora. I think that the African Union, because it is comprised of fifty-three member states on the African continent, should itself resolve to establish a protocol that says, "All Africans in the African Diaspora," and then define what they mean by Africans, "have a right to return to the African continent as their homeland and acquire citizenship." Every member state will enact laws and regulations within its own jurisdiction to ensure and facilitate that; then we have something we can work with, because I don't have to come to Ghana now on the right of return. I can go to Gabon. I can go to Kenya. I could go to Ghana, Congo. All I have to do is just follow the procedures that whatever country has for the application, under this claim, and make this claim.

The U.S. political prisoners are in jail, by and large, as "American citizens," subject to American jurisdiction and laws. But if we show that these individuals, first, have a right to resist what was being done to their people and that even if you criminalize that resistance and didn't recognize their right, you would have to recognize that they were a people who were taken into captivity and that you conferred citizenship on, without them asking. They have just as much right to renounce that citizenship and claim their original citizenship as they do to maintain the one they have been improperly given.

And if they have that right, then they can be transferred to member nation-states that you have treaties with, that you have a recognition with, to finish out their time. Look at Silvia Baraldini. Silvia Baraldini was a white activist who was incarcerated in prison because of activities with the armed anti-imperialist movement in America. She was an Italian citizen, but she hadn't lived in Italy at all. She was raised in America. But she claimed her Italian citizenship as a device to get out of doing time in the United States. Now Silvia Baraldini is in Italy, she's still under sentence, but she's free, basically, because if our political prisoners came here, the conditions of their confinement are totally up to us. They could be confined on a 500,000-acre estate, if we see so fit.

The thing is to provide a legal mechanism through which the U.S. political prisoner can be resolved to the satisfaction of the political prisoners, the movement, and to some degree the state that's holding them. Because the state that's holding them, although they're political prisoners, still takes them through the rituals of parole review, still takes them through the rituals of sentencing, of sentencing review, and applications and all that. So if they take you to a parole review, they're implying, okay, that there's a legal mechanism for you to be released under their guidelines. And you know that under parole, you can be released to another jurisdiction that will take you. That's part of the recommendations of parole. You know, you have a letter from the community saying that, you know, "We have a job for him, we'll look out for him." You know, "He's going to be taken care of, and we think that he's rehabilitated." The same letter could be written by a government, or by the African Union.

But right now, they have no claim to make to that government, and if the U.S. says, "Well, you're meddling in our internal affairs. What are you doing here? Don't even mention it." So they can't mention it. But, if there's a class action suit pending in the international court that says that we are members of this class, we're in a different position, especially if—in the context of a movement for repatriation—the forces we're fighting are "making atonement" for the slave trade, saying that we're their brothers. If this is true, then I should, as a repatriated Ghanaian, be able to file in civil court and say that my ancestors came from the Gambia. They were kidnapped by slavers and taken to the island of Antigua and Dominica, and then out of Dominica and Antigua, I had an uncle or aunt, and they migrated to Georgia, and so on. That's the basis of the class, that's the class action. It's not a U.S. citizen bringing a suit against its government, it's an African citizen bringing suit against the government that's held him in captivity for generations. And he would like to return to his original citizenship, and that's what the court has to determine: is this person, was this person in fact taken from his natural home against his will? And has, over a period of time, the government evinced a design to put him in prison, and he resisted this?

Of course, you know, on the United Nations charter now, you have a right to resist occupation, you have the right to resist enslavement. Slavery is illegal, and there's no statute of limitations on it. It doesn't say it's illegal back until last week, or the beginning of the twentieth century, it's illegal with no statute of limitations. Just like crimes against humanity. So that's why repatriation and this issue of right of return are important for the political prisoners. And this is an importance that I think that the average individual in the reparations movement, by and large, does not attribute any significance to. Not because they don't support our political prisoners, but because they're more focused on bringing reparations to the forefront of legal recognition, by countries, by states, by international institutions. So, they don't want to quibble and argue over whether homeboy is a criminal—because, you know, that's the first thing the State Department's going to say. "As far as these issues of political prisoners are concerned, we can assure that these individuals are mere criminals." I think that this reparations conference, although it might seem insignificant, may well be significant in terms of what it can represent, in terms of our consistency at every level. We have to make the issue of political prisoners clear at every level of principled struggle.

We have to say: "There *are* political prisoners in the United States." We have to make people pay attention to that. This is who they are. This is how their cases went. This is what's going on. What do you say as a reparations movement about these cases? What does the movement say?

When the universal law of return, and the universal right of return, is fashioned, there must be a clause in there that says, "Universal right of return extends to all political prisoners, and prisoners of conscience, who have been incarcerated in prisons and jails throughout the Diaspora for their beliefs, for their faith, and for their ethnicity and cultural purity." For repatriation, they should be able to just file a writ and say, "Look, I want to renounce my U.S. citizenship and claim my citizenship as a African citizen of the Gambia. And I have a letter from the Gambian mission saying that under the rules of the law of return, I have made that application and it has been accepted. And that Gambia will take full responsibility for my continuance of any type of legal sentence that I have to play out in the United States." Now the United States has to say yes or no. If it says "no," we've got a whole different type of follow-up campaign. If it says "yes," the political prisoners go home. That's why I think this issue of reparations and repatriation is important for the political prisoners. We have to establish a legal precedent for the release of our prisoners.

FOURTEEN

Women Are Africa's Hope: Pan-African Stories from Liberia, Cameroon, Mali, and the Diaspora

—————⇒❖⇐—————

Emira Woods
Lisa Veneklasen
Marianne Ballé
Moudoumbou
and
Roxanne L. Lawson

The Institute for Policy Studies—Foreign Policy in Focus (FPIF) codirector Emira Woods, originally from Liberia, writes and speaks extensively on contemporary issues in Africa. Marianne Ballé Moudoumbou, an activist from Cameroon who represents the Association of African Women for Research and Development (AAWORD), also serves as coconvenor of War Resisters International Africa Working Group. Roxanne L. Lawson, former Africa Program Associate of the American Friends Service Committee, is a lifelong activist for peace and justice. The following three excerpts, from an FPIF online article, from the fall 2006 Peaceworks *magazine special edition on Gandhi's Centenary, and from the March 2006 edition of* Peaceworks, *provide a sampling of recent reports of why the title remains all too true.*

Women Are Africa's Political Hope: Liberia Is Not the Only Female Success Story—Women's Power There Is Growing

Emira Woods *and* Lisa Veneklasen

Liberian president Ellen Johnson-Sirleaf addressed a joint session of the U.S. Congress in 2006. This historic honor, bestowed sparingly on international dignitaries, is a fitting tribute for

Africa's first democratically elected female president. But Ellen Johnson-Sirleaf is not an anomaly.

The African political landscape is being reshaped by women, generating hope for the future of the continent and raising the bar for democracy worldwide.

Few Americans would guess that the country that leads the world in political gender balance is Rwanda, where women make up half of the members of Parliament, a development that started in the mid-1990s. South Africa and Mozambique, also high on the list, are both countries with women composing more than 30 percent of their parliaments. This stands in stark contrast to the United States, where women make up only 15 percent of Congress.

African countries also have higher percentages of women in cabinet-level positions. In South Africa, thirteen out of twenty-eight are women, and in Rwanda there are nine women to twenty-two men. In the United States, there are six women in President Barack Obama's twenty-person cabinet.

One big factor in the rise of women's political power in Africa is affirmative action. Governments have set concrete targets for women's participation in political bodies. The newly formed Pan-African Parliament has also implemented affirmative-action measures to ensure a minimum of 30 percent representation by women, all of whom have been elected to office in their countries.

But African women's rising power is measured not just in numbers. In Liberia, the same women who bore the brunt of the country's more than two decades of war are the ones leading the struggle for peace and carving out a new economic and political path.

It was the Liberian women who crossed class, ethnic, and political lines to organize and sustain marches for peace and change over the past two years. Market sellers, students, farmers, professionals—women from all walks of life—marched daily in drenching rain and searing sun, often with their children on their backs, to demand the exit of their former leader, war criminal Charles Taylor, indicted by a special court in Sierra Leone, and to insist on an end to civil strife. Their efforts ushered in a period of peace that has now lasted more than two and a half years and opened the door to democracy.

After the 2005 election, when supporters of presidential candidate George Weah disputed the results and marched in the streets—again raising the specter of instability—it was women and leading religious leaders who engaged them in a dialogue and insisted on reconciliation and peace.

Of course, the real test for Africa's emerging female leaders is yet to come. Will they be able to translate leadership positions into a fresh agenda for peace, sustainable development, and democracy in the region?

In the case of Liberia, the challenges are daunting. A fresh agenda would mean mending the social fabric torn apart by twenty-five years of crisis and chaos in which 250,000 people were killed. A Harvard-educated economist, Johnson-Sirleaf, who was sworn into office in January 2006, should manage well a truth-and-reconciliation process that brings healing to a wounded society and holds key people responsible. A fresh agenda would also transform an economy that has relied on illicit activity for fourteen years—trade in diamonds used to finance wars; stolen timber; "raped rubber"; and the flow of illegal arms—into an economy that brings productive activity for the now 85 percent unemployed.

The critical role of women in that society must be recognized by giving them equal inheritance and land rights to allow them to fully and wisely use resources for their families and communities.

The U.S. Congress (and the Obama administration) should help give Liberia a chance at a fresh start by agreeing to cancel the country's external debts, accumulated under past dictatorships. Those debts, the equivalent of about 680 percent of the country's gross domestic product, undermine the capacity of the new government to tackle the problems of rising HIV/AIDS infection rates and a lack of functioning schools, electricity, and other infrastructure. Thirty percent of that debt is owed to the United States, which should not only forgive its share but also encourage other nations to forgive theirs.

The U.S. government should also use its leverage to ensure that U.S. corporations operating in the country act responsibly, paying proper fees, taxes, and wages; respecting labor rights; and protecting the environment. For example, Bridgestone/Firestone Inc. is now taking advantage of deals made with a former caretaker Liberian government as well as the desperation of many poor Liberians to profit from operations that employ child labor, destroy the environment, and violate other international standards.

There is much at stake for Liberia and the rest of Africa. But it's also a time to celebrate and support the region's newly emerging female leaders with a fresh agenda.

From Globalizing Nonviolence in an African Context

Matt Meyer

Marianne Ballé Moudoumbou, an activist from Cameroon who represents the Association of African Women for Research and Development (AAWORD), reminded us that globalization is not a recent phenomenon, but began with slavery, "Today, she stated, "we still face crucial issues regarding the connection between militarization and globalization. Refugees are the most obvious symbol and result of institutionalized racism and capitalism. So refugee emancipation has been a major priority for AAWORD, along with our work for the closing of all French military bases on the African continent." Noting that the Western powers don't want African people, or even the African Union, to have the power to help themselves, Marianne suggested that Africans must explore how they can empower themselves according to their own cultures and traditions.

As the sole African woman who serves as a member of the Women's Security Council in Germany (where she currently resides), Marianne discussed the ongoing work throughout Africa and among Africans living in Europe in support of United Nations Security Council Resolution 1325. The resolution, adopted in 2000, marked the first time the Security Council addressed the disproportionate and unique impact of armed conflict on women. Recognizing the undervalued and underutilized contributions women make to conflict prevention, peacekeeping, conflict resolution and peacebuilding, the resolution stressed the importance of women's equal and full participation as active agents in peace and security. "We have the power to protect our own people!" Marianne asserted. "We've been taught to be Anglophone against Francophone—but we are finding ways of working together. We must unite to make a better world."

—————⸙⸙⸙—————

Struggling toward African Self-Determination: A Report from the World Social Forum in Bamako, Mali

Roxanne L. Lawson

The World Social Forum is not an organization, it is a space. In Bamako, Mali, in January 2006 that space was, for the first time, truly Afrocentric. Bamako marked the first time that any World Social Forum could claim the majority of its attendees identified themselves as African or of African descent.

Until Bamako, fewer than 100 African nongovernmental organizations (NGOs) had participated in the previous incarnations of the World Social Forum (WSF), despite the vibrant regional and national Social Forum movements in Africa. The absence of African civil society at the WSF has been due, in the past, in large part to the expense of travel. Sponsoring WSF events on multiple continents this year was designed to rectify the absence of indigenous people and grassroots organizers at the WSF.

Mali, one of the poorest countries in the world, hosted the Polycentric World Social Forum, from January 19-23, ahead of those in Caracas, Venezuela, and Karachi, Pakistan (postponed due to the earthquake, at press time scheduled for March 24-29). Organizers estimated that approximately 15,000 people participated. This is the first step to root the WSF in Africa and mobilize the people of the continent. Locating the WSF in Bamako recognized that Africans and African descendants are those who have been the hardest hit by corporate globalization. Bamako offered progressive forces in Africa an opportunity to lead the way and offer African alternatives to global capitalism.

"Holding the WSF in Africa will increase African awareness as far as the link between our impoverishment and globalization. Also, Africans will feel more connected to the process because it is being held here," said Dr. Aminata Dramane Traore, a Malian author, political activist, former government minister, and one of the principal organizers of the Bamako Forum.

The Bamako Forum was indeed a place for members of civil societies to meet and share their different perspectives on global political economies. This was evident in the presence of groups from around Africa who came to Bamako to articulate their concerns; the Ogoni people from Nigeria, the Yaaku community in Kenya, and representatives of civil society from both Western Sahara and Morocco (which invaded Western Sahara in 1975 and has militarily occupied it since) were all able to make their case and educate people from other parts of the world about their struggles for self-determination.

This year's themes for all three Forums were focused on debt cancelation, antimilitarization, workers' rights, fair trade, food sovereignty and security, prohibition of patents on knowledge and living organisms, ending water privatization, and migration issues.

In Bamako, a particular emphasis was placed on the issues that are most central to the continent: odious debt, unfair trade that impacts food security, Africa's right to fight the HIV/AIDS pandemic, farming, the rights of migrants and "informal" workers, and the impact of all of these, through the lens of patriarchy, on the rights of women.

Activists discussed the limitations and inequities of the "Group of Eight's" 2005 debt cancelation plan and mapped out strategies for increasing recognition that Third World debt is illegitimate and should be repudiated. There were also discussions of post-World Trade Organization realities and trade disparities. Those present developed strategies for campaigns against Western farming subsidies, genetically modified organisms (GMOs), and bioprospecting.

Bioprospecting (which Vandana Shiva has called biopiracy) involves corporations filing patents on plants that have traditionally been used as medicines so that they can no longer be used. For example, the medicinal properties of the African yellow yam have been patented by Shaman Pharmaceuticals and Nigerian scientist Maurice Iwu. The utilization of natural resources in the context of capitalism was understood and articulated as a struggle for the right to life. Those who control the world's life-sustaining natural resources—such as food production, traditional and Western medicines, and water—control the lives (and deaths) of those who do not.

Issues of access and control in relation to the forum itself were also prominent in attendees' minds. While this Forum included village elders, local businesspeople, traditional healers, and the usual NGO types, and this represented a step forward, all were mindful that there is always room for more engagement.

Organizers admit that in the push to mobilize NGOs and their grassroots bases from across the continent, engagement of the local population suffered. For many who live and work in Bamako outside of the sphere of political organizing, the forum may have seemed like just another meeting of international corporate institutions.

This reality was due in large part to economics. To financially host the forum, the impoverished Malian government and the Africa Social Forum used most of their meager resources. As a result, they had very little money left over to sponsor the attendance of grassroots organizers from around the continent. Several private foundations sponsored representatives of grassroots women's organizations to attend the events in Bamako and helped to create the massive and stimulating presence of Africa's women at the gathering.

With the historic 2007 World Social Forum held in Nairobi, Kenya, during the same year that the world commemorated the 200th anniversary of the abolition of the transatlantic slave trade and the 50th anniversary of the independence of Ghana, it is clear that Africa is still on the move. The work done in Bamako early in 2006 helped paved the way for work that must intensify in the coming decades.

FIFTEEN

Matt Meyer

We Are Powerful: Working for Women and Change in Ghana
An Interview with Esi Sutherland-Addy

Ghanaian activist and academic Esi Sutherland-Addy is a senior researcher and professor at the University of Ghana at Legon, Institute of African Studies. A former deputy minister of higher education, Sutherland-Addy is also a specialist in women's studies and coeditor of the comprehensive Women Writing Africa: West Africa and the Sahel. *A leader and board member of countless regional and international organizations, she is also the eldest daughter of acclaimed playright and advocate Efua Sutherland and activist Bill Sutherland. Here, in an interview with Matt Meyer, she connects her own upbringing with her current work and concerns.*

MATT MEYER: What are your hopes and your fears about the current period?

ESI SUTHERLAND-ADDY: To begin with, I feel maybe too worried that young people today have bought into the notion of being individual, mobile citizens, who have a marketability around the world, who have skills, who think they can live anywhere in the world, and who are going out to gain material wealth for themselves. This turns people, at best, into amoral beings who are not interested in creating movements that confront the establishment, except insofar as it interferes directly with their aspirations to become wealthy. Now, this is a very pessimistic thing to say, but I don't think that it's just a Ghanaian thing. I think that a lot of young people around the world are caught up in this illusion that if they are able to get a big job somewhere, they are all right. And the unfortunate thing, of course, is that it has created a situation where not enough young people, in Ghana and in Africa in general, are involved in the wider global movements against, you know, the big global conglomerates.

Universities are not going on demonstrations because of that. They're not as involved in human rights issues as they should be. And for me, that's a failure of my generation; those are our children. Somehow we have not been able to pass the ideas that came to us from our parents on to our children. For me, that is one of the excruciating thoughts that goes through my mind every once in a while. Why or how did it happen that we were not able to pass this on?

We have got very skilled and dynamic young people. We've got young people who have a lot to offer. What we and they need is for that to be accompanied with a political alertness that leads it to action, where they will reject a system that is corrupt. Africa continues, in fact, to be a net exporter of these wonderful minds who are feeding into the first world their ideas about technology, management, and science. In a sense, something fantastic is happening in that, after independence, there has been a success in educating Africa. When you really look at who the doctors are, and the nurses and so on, then you begin to understand that something must have been done right. But what does it do for the majority of African people?

That's really the conjuncture at which I find myself when you ask that question. I may be being too harsh on our generation, but I think that there was so much given us—the work to end colonialism at the time of our parents. And what did we do with this awareness? Why have we become so indifferent? Having said that, I would also certainly say that a fight against colonialism is much clearer than a fight against economic globalization, surrounded by this consumerism.

Developing countries are in a space where we feel that we have to play catch-up. We can only do this by abandoning everything that we are. There's no other way out. People are caught in this, and there's deepening dependency and a loss of self-definition, an understanding of what it means to acquire health, what it means to educate oneself. All of these are now defined in terms of another. Of course, people from the first world countries are also caught up in this.

MM: Let's go backward a little bit and take a look at some of your own past, your own upbringing and the hopes that you had. Certainly your experience with your dad, but also with your mom—working in this bleak period in Ghana's history after the coup against Nkrumah and during numerous military regimes—taught you much about hope and struggle. You grew up during this globally bleak period, with colonialism perhaps mostly gone, but the entrenched fight for true economic independence just beginning. Yet you did not grow up in a bleak household.

ESA: I always say that we had a very special childhood—very privileged, not because we were materially wealthy at all, but in terms of the wealth of energies and the flow of ideas and the constant replenishment of hope and creativity. We got an awareness through the people around us, who were writing and who were waiting to struggle to sustain the freedom gained, and those who were willing to take things even a step further. We were around people like President Nyerere of Tanzania, and Nobel laureate Wole Soyinka—when he was sent away from Nigeria—used to come here all the time. We had this advantage of not only seeing that there was the possibility of hope, but being able to feel that we could do something about these possibilities. Most of the time, one sees that people don't feel that way.

In addition, my mom took us into the Ghanaian countryside on research trips to little villages. There we saw what a wealth of knowledge and creative skill there was, in spite of the poverty. And such generosity; I mean, you go to a small, tattered village, and when you are coming back, they give you tomatoes and peppers and charcoal and, you ask yourself, "How can these people?" It's just unbelievable. There we met the most creative dancers, poets, political thinkers. We would hear from these villagers political statements that could have come out of any of the great books that we use at the universities today.

By the time I went to university, I stood for president of my hall of residence. Later, when I went to UCLA, I got African Americans and Africans together to talk about why we weren't getting on better together. We stood up against the military regimes and joined the professional bodies. I wasn't highly political in the sense of joining a political cell, but I was generally political. It was an expectation from my upbringing, to feel that Africans are responsible for making the world aware of who we are and what we have to offer. One, therefore, does symbolic things: wearing African clothes or engaging in public speaking.

MM: Please describe some more of Efua's work and your own current work with the Mmofra Foundation, which she set up.

ESA: Without realizing it originally, my mom became the initiator of a new theater movement, one that refused to be dominated by European forms of theater and one that was searching avidly for an African idiom. She actively went out and looked for this idiom, to find people to reshape it into something that was not ethnically based, but combined whatever any ethnicity or any country had to offer to a Pan-African perspective.

This is something that made her famous not just in Ghana, but all over the continent and all over the world. It was basically taking the essence of the storytelling drama and the festival drama and creating theater out of that. She loved all the theaters of the world—Kabuki and Chinese theater, Greek theater, and so on. But she wanted everyone to see the marvelous stories and forms developed out of African theater. She wanted not only the world, but most importantly Ghanaians themselves, to see what they had.

So she started with an experimental theater on the beach. She built a people's theater in town. And she broke with the idea of theater as some kind of an elite experience. Eventually, though she started working for the University of Ghana, she convinced them that having an outreach program in town was very important. She worked with people who were amateurs: with people who were part of the elite acting group, but also with people from small towns and villages who were doing traditional Ghanaian storytelling dramas. She brought in aspects of the modern Highlife dancing, which was quite lighthearted in certain ways, but captured the new urban phenomenon.

Then she came to working with children in theater. Efua had a very, very strong belief that children were the greatest theater artists in the world, that all you had to do was to watch them play. No self-respecting writer, she felt, could do any writing for children unless they were willing and humble enough to let the children teach them. So she did just that—opened up the studio to children, had the children's theater program, and that program was also meant to deal with some of the things that really upset her, like people letting go of their traditions just because they thought they were being modern. She had a huge problem with people who wouldn't let their children speak Ghanaian languages because they felt that if you were properly cultured, you should be speaking French and English and so forth. She had these big battles on language, on cultural awareness, and on the environment. She loved all of Ghana's flora and fauna, so she worked on how to get children involved in environment through theater.

Her whole idea was that art should be both beautiful and functional. The crux was to get the right combination. People who had worked with her always said, "I could hardly read and write, and I came to the drama studio and I was taught how to read and write so that I could actually work from a script or change a plug, or do some wiring, do the lighting, do the makeup." All these ideals she had, she pumped through theater. Eventually, she ended up with this last major idea, which was the Pan-African Historical Theater Festival—PANAFEST. Her notion here was that those huge edifices along our coasts—the colonial castles that had been at the center of the Middle Passage slave trade—should themselves become the venues for dealing with the problems and turmoil that stays within people hundreds and hundreds of years later. She thought that a catharsis could be arrived at using theater, at festivals that would, in effect, take over these historic monuments. It was taken on as government policy and became what we know now as PANAFEST. Along with the drama, there was an educational component, there was research involved, and there was an aspect that involved letting people speak for themselves.

My mom set up the Mmofra Foundation to be a center that would support African children to be able to stand their ground within a world context and to be able to creatively help to advance their awareness of what they needed to make their own countries work better. She thought— why don't we make textiles that are for children's skins and that breathe, instead of wearing this synthetic stuff? Or why don't we have a doll that is an African doll, instead of buying these plastic dolls with straight hair. Why do our illustrators do such terrible drawings for children's books? She felt that children ought to be reading all the time, with books that would inspire and interest them.

MM: Let's shift now to your own work, as Deputy Minister of Education . . .

ESA: First, a quick background. In 1986, Ghana had been through a terrible time; we had the drought, we were hemorrhaging heavy in terms of teachers and nurses and other professionals; our classrooms were fifty percent empty. We had no chairs and we had no books, and it was just a very low time, not just in education, but economically as well. When Rawlings came to power, we were thinking, we've got to make some major shifts in order to change the situation, including some experimentation with new techniques.

We put together multilevel classes with one teacher, as well as a shift system so that the schools could have a twofold system—one set of classes in the morning and another in the afternoon. We asserted that every child in Ghana, whatever their background, ought to be able to get at least nine years of education, the content of which would involve both things that one does with one's hands as well as things that one does with one's head. We were committed to producing textbooks that would have illustrations reflecting gender parity and equality in them. We wouldn't allow pictures of a boy doing a science experiment while a girl insipidly smiles at him! We had an opportunity in the early part of the Rawlings government to say, "Look, okay, here we are, we are in a crisis. Let's try and resolve it."

We also, however, had to work within the context of the World Bank and the International Monetary Fund. One of the disappointments I think that we can now say we had was that we saw the problems, we had the facilities to analyze them, but we were hindered in our attempts at creating long-term, creative solutions. Education and the social sector are net losers of money, and this was something the World Bank didn't want to see. Logically, though, schools consume and don't produce money. We were, therefore, always battling in that context. It was very frustrating because we could get access to funding, but the money was mixed up in a World Bank philosophy that didn't agree with our goals. We got into a rut in which the ideals that we were promoting would hit a wall against our corporate sponsors.

Another disappointment was that we were not able to take our teachers along with us. Teachers thought that they were being imposed upon; they were not prepared to make the shift from writing everything on the board with the children learning by heart, to having a more interactive relationship with the children. A lot of our program was wonderful, but it needed the teachers. If there's one other thing that I regret, and still do think is an issue, is the difficulty in motivating teachers to see the validity of bringing older people from the community into the classroom. Someone who has a skill from the village should be brought into the school to do a skill program for students. How can we create an interface between school and society, between the nonformal and the formal aspects of educational life?

I think that we had an opportunity not only to define our problems properly, but to create new programs. We had a great deal of potential, but we were not able to achieve that potential. So we got an increase in numbers, but without a commensurate increase in quality. And we have paid for this. The infrastructure at the higher levels was being stretched, which shows that we were able to get the kids into schools. Once there, however, they wanted more. But we haven't been able to provide the next step.

On the whole, Ghana continues to be respected for the awareness and meticulous work we were able to bring to educational change. I'm proud of those things. Even the people from the World Bank had to admit to us later on that they couldn't fully control our efforts. They took the time to send nastier representatives, firmer people to try to regulate our work. Every time World Bank representatives left their time in Ghana, they would not sound at all like they sounded when they first came! One World Bank representative told us that he was asked by an officer: "What did those people do to you when you went to Ghana?!" In light of this work, I was made raconteur general of the fifth World Conference on nonformal education.

MM: How has that work led into your current work for the rights of women and with the Institute of African Studies?

ESA: When you find yourself as a token, and you go to a big meeting where there's only one woman in the room, and you say, "There should be more women in this meeting," it's telling when the reply is: "Oh, no-no-no-no. You represent all of them. You're too strong!" Even in the 1990s, I was very much aware that we had to get more girls and women into school. We know that women were and are the backbone of the agricultural sector in Ghana. In commerce, we're painfully aware of how little our potential is coming out because girls can't read or write. I got involved with the Forum for African Women Educationalists, which is this group of women ministers and vice-chancellors and so on. Our main aim is to get as many girls into school as possible. We were unabashedly saying, "We are powerful and we are going to get the girls in." We devised all kinds of strategies to reach these goals in an African manner. It's amazing what happens to the young girls once they get the confidence of a good education, and they're out there working in their communities.

Some of the other work I've done with women and on women, include support of an organization that's now ten years old called Farm Africa Solidarity. Farm Africa Solidarity is a peacebuilding organization throughout Africa that has tried to work in Rwanda and the Manu River region, in Guinea and Liberia and Sierra Leone. It has also worked at the level of the OAU, and AU now, to get parity for women. Our notion is not just to work in places where there's conflict, but to get into a position where women can insist that other women, the women who are involved and affected by conflict, must be at the table.

I'm involved on the board of the Open Society Initiative for West Africa, which works in support of developing democracies, They help to fund non-governmental organizations that educate for the promotion of democracy, for healthy responses to the HIV/AIDS crisis, and which even assist some government institutions in building peace commissions throughout West Africa. My primary area of work today is in the field of literature, on a project called the Voice of Women. Simply collecting materials and publishing them, showing what women really feel about polygamy, about doing chores in their homes, and so forth, is an exciting endeavor. When women gain a stronger voice in society, we all have reason for hope.

Sixteen

Traditions and Peace in Northern Ghana

Will Holloway

A 15-hour bus ride from Ghana's capital city of Accra, plus an additional 45 minute bumpy van ride from Tamale, lands you in Nanton. It is a small but thriving village of a thousand or more people from the Dagomba ethnic group of northern Ghana. Nanton is in the heart of the Kingdom of Dagbon, a centuries-old monarchy. The landscape is flat and parched with tall reeds and grasses parted occasionally by knarled shea and baobab trees. The houses are made from the dark brown rocky earth with cone-shaped roofs made from the reeds.

Each house exists within a larger compound, which includes the immediate and often extended family. Gender roles are fairly fixed in Dagomba culture. Most men are farmers, yet when not sewing seeds or tending their crops or livestock, they are pursuing their traditional roles in the village such as butchers, blacksmiths, drummers, imams, or healers. These roles are passed on from many generations back, and they are responsible for educating future generations. The women are usually responsible for processing the grain and other fruits and vegetables into food, and for general care of the household. They too have traditional roles that transcend day-to-day survival—including teaching the young girls to sing and dance. They pass along in-depth education about their ceremonial responsibilities.

Islam and traditional religion coexist relatively seamlessly, perhaps due in part to the fact that Islam had been introduced into Dagomba society slowly since Muslim traders first brought the religion from North Africa in the 1700's. The co-existence is perhaps best evidenced in rituals such as naming ceremonies, weddings, and funerals where the two traditions are in constant confluence with each other.

My research in Nanton focused primarily on determining the role of music within the larger culture. I found what I expected: that music is integral to almost every element of Dagomba social life. To discuss its meaning would almost be to discuss the meaning of the culture itself. Music is used to aide workers as they clear land; ceremonial songs and dances reference important battles and times of peace. The necessity of music at naming ceremonies and funerals indicates that music serves to both create and sustain community.

The master drummers, fiddlers, and praise poets of Dagbon are both storytellers and historians. They are steeped in the knowledge of the lineage of the Dagomba, who all claim to be descendants from one of two former chiefs. They have an acute knowledge of social relationships in their village, no matter how large. They typically use their skill to praise elders and other participants during ceremonies, but can be called upon at any time to praise and recant the history of an individual. During funerals, they facilitate the mourning process and assist the family with transitioning to life without the deceased. In essence, they are entertainers as well as messengers, healers and teachers.

One group drum song that is of particular importance to the Dagomba is the Takai. It signifies the creation of peace between the Dagombas and the Mossi, a neighboring ethnic group. As the history has been told, the Dagomba master drummers created this song to stop war after learning about a familial connection between the two groups. When performed with a corresponding dance, the song is both laden with the tension of battle, and the warm resolution of peace. The dancers carry metal "sticks" which represent swords. The dancers sway their bodies in motion to the beat of the drummers, who are in turn following and accentuating the movement of the dancers. As the drummers build rhythmic tension, the dancers spin, pause briefly and clash their sticks together. This represents the way in which the peace was achieved. According to the history, the chief drummers suggested striking sword against sword to indicate that they would not engage in battle.

Though the Dagomba have been involved in some conflicts since those long-gone days, Takai serves as an acknowledgement of the potential for peace. In Dagbon, music serves as the social glue, uniting the group with proverbs and lessons. Social order is maintained in part by the rituals which the musicians help to facilitate.

Could music be one of the primary tools to secure peace in the future? What are the implications of the use of music to unite groups in conflict? As music is indigenous to almost every ethnic, racial, national, and cultural group in the world, perhaps within it lies potential for connection, movement, resolution, and reconciliation.

Planting Critical Seeds for Cultures of Peace in Africa

Nancy Erbe
Chinedu Bob Ezeh
Daniel Karanja
Neba Monifor
George Mubanga
and
Ndi Richard Tanto

A contingent of international students in the Negotiation, Conflict Resolution and Peacebulding (NCRP) program at California State University, Dominguez Hills co-authored this paper with a little help from their Associate Professor. Based on the experiences of the authors in resolving conflicts in their native countries, the paper examines strategic ways to infuse peace perspectives within our cultural roots.

L ast year, a law review solicited my thoughts about, in their words, "pushing the envelope" with social justice and negotiating peace in a world dominated by power and violence.

Taking their language literally, one must ask how to effectively address contemporary obstacles to ensure that the message and, most importantly, the means, of justice is truly delivered to those in need. One answer—which may seem obvious to readers but is actually much too rare in practice—is to work with, empower, and support the conflict work of community members themselves. This chapter introduces five African professionals working within Cameroon, Kenya, Nigeria, Zambia, and the African Union. All are members of Diaspora and domestic circles intent on serving their communities through offering the best of conflict practice, including integrative bargaining (Raiffa 2003)[1] and restorative victim-offender mediation (Davies and Kaufman 2002).[2]

In a recently published book on South Africa's struggle, Nelson Mandela lauds a colleague, saying

> He developed a capacity for putting himself in the shoes of the enemy and thinking through a situation from the perspective of the enemy....(H)e taught the underground that it must respect rather than simply hate the enemy. If you hated the enemy, you dismissed him, depersonalized him, and as a result, you would always underestimate his ability to destroy you. On the other hand, if you respected your enemy, you never forgot how formidable he was....Hatred would destroy you; not the enemy.
>
> (O'Malley 2007)[3]

Renowned leaders like Nelson Mandela deservedly receive much attention and acclaim. What matters most, though, is that their hard-earned wisdom is actually practiced and spread. This article attempts to introduce a few lesser known inspirations working within—emerging voices with track records of success as well as innovative and practical plans. Barack Obama is only one of several contemporary visionaries with African roots. The authors highlighted here are, in turn, inspired by the emerging discipline of conflict resolution, a field that directly resonates with Mandela's quote above, teaching perspective taking—that the best negotiators know the power of thoroughly understanding their adversaries (Bevir 2006).[4] They will describe how to use restorative and facilitative mediation and integrative bargaining to advance some of the toughest, most troubling and costly conflicts facing their communities, nations, and continents: violent tribal conflict in Cameroon, the crippling intragroup and intergroup wounds and tensions from Britain's colonization of Kenya, the challenges of reintegrating child soldiers into viable, life-sustaining communities, and the debt crisis drowning their continent.

The authors see and describe contemporary conflict techniques as facilitating critical societal development in myriad ways. First, in-depth conflict analysis motivates resolution, raising awareness regarding the costs of continuing conflict and guiding conscious exploration and creation of alternatives. It further ensures inclusive process—that important stakeholders are identified and included. Equivalent conflict training for all concerned balances power and builds the capacity needed to proceed with collaborative problem solving. Truly impartial and skillful facilitation of interest-based negotiation builds essential trust and confidence—conflict by conflict, with every conflict solved to parties' satisfaction. Thus the foundation for bringing together conflicting parties is built.

Once a majority of community stands for peaceful conflict resolution and co-existence, political leaders and elders are more likely to follow their communities' lead. The authors agree that political and government stakeholders represent their greatest challenge, along with the multinational corporations who partner with these leaders and exploit community resources. They do not pretend that these are simple challenges with easy solutions. They strongly concur, however, that their societies are better prepared to confront these challenges with empowered mobilization of communities led by non- governmental and faith based networks. The authors also see much potential for grassroots community to mediate daily conflict and build "unity and diversity" through joint ventures (like the economic cooperative described in Cameroon) while rallying for responsive state institutions and leadership.

The African collective is inherently strengthened by its restorative conflict traditions as publicized to the world through South Africa's Truth and Reconciliation Commission. Victim-offender mediation that includes extended family and community and negotiates amends represents a long-standing African practice. Two authors call for harnessing this resource and proceeding with truth and reconciliation in response to erupting tensions in Kenya as well as the difficult task of reintegrating child soldiers.

As introduced and described later by author Ndi Richard Tanto, each vision exemplifies requisite reflective practice, that conflict techniques are tested and retested in the context of each particular conflict, challenge, and community, to ensure optimal and sustainable effectiveness. Impartial leadership must be prepared to persist over time in the face of political pressure. Three of the authors themselves represent the contemporary voice, influence, and power of the African Diaspora. They are the natural leaders for bringing the West's attention to and garnering Western support for what matters most.

A Call for Widespread Collaborative Conflict Transformation Training to Rebirth Peace

Most scholars and informed observers would agree that European colonialism had a devastating impact on Africa (Shah 2005).[5] Developed countries freely adjusted boundaries in treaties between one another to suit their administrative convenience without regard to the disparity between the groups being casually lumped together (Robbins 2002).[6] It is not far fetched to say that when the ruling colonialists left, their colonies were inadvertently rigged for failure from the very start. The artificial boundaries created within Africa brought together ethnic people without providing for cultural diversities. Nations were lumped together without regard to the fact that they were divergent and sometimes incompatible neighbors. The Human Rights Violations Investigation Commission (called "Oputa Panel"), the Nigeria equivalent of the South African Truth and Reconciliation Commission, as one instance, stated in its report submitted to the then President Olusegun Obasanjo that "the various ethno-communal groups in the country, including the major ones, complain of marginalization in the scheme of things" (Human Rights Commission 2002).[7] Most conflicts in former colonies, especially those in Africa, have been struggles to rebuild themselves and find new identities.[8] In the process, Africa has seen millions of its people slaughtered and millions more as refugees.[9]

An Insider Perspective on Contemporary Conflict in Africa

The simplistic approach to Africa's problem is to blame colonization for all its woes, but that would be wrong. African nations, despite the wrongs of colonization, have acquired a history—one that can be harnessed to cultivate a culture of "unity in diversity." While the various factions wrangle for control, the obvious fact that stands out is that they do not desire secession from the whole, but rather justice within the system. The solution lies in Africans beginning to ask each other as in the words of W. B. Yates in the poem, "The Second Coming," why events started: "Turning and turning in the widening gyre / The falcon cannot hear the falconer; / Things fall apart; the center cannot hold; / Mere anarchy is loosed upon the world...."

Fortunately, Africa has shown resilience in its ability to withstand the various conflicts that have beset it. Author Chinedu Bob Ezeh is of the school of thought[10] that for Africa to deal with its various conflicts, it must begin to look inwards and start developing conflict resolution mechanisms that address its peculiar conflict problems. While commending the African Union for its efforts in bringing peace to Africa, author Ezeh does not think it has done enough. It has not shown tenacity and resoluteness in addressing its various conflicts with a view to bringing them to an end immediately, or at least reducing them to a level of positive conflict that can be exploited for positive development.

Conflicts have always divided communities. Yet, not all conflicts are bad, as some level of conflict is required to instigate growth and development in Africa (Oetzel and Ting Toomey 2006).[11] The deep moral conflict that contemporary situations generate present opportunities to open to rich interpersonal learning, improved relationships, and creative collaboration.

Much of the conflict in Africa today is caused by power games (Akinyele 2000)[12] engaged in by the leadership who want to hold on to political power for as long as they can. The national question for most African countries in dispute is the issue of power and power sharing. In Sudan, Nigeria, Rwanda, and the Congo, the same recurring question always intrudes into the political, social, and human development. The question is inevitably who wields the political authority and controls the economic, natural, and human resources. All other conflicts, ethnic, economic, even environmental conflicts, subsume under the power frame.

Each side views the power struggle in terms of short-term, simplistic loss or gain: we are in power, so we must be gaining, or we are out of power; so we must be losing. This becomes an identity framing by the parties—a winner-takes-all identity frame. This more often than not leads to the mad desire to accumulate wealth by corrupt means while in power; thus creating further economic crisis. Predictably, the factions polarize and begin to characterize each other by reference to who they are or what they have done that has affected the other adversely. Relationally, struggles to ascend to power at all cost and sabotage those already in power follow, leading to the use of force and violence to achieve the desired goal. To achieve their ends, the political players have always relied on group, ethnic, religious, and sometimes military class affiliation. They seek a voice for their group, using any means possible: force, threats, moral and religious persuasions, and appeals to the sympathy of the populace in identifying with them in one way or the other. As the focus and goal of the leaders and the opposition become distorted, they lose sight of the whole frame, the succinct issue of what a nationality is in the true sense of the word. National development is lost to personal or sectional development.

Face-to-Face Communication Has Been Fruitful in the Worst of Scenarios

Author Ezeh wonders if we may be ignoring human beings' greatest gifts, ones setting us apart from other beasts, the gifts of communication and reason. Author Ezeh believes that the only way out of destructive power games is not to play it at all. He calls to change the trained incapacity for face-to-face confrontation described above, through empowering side-by-side joint problem solving throughout African communities.[13] He believes strongly that the destiny of people depends on individual decisions and actions—that one individual can truly make a difference in social conflict. As chief legal officer for the Anglican Church Diocese of Niger State, as one example, he was able to build critical and reliable alliances that allowed him to navigate the treacherous tensions of negotiating between Muslims and Christians.[14]

Communication can be a constructive instrument that socially defines conflicts, enabling parties to positively engage in meaningful exchange of information and understanding. Effective communication creates attentiveness within members of a group, enabling them to be willing to be influenced in the ideas of other members of the group,[15] thus creating bridge of proper perspective setting in conflicts. All help in reducing the incidence of conflict in the body politic.

There are situations where these principles of communication had been applied with success like the South African Truth and Reconciliation Commission and the Nigerian HRVIC (Oputa Panel). In the Nigerian case, the reconciliation of the factions of the Ogoni Four and Ogoni Nine was a high point in the commission's assignment. They were able to moderate a dialogue that enabled the warring factions to sign an accord that has held up to the present time. Moreover, the outcome helped empower the Ogonis, who after the peace accord were able to speak with a more powerful, united voice.[16]

Widespread Empowerment of Citizenry Is Critical

For the African continent to come out of its current myriads of conflict, there is need to bridge the theory-practice gap in conflict and peace studies. While there are skilled conflict transformation professionals in Africa and in the international agencies working in Africa, there has been too little gain in translating their experience into widespread community practice. Skilled professionals are usually outside zones of conflict. Their current practice is only coming in to deal with specific conflicts. The people that need their skills are found directly within the zones of conflict, with little or no valuable skill to enable them to deal with the situations that they face daily.[17] The few gains made in nationally and individually induced conflict resolution processes are soon lost in sectarian wrangling and power plays within the governmental system as well as lack of bureaucratic follow-through.

There is inevitably negative emotion associated with negotiation when it is based on positional bargaining. Consequently, people in conflict have often avoided negotiations as they tax the energy of the participants. If people are taught that there is an alternative, a collaborative style of bargaining that is "hard on the problem and soft on the people," it will help in enabling parties to overcome their phobia of conflict resolution. Promoting interest-based bargaining may, in author Ezeh's view, further emergence of factors necessary for the positive socioeconomic growth in Africa again.

Human rights, environmental protections, and conflict transformation policies are not achieved by accident, but through a well-thought-out planning process, rigorously achieved by the consistent monitoring and enforcement of laws, policies, and agreements reached after collaborative discussions aimed at such purposes. Collaborative efforts should be aimed at training people at the grassroots and professional levels, empowering them through skill training.[18] As the saying goes, it is time to teach the people to fish rather than giving the people fish when they are hungry.[19]

African citizenry and professionals need special training in effectively confronting and transforming relationships with their most powerful stakeholders, including their own political leaders, governments, and most, if not all, multinational corporations (hereinafter "MNCs"). For years, MNCs have been making huge profits from the natural resources of Africa; beginning with human goods in the form of slavery; then agricultural produce, timber, precious metals and stones, and finally oil and gas being economically exploited. When people feel the direct natural and environmental impact of destructive MNC operations, like the Ogoni and Shell BP conflict in Nigeria, and lack in requisite communication and negotiation skills, they have resorted to using the age-old method of brawn to express their frustrations and disaffection with long-standing systemic abuses. While such mobilizing has effectively unified them as a people and brought worldwide attention to their problems, it still has not advanced their critically needed economic development. Recently, Dr. Bernard Lafayette, one of Dr. Martin Luther King's colleagues in birthing the civil rights movement in the U.S., has recognized this need and flown to Nigeria to further train citizenry in non-violent resistance regarding outside control of African resources.

As things stand now, most of the skills required in the field are in the classrooms or conference venues, developing theories and building principles upon principles while those in need of the knowledge drown in ignorance. Quoting W. B. Yeats again, "...The best lack all conviction, while the worst / Are full of passionate intensity. / Surely some revelation is at hand / Surely the second coming is at hand...." If only we can merge our best in our learning with the passionate intensity of the innocent, dying in the ignorance and frustration of their un-knowledge, then surely the second coming will be at hand, the second coming of the reign of peace in Africa, the rebirth of the land of innocence.

A Real-World Case Study of Empowered Conflict Resolution and Democratic Peacebuilding: The Case of Balikumbat/ Bafanji and Bagam/Bamenyam Conflicts in West Cameroon

The conflicts between Balikumbat/Bafanji and Bagam/Bamenyam center on land. These conflicts started during the colonial period and persist due to the inability of the state to address them to the satisfaction of all parties. A multiplicity of maps defines village boundaries. Each village holds tenaciously to the map that gives it comparative advantage. The national Institute of Cartography, in trying to draw new administrative maps, most often reawakens some of the old conflicts as new administrative boundaries do not always respect the old ones. In situations of open clashes between communities, the government is very reluctant to demarcate boundaries. When it does, it gives scant attention to the traditional chiefs who have only observer status in the demarcation commissions.

Civil Society Provides Requisite Strategic Oversight through Reflective Practice

Effective conflict resolution is not spontaneous and sporadic. It takes time to prepare with the parties in conflict and to monitor every intervention, give feedback, and modify strategy where the need arises.[20] Principal challenges include bringing and engaging key leaders in long-term process, which first requires somehow reducing mistrust and building capacities of conflicting parties so they can effectively participate in the process.[21]

Before SeP took the challenge to mediate in the conflicts between Balikumbat and Bafanji and Bagam/Bamenyam in 1999, sporadic attempts had been made by the government and churches. While the intervention of the state was focused on enlisting leaders to end violence and destruction, that of the church appealed to their members to forgive each other and follow the example of Christ. These approaches were good in that they ended the violence. They were not sustainable and democratic, however, because the interests of the parties were not identified and addressed. Furthermore, the process did not involve all stakeholders.

SeP started its intervention with data collection and analysis of the conflicts. During this process, the major stakeholders, interests of the parties, and the beneficiaries of the situation were all identified. Information from this premediation stage helped to shape intervention strategy. The strategy consisted of training, creating space for dialogue, and direct mediation. It took six years of actions and reflections for a sustained peace to be achieved. During these six years, many lessons were learned about the process that can be useful in similar conflict situations in other communities and will be shared here.

Case-by-Case Success in Resolving Conflict Builds Necessary Community Confidence

Just as democracy depends on majority participation, conflict resolution/transformation depends on enjoying the confidence and participation of the majority. In the Balikumbat/Bafanji and Bagam/Bamenyam conflicts, the first trainings organized by the Ecumenical Service for Peace were to empower participants with knowledge of concepts of conflict and peace and nonviolent strategies in resolving conflicts. The objectives were to provide participants with a forum to vent their trauma from conflict and simultaneously win their support for the process. These first trainings were organized with the conflicting parties separately.

At the end of these trainings in the separate communities, structures referred to as Peace Committees were formed. The objectives of the Peace Committees were many, but most importantly they acted as forums for sharing of experiences and relay units in the field for sensitization of their community members on issues of conflict and peace and resolution of conflicts within the community. In some communities, there were more than one Peace Committee depending on the population and the geographical size of the community. Bagam had five committees. Bamenyam had one.

These committees became reflection centers par excellence in issues of conflict resolution and were co-opted by village chiefs to settle conflicts brought to the traditional councils for resolution. Community members identified committees as structures that settled community conflicts impartially. Many community members brought their conflicts to them rather than the traditional councils.

SeP monitored the process through monthly reports of the committees and organized field visits to discuss challenges. The successes registered by the committees in handling conflicts within and without the family made them very popular. Many community members wanted to join them. Since membership of the committees was conditioned by participation in a workshop in conflict resolution strategies, other workshops were then organized with the support of SeP to increase the membership of the Peace Committees in each village. In Bagam village, more than five hundred people were trained, including quarter heads, social group leaders, members of the traditional councils, and church leaders. After a year, the communities were sufficiently mobilized for peace.

Sustainable Conflict Resolution Depends on Equal Empowerment of the Parties and Eventually Bringing Them Together

Adequate empowerment of all concerned was crucial to the success of the conflict resolution process described here.[22] Equal empowerment of conflicting parties, or power balancing, puts them at the same level of knowledge on issues of conflict and resolution and facilitates rational and informed discussions of their conflict situation.

Once parties are sufficiently empowered, they must somehow be skillfully brought together. While the first workshops were organized per community, the second series of workshops were organized for Peace Committee members of the conflicting communities. The organization of second workshops with conflicting parties was a serious challenge. For victims of violence who saw their property destroyed, lost dear ones, and boycotted roads and services in each other's community, to come together for three to five days to attend a workshop was a major step in the process.

Focus during these second workshops was on continuing empowerment through training in mediation skills and facilitating peace building through analysis of the conflict by the parties, and development of scenarios for resolution and mediation. The cost/benefit analysis tool proved very effective. After analyzing their conflict's impact, participants became acutely aware of what they were losing because of the conflict. This motivated them to work for resolution.

These second workshops brought together conflicting parties to begin reflecting on their problems, commit themselves to the peace process, and make proposals for possible solutions. This working together, analyzing their situation together, helped to clear misunderstanding between them, reduce stereotypes and reestablish relations. Facilitated process built a common understanding and vision for the conflict. That vision focused essentially on the future of their relationship and not the past with its tribulations. It was during the second workshops, which took place in Balikumbat with the participation of Balikumbat and Bafanji, that the idea of exchange visits between conflicting communities was proposed and accepted as a good strategy to rebuild relationships and communication between conflicting parties.

After the series of second workshops, the participants were sufficiently empowered to monitor and mediate most of their conflict without assistance. SeP continued to monitor from a distance but waited for parties to initiate consultation when difficulties arose.

Exchange Visits Reestablished Relationships and Began Rebuilding Trust

The second workshops described above stimulated large-scale mobilization for exchange visits between conflicting communities. In the Balikumbat and Bafanji conflict, the first visit was organized in Bafanji. The Peace Committee mobilized the entire village to prepare to receive the Balikumbat people at its market square. Committees were formed to take care of reception, feeding of guests and programme/activities of the visit. This first exchange visit brought together over five hundred people at the market square. The Peace Committees presented reports of their activities, successes and challenges, and orientations for the future. The administrative authority, SeP, and the church all made commitments to the process. The exchange visit was further characterized by singing, sketches, and feasting. This communion of people, who were enemies for years, opened a new chapter in the peace process. Those who were skeptical about the outcome of the peace process joined the crusade for peace.

One of the events that marked the first exchange visit (Bafanji) was the testimony of a mother (Mary lum) who saw the nurse that helped her birth twins at the Balikumbat Health Center just on the eve of the 1995 war. She gripped the nurse with tears of joy, hurried to her house and brought the twins who were already seven years old.

This testimony was followed by many others. Participants could talk freely on the war without pain, a pointer to the fact that they had forgiven the past. The exchange visit marked the beginning of informal visitations between the people of the conflicting communities. Other exchange visits were organized with the same popularity.

In addition to playing a great role in mobilizing people for the peace process, the exchange visits helped rebuild broken relationships, commit community leaders and administrators to the peace process, and reestablish communication as well as promote communal use of social services like schools, hospitals and roads in each other's community.[23] The exchange visits further permitted SeP to evaluate the progress made by the parties and identify issues needing attention to facilitate the process.

Direct Mediation with Chiefs Has Been Necessary along with Empowered Citizenry to Move from Positions to Interests

Mediation is a very delicate balance. If the mediator is identified as taking sides with one of the parties, the process is frustrated. Instead, the mediator must be impartial. Impartiality encompasses lack of bias and inclusive treatment of all voices concerned with a particular conflict. When done appropriately, mediation responds to the needs and interests of all stakeholders, including the most marginalized and contentious, in equivalent ways, balancing power[24] so that all have an equal opportunity to be heard. In contrast, ineffectual conflict process around the world routinely excludes one or more significant interests; often mirroring the political tactics that incite ethnic conflict.[25] Without impartiality, mediation and other conflict process can easily become pawns for powerful interests.

To mediate with leaders who hold steadfast on their positions is a serious challenge. Working with community members has been much easier than working with the chiefs. Direct mediation is important because the interests of the chiefs often differ from the interests of their populations. A chief might just need political power, for example, and his people are held hostage in conflict unless ways are found to persuade the chief that serving his people's interests also secures and builds political power. The communities usually seek their interests, or underlying needs, while the leaders are prone to taking entrenched positions, seeking power rather than environments conducive to running farms without fear of destruction, as one common example.

One of the achievements of the exchange visits described earlier was the fact that it made the chiefs who considered themselves all powerful follow in the steps of their people. The chief of Balikumbat village, Doh Gah Gwayin, who was not prepared for the peace process, discovered that his quarter heads and traditional council members were very involved in the process and he had to join the bandwagon. In the Bagam/Bamenyam conflict, it was during an exchange visit that the chief of Bagam, Simo Tankeu Jean Marie, declared before hundreds of people from the conflicting villages that "people can make mistakes and can repent when they are made to recognize the mistake." He made it clear that he was ready to change and to promote peace in the subdivision.

Direct mediation between the chiefs themselves has been an important stage in the conflict resolution process in the Bagam/Bamenyam conflict. SeP facilitated several mediation efforts. SeP used the office of the divisional officers, who are the direct administrative heads of the chiefs, to convene the meetings. During these meetings, SeP facilitated discussions. The meetings and discussions were very hostile at the beginning with the Fon of Bamenyam refusing to take part in entertainment after the meeting on the excuse, "The pot is still on the fire." By this, he meant that there was still tension between the parties, making it difficult for any form of sharing to take place. During the last meeting that was held, the two chiefs accepted concessions,[26] and the chief of Bamenyam, Moko Moko Pierre, could now participate in the entertainment. He even remarked, "If you carry a basket of maize on your head and fall, you cannot recover all the grains." This was indication that with the concessions made, the tension between the two parties had reduced, and he was ready to share in the feasting since according to him, "The food is now ready and can be eaten."

Community Consensus Has Prioritized the Importance of Establishing Communal Projects for Socioeconomic Empowerment; Going Further Will Require State Collaboration

In the situation of Balikumbat and Bafanji, when the Peace Committee members saw that relations between them had normalized, they brought up an idea to form a farmers' federation, bringing together the parties. After a series of reflections on the structure of the federation, the Balikumbat subdivisional Integrated Farmer's Federation was formed to promote agriculture and seek funding and markets for members' produce. The leadership of the federation as well as the hosting of meetings of the federation rotates between the two communities. This has helped to reinforce relationships and build a common vision for the villages.

Within the last five years, the peace committees are still very vibrant in villages, peace forums that bring together peace committees are still operational, and no incidences of conflict have been reported. All the issues that led to the conflicts, however, have not been addressed. The roles of the administration, the chiefs and the elite remain major challenges.[27] Nonviolent strategies have proved effective in transforming negative conflict interactions into cooperative and positive interactions. Nevertheless, much still needs to be done for this approach to be endorsed and supported by the government. The government has to revisit its land tenure systems and exercise authority over land rather than leave land issues in the hands of traditional rulers. The future of peace in Africa lies in the recognition of the role of the civil society in conflict transformation and the collaboration of the state.

Victim-Offender Mediation, of the Best of Truth and Reconciliation, Can Immediately Help with Intratribal and Intertribal Conflict in Kenya as well as Empower Justice in the Form of Economic and Other Critical Development

As a Kenyan theologian, Pastor Daniel Karanja[28] has a vision for restorative justice in Kenya, specifically a truth and reconciliation commission mirroring the South African experience and incorporating integrative negotiation as well as victim offender mediation. Lessons learned from similar commissions will be utilized as resources. He has assessed truth and reconciliation (Lerche 2000)[29] as the best way forward in dealing with atrocities committed by British colonialists against the Kikuyu people in Kenya and the resultant intragroup and intertribal tensions within the third and fourth generations for all concerned (Elkins 2005).[30] Pastor Karanja sees truth and reconciliation, providing an "appropriate forum to process deeply hidden anger to prevent future violent retaliation" (Karanja 2008).[31] Like author Ezeh, Pastor Karanja encourages working with stakeholders to realistically assess their BATNAs([best alternatives to a negotiated agreement). Violence can be prevented if parties are empowered, made aware of their BATNA early enough before the conflict explodes to uncontrollable proportions, and encouraged to create even stronger, more desirable, alternatives if at all possible.

Kenya's Conflict

In December 2007, Kenya held a fiercely contested general election followed by unbelievable intertribal violence. Intense negotiations led by former UN Secretary General Kofi Annan and backed up by international pressure saved the country from disintegrating into the likes of the Rwandan genocide.[32] The postelection violence was just a tip of a hidden iceberg of postcolonial, unfair land ownership policies, tribalism-based political and economic control of resources, and intertribal campaign rhetoric rivalry by both political camps. The president appointed a commission of inquiry headed by a former South African judge, and the team has been conducting open fact-finding hearings across Kenya. The commission's report concludes that, overall, the votes were not stolen in favor of one side; however, negative civil society activism through the mass media planted the first seeds of violence. Civil society members prior to the elections alleged that the government had already planned to steal the elections and had planned "official" violence to cover up their sinister motives. The debate of whether these conclusions are trustworthy continues. With such a questionable ethical stance, the civil society has some work to do. Unfortunately, the truth and justice reconciliation process promised during the negotiations has not yet been formed.[33] Fighting politicians formed a government of national unity to protect their selfish interests while the masses wallow in despair, disease, poverty, and estrangement from the very government their parents and family members died for. There are still some internally displaced people (IDPs) eight months after the chaos. The seeds of suspicion and mistrust planted during the violence could only be uprooted by a long-term process of direct engagement between the affected tribes addressing the root causes of intertribal mistrust and violence. Leaders must be challenged to persuade their followers before, during, and after the elections that no one wins in violent conflict.

A Vision for Truth and Reconciliation Beginning with Intratribal Tensions

Pastor Karanja plans to first educate and rally clergy to build the capacity for negotiations from within before seeking regional and international support.[34] Indigenous traditional methods of negotiation[35] provide foundational support. Once a Kenyan Truth and Reconciliation Commission (TRC) is convened, it would begin by addressing intragroup conflict resulting from Britain's divide and rule policy. Colonial-related wounds that have never been addressed must be the starting points in order to acknowledge the immense nature of the tribal-based bias and prejudice that leads to generational violence. Encouraged is face-to-face negotiations between the Kikuyu who believe that they did bear the heaviest burden of leading the Mau Mau war against Britain and hence assume a sense of entitlement and privilege ahead of the loyalist Kikuyus and other tribes. Other tribes do not take this assumption lightly and hence dislike the Kikuyu domination in the country.

Author Karanja stresses the importance of impartial and sincere dialogue where pain is acknowledged and heard and losses deeply honored. Victims need a safe place to tell their stories, grieve their losses, and hear offenders take responsibility for the harm they have committed in order for healing to commence (Evenson 2004).[36] Ideally, new perspectives form. Perhaps the victim is able to see the perpetrator as vulnerable and in need of care and compassion for the first time. Optimally, individual and group identities are transformed (Stengel 2008).[37] While care must be taken not to rush the process of forgiveness, parties could do well to remember the words of Archbishop Desmond Tutu, "Without forgiveness there is no future."

One conflict resolution tool necessary to creating the safe space described above is the inclusive selection of impartial facilitators, investigators, and mediators for the truth and reconciliation process so that all concerned are satisfied and willing to proceed with some degree of trust. Daniel Karanja is satisfied with the approach South Africa took here, convening a qualified panel of commissioners who openly shared the process and resultant information with their publics.

Another conflict resolution tool Pastor Karanja recommends for creating the safe, vulnerable space described above is negotiation of process parameters, or ground rules, such as respect for others as well as detailed response to anticipated outbursts of anger (Erbe 2003).[38] Ground rules are process principles and boundaries agreed to by parties to a conflict process. They can be negotiated to effectively respond to angry outbursts and other conflict escalation. They can also craft uniquely effective multicultural process.

The preparation process of all key participants will be critical to the success of Kenya's TRC. For example, understanding the Mandela eight secrets of leadership [39] will empower the participants as well as motivate win-win outcomes.

This conversation is necessary as all sides dig deeper to slowly rebuild trust through small agreements genuinely addressing the needs of those present, followed by the consistent implementation necessary to demonstrate trustworthiness. After shared acknowledgment of victimhood (underlying their intragroup conflict) and requisite trust building, it is anticipated that the Kikuyu people will be ready to explore the victim offender mediation process.[40]

Traumatized angry victims, intent on revenge and punishment for their perpetrators, need an opportunity to examine and evaluate which options are realistically available to them. If they consequently determine that a meeting with their offender is of value to them, they are then able to negotiate on behalf of their needs and interests. An offender may agree to responsibility for the harm caused, even some form of punishment, or offer to repair harm (physical, emotional, and psychological) in ways that are unexpectedly attractive and healing to victims.

Repair of Harm Must Prioritize Community Development

Pastor Karanja further elaborates his thoughts about the lessons learned from South Africa's experience and other, more recent, truth and reconciliation. Most importantly, he promotes community, rather than individual, reparations—repairing harm in ways that advance the educational and economic status of the communities injured, thus avoiding complex disputes and ongoing tensions over amounts of individual reparations (Esman 1997).[41] He is quite critical of how Western perpetrators, often coconspirators with and beneficiaries of international crimes have not been held accountable for repair of harm.[42] He also hopes to avoid a small, elite group of well-connected Kikuyu people benefiting to the detriment of many as happened in Kenya following independence. Families of former Kikuyu colonial loyalist politicians who were supporting the colonialists carved out thousands of acres of land at the expense of the majority poor Mau Mau warriors and their families who had fought for independence.

A recent report on development assistance aimed at ending ethnic conflicts found out that while there are no formulas for resolving ethnic conflict, the natives must be engaged fully in deciding what is fair and equal distribution of resources. Identifying mutual interests and building consensus will go a long way in building sustainable community.

Learning from and Building on Past Truth and Reconciliation

Unanswered and to be explored is the question of how to avoid retraumatizing victims during the TRC process. Employing the skills of professional pastoral caregivers to be available during the TRC process could provide the emotional and psychological counseling necessary and absent during the South African TRC.

Pastor Karanja is further searching for ways to avoid a repeat of the isolation and harassment that occurred to women participating in Rwanda's Gacaca courts when they came forward to testify against their perpetrators. All participants could be requested to sign an agreement guaranteeing the safety of all participants and freedom from all forms of intimidation before, during, and after the process.

Civil Society and Faith-Based Communities Must Hold Government Accountable for Transformation of Relationships

Like what has been described by the other authors of this chapter regarding their governments, the government of Kenya is a tough stakeholder. Its past track record with commissions of any kind is foggy and shrouded with secrecy. Unless faith-based communities and civil society members take full responsibility and hold the government accountable, this TRC process will be just another empty drill without meaningful results (Wainaina 2008).[43] The lessons learned from South Africa are vital and should be considered each step of the way for the Kenyan process to succeed. Reconciliation must move past the mechanics of conflict resolution and literally focus on healing and repairing broken relationships. Understanding the woundedness of each participant and the shared desire for wholeness and restoration could overcome all barriers and roadblocks of self-interest. The chapter of violence, death, and destruction may never be permanently closed, but this process will provide a new vocabulary for telling the story to succeeding generations in a way that will prevent future fractures from occurring and taking these communities through the same cycle of violence over and over again.

Reintegrating Child Soldiers through Engaging Communities in Victim-Offender Mediation of Restitution/Amends that Embrace Indigenous African Tradition

One of the greatest challenges in postwar recovery and reconstruction is effectively rehabilitating and reintegrating former child soldiers into productive sectors of society.[44] Since the end of Liberia's civil war in 1998, both local and international nongovernmental organizations (NGOs) have been running a series of programs to rehabilitate thousands of former child combatants. Scholars describe and evaluate their work as combining family reunification, access to education, skill training, health service, and psychological recovery (Shepler 2005).[45] Family and community mediation have been instrumental to these rehabilitation and reintegration efforts, bringing whole families, traditional authorities, and the church into the rehabilitation process. While much has been achieved through these processes, there is an overall feeling that progress has been slow (Druba 2003).[46]

Research concluding that inadequate social institutions hinder reintegration of child soldiers mirrors the condition initially attributed as responsible for child soldiers: lack of political will on the part of regional governments and the international community to enforce and respect legal instruments governing the involvement of noncombatants, especially children, in warfare. International legislation regulates the protection of children in conflicts. Yet law alone has not been enough to prevent the involvement of children in war in the face of present-day trends in weapon manufacture. Modern weapons are light to carry and easily operated by children as young as ten years. Children with little or no education, poor economic backgrounds, and broken homes are the most vulnerable to forceful enlistment, especially refugees. These same children struggle with rehabilitation.

Yet, once again, as stressed repeatedly by earlier authors, African communities have informal options for addressing their needs that can be exercised while waiting for and working on strengthening social institutions. This is particularly true when discussing the reintegration of offenders into families and broader communities. (The latter is especially important when viable families no longer exist.)[47]

Author Mbonifor concurs with scholars who attribute the slow pace of rehabilitation to overemphasis on economic rather than psychological recovery. He believes that while providing livelihood for these children is indispensable, repairing their "damaged self" can do more for effective reintegration. He proposes that victim-offender mediation incorporating African restorative traditions be added to the family and community mediation processes currently being used. Author Mbonifor sees contemporary restorative justice processes of victim-offender encounter, public forgiveness, restitution, community service, and truth and reconciliation as ripe for blending with native African forms of restitution, forgiveness, and ritualistic cleansing.

Restitution and public forms of forgiveness are not new to most traditional African communities. The only new thing being promoted here is that these forms of restoration be used with child soldiers. Traditional societies have reserved them for notorious adult criminals like murderers, thieves, adulterers, sorcerers, and others who have gone terribly against public norms and then sought repentance and forgiveness from their societies.

It is important to first explain the relevance, process, and consequence of the traditional form of public repentance/forgiveness and restitution in the form of community service within an African context. African offenders are expected to actively seek forgiveness and restitution. They are strongly motivated to do so because they well understand the consequences that will befall them should they chose to stay with the blood of innocent people on their hands. It is safer and cheaper to offer to do community service than to wait and be ostracized or exiled from their communities. Even in moderate cases, no one will marry from a family whose father, mother, or sibling has once spilled human blood or been involved in a crime of similar magnitude.

In most of Northwest Cameroon, traditional and ritualistic ceremonies are organized, mostly in public squares, where whole families and communities turn out to witness the purification and readmission of previously "bad birds" of the society. At these events, all family members are cleansed from the humiliation brought by the evil acts of their loved ones. Most important to understand is the community-centered approach. The collective system in most of these traditional societies stipulates that though crime may be the direct blame of the individual offender, the container community within which the offender was born and nurtured shares in the culpability for the offense. Consequently, child-soldering is a crime against the entire community by an important segment of the same community.

The offending and offended community can even go beyond the family. Just like other traditional systems in many parts of the world, traditions in

North West Cameroon revere children as the collective wealth and even the engine of society. In return, a teenage boy or girl is expected to give the same respect to neighboring parents or seniors as he or she would accord to parents. This same reverence further means that a juvenile offender not only humiliates the immediate family but also the offender's neighbors and entire community. This African belief is distinct from the conclusion of some pro-children's rights authors who attribute child-soldering largely to failed societal responsibility. Western scholars generally see young ex-combatants as victims of neglect by their families and societies. The African family system belief, however, is that children are supposed to be good, respectful, and hardworking. There is no justification for crime, no matter the circumstances. Thus, irresponsibility like a choice to fight in war and kill must be forgiven for children to be accepted back by their families and society in general. Even if the Western and international worlds do not agree with giving children themselves the blame for infant soldiering, understanding the African perspective helps in understanding the importance of giving the children opportunity to regain their lost image of goodness by offering to pay a price for it by appearing in public and doing community service.

At the same time, children's families, immediate and extended, share in some degree of culpability. Thus, they, too, must be prepared to seek forgiveness and make amends. Including these traditions in current efforts at mediation would likely facilitate integration of child soldiers.

Negotiating and Mediating Africa's Debt Crisis

Most of the world now understands that Africa's debt and health crises have escalated to breaking points (Sachs 2005).[48] Out of the forty-one heavily indebted poor countries in the world, thirty-three are in Africa (Stewart et al. 2003).[49] Countries are paying more toward debts than to health care and other essential domestic services.[50] On average, African countries are spending eight times more repaying foreign debts than funding domestic social services. For every one dollar that poor African countries get in grant aid, they pay back fifteen dollars on debts (Paul and Valley 2006).[51]

In response, author Mubanga hopes to use his negotiation and mediation skills and knowledge to persuade international leaders and lenders to consider several options for debt relief rather than simply insist on current requisite conditions.[52] The options he promotes include: (1) bankruptcy as an option for African countries, (2) tracing and freezing the accounts of corrupt African leaders outside of Africa by the G8, IMF, Paris Club, and

World Bank when these accounts contain loan money stolen from African people, and (3) flexibility in the conditions that poor countries in Africa must meet to qualify for debt relief, including removal of conditions under certain circumstances.[53]

Mediating—Exploring a Bankruptcy-Like Approach

Living in the U.S. has given author Mubanga an opportunity to observe big companies in the U.S. survive total collapse after applying for bankruptcy. The companies must first reach a critical stage, similar to the one seen in Africa, accumulating overwhelming debts. A considerable number of American companies learn from their mistakes and do very well after reorganizing themselves while being protected by bankruptcy law. The author is not a lawyer. He envisions, however, that African leaders might make it clear that they have reached bankruptcy-like status and are prepared to negotiate debt repayment.[54] This is very much like the beginning of Columbia economist Jeffrey Sachs's work with countries like Bolivia that were at the point of bankruptcy.[55]

Negotiating Help in Effectively Tracing Funds Stolen by Corrupt African Leaders

Another issue ripe for negotiation with lenders would be support for effectively tracing funds that have been absconded by corrupt African leaders. Most of the money loaned to African countries, a reported $140 billion since independence, has been taken by such leaders and hidden in foreign accounts.[56] Those who hide their money abroad are given immunity for over two hundred years, for example, Switzerland has not allowed the disclosure of banker information.

Despite obstacles, African governments are finding creative approaches to trace such funds that promise some success. Support from international lenders would likely heighten progress here. The Kenyan government led by President Kibaki, who took over from Arap Moi, for example, hired an American company, Kroll of New York, to trace these funds. The company has made shocking revelations and forced many high-ranking judges to resign.

Once corrupt leaders die, purportedly money is even harder to trace. Mobutu Sese Seko, former president of Zaire, which is now Democratic Republic of Congo, is one of the African leaders who kept billions of dollars in foreign accounts. After his death, the government of Congo DRC failed to trace the funds. Likewise, Sani Abacha (former president of Nigeria) took billions of dollars, which he kept in separate accounts abroad. When he died in office in 1998, the Nigerian government initially could not trace the money. Yet, amazingly, after constant pressure from the new president, Olusegun Obasanjo, Switzerland returned $1 billion of the stolen money to Nigeria.

Mediating—Negotiating Options to the Debt Crisis that Truly Work

As mentioned before, excessive reliance on outside experts who attempt to act for the parties rather than empower them to act on their own behalf has not worked. This is typical of what is happening in Africa. Instead of negotiating with African leaders[57] mutually beneficial ways to resolve the debt crisis, the World Bank and the IMF set up the standards to be followed. The World Bank and the IMF, for example, came up with the idea of canceling debts for heavily indebted African countries that registered growth and reduced poverty. This did not work. Even though cancellation of debts was done in good faith, in April 2001 the IMF and the International Development Association (IDA) issued a joint paper conceding for the first time that debt cancellation was not benefiting poor African countries. The policies that the countries were required to meet to qualify for debt cancellation resulted in negative growth and a sudden increase in poverty (Gunter and Nureldin, 2005).[58]

Yet another program was introduced in spring 2005 that allowed the IMF and World Bank to guide poor African countries on how to remain above the 150 percent debt-to-export ratio for ten years or more. Out of the thirty-three heavily indebted countries in Africa, only Malawi and Niger are on course. The other thirty-one countries have failed to reach the goals.

Author Mubanga concurs with the World Bank and IMF idea of canceling Africa's debts. The results would have been different, however, if officials from the World Bank and the IMF had sat down with representatives from Africa to explore common grounds/interests, share and create mutually agreeable reasoning, and build future relationships. Facilitative mediation could clearly guide such good faith, collaborative problem solving. At its best, it facilitates broad participation among diverse interests for consensus-building and sustainable resolution. The IMF is already intimately acquainted with such mediation. Years ago it created an ombudsmediator office in response to harsh civil society criticism of its support for mining operations in Peru. That office has already mediated community process similar to what is being proposed with African leaders here.

Mediation would give African leaders the important opportunity to educate their lenders about the specific reasons they are defaulting on debts. African countries are failing to repay debts on time for a variety of reasons. The major one is drought. Countries like Uganda, Kenya, Tanzania, and Ivory Coast, just to name a few, depend on agriculture exports. Once they are ravaged by drought, their major source of earning much needed dollars for repaying debts is crippled. The countries end up defaulting on their loans, resulting in the devaluation of their currencies. When the local currency is devalued, the price of imports increases and the price of exports is reduced very low, resulting in stagnant domestic growth. Negotiation would facilitate troubleshooting of this mutually harmful cycle and brainstorming options so that both African and lender interests are satisfied.

Negotiating through face-to-face mediation would also give African nations and lenders a chance to discuss the challenges involved with meeting conditions that qualify African nations as heavily indebted poor countries (HIPC). To qualify for HIPC status, poor nations must drop subsidies for basic commodities, eliminate trade tariffs, and open their markets to free trade. With unrestricted access to African economies, foreign companies flood their markets with cheap goods that wipe out local industries. Instead of supporting independence and development, to many Africans, HIPC appears to foster increased dependence and perpetual underdevelopment.[59]

Author Mubanga concurs with his coauthors in the importance of creating truly trustworthy and impartial oversight, guidance, and reflective practice throughout Africa to review loan applications and ensure that the vast majority of development aid reaches those intended and in most need. He proposes a panel with representation from all concerned—perhaps like an international arbitration panel, with all stakeholders agreeing to its members. Muhammed Yunus, of the Graneen Bank, has found the poorest of women to be quite trustworthy. They would also provide intimate community and cultural understanding. A development or financial member of this panel could ensure that a hospital is actually built, for example, before giving money for a school.

Conclusion

UNESCO defines the culture of peace as

> the culture that promotes peaceable diversity....The ceaseless culture creating activity that characterizes the social body involves interaction at every level, from the intrapersonal...to

the interpersonal—in household, neighborhood, community, on through successive levels of civic organization through city to the United Nations....Because there is a constant interpenetration of levels, the societal capacity for aggression or peacebuilding depends on patterns developed in every domain....[60]

These authors remind us of the resilience of the African spirit, seeing and strategizing practical paths for hope in the face of violent ethnic eruption and repeated betrayal. As seasoned practitioners of many years, representing law, medicine, theology, education, and community development, and students of conflict and peace, they are able to guide the international community with specific ideas that they see bearing fruit.

All agree that truly impartial oversight and direction is critical to confidence building, the inclusive conflict mechanisms necessary to create "unity in diversity" for sustainable problem solving, and transparency and accountability in the use of funds. Several recommend the conscientious reflective practice exemplified by author Tanto's work in Cameroon. Like Columbia economist Jeffrey Sachs's diagnostic economics, African conflict and peace must be analyzed and evaluated case by case, relationship by relationship, and practice by practice.

Most commend integrative rather than positional negotiation tactics. They ask that the communities in conflict be empowered themselves in conflict analysis, including sophisticated evaluation and creation of alternatives and identification of underlying interests rather than being expected to rely on the sporadic intervention of skilled outsiders. At times, of course, skilled mediators may still prove instrumental to moving forward, as once again exemplified by author Tanto's decade of African mediation and Kofi Annan's recent mediation in Kenya. Leaders and communities must somehow be persuaded to participate in collaborative conflict work.

Africa has a long and revered tradition of restorative justice, or victim-offender mediation, introduced to the world through South Africa's Truth and Reconciliation Commission. Reflective practice allows for imperfections—new lessons can be learned and tested with each new attempt. Progress occurs through the inner strength to honestly reflect and the collective determination to keep building on what works.

None of these authors proposes an easy answer or panacea. They acknowledge that they need international support in confronting elites, political leaders, governments, and multinational corporations whose self-interest "holds communities hostage." At the same time, they see contemporary conflict techniques empowering and mobilizing communities to do what they can to meet their immediate needs and interests. Joined by skillful and devoted civil society and faith-based networks, author Tanto reports that even political leaders can be moved to serve their community interests.

Notes

1. See Howard Raiffa et al., *Negotiation Analysis: The Science and Art of Collaborative Decision-Making* (Cambridge, MA: Harvard University Press, 2003): 191. Integrative, or interest-based, negotiation was made popular by Roger Fisher and William Ury in their classic *Getting to Yes: Negotiating Agreement Without Giving In* (Penguin Books, 1991). Rather than the more common distributive bargaining, where parties simply divide what is being negotiated, usually through a series of concessions, integrative process leads parties in "expanding the pie" through conflict analysis of underlying interests and creative options evaluated with principled criteria to optimize outcomes for all concerned. See Nancy Erbe, "Appreciating Mediation's Global Role in Good Governance," *Harvard Negotiation Law Review* 11 (2006): 355, 386-89 ("Parties might ask for example 'How can we (both) protect infants and generate ore simultaneously...?'")

2. Broadly defined, mediation is any force outside of a conflict that helps with the negotiation, resolution, and transformation of that conflict. For this chapter, mediation is defined as "facilitated face-to-face dialogue...allow[ing] communication, understanding, rehumanization of the enemy, reframing of the conflict as a shared problem to be solved[,]...moving towards inclusive processes of mutual empowerment...in a way that respects the interests, needs and values of all." John Davies and Edward Kaufman, *Second Track/Citizens' Diplomacy* (Lanham and Oxford: Rowman and Littlefield, 2002). Restoration represents a completely different approach to criminal justice than the better-known retributive justice. It is defined by one leader in the field as "a systematic response to wrongdoing that emphasizes healing the wounds of victims, offenders, and communities caused or revealed by crime. [Restorative practices]...respond to crime by: 1) identifying and taking steps to repair harm, 2) involving all stakeholders, and 3) transforming the traditional relationship between communities and their governments in responding to crime." Lynette Parker, "Restorative Justice: A Vehicle for Reform?" (paper presented at the annual meeting of Latin American Studies Association, Las Vegas, Nevada, 2004). Truth and reconciliation commissions are the most widely known example of restorative justice. *Contra* N. Erbe, "Appraising Surge in Legal Scholarship Regarding Restorative Justice and Discovering Lenses to the South," *BePress Legal Series (2005)*, http: law.bepress.com/cgi?article+2750&context=expresso (arguing that truth and reconciliation commissions represent hybrid justice, combining retributive and restorative approaches to justice for highly pragmatic reasons, such as the need to force

the most powerful offenders, like the Catholic church, to dialogue through cost prohibitive lawsuits and embarrassing publicity).

3. Padraig O'Malley, *Shades of Difference* (Penguin Group, 2007).

4. Mark Bevir, "Negotiation," in *Encyclopedia of Governance* (Thousand Oaks: Sage, 2006): 593. Conversely, in multiple studies, the worst negotiators and facilitators of cross-cultural process are described as poor and judgmental listeners lacking deep understanding. Nancy Erbe, "The Global Popularity and Promise of Facilitative ADR," *Temple International and Comparative Law Journal* 18 (2004): 343-89; Andrea Kupfer Schneider, "Shattering Negotiation Myths: Empirical Evidence on the Effectiveness of Negotiation Style," *Harvard Negotiation. Law Review* 7 (2002): 143.

5. Anup Shah, *Conflicts in Africa* (2005). http://www.globalissues.org/Geopolitics/Africa?Intro.asp#TheLegacyof EuropeanColonialism.

6. Richard H. Robbins, *Global Problems and the Culture of Capitalism* (Boston: Allyn and Bacon, 2002); Bob Geldof, *Why Africa?* http://www.data.org.

7   The Human Rights Violations and Investigation Commission (report submitted to the president, Nigeria, May 2002). Marginalization is one of the results of a tit-for-tat response to the nasty tactics of destructive power games, polarizing the parties and ensuring that they work at opposite ends rather than from constructive common interest-oriented, principled bargaining approaches to conflict. It finds justification in reciprocity of response, but ultimately generates a continued hostility and at best a stalemate that refuses to take actions based on objectivity and consideration for the other's point of view.

8. Boundaries of the African countries were arbitrarily set by the colonial masters without regard to tribal and cultural affinities or differences. Persons of the same affinities found themselves in different administrative locations, while persons of dissimilar affinities were lumped together, thus creating conflicts through quests for familial mergers, and nonfamilial separations, leading to expected intra- and interboundary agitations.

9. The acknowledged international responsibility to protect countries whose governments fail to protect post-Rwanda is critical to future peacebuilding throughout Africa and will be mentioned in this paper as relevant to specific plans; e.g., Kofi Annan's recent mediation in Kenya.

10. Chinedu Bob Ezeh is an attorney with over twenty years' experience whose practice in Nigeria included acting as ombudsperson.

11. John G. Oetzel and Stella Ting Toomey, *The Handbook of Conflict Communication* (Thousand Oaks: Sage, 2006): 391.

12. R. T. Akinyele, "Power Sharing and Conflict Management in Africa: Nigeria, Sudan, and Rwanda," *Africa Development* 25 (2000). The power game is a manipulation engaged in by political leaders who seek to dominate their opponents. In turn, the opponents feel that they have no choice but to join in the confrontation. The game of dominance progresses to the detriment of the populace, who become the pawns in the power game. William Ury, *Getting Past No* (New York: Bantam, 1993), postulates that the game works

by a threat to the other side through force or coercion, with the hope they will back down. The negative result, however, is that unless you have decisive power advantage, the other party usually fights back, reverting to anger and hostility, clinging more stubbornly to positions, and becoming increasingly resistant to reaching an agreement.

13. The first victim of the power game described above is the objectivity in the face of a conflict that is needed to negotiate effectively. Power games depend on reacting to threat or pressure of the other side. In response, the most powerful weapon is not reacting, taking a dispassionate and objective bird's-eye view of the problem, and using generous tit-for-tat in defusing the toxicity of nasty tactics in a conflict situation.

14. Author Ezeh has successfully practiced "generous tit for tat" in the face of nasty tactics. Instead of reciprocating in kind and escalating destructive conflict, he has committed to principled negotiations, gently and firmly taken care of himself in the face of attack, and nevertheless shown respect for the person of the attacker, thus improving his relationship with the attacker, but even more so, establishing his community profile and reputation as a person of moral integrity.

   Jeffrey Sachs is another contemporary example of a spokesperson promoting the negotiation strategy of generous tit for tat as key to avoiding disastrous confrontation. Exercising this strategy, a negotiator adopts the position of cooperation as long as the other negotiators do. If a party begins to cheat, attack, or otherwise not cooperate, however, the first negotiator also stops cooperating to let the other know the consequence of noncooperation. At the same time, the first negotiator generously forgives by not reciprocating in a nasty way. Instead, the door for cooperation is left open. The first negotiator may even generously "extend" the olive branch of renewed cooperation in the hope of enticing others to resume cooperation.

15. Morton Deutsch, Peter T. Coleman, and Eric C. Marcus, *The Handbook of Conflict Resolution* (San Francisco: Jossey-Bass, 2006): 27.

16. In 1995, the government of Nigeria under the military dictatorship of General Sani Abacha, executed nine young men from the Ogoni tribe of Nigeria for the alleged killing of four elders of Ogoniland. The Ogoni nine had been protesting the activities of the multinational oil companies (especially of Shell BP) on their land, the marginalization of the Ogoni people (whose land produced close to 35 percent of the total crude production of Nigeria) in the sharing of the revenue by the government, and also the negative and environmentally destructive procedures adopted by the Shell BP in oil exploitation and production in the region. The Ogoni crisis ended with the murder of the four by irate youths and the resultant lopsided trial and judicial murder of the nine by the federal government. It is instructive that full oil exploration has not been restored in Ogoniland since the incidents.

17. In teaching his course in African Conflict Resolution at George Washington University, former ambassador David Shinn concurred with author

Ezeh's observation, stating that the grassroots community has generally been neglected with conflict efforts or, in his words, is "one of the most underutilized." *See* http://www.gwu.edu. He notes a few exceptions, referring readers to Creative Associate International, Inc, for its listing of indigenous conflict work and mentioning the Women Waging Peace project at Harvard.

18. BATNA is one example of empowering negotiation tactics made popular by Fisher and Ury of Harvard's Negotiation Project. BATNA is the acronym for Best Alternative to a Negotiated Agreement and represents a party's walkaway alternative at a negotiation table. Parties can be empowered through encouragement to actively create "best alternatives." Awareness of BATNAs can further motivate parties to be more responsive to needs/interests and maximize assets while negotiating.

19. In the Cameroon, as a result of the conflict arising between the Bafanji and Balikumbat villages, Ndi Richard Tanto and his team of Ecumenical Service for Peace, SeP, pioneered a novel process of training the parties in mediation and negotiation skills rather than mediating the problem for them. They thus created a well pool of people who not only aspire to peace, but also are skilled in the process of achieving peace. This resulted in the achievement of lasting peace in an area that otherwise was known for its recurring conflicts. This is similar to the process author Ezeh is designing and implementing in Nigeria through the training of Anglican priests to be veritable agents of grassroots peace processes and initiatives. The scheme is called the Anglican Peace Initiative, under the leadership of the charismatic Anglican Primate of the Church of Nigeria, Anglican Communion. Since the priests have widespread ministry services all over Nigeria, touching most grassroots areas of the country, this training is intended to create much needed peace ambassadors at the grassroots in Nigeria, who have their fingers on the conflict pulse of the country, thus reducing incidents of violent conflicts from erupting periodically as is constantly the case at present.

20. Author Tanto describes reflective practice—the fundamental conflict technique for evaluating and ensuring case-by-case effectiveness. Ndi Richard Tanto is a mediator in Northwest Cameroon who has worked with the Ecumenical Service for Peace (SeP) for many years.

21. Howard Wolpe and Steve McDonald, "Democracy and Peace-Building: Rethinking the Conventional Wisdom." http://www.wilsoncentre.org.

22. Wolpe and McDonald argue that there has been a missing link in the traditional approaches to peacebuilding. That key link is the building of capacities of key leaders to facilitate the peace process. In author Tanto's effort to resolve the conflicts in West Cameroon, capacity building was a key component. Leaders were trained to carry the process forward by analyzing the conflict and developing possible scenarios for peace.

23. According to Susan Mckay and Dyan Mazurana, exchange visits bring opposing factions together to build a culture of peace based on the development of self-esteem and dialogue. Susan Mckay and Dyan Mazurana,

"Impact and Limitations of Media Technology," www.ifuw.org/peace/peace-building/raising-womens-voices.html.

24. In one study of cross-cultural conflict process in four regions of world, inclusive process facilitated by an open-minded and encouraging, or engaging and concerned, third-party facilitator was the top recommendation for a quality experience.

25. The external evaluation team of the International Monetary Fund ombuds-mediators found that nongovernmental organization watchdogs are often necessarily to safeguard third-party impartiality and independence.

26. This is a classic example of how extending an olive branch can work in the generous tit-for-tat negotiation strategy described in footnote 15.

27. Questions on ownership of land in Cameroon are very complex. The land tenure system designates all land in Cameroon as state land. Land is managed by the Ministry of Territorial Administration through its decentralized structures. The closest administrator of land to the population is the divisional officer popularly called "chef terre" or "the leader in charge of land." He works closely with village chiefs, referred to as "axillaries" of the administration in the management of the land. By law, there is a hierarchy of power from the minister of territorial administration to the village chief. While the first three categories of actors: minister, senior divisional officer, and the divisional officer have the authority to use their power to demarcate land, the chiefs have only consultative powers.

   The situation described above is what obtains in principle. In practice, however, the chiefs are the real owners of the land and can go as far as waging a war on whoever threatens their authority over land. All the conflicts that have occurred in Western Cameroon within the last fifteen years have been due to a disregard of state authority over land by the chiefs. The Balikumbat/Bafanji, Bagam/Bamenyam, Bali/Bawock, Mbessa Oku conflicts are all due to the insubordination of traditional chiefs to constituted authority. In the Oku/Mbessa conflict, for example, the state planted pillars to demarcate the land and the chief of Oku ordered for the pillars to be removed.

   In the Bali/Bawock conflict, the administrative authority of Mezam wanted to solve the problem by demarcating the frontier between the two villages. The 2nd Assistant SDO Muma Charles, who went to the field to examine possibilities for the demarcation, was chased from the area on the instructions of the chief of Bali Fon Galega. The Bali people went as far as taking the senior administrator to court for infringing on the chief's land.

   Insubordination can be understood against the background of the democratic practice in Cameroon. Democracy in Cameroon means rule of the majority at all cost. For that reason, political parties, in their struggle to win political power or stay in power, put in place mechanisms to ensure majority vote at all costs in every election. Village chiefs have therefore been hotly sought by political parties because they have the power to mobilize and influence their subjects at the local level to vote for one party or the other.

Victory in an election could well be a result of the ability of a political party to win the support of the village chiefs. As such, these chiefs stand in a vantage point to bargain for facilities from political parties, and the party that wins due to their support gives them a free hand in issues of land as compensation for votes. That was the case with the Balikumbat/Bafanji conflict wherein Fon Doh Gah Gwayin rigged elections, got the only CPDM party seat of the twenty seats in parliament for the North West Province, and invaded Bafanji, which largely voted for the opposition SDF party.

28. Daniel Karanja is a theologian from Kenya who has published on oppressive tribal and cultural practices like female genital mutilation and the needs of women living in communities of oppression. He is currently engaged in developing a faith-based conflict resolution curriculum for Kenya—laying the foundation for Truth and Reconciliation, first within his own community.

29. Charles O. Lerche III offers this definition of reconciliation—"…Reconciliation is currently essential to the construction of sustainable peace. It can be defined as a profound process of dialogue between conflicting parties, leading to the recognition of the "*other*," and respect for his or her differences, interests and values … the action of restoring broken relations … the acknowledgment of the dignity of victims long ignored. It restores the individual's capacity to take hold of herself and to manage the future and herself in that future. It restores the capacity to live with or alongside the other. It allows us, while remembering, to bring closure to a chapter in our past. It enables us to live in the present, making our life as a nation and our lives as individuals in a shared future. It always remains a never-ending process" (citing Commissioner Wynand Malan of the South African Truth and Reconciliation Commission). Charles O Lerche III, 'Truth Commissions and National Reconciliation: Some Reflections on Theory and Practice," *Peace and Conflict Studies* 17 (May 2000).

30. For probably one of the best-detailed historical accounts of the British atrocities in Kenya, see Caroline Elkins, *Imperial Reckoning: The Untold Story of Britain's Gulag in Kenya* (New York: Holt, 2005). In 2006, Elkins was awarded the Pulitzer Prize for General Non-Fiction for her work in Kenya. She eloquently details how the British imperialists maltreated the Gikuyu people of Central Kenya. She is currently an associate professor of history at Harvard University in the Kennedy School of Government.

31. Daniel Karanja, *Final Portfolio* (2008).

32. Kofi Annan, former UN secretary general, successfully negotiated a power-sharing deal between the current Kenyan president and his opponent—now the prime minister under the new agreement—due to his ability to discern the immediate and long-term interests of the parties and persuade parties through reviewing the costs of continuing conflict: rising violence/destruction of life and property. The Kenyan public seemed quite comfortable with Annan's team of qualified and experienced expert negotiators. Unfortunately,

the root causes of these postelection violent acts have yet to be addressed, and hence there is urgent need for a full-fledged truth and reconciliation commission.

33. The mission stated—"AN ACT of Parliament to establish a Commission to seek and promote justice, national unity, reconciliation and peace among the people of Kenya by inquiring into the human rights violations in Kenya and recommending appropriate redress for persons and communities who have suffered injury, hurt, damage, grievance or those who have in any other manner been adversely affected by such acts and omissions." Soon after this draft was presented to parliament, the parliamentarians were distracted by the 2012 presidential succession debate. Unless the faith-based communities take charge of this issue in a united, interfaith approach, the TRC will remain where it is right now.

34. Faith-based communities have both grassroots, regional, and national networks in place. For example, the Anglican Church of Kenya has an established justice and peace department including a research unit that has published on problem solving. The Catholic Church of Kenya, too, has a robust justice and peace unit staffed by professional experts familiar with local, national, and international issues. Building liaison with these and other interfaith-networked organizations will add to the already excellent efforts going on in Kenya.

35. There are known African methods of reconciliation and healing that could immensely help in this process. Cultural awareness of tribal and ethnic underlying interests cannot be ignored if conflicts are to be resolved. The role of formally recognized elders and their time-tested expertise in bringing two warring sides together especially among pastoralists competing for dwindling water and grazing areas must be embraced. Author Karanja's father, as one example, was village chief. Every Monday, he gathered with recognized elders to hear grievances from various parties and decide accountability and punishment. This system worked since the village concept of justice recognized that the complainant and the offender belonged to the village before and after the punishment. Rehabilitation was deeply ingrained in this village judicial process. John Mbiti, an African philosopher, explains the necessity of communal understanding even in conflict resolution, "... I am because we are ... because we are therefore I am." Parties understand that life is intricately held together and interlinked between families, villages, and regions; hence, conflicts must be resolved through the involvement of the entire community. For more details, see Josiah Osamba, "Peace Building and Transformation from Below: Indigenous Approaches to Conflict Resolution and Reconciliation Among the Pastoral Societies in the Borderlands of Eastern Africa." http://www.accord.org.za/ajcr/2001-1/accordr_v2_n1_a5.html.

Mr. Osamba is a lecturer in the Department of History at Egerton University, Njoro, Kenya, studying toward a Ph.D. in dispute resolution as a

Fulbright Junior Scholar at Nova Southeastern University, Fort Lauderdale, Florida.

36. Elizabeth M. Evenson, "Truth and Justice in Sierra Leone: Coordination Between Commission and Court," *Columbia Law Review* 104 (2004): 730.

37. Richard Stengel, "Mandela, His 8 Lessons of Leadership," *Time Magazine* (July 21, 2008). Rule 8 states "Keep your friends close—and your rivals even closer." Mandela truly expressed care for his enemies. He invited them to social events, called them during their birthdays, and attended family funerals. Building trust must be the foundation to quell strong feelings of revenge. In violence, there is no winner; all sides lose. Learning as much as possible about the other side, likes, dislikes, favorite routines, can move relationships to new and healthy levels where communication barriers are broken.

38. Nancy Erbe, *Holding These Truths: Empowerment and Recognition in Action (An Interactive Case Study Curriculum for Multicultural Dispute Resolution)* (Berkeley: Public Policy Press, 2003): 149.

39. Richard Stengel stated the following eight lessons of leadership from President Nelson Mandela during an interview marking his ninetieth birthday celebration: 1) Courage is not the absence of fear—it's inspiring others to move beyond it, 2) Lead from the front-but don't leave your base behind, 3) Lead from the back—and let others believe they are in front, 4) Know your enemy—and learn about his favorite sport, 5) Keep your friends close—and your rivals even closer, 6) Appearance matters—and remember to smile, 7) Nothing is black or white, 8) Quitting is leading, too. These enduring principles of leadership, especially at the negotiation table, will eliminate positional and inefficient negotiation ushering integrative win-win outcomes for all.

40. Ideally, present day generations of former British perpetrators will be moved by Gikuyu stories, feeling empathy and a genuine desire to make amends. Amend-making will benefit by applying the four principles of negotiation offered by Fisher and Ury: 1) separate the people from the problem, 2) focus on interests rather than positions, 3) generate a variety of options before settling on an agreement, and 4) insist that the agreement be based on objective criteria. Such a sense of balance and fairness between third and fourth generations who did not directly engage in this conflict provides an optimal environment to address sensitive matters with an objective and solution focused manner. Cross-cultural intelligence will be an added advantage when these two sides gather.

41. Milton J. Esman, "Can Foreign Aid Moderate Ethnic Conflict," *Peaceworks* 13 (March 1997).

42. For example, a 2002 lawsuit accused several corporations and banks of aiding and abetting South Africa's apartheid government.

43. A similar warning was issued by Ndungu Wainaina (director, International Centre for Policy and Conflict, a member of the Kenyans for Peace with Truth and Justice Coalition), *The Daily Nation* (May 17, 2008*). "*…Vigilance, after TJRC submits its reports, is critical, given the fact that previous

commissions have not addressed issues of impunity. Many such are still gathering dust in government offices. How do you compel the government to ensure that the recommendations are followed to the letter? How do you ensure that victims get justice? There are major questions and skepticism towards the roles of TJRCs in meeting their goals. Huge differences in understanding and expectations of the process exist between the elites and the communities. TJRCs across the world are notorious in their failure to implement their recommendations. This has led to rare attainment of the expected moral regeneration of the society. The ethnic and political divisions look even more set to make the work of TJRC more difficult in Kenya. The government and its agencies as well as the citizens must behave in a manner to further the ideals of such a process. However, as long as previous injustices continue being replicated in Kenya, such as the gross human rights violations like extra-judicial killings and torture, then TJRC may not succeed. It would easily turn into another conflict resolution mechanism. The truth-seeking process is unfinished business that provides a foundation for the transformation of the state. It is only a step in the process of addressing long term and short term issues."

44. Author Neba Monifor is one of Ndi Richard Tanto's neighbors and colleagues, a historian, teacher, and community activist.

45. S. Shepler, "The Rites of the Child: Global Discourses of Youth and Reintegrating Child Soldiers in Sierra Leone," *Journal of Human Rights* 4 (2005): 197-211; F. Faulkner, "Kindergarten Killers: Mortality, Murder and the Child Soldier Problem," *Third World Quarterly* 22, 4 (2001): 491-504.

46. V. Druba, "The Problem of Child Soldiers," *International Review of Education* (2003): 48 (concluding that rehabilitation and reintegration are greatly hampered by lack of funds and inadequate personnel and social institutions).

47. The challenge of refugee children is more complex.

48. Jeffrey D. Sachs, *The End of Poverty* (New York: Penguin, 2005): 81-82, 89, and 203 (describing how development aid has fallen in the last decade as diseases like AIDS and malaria have been endemic and how the IMF and World Bank have failed Africa).

49. Frances Stewart, Sanjaya Lall, and Samuel Wangwe, *Dead End to Development, Alternative Development Strategies* (New York: St. Martins Press, 2003).

50. George Mubanga is a journalist and radio commentator from Zambia who helped lay the foundation for South Africa's Truth and Reconciliation process through quietly meeting with communities and persuading their participation. Africans living in Africa have benefited from several programs designed by organizations and countries in the Western world that aim at improving the standard of living. Volunteers from Scandinavian countries, the United States, and Japan are playing a critical role helping millions of disadvantaged Africans and orphans who have lost their parents from AIDS

as one instance. S. Adepoju and R. Stewart, *African Study Review* 38, 1 (April 2001): 103-74.

51. B. S. Paul and R. Valley, "Gleneagles Did Succeed," *New Statesman* 135 (2006): 4-26.

52. Economist Sachs, like authors George Mubanga and Ndi Richard Tanto, promotes a clinical, or case-by-case, diagnostic evaluative approach, exemplified by conflict resolution's reflective practice, rather than a "one size fits all" approach to financial recovery.

53. Journalist Mubanga plans to use the conflict cost/risk/benefit analysis tool to explore the dire need for these options in a documentary film.

54. Author Mubanga would appreciate hearing from bankruptcy lawyers concerned with the African debt crisis who could educate him about contemporary bankruptcy law/proceedings and help him explore possible correlations and avenues for African countries. He is particularly interested in learning more about Chapter 15, which incorporates the Model Law on Cross-Border Insolvency drafted by the United Nations Commission on International Trade Law (UNCITRAL) in 1997. The law allows U.S. courts/judges to issue subpoenas (orders) as circumstances dictate on bankruptcy proceedings that involves foreign countries. The main consideration of U.S. courts/judges when handling cases of this nature depends on whether the conduct of a creditor/debtor violates laws of public policy in the United States and does not conform to basic rules of procedural fairness.

55. Sachs had studied the Great Depression and mechanisms to help "extricate countries from bankruptcy." Jeffrey Sachs currently acts as an impartial, trusted outside adviser to many countries in such crisis.

56. M. Lancet, "Making Healthy a G8 Priority," *Spotlight on Africa* 368 (2005): 311-29.

57. Due to problems with corrupt African leaders described earlier, author Mubanga proposes forming an independent body with representatives from all African countries. This will be done in consultation with the African Union, which is the mother body of all African countries. The officials will be accorded responsibilities that range from screening of loans given to African countries to implementing proper usage and coming up with affordable payment plans with lenders. Its purpose would be impartial oversight, providing transparency and accountability to ensure good faith.

58. Gunter G. Bernhard and Hussain M. Nureldin, *African Development Review* 17, 3 (December 2005): 461-92.

59. Author Mubanga hopes to produce a television documentary looking at what it takes for a poor country to qualify for debt cancellation and the effect of delaying until a country reaches heavily indebted poor country status to qualify for debt cancellation. The documentary will compare conditions prevailing before countries qualified for debt relief and ask: has the situation changed for better or worse?

A portion of the documentary is going to look at the possibility of unifying the countries of Africa into one entity, the United Nations of Africa (UNA). Uniting the countries of Africa into one dominant force may have many advantages. This is evident in the United States of America, where most poor states, like Louisiana, survive major catastrophe after receiving funding from the federal government.

Some politicians in Africa may feel uncomfortable with people discussing openly the current situation in their countries and may persecute them. To prevent this, before the start of recordings, author Mubanga will spend time educating local political and religious leaders on the importance of the documentary. He will make it clear to the local politicians that allowing people to speak freely in this documentary may be key to getting vital information that may guide officials from various lending institutions to change their stance on Africa's debts.

60. Elise Boulding, *Cultures of Peace: The Hidden Side of History* (Syracuse, NY: Syracuse University Press, 2000) (emphasis added).

EIGHTEEN

Positive Peacemaking and the Women of Nigeria

Ifeoma Ngozi Malo

Conflict is inevitable because it can originate in individual and group reactions to situation of scarce resources; to division of function within society; and to differentiation of power and resultant competition for limited supplies of goods, status, valued roles and power-as-an-end itself. [1]
—C. R. Mitchell (1989)

With a population of well over 120 million people, Nigeria holds the record as the most populated country in Africa. Apart from its membership with the OPEC community, Nigeria is also considered a major player among oil-producing countries around the world. [2] The discovery of oil in Nigeria has brought with it the twin-edged sword of suffering and pain, and yet it has brought profits, too. Whereas Nigeria's oil was meant to be a blessing, it has assumed the vestige of a curse to the Niger Delta people. The continuous conflict in the oil-producing communities of the country has given a pathetic turn to the events in the Niger Delta. Since the first major oil spill at Shell's Jones Creek on October 17, 1998, [3] there have been many other major oil spills in the region. The Niger Delta region holds the record for some of the worst environmental pollution in Nigeria, if not the world. Farmlands have been destroyed, rivers polluted, villages sunk by flood, shrines desecrated, bodies of dead relatives carelessly exhumed and ground up by construction companies' bulldozers, women and children killed in avoidable pipeline fires, and harmless protesters callously killed by agents of the federal government.

All this pointedly raises concerns among the local communities who have their means of survival and the environment threatened by the activities of multinational corporations like Shell, Chevron, Mobil, Texaco, and Agip. The situation in the region is deplorable, and vivid accounts exist of the pains, deprivations, and detailed stories of oppression suffered by communities in the area. This is all due to the deplorable extractive activities of multinational oil companies (MNCs) in their oil exploration activities and repressive style used to squelch any complaints. However, little has been done to redress the wrongs, and the situation only worsens each day. This article seeks to examine the role and motivation of women in the struggle for better living conditions and an end to exploitation in their communities.

Brief Overview of the Niger Delta

The population of the Niger Delta is estimated to be about ten million people and continues to grow at about three percent a year. This number makes up about 14 percent of Nigeria's overall population. There are more than forty ethnic groups in the area with links to the linguistic groups of Ijaw, Edo, and Igbo.[4] The Niger Delta is one of the world's largest wetlands, and the largest in Africa. The Niger Delta is rich in both renewable and nonrenewable natural resources such as oil, gas, bitumen, nontimber and timber forest products, wildlife, and so on. Ninety percent of the total revenue for the Nigerian government is generated from oil and gas exploration.[5] Even before the discovery of oil in the Niger Delta, it served as a transit route for a lot of trading activities from the slave trade to the palm oil trade, as it was located on the coastal line of the midwestern region of Nigeria.

These perceived advantages of the Niger Delta area also turned out to be the source of many conflicts leading to the continuous bloodshed and sorrow for many families in that region. Due to its strategic location at the heart of the Nigerian oil- and mineral-producing areas, it experienced tremendous growth in population and importance, being the major oil-producing region for the entire country. Warri and Port-Harcourt, two of the oil-rich towns in the Delta, played host to two of Nigeria's four refineries and both refineries remain the only ones with the joint capacity of a daily output of 50 percent of the total regional production.[6] However, this output has greatly declined to just below 30 percent per day in recent times, due to the instability and highly volatile nature of the region.[7] All the other refineries are moribund from lack of maintenance.[8] For instance, in late September 2004, news reports were filled with the outbreak of hostilities by competing youth militia groups in Port Harcourt, one of the major towns playing host to oil workers and companies.[9]

The Niger Delta is the most prominent region among the oil-producing areas of Nigeria. The territory known as the Niger Delta comprises six states—Rivers State, Delta State, Bayelsa State, Edo State, Cross River State, and Akwa Ibom State. The occupations of the local people in the Niger Delta include fishing, peasant farming, small-scale trading, and local income-generating projects. The men are considered the breadwinners in the traditional Niger Delta home, but in reality the women make immeasurable contributions to their families and communities. The women care for the family; they trade, fish, and undertake peasant-farming activities. Their tasks are both productive and reproductive, while the men mostly climb palm trees to get palm wine, build canoes, and operate commercial speedboats around the area.[10]

Historical Background to the Crisis

Examining the history of this conflict requires exploring the colonial roots of the ethnic rivalry and the consequent political dimensions that impacted on the disputes between the parties as a result of the British intervention.[11] Part of the root cause can be attributed to the failure of British colonial policies in the area. Long before the arrival of Europeans in the coastal areas of the Delta, the three indigenous communities of Itsekiri, Ijaw, and Urhobo lived independently of one another in relative peace. The British, who eventually gained control of the area, ushered in an administration that brought together these culturally different people into the same political unit purely for commercial ends, without regard for the lack of cultural affinity and common will among those involved.[12] According to Horowitz, "Such a society... held together by the dint of the force of colonial power, is inherently a precarious and unstable social form."[13]

One major barrier to the stability and development of the area is the contention over land rights. The question of who owns the land and who is entitled to the rents accruing from them has added many twists to this conflict and has become the subject of endless litigation and a series of government commissions since the beginning of the twentieth century.[14] The issues leading to the conflict in the Niger Delta have also created conflicting claims of ownership by the three dominant ethnic/cultural groups, and this in turn has exacerbated the conflict. The claims and counterclaims, which have triggered hateful conflicts in the Niger Delta and backlash against government forces and oil companies in that region today, are numerous. The new round of efforts to control land by the indigenous people of Warri is the bane of the current conflict. As Rodolfo Stavenhagen asserted, "Land is not only an economic factor of production; it is the basis of [their] cultural and social identity; the home of ancestors, the site of religious and mythical links to the past and to the supernatural."[15]

Due to the opportunities presented by the oil business, people flooded to the Niger Delta region from every part of the country and indeed the world (including expatriate oil company workers) "in search of the golden fleece." This resulted in heightened stakes for land and the bitter contest by the three major ethnic groups in the region, namely the Ijaws, Itsekiris and Urhobos, for ownership of this oil-rich region known as Warri. However, the conflict that has dominated the relationship among these three ethnic groups in Warri has heightened the hostilities among the various cultural groups. Thus the crisis in the Niger Delta can be attributed to the struggle to dominate local politics. The conflict is in part centered on the use and distribution of community land rights in the region, but has also extended to the activities of oil exploration by multinational corporations in the host communities.

The Dispute in the Niger Delta

> Globally, human existence seems to be at risk not only because of such social aberrations like mutual mistrust and hatred, insecurity, ethnic chauvinism, language differences, religious fanaticism, intra and interstate conflicts, but also because of man's inability to predict, manage and control intending disorders.[16]
>
> —Onduku Akpobibibo

Prior to the outbreak of hostilities and violence, the Niger Delta was a multiethnic embodiment of quiescence, where everyone was welcomed to live or do business. Due to its strategic location at the heart of the Nigerian oil-producing areas, the Niger Delta experienced tremendous growth in population and importance for the country.[17] "As the growth in oil business turned the Niger Delta into a land of opportunities, people flooded the area from all parts of the country and indeed the world in search of the golden fleece."[18] People from diverse backgrounds, including foreign nationals, were known to have lived together in relative peace and harmony.[19] Besides the three ethnic groups that lived in Warri, there were other ethnic groups indigenous to Delta State like the Delta Ibos and the

Isokos and even nonindigenous tribes like the Yoruba Hausa and Ibo; all these settled and made a home in the Niger Delta region.[20]

It is quite true that the Niger Delta region had always had its share of skirmishes and conflict. However, never in its history had there been this much bloodshed with warring youth militias ready to die for their various causes.[21] The mayhem that has engulfed the region since the early 1990s and that continues today has been unprecedented since Nigeria's civil war.[22] Indeed, it has been suggested in many forums that the Niger Delta region currently operates as a different entity within Nigeria.[23] The warring factions have become a law unto themselves while operating under the guise of ethnic militia groups.[24] This has turned the area into a war zone and has made it perilous for its inhabitants, including entire families.[25]

Yet there exists another type of dispute, which has its root in the natural resources derived from this area.[26] Crude oil from this region accounts for nearly 85 percent of the country's revenue, and yet this same revenue causes the division among the oil-exporting communities.[27] This has turned out to be the leading source of continuous conflict, bloodshed, and sorrow to many families in that region. Almost four decades of strife reached its peak in the early 1990s,[28] and the conflict continues today.

The Oil Companies vs. Oil-Producing Communities

Despite the depletion of both human and natural resources by multinational companies, there has been no meaningful development for the people living in those communities. And despite its considerable natural resources, the Niger Delta remains one of the poorest and most underdeveloped parts of the country.[29] The inhabitants, 70 percent of whom still live a rural subsistence characterized by a total absence of such basic facilities as electricity, pipe-borne water, hospitals, proper housing, and good roads, are weighed down by debilitating poverty, malnutrition, and disease.[30] All this pointedly raises the issues of resource control and the use and management of oil resources by the federal government to the exclusion of the local communities.

It appears that the people have not benefited from oil resources and reserves that exist in the area. Worse still, the richly endowed environment remains under debilitating assault from unending gas flares, unmitigated oil spills, land seizure, and river and air pollution by multinational oil corporations.[31] An example is the case of the village of Oloibiri in the Ogbia Local Government Area of Bayelsa State, where the first oil well was drilled more than fifty years ago. Today, the inhabitants of this community are left with nothing but damaged farmlands and polluted rivers, with no electricity, potable drinking water, or other basic social amenities.[32] Similar to the Oloibiri situation, many residents of other oil-bearing communities continue to live in primitive conditions, alongside the high-tech facilities of the multinational corporate community that they host.[33]

The guilty multinational corporations like Shell, Chevron-Texaco, Exxon-Mobil, Shell Nigeria, and Agip continue to threaten the residents' basic livelihoods on a daily basis.[34] The environmental situation in the region remains deplorable, and there are vivid accounts of the pains, deprivations, and oppression to which the people of this region are subjected to every day.[35] Added to these problems are the repressive measures of the federal government, which has sided more with the oil corporations than with the host communities demanding better living conditions.[36] As the situation worsened each day, and the degradation of the environment and sources of livelihood continued, the conflict naturally escalated and set the stage for more opposition by the ethnic militias.[37] This time, the heat was turned up on the oil companies, which had been fingered as complicit in stoking the embers of hate among the communities. This included targeting their perceived collaborators within the communities as well as government agents sent to protect the oil facilities and their employees.[38]

The communities have also realized that the oil companies have been playing a big part in the local politics for many years now, generating the conflict in the region. As a result, local residents' opposition and agitation for better compensation for destroyed land and livelihoods took a violent turn. Daily news from the region was replete with vandalized oil pipes and terminals, as well as kidnapping of high-level oil company workers, particularly expatriates.[39] This further heightened the area's security problems, and the federal government increased the troops posted to the area. However, the soldiers' intervention led to a witch-hunt in the Niger Delta communities and an all-out war with the youth militias in these areas.[40]

The result of these conditions is that the oil-rich region became a community filled with different ethnic militias, each expressing its grievances through violence against both the security forces and the oil companies. The youth militias evolved new ways of dealing with their enemies through violent opposition, kidnapping of oil multinationals' staff, hijacking, blockades, and seizures of oil facilities.[41] The security situation in Warri was unsafe, compelling many people and businesses to move out. For instance, many of the oil companies moved to Port Harcourt, which was considered safer than Warri city for oil businesses in the zone.[42] But then the security situation in Port Harcourt also took a turn for the worse. Since newspapers filled with reports of hostilities between competing youth militia groups, many businesses also closed in the once-serene garden city.[43] This is a recent development, as Port Harcourt had been considered the safest oil-rich city of the area, but today it suffers the volatility for which the Warri community was formerly known.

Organized Opposition in the Niger Delta

There are many documented accounts of environmental pollution and degradation in the Niger Delta area. For example, in their report on the Niger Delta conflict, Moesinger and Maglio explain the destructive impact of pollution by the oil companies and how this greatly impoverished the local communities. They write:

> Indigenous groups are actually further impoverished due to environmental degradation from oil production and the lack of adequate regulations of multinational companies as they become more vulnerable to food shortages, health hazards, loss of land, pollution, forced migration and unemployment. These affected groups include [the] Ogoni. The welfare of these various groups has been completely neglected by the ruling military regime and the multinational companies.[44]

John Agbonifo, writing on the Ogoni crisis, quotes an Ogoni man's summation of the situation in the community:

> Before, life was good, food was in abundance, life was easy, and productivity on the farm was quite enormous. I am shocked to observe the incidence of the arrival of Shell and the decline of our productivity. Plants are now dying, land is flooded, fishes are killed. We do not understand these things; our lives are becoming unbearable; we have diseases on our body and on our skin any time we go into water.[45]

The Ogonis of Rivers State in Nigeria were one of the first peoples to have an organized, grassroots mobilization in the early 1990s.[46] Turner explains that in 1990, nine Ogoni associations formed the Movement for the Survival of the Ogoni People (MOSOP).[47] This mobilization arose against the background of communal frustration, which brought about their struggle for self-determination and resource control in the Niger Delta. They issued the Ogoni Bill of Rights, which gave a detailed set of demands for environmental cleanup, a greater share of oil revenue, and participation in the determination of issues that affect their lives.[48]

The Nigerian state and the multinational oil corporations ignored this Bill of Rights, and therefore the Ogoni staged an unprecedented protest against Shell on January 4, 1993. Two important demands were for reparations and the right to refuse further oil production in Ogoni land. Human Rights Watch (1999) reported that this movement was a statement to the world about the practices of multinational oil corporations and the Nigerian government.[49]

The Nigerian state and the multinational oil corporations ignored this Bill of Rights, and therefore the Ogoni staged an unprecedented protest against Shell on January 4, 1993. Two important demands were for reparations and the right to refuse further oil production in Ogoni land. Human Rights Watch (1999) reported that this movement was a statement to the world about the practices of multinational oil corporations and the Nigerian government. The controversy heightened in 1994-1995. Protests were successful in closing down oil plants. Women were actively involved in coordinating these mass, grassroots protests, and they marched alongside the men during this struggle.[50] Ken Saro-Wiwa and his MOSOP group were considered worse than a nuisance by the government for organizing such a huge revolt. They were met with state violence, actively abetted by the multinational giants.[51] In November 1995, the Justice Ibrahim Auta Military Tribunal, a kangaroo court set up specifically to find the accused persons guilty, convicted Saro-Wiwa and seven colleagues for murder. All eight were executed on November 10, 1995.[52]

The wrongful conviction, detainment, sentencing, and subsequent death by hanging of the Ogoni 8, as they were called, elicited worldwide condemnation and protest, as it was done with the hope of destroying the will of the Ogoni people. Their fight was to hold the oil companies accountable for destructive activities and double standards. The backlash following the hanging of the Ogoni 8 against such companies as Chevron-Texaco and Shell led to further repression of anti-oil protests.[53] The oil companies were also known to have silently supported and provided logistics and equipment for the trial of the Ogoni 8.[54]

MOSOP gave much organizational impetus to other Niger Delta social movements. Thus began a series of mass protests from the mid-90s by other similarly affected communities around the oil-producing areas. Beginning with the Ogoni Bill of Rights in 1990, the ethnic nationalities of the Niger Delta slowly began to assert their rights and demand compensation for the destruction of their environment. This was an attempt by the different groups to declare their intention and determination to reclaim their human dignity and fundamental rights. These declarations included the Ogoni Bill of Rights,[55] the Kaiama Declaration,[56] the Aklaka

Declaration of the Egi People,[57] the Oron Bill of Rights,[58] the Warri Accord,[59] the Ikwerre Declaration,[60] Resolutions of the First Urhobo Economic Summit,[61] Demands of the First Niger Delta Indigenous Women's Conference for Women of Bayelsa State,[62] and the Gambia Accord.[63] Each declaration by the different groups formed the basis for the struggle for self-determination and represented the struggle and quest for control of resources by each nationality.

Many of these demands resulted in struggles and armed warfare among the restive youths in the region. News reports across the three core states of the Niger Delta—Delta, Bayelsa, and Rivers States—revealed how the instability in the region had translated into violent political, socio-economic, ethnic, and communal conflicts. In the cities in particular, there was a resurgence of ethnic animosities, leading to considerable violence and destruction among the ethnic groups.[64] The conflict revolved mainly around issues of political representation, land, political justice, and the social contract.

The Niger Delta Women

The above scenario set the stage for the participation of women in the struggle in this region. However, unlike the men, their protests and demonstrations were not against each other, but rather a collective act of solidarity as mothers, daughters, sisters, and aunts who had long been affected and ignored in the region's protracted conflict.[65] Sokari Ekine, a notable female activist who has worked closely with Niger Delta women, likens the condition of those women to that of women under siege in a war.[66] Ekine reports that Niger Delta women are known to suffer great hardships, especially from the warfare that continues to take place in their communities.[67]

Furthermore, there are reports and accounts of victimization and brutalization of the women and children in these communities by security details hired by the oil companies for protection.[68] The women are also known to be subjected to rape, military prostitution, and physical abuse by soldiers and police details under federal authority. As a result, many are forced to flee their homes in distress. The majority of the people in the Niger Delta are in no way gainfully employed because their source of livelihood has been taken from them; they are neither compensated for their loss of income nor do they benefit from the presence of the multinational companies in their communities. Less than five percent of the people in the Niger Delta work for these companies, and, for women, the figure is less than one percent. The number of able-bodied men in the area has been depleted by the many killed during violent confrontations between government forces and the communities.[69]

In the past decade, highly negative reports by environmental groups about environmental conditions in the Niger Delta have become very public. This is primarily because human rights groups joined forces with people in the local communities to expose the deeds of the oil companies. This has significantly raised the awareness of the communities in which the resources and environment are exploited. Environmental groups also detailed the connivance of the Nigerian military government with the oil companies in covering up oil spills and other environmental hazards.[70] The reports documented the horrifying killings of residents' sons, husbands, and fathers by state agents, raping and killing of young females, destruction of the ecosystem, desecration of sacred sites, and total neglect and impoverishment of the people whose lands produce the wealth that sustains the rest of the country.[71]

Despite all of the exposure of the problems facing the Niger Delta people, their situation remains largely unchanged. Many of the cries by these oil communities are muffled because they lack access to the Nigerian media, which are controlled and regulated by the federal government. The communities also lacked the resources to fight the multinational corporations through established channels, especially since the regulatory bodies and laws regulating oil company activities actually favor those companies.[72] Furthermore, little or no environmental impact assessment has been conducted, leaving the actual level of damage in these areas undetermined. The Niger Delta communities appeared to have no other choice but to take matters into their own hands.[73]

Women's Participation in the Resource Control Struggle

Throughout Nigerian history, there have been numerous powerful illustrations of the strength of women's political agency. Women's movements and organized protests are traditionally rooted in the country's historical development. The Nigerian state structure was created and enforced by Western-influenced patriarchal agents who sought to restrict women's political and economic agency.[74] Opposition to oppression and subjugation by constituted authority appeared in pre-colonial times and expanded throughout colonialism, military regimes, and "democratic" transitions. Historical analysis reveals that women's post-colonial initiatives have consistently challenged the discriminatory structures of the state. Specifically, the mid-1980s marked a strategic political shift of women's activism against the patriarchal state. The instability of the 1990s and early 2000s has existed in Nigeria as a direct result of the State's perpetuation of exclusionary structures.[75]

Heather Turcotte, a researcher on women political movements in Niger Delta, argues that historical research has shown that Nigeria's male political elite appropriated oil production exclusively for their own benefit. This male elitist group harnessed the highly profitable resources accruing from the oil proceeds for its own personal advantage, thus making it easy to subdue the women and ethnic minorities from the oil-producing region into complacency.[76] Turcotte further reveals that at some point in its history, control of resources in the Niger Delta communities became a major target for women's resistance. This resistance by the women extended and permeated significant portions of 'political, economic, and social discourses", and "used the institutionalization of oil as a political power tool."[77] The struggle also significantly altered "the relationship between women, their communities, the state, and the international sphere."[78]

The history of the Niger Delta women has always been one of community participation. In many of these communities, women are the custodians of the culture and the active members of society. This dynamic was no different in their struggle against the multinationals and state aggressors, in which they have sometimes had to pay huge prices for their activism.[79] Soldiers and police have been known to systematically terrorize entire communities, assaulting and beating women and children indiscriminately with the aim of damaging and humiliating or destroying these communities. Due to the long drawn-out conflict among the men folk in the region, the majority of people left in the villages are women, children, and the elderly. As a result, when a village comes under attack, these groups of people are the most affected.[80]

The Nigerian state and their international cohorts have acknowledged the recent re-emergence of women's movements in the Niger Delta region. In recent times, the news media has been agog with the historic political role of the Niger Delta women's strategic resistance against an oppressive regime that promoted the dictatorial industry of petroleum.[81] These women suddenly shunted aside their male youths, marched onto the frontlines, and became the hostage-takers of oil workers in the region.[82] This supports the assertion that women, when well organized, have substantially affected and contributed to the political, economic, and social structures of Nigeria.[83] History is replete with early accounts of female participation in the Niger Delta struggle. Around the mid-1980s, various groups of women from the Niger Delta region began protesting against the state's dominant industry of petroleum. The protests consisted of well-organized social opposition against oppression.

For instance, in 1984, Ogharefe women stormed the production site of the U.S. corporation Pan Ocean. In March 1986, Bonny Island women held officials of the multinational oil corporation Shell hostage for two days. In April 1986, Egbema women of Imo State infiltrated Shell's platform and largely halted production. In August 1986, 10,000 Ekpan women fiercely demonstrated against the Nigerian National Petroleum Corporation (NNPC) refinery.[84] These massive social protests, led by Niger Delta women, were significant contributions to the beginnings of an international oil movement. Demanding that multinational oil corporations take responsibility for their discriminatory practices that had been destroying and debilitating the Delta since oil exploration began in 1907, these groups of Niger Delta women used their historic political influence to challenge the Nigerian state structure.[85]

As previously mentioned, the Movement for the Survival of the Ogoni People led by Ken Saro-Wiwa made headlines around the world and achieved massive international appeal.[86] According to Turner, women were active in the Ogoni movement through the Federation of Ogoni Women's Associations and were major participants in the January 4, 1993 oil protests in which 300,000 Ogoni protested against Shell's action in Ogoni-land. Turner also explains that for the first time the Ogoni governing organ officially accepted women and youth as full participants within it.[87] Turner quotes Diana Wiwa regarding women's involvement in the Ogoni movement:

> …a lot of the movement was based on the stories he [Ken Saro-Wiwa] had collected over the years about what the women complained about… so we supported Ken, the feminist. Ken was very well supported because he was very furious about [the erosion of] women's rights.[88]

The participation of Ogoni women in the struggle for better living conditions appeared to have provided the impetus for broader opposition by women in the Niger Delta. On July 8, 2002, Itsekiri women from Ugborodo in the Warri area of Delta state marched to Chevron-Texaco's multibillion-dollar tank farm and terminal in Escravos and took over the facilities for ten days. The women held all the workers in the area hostage and refused to leave until all their demands were met. Their overall demands amounted to three major requests: employment opportunities for their children, greater economic empowerment, and enhanced development of infrastructure in the area. While it lasted, the blockade disrupted the production of an estimated 500,000 barrels of oil per day. Some 800 workers remained trapped in the terminal, although the protesting women later released 400 of their colleagues as a good-will offer.[89]

The standoff with the women ended after the oil company and the Ugborodo community signed a memorandum of understanding. Under its terms, the Nigerian National Petroleum Corporation/Chevron Joint Venture pledged to redress the community's grievances. Specifically, the agreement included regular offers of jobs to the people, establishment of income- and wealth-generating schemes, and the provision of school blocks, town halls, electricity, and potable water.[90]

Yet there was no immediate respite to this new wave of revolutionary protests that were suddenly springing up.[91] Nine days into the invasion of Escravos by Itsekiri women, Ijaw women from Gbaramatu (also in the Warri area) nonviolently seized and occupied four flow stations belonging to Chevron-Texaco.[92] They came chanting slogans such as, "Gbaramatu kingdom has nothing to show for over thirty years of the company's existence."[93]

The women's occupation of the Abiteye, Makaraba/Otunana, Dibi, and Olero Creek flowstations cost Chevron-Texaco an estimated 110,000 barrels per day of oil production. The company extracts more than 400,000 barrels of oil per day from the Niger Delta, the vast majority of which is processed at the Escravos facility. Communities around these facilities continue to be plagued by oil spills, which destroy their fishing economy, and gas flaring, which causes acid rain, skin diseases, asthma, and other negative health effects. Not only have their traditional economies been destroyed by oil operations, but very few jobs, economic opportunities, or social services exist in the affected areas.

Representatives of the women negotiated and reached accords with Chevron-Texaco officials at the Abiteye flow station. They signed a memorandum of understanding outlining various conditions that the oil company must meet in order to continue production. Demands were made for compensation for the negative impacts and environmental degradation from Chevron-Texaco's oil activities.[94] Although the company conceded on several demands, with further negotiations scheduled to take place the following month, the conditions of the Escravos "agreements" only foreshadowed the usual nature of Chevron-Texaco's empty promises.

Forms of Protest and Opposition

In the past, response by oil companies to the demands of the host community, irrespective of the nature of the protests, were usually violent attacks on the demonstrators. This was made possible through the heavy reliance on military and police agents.[95] However, the Chevron-Texaco protest by the women was different as there was no violence following their takeover of the oil terminals. The wave of peaceful mass demonstrations by the women from affected communities successfully halted the operations of a multinational oil company like Chevron-Texaco in the Niger Delta for nearly two weeks. What started as a single action of opposition by 150 women from villages surrounding the Escravos oil terminal grew to over 3,000 women joining in a non-violent direct occupation of four other Chevron-Texaco facilities in the Niger Delta.[96]

The demands of the protesting women were not unlike those that had been made in the past by the youth and male activists against the oil multinationals operating in the area. Their demands included jobs, education services, health services, and economic investment in their communities. The women were particularly miffed that there was little to show for the years that oil had been drilled in their communities. What's more, the reckless pollution of their environment ensured that they had become endangered species in their own homes. The women also accused Chevron-Texaco of having a long record of failing to follow through on its commitments to affected communities. As if to confirm these allegations, the company almost immediately began to renege on the "agreements" made in ending the Escravos occupation.[97]

The nature of the occupation by the Niger Delta women is essential in analyzing the success of their mission. It is important to note that the form of the opposition has provided the impetus for a number of similar occupations by women and elderly persons in other oil communities around the Niger Delta.[98] Armed with only food and their voices, these village women carrying their children on their backs occupied the various oil facilities and the terminal for weeks. They barricaded a storage depot, thus blocking docks, helicopter pads and an airstrip, which covered all the entry points to the facility. Their presence prevented well over 700 workers from working or leaving the premises until the company agreed to certain conditions.

The company agreed to accede to most of their requests and even worked out the modalities for the implementation of those agreements. For instance, the company agreed to hire twenty-five villagers over five years and to help build clinics, schools, and fish and chicken farms. Today, the general opinion is that the agreements reached with the women did little to change these situations. The multinationals seem to have lapsed into their lackadaisical attitude once the women ended their occupation of the oil terminals.[99] However, the actions of the women in getting the oil companies to listen and negotiate with them and even accede to some of their requests are by no means small achievements. These are even more major achievements given that the many years of war and violence in the area had not achieved similar results.[100]

Toward the end of Escravos standoff, troops from the Nigerian Army were moved to the flow stations to prevent any acts of vandalism. They were reportedly given explicit instructions not to molest the protesting women.[101] These women, like their forebears in the early '80s, used dance, song and the threat of nakedness to block and intimidate both the company operatives and their security details.[102] Furthermore, the military and police forces sent by the state to squelch the protest were also unsuccessful, as the women threatened them with the same ammunition. Nakedness, dance, and song have been effective historic power tools that express and enforce women's political agency and effectiveness within the community.[103] These means of protest ensured that the women continued to disrupt the state's oil production for the length of time that they did.[104]

The people of the Niger Delta are very traditional. Destruction of their environment equates with destroying the source of their livelihood. Their small-farming and fishing activities permeate every vestige of their life, and their various colorful festivals are their heritage and their identity. The local people, particularly the women, believe in their culture, and they tend to promote this culture in everything they do. However, this same culture could also be used as a means for reprimanding offending members of the community or those who take the hospitality and simplicity of the local people for granted.

For instance, dance is considered a strong communication tool in many traditional societies in Nigeria. It is a well-understood cultural tool for passing messages among members of a society. The Niger Delta women protested their conditions with the use of dance. Judith Hanna, writing on the use of dance and protest in opposition, writes that the historic use of dance in Nigeria is symbolic of the identity or culture of any community.[105] Traditionally, dance was a social outlet performed by both men and women within the village community for important ceremonies such as births, deaths, harvests, religious celebrations and other notable community events. Hanna further explains dance as a political and powerful instrument of communication: "The body, the instrument of dance, is the first means of human power, with which everyone can identify."[106]

Heather Turcotte, writing on the political expression of dance, argues that in a "shame-oriented society," dance assumes the "ultimate means of social control." Women used dance to express grievances within the community,[107] and in protests such dance involve heavy stamping of feet on the bare floor to show their fury.[108] This was exactly what the Niger Delta women did, using dance to assert their political grievances. During their occupation of the oil facilities, they had come up with dances specifically aimed at ridiculing the workers in the companies. Most of these dances were accompanied by songs and chants taking aim at the heads of these multinational companies.[109] The jibes in their songs were couched in satirical lyrics to accompany the dance in order to further lament the severity of the grievance and protest. Women would dance en masse, singing songs laced with such sardonic humor and sometimes highly embarrassing songs to enforce public ridicule of community members at fault.[110]

Public ridicule was and still is taken seriously and quickly acted upon by the offenders in order to avoid further defamation against the accused. Their numbers notwithstanding, the Niger Delta women who had taken over the facilities at the oil terminals were able to utilize this tool against the offending oil companies. They were armed with little more than their songs and dance, but were able to get their demands on the table by merely exercising this familiar yet weighty form of social control.[111] Even oil company staffs that were not of Niger Delta origin must have sensed the fury behind the voices and the spiritual movements of the women. Those who did sense this fury would have been educated on the import of the women's actions by those who are more knowledgeable about such matters.[112]

Another form of protest used by the women in the Niger Delta was the threat and use of nakedness. Historical accounts of female opposition show that this form of protest was common to women in eastern Nigeria. For the eastern communities, nakedness in public is considered a "serious and permanent curse" capable of causing physical, economic and political impotency among the men for whom the women disrobe.[113] Such a threat of nakedness usually creates serious alarm among the men folk who are guilty of provoking such a threat, since such an exhibition is usually considered an extreme and weighty form of demonstration. To warrant this, such women must have been pushed to their limits, and before it gets to the stage of stripping, male offenders often push for hasty negotiations in order to avoid the debilitating effects of this type of women's protest.[114]

This strategic tool stripped the offender of all credibility in the public and private spheres. No men, even those from outside the communities, ever questioned the use of nakedness—they feared it.[115] Women would also storm the compounds of men they had grievances with and hold their offenders hostage. They refused to let the offender leave and continued to dance, sing and threaten the offender with nakedness. In some cases, they would physically sit on the offender with clothed (and sometimes unclothed) behinds.[116] However, the threat of or actual use of nakedness as a form of protest is never made lightly in order not to diminish its potency. Indeed, before any such action is undertaken, the women issue a warning to the offenders on their proposed course of action. When such threat is issued, the offenders usually request a peace meeting with the women to prevent such a course of action. There is also a myth surrounding this use of nakedness that suggests that for those men for whom this form of protest is used, death is sure to come knocking at their door a year from when the stripping occurs.[117] Women's groups tend to use the method only when their oppressors have pushed them to their limits, and they see no other alternative to get their oppressors to redress a wrong.[118]

In the case of the Niger Delta women, they had reserved this tool only for when there were attempts by state agents and security guards of the multinational to dislodge them from their campsites in the oil terminals. Reports have it that the women stripped themselves of the clothing both as a way of placing curses on their adversaries and to shame the security details who had come to disturb their peaceful protests.[119] It was no surprise then when various accounts of the standoff at Escravos reported that those men who were present when the stripping began had to run away, with some of them leaving their guns and ammunition behind in order that the curse that follows such action would not befall them.[120] Due to the similarities in culture and tradition among many societies in Nigeria, the relationship between the local security personnel and the women could be likened to sons and mothers or brothers and sisters. As a result, they were unlikely to stay and see their grandmothers, mothers, sisters, and daughters go completely naked in order to get what was rightly their due from an oppressive corporate entity.[121] The thought alone was enough to make them rethink their actions.

Conclusion

The shaming element resulting from all three means of protest—singing, dancing and stripping—are each considered quite strong in their own right. Particularly, the curse that emanates from stripping is considered quite catastrophic. In the case of the Niger Delta women, these means of protest were effectively used to keep the military and police away for as long as it took for their demands to be met. They were able to use this as an effective negotiating tool, while totally disarming the possible use of violence in their dislodgment. Male workers in the oil company were also not in a hurry to see such sights and were willing to stay hostage until the women were satisfied. This nonviolent method further supports the assertion that there are indeed innovative nonviolent means capable of achieving more results. Furthermore, it is clear that violence is a cycle that perpetuates itself through counter-violence. As history has shown repeatedly, it solves little and creates more problems. I personally find it ironic that after a series of violent actions, parties usually find it expedient if not necessary to come to the negotiating table. This suggests that despite the violence that exists, peaceful negotiations remain imperative for any form of lasting peace to hold water among the disputing parties.

Kingsley Osadolor, in his commentary on the "rise of the women in the Niger Delta,"[122] suggests that the current radical stance of the Niger Delta women might color the very nature of future agitation. Such agitation, he states, will go beyond the Niger Delta communities to the Nigerian state as a whole, especially if the current state of affairs in the entire country remains unchanged. Osadolor further notes that the male members of the Niger Delta communities appear to have "beaten what is obviously a strategic retreat, and that the women have become the Amazons."[123] He asserts that one of the most important factors in the protest employed by the women was the absence of any violence. Osadolor notes that the women fired no shots nor did they need to throughout the length of their standoff with the oil companies.[124] This can be considered a major success and no small victory, especially in light of the responses to prior protests and opposition in that area.

Part of the defiance shown by the women is also predicated on the fact that environmental degradation in the Niger Delta is not limited to the activities of the oil companies, but also includes reckless deforestation by multinational logging companies and destruction of the ecosystem by the execution of construction projects without proper environmental impact assessments.[125] There have been a series of accusations by human and environmental rights groups against the oil companies for employing double standards. The oil companies are constantly accused of damaging practices in Nigeria that would never be permitted in North America or Europe where they are headquartered. Instead of a better life, the armed enforcement actions by the Nigerian federal government have meant more penury for the oil-producing regions.[126] The case of state-sanctioned brutality was also the situation that necessitated the actions of the Itsekiri and Ijaw women. Furthermore, the "useless token measures adopted by succeeding governments to redress the inequalities so manifest in the oil-producing states were incapable of bringing succor to the people."[127]

It is therefore the nagging issues of resource control management that lie at the core of the agitation by the Niger Delta women. In the 2002 federal appropriation bill, very little was allocated to take care of the Niger Delta indigenous people, compared to what was voted for the Federal Capital Territory and the presidency. Currently there is renewed agitation by oil-producing states in the country seeking a 25 percent derivation formula from the country's federal budgetary allocation.[128] While this has been met with opposition by some sections of the country, such an allocation might be required to jump-start genuine wealth-creating opportunities for indigenous people of the oil-producing states.[129] Itsekiri and Ijaw women, by their actions, have thrown new challenges to women in the region, and similar actions of these sorts have continued to emerge all over oil- producing communities. Women throughout the Niger Delta no longer seem willing to sit back, instead feeling compelled to act not only to save their heritage but also to protect the future of children all over the world, they have decided to join the fight for better living conditions in the Delta.[130]

Women's groups in the Niger Delta continue to push forward women's "well-being" by addressing issues of violence against women, environmental degradation, and official inclusion of women in political and economic structures.[131] Traditional organizations have shifted to incorporate international organizations as part of this movement for justice. The continuing lack of "democratic" accountability by male elites prolongs the process of obtaining justice and security within the Niger Delta region. Annie Brisibie, president of Niger Delta Women for Justice, claims that women still retain the ability to rally and organize against their opposition post-Nigerian "democracy." However, she states that "the amount of money being spent" by the government in perpetuating the instability and violence in the area continues to rise.[132]

Women's resistance in the Delta has grown into a movement and is aided by its alignment with international actors in a larger human rights and environmental protection movement that could possibly pressure the state into meeting the needs of its citizens. As a result, international human rights groups have joined forces in calling on democratic nations to take action against the oppressive nature of the Nigerian government in dealing with the oil communities.[133] The nonviolent takeover by the Niger Delta women of the oil facilities put the spotlight on the abusive practices of the Nigerian government and oil companies and gained some international exposure for this struggle.[134]

With the proliferation of nongovernmental organizations (NGOs) in the oil-producing states, future plans of action will likely involve a larger role for women. The actions of the Ijaw and Itsekiri women have buoyed the spirit and stamina of women in other communities in the oil-producing areas. This is evidenced by the swelling numbers of nonviolent takeovers of oil facilities in the area by a number of women on the front line of the struggle for a better life and a better community. Osadolor writes that quite apart from the inherent challenge it poses, the lead provided by the Itsekiri and Ijaw women is a rebuke of the "often-puerile lipstick approach to agitation by other women's groups."[135] He writes further:

> Rather than seek more political positions for women and in a vicious cycle so they can join the ranks of the oppressors, the Delta women are at the barricades campaigning for the dividends of good governance. By their actions, they are rebuking the overdressed and over-made-up first ladies and other unconscionable spendthrifts who squander the country's resources while the country is being ravaged by disease and poverty. It is not far-fetched to read into these events a dress rehearsal for people's power. Have our women elite forgotten what happened to Queen Marie Antoinette of France?[136]

Writing along similar lines, William Sutherland and Matt Meyer argue that "power and the shifting and balancing of power dynamics" are synonymous with revolutionary change.[137] This point states the obvious, but it is the nature and form in which such shifts occur that makes the difference. Sutherland and Meyer state that in a number of cases, some form of nonviolent action usually precedes armed struggle.[138] Yet, if this were the case, it seems almost ironic that such actions usually end back up at a negotiation table. It therefore becomes imperative that people and communities all over must explore new and original nonviolent means of resolving conflict so that they become ingrained in society.

The forms of resistance used by the Niger Delta women embodied this factor, as they used only weapons bestowed upon them by nature and through their own ingenuity. The advantages and potency of these methods far surpassed any other means of opposition used by the men and youth militias in the communities. To further advance the argument of the potency of a nonviolent movement, Sutherland and Meyer quote Gene Sharp, another scholar, as stating that:

> Nonviolent action is capable of wielding great power, even against ruthless rulers and military regimes, because it attacks the most vulnerable characteristics of all hierarchical institutions and governments: dependence on the governed.[139]

I guess the Niger Delta women through their revolutionary methods of protest proved him absolutely right.

Notes

1. I. S. Imobighe, C. O. Imobighe, C. O. Bassey, and J. B. Asuni, *Conflict and Instability in the Niger Delta: The Warri Case* (Ibadan, Nigeria: Spectrum Books Limited, 2002): 15.

2. Nigeria is considered the sixth largest producer/exporter of oil worldwide.

3. Annie A. Brisibe, "African Tradition: The Identity of a People, with Special Focus on Globalization and Its Impact in the Niger Delta," C.O.O.L. Conference, Boston, March 18, 2001. http://www.ndwj.kabissa.org/ArticlesResearch/AB2/ab2.html (accessed June 23, 2004).

4. Ibid.

5. Ibid.

6. John Agbonifo, "The Colonial Origin and Perpetuation of Environmental Pollution in the Postcolonial Nigerian State." http://lilt.ilstu.edu/critique/fall2002docs/jagbonifo.pdf (accessed February 7, 2004).

7. O. Edevbie, "Who Owns Warri? The Politics of Ethnic Rivalry in the Western Niger-Delta Region of Nigeria," Urhobo Historical Society, November 2003. http://www.urhobo.kinsfolk.com/Conference/FirstAnnualConference/ ConferenceMatters (accessed October 27, 2003).

8. J. G. Frynas, *Oil in Nigeria: Conflict and Litigation Between Oil Companies and Village Communities* (Hamburg LIT, 2000).

9. For more information on the new rebel movement in the Niger Delta, see the BBC Africa news article at http://news.bbc.co.uk/2/hi/africa/3713664.stm. See also the Reuters News article on the Niger Delta opposition at http://www.alertnet.org/thenews/photoalbum/1096458645.htm?_lite_=1.

10.. Brisibe, "African Tradition" (see n. 3).

11. Edevbie, "Who Owns Warri?" (see n. 7)

12. Ibid.

13. Donald Horowitz, *Ethnic Groups in Conflict* (Los Angeles: University of California Press, 1985): 136.

14. Ibid.

15. Rodolfo Stavenhagen, *The Ethnic Question, Conflicts Development, and Human Rights, Japan* (United Nations: University Press, 1990): 100-1.

16. Akpobibibo Onduku, "Sustainable Development as a Strategy for Conflict Prevention: A Case of the Niger Delta." http://www.ogele.org/features/features_nigerdelta.html (accessed October 22, 2003).

17. Imobighe et al., *Conflict and Instability in the Niger Delta (see n.1)*.

18. Ibid.

19. Ibid. See also Brisibe, "African Tradition" (see n. 3).

20. Imobighe et al., *Conflict and Instability in the Niger Delta* (see n. 1).

21. Ijaw Council for Human Rights (ICHR), "The Many Worrying Wars of Warri," www.nigerdeltacongress.com (accessed October 27, 2003).

22. Ibid.

23. Ibid.

24. Ibid.

25. A. Salihu, E. Okon, and N. Sow, "Enhancing the Capacity of Women Leaders of Community Organizations to Contribute Towards Peace Building in the Niger Delta Region of Nigeria," as cited in *Needs Assessment Report: Niger Delta, Nigeria,* July 12-20, 2002, http://www.international-alert.org/pdf/pubwestafrica/niger_delta_needs_assessment.pdf (accessed September 2, 2004).

26. Edevbie, "Who Owns Warri?" (see n. 7).

27. Nisirimovu Anyakwee, Executive Director, Institute of Human Rights and Humanitarian Law, in "Poverty in Wealth: Report on the People of the Niger Delta and the Display of Poverty in Wealth" (Port-Harcourt, September 2000): 3.

28. Imobighe et al., *Conflict and Instability in the Niger Delta* (see n. 1).

29. Salihu et al., *Needs Assessment Report* (see n. 25).

30. Okonto and Douglas, as cited in Salihu et al., *Needs Assessment Report* (see n. 25).

31. Ibid, p. 9.

32. Onduku Akpobibibo, *The Lingering Crisis in the Niger Delta: A Field Work Report.* http://www.peacestudiesjournal.org.uk/docs/OilConflict.PDF (accessed November 20, 2003).

33. Nisirimovu Anyakwee, Executive Director, Institute of Human Rights and Humanitarian Law, in "Poverty in Wealth: Report on the People of the Niger Delta and the Display of Poverty in Wealth" (Port-Harcourt, September 2000), p. 3. As cited in Akpobibibo, *The Lingering Crisis in the Niger Delta* (see n. 32), p. 3.

34. See NDDC, *NDDC Profile* (Port-Harcourt, 2001).

35. Emem J. Okon, *Report of the Niger Delta Women for Justice (NDWJ) on the Delta Women Siege on the American Oil Company, Chevron-Texaco in Delta State of Nigeria,* Doifie Ola, ed. (2002).

36. Brisibe, "African Tradition" (see n. 3).

37. Okon, *Report of the Niger Delta Women for Justice* (see n. 35).

38. Brisibe, "African Tradition" (see n. 3).

39. Akpobibibo, *The Lingering Crisis in the Niger Delta* (see n. 32), p. 3.

40. Sam Amadi, *Still the Circle of Poverty: A Report by the Social and Economic Rights Action Center (SERAC) on the Economic Livelihood and Political Empowerment of Oil Communities in the Niger Delta,* 2004. See also Imobighe et al., *Conflict and Instability in the Niger Delta* (see n. 1).

41. It became common practice for young militia groups to kidnap expatriate oil workers and contractors working within the oil fields located in the communities before they are released in exchange for a huge ransom. In February 20, 2005, a Korean oil expatriate staff member working with Daewoo Nigeria

was taken hostage. Reports say that he was released in exchange for a huge ransom running into millions of *naira* (Nigerian currency) by his company and the Korean consulate.

42. The Anglo-Dutch oil company Shell Petroleum also relocated its administrative headquarters to Port-Harcourt.

43. George Esiri, Reuters Alert (ref: POR01/2004). http://www.alertnet.org/thenews/photoalbum/1096458645.htm?_lite_=1 (2004).

44. For more on this point, see "TED Case Studies: Ogoni and Oil." http://www.american.edu/TED/OGONI.HTM.

45. Vincent Amanyie, *The Agony of the Ogonis in the Niger Delta* (Bori, Nigeria: Fredsbary Printers and Publishers, 2001): 23, as cited in Agbonifo, "The Colonial Origin and Perpetuation of Environmental Pollution" (see n. 6).

46. Terisa Turner, "Why Women Are at War with Chevron: Nigerian Subsistence Struggles Against the International Oil Industry," *Journal of Asian and African Studies* 39, 1-2 (2004): 63-93. See also http://www.uoguelph.ca/~terisatu/counterplanning/c3.htm and http://jas.sagepub.com/cgi/content/refs/39/1-2/63.

47. Ibid.

48. "Ogoni Bill of Rights." http://www.nigerianscholars.africanqueen.com/docum/ogoni.htm.

49. Amanyie, *The Agony of the Ogonis*, p. 23 (see n. 45).

50. Terisa Turner, "Oil Workers and Oil Communities: Counter Planning from the Commons in Nigeria" (1997). http://www.uoguelph.ca/~terisatu/counterplanning/c3.htm (accessed March 5, 2002).

51. See Ken Saro-Wiwa, *A Month and a Day: A Detention Diary* (New York: Penguin, 1995) for early information on the MOSOP movement. See also Chris McGreal, "Ken Saro-Wiwa: Not Entirely Innocent?" *Mail and Guardian*, http://www.rchive.mg.co.za/NXT/gateway.dlll.

52. The military tribunals were constituted by the military dictatorship of General Sanni Abacha. Even after the death of the Ogoni Eight (as Saro-Wiwa et al. were known), the militarization of Ogoni land and the decimation of the Ogoni people continued for a long time.

53. Agbonifo, "The Colonial Origin and Perpetuation of Environmental Pollution" (see n. 6). See also Amadi, *Still the Circle of Poverty* (see n. 40).

54. Frynas, "Oil in Nigeria" (see n. 8).

55. See "Ogoni Bill of Rights." http://www.waado.org/NigerDelta/Rights-Declaration/Ogoni.html.

56. See the Kiama Declaration from the Ijaw Resource Center. http://www.ijawcenter.com/kaiama_declaration.html. See also http://www.dawodu.net/kaiama.htm.

57. See the Aklaka Declaration. http://www.waado.org/NigerDelta/Rights-Declaration/Oron.html.

58. See "Ogoni Bill of Rights." http://www.waado.org/NigerDelta/Rights-Declaration/Oron.html.

59. See the Warri Accord. http://www.ndwj.kabissa.org/Declarations/declarations.html.

60. See the Ikwerre Declaration. http://www.ndwj.kabissa.org/Declarations/declarations.html.

61. See Resolutions of the First Urhobo Economic Summit. http://www.ndwj.kabissa.org/Declarations/declarations.html.

62. Demands of the first Niger Delta Indigenous Women's Conference for Women of Bayelsa State (1999). http://www.ndwj.kabissa.org/Declarations/declarations.html#Demands.

63. See the Gambia (Women's) Accord. http://www.ndwj.kabissa.org/Articles-Research/GambiaAccord/gambiaaccord.html.

64. See the BBC Africa website for a detailed sequence of the Niger Delta conflicts. See also Akpobibibo, *The Lingering Crisis in the Niger Delta* (see n. 32). See also ICHR, "The Many Worrying Wars of Warri" (see n. 21).

65. See Sokari Ekine, "Women in the Niger Delta: Violence and Struggle" (1999). http://www.ndwj.kabissa.org/ArticlesResearch/Sok1/sok1.htm#ViolenceStruggle.

66. Ibid.

67. See also Akpobibibo, *The Lingering Crisis in the Niger Delta* (see n. 32). See also Ekine, "Women in the Niger Delta" (see n. 65).

68. Ekine, "Women in the Niger Delta" (see n. 65).

69. Ibid.

70. ERA Annual Report. http://www.eraction.org/index.php?page=modules&name=articles&action=view&artid=35.

71. Ekine, "Women in the Niger Delta" (see n. 65).

72. Salihu et al., *Needs Assessment Report* (see n. 25).

73. This opinion is popularly held by various groups in the Niger Delta. See Amadi, *Still the Circle of Poverty* (see n. 40).

74. Heather March Turcotte, "Beneath the Oily Surface: Women's Political Movements Against the State and Oil in Nigeria," ed. Mercier Laurie and Gier Viskovatoff Jaclyn. Working Paper, San Francisco State University, 2002. Under review for paper in *International Anthology on Gender, Gender Relations, and Women's Activism in Mining Communities.* http://www.isanet.org/noarchive/turcotte.html (accessed July 8, 2004). See also http://www.kabissa.org/ndwj.

75. Ekine, "Women in the Niger Delta" (see n. 65). See also Brisibe, "African Tradition" (see n. 3).

76. Turcotte, "Beneath the Oily Surface" (see n. 74).

77. Ibid. See also Ekine, "Women in the Niger Delta" (see n. 65). See also Brisibe, "African Tradition" (see n. 3).

78. Turcotte, "Beneath the Oily Surface" (see n. 74).

79. Ekine, "Women in the Niger Delta" (see n. 65). See also Amadi, *Still the Circle of Poverty* (see n. 40).

80. Ibid.

81. Ibid. See also Turcotte, "Beneath the Oily Surface" (see n. 74).

82. Kingsley Osadolor, "The Rise of the Women of the Niger Delta," *Commentary, The Guardian* (Independent), Lagos, Nigeria, July 24, 2002.

83. Salihu et al., *Needs Assessment Report* (see n. 25).

84. Ekine, "Women in the Niger Delta" (see n. 65). See also Okon, *Report of the Niger Delta Women for Justice* (see n. 35).

85. Turner, "Why Women Are at War with Chevron" (see n. 46). See also http://www.uoguelph.ca/~terisatu/counterplanning/c3.htm.

86.. Saro-Wiwa, *A Month and a Day* (see n. 51). See also Ken Saro-Wiwa, *A Forest of Flowers: Short Stories* (Port-Harcourt: Saros International, 1986). See also Human Rights Watch (1999).

87. Turner, "Why Women Are at War with Chevron" (see n. 46). See also Turcotte, "Beneath the Oily Surface" (see n. 74).

88. See Turner, "Why Women Are at War with Chevron" (see n. 46).

89. Osadolor, "The Rise of the Women of the Niger Delta" (see n. 82).

90. Ibid.

91. Ibid.

92. Ekine, "Women in the Niger Delta" (see n. 65). See also Okon, *Report of the Niger Delta Women for Justice* (see n. 35).

93. Ibid. See also Turcotte, *"Beneath the Oily Surface"* (see n. 74).

94. Turcotte, "Beneath the Oily Surface" (see n. 74).

95. Ibid.

96. Ibid.

97. Ibid.

98. Ekine, "Women in the Niger Delta" (see n. 65).

99. Turcotte, "Beneath the Oily Surface" (see n. 74).

100. Okon, *Report of the Niger Delta Women for Justice* (see n. 35).

101. Osadolor, "The Rise of the Women of the Niger Delta" (see n. 82).

102. Tania Branigan and John Vidal, "Naked Power Play from the Mamas—Niger Delta Women Have Issued the Ultimate Threat: Meet Our Demands or We Strip," *The Guardian* (Independent), Lagos, Nigeria, July 27, 2002.

103. Turcotte, "Beneath the Oily Surface" (see n. 74).

104. Ekine, "Women in the Niger Delta" (see n. 65).

105. Judith Hanna, "Dance, Protest, and Women's 'Wars': Cases from Nigeria and the US," in *Women and Social Protest*, ed. Guida West and Rhoda Blumberg (New York: Oxford University Press, 1990).

106. Ibid.

107. Ibid. See also Turcotte, "Beneath the Oily Surface" (see n. 74).

108. My research on the use of song and dance in many communities in southeastern Nigeria shows that these means of protest are very common and very potent. Songs and dance are also useful in creating a spirit of camaraderie and strength of resolve among the women in pressing home their demands.

109. Turcotte, "Beneath the Oily Surface" (see n. 74).

110. Hanna, "Dance, Protest, and Women's 'Wars'" (see n. 105).

111. Turcotte, "Beneath the Oily Surface" (see n. 74).

112. Ibid. See also Terisa Turner, "Women's Uprising Against the Nigerian Oil Industry in the 1980's," *Canadian Journal of Development Studies* 14, 3 (1993): 329-57.

113. Terisa E. Turner and M. O. Oshare, "Women's Uprisings Against the Nigerian Oil Industry," in *Arise! Ye Mighty People! Gender, Class and Race in Popular Struggles*, ed. Terisa Turner (Trenton: Africa World Press, 1994): 141.

114. My maternal grandmother from southeastern Nigeria recalls two occasions in the early 1940s when the women in her village had to use their bodies as weapons in their fight against oppressive trade taxes. These measures were taken after a series of complaints about these taxes had gone unheeded by the responsible parties.

115. For discussion on the use of dance and the body in power politics, see Jane Cowan, *Dance and the Body Politic in Northern Greece* (Princeton: Princeton University Press, 1990), as cited by Heather March Turcotte, "Beneath the Oily Surface" (see n. 74).

116. Turcotte, "Beneath the Oily Surface" (see n. 74).

117. Apart from stripping for the offending party(ies), women are also known to sometimes take the offending party hostage after they have visited their nudity on him and continue to keep him hostage until all their demands are met. See also Turcotte, "Beneath the Oily Surface" (see n. 74), and Ekine, "Women in the Niger Delta" (see n. 65).

118. From my grandmother's account, not only was the threat carried out by women in the village, it was also a potent weapon used to reverse the taxes that had been previously imposed on them. The guilty parties who witnessed the stripping were said to have lost their lives exactly one year after the stripping occurred as a consequence of the sight they witnessed when the women came knocking on their doors with no stitch of clothing on their bodies.

119. Turcotte, "Beneath the Oily Surface" (see n. 74), and Ekine, "Women in the Niger Delta" (see n. 65).

120. Michael Peel, "Nigerian Women Win Changes from Big Oil—Women Making History News," *Christian Science Monitor*, December 8, 2002. http://www.csmonitor.com/atcsmonitor/specials/women/world/world081202.html. See also Branigan and Vidal, "Naked Power Play from the Mamas" (see n. 102).

121. Doran D'arcy, "Nigerian Women Take on Oil Corporation—and Win," *The Namibian,* July 17, 2002, http://www.namibian.com.na/2002/july/africa/02726ACCD6.html .

122. Osadolor, "The Rise of the Women of the Niger Delta" (see n. 82).

123. Ibid.

124. Ibid. See also Ekine, "Women in the Niger Delta" (see n. 65).

125. Brisibe, "African Tradition" (see n. 3).

126.. See also Ekine, "Women in the Niger Delta" (see n. 65).

127. Ibid. See also Turcotte, "Beneath the Oily Surface" (see n. 74).

128. Emmanuel Aziken, Hector Igbikuowubo, and Austin Ogwuda, "South-South, North Stand-off on 25% Deepens," *Vanguard Nigerian News,* June 22, 2005.   http://www.vanguardngr.com/articles/2002/headline/f122062005.html .

129. Osadolor, "The Rise of the Women of the Niger Delta" (see n. 82).

130. Nigeria Today Online reported on December 13, 2004:

"Hundreds of Kula villagers including women and children stormed three oil platforms operated by Shell and Chevron-Texaco on Sunday [the day before], hitting oil output and trapping over 100 workers briefly. Preliminary talks between Kula community and officials of Rivers state government had failed to end the dispute over jobs and development, local chief Anab Sara-Igbe said. After a first meeting in the state capital Port-Harcourt, the protesters insisted that senior government officials visit the remote fishing village at the southern tip of the Niger Delta to see conditions for themselves. 'The delegation sent was of a very low rank,' Sara-Igbe said. 'The facilities will remain shut until we meet and dialogue with Mr. President or his representatives who must not be less than a cabinet minister in rank.' Sara-Igbe said another meeting was slated for this week, adding that militants would stay around the platforms to ensure production was not restarted."

131. See Turcotte, "Beneath the Oily Surface" (see n. 74).

132. Brisibe, "African Tradition" (see n. 3).

133. Amy Goodman and Jeremy Scahill of Pacifica Radio's "Democracy Now!" program (http://www.democracynow.org) reported on October 1, 1998, that on May 28, 1998, the day after the president made his speech on the African Growth and Opportunity Act, Chevron was involved in political oil killings. The Chevron Company transported Nigerian soldiers, in company vehicles, to the Parade oil platform where activists were protesting. Two protesters were shot to death, others wounded, and eleven imprisoned. As cited in Turcotte, "Beneath the Oily Surface" (see n. 74).

134. Turcotte, "Beneath the Oily Surface" (see n. 74).

135. Osadolor, "The Rise of the Women of the Niger Delta" (see n. 82).

136. Ibid.

137. Bill Sutherland and Matt Meyer, *Guns and Gandhi in Africa: Pan African Insights on Non-Violence, Armed Struggle and Liberation in Africa* (Trenton, NJ: Africa World Press, 2000): 266.

138. Ibid., p. 269.

139. Gene Sharp, as cited in Meyer and Sutherland, *Guns and Gandhi in Africa* (see n. 137), p. 266.

NINETEEN

Equipping the New African Peacebuilder: A Case for African Peacebuilders to Stand in Solidarity against Several Empires

Titus K. Oyeyemi

Introduction

In this article, the writer would like to discuss and trace the reasons why violence persists in Africa to a strange causality: the legacies of different empires. These empires are not limited to physical foreign or indigenous kingdoms, governments, authorities, or principalities, but include cultural, religious, language, economic empires that control or have controlled the lifestyles of the Africans in the past, present, and future. In addition to identifying these empires and the barriers they pose to true development, progress, and peace in Africa, some solutions will be offered on how Africans could proactively overcome the resulting strangulating and persistent conflicts. This article, in addition to many of its kind that this author has written, is targeted at young Africans who need to pay some attention to the past history of Africa with a view to analyzing what has persistently gone wrong and to encourage them to employ their modern and educated minds to liberate and move the continent and her people forward into another glorious era.

Africa, Where Cometh War amidst Thee?

James, the Elder, of the Judeo-Christian Church in Jerusalem, asked the question in his

Epistle: "From whence come wars and fighting among you: come they not hence, even of your lusts that war in your members?"[1] Vernard Eller, reflecting on the question asked by James, traced war and violence to the book of Genesis in his book *War and Peace from Genesis to Revelation,* beginning with the account in Genesis, Chapter 4, of how Cain killed his brother, Abel, following the expulsion of their parents from the Garden of Eden.[2] Treating the same subject but with elaborate analysis, Marc Gopin searched for the causes and effects, problems and solutions, to war and violence in his book *Between Eden and Armageddon.*[3] In his medieval work, *The Reconquest of Africa,* Procopius (534 A.D.) gave us a detailed account of how Belasarius, Emperor Justinian's great general, overthrew the Vandal Kingdom to reconquer Northern Africa.[4] The work of Chancellor Williams entitled *The Destruction of Black Civilization—Great Issues of a Race from 4500 B.C. to 2000 A.D.*[5] and the work of George G. M. James, *Stolen Legacy,*[6] are some texts to turn to if we are to find out how war, violence, and hostilities came to Africa from antiquity to our own present days. To understand the position of Africa from prehistoric periods, Williams presented a table of the dates when towns/cities were founded (Table 1).

Table 1: Table of Dates When Towns/Cities Were Founded

Towns/Cities	Date Founded
Nowe (Thebes)	Prehistoric
Memphis	3100 B.C.
Babylon	2100 B.C.
Jerusalem	1400 B.C.
Athens (Village)	1200 B.C.
Rome (Village)	1000 B.C.
Antioch	400 B.C.
Athens (City)	360 B.C.
Rome (Town)	250 B.C.

Williams explained, "For generations Memphis was almost entirely an all-African city, with white Asian villages slowly growing up around the outskirts. For the Asians were a very smart and very cunning people. Once conquered, they feigned complete and humble acceptance of African rule."[7]

Historians still consider Ethiopia as the location of Ancient Africa with Egypt as the oldest daughter of Ethiopia (Table 2).

Table 2: Ancient Africa

North African Ancient Empires
African (Egyptian) Dynasties/Empires
before Asian and European Conquests
Egypt: Ethiopias Oldest Daughter
Egypt: the north-eastern region of Ethiopia
Lower Egypt: Chem: Northern Ethiopia
Upper Egypt: Nubia or Sudan: Southern Ethiopia

According to Williams, Egypt was occupied by foreign rulers for a total of 2,986 years, between 4,000 B.C. and 332 B.C. (see Table 3).

Table 3: Years of Foreign Rule over Egypt

Foreign Ruler	Years
Jewish	500
Assyrian Interludes	Interludes
The Persian	185
The Greeks	274
The Romans	700
The Arabs	1,327
Total years of foreign rule over Egypt	2,986

So if Egypt was to be taken as a model for Africa, then Africa can be said to have known over 4,000 years of foreign rule. What this means for Africans is that whether at home or in Diaspora, they have always been subjected to foreign rule. And perhaps it is the struggle to shake off this yoke that has contributed to incessant violence for the Africans. Williams gave the account in the following manner:

> Where Asia and their mulatto offspring gained control, the Black Africans migrate southwards. The picture was generally the same from 4,000 B.C. onward. In the Asian-held areas in the north, the Blacks had hard choices to make. As elsewhere on the continent, they had the choice of remaining slaves; or if they were well-to-do members of the professional classes: architects, engineers or skilled craftsmen, they could remain, become integrated in Asian society, be classified as "white" and

even hold high positions; or finally, they could reject integration into Asian culture and migrate southwards.[8]

As a result of this southward migration, Williams continues, "a number of African tribes four thousand miles south from Egypt still claim Egypt as their ancestral homelands."[9]

The Stolen Legacy

The object of George G. M. James's work *Stolen Legacy* was to show that the purported Greek philosophy was indeed stolen from Ancient Egypt or at least was the offspring of ancient Egyptian philosophy. James claimed that the teachings of the Egyptian Mysteries reached other lands centuries before it reached Athens and that the chronology of Greek philosophers is mere speculation.[10] James pointed out emphatically that pre-Socratic philosophers were educated by the Egyptians and that Athenian philosophers like Socrates, Plato, and Aristotle were educated in the curriculum of the Egyptian Mystery System.[11] The effects of the conquest of Egypt by Alexander the Great gave people like Aristotle, a tutor of Alexander, unfettered access to the royal libraries, museums, and temples of Egypt. James explained this as follows:

> Just as in the invasion of Egypt by the Persians, the invading armies stripped the temples of their gold, silver and sacred books; and just as in the capture of Athens by the Romans, Sulla carried off the only library of books which he found; so it is to be expected of Alexander the Great, in his invasion of Egypt. One of the first things he and his companions and armies would do would be to search for the treasures of the land and capture them. These were kept in temples and libraries and consisted of gold and silver out of which the gods and ceremonial vessels were made, and sacred books and manuscripts kept both in libraries and in the "Holy of Holies" of Temples.[12]

James went on to write:

> It is therefore an erroneous belief that the Greeks, on Egyptian soil, and through their own native ability, set up a great university at Alexandria and turned out great scholars. On the other hand, since it is a well known fact that Egypt was the land of temples and libraries, we can see how comparatively easy it was for the Greeks to strip other Egyptian libraries of their books

in order to maintain the new Library at Alexandria, after it had been already looted by Aristotle and his pupils.[13]

Ancient Africans Were Empire Builders but the Invasions Were Brutal

Ancient Africans built and rebuilt empires as they lost them to foreign and invading armies. They lost both Upper and Lower Egypt and their beloved Memphis and Thebes; thus Ethiopia's border was pushed below the First Cataract at Assuan.[14] Williams talked about more and more invasions:

> Other invasions came. The Persians under Darius the Great took over, and their domination of Egypt lasted from 525 to 404 B.C., with the assistance of Greek mercenaries.
>
> They [Africans] returned in 343 B.C. to re-establish their rule, but again for only a relatively short duration. Alexander reached Egypt in 332 B.C. on his world- conquering rampage. But one of the greatest generals in the ancient world was also the Empress of Ethiopia. This was the formidable black Queen Candace, world famous as a military tactician and field commander. Legend has it that Alexander could not entertain even the possibility of having his world fame and unbroken chain of victories marred by risking a defeat, at last, by a woman. He halted his armies at the borders of Ethiopia and did not invade to meet the waiting black armies with their Queen in personal command.[15]

But Africans built other ancient empires in the west, east, central, and south of Africa and shown in Table 5 below.

Table 5: African Empires before European Encroachment in 1800

South, East, Central	West
The Great Zimbabwe	Ancient Ghana,
The Kongo	Kanem
The Zulu	Mali
	Songhay
	Hausa States
	Asante
	Ife and Benin

1830 and the Beginning of Politics for Africa

History 101 teaches us that Africa had ancient empires that were similar in characteristics to the kingdoms (regna) that succeeded the Old Roman Empire, but widely dissimilar in opportunities. However, according to Professor Basil Davidson, the renowned British historian and the world's leading expert on African historiography, "history stops for Africa in 1830; and after that it's politics."[16] Several significant reasons might have led Davidson to select 1830 as the end of history for Africa and the beginning of politics not by indigenous Africans but by Europeans. Perhaps the major reason was that the Abolition of the Slave Trade Act, passed in 1807, became legalized in 1833.[17] This period was followed by the intense and violent scramble for Africa leading to the partition and eventual colonization of Africa among the seven European countries in 1884,[18] the Boer War in South Africa (1899-1902),[19] the more than three decades of native Africans fighting to resist European encroachment, and the postindependence struggles that plunged Africa into deadly chaos, violence, and war. The year 1830 was also a good time to take stock of how Africans had come along in the history of humanity dated back to antiquity, medieval times, and the direct or indirect effects of the Italian Renaissance of the 1400s and the 400-year-long spell of the slave trade, when one part of the world was developing and another was destroying.

There is more than one way to evaluate the effects of the Abolition of the Slave Trade Act of 1833 on the world economy. For the Europeans, the Act destroyed 400 years (1440-1840) of trading in Africans as mere commodities and their access to free slave labor. But it cost the British government a fortune to stop the Atlantic slave trade. Apart from the vast public funds spent to stop the slave ships and their captains on the high seas by the Royal Navy, the British government paid huge compensations to slave owners. The Bishop of Exeter, for example, was paid 12,700 pounds for his 665 African slaves by the British government.[20] The reason for the scramble for lands in Africa by the imperialists was therefore not far-fetched; if they could no longer take the Africans as slaves, they could occupy their lands.

Another way to look at the situation was the loss of revenue to the African elites, kings, warlords, and rulers, who had benefited from the false wealth that resulted from the slave trade. Though there was abundant evidence to support the fact that the Africans resisted European encroachment, the battles were lost to conquest or promises of compensations. For their part, the Europeans—who believed they had come to own African land either through payments, compensations, conquests, or outright thieveries— claimed a justification to the occupation until the nationalists, mostly Western-trained and -educated young Africans, began political uprisings immediately after World War II.[21]

Understanding Violence in Postindependence Africa

Violence in postindependence Africa may never be understood except through attention to how the violence came to be in the first place. World leaders—and anyone for that matter, including the UN—who wants to work or labor for peace in Africa must shift their focus and perception beyond colonial Africa to a new Africa that is beyond colonial geographical boundaries. Until the planners begin to use a different demographic approach, one that will see not Nigerians, Ugandans, or Kenyans, but one that will plan for Africans in Nigeria, Africans in Uganda, and Africans in Kenya, we may never be able to overcome violence in Africa. One thing that this approach will help us to discover is that most of the problems encountered by one part of Africa are similar to those of another part. These problems can be regarded as the legacies of various empires:

- The legacies of the ancient empires
- The legacies of the slave trade empires
- The legacies of the colonial empires
- The legacies of the ethnic and language empires
- The legacies of the empire of religions
- The legacies of the empire of multinational organizations
- The legacies of corruption and social ills and their empires

Every one of the above named empires left their legacies and stamps on life in Africa and upon Africans. Let us consider two of those empires— the empires of the slave trade and the colonial empires. Remember that we are dealing with their legacies and by identifying their legacies, we can understand the impact they have on present situations in Africa.

The Legacies of Slave Trade Empires

The legacies of the slave trade can be examined in three different periods: before, during, and after. Or we can review the situation before, during, and after the abolition of the slave trade.

Before Abolition

In the 400 years (1400-1800 A.D.) that the Atlantic slave trade lasted, and coupled with the effect of the Arab slave trade connections, over forty million Africans were forced into slavery outside Africa.[22] Not everything that happened to Africans and Africa during this period can be represented in this work. One thing is common, however: Africa was denuded of able-bodied men and women who could have meant progress for the continent. Like the Assyrian wars that exiled the nobles and the intelligent and left the poor and the weak on the land, the same thing happened to Africa. Can you imagine that someone of the status and caliber of Leo Africanus (formerly known as Al-Hasan bin Muhammed al-Wazzan al-Fasi) was once sold into slavery, freed after baptism by Pope Leo X, and then com-missioned to put together a survey of his knowledge of the continent of Africa? He might have been the first chancellor of the African University at Timbuktu.[23]

Before abolition, therefore, Africans became mere commodities and chattels to be owned. They were traumatized. But most importantly, the slave trade gave an erroneous impression of wealth to the African elites, kings, and warlords.

The legacy today is that every African who came to power either through royal heritage, militarism, or politics, still exhibits the error of lining their pockets with public funds.

During Abolition

Though the Abolition of the Slave Trade Act was passed in the British Parliament in 1807, "British captains who were caught continuing the trade were fined 100 pounds for every slave found on board. However, this law did not stop the British slave trade. If slave ships were in danger of being captured by the British navy, captains often reduced the fines they had to pay by ordering the slaves to be thrown into the sea."[24] This was also a period referred to as "captured and recaptured." The slaves, who were captured from their native lands, were recaptured on the Atlantic Ocean by the British navy, which was patrolling and policing the slave routes. The recaptured slaves were deposited at designated places such as Freetown in Sierra Leone, founded in 1799 by the British as a land for freed slaves returning to Africa. Monrovia in Liberia was another depot from slave progenies arriving from the United States in 1820.[25] Short of being a refugee camp, the resettlement program was in itself a tedious event in the life of Africans. However, because these returning Africans had received Western education, they were soon incorporated into the nationalist movements for independence for their various countries.

After Abolition

After abolition of the slave trade, the freed Africans had to piece their lives together, but at a changed level that they still have not thoroughly mastered and may never master. For every one of them caught in the melee of slavery and euphoria of freedom, life had to start again as if in childhood but with the needs of adulthood. Since I did not live in that time, I cannot experience but only imagine the confusion in the atmosphere. Surely, it would have resembled the aftermath of Hurricane Katrina when the displaced had to be transported to distant lands and accommodated in Astrodomes. Fortunately, for some, they were quick to rehabilitate, trace, and reunite with their native kin; but they had to deal with their inner-borne hostilities for the kings and warlords who had sold them into slavery in the first place. The effect of these hostilities was realized down the road, some 100 years later, when the Western-trained freed slaves began to agitate for and claimed independence from the colonial masters.

The Legacies of Colonial Empires

The seeds for colonialism, racism, geopolitics, and African dictatorship were sown, cultivated, and grown in the years before and up to the twentieth century. The ripened fruits and bitter tastes were, however, reaped in the 100 years between 1900 and 2000 A.D.

Basil Davidson, writing in his book *The Black Man's Burden—Africa and the Curse of the Nation-State*, captured the whole colonial experience like this:

> The whole great European project in Africa, which stretched over more than a hundred years, was questionable and futile; it constituted a vast obstacle thrust across every reasonable avenue of African progress out of preliterate and pre-scientific societies into the "modern world." It achieved the reverse of what occurred in Japan made aware of the need to "catch up with the West." It taught that nothing useful could develop without denying Africa's past and without a ruthless severing from Africa's roots and it encouraged a slavish acceptance of models drawn from entirely different histories.[26]

The adverse effects of colonization lingered on before and after independence in the 1960s. Loss of self-rule and self-respect, racism, a victim mentality, and divide-and-rule were common abuses of colonialism. Because the African's labor was so cheap, he or she became so disoriented and noncommitted that his or her nonchalant attitude was unfortunately mistaken for laziness. Tax revenue was introduced in colonial Africa for two reasons: to meet public administrative expenses and to force the "lazy" African to work in the Europeans' plantations to earn income to pay the tax imposed; otherwise, his/her livestock would be confiscated to pay the taxes.

The postindependence adverse effects are what we are still grappling with today in Africa. Independence, instead of producing national leaders, often produced ethnic saviors and tribal warlords. When the struggle for independence became so intense that colonial masters were faced with imminent release from governing their African empires, they considered returning the lands to the traditional rulers from whom they took the lands in the first place. But the Western-educated would have nothing to do with that idea; having been selected, they did not want to be neglected or rejected. They used their literate prowess to outwit the illiterate kings and rulers. The new political leaders, bent on reaping the fruits of their labors, threw all caution to the winds and instead of leading were dealing with their new countries. Within the first ten years of attaining independence, all African Free States had fallen into the hands of military rulers, trained by erstwhile colonial masters, who in turn became their puppets. Unlike Alexander the Great, who came, saw, and conquered, the young military rulers in Africa came, saw, and plundered and practiced not only "divide and rule," but "divide and destroy." The aftermath was the youth indiscipline within the military brass that multiplied coups, insurgencies, and rebellions all over Africa, not for national cohesion but for corrupt gains and ethnic supremacy.[27]

Colonial Legacies and Barriers to Regional Peace and Cohesive Economic Development

Barriers to regional peace and cohesive economic development in the twenty-first century can be traced to prehistory times, the medieval period, the Renaissance, modern and postmodern eras, and even the fledging globalization. Before looking at these barriers, let us take a look at the Empires of the seven European countries that colonized Africa (Table 6).

Table 6: European Empires in Africa and Dates of Independence

French African Empires			
Country	Date of Ind.	Country	Date of Ind.
Algeria	1962	Gabon	1960
Benin	1960	Guinea	1958
Burkina Faso	1960	Madagascar	1960
Cameroon	1960	Mali	1960
Central A. Rep	1960	Mauritania	1960
Chad	1960	Morocco	1956
Comoros	1975	Niger	1960
Rep of Congo	1960	Senegal	1960
Cote D'Ivoire	1960	Togo	1960
Djibouti	1977	Tunisia	1960

German African Empires	
Country	Date of Ind.
Namibia (1920)	1920
Tanzania (1961)	1961
Zanzibar (1963)	1963
Co-ruled by Britain and now part of Tanzania	

British African Empires			
Country	Date of Ind.	Country	Date of Ind.
Botswana	1966	Seychelles	1976
Egypt	1922	Sierra Leone	1961
Cameroon	1960	Somalia	1960
Eritrea	1952	South Africa	1961
The Gambia	1965	Sudan	1956
Ghana	1957	Swaziland	1968
Kenya	1963	Tanzania	1961
Lesotho	1966	Uganda	1962
Malawi	1964	Zambia	1964
Mauritius	1968	Zanzibar	1963
Nigeria	1960	Zimbabwe	1980

Portuguese African Empires	
Country	Date of Ind.
Angola	1975
Cape Verde	1975
Mozambique	1975
Sao Tome and Principe	1975

Belgian African Empires	
Country	Date of Ind.
Burundi	1962
Congo DR (former Zaire)	1960
Rwanda	1962

Italian African Empires	
Country	Date of Ind.
Eritrea	1941
Claimed by Ethiopia	1993
Libya	1943
Allied Administration	1951
Somalia	1960
Co-ruled with Britain	1960

Spanish African Empires	
Country	Date of Ind.
Western Sahara	1976
Equatorial Guinea	1968

For convenience of analysis, discussion in this section will be limited to the colonial legacies. I will use the case of the Economic Community of West African States (ECOWAS), founded in 1975, as an illustration.

"Before the coming of Europeans," wrote Adebayo Adedeji, "West Africa had been the home of some of the most remarkable achievements of early black civilizations, with such illustrious empires as Songhay, Mali, Ghana, the Sokoto caliphate, Benin, and Oyo."[28] However, by the time of the African partition in 1884, sixteen distinct countries had evolved from those ancient empires. Four of those countries became British colonies, and they now speak English as their official language. The remaining twelve countries became French colonies, and they now speak French as their official language. Adedeji mentioned that the need to integrate the West African region was first discussed at the "fifth pan-African congress held in Manchester, England, in October 1945."[29] But after the dismantling of colonialism, when the integration of West Africa was brought up again for discussion in 1972, "Senegal's Leopold Senghor and Guinea's Sekou Toure were at opposite ends of the integration spectrum."[30] Senghor was reported as saying that before Francophone West African states could cooperate with their Anglophone counterparts, two conditions must be satisfied: (1) West Africans must be fluent in both French and English, and (2) the West African subregion must be extended geographically to Kinshasa to bring the Democratic Republic of the Congo (then called Zaire) into the proposed economic community. Adedeji explained, "Like France, Senegal has never been able to hide its fear of a strong Nigeria dominating West Africa. Senghor's idea of including Zaire in ECOWAS was an attempt to balance Nigeria's strength."[31]

Nonetheless, the formation of ECOWAS went ahead and the economic community was established in 1975, but today the community is weakened and in disarray. In 2000 it was reported that with the backing of the French government, the eight Francophone West African countries established their own economic community, named Union Monetaire Ouest Africaine (UEMOA), and that the community was "being hailed in the West as the most impressive cooperation entity yet seen in Africa."

Why did I use this story? It can be seen from the illustration above that several barriers are actually militating against regional peace and cohesion in Africa. Here we can see the effect of the unfinished business of colonialism, language impediments, inability to outgrow past differences, regional and communal conflicts, shaky foundations for independence, fear of domination, lack of trust, military implications, and external influences. As it was for the subregion, so it is for the subsectors and subcultures of individual countries in Africa.

Overcoming the Empire of Languages

It is true that Africans speak thousands of languages and dialects. In the opinion of this writer, the language problem is the easiest to overcome by Africans if the leaders and the people are serious. Language is a barrier that Africans can easily overcome within a span of thirty years. Before the occupation by the Europeans, some threads of language linked almost the entire African continent. The major language families[32] are Afro-Asiatic, Austronesian, Indo-European, Khoisan, Niger-Congo, and Nilo-Saharan. Another language pattern presents itself for easy adoption by Africans. It can be seen from Table 6—European African Empires—that the French and the British colonized the major parts of Africa, with their colonies grouped closer to one another.

For example, of the sixteen countries in West Africa, only four speak English; the official language of the rest is French. Similarly, in East, Central, South, and North Africa, except for pockets of Arabic, Portuguese, and Italian, the larger former British colonies speak English as their official language. President Leopold Senghor of Senegal spotted this possibility and called attention to it when ECOWAS was being founded. If that call had been heeded at that time, thirty years ago, it might have been possible to have overcome the language barrier in Africa by now. It is not too late anyway. African leaders can adopt a policy where every child of five will learn two languages at school, French and English. This will in no way affect the Africans' mother tongues; it might even strengthen them.

In his thesis and forty-course curriculum for the structured peace education, Oyeyemi included a course that can accommodate this possibility.[33]

Making a Case for Equipping a New African Peacebuilding

Many commentators on African conflicts, violence, and wars are quick to point to lack of leadership, illiteracy rates, and underdevelopment as some of the causes of unpeace in Africa. Most of the trained peacemakers or peace workers who are coming from the Western world think that if they can train new leaders, increase the literacy rate, and help to promote development, the violence will go away. This approach has not worked in the past, is not working in the present, and it may not work in the future. This writer believes that a deliberate effort has to be made to deal with the fundamental sources of conflict, violence, and wars in Africa. Those fundamental sources are described here as empires. Like someone going up against an empire, everything that makes the empire a stronghold must be understood in order to pull down the stronghold. The empires that will be listed here are what sustain strongholds of violence in Africa. They need to be dismantled if peace is to reign supreme in Africa:

- the ancient empires
- the slave trade empires
- colonial empires
- regional empires
- ethnic and language empires
- the empire of religions
- the empire of multinational organizations
- empires of corruption and social ills

The Structured Education for Peace

History and other social subjects or courses that threaten the above empires in their course of study tell stories, interpret stories, and usually leave the readers to form their own judgments or develop their own opinions. Those courses or subjects are taught mostly for knowledge but not with a view to propose or recommend solutions. Similarly, most recent and contemporary investigative reports identify the problems but when it comes to offering a solution, they do it in such a blanket form that it is difficult to assign responsibility or allocate resources that can be easily accounted for by anyone. Many reports are written in high academic language that the middle actors who actually need to know and use them cannot because they do not understand them. At the other extreme, most of those reports are good for research only and when not in use gather dust on the shelves. The time has come to invest in a peace education that will reach down to the grassroots. Serious thought must be given as to how the plans for action can become the common property of the overall public.

A structured education for peace, as envisaged by this writer and being promoted by African Projects for Peace and Love Initiatives (APPLI), employs both the historic and contemporary knowledge and uses them to develop appropriate solutions that could empower the Africans for action by proactively preventing the repetition of those events that had led to unpeace experiences in the past. The structured education for peace is designed to address cognitive issues at various levels—African past, present, and future—by applying religion, sociology, philosophy, psychology, peacebuilding praxis, and sufficient dosages of economics, political, and environmental studies.

In designing and developing structured education for peace, we gave consideration to the fact that every subculture of the African grassroots community must be educated in the art of peacebuilding. For this reason, different parts of the structured education for peace are age-related: beginning from the kindergarten to the postsecondary educational level. Individuals who wish to become professional peace workers or who are interested in making a career in peacebuilding can follow a set pattern of training and become proficient in peacebuilding.

In their March 2005 report entitled *Our Common Interest*,[34] the Commission for Africa, set up by British Prime Minister Tony Blair, gave the following reasons why preventing violence in Africa would be better than intervention:

- The right to life and security is the most basic of human rights. Without increased investment in conflict prevention, Africa will not make the rapid acceleration in development that its people seek. Investing in development is itself an investment in peace and security, but there is much more that should be done directly to strengthen conflict prevention.

- Violent conflict has killed and displaced more in Africa than in any other continent in recent decades. [This writer has come up with a statistic that shows that over 17,000,000 Africans have been killed by war-related violence since 1950.] This has driven poverty and exclusion, undermined growth and development, and deprived many of their right to life, liberty, and security as enshrined in Article 3 of the Universal Declaration of Human Rights.

- Violent conflict causes huge human suffering and denies many Africans their most basic rights to life and security.

- Violent conflict and insecurity undermine development. It increases poverty; reduces growth, trade, and investment; and destroys vital infrastructure and human capital through death, injury, and displacement. Violent conflict encourages high levels of military expenditure, diverting resources away from development.

- Violent conflicts, once sparked, can create intractable and ongoing tensions that are very difficult to resolve.

- Reacting to conflict is more expensive for the international community than preventing it. If the international community reacts to a crisis, it tends to be through deployment of peacekeepers or humanitarian assistance.

For these reasons, it can be seen that the time is ripe for a considerable investment to be made directly in proactive peacebuilding and conflict prevention. With adequate support, the proactive peacebuilding projects of APPLI could contribute tremendous progress toward conflict prevention in Africa.

Sociocultural Adjustment Program and the Call for Change

Culture drives, determines, or shapes the lifestyles of people all over the world. Pope John Paul IV, in his speech to the Fiftieth General Assembly of the United Nations on October 5, 1995, explained that "different cultures are but different ways of facing the question of the meaning of personal existence."[35] This in a way explains the individual human rights to life and security. Africans—individual, group, community, and ethnic— ought to cultivate a new lifestyle by making some sociocultural adjustments that will promote grassroots peacebuilding. A deliberate and systematic approach must be engaged that will strategize meaningful efforts to achieve this goal.

As good as any education can be, it cannot be sufficiently good unless the educated decide to pursue what is good with his or her good education. There is no doubt that a large population of Africa is not well educated, but those who are well educated are in sufficient numbers to lead the continent out of decadence. Instead of adjusting socioculturally and encouraging others to do so, several educated Africans would rather Anglicize or Francicize, holding in derision their African heritage.

As with the educated biblical Moses, meaningful liberation may never come to Africa unless the educated Africans are prepared to till the soil with the tillers, plant the seed with the planters, and reap the crop with the reapers. This is both a principle and a metaphor. Let the educated assume the responsibilities of mentoring the people. Let them show the tiller how to till better, the planter how to plant better, and the reaper how to reap better. Let them show the masses that they can be trusted with responsibility and counted upon for honesty and accountability. Let them replace their rogue's mentality with a growth mentality. Let them overcome religious bigotry and ethnic dichotomy. Let the rulers rule and let the leaders lead. What Africans need to develop is character, not conflicts. Who will wake Africa up from its slumber? Who will give Africa the new spirit of peacebuilding?

Conclusion

Africa needs new, visionary teachers. Those who can look back and figure out what went wrong in the past, look at the present and see what is going wrong, stave their hands at what is at stake, visualize the future, and navigate the journey ahead. New leaders like Moses, who in spite of having spent forty years enjoying the pleasures of the palace, knew no freedom until his people were freed. Those who, like the biblical patriarchs, first go to the wilderness to learn enough wisdom to liberate their own people. Africa needs transformational leaders who can midwife development and progress through positive and peaceful changes. As a part of his vision for Africa as the Future Land of Peace, Oyeyemi penned a poem, part of which reads:

Let Africa arise now with the rising of the sun
Like the parts of a body, let the tribes unite and function together ·
To give Africa meaning and purpose
For the future of Africa is precious,
Let's together cherish her presence.

We love Africa, We seek her future peace
Nations and tongues may differ, but we are all the same
With Peace and Love Africa will be great
We Love Africa, the Future Land of Peace.

Bibliography

Abdullah, I., and I. Rashid. "Rebel Movements." In *West Africa's Security Challenges—Building Peace in a Troubled Region*, edited by Adekeye Adebajo and Ismail Rashid. Boulder, London: Lynne Rienner Publishers, 2004.

Adedeji, A. "Ecowas: A Retrospective Journey." In *West Africa's Security Challenges—Building Peace in a Troubled Region*, edited by Adekeye Adebajo and Ismail Rashid. Boulder, London: Lynne Rienner Publishers, 2004.

Adeola, F., K. Y. Amoako, N. K. Baker, et al. *Our Common Interest—Report of the Commission for Africa*. 2005, pp. 157f.

BBC World Service. "The Story of Africa—Between World Wars (1914-1945)." http://www.bbc.co.uk/worldservice/africa/features/storyofafrica/index_section13.shtml (accessed October 3, 2005).

Davidson, B. *Let Freedom Come—African in Modern History*. New York: The Atlantic Little Brown, 1983.

Davidson, B. *The Black Man's Burden—Africa and the Curse of the Nation-State*. New York: Times Books, 1992.

1833 Abolition of Slavery Act . http://www.spartacus.schoolnet.co.uk/Lslavery33.htm (accessed October 25, 2005).

Eller, V. *War and Peace from Genesis to Revelation—King Jesus Manual of Arms for the Armless—Christian Peace Shelf Selection*. Scottsdale, PA, 1981.

Gopin, M. *Between Eden and Armageddon*. New York: Oxford University Press, 2000.

Guestbook. *Anglo Boer War Museum*. http://www.anglo-boer.co.za (accessed October 25, 2005).

James, G. C. M. *Stolen Legacy*. USA: African American Images, 1954, reprinted 2001.

Koeller, D. W. *Liberia Is Founded by Freed Slaves 1821*. http://www.thenagain. info/WebChron//Africa/Liberia.html (1996-1999).

"Leo Africanus." From Wikipedia, the free encyclopedia. http://en.wikipedia.org/ wiki/Leo_Africanus (accessed October 28, 2005).

Okumu, W. A. J. *The African Renaissance*. Asmara, Eritrea: Africa World Press. 2002.

Oyeyemi, T. K. *Equipping the New African Peacebuilder—Curriculum for Structured Education for Peace* (unpublished, 2004).

Pope John Paul II, "Speech to the Fiftieth General Assembly of the United Nations, New York, October 5, 1995." http://www.catholic.net/RCC/hsmission/speech.html (accessed October 25, 2005).

Procopius. *History of the Wars*, IV, ix, trans. H. B. Dewing. New York: C. P. Putnam's Sons, 1916: 279-83. In the Internet Medieval Source Book. http://www.fordham.edu/halsall/basis/proco-anec.html (accessed October 25, 2005).

Williams, C. *The Destruction of Black Civilization—Great Issues of a Race from 4500 B.C. to 2000 A.D.* Chicago, IL: Third World Press, 1987.

Notes

1. James 4:1.
2. Vernard Eller, *War and Peace from Genesis to Revelation—King Jesus Manual of Arms for the Armless* (Scottsdale, PA: *Christian Peace Shelf Selection*, 1981).
3. Marc Gopin, *Between Eden and Armageddon* (New York: Oxford University Press, 2000).
4. Procopius, *History of the Wars*, IV, ix, written 534 A.D., translated by H. B. Dewing (New York: C.P. Putnam's Sons, 1916), 279-283. In the Internet Medieval Source Book, http://www.fordham.edu/halsall/basis/proco-anec. html (accessed October 25, 2005).
5. Chancellor Williams, *The Destruction of Black Civilization—Great Issues of a Race from 4500 B.C. to 2000 A.D.* (Chicago, IL: Third World Press, 1987).
6. George G. M. James, *Stolen Legacy* (USA: African American Images, 1954, reprinted 2001).
7. Williams, *The Destruction of Black Civilization* (see n. 5), p.67.
8. Ibid., p. 61.
9. Ibid.
10. James, *Stolen Legacy* (see n. 6), p. 14.
11. Ibid., p. 131.
12. Ibid., pp. 445-46.
13. Ibid., p. 46.
14. Williams, *The Destruction of Black Civilization* (see n. 5), p. 118.

15. Ibid.

16. Basil Davidson, *Let Freedom Come—African in Modern History* (New York: The Atlantic Monthly / Little Brown, 1983).

17. *1833 Abolition of Slavery Act* , http://www.spartacus.schoolnet.co.uk/Lslavery33.htm (accessed October 25, 2005).

18. *The Scramble for Africa,* http://purpleplanetmedia.com/bhp/pages/scramble.html (accessed October 25, 2005).

19. Ibid.

20. *1833 Abolition of Slavery Act* (see n. 17).

21. BBC World Service, "The Story of Africa—Between World Wars (1914-1945),"http://www.bbc.co.uk/worldservice/africa/features/storyofafrica/index_section13.shtml (accessed October 3, 2005).

22. W. A. J. Okumu, *The African Renaissance* (Asmara, Eritrea: Africa World Press, 2002), 22.

23. "Leo Africanus," Wikipedia, the free encyclopedia, http://en.wikipedia.org/wiki/Leo_Africanus (accessed October 28, 2005).

24. *1833 Abolition of Slavery Act* (see n. 17).

25. D. W. Koeller, *Liberia is Founded By Freed Slaves 1821,* http://www.thenagain.info/WebChron//Africa/Liberia.html (1996-1999).

26. Basil Davidson, *The Black Man's Burden—Africa and the Curse of the Nation-State* (New York: Times Books, 1992).

27. See Ibrahim Abdullah and Ismail Rashid, "Rebel Movements," in *West Africa's Security Challenges – Building Peace in a Troubled Region,* ed. Adekeye Adebajo and Ismail Rashid (Boulder, London: Lynne Rienner Publishers, 2004).

28. Adebayo Adedeji, "Ecowas: A Retrospective Journey" in *West Africa's Security Challenges—Building Peace in a Troubled Region,* ed. Adekeye Adebajo and Ismail Rashid (Boulder, London: Lynne Rienner Publishers, 2004), 21.

29. Ibid, p. 22.

30. Ibid, p. 29.

31. Ibid.

32. "Languages and Religion," http://www.africanculturalcenter.org/5_3languages_religion.html, October 3, 2005.

33. T. K. Oyeyemi, *Equipping the African Peacebuilder – Curriculum for Structured Education for Peace* (unpublished, 2004).

34. F. Adeola, K. Y. Amoako, N. K. Baker, et al., *Our Common Interest—Report of the Commission for Africa,* 2005, pp. 157f.

35. Pope John Paul II Speech to the Fiftieth General Assembly of the United Nations Organizations, New York, October 5, 1995. http://www.catholic.net/RCC/hsmission/speech.html (accessed October 28, 2005).

TWENTY

Narratives of Ufulu: Pan-Africanist Autobiography and the Global Peace and Justice Movement

Steve Sharra

Introduction

This chapter discusses four autobiographical and biographical accounts that create an unexplored confluence of currents that involve African and African American struggles against global injustice. That confluence contributes a hitherto little studied Pan-Africanist perspective to the discourse of the global peace and justice movement. The chapter starts with the autobiography of Masauko Chipembere and an account of his education in the then Nyasaland (now Malawi), the then Southern Rhodesia (now Zimbabwe), and at Fort Hare University College. Fort Hare has a history inspired by African American struggles for racial justice in the United States of the late 1800s to the 1900s, a connection that also ties John Chilembwe, a Malawian anticolonial and antiracist pioneer, to W. E. B. DuBois, Ghana's Kwame Nkrumah, Kanyama Chiume, and Masauko Chipembere. This chapter explores the linkages among these personalities and the Pan-Africanist goals they pursued for "Ufulu," the Chichewa word for self-rule/independence/freedom. The linkages connect the African continent to North America, covering Malawi, South Africa, the United States, and Ghana. The chapter closes with a consideration of the relevance of Pan-Africanism to ongoing struggles for people of African descent in Africa and the Diaspora. This chapter is fashioned in the spirit of Pan-Africanist contributions to the global peace and justice movement, as pioneered by W. E. B. DuBois at the start of the twentieth century, and kept alive today through the work of Bill Sutherland, Matt Meyer, and Elavie Ndura-Ouédraogo, among other scholars. This present volume, a sequel to Matt Meyer's and Elavie Ndura-Ouédraogo's 2009 volume, is a continuation of that spirit.

Pan-Africanist Auto/Biography

Two autobiographical accounts, and one biographical account, addressing Malawi's struggle for independence from British colonialism, embed Malawian narratives into Pan-Africanist conceptualizations of peace and justice as they relate to anticolonial struggles. Henry Masauko Chipembere's (2001) autobiography *Hero of the Nation: The Autobiography of Henry Masauko Chipembere*, was published posthumously, edited and introduced by Robert Rotberg, after Chipembere's death in 1975 in the United States.[1] Kanyama Chiume's *Autobiography* (1982) was published at the height of the Malawi dictatorship from which he had fled in 1964.[2] Chiume returned to Malawi in 1994, after the demise of the dictatorship and the introduction of multiparty politics. He died on November 21, 2007, in New York, a day before his 78th birthday.

But the story of the struggle for Malawi's independence from colonialism goes back to the beginning of the twentieth century. A biography of John Chilembwe and his 1915 uprising describes Chilembwe's inspiration for racial justice from his collaboration with African American preachers, in a background strongly influenced by the scholarship and activism of W. E. B. DuBois, among others.[3] DuBois's long life saw him take part in the formative stages of Ghana's independence as the first sub-Saharan African country to liberate itself from British colonial rule.[4] The struggle for independence from colonial rule in many African countries is explored in this study for purposes of exploring Pan-Africanist contributions to the global justice movement. It is one of many struggles against historical and global injustices visited upon Third World peoples.

Both Chipembere and Chiume foreground their educational experiences in different parts of southern and eastern African, demonstrating how their education opened up for them avenues for articulating the evils of European colonialism. They both obtained university degrees, in South Africa and Uganda, respectively, in the mid-1950s, and returned to Malawi where they became actively involved in the efforts to secure independence for Malawi. Of particular note was how their education equipped them to join the struggle for freedom and justice for their people.

In South Africa and Uganda respectively, Chipembere and Chiume went to college together with a generation of other Africans who also went on to take up leadership positions in their countries' struggles. Thus the struggle against colonial injustice in other parts of Africa was tied to the struggle against apartheid in South Africa, in which a minority settler regime imposed itself on the majority African population and made them second-class citizens on their own land. These struggles on the continent of Africa were themselves tied to larger struggles waged by people of African descent especially in the Americas as well as in Europe, where they formed an important Diasporic formation.

An Education for Emancipation and Consciousness: Henry Masauko Chipembere

Hero of the Nation (2002) is Chipembere's first-person narration of his life, from birth through the intense period of the struggle for Malawi's independence. Chipembere died before he could finish his autobiography. Despite providing several flash forwards going beyond Malawi's independence and his exile in the United States in the seventies, Chipembere's narrative structurally ends in 1959, leaving out the vigor and intensity of the next five years leading up to Malawi's independence in 1964. Nevertheless, Dr. Rotberg has included eleven speeches Chipembere made, including the one he made on September 9, 1964, with which he announced his resignation from the cabinet during what became known as the Cabinet Crisis, barely two months after independence on July 6.

As autobiography, the writings examined in this study and the lives of antiracist and anticolonial struggles merge the arbitrary distinctions that divide the various movements formed by people of African descent around the world to fight for justice both at the local level as well as the global. Their stories, both ordinary and extraordinary, resonate with the lives of many people of African descent who have to deal with many of the social, cultural, political, and personal contexts of identity formation and redefinition that these autobiographical accounts detail. They are accounts that raise questions about characterizations of Black and African identities, the role of education, the type of education, Pan-African cultures and traditions in the shaping of individuals. They defy representations of Blacks as passive or complicit in the colonial project. They depict Africans taking on the forces of racism, imperialism and colonization to carve out a future for African countries and people of African descent around the world.

While Chipembere writes with simple, straightforward prose, his narrative has buried underneath it a powerful unraveling of conscientization, the building of a political consciousness that interrogates race at a time when the white British colonial administration and the missionary establishment had taken over local control. Chipembere's application of his academic training was far from the transmission model where, as Paulo Freire cautioned, knowledge is seen as being poured into the passive mind of a pupil.[5]

At the age of 14, Chipembere was sent to a boarding school, Malosa Full Primary School, in the year 1944. During that time he witnessed the transplanting of British conservative ideals of elitism among the African Christians brought by Anglican missionaries, who propagated a Britain-is-best attitude. Boys returning home from Malosa carried with them that elitism, dressing and behaving in manners taken after their British teachers. At home, their families gave them the royal treatment, not allowing them to help in the farms or do menial domestic chores, which was seen as taking away from their dignity. "They were now *azungu* (whites), and therefore superior."[6]

Coming very early on in the autobiography, the choice by Chipembere to present this observation in such racially conscious terms points to his growing awareness of the white supremacist culture that had taken hold in the society in which he was growing up. Looking back at the hard work his teachers put into their teaching at Malosa, he hypothesized that the missionaries, in general, worked for the benefit of the white cause, with the realization that "wherever the African students went, they would be working for the White man and helping him to make greater wealth or to rule Africa effectively."[7] Chipembere's use of the term "make greater wealth" can be read against standard claims that the colonial project was a humanitarian one, which left Africa better off than when the Europeans found it. Africa produced a lot of wealth for Europe, in a process that impoverished Africa and its prospects for a more prosperous future.[8] Whether Chipembere saw this during his student days at Malosa Primary or later in his reflections as he wrote his autobiography, the proliferation of poverty in postindependence Malawi makes Chipembere's observation more pertinent in today's Malawi, sub-Saharan Africa, and indeed in many parts of the global North and South, where wealth continues to be divided among the ruling classes and their inner circle. Whereas the wealth Africans created during the colonial times went to entrench a system that worked against their interests, today's wealth continues servicing international debt and lining the pockets of the ruling clique, to the continued impoverishment of ordinary people.

In 1948, Chipembere moved on to Blantyre Secondary School, established seven years earlier as an achievement of what Chipembere termed

"African nationalism."[9] The Nyasaland Native Association (NNA), a body formed in 1944 as the umbrella organization of various local and ethnic associations, made constant requests to the missionaries and the colonial administration to build the school. Chipembere's mention of the role of the NNA in the building of the school serves to demonstrate the pioneering role Africans had in defining their own destinies and making the best of a situation of struggle against foreign domination. That this role entailed exploiting opportunities made available by the missionary and colonial presence testifies to the entrepreneurial spirit of the Africans to blend their aspirations with those of the colonialists and forge new possibilities. This is not the same as saying that Africans consented to foreign rule and participated in their own oppression, as some scholars, working in a particular vein of postcolonial scholarship, have argued.

Chipembere's experiences at Blantyre Secondary School continue in the direction of a political consciousness about the British colonialists' racism against Africans. He describes the principal of the school, Geoffrey Tozah Pike, as an "imperialist" who "believed in the superiority of the British people."[10] Chipembere quotes Pike as often repeating the remark, "I was treated with respect everywhere because they realized that I was an Englishman." In expressing his annoyance at an individual student, Pike would use the words "an example of a typical African fool," while extending his ridicule to the entire African race. But as with all characterizations of people based on difference, Pike and his wife, also a teacher at the school, had their own contradictions. Pike's wife singled out Chipembere as different from the rest because of his ability to think hard, and Pike himself once attributed Chipembere's malaria-induced tendency to appear lost and in thought to too much intelligence, telling him: "Your trouble, Chipembere, is that you are very intelligent and like all intelligent people you think too much."[11] Chipembere is quick to add in his narrative that although he didn't accept that generous characterization later in life, it wrought wonders for him, giving him a huge morale boost at thinking of himself as in possession of a "superabundance of intelligence."

That colonialism had its humanizing moments can also be seen in Pike's uncharacteristic acquiescence in a potentially explosive situation in which Chipembere led a food boycott after the students suspected the boarding master, an African, of embezzling their food. Food rations at the school had been reduced, in large part due to a countrywide famine in 1949. However the British teachers also harbored the notion that the students were better fed at school than at home and went ahead with the decision to reduce the rations, believing the students would still be content. On the afternoon that Pike uncharacteristically listened to the students and promised to improve the food situation, the school was being visited by Arthur Creek Jones, the secretary of state for the colonies, widely known as a radical, pro-African cabinet minister for the ruling Labor Party in Britain. Chipembere remarks that Jones "was not the type of politician who could be allowed to see an angry African student food strike," a situation that could have led to Pike's removal from his position. Mr Pike exuded a conciliatory attitude that day, on account of his pro-African superior, yet another example of the inherent contradictions in the unfolding of the colonial project.[12]

The political education of Chipembere took different forms, from his primary school, secondary school, and up to his university days at Fort Hare in South Africa. At Goromonzi Secondary School in the then Southern Rhodesia, Zimbabwe today, where he went in 1950, he singles out the debating society as an entire form of education in itself. He was elected secretary of the society and was thus entrusted with the taking of notes, which necessitated close attention to everything that was said. The student body at Goromonzi was a hotbed for political consciousness, precipitated by the racism that had a turning point in the 1930 Land Apportionment Act, which had divided land into black and white areas. [13]A footnote at the bottom of the page states that in 1931, 50,000 white settlers controlled 48 million acres, while a million Africans were left to share 28 million acres.

Chipembere credits Gideon Mhlanga, an African teacher at Goromonzi, who he says played a big role in his political education, although at the time Mhlanga was considered moderate and elitist. Chipembere observes that what he learned from Mhlanga highlights the need for African youths to be taught by African teachers to the extent possible, while also noting that teachers from other cultures can provide a rewarding experience to students. From a pedagogical point of view, a healthy, sensitive balance between local teachers and those from other cultures and countries would go a long way in opening up young people's minds to pertinent local issues as well as global ones.

Chipembere also recounts an experience at Goromonzi that gave him the resolve as to what he would dedicate the rest of his life to. He was riding a bicycle one day when a white man with his wife demanded, in the local Shona language, that he remove his hat, as was the expectation of every white man upon meeting a black person. Chipembere didn't speak or understand the Shona language, whereupon the man started beating him up with his walking stick. Chipembere describes the experience as a baptism with fire. "I was now convinced that the White man in Africa hated and despised Africans and wanted to perpetuate a relationship of master and serf between himself and black people. I resolved I was going to dedicate my life to the destruction of white domination and the achievement of self rule by the African people."[14]

Chipembere entered Fort Hare University College in South Africa in 1952, where he further credits higher education with equipping him and other Africans with the intellectual energy and leadership to fight the racist white settler regime in southern Africa. His curriculum at Fort Hare was heavy on political philosophy, including Plato, Aristotle, Machiavelli, Locke, Rousseau, Voltaire, Hegel, John Stuart Mill, and Marx and Engels. Marx and Engels's *The Communist Manifesto* was required reading right in the first year. This was also a time of great political agitation against racist rule in South Africa, and Chipembere became actively involved in local student politics.

In addition to the academic curriculum he underwent at Fort Hare, Chipembere also presents a brief history of how the university came into being. He writes that Fort Hare was established in 1916, due to the pioneering efforts John Tengo Jabavu, an African leader who was inspired by the African American educator and leader Booker T. Washington. It was South Africa's first university built for African students, who were denied a university education in the existing white institutions. The inspiration for the establishment of Fort Hare University makes a pertinent connection between the aspirations of African peoples on the continent and those of African people outside the continent. With Chipembere's education at Fort Hare, the binding ties are cast even wider to underscore the intertwining of the fates of African peoples on and outside the continent.

Where it is not too clear what specific curriculum content and pedagogy triggered Chipembere's anticolonial and antiracist struggle starting in primary school, a number of factors can be extrapolated from his narrative. His general experiences growing up as a missionary child, his teachers at Fort Hare, the curriculum, and a politically heightened atmosphere and awareness in South Africa all combined to further strengthen his resolve. That his missionary upbringing served the opposite purpose of radicalizing his beliefs in the eyes of his father and the British missionaries is another example of the contradictions and inconsistencies of effects and consequences inherent in the colonial enterprise. Bidding farewell to Chipembere in prison in 1961, an Anglican missionary, Bishop Thorne, took responsibility, while regretting it at the same time, for how Chipembere turned out. Bishop Thorne was the one missionary Chipembere says knew more than any other missionary and who was held in the same esteem as the governor of the protectorate. He was also considered a good friend of Chipembere's father. Having paid for some of his education, the bishop, Chipembere believes, was aware of Chipembere's highly developed political consciousness and how the church's role as a partner in the colonial administration had influenced Chipembere against white settler rule.

A reading of Chipembere's focus on the growth of his racial and political consciousness and his awareness of the evils of colonialism is central to understanding the medium of autobiography and the insights it allows into the formation of his Pan-Africanist consciousness. Chipembere is faithful at recounting specific details of acts of racial prejudice perpetrated by whites against blacks, showing how his devotion to the fight for self-rule was strengthened with each specific incident.

One would expect the racialist dimensions of the political scene to be resolved by the coming on the scene of a respected Malawian and nationalist, Dr. Hastings Kamuzu Banda, who later became the country's first postindependence leader. However Chipembere's autobiography demonstrates how Kamuzu's own racialized views of black Malawians catalyzed a breakdown of the momentum achieved at independence, leading to what became known as the Cabinet Crisis of 1964, three months into independence. The consequences of this breakdown reverberated across the efforts built by other Pan-Africanist leaders elsewhere on the continent to make independence from colonialism meaningful for all Africans, as had been the vision of Kwame Nkrumah.

John Chilembwe and the 1915 Uprising

Chipembere avoids romanticizing an otherwise bitter philosophical disagreement between Booker T. Washington and other African Americans, most notably W. E. B. DuBois, who saw Washington's nonresistance approach to racism in America as effective only to an extent. But the African intellectuals Chipembere met and admired at Fort Hare themselves had ties to African American intellectuals, whom they actually met in their various journeys.

The inspiration coming out the era of Washington and DuBois also provides other layers of Pan-Africanist connections working in conjunction with other European and Americans who supported the liberatory efforts of Africans in Africa and in the Diaspora. Some of the names associated with Fort Hare from its early days in the early 1900s had shared synergies with African Americans, such as John Dube. According to Nelson Mandela in his autobiography, *Long Walk to Freedom*, Dube was a black South African who became the first president of the African National Congress when it was formed in 1912.[15] At the turn of the century, Dube visited the United States and made acquaintances with African American leaders and pastors. At that very time, a Malawian who would later become a pastor and also an antiracist and anticolonial leader, was also in the United States. That Malawian was John Chilembwe, whose story is chronicled in a biography first published in 1958.[16]

According to Shepperson and Price, John Chilembwe met with John Dube in Virginia, in the United States, at a time when African Americans were experiencing reversals in their civil rights earned following the American Civil War and emancipation from slavery.

Chilembwe was taken to the United States by Rev. Joseph Booth, a British pastor who had come to South Africa, and later to Nyasaland, to throw in his lot with the Africans in their struggle against colonial occupation. Chilembwe worked for Booth as a young boy, eventually helping pay for his passage to Virginia where he enrolled at Virginia Theological Seminary, an African American Baptist seminary in Lynchburg, Virginia. Chilembwe established his own connections with African Americans, and when he returned to Nyasaland after his pastoral training in Virginia, a number of African American ministers followed him.

Shepperson and Price write that Chilembwe experienced the full force of racism in America. At one time he had stones thrown at him by white youth when they saw him and Booth walking together. Chilembwe witnessed the disenfranchisement and denial of civil rights to African Americans in Virginia and other states. They write he also witnessed lynchings and other kinds of racist violence routinely visited upon black people in America. No record is known as to what Chilembwe read and studied in America, but Shepperson and Price point out that Chilembwe could not have remained unaware of what African American scholars and writers such as W. E. B. DuBois were writing and publishing, "with the aim of boosting the racial consciousness and pride of the Negro."[17] Chilembwe continued receiving publications from his African American compatriots when he returned to Nyasaland.

Shepperson and Price write that at the time Booth and Chilembwe arrived in America, "a wider movement of cultural nationalism," known then as Pan-Africanism as it is still known today, was gaining momentum. More than a century later, the definition of Pan-Africanism has changed little. At that time, Pan Africanism was understood, in Shepperson and Price's words, as "an attempt to find the general elements in the problems of Negroes of all countries, and to remedy them through multi-national Negro action." They quote W. E. B. DuBois as having said in 1897 that if "the Negro were to be a factor in the world's history, it would be through a Pan-Negro movement."[18]

Chilembwe's three-year stay in America, building close alliances with African American leaders in person and through their writings, must have contributed to Chilembwe's own sense of the racial oppression black people suffered both in Africa and in the Diaspora. He must have read about slave revolts, of which Virginia had more than a fair share, according to Shepperson and Price. As he was leaving Africa to come to America, Chilembwe's family and compatriots had asked him to find out how the long-gone sons and daughters of the continent, whom they knew had been taken from the continent during the slave trade, were faring.

When Chilembwe returned to Nyasaland, he used his sermons to preach about racial equality and self-determination. The British colonial administration was in the habit of enlisting Africans to fight in British wars. In some wars, Africans from the region were made to fight against other Africans, as in the Ashanti War of 1900 and in British campaigns in Somaliland around the same time. African soldiers were also enlisted to fight alongside the British in World War I, which Chilembwe protested bitterly, to the point of leading an armed rebellion, which came to be known as the Chilembwe Uprising of 1915. This was in addition to other grievances Africans had against their treatment at the hand of the British colonial settlers. Chilembwe's role in the struggle for social justice for Africans in Africa, the alliance and support of African Americans in this pursuit, completes a circuit in which a Pan-Africanist consciousness offers an approach for addressing problems of injustice affecting people of African descent in Africa and in the Diaspora.

DuBois, Pan-Africanism, and the Global Peace Movement of the Early 1900s

The development of a Pan-Africanist consciousness as an intellectual approach to addressing problems facing people of African descent owes a great deal to the scholarship and activist work of W. E. B. DuBois. DuBois combined a Pan-Africanist perspective to a peace philosophy that connected the quest of Africa's independence to people of African descent and Third World solidarity. For DuBois, the struggles of African peoples on the continent and in the Diapora were the struggles of Third World people around the world, united in their experience of European racism and colonialism. In 1923, DuBois wrote in an edition of *The Crisis*, a magazine he edited:

> Peace today, if it means anything, means the stopping of the slaughter of the weaker by the stronger in the name of Christianity and culture. The modern lust for land and slaves in Africa,

Asia, and the South Seas is the greatest and almost the only cause of war between the so-called civilized peoples.[19]

DuBois put the same amounts of energies into the global peace movement as well as into Pan-Africanism. In a paper titled "Work for Peace," in his *The Autobiography of W. E. B. DuBois*, DuBois starts off by looking back to how he became interested in the study of Africa. By the time of his generation, toward the end of the nineteenth century, the acquaintance of African Americans with Africa was neither through the direct presence of Africans who had been born in Africa and had been enslaved and brought to the Americas, nor through the passing on of the knowledge to children of former slaves. DuBois writes of "much distaste and recoil" about Africa among African Americans, "because of what the white world had taught them about the Dark Continent. There arose resentment that a group like ours, born and bred in the United States for centuries, should be regarded as Africans at all."[20] His own grandfather was "particularly bitter about this." DuBois says his interest in Africa was by "logical deduction," which he describes in the following terms:

> I was tired of finding in newspapers, textbooks and history, fulsome lauding of white folk, and either no mention of dark peoples, or mention in disparaging and apologetic phrase. I made up my mind that it must be true that Africa had a history and a destiny, and that one of my jobs was to disinter this unknown past, and help make certain a splendid future. Along this line I did, over a stretch of years, a great deal of reading, writing, research, and planning.[21]

DuBois's dedication to issues of global peace included his participation in the Cultural and Scientific Conference for World Peace, which took place in New York City in March 1949, the World Congress of the Defenders of Peace in Paris in 1950, and the formation of the Peace Information Center. DuBois even campaigned for a U.S. Senate seat for New York in 1950, on the American Labor Party ticket, as a peace candidate. His participation in the campaign, which he lost, was quickly followed by an indictment from the U.S. Department of Justice against the Peace Information Center as well as DuBois himself. He was arrested and charged with the alleged crime of being an agent of a foreign government. The trial attracted worldwide attention and condemnation against the U.S. government, and after a protracted trial process lasting nine months, the judge threw the case out, and DuBois and his colleagues in the Peace Information Center were freed.

By the time DuBois was working in the global peace movement, his dedication to Pan-Africanism was several decades old. It included organizing and participating in the Pan-African Congresses, the first of which took place in 1919. Four more congresses would be convened, leading up to 1957 when DuBois symbolically handed over the torch of Pan-Africanism from the Diaspora to the mother continent. The occasion was the crowning of Ghana's independence, which, ironically, DuBois failed to attend. His passport had been impounded by the U.S. government. However, DuBois wrote a letter to Nkrumah, in which he passed on the torch of Pan-Africanism to Nkrumah, to Ghana, and to Africa.

Ghana And Pan-Africanism in Malawi: Kanyama Chiume

At the point that Ghana was achieving its independence in 1957, Malawi's own struggle was heating up. The confluence comes full circle with the autobiographies under study here, illuminating connections and influences from DuBois, Chilembwe and Jabavu at the turn of the twentieth century, to Malawi's own independence in 1964. Woven into the fabric of the narratives are stories that construct a Pan-Africanist trail that passes through Malawi, South Africa, the United States, and Ghana, among other nations.

Chilembwe's 1915 Uprising planted the seeds for a yearning to break free from colonialism, and throughout the following decades Africans kept searching for ways to liberate themselves from racial oppression and injustice. Upon finishing his university education in Fort Hare, Chipembere picked up from where Chilembwe and others had left off and took Malawi's struggle for independence to new heights. Ghana's president Kwame Nkrumah and his articulation of Pan-Africanism were to become important elements in Malawi's eventual triumph over colonial rule.

Dr. Hastings Kamuzu Banda, Malawi's first president, spent a good part of the 1950s in Kumasi, Ghana, where he became very close to Dr. Nkrumah. They had first known each other in London, where Dr. Banda had been practicing medicine. Dr. Nkrumah would eventually become actively engaged in Malawi's own struggle for independence from the British. Kanyama Chiume's autobiography gives an elaborate and inspiring account of the support Malawians received from many Africans on the continent, particularly from Nkrumah and Ghana.

In his *Autobiography*, Chiume describes a visit he made to London in 1959, as part of ongoing moves to source financial and material resources to aid Malawi's independence efforts. Upon learning of his presence, Nkrumah sent £100 to help in the work Chiume was doing in London.

Nkrumah followed up on that offer with an air ticket to Chiume so that on leaving London, Chiume should fly directly to Ghana to continue strategizing and mobilizing resources to aid Malawi's freedom struggle. In Ghana, Chiume was given a triumphant welcome and "was carried shoulder high amidst shouts and placards to the effect that a Nyasalander murdered is a Ghanaian dead."[22]

And more support from Nkrumah and Ghana was yet to come when Kanyama met with Nkrumah:

> When I saw Nkrumah personally he was most vehement in his denunciation of imperialism in Nyasaland. Since the Devlin Commission had already been appointed, and we were determined to defend our colleagues in detention, he offered £10,000 to cover the defence costs. In addition, he placed at our disposal the services of an able Ghanaian lawyer, Mills Odoi, to accompany whoever we chose to go to Central Africa for the purpose.[23]

When Chiume met Nkrumah again in early 1964, Nkrumah could not have been more forthright and passionate about the significance of Pan-Africanism:

> Nkrumah talked about the urgent need for an All-African government. "Many of our troubles, Chiume," he emphasized, "are due to the fact that we are not united. We must have a continental government to prevent the further balkanization of Africa and, as far I am concerned, when Malawi is finally free and only seven of us are ready, we should just plunge into it. Others will follow."[24]

In the self-government days running up to full independence in 1964, Kanyama Chiume held the external affairs portfolio. This enabled him to travel widely in his capacity as cabinet minister, a position from which he never failed to advocate for Malawi, and Africa and Pan-Africa. More than any other Malawian politician, with the exception of Masauko Chipembere, Chiume had a deeper understanding of the role Pan-Africanism was playing in the emancipation of Africans on the continent and in the Diaspora. He toured the United States in 1963, and his entourage successfully arranged for a meeting with Reverend Dr. Martin Luther King, Jr. However, King had to cancel at the last minute and without prior warning, going to Louisiana to attend to an urgent matter. They requested a meeting with President John F. Kennedy and his brother Robert Kennedy, but were unable to meet them. They were, however, able to meet with Dr. Ralph Bunche, the 1950 Nobel

Peace laureate, the first person of color to ever win the Nobel Peace Prize. Chiume's stay in America emboldened his Pan-Africanist outlook, at once observing the racist society Black Americans lived in, and the effects that racism had on their identity struggles. Chiume wrote:

> But the majority were treated as though America was not their real home, and they were made to believe that they had no past, no heritage and no history. His African forebears were presented to him as savages who had sold him into slavery. He was discouraged from finding his identity in Africa and yet the struggle he was waging in his adopted country was basically the same struggle that his African brothers were waging. While Africa remained in bondage, I felt, so would the Afro-American remain oppressed in the USA. His real hope for the future lay in him discovering who he was. The black scholar must help rewrite Africa's history, and the black educationalist must impart the truth about our great continent. In this renaissance the Afro-American and the African must work together.[25]

Chiume made sure to bring this message back home from the United States, but he was doubtful if Dr. Banda, who himself had spent many years going to school in the United States, shared this worldview. Dr. Banda was far more interested in consolidating his political relationship with white colonialists in Southern Africa, including the Portuguese in next-door Mocambique, and in South Africa. This incensed Malawi's neighbors, including Tanzania's Julius Nyerere and Zambia's Kenneth Kaunda, who agreed with Chiume and the other Malawian cabinet ministers that Banda's liaisons with settler colonies in the region was a betrayal of the struggles the Africans in these countries were fighting against their oppressors. The differences between Dr. Banda and his cabinet ministers grew and became irreconcilable three months after Malawi officially got its independence in 1964. Over the years, Chiume would acquire the unenviable accolade of being Dr. Banda's "Enemy Number One."

Conclusion

DuBois's scholarly and activist work merged Pan-Africanist consciousness and the global peace movement. The liberation of African and other Third World countries from European colonialism was a major step in ending the racial aspect of global injustice. New forms of racial injustice have sprouted, aided by the financial and economic control that rich countries have on African and other Third World countries. The old struggles against colonialism served their purposes at the time, but the spirit of Pan-Africanism met obstacles that prevented it from asserting its relevance in a postcolonial context. Yet, the kind of consciousness that Pan-Africanism promoted is equally relevant today, as Paul Zeleza (2007) writes in a recent keynote address:

> It is becoming increasingly clear, or it ought to, to African policy makers and intellectuals that the Diaspora and Pan-Africanism may constitute the most reliable vehicles for enhancing Africa's presence in the world system. The Pan-Africanism of the twenty-first century must take the Diaspora option seriously, which requires devising creative strategies for knowledge and skill circulation, the formation of national, regional, and continental knowledge networks that facilitate brain mobility, from academic exchanges to consultancies and temporary return migrations, to the transmission of information and vigorously defending Africa which is routinely defamed in Euroamerica with little social cost. In short, the Diaspora, both the historic and contemporary, constitutes Africa's eyes and ears in the world, the interpreter of the world to Africa and Africa to the world. It is indispensable to the globalization of Africa and the Africanization of globalization.[26]

The autobiographical and biographical experiences of Africans and African Americans discussed in this chapter capture important epochs in the endeavors of people of African descent to determine their destiny. It is important to note the role that the education of Chipembere, Chiume, and other leaders played in shaping their Pan-Africanist worldview. That worldview has never been adequately reflected in the curriculum and educational policy in our schools today, with the result of the loss, for good or for worse, of the lessons that Pan-Africanism taught us. For the seeds to bear sweet, ripened fruit, there is no better place to cultivate than the school curriculum and teacher education programs.

Through these narrative accounts, we begin to consider how the major struggles of people of African descent contribute Pan-Africanist concepts of peace and justice to the global peace and justice movement, which is bedeviled, according to Marvin Berlowitz, by dominant Eurocentric biases.[27] A major development in the Pan-Africanist contributions to the movement has recently come from Bill Sutherland and Matt Meyer[28] and Matt Meyer and Elavie Ndura-Ouédraogo.[29] The narratives help us see how the yearning for world peace has a global constituency and how the lived experiences of Africans and African Americans are an important narrative of that constituency.

319

Notes

1. Henry Masauko Chipembere, *Hero of the Nation: Chipembere of Malawi: An Autobiography*, ed. Robert Rotberg (Blantyre, Malawi: Christian Literature Association of Malawi, 2001).

2. Kanyama Chiume, *Autobiography of Kanyama Chiume* (London: Panaf Books, 1982).

3. George Shepperson and Thomas Price, *Independent African: John Chilembwe and the Nyasaland Rising of 1915* (Edinburgh: Edinburgh University Press, 1958).

4. W. E. B. DuBois, *The Autobiography of W. E. B. DuBois: A Soliloquy on Viewing My Life from the Last Century of Its First Decade* (New York: International Publishers, 1968).

5. Paulo Freire, *Pedagogy of the Oppressed* (Continuum: New York, 1970).

6. Chipembere, *Hero of the Nation*, 81.

7. Chipembere, *Hero of the Nation*, 85.

8. Walter Rodney, *How Europe Underdeveloped Africa* (Washington, DC: Howard University Press, 1971). See also Joseph Inikori, *Africans and the Industrial revolution in England: A Study in International Trade and Economic Development* (Cambridge/New York: Cambridge University Press, 2002).

9. Chipembere, *Hero of the Nation*, 87.

10. Ibid., p. 88.

11. Ibid., p. 91.

12. See Simon Gikandi, *Maps of Englishness: Writing Identity in the Culture of Colonialism* (New York: Columbia University Press, 1996).

13. Chipembere, *Hero of the Nation*, p. 98.

14. Ibid., p. 105.

15. Nelson Mandela, *Long Walk to Freedom: The Autobiography of Nelson Mandela* (London: Abacus, 1994), 742.

16. George Shepperson and Thomas Price, *Independent African*.

17. Ibid., p. 102.

18. Ibid., p. 103.

19. DuBois, *The Autobiography of W.E.B. DuBois*, p. 348.

20. Ibid., p. 343.

21. Ibid., p. 343.

22. Kanyama Chiume, *Autobiography of Kanyama Chiume*, p. 122.

23. Ibid., p. 122.

24. Ibid., p., 167.

25. Ibid., p. 163.

26. Paul Tiyambe Zeleza, The Contemporary Relevance of Pan-Africanism. http://zeleza.com/blogging/u-s-affairs/contemporary-relevance-pan-africanism. Keynote address, *Launch of the Kwame Nkrumah Chair in*

African Studies, Institute of African Studies, University of Ghana, Legon, September 21, 2007.

27. Marvin Berlowitz, "Eurocentric Contradictions in Peace Studies," *Peace Review 14, 1 (2002): 61-65.*

28. Bill Sutherland and Matt Meyer, *Guns and Gandhi in Africa: Pan African Insights on Nonviolence, Armed Struggle and Liberation in Africa* (Trenton, NJ/Amara, Eritrea: Africa World Press, 2000).

29. Matt Meyer and Elavie Ndura-Ouédraogo, *Seeds of New Hope: Pan-African Peace Studies for the Twenty-First Century* (Trenton, NJ/ Asmara, Eritrea: Africa World Press, 2009).

TWENTY ONE

Gail M. Presbey

Security through Mutual Understanding and Coexistence or Military Might? Somali and U.S. Perspectives

Introduction

During the last two decades, Somalis have seen their country ravaged by internal wars and external aggressors. To a large extent, religiously and ethnically homogenous (with small ethnic minorities of Somali Bantu and Sudanese Somalis), Somalia was nevertheless ravaged by internal divisions based on clan affiliation during the 1990s.

The struggle for control of national government was the rationale for United Nations forces to intervene in 1993. U.S. Admiral Jonathan Howe drew UN forces into combat when he became embroiled in taking sides while trying to fix the outcome of the power struggle. This resulted in the notorious "Day of the Rangers," when over 1,000 Somalis and eighteen U.S. service personnel were killed. Shortly afterward, the U.S. pulled its troops out of Somalia. The deteriorating situation led many Somalis to leave their country, settling in the Dadaab refugee camp just across the border in Kenya.

This chapter spans two decades of Somalia's recent troubles. It will try to grasp what went wrong with the military approach to Somalia's problems during the 1990s, drawing on Mark Bowden's extensive interviews with both Somalis and U.S. military personnel related in his study, *Black Hawk Down*. The chapter will try to clarify a distorted picture of the situation given in the U.S. media and in the film version of *Black Hawk Down*. It will then contrast this military perspective with the work for conflict resolution and peace education at the Dadaab refugee camp. Here I will draw on interviews I conducted with refugees during 1999 as part of a study done in cooperation with the Office of the United Nations High Commissioner for Refugees (UNHCR) on behalf of CARE International of Kenya, the nongovernmental agency in charge of running the camp. I found that many Somalis had significant insights into the problems of their country. They only lacked a way to catapult their wise leaders into positions of power where they could enact sane and constructive policies. Just as with Bowden's book, listening to the voices of Somalis is the source of key ideas needed to solve their problems.

The chapter ends with an update to recent events in Somalia, especially during the last couple of years. Once again, Somali voices have gone unheeded and the United States has intervened through its proxy, Ethiopia, in a way that shows they do not understand the situation on the ground in Somalia. Somalis are still suffering because of this misunderstanding. At the heart of this problem is a U.S. foreign policy that is short sighted in its goals of protecting its own position of global dominance and ignoring real security that comes with citizens of their respective countries having basic needs met, democratic control of their governments, and demilitarization.

Bowden's *Black Hawk Down*

Mark Bowden's book, containing extensive interviews with both Somalis and U.S. service members stationed in Somalia sheds light on the political situation that came to a head on October 3, 1993, known as the "Day of the Rangers." The central Somali government had come undone, and various faction leaders were each taking military arms to lay claim to the whole country. It certainly was a humanitarian crisis. The problem was how to intervene in a way that saved lives and did not exacerbate the problem. The United Nations called for troops and U.S. Admiral Jonathan Howe was put in charge. However, the U.S. personnel apparently lacked the understanding of the Somali context needed to help the situation.

The service members and their commanders had grossly underestimated the enemy. U.S. forces went into the heart of General Mohamed Farrah Aidid's support area in Mogadishu in broad daylight, presuming they could accomplish their mission of catching Omar Salad and Mohamad Hassan Awale within a couple of hours. But going into a crowded area of a city where people were still very heavily armed (considering the civil war still in progress) caused Somalis to want to fight the intruding Americans. Their being under attack and outnumbered caused the U.S. service members to quickly discard the rules of war; they began to shoot at anyone, even into crowds.[1] Black Hawk and Little Bird helicopters armed with automatic weapons shot into crowds overhead, turning these crowds within minutes into "a bleeding heap of dead and injured."[2] In less than twenty-four hours, eighteen U.S. service members and 500 to 1,000 Somalis had been killed to abduct the two lieutenants. The president and other military officials bemoaned the fact that the price had been too high. But which price? One gets the distinct impression that the "high price" refers to the eighteen U.S. service members and not the more numerous Somali deaths.

Bowden's book is intended to educate the reader, who is presumably in the same shoes as the Rangers: "None of the men . . . knew enough to write a high school chapter about Somalia. They took the army's line without hesitation. Warlords had so ravaged the nation battling among themselves that their people were starving to death."[3] U.S. forces were supposed to be in Somalia on a peacekeeping mission for the UN. They got involved in trying to arrest General Aidid's top ranking military men because Aidid had been opposed to the power-sharing plan the UN had for a postwar Somalia.[4] Indeed, the U.S. public's shock at the public display of the killed U.S. soldiers was due to their belief that the troops were there only to "feed the hungry," and they had not known that, since the Abdi House killings by U.S. troops on July 12, Aidid was "at war" with the U.S. In fact, before October 3, the U.S. had already conducted six missions or raids with mixed success.[5]

Mickey Kaus, drawing on Oakley's book, explains further why, by October 3, most Somalis were united behind Aidid and against the U.S. intervention. As he explains, the UN operations there happened in two phases. Phase I, mostly successful and very important, was an emergency feeding operation. At that point, troops were stationed there to oversee the food distribution process. But later, a Phase II "nation-building" project began. The UN wanted to oversee a power-sharing version of national unity in Somalia, but Aidid felt that since he had done the most conquering, he should be in power. Aidid and his SNA forces began to think that the UN opposed them in favor of Siad Barre's ethnic group, the Darod. These suspicions were reinforced when the UN closed down Aidid's anti-UN radio station, while allowing a rival, Ali Mahdi, to operate his station. When twenty-four Pakistani UN troops showed up to "inspect" the radio station, Aidid loyalists suspected them of foul play and killed them. The UN, concerned about discouraging the precedent of attacking UN peacekeeping troops, decided to launch a manhunt in search of Aidid and his leaders.[6]

However, Bowden reported an earlier tragic incident that most surely played a role in Somali reluctance to cooperate with the U.S. and the UN. On July 12, 1993, fifty to seventy clan elders and intellectuals, who had met at Abdi House to discuss Howe's peace initiative, were killed when the venue of the meeting was bombed. Bowden includes the testimony of Mohamad Hassan Farah, who witnessed sixteen TOW missiles (capable of piercing the armor of a tank) being fired at the building.[7] He also reports that Howe said that only twenty people were killed and all had been in Aidid's military leadership. Thus, the UN and Somali accounts had vast discrepancies.[8] (The massacre was also covered by *Washington Post* reporter Keith Richburg.)[9] Targeting Aidid loyalists may have increased the perception, cited by Farah, that the U.S. was against Aidid and the Habr Gidr clan and was favoring a rival clan, the Darod, from which the former leader Siad Barre hailed.[10] With such perceptions running rampant, asking an embattled clan to accept the help of a group that has been bombing their leaders was difficult at best.

In 1993, the U.S. considered its military response to be a grave error—a failure. It resulted in the forced resignation of top military officials. However, Bowden did not want this story to be buried. He pieced together the story of the battle and put a new spin on it, one that the U.S. military did not dare: he decided that the men involved were unsung heroes and should be a source of pride for the nation. He wrote a series of stories for the *Philadelphia Inquirer*, put together a website and documentary video, and created a best-selling book, *Black Hawk Down: A Story of Modern War*.[11] That account has become a top draw at movie theaters with director Ridley Scott's film production based on the book.

How do the U.S. service members come out looking like heroes, after blatantly discarding the "rules of war" by shooting indiscrimately? Three main factors in the book and film contribute to this spin. First is the focus on the solidarity that soldiers have with each other; this is presented to civilians as a model for their behavior. Second, the Somalis are described as subhuman animals, living in a city that has not yet seen "civilization." Descriptions seemingly right out of Joseph Conrad's *Heart of Darkness* make it difficult for viewers to empathize with Somalis who are hurt or killed, since they are encouraged instead to take the U.S. point of view and to empathize with the threat that the service members felt. Third, the reasons for the U.S. presence in general and action in particular either are not mentioned or are presented as justified and righteous. Somali society is presented as so chaotic and distasteful that viewers can only imagine that the Somalis should submit to U.S. or UN rule rather than to attempt self-rule.

Bowden's epilogue causes us to question his claimed "neutrality." While he states critically that the U.S. should not have taken sides (against Aidid) in the civil war, he argues that once the U.S. had decided to get involved, it should have seen its project through to the end.[12] He notes that many service members were disappointed that they could not have stayed and finished the battle for Somalia's next government.[13] Bowden claims that he wrote the book for these American soldiers.[14]

Bowden also concludes with harsh words for Somalia. He thinks that the UN forces were there as an effort to help Somalia rebuild a unified national government. By fighting with U.S. forces (and targeting Pakistani forces on June 5, 1993, also part of the UN team[15]), Somalis rejected outside help without being able to resolve their problems on their own. He argues, "without natural resources, strategic advantage, or even potentially lucrative markets for world goods, Somalia is unlikely soon to recapture the opportunity for peace and rebuilding afforded by UNOSOM (United Nations Operation in Somalia). Rightly or wrongly, they stand as an enduring symbol of Third World ingratitude and intractability . . . they've effectively written themselves off the map."[16] Bowden falls short of saying what the Somalis did was "wrong" in a moral sense, but he judges them as shortsighted and far from pragmatic, missing their golden opportunity.

While Bowden calls the Somali death toll "catastrophic," it is not in the context of condemning the U.S. troops for discarding rules of war and causing the high casualties. One gets the impression that discarding such rules is one of the things about war that cannot be changed, a lesson that the young Rangers finally learn by experiencing a real war. Rather, he makes the remark in the context of calling Somalia's victory against the U.S. forces "hollow," almost as if it is the fault of Somalis themselves that their death toll was so high. Aidid could have been spared these casualties if only he had cooperated with the UN plan from the beginning.[17] No wonder the military loves this book. When the pilot, Durant, makes a comment on videotape during his captivity that things "have gone wrong" in Somalia because too many innocents were killed, he later felt bad about saying it and wished he had not.[18]

Bowden, nevertheless, does history a great service by going to the area soon after that fateful day to collect Somali testimony. He notes that he and photographer Peter Tobias were the only two Americans who ever came back to Mogadishu to piece together the story. He encouraged at-first reluctant Somalis to cooperate with his investigation by arguing that in this way, their story would reach a wider audience,[19] Bowden claims that the book is meant to represent both sides; when he represents the U.S. service members' views that the Somalis are diminutive humans, he is careful to note that the descriptions are how they were perceived and not necessarily how they really are. But the scenes in the book where Somali eyewitness accounts are reported are all missing from the film. We can only regret that the film did not use the material from Somalis in creating a more multisided perspective on the military engagement.

Some Somali perspectives in the book describe those who were going about their daily business and were then interrupted by the sudden outbreak of U.S. gunfire. In the case of Kassim Sheik Mohamad, his garage was bombed and his employees killed. Mohamad and others tried to bury the dead by the end of the day, according to Islamic practice, but U.S. helicopters routinely scoured the local cemetery near Mogadishu to shoot at them.[20] Ali Hassan Mohamad saw the Rangers as "cruel men who wore body armor and strapped their weapons to their chests and when they came at night they painted their faces to look fierce."[21] After witnessing the Rangers kill his brother, Mohamad decides he must take up arms and fight the Rangers.

Some Somalis recorded in the book are given a chance to reflect, sharing their ideas with the reader. Bashir Haji Yusef was educated in the U.S., so as he watched the fighting, he reminded himself that most Americans have no idea what their soldiers did abroad. In other words, he was able to sort out his angry condemnation of the soldiers' actions from a broader condemnation of all U.S. citizens.[22] But his reflection also challenges the reader, who is now learning of the actions of their armed forces. This is one of the rare passages where a Somali viewpoint is able to challenge, indirectly, the U.S. perspective. The book also highlights the tireless work of surgeon Abdi Mohamed Elmi. In the morning, his 500-bed hospital was mostly empty. By the end of the day, it was overflowing with the wounded, and Elmi had to perform surgeries one after the other with no time for rest.[23] In contrast, in the film, we never see Somalis past the second in which they are pierced with a bullet.

Some of the Somali testimony included in the book succeeds in blurring the "us-them" dichotomy temporarily. The book quickly mentions that friendly Somalis helped a crew of a crashed Black Hawk helicopter to escape.[24] The website photo page shows Yousuf Dahn Mo'Alim, who saved the pilot Durant from an angry mob and then was shot by U.S. gunfire.[25]

When Abdiaziz Ali Aden saw a Super Six One helicopter crash, nicking the corner of his roof, he was curious to see the U.S. soldiers emerge. But when he saw them, he concluded that they did not look human, since they were covered in body armor, goggles, and helmets.[26] So, while the Somalis were portrayed as subhuman and animal-like, the U.S. service members also lacked humanity, but because they merged with machine and armor. Somalis, when they got their hands on such U.S. soldiers, liked to unmask and de-armor them. For example, when they found the pilot Durant, they tore his clothes off, looking for concealed weapons.[27] That Somalis were able to commit cruel acts is also part of the story—not all were innocents. Hassan Yassin Abokoi saw a mob descend on U.S. service members who had been in a crashed helicopter. "He saw his neighbors hack at the bodies of the Americans with knives and begin to pull at their limbs. He then saw people running and parading with parts of the Americans' bodies," as if they were trophies.[28] Of course, there is also the infamous image of Black Hawk crew chief Bill Cleveland's corpse being dragged naked through the streets by a gloating crowd of Somalis.[29] Certainly, this glee about the dismemberment or the exposure of a dead body is deplorable. But the U.S. side also mutilated bodies, not with hand-held knives but with automatic weapons. Bowden describes how the Rangers laughed when one woman was shot so severely she "no longer even looked like a human being."[30]

In addition to valuable insights from the collections of interviews with Somalis that they collected, Bowden and Tobias also provide valuable insights from their candid interviews with U.S. service personnel. Reading the book, one notes that many U.S. servicemen are introduced to the reader first by a description of their looks. They are always muscular, the epitome of manhood. In a vain society such as ours, to possess bulging muscles is a sign of one's self-discipline and strength. The Somalis, on the other hand, are nicknamed by the U.S. service members as the "Skinnies," suggesting that their extreme thinness means that they are worthless.[31] The book also explains how U.S. service members note that Somalis do not work. "The people here, it seemed to Stuecker, just lounged, doing nothing, watching the world go by outside their shabby round rag huts and tin shacks. . ."[32] Indeed, the main event in town was lining up by the thousands to get handouts of free food from aid agencies. Knowing prevailing U.S. values, finding out that Somalis did not work and instead received aid, is a sure way to undermine their human dignity; they're the international version of "welfare scum." Bowden makes the service members' judgment clear: "they all felt sorry for the kids. For the adults they felt contempt."[33]

Just as U.S. civilians presume that welfare scum are "on drugs," so the book describes Somalis who chew *khat*, an amphetamine, which makes their teeth look black and orange and makes them "look savage, or deranged."[34] Never mind that the Somalis have suffered a long war with dire food shortages and that *khat* also numbs the pain of hunger and gives one energy to move when one is severely undernourished; all these signs of poverty and coping with hunger (thin bodies, dependence on food aid, and chewing *khat*) mark the distance between the young, strong, and well-fed "full" human beings and their diminutive "shadows."

The city of Mogadishu is also presented as a primitive, premodern city. Speculation in the book about how human life is even possible without running water, electricity, and an operating sewage system abounds. At the beginning of the book, before the Rangers descend, Bowden describes the city as "a catastrophe, the world capital of things-gone-completely-to-hell." Everything of value had already been looted, he notes. "Every open space was clotted with the dense makeshift villages of the disinherited."[35] Bowden said U.S. service members looked at Mogadishu and thought of the "Mad Max" movies, a land after the "end of world" run by armed gangs, and that they, the U.S. Armed Forces, represented the "civilized world" sent to straighten things out.[36] We later hear that retired U.S. Admiral Jonathan Howe, in charge of the UN mission in Mogadishu, said of Somalia, "Here was a country not just at ground zero, but *below* zero."[37] Of course, a place that is already "below zero" cannot sink further; if it has nothing, one does not have to worry about, or justify, destroying the last remnants. Anything would be an improvement.

The film tries to correct the one-sidedness of the comments found in the book about Somalis and Mogadishu. At the beginning of the film, a Somali arms merchant who sells guns to Aidid, named Atto, is captured and jailed at the U.S. base. You hear one soldier ask the other, "What do you think of him?" The soldier replies, "Urbane, sophisticated." That being the first U.S. description of a Somali in the film, the comparisons to *Heart of Darkness* that jump out from the book are muted or left unsaid; in a sense, they are "covered up," to make the film look more politically correct.

Americans often like to think of themselves as rooting for the underdog or giving credit to those who are trying hard. The Rangers and Delta Force crews' meeting with stiff resistance in the beginning makes them temporary underdogs. Soldiers in tough situations are helped by helicopters. The superior fighting power of the helicopters is demonstrated several times in the film by focusing on the cascade of empty bullet shells that falls from the helicopters as they hover overhead, sometimes showering the U.S. troops below. Later, when the Black Hawk is shot down, Bowden explains: "It was more than a helicopter crash. It cracked the task force's sense of righteous invulnerability."[38] Part of the story Bowden wants to tell is how the Rangers become human by feeling their vulnerability. He earlier described how Rangers had never been in real battle but only practiced and how they yearned to be in a real battle; but when they actually got to fight in Mogadishu, it was disorienting.[39] How much have they changed because of their experience? Even after the fighting, the men assert that it feels to them as if they had been in a movie that could not have been real.[40]

Ways in Which the Film Diverts from the Book's Message

The context during 2001-2002, in which it was decided that this book should become a film, is important to remember. The new post 9-11 context and the beginning war in Afghanistan made some Americans want to present the story to America.

Being the world's only remaining superpower after the demise of the Soviet Union, the United States has been trying to redefine its geopolitical position. Powerful military contractors lobby to ensure that the end of the Cold War does not mean the end of weapons procurement or military spending. No longer poised to fight against a mighty adversary, the U.S. now engages in wars with relatively small and weak countries. How does the U.S. avoid looking like a thug in such confrontations? Since 9-11, the answer is simple: the seemingly small, weak, secret terrorist groups around the world are portrayed as actually mighty and bent on grave destruction, requiring vigilance at home and abroad, an unlimited military budget, and U.S. troops, with far superior military technology on their side, are the poor, embattled "good guys" just trying to help others. A pattern of U.S. military adventures against small, impoverished nations had asserted itself long before 2001, including Vietnam, Grenada, Panama, Iraq, Somalia, and the bombings of Libya and Sudan. Since the pattern may continue, films like *Black Hawk Down* psychologically desensitize U.S. citizens to such endeavors so that their discomfort at being the global bully will be minimized.

A headline story in *U.S.A. Today* about the war in Afghanistan drew a direct parallel between the fighting in Afghanistan and the film *Black Hawk Down*. Reporter Jonathan Weisman ponders in the third paragraph of his article, "When the history of the war is written, the traumatic battle in the mountains around the Shah-e-Kot Valley will be remembered as a testament to heroism: A bloodied, outnumbered band of U.S. service members held off a determined al-Qaeda force on frigid rocky terrain at least 8,000 feet above sea level. Call it *Black Hawk Down* in the snow."[41] Why would a reporter so soon interrupt his recitation of the facts of the battle, to suggest to readers that they should project themselves to a point forward in history, where their judgment, mimicking the judgment of the film, will decide that today's U.S. casualties in Afghanistan were heroes? This reporter is not the first to suggest that the film has a message, not only about history, but also about the current U.S. war on terrorism. In its most general terms, the message is: support our troops and do not question the war's intent or methods.

The claim that the U.S. casualties at Shah-e-Kot were similar to those in *Black Hawk Down* is due in part to their helicopter being shot down. But in what sense were the troops "outnumbered"? There were twenty-one service members in the helicopter, who were fired upon once they were downed. Through use of mobile cameras mounted on aircraft, Pentagon officials say they saw "a large number of enemy forces" advancing on the crash site. Overall, the same article explains, several hundred al-Qaeda fighters opposed 2,000 U.S. and allied troops. The article also explains, "within minutes, Air Force F-15 and F-16 fighter bombers were on the scene, pounding al-Qaeda positions and trying to drive back the enemy." They were shortly joined by Air Force AC-130 gunships, equipped with Gatling guns and howitzers, "which can blast out as many as 1,888 rounds a minute." But the journalist's eye trains us on the movement of the dozen or so vulnerable U.S. service members, searching for safety behind rocks, because to focus on the larger overall imbalance of power (air surveillance, F-15 and F-16s, and AC-130s) might be disquieting; it would reveal the U.S. as international bully.

Having had a glimpse of the Pentagon Papers, we know that the U.S. government and the Pentagon are particularly concerned with the image the United States projects at home and abroad. To win a battle but lose the public relations spin on the battle would mean, in effect, losing the war.[42] The U.S. hires specialists in military propaganda to ensure that the war is seen from the point of view that the government promotes. One could hope that, with freedom of speech in America, journalists could ferret out the facts and unmask blatant propaganda. Certainly, some journalists are dedicated to doing so; but other journalists get swept up in the same patriotic fervor as the general public.

Film reviewer Neil Gabler notices how *Black Hawk Down* departs from earlier war films, such as those during World War II that emphasized that the U.S. had a clear moral imperative and those made about the Vietnam era when the moral cause evaporates. Instead, "The rangers' obligation is to one another—to make sure their friends and fellow troops survive . . . in *Black Hawk Down* the battle becomes the cause, and the cause is the individual. As one soldier in the film puts it: 'It's about the man next to you. That's it.'" He thinks the film reflects recent trends of accepting unquestioningly the authority of the government as it chooses its wars and causes.[43]

Just as Gray noted about his experience in World War II, the camaraderie between soldiers intensifies as they face danger together.[44] The intoxicating feeling of overcoming individual isolation and merging into a "team," a "fighting unit," is so overwhelming that service members often look back on such moments as the high points of their lives. In the book, Private Kurth goes through the same emotions in miniature, which the readers are encouraged to share. One minute he is thinking he is in hell on earth and is ready to quit the service; the next minute he wants to re-enlist, for as he says, "Where else am I going to get to do something like this?"[45] The quick-paced, ever-changing war scene gives excitement never to be found in the humdrum existence of middle-class American life or life in the barracks back home.

The film has been the subject of protests in New York City; the group A.N.S.W.E.R. (Act Now to Stop War and End Racism) argued that it presents the war as a "race war," and *Village Voice* film reviewer Geoffrey Gray notes that while there were only two African-American soldiers stationed in Somalia, the starkness of white U.S. soldiers fighting against Africans plays into Ridley Scott's racist film aesthetic.[46] The film depicts one African American soldier who is around while Eberhart, the commander of a small unit, explains that he is not sure he agrees that the U.S. should be fighting in this war and that he respects the Somalis. After Eberhart speaks, the African American solider accuses Eberhart of being a starry-eyed idealist and then quickly espouses some realpolitik. So how can it be a race war if the African American soldier is not critical, while only the starry-eyed white idealist is? The film does not address the role of racism on an international scale, although it is an aspect of the film that has impressed and stunned critics and viewers. Film reviewer David Brooks, however, cites a Somali viewer, Mohamad Ali Abdi, who argues that in the film, "the reality of the Somali character is captured," especially "the crazy way Somalis just kept on fighting."[47] If Abdi's statement is accurate, then it may be that the racism of the film has to do not so much with distortion of the scenario as it does with providing accurate, snapshot glimpses into that reality without providing the context in which those snapshots can be understood—for example, the motivation for Somalis to fight so fiercely against the U.S., especially when they were technologically overwhelmed.

Bowden never mentions that the unacceptability of the carnage (U.S. and Somali) is the lesson to be learned from the failure of the military involvement. Indeed, if the recent war in Afghanistan is an example of lessons learned and applied, it seems that the only lesson learned is that U.S. casualties must be minimized, not necessarily those on the other side. When Bowden explains, "What happened to these men in Mogadishu comes alive every time the U.S. considers sending young soldiers to serve American policy in remote and dangerous corners of the world,"[48] this makes clear that the Pentagon is only counting the loss of U.S. lives and not the overall loss of lives. On his website, Bowden explained to a reader,

"The reality of war ought to give the public and our leaders appropriate pause before risking the lives of American soldiers. . . . One reason I think troops were committed in Mogadishu was the heady feeling that followed the Gulf War, which looked nice and antiseptic on all those videos on CNN."[49] As Bowden explains, the Rangers were "shocked to find themselves bleeding on the dirt streets of an obscure African capital for a cause so unessential. . . ."[50] While the cause was supposedly the noble one of helping Somalia reconstitute its government, the cause was not important enough to justify loss of U.S. lives.

Kaus reports that the Rangers had accepted the fact that casualties are part of their job and were frustrated with Clinton for calling off the project. While mourning the loss of eighteen of their men, they considered the battle worthwhile because the *ratio* of casualties was favorable to the U.S. However, Kaus cautioned, "[w]ith such a favorable 'exchange ratio,' Phase II of the Somali mission was rapidly approaching destroy-the-village-in-order-to-save-it territory."[51] In a similar parallel, military officials describing the recent battle in Shah-e-Kot, Afghanistan, which resulted in seven U.S. deaths, were quick to note, "In the larger operation, the enemy death toll is far higher." They explained that forty to fifty al-Qaeda fighters besieging the downed Americans were killed.[52] The entire operation in Afghanistan has resulted in few U.S. casualties, while civilian Afghan casualties were estimated to be about 3,800.

Bowden argued that the battle shows the limits of what force can accomplish. For example, force alone could not install a democratic government in Somalia.[53] But if this is so, would not sending a different deployment to Somalia, a nonmilitary force, have been better? If people cannot be forced by gunpoint into living in peace with each other, what kind of help would be more helpful? Kaus argues that if Bowden deduced that military might alone would not bring the hoped-for democracy, then his advice that Clinton should have gone ahead and finished the plan to undermine Aidid's power would have been pointless—even its ultimate "success," at the price of more lives, would have been a failure.

Kaus notes that the film ends on a note of defeat. We see the caskets of the dead service members, and we get the distinct impression that nothing has been solved in Somalia.[54] Yet the film comes at a time when the U.S. government wants people to acquiesce or support the use of troops around the world to fight the war on terrorism. Gabler argues that the film will be seen as calling for renewed pride in U.S. forces and signals U.S. citizen's preparedness to see them engage in combat.[55] Rather than caution regarding jeopardizing the lives of U.S. service members (let alone noncombatants of other countries) as Bowden claims was his intention, the film may renew the commitment for U.S. intervention abroad and possibly in Somalia itself.

Insights of Refugees

Far away from the halls of Hollywood, Somali refugees have had their own experience of Somalia's troubles and their own insights into solutions. Not framed by the same issues of the U.S. projecting its image and maintaining respect and fearsomeness, Somalis are concerned about their country because they want to live in it. Just as Bowden's interviews with Somalis in Mogadishu after the "Day of the Rangers" are valuable, so also did I find great value in being able to converse with refugees who gave their unique perspectives.

With the help of Chaungo Barasa, Head of Water Engineering for CARE International–Kenya at the Dadaab refugee camp (himself a keen interviewer due to his experience in Odera Oruka's sage philosophy project in Kenya), I was able to interview sixteen refugees at Dadaab's three camps (Ifo, Dagahaley, and Hagadera) who were involved in peace education and other constructive endeavors at the camp. Interview topics included sources of conflict and solutions to conflict on interpersonal, refugee camp, national, and international levels. For these purposes, I will focus on their insights to solutions to their national problem, but I will also bring in the other categories as they are helpful to shed light on the national problem.

Causes

The Somali community has done a lot of reflection on what caused the war in Somalia. Hassan analyzed the situation as stemming from the perennial struggle of pastoral communities for grazing lands. In the past, communities might steal camels from each other; elders would be called in to negotiate and to suggest return of camels when necessary. Contemporary conflicts are graver because they involve struggle not for tangibles like camels, but for intangibles like power, advanced weapons, and desire for wealth. Competing warlords get people to fight along tribal lines, due to lack of education.

Yussuf continued this topic of how traditional struggles over grazing land and livestock formed a background for contemporary problems in Somalia. Uneducated people did not always respect their neighbor's requests, which could lead to conflict. He gave an example of a recurring situation, in which a family living near him had an odiferous dead cow or donkey. When he complained and asked the family to bury it, they said, "It does not concern you; we are going to beat you up, or we are going to detain you." He attributes such attitudes and ways of speaking to lack of education. Yussuf is worried about practices of tribalism resurfacing in Somali politics. He describes Somalia as "a big tribe which has divided itself." Somaliland, Gede, and Jubberland are divided tribally, each with their special diet, even though many immigrants may live there. Political parties go along tribal lines. He thinks that due to lack of education, war-lords do not understand how tribalism will hurt them. In his estimation, the elders were cooperating with the warlords, that the warlords had elders in their "pockets," and because of this, the elders were not filling their traditional role of passing wisdom to the next generation.

Abdullahi spoke at great length and with considerable depth about the problems of his country. He began by outlining what he considered to be four kinds of governments, based on scripture, colonial law, dictatorship, and democratic/ parliamentarian constitution. He wanted to focus on the problems of dictatorship. A dictator who unfairly rewards his loyal fol-lowing while oppressing others will inevitably become unpopular and be overthrown. But at the time of the overthrow, a new leader can either unify the country and take it to prosperity, or become a factional leader who divides people and encourages strife. He says that the latter happened in Somalia. Factional leaders encouraged looting of weapons and other goods as they encouraged their followers to fight other groups. Those who are unqualified to become leaders are nevertheless political opportunists who use weapons and fighting to grab power positions. As he explains, "The only thing the political leaders know now is how to use the gun against civilians." They put illiterate people in positions of power because they are easier to manipulate. In the mayhem, intellectuals and families fled from the strife. He thinks that educated people know the dangers of civil war and so would have been more careful.

Abdullahi complained about what he thought was international apathy toward the plight of Somalis. He said that leaders in the community who were in the camps were willing to work with international agencies, which were serious about helping Somalia. He further noted that when Somali intellectual leaders went to peace talks in Kenya, it was hard for them to understand the faction leaders. Often the faction leaders agree to work for peace, but later they do not implement the policies. Abdullahi noted that the faction leaders come to Somalia with funds and attract people to their movements because of funds. A solution would therefore involve defund-ing the faction leaders and funding alternatives based on international groups working with community leaders.

Amina described the struggles and frustrations of living in a refugee camp. While all human beings want security—their basic needs like food, shelter, and health—the refugees did not have these basic needs secured. Life is precarious and every day is a challenge. Refugees listen to the radio and are disheartened to hear that the fighting between clans is continuing in some areas. Asked about the cause of conflict in her country, she said, "The war-lords haven't understood the goodness of their people. . . The majority of Somalis, although many have died because of war . . . but the few remaining, the majority are women and children with no fathers, and children who are orphans, who miss their fathers and mothers. And they would all like to have peace in their country."

Amina further explained that the bad situation continued because old men who should be leaders had no money, so they could not attract the youth, who will fight for those who promise them riches. She is frustrated that sons will ignore the counsel of their mothers and join wars. In her own words, she said:

> The conflict is there in Somalia because of the war-lords; they still have not understood the goodness of their people, because each and every one of the war-lords wants to have power, wants to be the president of the country, and he does not want the others to be president. They are all selfish, each wants everything for himself. . .War-lords use publicity and often like to talk about tribal issues. In Somalia these war-lords are divided into tribes and clans. So war-lords usually use youth from their tribes and they attract them with something which youth like . . . they tell them, "we're fighting with the other tribe and they want to overtake our town, they want to do this to us, so we should fight with them." So that would be the tactic usually used. Old men who are supposed to be doing reconciliation and peace, now he has nothing, he is very poor back home in Somalia and here... all the resources are in the hands of the war-lords. The youth are with the war-lords because the war-lords are getting a lot of money [sic].[56]

Amina thinks that the solution to this problem is to have the international community help in cutting off the flow of weapons and funds to the warlords. We can see in her analysis an apt expression of the role of manipulation of ethnic and clan issues for personal gain and political power. The conflict is not really about ethnicity; tribalism is a ruse to get people motivated to fight.

Ethiopian refugees also reflected on the situation of their country. Bekele argued that in Ethiopia, tribalism and favoritism cause conflict.

People are not allowed to practice religion and morality as they wish. Abebe said that leaders are ambitious and will do anything to get a plot of land. Tsefaye reiterated, arguing that it is the same in Somalia; each warlord wants his personal benefit. He also opined that the U.S. Armed Forces being driven out of Somalia was unfortunate.

Some people emphasized the way in which people are misled to believe that they must hate enemies. Bekele said that wars begin when an ideology is imposed on people. Individuals may have independent ideas, but under peer and government pressure, persons will feel compelled either to hide their disagreement or change their views to fit the reigning ideology. The purpose of the ideology is always to be able to exploit some party. He gave the European colonizing of Africa and later the Cold War as examples of ideologies intended to exploit people. Tsefaye noted that the process of defining enemies begins very early. As children, they have been told that people from other countries are bad. This creates a predisposition that makes being manipulated to fight later easier. Hassan argued that the lack of education is the key cause of war since because of it people are easily manipulated.

Wani stated what is widely believed to be the case, that in both Sudan and Somalia, the leaders are dictators and they use their dictatorial powers to cause wars. But others noted that the cause of conflicts has to do not only with the perpetrators themselves, but also with the reluctance of others to get involved in helping to avoid the conflict or the inability of well-meaning parties to be effective in helping. Abebe bemoaned that the OAU was powerless to help resolve his and other countries' problems because leaders of government and rebel troops disregard its advice. Abdullahi went so far as to say that there is an "international conspiracy" to lose interest in Somalia's problems; he came to that conclusion because he noted that no country will help his country.

Solutions

Bekele explained bluntly that the greedy ones must go. Abdullahi argued that since the problems had economic roots, a solution would have to involve funds to compete with the faction leaders. Abdullahi said that the international community must finance peace because, he charged, right now they are the ones who are funding war. Whether factional leaders succeed depends on their finances, and they are getting their finances abroad. He argued that the supply of weapons to Somali factional leaders must be stopped. The international community must stop supplying weapons to faction leaders; community groups must employ youths so that they do not turn to faction leaders for survival.

Amina also asserted that the international community should stop giving weapons to the Somali warlords. In the meantime, while she is in the camp, she organizes with others to improve conditions in the camp. She is part of a security committee, organized with block leaders, to prevent any fights that might escalate. She also works to discourage practices of wife beating and to help families stay together because break-ups are hard on the children. She is also on the antirape committee, which helps victims get support from social services, hospitals, and the police. The committee also organizes women so that they can travel in groups to lessen their vulnerability when they gather firewood. Her insights into conflict and its solutions certainly conform to the motto, "Think globally, act locally."

Hassan argued that there should be education, which would help people to understand the causes of conflicts. Such education would be an important first step in being able to avoid or stop conflicts. Hassan is involved in peace education for children at the camp. He teaches children to understand the root causes of conflict, whatever the level. He explains, "What is the conflict? Are the people in the problem acting out their feelings, or are they hiding their feelings behind another argument...? What does each person in the conflict need? What is stopping them from getting what they need?" The goal of negotiations is for both sides to be happy with the outcome. Hassan explains that when one listens respectfully to the other in a conflict, emotional agitation may calm as they see they are being taken seriously. Hassan explains how these basics of conflict resolution intersect with Somali culture. He says it is part of Somali culture that when there is a conflict, others get involved. When children are in conflict, elders will step in. Traditionally, the parties brought in (for example, parents) would be highly agitated and aggrieved. Nevertheless, they would be motivated to seek redress. Under the current circumstances, however, it is a challenge for Hassan and others teaching conflict resolution to encourage parties to become calm in order to solve their problems.

Hassan explains that the peace education program at the camp has been promoting its views by teaching children peace songs, which have verses like: "We are fingers of one hand, come and join us in our quest for unity." There are songs the goal of which is mutual understanding among the different groups within Somalia and to undo ethnic and racial hatreds. Hassan also teaches the children peaceful games that do not use violence. There is also a need to address textbooks used in school that contain derogatory accounts of Somalia's neighbors. Hassan explains that based on his study of civics, he concluded that Ethiopians were "like wild animals which eat people"; but when he got to the camp, he found instead that "Ethiopians are absolutely very logical people, civilized and normal people, and now we are friends." He does not want the next generation to be subject to the same miseducation he had suffered.

While he teaches children at his camp, he sees the need for learning the lessons of creating peace, not only in the camp, but between nations and people, as for example between Palestinians and Israelis. As he explains, "peace is an international requirement."

Tsefaye pointed to the role of poets. He suggested that people compose verse to discourage people from fighting. He himself wanted to write a book; he thought that writing poetry and books would get the message of peace out to many people and have a good influence.

Analysis

Overall, the Somalis with whom I spoke saw their country's problem in a larger international and longer historical context than the usual focus on the immediate situation. They explain how different groups—the warlords, the intellectuals, the elders, the uneducated, the youth—all play different roles and together make up the Somali situation. Their solutions call for deeper understanding and deeper cooperation among all the stakeholders. The interviews include a wealth of information, which can be explored in depth and become the basis for future action to improve small communities as well as international relations.

Amina's insights are just one example of political wisdom. Focusing on questions of which companies or countries supply the weapons or the funds to buy the weapons, and then pressuring those sources to cut off their supply of weapons, would be a major step in de-escalating conflict in the area. A follow-up step would be to collect and destroy the guns already held by the general population, especially in war-torn areas. Control of arms proliferation is already an important project for the United Nations as well as NGOs. Since youth are attracted to join armed forces through promise of pay, or even just food, there is a need for alternative programs for youth, where they can be kept busy developing their skills in positive ways. Then the armies of the warlords would not look as alluring.

Quite a few of those interviewed emphasized the role of ideology—of governments or movements popularly picturing their enemies as inferior to themselves. Many media analysts and conflict resolution and peace studies advocates have explored this theme. Louis Kriesberg notes that our concept of self (individual or group) as superior or chosen by God can have the destructive tendency to harm others seen as inferior or evil.[57]

Michael Nagler, when trying to fathom the flare-up of ethnic tensions in Rwanda and the former Yugoslavia, often finds that just prior to a break-out of ethnic violence, one can find that some aspect of the media had been stirring up ethnic hatred in its news coverage, encouraging perceptions of the enemy as intolerable in some way. Nagler speculates that a key ingredient for a more peaceful world would be the media working to shed light on the sources of conflict and covering positive examples of when conflicts are solved.[58] He also echoes Hassan's insistence that much violence stems from ignorance. Nagler suggests that of the models that could be used to study and understand the causes of and solutions to violence, the one he finds most helpful is to understand violence as the result of ignorance, which can be lessened or abated by education.[59]

While refugees may come up with solutions and tactics already known by professionals who have written books, insights that come from their own communities and not just books are more likely to be accepted and implemented. Taking stock of the resources of those in one's own community is certainly the first step in improving conflict situations at whichever level they might occur, whether interpersonal or international.

Somalia as "Political Football" in Other Countries' Agendas

While one crucial aspect of Somalia's problems has to do with their negotiating their internal difficulties, Somalis have had an additional layer of problems from often being treated as a political football by larger countries with their own separate agendas, which do not have Somali thriving at the heart of their concerns. This problem goes back a long way. During the Cold War, Somalia was a client state of the Soviets, while the U.S. backed Haile Selassie in Ethiopia. But in 1975, when Haile Selassie was toppled by leftist Mengistu Haile Miriam, who then allied himself with the Soviets, the United States decided to court Somalia's Siad Barre. Military support kept Barre in power until 1991, when the U.S. withdrew its support after the fall of the Berlin Wall and Soviet power diminished. Barre was immediately overthrown by clan-based militias. During this entire Cold War period, it could be argued that Somalis were prevented from having a government that reflected their values and collective wishes.[60]

During the 1990s, there was factional fighting, and the United Nations got involved in trying to bring humanitarian aid and governmental stability (with the "Black Hawk Down" episode being just part of that years-long experience). General Aidid, and, upon his death in 1996, his son Hussein Aidid, struggled for dominance in the region. The Rahanweyn Resistance Army also fought for power and territory, capturing Bay and

Bakol in 1999. A peace conference held in Djibouti in 2000 created a Transitional National Government, formed in Ethiopia, while its base was in Baidoa. Somaliland seceded. A peace process in 2002 led to the formation of a Transitional Federal Government in 2004, led by Abdullahi Yusuf Ahmed.[61] But this TFG was experienced as ineffectual by many Somalis, who were tired of disorder in their governments. It also never gained the extent of legitimacy it needed to be effective. A popular movement called the Union of Islamic Courts began to gain support and to control many parts of Somalia.

What are reasons for conflicts between clans that dominated Somalia during most of the 1990s until recently? A study of the role of fights over resources was done by Christian Webersik, a postdoctoral fellow with the United Nations Institute of Advanced Studies. He noted that Bay and Bakol are the breadbasket of Somalia. Cereals come from Bay, while Lower Shabelle provides bananas. Faction leaders fight for control of resources and the means of trade such as seaports and airfields. Referring to resource scarcity theorists Johan Galtung and Paul Collier, he explains that the availability of lootable resources can prolong conflicts, not only providing needed supplies for fighting but also becoming the reason to continue fighting (to win the prize of future resource control). Other resource issues include a profitable trade in charcoal that continues during government neglect (since there are no environmental limits on deforestation) and the profits made from selling arms. Hotel managers and shipping agents profit from NGOs bringing aid during Somalia's crisis, and the lack of law and stability brings profits to security companies, which must therefore be hired to protect NGOs and their shipments.[62] Those who profit from this kind of instability do not necessarily want peace restored.

Martin Doornbos explains that in Somalia there are many groups opposed to the reemergence of a centralized state. Through lengthy, painstaking negotiations over recent years, by 2002, they concluded that they would prefer a loose federation (similar to Switzerland or the United Arab Emirates), to minimize chances that one clan or subclan would dominate the whole. While such an arrangement would be unconventional in the African context, Doornbos opined that it would be the best working model for Somalia. However, the UN and the European Union were still trying to institute a government of national unity. Prime minister of the interim national government, Galaydh, on October 19, 2001 pledged to the UN Security Council that he would support the war on terror, but Somalis soon rejected him and his cabinet. However, after 9-11, all neighboring states and the OAU (Organization of African Unity), EU (European Union), and UN supported the old and status quo concept of a centralized national government. Doornbos fears that other nations' and organizations' agendas will override Somalia's attempts at solving the nation's problems.[63] It seems that the U.S.-led "war on terror" will put U.S. security first, even at the cost of continuing to destabilize Somalia.

The situation in Somalia dramatically worsened during 2006-2008. The Union of Islamic Courts (UIC) gained popularity and territory in 2006, taking over Mogadishu and much of central and southern Somalia. Many Somalis felt some relief from the chaos that had been present due to the ineffective central government. The problem is, both the United States and Somalia's neighbor Ethiopia could only see the UIC through the lenses of their own concerns. They did not want an Islamic-based government in Somalia due to their own fears. The U.S. thought that the UIC could open Somalia to al-Qaeda's influence. Seeing that Ethiopia also had its reasons to oppose an Islamic government in its neighbor (since it was working to quell similar sentiments within its own country), the two cooperated to militarily oust the UIC.

Ever since the U.S. embassy bombings in Kenya and Tanzania in 1998, and increasingly since the September 11, 2001 World Trade Center and Pentagon bombings, the U.S. has increasingly seen all developments in Somalia through the lens of its "war on terror," and because of this has often misjudged situations and neglected the impact of their decisions on the Somali people. Sharif Nashashibi, chair of Arab Media Watch, notes within the context of East Africa, Somalia and Sudan are the only two countries that have not yet cooperated with U.S. policy agendas. Ethiopia has had an interest in ensuring that Somalia remains weak, for a united Somalia could begin troubles with Ethiopia's three million ethnic Somalis. Occasionally over the past few years, Ethiopia has conducted military maneuvers within Somali territory. Now Ethiopia claims that terrorists are hiding within Somalia and is requesting that the U.S. do something about it.

In his 2002 State of the Union address, George W. Bush mentioned Somalia as a possible stronghold for terrorists and therefore a potential target for the U.S. However, no one from the U.S. Embassy staff had visited Somalia since September 11, 2001, and no evidence of terrorist activity had been reported in the country. In the meantime, the U.S. closed down the Barakaat, which was a telephone and banking system used by Somalis abroad to send $300–$500 million per year back to family members living in Somalia. The U.S. argued that the system was used by al-Qaeda terrorists; but its closing puts untold hardship on many Somalis.[64] Sarah Bayne, in a briefing paper presented to the European Union on January 9, 2002, argued that the closing of the Al-Barakaat created economic shock throughout the country. She noted that in Somalia, total Diaspora remittances exceed the value of exports and international aid. Earlier, livestock had been a key export, but it had been recently banned because of Rift Valley Fever. Therefore, cutting off the flow of remittances was akin to severing a lifeline. The U.S. has also declared Al-Itihaad to be a terrorist group. It is true that Al-Itihaad did fight to establish an Islamic state from 1991 until its defeat by Ethiopian forces in 1997, but in the meantime, it has become the country's leader in providing education, health, and welfare services, so its shutting down would also lead to the misery of many in Somalia. The UN has declared that Al-Itihaad was not engaged in terrorist activities. Bayne argues that, by closing both Al-Barakaat and Al-Itihaad, the current U.S.-led strategy toward Somalia carries enormous risks to long-term prospects for peace and stability within the country and ultimately will become counterproductive.[65] She is also concerned that now faction leaders will use the threat of Islamic militancy to manipulate international donors.[66]

The U.S. has also not always had the best influence on fragile peace processes. When a peace process sponsored by the UN had as its goal the creation of a multiethnic Somalia, some faction leaders (including Aidid's son Hussein, who was a U.S. marine) walked out, assured that they had backing from the U.S. and Ethiopia.[67] Such developments lead one to believe that the U.S. is not pursuing the most peaceful agenda, but rather one that will ensure the allegiance of the new Somali government with U.S. policy. Nashashibi states, "Thus when one sees the regional gains made by the U.S. in its wars against Iraq and Afghanistan, it is not difficult to draw parallels to Somalia, and to understand the deep-rooted fear and suspicion in the Arab and Muslim worlds that behind the 'war on terror' is a strategy of attaining regional dominance and compliant allies regardless of local and humanitarian consequences."[68]

During 2006, the Islamic Courts became a formidable alternative to the (covertly) U.S.-backed transitional government and local military strongmen who had carved Mogadishu into their personal territories. The UIC seized control of Mogadishu in June 2006, dismantling roadblocks, reopening the airports, repairing streets, and bringing peace to the city. Many clan elders were relieved to see peace restored and so backed UIC-aligned militias. Soon the transitional government had little power outside of its base in Baidoa.[69]

While the U.S. State Department was not in favor of military intervention in Somalia, General John Abizaid arrived in Addis Ababa on December 4, 2006 to make a courtesy call to the Ethiopian Prime Minister Meles Zanawi. The official story is that Ethiopia decided to have its armed forces enter Somalia on December 24, 2006, but they had been aided by U.S. Intelligence prior to the invasion, which gave them information on the position of the Islamists they wanted to fight. According to Peter Pace, head of the Joint Chiefs of Staff, the U.S. justified its involvement, including sending advisers with Ethiopian forces and its eventual use of air strikes using "the Pentagon's authority to hunt and kill terrorism suspects around the globe, a power the White House gave it shortly after the September 11 attacks."[70] The Pentagon uses its outpost in Djibouti as a base for Special Operations Missions that involve Delta Force and other elite fighting forces, and that base was able to aid Ethiopia in this context.

While officials from Washington have characterized the Ethiopian invasion of Somalia as a response to Somalia's aggression, and while some Somali leaders had used aggressive and threatening language, *New African* columnist Cameron Duodu argues that the proper response to verbal provocation would have been to complain to other countries and work through the African Union to address the problem.[71]

On Christmas Eve of December 2006, Ethiopian forces, with the backing of U.S. forces and Somalia's transitional government, entered Somalia to topple the UIC. The U.S. used helicopter gunships in air strikes and in what they termed "mopping up" operations. The European Union condemned the invasion. Kurt Shillinger, a South African Institute for International Affairs expert in terrorism, stated that the U.S. would be better off if it concentrated on governance-building processes rather than military actions that could lead to the further collapse of Somalia and bring about exactly what the U.S. was hoping to prevent.[72] In fact, this military action could be an example of "preemptive" war against al-Qaeda, because the argument was mainly that conditions were ripe for al-Qaeda's entrance. But different parties to the fight had different estimations of whether al-Qaeda really had a significant presence in Somalia. Somalia's foreign minister Ismail Mohammed Harre said that his government had been fighting with *jihadi* forces, who had blood on their hands—real international terrorists.[73] But others say that while there may be many sympathetic to al-Qaeda, the UIC was not connected to international terrorists. A *Le Monde* editorial charges that the U.S. confuses "terrorism, jihadism, and Islamism" and by conflating these categories, mobilizes men to take up arms against Ethiopian forces.[74]

The December 2006 military intervention involved the cooperation of the U.S., Ethiopia, the Somali transitional government, and Kenya, which sealed off its border and captured those who tried to flee across into Kenya. Human rights groups say that Kenya arrested about 150 people and sent eighty of them back to Somalia and Ethiopia in what they charge was a

U.S.-planned case of extraordinary rendition. Among those held incommunicado was U.S. citizen Amir Mohamed Meshar, flown from Nairobi to Baidoa on February 10, 2007. The Muslim Human Rights Forum challenged the Kenyan government in court. Under a judge's order, authorities showed that eighty detainees had been transferred to Somalia and Ethiopia on three chartered flights on January 20 and 27 and February 10. Those flown to Ethiopia were Ogaden and Oromo fighters who joined Somali's Islamists in fighting against Ethiopian troops. There were grave issues about the violations of human rights involved in renditions such as these.[75]

In addition, Prime Minister Ali Mohamed Gedi and Deputy Prime Minister Hussein Aidid had a difficult task of convincing Somalis of the legitimacy of the transitional government since they were reliant on Ethiopian forces and, as time went on, African Union peacekeepers (from Uganda and Nigeria) to stay in power and so were easily seen as beholden to foreigners, not Somalis. In the meantime, the anarchy that reigned before the Islamic Courts took power returned, so that business people were back to having to pay bribes and protection money in a chaotic context.[76]

In its further attempts to influence politics by proxy, the U.S. hired DynCorp International to help with the peacekeeping mission in Somalia. DynCorp then hired 1,500 Ugandan troops as peacekeepers, who were greeted with mortar attack and firefight upon their landing.[77]

Members of the Islamic Courts found asylum in Eritrea, which extended support to them in hopes of thwarting their common rival, Ethiopia. From his base in Asmara, Islamic Courts leader Sheikh Hassan Dahir Aweys argued that Somalia's transitional government (which cooperated with Ethiopian and U.S. forces) were traitors to Somalia. He criticized the Bush Administration's involvement in Somalia (commenting, "Bush thinks that he is in charge of the world") and insisted that Somalia had to be liberated from Ethiopian troops.[78]

Fighting continued throughout 2007, with several hundred killed in April. Those fighting the Ethiopian forces had been "flattened under a deluge of fire," said a reporter from Le Monde. Ethiopian and transitional government forces went door-to-door in Mogadishu, breaking in and searching for fighters and weapons, making the city unlivable. The security situation worsened. By November 2007, it was reported that the Ethiopian forces engaged in targeted and blind assassinations and "fire on passersby and opened tank fire on residential neighborhoods and the Bakara market."[79] By the end of the year, Elman Human Rights Group (the oldest human rights organization in Somalia, then banned by the transitional government) charged that 5,960 Somali civilians had been killed during

2007; over 700,000 people were displaced by the fighting.[80] By December 2007, some 200,000 refugees were in a makeshift camp called Mustahil, which was located on a road from Mogadishu to Afgoye. UN relief aid had to get through checkpoints that extorted payments.[81] Oxfam warned of a grave humanitarian crisis. Cereal prices increased by 500 percent, rice tripled, and fuel prices soared. Oxfam predicted 2.6 million people would be in dire need of assistance.[82]

Staying just offshore, U.S. naval forces fired two Tomahawk cruise missiles from a submarine into Somalia on March 3, 2008. Pentagon specialist Bryan Whitman explained that they were aiming at a "known Al-Qaeda terrorist," Kenyan Saleh Ali Saleh Nabhan, who was wanted for questioning in terrorist attacks within Kenya in 2002. Somalis say that the missiles hit and killed three civilians, three cows, one donkey, and destroyed a house. Somalis protested the bombings. U.S. forces had already fired into Somalia several times in 2007.[83]

The Senlis Council argued that frustration with war and unemployment was fueling the insurgency against Western forces. What was needed in the area was jobs and democracy, not more war against terror.[84] Both the International Crisis Group (Brussels) and the Center for American Progress (Washington, DC) contributed to a report called "Somalia: A Country in Peril, a Foreign Policy Nightmare," which charges that "U.S. counter-terrorism policies have . . . generated a high level of anti-Americanism and are contributing to the radicalization of the population."[85] Authors reported that the situation in Somalia in 2008 exceeded any possible worst-case scenarios that regional analysts had thought up prior to the Ethiopian invasion. The report points to the fragile peace begun by the signing of the "Djibouti Agreement" in August 2008, in which moderates from both the transitional government and opposition had cooperated. However, more extreme armed groups like Islamist Shabaab were not been on board and could undermine the agreement's success. Ken Menkhaus and Chris Albin-Lackey, who presented the report, argued that the moderates in Somalia had to be strengthened and supported, but that U.S. policies, especially its putting Shabaab on a list of terrorist groups, have "actually worked to strengthen and embolden hard-liners", resulting in "the exact opposite of what we set out to achieve," according to Menkhaus.[86]

The United States seems to have continued its policy of ignoring Somalia's grave humanitarian problems, while continuing to intervene (albeit now through proxies like Ethiopian troops) whenever it decides U.S. security is at risk. As a result, horrible conditions fester, but if they ever spawn what the U.S. considers a dangerous response, it squelches that response, leaving horrible conditions neglected. Is this a smart way to fight the "war on terror"? Under these conditions, Somalis' dreams of having a livable country will be forever postponed.

If the swooping down of elite forces (in tandem with their proxies) is the new way in which the U.S. hopes to engage others in war around the world, with expensive technology, intent on saving U.S. lives while being willing to jeopardize the lives of others, we need to find alternatives quickly. Surely, such methods cannot ensure peaceful reconstruction of war-torn peoples. They also jeopardize noncombatant immunity and human rights. The popularity of the film *Black Hawk Down* may bode ill for the conscience of our nation. Films like this therefore become the sites of contestation: who will win the hearts and minds of U.S. citizens, and for what cause?

Acknowledgments

I would like to thank Chaungo Barasa and support staff at CARE International of Kenya, especially Wayne Nightingale and Marangu Njogu, for arranging a series of interviews with refugees at Dadaab during 1999. Also, thanks to UNHCR for granting permission for the study. I would also like to thank the J. William Fulbright Foundation for a Senior Scholar position at the University of Nairobi from 1998–2000, which made my participation in this research possible. The names of the refugees quoted in this article have been changed to protect their identity.

Notes

1. Mark Bowden, "A Defining Battle" (1997). http://inquirer.philly.com/packages/somalia/Nov16/rang16.asp.
2. Mark Bowden, *Black Hawk Down: A Study of Modern War* (New York: Penguin, 2000), 49.
3. Ibid., p. 10.
4. Bowden, "A Defining Battle."
5. Ibid.
6. Michey Kaus, "What *Black Hawk Down* Leaves Out: That Somali Raid Really Was More a Debacle Than a Victory" (2002), http://slate.msn.com/?id=2060941&device=, accessed 22 October 2008.
7. Bowden, *Black Hawk Down*," p. 72.
8. Bowden, "A Defining Battle."
9. Kaus, "What *Black Hawk Down* Leaves Out."
10. Bowden, *Black Hawk Down*," p. 71.
11. Ibid.

12. Ibid., p. 355.
13. Ibid., p. 329.
14. Ibid., pp. 345-46.
15. Bowden, "A Defining Battle."
16. Bowden, *Black Hawk Down*," p. 334.
17. Ibid., p. 333.
18. Ibid., p. 321.
19. Ibid., p. 333.
20. Ibid., p. 278.
21. Ibid., p. 30.
22. Ibid., 75.
23. Ibid., pp. 289-90.
24. Ibid., p. 61.
25. Bowden, "A Defining Battle," photo page.
26. Bowden, *Black Hawk Down*, p. 81.
27. Ibid., p. 196.
28. Ibid., p. 195.
29. Ibid., pp. 260, 292.
30. Ibid., p. 217.
31. Ibid., pp. 8-9.
32. Ibid., p. 50.
33. Ibid., p. 51.
34. Ibid.
35. Ibid., p. 7.
36. Ibid., p. 10.
37. Ibid., p. 92.
38. Ibid., p. 80.
39. Ibid., pp. 8,18.
40. Ibid., pp. 345-46.
41. Jonathan Weisman, "Deadliest Day for U.S.," *USA Today* (March 6, 2002).
42. Hannah Arendt, "Lying in Politics: Reflections on the Pentagon Papers," in *Crises of the Republic*, ed. Hannah Arendt (New York: Harcourt, Brace, Jovanovich, 1972).
43. Neal Gabler, "Seeking Perspective on the Movie Front Lines," *New York Times* (January 27, 2002, Week in Review).
44. Glenn J. Gray, *The Warriors: Reflections of Men in Battle*. 2nd ed., with introduction by Hannah Arendt (New York: Harper and Row, 1970), 26-29.
45. Bowden, *Black Hawk Down*," p. 246.
46. Geoffrey Gray, "Review of *Black Hawk Down*," *Village Voice* (6 February 2002).

47. David Brooks, "Black Hawk Down," *Journal of the Anglo-Somali Society* 31 (2002), 57.

48. Bowden, "A Defining Battle."

49. Bowden, Reply 11/20/97, http://inquirer.philly.com/packages/somalia/ask/ask1.asp.

50. Bowden, "A Defining Battle."

51. Kaus, "What *Black Hawk Down* Leaves Out."

52. Jonathan Weisman, "Deadliest Day for U.S.," *USA Today* (March 6, 2002).

53. Bowden, *Black Hawk Down*, p. 342.

54. Kaus, "What *Black Hawk Down* Leaves Out."

55. Gabler, "Seeking Perspective on the Movie Front Lines."

56. Interview by the author, with Amina (name changed), Dadaab refugee camp, May 1999. Included in report, "Conflict Resolution at Dadaab Refugee Camp," submitted to CARE Kenya, 17 August 2001.

57. Louis Kriesberg, *Constructive Conflicts: From Escalation to Resolution* (Lanham, MD: Rowman and Littlefield, 1998), 11.

58. Michael Nagler, *Is There No Other Way? The Search for a Nonviolent Future* (Berkeley, CA: Berkeley Hills Books, 2001), 19, 27, 36, 126, 165, 169.

59. Ibid., p. 57.

60. Najum Mushtaq, "Anatomy of an Unending Conflict," *New African* (February 2007): 26.

61. Christian Webersik, "War Over Resources? Evidence from Somalia," *Environment* 50, 3 (May/June 2008): 51.

62. Ibid.

63. Martin Doornbos, "Somalia: Alternative Scenarios for Political Reconstruction." *African Affairs* 101 (2002): 93–107.

64. Sharif Nashashibi, "Target Somalia: A Hidden U.S. Agenda?" (8 January 2002) http://www.netnomad.com/hiddenagenda.html, accessed 22 October 2008; Donald G. McNeil, "A New Scrutiny of Somalia as the Old Anarchy Reigns," *New York Times*, February 10, 2002.

65. Sarah Bayne, "Somalia and the Fight Against Terrorism: Recommendations to the E.U.," *Journal of the Anglo-Somali Society* (Spring 2002): 37-40, quote from 38.

66. Ibid., p. 39.

67. Nashashibi, "Target Somalia: A Hidden U.S. Agenda?"; McNeil, "A New Scrutiny of Somalia as the Old Anarchy Reigns."

68. Ibid.

69. Rob Crilly, "Uneasy Shift in Somalia," *Christian Science Monitor* 99, 24 (December 29, 2006).

70. Mark Mazzetti, "Pentagon Sees Move in Somalia as a Blueprint," *New York Times* (January 13, 2007).

71. Cameron Duodu, "Somalia: Why the New American 'Blueprint' Is Dangerous for Africa," *New African* (February 2007): 48–49.

72. Scott Baldauf, Mike Pflanz, Christian Mike, "U.S. Takes War on Terror to Somalia," *Christian Science Monitor* 99, 31 (January 10, 2007).

73. Shashank Bengali and Jonathan S. Landay, "U.S. Allies in Africa May Have Engaged in Secret Prisoner Renditions," *McClatchey Newspapers*, March 13, 2007.

74. "Descent into Hell," editorial, *Le Monde*, November 14, 2007.

75. Bengali and Landay, "U.S. Allies in Africa May Have Engaged in Secret Prisoner Renditions."

76. Rob Crilly, "Somalia Tense After Islamists Vanish," *Christian Science Monitor* 99, no. 26 (3 January 2007).

77. Matthew Lee, Donna Borak, Pauline Jelenik, and Salad Duhul, "U.S. Hires Military Contractor to Support Peacekeeping Mission in Somalia," *Associated Press* (March 7, 2007).

78. "We Are Going to Liberate Somalia," *Mail and Guardian* (May 22, 2008).

79. Jean-Philippe Remy, "A War with No Front and No Rules Hammers the Devastated Somali Capital," *Le Monde* (November 14, 2007).

80. "5,960 Civilians Killed in Mogadishu in 2007," *Associated Press* (December 2, 2007).

81. Shashank Bengalli, "Somalia Descends into Africa's Worst Crisis," *McClatchey Newspapers* (December 13, 2007).

82. Xan Rice, "Rising Food Prices Pushing East Africa to Disaster," *The Guardian UK* (July 24, 2008).

83. Jeffrey Gettleman and Eric Schmitt, "U.S. Forces Fire Missiles into Somalia at a Kenyan," *New York Times* (March 4, 2008).

84. Damien McElroy, "U.S. Wars Have Helped Al-Qaeda," *The Telegraph UK* (June 26, 2008).

85. Jim Lobe, "U.S. Policy Risks Terrorism Blowback in Somalia," *Mail and Guardian* (September 5, 2008).

86. Ibid.

Perspectives on a Demobilization Center in Merka, Somalia

Nasri H. Adam

Somalia is a homogeneous society with one tribe, one language, one religion, and one culture. Somalis have a nomadic society and generally lead very democratic and independent lives. Many live in the rural areas and have their wealth in animal rearing, camels in particular. After independence in 1960, Somalia had nine years of a democratic government system with elections. In 1969, the military took power in a coup d'état. For twenty-one years, Somalis lived under an authoritarian regime that was eventually ousted in 1991 by guerrilla opposition groups from all regions.

To date, Somalia remains without a formal governing structure!

The conflict that began in 1990 affected Somalis living in East Africa in very personal ways. The neighboring countries believe that we Somalis are different from our neighbors—those in the North Eastern Province of Kenya, in the Zone Five region of Ethiopia, and Djibouti. Although we were unaware of the prevalent politics in Somalia, its effects rippled down to those of us living in Nairobi, Kenya's capital. All Kenyan Somalis had to undergo a screening process to determine their citizenship.

This chaos was taking place at about the time I completed my high school education. I was thinking what a great world this was, having dreams of what I wanted to be and places I wanted to go in the near future. Somalia was one of those places.

Although only one side of my family was from there, there was a clear distinction for me about my Somaliness. Even though I was born and raised in Kenya, in a different culture and environment, I saw and still see myself as a Somali.

However, there was a different aspect of Somalia that I was unaware of: clan/tribal politics. This is a very crucial aspect when conflict starts and when it is clan- or tribe-based. Then issues of identity come in, and the entanglement is much deeper than outsiders can understand.

By 1991, I knew that things would not be getting better and that families were seeking refuge in their relatives' homes in Kenya and elsewhere. My urge to travel to Somalia and contribute to the humanitarian cause was strengthened by what I kept hearing from my cousins and friends who had managed to safely escape to Kenya. I was living and working in Nairobi, having access to social amenities and security, yet unsatisfied with where my life was heading. I hated seeing the suffering, starvation, and chaos shown by the media. I wanted to know what was being done to alleviate the situation of the Somalis, who had no government, security, infrastructure, or access to services such as health and education.

Finally, in 1994, I managed to travel to Mogadishu, Somalia's capital. What did I expect? Definitely not the destruction shown by gaping holes in all buildings, deserted neighborhoods, and remnants of main streets. Other parts of the town were completely overcrowded, and conflict seemed non-existent. An example was the main markets, where business life is almost normal, with only occasional sounds of gunshots.

What caught my attention were the weapons on the streets, carried mainly by young men of varying ages. Several vehicles armed with machine guns, driven by men with bazookas and rifles, cruised around the streets and neighborhoods, looking for only God knows what.

Generally, these young men are heavily armed and either "work" independently or in groups, but usually with a vehicle. They are either affiliated with a faction leader or are freelancers. Their plight is complex and unknown to many. They are known as Moryaans, or militias.

I came to be involved with this group of young men through IIDA, a nongovernmental organization that I volunteered with over a three-year period.[1] IIDA—one of many women's organizations in Somalia—worked to bring about peace and to assist Somalis in rebuilding their communities. In particular, IIDA designed a pilot project to examine how the issue of militias and security within Merka could be tackled.[2] In partnership with an Italian organization, the Coordinating Committee of the Organizations for Voluntary Services (COSV), the Demobilization Program was implemented, with its main objective to reintegrate militia members into civil society. The program began in May 1997, funded by the European Commission under its Peace-Building Program.

Clearly, this was a big challenge in a country where there was no central government or any local authority to enforce law and order except traditional clan structures. It was also an opportunity for those involved in making peace a reality. And it was a one-of-a-kind initiative, since no such program had been previously implemented in Somalia.

When I realized the implications of the program and became part of the team, I felt overwhelmed. I wondered whether these young men could possibly be as horrible as everyone claimed they were. I pondered how we could ensure a working relationship with them, given that they had been their own bosses for so long, with no respect for authority.

The Demobilization Program planned to enroll 150 militia members from the ages of 18 to 30. They were to come from the Lower Shabelle region, and a larger quota was given to those from Merka, the regional town. Four of us were to carry out interviews of the militiamen who would be coming to the IIDA Center. We prepared a questionnaire seeking information such as:

Place of birth, and why you left home.

Your educational level.

When did you join the conflict, and which conflict did you join, the effort to oust the government, or the interclan conflicts?

What were your dreams?

Are there things that you would like to accomplish? If so, how? If not, why not? And what could help you accomplish these things?

This information helped create a biography of each of the incoming students, and their educational level determined the curriculum.

The Demobilization Program planned to include basic education (mathematics, literacy, science, geography, Somali, English, and civic education), vocational training (agriculture and fishing), and extracurricular activities (basketball, football, and assistance in Merka's hospital and sanitation program).

The implementing organizations looked forward to creating behavioral change among the militia members. We hoped they would become peace activists as a result of being in the program, which would enhance security and have a positive influence on the other militias still on the streets. The presence of the program would allow the community to work and be part of the demobilization center, through facilitation and discussions among the militia members and community members. Athletic competitions between the center team and the town were also held to allow for the social reintegration of the militia members.

The citizens of Merka realized the potential of this program and that we could all work together to develop programs that would serve the needs of the community by involving this particular group, the members of which were outcasts from their own society. The expectations of the organizations and community were very much interlinked, and this enhanced the support and working relationship among the parties.

The militia members were a different story. They were very suspicious of our intentions, and many told us that they felt naked without their guns and susceptible to attacks from other militias. Their guns were their identity! The decision to hand over their guns—a prerequisite to their joining the demobilization center—proved difficult for many in the beginning. They demanded to know what they would get in return and for how long. At such times we emphasized their current options: die or kill someone else in the name of so-called defense tactics or have hope of a better future, including what is being offered at the center. We also had a lot of help from community members, who identified the "worst" and most feared of the militias. Family members were also involved in persuading militia members to take advantage of the opportunities offered at the center. With all the community efforts and support and our continuous involvement in assisting the community in this particular region, our work and the center proved a success within the first few months.

We discovered that many of the militia members had been left homeless, far from their families, and had resorted to arms to defend themselves. With a lot of pressure from their clan elders, others confessed to witnessing the killings of close family members, mainly fathers, uncles, or elder brothers. Many of the younger ones got involved due to peer pressure and were later forced to defend their clans during the interclan conflicts.

During my time at the center, I discovered that many of the students had stayed in the militias because they had been desperate to survive. Following the clan-based faction leader provided the young men with food, personal security, pocket money, and shelter, in addition to being with their peers. What went to their heads was the sense of power. They were the ones who controlled things. This was very true!

Some worked for family members who ran businesses, and they could not break away. One of the students mentioned that Mafia activities took place, and they were at times sent to eliminate individuals. They felt bound to those in charge; otherwise, where would they go and how would they survive?

Talking to the ex-militia students brought a lot of things into perspective for me. Young people in all times of conflict become pawns, are brainwashed through clan/tribe/ethnic politics, and fight for things they don't understand. Many wish they had realized the impact of their acts and hope that they will be given another chance. As yet, we continue to condemn them within our communities. Through the media and in our writings, we keep referring to them as hooligans going on gun sprees!

Many of the students at our center were not only traumatized, but also sick. Many had tuberculosis, and the center treated them. The compassionate nature of the support staff, the teachers, and the administration has been commendable. The students never expected to be shown respect and consideration or to have people concerned with their welfare. We all felt a change in attitude among the students who were ready to listen and willing to learn. There were a few who still felt that they could not follow the center rules, but after three months they, too, became part of the larger group.

I had taken the learning process for granted, but witnessing these students struggling and asking questions, I realized the importance of this program. It gave inner power to the students to excel and to discover who they were intellectually. The students organized sessions for debates, and we facilitated the process to have productive discussions. It was with a lot of emotion that I was able to compare the initial interviews of the militia members and their participation in the activities within the center several months later.

It is satisfying to me and the teachers when a student tells us that he can now read and write his own name and read the local newspaper and that during his break time he wants the teachers to answer some of his questions. This was a very normal environment to us in the center, and I kept forgetting the security issues around the country, the lack of education for most Somali youth, and the lack of infrastructure.

In this small town of Merka, an impossible program in a country that has defied normal structures is a success, and a second group of militia members will be enrolled, while the first group will be assisted in starting agricultural and fishing businesses.

I am very proud to have been part of this first demobilization center in Somalia and hope that it is not the last.

Conflict is not something that we can all understand, and it is worse when it is armed conflict. It creates a lot of negative aspects, but it can be positive to challenge the potential of community members in rebuilding their lives. Through all the chaos, we need to pay close attention to the young and offer them opportunities so that they do not later take to the streets and kill. If the young Somali militia member had no access to a gun, his life would be different, but now he feels that without it he has no life! The proliferation of arms, especially in countries that are suffering, is inhuman. Somalis are dying from cholera outbreaks and malnutrition; there is no reason we should die from stray bullets or mortars being fired at innocent civilians!

> "War destroys today's generation.
> Peace builds tomorrow's generation."

Notes

1. The IIDA women's development organization was established in 1991. Its name stands for "celebration" in Somali, with particular reference to a name given to a baby girl born on festivity day.
2. Merka is a coastal town 75 miles south of Mogadishu.

Rethinking the Nation in Post-War Reconstruction in Niger Republic

Ousseina Alidou

Many civil wars on the continent of Africa have been triggered by forces that are essentially politico-economic in nature. Yet, a good if not an overwhelming proportion of these violent conflicts came to assume an ethnocultural articulation that exacerbated their viciousness and delayed their resolution. In the process, the ethnocultural sometimes came to be "imagined" as a cause in its own right. As a result, while peace efforts in such a war situation must certainly address the root politico-economic causes, ethnocultural considerations often need to be an integral part of the package if the gains of conflict conciliation are to endure.

It is this ethnocultural dimension of the war situation that my essay is intended to explore, with specific reference to the so-called "Tuareg Rebellion" and its aftermath. This refers to the civil war that took place between the 1980s to the 1990s in the West African Republic of Niger. I shall pay particular attention not only to the ethnocultural face of the war, but also to how the question of ethnocultural identity came to be tackled in the postwar (re)construction of the nation itself, drawing my examples specifically from humanistic data, critical analysis including interviews with Tuareg women who played key roles in and during the conflict and its aftermath resolutions, and folkloristic and literary productions.

The "Tuareg Resistance": The Politico-Economic Background

Between 1985 and 1990, the Tuareg—a nomadic, pastoral people inhabiting the Sahara—launched sporadic attacks from their military camps in Libya and Algeria with arms supplied by France, Germany, and other foreign countries. These attacks provided grounds for the Nigerien government to implicate all Tuareg indiscriminately and to order the national armed forces to lead a merciless crackdown on Tuareg civilians. Both the Tuareg rebels and the national armed forces operating in the north of the country violated the human rights of innocent Tuareg and other ethnic groups. The appalling silence of the rest of the population aggravated their fate.

The causes of this conflict are partly political and partly economic. Among the Tuareg themselves, there are those who believe that the entire problem could be traced back to the colonial division of the country. In the words of Agaisha—a leading female activist in the conflict situation interviewed in December 1998 and 2000—for example:

> Well, the Tuareg problem is really a vast problem which does not evolve from the present. The Tuareg problem began with the colonizer. If there is someone who created the Tuareg problem, it is maybe the colonizer because the Tuareg are herders who are always mobile. They were nomads who do not know these problems of borders. A nomad can move from Niger to Mali. For him he is always at home. He can go from Mali to Algeria, this is still home for him. However, now with the problems of [national] borders, there is of course a limit: Tuareg from Niger must remain in Niger. If you want to cross to Algeria, you must possess a national identity card, a concept they don't understand. They don't understand the concept of a national identification card, let alone that of a passport. Therefore, this is the problem. It is an old one and I think the issue has been the focus of well-documented studies over the years.

Thus, the impact of European colonial balkanization of Africa, leading to the creation of the modern nation-states, is what, in Agaisha's assessment, accounts for the crisis confronting nomadic Tuareg populations in whichever postcolonial state they may be regarded as citizens of and more particularly in Niger Republic. The colonial border configuration stripped them of their cultural and survival rights to have access to natural resources (water, herding sites, animals, etc.); broke the cohesion of a unified ethnic group by scattering it to several distinct "sovereign countries," thereby imposing new "national" identities on each disjointed unit of the old entity; and confronted the pastoral groups with the challenge of adjusting to the demands of colonial structures and integration into the mainstream of a new sociopolitical and economic order.

The quest for green herding areas often led to the development of tensions with other native agricultural sedentarian communities sharing and competing for the same natural resources. Numerous tragic conflicts were registered as herds of pastoral groups invaded agricultural lands in response to severe, long-lasting periods of drought and lack of natural resources for survival in the newly designated pastoral lands.[1] At the international level, nation-states led not only to the political and cultural marginalization of nomadic Tuareg populations (and other nomadic groups, including the Tubu), but also to their being perceived as "violators" of legal national and international immigration regulations. Lack of adequate understanding of the laws due to the high rate of illiteracy in Western education arising from nomadic resistance to assimilation into the new colonial and postcolonial social order made the Tuareg particularly vulnerable to such criminal charges of the immigration kind. The colonial borders, in other words, became a source of great tension in the system of livelihood for the pastoral groups and, therefore, of potential violent conflicts both within the nation and across the nation.

In addition to the border factor, however, there were several politico-economic developments within Niger that contributed to the eruption of the Tuareg resistance. From 1960 to 1991, the political leaders of successive civilian and military regimes in Niger sustained their authority through an excessively authoritarian and centralized system of government. The leaders maintained patron-client relations with organized social groups—such as the union of civil servants and the student organizations—which had the potential to oppose state authority.[2] Both regimes marginalized rural farmers and nomadic and/or nonnomadic pastoralists. The most alienated groups, which were excluded from formal participation in the national decision-making process, were the nomadic Tuareg, Tubu, Fulani, and Arabs, as well as almost all women.

The various regimes neglected the development of rural economies and, worse, misappropriated international foreign aid allocated to Sahelian regions that were severely affected by prolonged drought and famine. Moreover, the revenues generated by uranium and coalmines benefited mainly the ruling political leaders who used them to maintain power by satisfying the interests of the urban professional middle class and students. At the same time, the regimes ignored the basic survival needs of the people who produced the mineral wealth.

Severe famine and lack of government assistance forced many nomadic populations to abandon their rural settlements and seek assistance in the towns. The Tuareg were the most seriously affected, and the years 1984–1985 saw the mass exodus of nomadic Tuareg and Fulani whose livestock had been decimated by the drought. They moved south toward the cities and north into the neighboring countries of Algeria and Libya. The failure of their own government to assist them and their bleak future made thousands of frustrated Tuareg and Tubu vulnerable to Mu'amar Qaddafi's imperialistic designs, which were couched in revolutionary rhetoric. They became easy prey to his guerrilla force and were at the service of his expansionist interventions in the region. Similarly, border disputes between Niger and Algeria led the Algerian government to organize a Tuareg insurgency against Niger.[3]

Libya and Algeria finally expelled Tuareg refugees from their territories and forced them to return to Niger. This expulsion came at a time of intense sociopolitical crisis resulting from economic austerity, which was precipitated by a number of factors. These factors included the fall of uranium prices, France's disengagement from Niger, and the antisocial measures of economic redress imposed by international donors through structural adjustment policies. This crisis triggered painful disappointment and disillusion with the promises of an all-inclusive national integration made by President Ali Saïbou in the late 1980s.

The Saïbou regime became conscious of the military training received by a significant number of returning Tuareg and was extremely suspicious of them. The regime's authority was already weakened by the opposition of the middle class and student organizations, which saw their interests compromised by the economic austerity measures imposed by the International Monetary Fund and the World Bank. Against this backdrop, Tuareg men and women became the target of harassment and repression and were subjected to mass political arrests and brutalization. Once more they were regarded as unfit outcasts in their own country.

By 1991, Niger's political crisis led to national fragmentation with three consequences: the marginalization of northerners—especially nomadic Tuareg who resisted being mainstreamed into the national order; the increasing loss of the sympathy of groups representing the mainstream or center for the plight of marginalized Tuareg; and the exacerbation of stresses and tensions at the national level. The resulting rebellion was the response of the marginalized to their plight when no other solution seemed open to them.

The Ethnocultural Dimension of the Conflict

These politico-economic dynamics were from the very beginning compounded by issues of ethnocultural identity. The population of Niger, estimated at over ten million inhabitants, is often described as multiethnic in composition. The ethnic groups include the Hausa (50 percent), the Zarma-Songhay (22.8 percent), the Fulbe/Fulani (10.4 percent), the Kanuri (8.5 percent), the Tuareg (3 percent), and the Tubu (0.5 percent). The rest is comprised of a small host of ethnic minorities that include the Schwa-Arabs, the Gurmance, and the Buduma. Of this total population, about 50.4 percent are women of whom 42 percent are between the age of 15 and 42. These are the figures that are provided by the national census.

As much as the census record—itself a product of European colonial conceptions of African identities—has categorized the population into seemingly discrete ethnic and religious units, it masks and distorts the reality of ethnocultural dynamics and composition of the nation. "Hausaness," for example, which is said to cover about a half of the demographic map of the country, has always been a multiple and shifting identity. Within it are elements from various ethnoregional sources and, though regarded as essentially Islamic, its religious face has been equally inclusive of Hausa of other faiths (African traditional spiritualities and Christianity, be it Catholicism or Protestantism). Numerous people of "Hausa" origin are, for all practical purposes, regarded and see themselves as "Zarma." The Mauri/Mawri (Maouri) are an example of such a group that can claim to be both Hausa and Zarma, or of a new ethnicity. The people of Ader in Tahoua Department (southeastern and central Niger) and Abzin in Zinder (in Eastern Niger) and Agadez Departments (Northern Niger) and Ingall in Agadez manifest a similar complexity at the intersection of Tuaregness, Hausaness, Fulaniness, or Zarmaness within the Saharan-Sahélien space. Yet, the Mauri, the Adarawa (from Ader) who claim ties to both Hausas and Tuareg—as the saying in Hausa goes, *Ba'adare duk Buzu ne* (meaning any person of Ader is a Tuareg)—the Damagarawa (from Zinder) who are originally Kanuri-speaking people linguistically and culturally assimilated to the Hausa, , and the Isawaghan (from Ingall in Agadez) whose native language Tasawaq is clearly Creole-based of Songhay and Berber[4] and who claim historical ties to the old Songhay Empire of Kankan Mousa and Arab-Berber ancestry, are but the more obvious articulations of Brassage Sahélien, i.e., ethnocultural blending. The popular dance song, Tigyedima "Drum" by Abdoul Salam in which he addresses the complexity of a man and his lover's identity is a great appraisal of both the scope and dynamism of Niger's cultural and ethnic Brassage.

It is indeed true that the notion of an ethnic group in "purist" terms has been relatively new to the relational universe of the people of Niger of old and new cities, and its articulations in the modern nation-state are often linked to the opportunistic politics of power stimulated initially by European colonial agendas and carried over, subsequently, into the postcolonial dispensation. The average Nigerien, especially in the urban and in the semi-urban spaces, embodies the many-in-one and, depending on the context, can be simultaneously Tuareg, Fulani, Hausa, Zarma, and so forth, without implying a crisis or a confusion of identities. Furthermore, in most Muslim family formations where polygamy is common, complex ethnicities for a single family must be expected for individuals within the family. For example, while children could share one ethnic thread through a fatherline, the same children of the same father could diverge on ethnicity through their motherline if their father's wives are of different ethnicities. Family cultural and ethnic Brassage (blending) is a condition resulting from the predominance of Islam across ethnic groups in Niger, government's appointment of civil servants in various parts of the country that often differ from one's original "ethnic" base, and other forms of rural-urban exodus.

It is significant that Niger is located in the Sudanic belt, a region that covers the entire area from Senegal in West Africa to the Red Sea in Northeast Africa. This area has a rich history and remarkable linguistic, cultural, and ethnic patterns of interactions with both populations in the southern fringes of the Sahara, commonly referred to as the Sahel, as well as those of the central and northern fringes of the Sahara, which are dominated by Arab and Berber populations. Lying just in the central and southern fringes of the Sahara desert, for thousands of years the Sudanic Belt (Sahelian region or western Sudan and the Eastern Sudanic Belt) served as a link between the so-called Sub-Saharan Africa and the worlds of the so-called North Africa and the Mediterranean. In this long period, the region has been a source of trade, religious interaction, and labor migration to North, East, and Atlantic parts of Africa, leading to multiple formations of Diasporic communities that have continued to shape its complex identity. The works of Abu Manga and Yamba are fascinating analyses of the Arabized Hausa-Fulani populations in contemporary Sudan Republic, a country that is sometimes considered a part of the Middle East. This complexity was later compounded by French and British colonial rules and their postcolonial aftermath.[5] Although both French and British colonialisms aimed to stabilize African populations in their conquered territories, they did not succeed. In fact, populations at the border of Niger and Northern Nigeria, for example, were crossing boundaries throughout the colonial period. For example, families in the "borderland" resisted colonial attempts to split them and continue to do so to the present day through creative mechanisms to subvert the legitimacy of these colonial demarcations of territories, a legacy that now defines postcolonial national boundaries and citizenships. Clearly, then, Brassage Sahélien in Niger is a child of several millennia of sociocultural, political, and economic history of this wide region.

This fact of Brassage Sahélien is clearly demonstrated in the identity of Agaisha, who narrates her family lineage in the following words:

> I was born in 1960 in Tigida-n-Adagh in the county of Tchi-rozerine in Agadez department. My mother is Targui (female Tuareg) and my father is Hausa-Ba'adare from Tahoua. My father told me that if I am asked about his ethnic background I should say he is a sedentarian Tuareg because the Ba'adare are originally Tuareg who became Hausa through the sedentarisation process and intermarriage. His mother is Targui from Talamses and his father is Ba'adare. My father was a forestry officer. He and my mother divorced and I stayed in the village with my maternal grandmother until I was seven when I joined my mother who was living in Tudu after the divorce. I learnt Hausa there with the other children.

Reflecting on her first marriage, which took place in Tudu, Agaisha reveals more of her feelings about the meaning of Nigerien identity:

> My first husband was in the military. He is from Ader, a Ba'adare [pause] But he himself is quite a mixture [laugh] Well, his mother is Ba'adara, but his father is from Dancandu, so he is Zarma [laugh] His father is Zarma and his mother is from Tahoua Hausa-Ba'adara. And here we are—he married me, a Tuareg [laugh] This is quite a distinctive characteristic of Niger [laugh] There is this Brassage [blending] [pause] This is Niger....The Brassage is even the advantage of being Sahélien, that is Nigerien, because all people are interrelated and one feels at home wherever one is. There is no one ethnic group today that can claim it is only Hausa or Tuareg [pause] That is the fact...not being mixed does happen, but...that is how I describe the common Brassage [pause].

This paradigm of identity, however, was severely challenged and in some cases even supplanted by the European colonial intrusion. As indicated earlier, in place of the fluidity and multiplicity of identity, it now imposed a rigidity, especially, through the institution of census and identity cards. Nigeriens were now forced to think of themselves in exclusive and purist ethnic terms as either Hausa or Zarma or Tuareg or Fulbe, etc. The fact of Brassage no longer had any place in the colonial construction of Nigerien identity, and those of Brassage Sahélien identity—like Agaisha—had now to splinter their "blood" into its constituent strands and were forced to chose one, but not the other.

In addition to this narrow ethnicization of the Nigerien society, the colonialists also tried to impose a racial hierarchy. Nigeriens were suddenly structured along a racist European paradigm of skin pigmentation, with the typical division between Whites and Blacks, no matter how much of a misnomer such terms were in the Nigerien context. The use of racist concepts, Abdou Moumouni points out, was a clear tool intended to reinforce the colonial policy of divide and conquer among African people. This language of racial categorization was very explicit in the colonial curriculum outline for elementary education:

> Elementary level: what were our ancestors. What are they today. What do they owe to the French. Simple general concepts on France and the French.

> Advanced Elementary level: French West Africa in the Past. Invasion of Black Africa by the White race: Fulani (Puular), Berber [Tuareg], Arabs, Moroccans, Europeans, French. Colonial genius and French civilization. The great eras of their history. Their institutions. Their inventions. Their civilizations. Foundations of colonial empire. Commercial societies. Contacts between French and Black Africans up to the end of the 19th century.

Nigeriens were now thus initiated into thinking about their identities not in cultural terms, as had been the custom, but in colonial, Eurocentric terms of race and color. The Fulani and Hausa, for example, were no longer brothers and sisters of each other, but members of separate races altogether!

This Black-White distinction in the identitarian landscape of postcolonial Niger was very significant in planting potential seeds of discord. As Bill Ashcroft has noted:

> …"Black" and "White" have become the most powerful signifiers in the contemporary racial landscape. No two words have had the momentum and catastrophic consequences of the words "white" and "Black": no two words so completely encompass

the binarism of western culture or have such profound cultural ramifications.[6]

In the final analysis, then, the French did for Niger what the Belgians did for Rwanda and Burundi—as Mamdani[7] explains—in terms of the racial construction of the people of these two parts of Africa.

With this background, therefore, when the "Tuareg Armed Rebellion" broke up, it was easy for some Tuareg ideologues of the war to draw on these racist colonial categories to feed the war machine. For them, the very marginalization of the Tuareg was now presented as a plight of a racial minority, rather than as part of a regional disenfranchisement that is recurrent and peculiar to the postcolonial state. Of course, some of the Tuareg elite beat this racialist drum of nationalism—further supported by European media representation of the conflict—to serve their own class interests. In the process, they wiped out of the face of Agadez and Tahoua regions the presence of other indigenous groups like the Fulbe, Hausa-Adarawa, Arabs, and the Isawaghans (Ingall Borey "northern Songhay people of InGall"), who were sharing the same fate as the Tuareg. In the final analysis, therefore, what started as a legitimate struggle for the economic and the political reorganization of the society quickly assumed a racial divide that made it particularly difficult to resolve by building alliances with members of other groups who were sympathetic to the Tuareg cause.

The Aftermath of Civil War

After several years of negotiations, a peace agreement leading to the end of armed struggle was finally signed between the government and the Tuareg combatants on April 24, 1996. The spirit of reconciliation that led to the final resolution of the conflict was, of course, partly inspired by the momentum for democratization and pluralism that engulfed the nation in the 1990s onward. In addition to the more popular demand for democracy and the rule of law, ethnic, religious, and sexual constituencies that had hitherto been marginalized and disenfranchised took advantage of this new political space to advance their own struggle for greater socioeconomic and political representation and parity in the nation. In other words, the new political climate in the nation induced both the besieged regime that had come under increasing pressure from both local and international communities and the embattled Tuareg to see the moment as a window of opportunity for the negotiation of a peaceful resolution to the armed conflict.

An immediate concern of the two parties in the peace accord was the demobilization of the Tuareg combatants and their reintegration into the national military and paramilitary programs. Unfortunately, however, kinship and class factors came to blur the question of who should be integrated first among the Tuareg ex-combatants and victims. According to Agaisha, our Tuareg activist interviewee, of the one thousand jobs created in the process of reintegration, only eleven went to women, who were admitted into professional public schools—as part of the new reconstruction opportunities created specifically to cater to the Tuareg community. Most of the posts in government and state institutions were also allocated to the male Tuareg elite and their relatives, leaving thousands of ex-combatants empty-handed and bitter. The Tuareg women became even more acutely marginalized as the forgotten sister comrades:

> In this integration business, the Tuareg women saw it all [pause]
> We fought and risked our lives just like men and sometimes
> even thousand of our children including my daughter failed
> school and could not be admitted in school because we don't
> speak Arabic. So they stayed home for two and three years doing
> nothing and forgetting the little they learnt in French before
> the exile. But now we, the women and the children are thanked
> with nothing. Even the eleven women who got something had
> to suffer in order to be heard [pause] Well the Tuareg women
> must rely solely on themselves for any possibility of survival and
> empowerment. But we will never forget or give up on asking
> them, the male comrades, our share...

As argued in Turshen and Alidou,[8] where rehabilitation and reeducation of ex-combatants were undertaken, they were implemented within the framework of established patriarchal and militaristic culture. In the case of Niger Republic, it is important to bear in mind that the whole process was conceived by a military regime that violated the right of the citizens of the country to a democratically elected government. Furthermore, the use of the ex-combatants in the military and paramilitary sectors only intensified the militarization of a society that already suffered extremely from decades of authoritarianism and military dictatorship. In moments of crisis, military training has been the source of terror against women and civilians when the state could not meet the material needs of its military personnel. This danger was even more horrifying when one extends the analysis to the bitter unintegrated and trained ex-combatants.

The war aftermath experience and the betrayal of Nigerien women by the new "reconstruction regime" forged a new consciousness among Tuareg women within postwar Niger Republic. Seeing that the male-controlled state, combined with the economic limitations of an already patriarchal government, could not sufficiently provide opportunities for women, the women decided to conceive and act on their own initiatives. As Agaisha contends:

> Wartime and aftermath conditions have forced the Tuareg women to resist the dependency ties imposed upon them by men before the uprising and to pave creative ways for self-empowerment by exploiting all the resources at their disposal. We have created women's arts cooperatives which generate money to support ourselves and our families. When the men saw our success and asked to be part of some of them, we made it a clear condition that a woman must remain the principal manager of the cooperative. This did not please some of the men, but they can't do anything about it. They are women initiatives and they must be headed by women. We too are capable and we are tired of letting them run our lives…

These new spaces for women's agencies and empowerment in the aftermath of the Tuareg war created conditions for women to be in the forefront of the antiwar movement in the country. In fact, the Tuareg women who participated in the Dakar 1998 workshop on "Women and the Aftermath of Civil Wars in Africa" proceeded, upon their return to Niger, to establish the Nigerien chapter of the Coalition of African Women Against War.

In addition to the issue of demobilization, the terms of the Peace Accord included: (a) administrative decentralization; (b) maintenance of security in the Saharan regions affected by the armed conflict; (c) the socioeconomic (re)integration of the ex-combatants by way of providing educational and job opportunities; and (d) stimulation of economic development of the pastoralist regions affected by the current droughts, famine, and armed conflict. As the table below indicates, the Nigerien government was able to make substantial progress in the provisions of terms (a), (b), and (c) with the financial assistance of international funding agencies—including UNDP, French Cooperation, and the World Bank.[9]

Units	Number Predicted	Number Integrated	Remaining
Nigerien Armed Forces	274	274	0
Gendarmery	66	66	0
Saharan Security Forces	1,602	1,602	0
Republican Guard	91	91	0
Police	107	107	0

Units	Number Predicted	Number Integrated	Remaining
Custom	120	120	0
Forestry/Fauna Guard	112	112	0
Sub-Total 1	2,372	2,372	
University	152	152	0
Middle School/ High School	160	140	20
Teacher Training School	84	84	0
School of Public Health	65	65	0
School of Administration and Husbandry Kollo	61	61	0
Civil Servants	7	7	0
Ministry of Education	73	63	10
Ministry of Health	40	36	4
Sub-Total 2	642	608	34
TOTAL	3,014	2,980	34

The same international agencies, however, were unwilling to invest in the economic restimulation of the pastoral regions from which the Tuareg movement erupted. In other words, the agencies poured money to integrate the ex-combatants into the military and paramilitary arms of the state—thereby reinforcing the militarization of the nation, but would not commit any funds to redress the regional inequalities that precipitated the conditions of the conflict in the first place. This burden was left to the now impoverished government that lacked the material means to deal with the root (i.e., economic) cause of the civil war. It is precisely in protest against this policy of intensified remilitarization of the nation in the aftermath of the civil war that the Coalition of Nigerien Women Against War (CFNCG) chose an iconographic symbol—of a woman, with a baby on her back, breaking a gun into two as she would a stick of firewood—representing their philosophical vision of national reconstruction.

If the international donor agencies and the Nigerien state failed the Peace Accord in its most fundamental, economic provision, the rank-and-file citizens of the nation did not give up hope. On the contrary, they began spontaneously to organize themselves as individuals, as community groups, to find creative ways of economic revitalization of the regions. The most promising of these initiatives have been in the form of small businesses in leather craft, jewelry, and tourist-oriented services. Invariably, women have been an integral part of many of these ventures.

The Cultural Dimension of Reconstruction

Even as some of the terms of the peace accord were being violated by the elite of both sides, it was clear to the majority of Nigeriens that the sustenance of peace in the nation could benefit significantly from cultural "projects" of one sort or another. Some of these were government sponsored and others were products of private individual and group responses. For example, in September 25, 2000, the government organized a major cultural festival called "Flamme de la Paix" (Flame of Peace). This national event was intended to celebrate and reinforce the spirit of national reconciliation. Among the many activities presented at the forum were dramatic, dance, and musical performances; carnivals; literary and other presentations, most of which were intended to underscore the shared historical and cultural experiences of the peoples of Niger.

More spontaneous and more profound in effect, however, were initiatives undertaken by individuals and community groups outside the government. Particularly significant in this period were productions in folklore and literature. The relationship between folklore/literature and the state has always been an ambiguous one. The state often draws on folkloric and literary traditions to legitimize itself and its actions. At the same time, however, it moves swiftly to clamp down on any artistic expression that appears critical of the state. [10] Under the regime of the late General Seyni Kountché, for example, griots, singers, and performers were prohibited from mentioning the names of contemporary political figures, especially if the lyrics had a critical tone. The political content in arts that remained uncensored was the type that celebrated the nation—building ideology of the government of the day—Société de Développement (participatory development) in the case of the General Seyni Kountché era.

With the democratization momentum of 1990s onward, however, there has been greater freedom of artistic expression. This has allowed singers, performers, and writers not only to be openly critical of the state at times, but also to challenge the conduct of the leadership by name.

One such singer who has risen to popular celebrity in recent time is Abdoul Salam, a graduate of the English Department of Abdou Moumouni University and currently a high school teacher in Niamey, the capital city. He is himself Tuareg of mixed origins and a fluent speaker of Tamajaq language. Though, "lettered" in Qur'anic, French, and English media, Abdoul Salam has been remarkably sensitive to the place of orality in popular consciousness, especially as it relates to the identity of the nation. As a result, most of his songs are heavily rooted in the dance-song genre of orality and performance, and their lyrics are often crafted in a variety of local languages, maintaining the beat and rhythm of the oral essence of various ethnic groups.

Of particular relevance for our discussion of postwar reconstruction, is his song entitled "Unité Nationale" (National Unity) which is reproduced below. Since its release, it has remained a major hit in the country, serving to inspire the population toward national reconciliation.

The Peace Dance Song of Abdoul Salam

Unité Nationale

French language—Unité nationale, Unité nationale, Unité nationale, Unité nationale

Tamajaq language—Hausa language—French Eheee ehehehe ehe Hayma ne / ehe hayma ne Ehe zancen unité nationale

Hausa Language—Zancen unité nationale zancen kowa Zancen unité nationale zancen kowa

Ya shahi yara, ya shahi uwayen yara Ya shahi yara, ya shahi uwayen yara

Bay bar maza ba, bay bar mata ba Bay bar maza ba, bay bar mata ba

Maza na Nijar da mata na Nijar da yara na Nijar Ba zama muke ba don babu lokaci ne Mu je mu Nyame inda manya suke Manya siyasa mu gwada musu kukanmu tsohin talakkawa

"National Unity"

National unity, National unity, National unity, National unity

Eheeee ehehehe ehe Oh! My heart! Oh! My heart! Oh! you [the listener] National Unity

Talking about national unity is everybody's business Talking about national unity is everybody's business

It concerns children, it concerns the children's parents It concerns children, it concerns the children's parents

It does not exempt men, it does not exempt women It does not exempt men, it does not exempt women

Men of Niger, Women of Niger and Children of Niger We shan't [idly] sit because there is no time Let's go to Niamey where the leaders are To present the political leaders our cries and the elderly poor, too

Zancen siyasa ba hushi ake ba ba
hwada ake ba Zancen siyasa ba
hushi ake ba kuma ba gaba ake ba
Hushi da gaba ba alheri ba ne ba
Hushi da gaba ba alheri ba ne ba

Political engagement does not
mean getting upset or getting
into fights Political engagement
does not involve getting upset or
holding grudges Getting upset
and holding grudges don't lead to
any happy outcomes Getting upset
and holding grudges don't lead to
any happy outcomes

Ku dibi Laberiya irin haka inda
ta kai su Ku dibi Kongo irin haka
inda ya kai su Ku dibi Seriya
Lewon irin haka inda ya kai su
Ku dibi Burundi irin haka inda ya
kai su

See what happened to Liberia,
[see] what these kinds of things
have led them to. See what happened to Kongo, [see] what these
kinds of things have led them
to. See what happened to Sierra
Leone, [see] what these kinds
of things led them to. See what
happened to Burundi, [see] what
these kinds of things have led
them to.

Mu dibi kanmu in kasan nan
muke so Ku dibi kanku in kasan
nan kuke so Mu dibi kanmu in
kasan nan muke so Ku shirya
kanku in kasar nan kuke so

Let's be self-reflexive if it is this
nation that we love Be self-
reflexive if it is this nation that
you love Let's be self-reflexive if
it is this nation that we love Unite
your minds if it is this nation that
you love

Tanja Mamadu da kai muke
Maman Usmanu da kai muke
Mahaman Yusuf da kai muke
Hamid Aghabit da kai muke
Mumuni Jarmakoy da kai muke
Akoli Daweyl da kai muke Duk
yen siyasa da ku muke

Tanja Mamadu, you are the one we
are addressing Maman Usmanu,
you are the one we are addressing Mahaman Yusuf, you are the
one we are addressing Hamid
Alghabit, you are the one we are
addressing Mumuni Jarmakoy,
you are the one we are addressing
Akoli Daweyl, you are the one we
are addressing All of you political leaders [are the ones we are
addressing]

Mu shirya kanmu, mu shirya kanmu in kasar nan muke so Mu shirya kanmu in kasar nan muke so Mu shirya kanmu in kasar nan muke so

Let's bring our minds together, let's unite if it is this nation that we love To unite if it is this nation that we love To unite if it is this nation that we love

French language—

Unité nationale, Unité nationale, Unité nationale, Unité nationale

National unity, National unity, National unity, National unity,

Code Switching- Dialogue Mode French-Tamajaq-Hausa-Zarma T: Muhammad, ehe, ga shi wannan Muslim shina fadi unit, na warla? [Hausa-Tamajaq] Z: Unite ga ti ir ma ker di [Zarma] T: In rike ka? [Hausa] Z: Manti wodi. [zarma] T: To mine ne? [Hausa]

T: Muhammad, what does this Muslim [fellow] mean by unity, unity? Z: Unity, means we should hold each other. T: That I hold you? Z: I don't mean that! T: Ok, What does it mean? Z: That we be of the same mother and same father! T: That we be of the same mother and same father?

Z: Ir mate ?a fo da baba fo! [Zarma] T: Mu zam uwa dai da uba dai? Yar wallah! Wanga bazabarme akwai dan wayo gare ka. Ashe!   Lissafi gare ka. Ke nan mu yi rawan t?nde tare,   mu ci kopto tare! Dan kasa wanga shi ne ya hi ...muna duka alheri [Hausa] Tamajaq Language—Eheeeee ... eheheheeeeeee Eheeeee ...ehehe- heeeeeee Hayma ne ehe haymane hayma ne unit nationale Betuni unit nationale, betun unite nationale Betuni unit nationale betun nakiyan Wurtoya barbaran, Wurtoya bar- baradan Wurtoya bararan Wurtoya yahmedan akiccin dodan

Oh! Zarma fellow you are smart at times, arent you? Indeed, you do analyze well. So it means we can dance to the Tuareg dance-poetry together and eat spinach together! This way is the best for all the citizens of this country [nation].

Eheeeee ...eheheheeeeeee Eheeeee ...eheheheeeeeee Oh, My heart! Oh, My heart! Oh! you [the listener] National Unity Talking about national unity is everybodys' business It does not exempt children, it does not exempt the parents It does not exempt men nor women.

The song opens by foregrounding the theme of national unity as one of great urgency needing the attention of every citizen of the country, including, most importantly, politicians whose "vocation" it has become to engage in trivialities and personal bickering. It then proceeds to invoke the horrific examples of war-torn African countries, as a result of the failure to forge a transethnic national consciousness. Accordingly, the "love of the nation" itself comes to be pegged to the willingness of citizens to engage in a self-reflective exercise of interrogating the "narrow" forms of the ethnic identification in favor of the more embracing postcolonial nationhood. In this regard, the artist challenges individual leaders of ethnic- and/or class-bound political parties to invest their energies positively to finding solutions to the problems facing the different constituencies of the disenfranchised majority in order to maintain the integrity of a healthy nationhood. This exhortation of the political elite is made in the context of a tradition in which ethnicity is used divisively to further political ends even as these elites themselves are products of ethnocultural blending.

On the surface of it, the theme of national unity in Abdoul Salam's song almost seems to betray a certain acquiescence to the colonially inscribed terms of ethnic identification, which, unchecked, in the artist's opinion, can lead to the kind of genocidal horrors that bedeviled countries like Burundi and Rwanda. At another level, however, Abdoul Salam seeks to inscribe a new understanding of Brassage Sahélien of a person tied to multiple ethnic threads, one in which Nigeriens can belong to a multiplicity of ethnocultural entities all at once. He demonstrates this possibility by highlighting the place of language and Islam in shaping Nigerien identity. The larger portion of the lyrics of the song is in Hausa language, the predominant lingua franca of the nation. Yet, the title of the song, which cuts across the rest of the song and constitutes its main theme, is in French, a language of French-educated elite who comprise less than 10 percent of the overall population of Niger Republic. It is precisely this anomaly that becomes the subject of the satirical and penultimate stanza that has a dialogic format.

In this particular satirical stanza, a Tuareg asks his Zarma banter-sibling using code-switching between Tamajaq and Hausa: "Muhammad, what does this Muslim mean by "Unité (unity), unité?" This question raises a number of issues: First, it exposes the enduring problem of an entrapped elite trying to communicate issues of great national importance in an "alien" language that is still inaccessible to the majority of the citizenry. Indeed, even for a phrase like "national unity" the only thing that the Tuareg inquirer could remember is the word "Unité." This is not only a measure of people's incomprehension of the French language, but also the distrust that such exclusionary modes of communication inculcate in their minds.

It is equally significant that the Tuareg inquirer identifies the singer by his religious affiliation as the "Muslim" fellow, and not by an ethnic or regional designation. What is clearly happening here is the emphasis on Islam as a shared religious and cultural heritage across the "ethnic divide." Even as the artist is talking about national unity, the Tuareg inquirer has already identified an existing thread of historical and cultural experience that binds the nation, that is Islam. So, what "Unité" beyond that forged by Islam are we talking about, wonders the Tuareg.

The Tuareg's interlocutor is of Zarma background. In fact, he refers to him as "D'an Bazabarme" meaning "son of Zarma." The Zarma man's response is primarily humorous and conveyed in the Zarma language. The entire dialogue is coached in a style and tone that draw from the tradition of a joking relationship that historically framed the interaction between many ethnocultural groups in the country, but more especially between the Zarma and the Tuareg. In addition, the dialogue takes place in three different indigenous languages—Hausa, Tamajaq, and Zarma—without impeding communication. In essence, then, Abdoul Salam challenges those who advocate French as the national language of the country and who regard the multiplicity of indigenous languages as a barrier to transethnic communication. On the contrary, the dialogue in the song between the Tuareg and the Zarma not only treat French as alien and incomprehensible, but it celebrates multilingualism as a bridge rather than a barrier to national unity.

After several attempts by the Zarma man to offer a metaphorical interpretation of what "Unité Nationale" means, it finally dawns on the Tuareg man that "Unité Nationale" suggests that "We can dance and eat Kopto [spinach] together." Symbolically, in Zamra culture, Kopto is a staple dish of the common person. This definition of "Unité Nationale" sees the process of sharing national resources, no matter how meager they may be, as fundamental for the construction of national unity. It is a process by which people can connect in celebration as in mourning, in abundance as in hardship.

The last stanza of the song is entirely in Tamajaq language. It is the kind of chorus that again calls for everyone in the nation to make the quest for national unity a central concern of their lives. Tamajaq, of course, is the language of the Tuareg people who engaged in armed resistance against their marginalization and disenfranchisement in the nation. Through the use of Tamajaq in the song, therefore, Abdoul Salam shows both his disapproval of Tuareg disenfranchisement and gives them a voice as partners in the search for national unity.

In the final analysis, then, even if the nation has come to be conceptualized in ethnolinguistic terms reminiscent of the colonial legacy, the song "Unité Nationale" emphasizes the necessity of reaching out to each other, drawing on historical connections that bind the people. Yet, these linkages ought not to be established in a manner that is uncritical of the distributive inequalities existing in the nation. It is only a transethnic consciousness rooted in distributive justice that can be a fabric for a new national tapestry of identity in the aftermath of the armed conflict.

In addition to the type of folkloric genres represented by Abdoul Salam's song above, which are targeted for the wider audience, there have also been relevant literary productions targeted specifically at the young in schools. A good example of these postwar reconstructive attempts in the cultural arena is the novella by Muhammad Aghali written in language Tamajaq and entitled (*Sister of Shado or the Price of Tolerance*). This novella was ranked highest among the literary texts in language Tamajaq intended for schools. As a result of its success, it has been listed for translation in other local languages used in schools as well as in French. The summary of the novella presented by the 2003 literary competition is as follows:

> Wars are born in people's minds, therefore the value of peace must be in the minds of people." Two children, a boy and a girl, live innocently according to the gifts that a war-torn land offers them. A group of refugees coming from Shada arrives in Kataka. While Shada is the land of the girl, Kataka is the hometown of the boy. It happens that life binds the two youngsters by a great friendship. The father of the boy is the military commandant who must manage the flux of refugees from Shada and these are grouped into two categories. One category is sent to the prisoner camp since it includes the people not supported by the government of Kataka, whereas the other category is sent to a safe heaven where its members were able to recuperate strength before returning to the front.
>
> Unfortunately, the young girl and her parents belonged to the "cursed" category. Thus begins the torment of the commandant who was torn between his duty and passion for these two young children and friends. After long soul searching, he is seized by the "flame of reason, love, passion and love of one's neighbor and disregard for fictive barriers that human evil implant in humanity.[11]

Further, the jury of the literary competition commented:

> Although this novella was initially conceived as children's literature, it also calls for adults' consciousness on injustices and intolerance which they produce in the system of governance.[12]

Through this type of children's literature, then, cultural activists are trying to shape a new consciousness of Nigerien nationhood by infusing the educational curriculum for the young of the society with a content that is sensitive to issues of equality and distributive justice.

Conclusion

I began this essay by giving a description of the "Tuareg Rebellion" in Niger Republic and its root politico-economic causes. In the process, I also demonstrated how the attempted racialization of Nigerien society by French colonial ideology came to feed the "ethnic" war machine in the postcolonial dispensation in spite of the tradition of Sahelian Brassage that had defined this Sahelian space for centuries. Under the circumstances, one is bound to agree with Mahmood Mamdani that at times "racial differentiation can be an attempt to biologize and rationalize class [or group] differences at a time of crises."[13] Such ideological exercises of "biologizing" class (or group) differences are often undertaken by those in power. But in the case of Niger, it was some of the elite of the marginalized Tuareg who initially resorted to the "race" card to give further legitimacy to the conflict. In the meantime, the state, too, resorted to the same principle of biological determinism in its repressive hunt for the Tuareg combatants and their sympathizers.

The peace accord signed between the leaders of the Tuareg Armed Resistance and the government was a comprehensive one. Yet, its greatest success was in the integration of the Tuareg ex-combatants into the nation's units of the national armed forces—militarizing the society even further. In the more crucial sphere of the economy, the Peace Accord ended up relying on the resourcefulness and ingenuity of the affected citizens themselves.

At the same time, there have been some great cultural initiatives seeking to reinforce the spirit of peace by cultivating the citizens' awareness not only of the horrors of war but also of their shared history and shared destiny as sources of a shared identity. To the extent that the economic problems that triggered the conflict are yet to be resolved, these cultural productions could serve a palliative function, masking the failure of the state and international agencies to intervene effectively in the economic reconstruction of the war-torn regions. On the other hand, some of the cultural activities, like Abdoul Salam's song and the novella, have the potential to serve as ideological inspiration for yet another phase of militant resistance. For as much as they continue to preach the gospel of peace and unity, they have left no room for doubt that the only path for an enduring peace and a united nation is the eradication of inequality in the material well-being of the citizens of Niger Republic.

Notes

1. Robert Charlick, *Niger: Personal Rule and Survival in the Sahel* (Boulder, CO: Westview Press, 1991).

2. Ibid.

3. Ibid., 141-42.

4. Ousseina Alidou, "Popular Drama in Hausa Culture and the Politics of its Appropriation," in *African Visions: Literary Images, Political Change and Social Struggle in Contemporary Africa,* eds. Cheryl Mwaria, Silvia Federici, and John McLaren (Westport, CT: Greenwood Press, 2000), 193-208.

5. William Miles, *Hausaland divided: Colonialism and independence in Nigeria and Niger* (Ithaca: Cornell University Press, 1994).

6. Bill Ashcroft, "Language and Race," *Social Identities* 7, 3 (2001): 311.

7. Mahmood Mamdani, *When Victims Become Killers: Colonialism, Nativism, and the Genocide in Rwanda* (Princeton: Princeton University Press, 2001), 76-102.

8. Meredeth Turshen and Ousseina Alidou, "Women and war," *Bulletin of Africa Concerned Scholar: Women and War* 55/56 (1999): 1-5.

9. Republic of Niger, "L'Avènement des conflits récents au Niger: Cas de la rébellion armée." Report of the High Commission for .the Restoration of Peace, Office of the President, June 2001: 6-7.

10. Alidou, Popular drama in Hausa culture and the politics of its appropriation. 2000: 201

11. Translated from Malam Garba Mamane, *Summary of the 2003 Literary Competition Texts,* (Niamey: PEB2-GTZ, 2003).

12. Ibid.

13. Mamdani, *When victims become killers,* 77.

TWENTY FOUR

A Promise for the Future?
Student Crisis at the University of Buea, Cameroon

Molem
Christopher Sama
and
Debora
Johnson-Ross

Abstract

Cameroon is at the crossroads of West and Central Africa and, by virtue of its tricolonial heritage, designates English and French as official languages, German having been superseded. The two official languages have engendered a complex duality at almost every level of society, particularly within the highly centralized government. The higher education system reflects both the centralization of the administrative process and the "split personality" it fosters. There are six state-funded universities in Cameroon. The University of Buea (UB) is the only one to proudly proclaim an Anglo-Saxon character.

The University of Buea, true to Cameroon's dual nature, is both a point of pride and a source of conflict to the state. Following the Anglo-Saxon tradition and located in the English-speaking South West Province, UB attracts mostly Anglophone students. As its competitiveness and educational standards have been proven, increasingly more Francophone students seek admission. The university has been relatively peaceful until recent times during which student demonstrations have occurred each academic year since 2005. These strikes may be attributed to a variety of factors including growing student political organization and sense of empowerment, along with the lack of adequate university funding and resources. In addition to these factors, the growing Francophone preference for English-language education has acted as a catalyst for competition as limited spaces in the university increasingly go to Francophones. The situation became more complex when in the November 2006 UB student strike, both Anglophone and Francophone students demonstrated. The strike was highly politicized, ultimately resulting in two student deaths and the demotion of the vice chancellor.

Introduction

In his 2002 article on student strikes in Cameroon, Piet Konings argues that Cameroonian students played an "exceptional" role in Cameroon's political liberalization process from 1990 to 1996, particularly at the University of Yaoundé[1]. (Konings, 2002: 181). A major emphasis of Konings's argument involves the tensions between the autochthonous Beti students who called the Centre Province home and the Anglophone and Bamileke "stranger" students who were rendered somewhat ineffective in struggles against the state because of protracted infighting. The fact that the University of Yaoundé was the single state university during most of this time period was crucial because students had little space in which to maneuver, both literally and figuratively. The university's infrastructure was deteriorating; classes of 1,000 or more students in venues designed to hold half that number were common; and structural adjustment programs (SAPs) severely constrained the financial resources needed to improve the state of higher education in Cameroon. By 1993, however, the university system was expanded with the establishment of six regional universities—Yaoundé I, Yaoundé II, Dschang, Ngaoundere, Douala, and Buea. This restructuring of the university system has engendered a number of changes, not the least of which are the ways in which groups of students relate to one another and the ways in which they communicate with the state. The University of Buea strike of November-December 2006 was marked by violence on the parts of students and the state as in previous strikes, but it was also characterized by student action based not on ethnic differences, but on solidarity against the state. This chapter reports on a survey that attempted to illuminate student motivation for this particular strike and the ways in which it may mark a new period in Cameroon's political evolution.

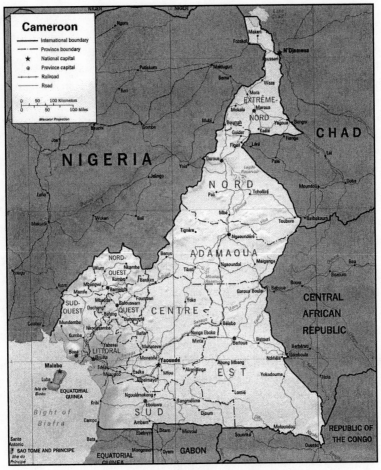

Map of Cameroon[2]

The Setting

The University of Buea (UB) is the only English-speaking university in Cameroon, as well as in the Central African subregion, and thus holds a special status within the university structure. It is one of the few government institutions at which all who enter conduct business largely in English. Although both English and French are official languages of the state, it is common to conduct government-related business in French (although the situation is becoming more balanced between English and French incrementally, at least in the Anglophone provinces—South West and North West). The University of Buea student body has grown exponentially from approximately 3,000 in 1995 to nearly 15,000 in 2006.

UB's growth can be attributed to three factors—increased access to higher education in general; UB's reputation for providing a solid education; and growth in numbers of Francophone students desiring to be educated in English. The resources available for UB have not increased to levels commensurate with the institution's needs, however, and students consistently complain about the fees and inadequate facilities they endure. It would be quite easy in this context to suggest that students decided to strike for these reasons, but such a suggestion would be woefully insufficient. Klopp and Orina argue that student struggles are "fundamentally linked to wider struggles to democratize the state and economy."[3] The results of the UB student survey reported herein support this view.

In November 2006, UB opened the first medical school in the English-speaking provinces of Cameroon. Admission to the medical school was to be based on a written examination, followed by an interview. The written examination was announced by the Ministry of Higher Education and was held without incident. The results of the exam were announced and published by the vice chancellor (VC) of the University of Buea.[4] The announcement also included notification of those who were to be interviewed on the basis of attaining a predetermined grade on the examination. At this point the minister of higher education took exception to the vice chancellor's announcement. Since the written exam had originally been announced by the minister of higher education, it was considered his prerogative to announce the results. The results announced by the VC were retracted and the list of students to be interviewed for admission was revised. Additional names were added to inject "regional balance" into the admissions process, according to the Ministry. Significantly, this was the first time that "regional balance" was publicly promulgated as a state policy. The minister of higher education issued a press release that stated in part:

> ...the list of eligible candidates to sit the oral part of the examination [was] composed of 127 anglophone candidates and no francophone candidate, whereas out of the 870 candidates who sat for the written part of this examination, there were 292 francophone candidates, that is 33.56% of the total....As a result...26 best francophone candidates were added by the Jury to the list of eligible candidates to sit for the oral part of the examination, without suppressing a single name of successful anglophone candidates, thereby bringing the total number of candidates eligible to sit for the oral part of the examination to 153.[5]

Dibussy Tande also reported:

And when the final list of the 85 successful candidates was made public, an accompanying press release stressed that the list was driven by "regional balance" considerations. For the first time in the history of public examinations in Cameroon, official results included a detailed breakdown of the linguistic and provincial origins of the successful candidates:—25 Francophones were admitted against 60 Anglophones with the following provincial breakdown: 39 students from the Northwest province; 21 from the Southwest; 6 for [sic] the Western province; 4 from Adamawa; 4 from the South; 4 from the Center, 3 for [sic] the North; 2 from the Littoral; 2 from the Far North, and 3 from the East.[6]

During the same time period, however, the University of Douala Medical School admitted its first class with no mention of the regional balance "policy" and one lone Anglophone successfully negotiating the admission process. Tande also noted:

> Although the Minister insisted that this balance was in conformity with texts governing Higher Education in Cameroon, it was definitely not in conformity with the ministerial decision signed by the same Minister in August 2006 organizing the examination into the UB medical school.
>
> According to Article 10 of the decision: *"A l'issue de l'étude du dossier et des épreuves écrites, le jury dresse et publie par ordre alphabétique la liste des 72 meilleurs candidats admissibles à l'épreuve orale."* (i.e., after the review of student files and the written examination, the jury shall publish, in alphabetic order, the list of the **best 72 candidates** eligible to take part in the oral exams).
>
> According to article 12 (1) of the same decision, *"à l'issue de l'entretien, le jury établit une liste des candidats proposés à l'admission au concours par ordre de mérite en tenant compte des notes obtenues aux trois épreuves"* (i.e., after) the orals, the jury shall establish a list of candidates proposed for admission **by order of merit** (*emphasis Tande's*).[7]

At UB there were a series of rumors claiming that the names added to the interview list were those of individuals who had special consideration particularly as merit was expressly dismissed by the minister. It is unclear whether or not students had access to the minister's statements, but their perceptions were paramount. Students widely perceived the Ministry's actions as the perpetuation of a corrupt system of patronage and cronyism. They felt that applicants who had met the predetermined mark should be granted interviews regardless of place of origin or family status. Another important factor was that UB students had just that semester been granted the privilege of reconstituting the student union. The newly empowered student leaders seized upon the medical school admission process as an issue around which to coalesce. They approached the university administration with a list of demands and a request for negotiations. Unfortunately for the students and the university administration alike, neither had the level of autonomy they thought they had in the situation. They were willing to talk to one another, but officials at the level of the state had no intention of entertaining discussions with the students. As with previous student expressions of dissatisfaction, the Cameroon government reacted with force against students who had taken to the streets. The students themselves had damaged university buildings and vehicles among other property. They threw professors out of classrooms and suggested that they leave campus in order to remain safe. The students locked the gates of the university and prevented anyone from entering the campus by the second or third day. Once they realized that this strike was going to be protracted, many students left student hostels, traveling home or staying with family and friends away from the university area.

The government's reaction to the students was overwhelmingly harsh. Police and military were brought in, beatings and vicious assaults took place, and live bullets were used against the students. The fact that live bullets were used by the government forces was viewed as a direct assault against UB. In student demonstrations that had occurred in other provinces, rubber bullets and less final strategies were used to quell the students.

Unlike previous student strikes in Cameroon, media and newly accessible technologies became very important. Even when the government made claims of no injuries and calm at university junction, a new, independent television station, STV, interviewed injured students and bystanders for immediate broadcast. Additionally, Internet-savvy students and local citizens uploaded photographs, maintained blogs, and emailed fellow Cameroonians updated information on a regular basis. The Internet version of *The Post* newspaper provided daily updates (www.postnewsline. com).[8] These media outlets, which fell outside of government oversight, made it supremely difficult for the government to control both the content and flow of information to the public as they had in the past.

One unexpected outcome of the strike was a sympathy strike staged by predominantly Francophone students at the University of Douala. Students supporting one another's causes is not unique. In 2005, Anglophone students from UB took to the streets in support of a student uprising at the University of Yaoundé I.[9]

The Survey

A number of questions were raised by those students who chose to participate in the strike and those who chose to observe from the sidelines. How did they make their decisions? What was the substance of these differences? Were they based on ethnic origins and class as many observers assumed? A survey of randomly selected students was conducted in an effort to understand more about UB students and their motivations with respect to the strike. The findings are detailed herein.

Nearly half (48 percent) of the students interviewed were second-year university students (in a three-year curriculum), and a majority (65 percent) were students in the Faculty of Social and Management Sciences, which is UB's largest faculty with approximately one-half of the university's student population. All of the respondents fell between the ages of 20-24, with males numbering slightly higher at 54 percent and females at 44 percent (and 2 percent no response). Of those who responded to a self-identification query, 89 percent were Anglophone and 10 percent were Francophone. An interesting picture emerges as we note that 57 percent of the respondents were from the North West province, the home base of the government's major opposition, the Social Democratic Front (SDF). Only 26 percent of the students were from the South West province where UB is located, but home to a vocal secessionist movement. Ten percent of the students were from the West, and 3 percent were from the Littoral and other provinces. It appears that 83 percent of the respondents were from the Anglophone provinces (North West and South West), even though 89 percent reported being Anglophone. Similarly 13 percent were from Francophone provinces while 10 percent identified as Francophone. The small disparities in these numbers may be attributed to the relocation of civil servants and movement for employment purposes. It is common for children to be raised in Anglophone or Francophone regions by parents whose homes of origin are elsewhere, resulting in the "stranger" phenomenon. Someone may be considered a stranger in spite of having spent a lifetime in a community because her or his parents came from a village in another province. That village is considered her home even if she has visited it only once in her life.

Despite the fact that 90 percent of the respondents had English as the first language of instruction and 7 percent were first taught in French, 85 percent of the students earned the General Certificate of Education "A-levels" (GCE in the British educational system) as the qualification for entering university and 13 percent held the BAC or baccalaureate (French system). These results suggest that approximately 5 to 6 percent of Anglophones were educated in the French tradition. It is clear that a majority of the students who participated in the survey were of Anglophone heritage. It is also clear that students of Francophone heritage are able to freely attend UB.

Economic status was also a key demographic for the respondents. School fees and other support were provided by parents for 56 percent of the respondents. Another 19 percent were supported by relatives other than parents. This means that 25 percent of the students were either supporting themselves or did not report their sponsorships on the survey. Of all the students, only 7.5 percent had any form of scholarship. The situation of today's students is far different than university students prior to 1983 who received bursaries from the government that covered their educational expenses. The era of structural adjustment programs put an end to this policy and has also led to increased unemployment and diminished expectations for university graduates.

Even students with sponsorships struggle to make ends meet. Fifty-eight percent of the respondents receive an allowance ranging between fcfa 100,000-500,000[10] per annum, and 35 percent receive less than fcfa 100,000 for the same time period. Of the total, only 22 percent (all women) of the respondents lived in the university hostel. A quite large 76 percent reported living off campus with 60 percent paying rent of fcfa 10,000-20,000 per month and 10 percent paying less than fcfa 10,000. If a student received an allowance of fcfa 200,000 per year and paid fcfa 15,000 for rent for ten months of the year, she would have only fcfa 50,000 remaining for food, clothing, photocopies, and textbooks (when available). Many Cameroonians are experts at stretching a franc but at some point in time, this hypothetical student may have to make some difficult choices about the use of her money. This example began with an allowance of fcfa 200,000, but 35 percent of the respondents received less than fcfa 100,000 per year, meaning they would fare worse financially. More significantly, most students pay a registration fee of fcfa 50,000 per academic year. If the student's sponsors expect the university fee to be paid from the allowance, the student is in an even worse financial position. The hypothetical student would have no funds remaining once the school year begins because most landlords charge students the entire year's rent upon occupancy. This simple illustration at the individual level supports the accounts of larger systemic financial ills in Cameroon's higher education system addressed by Nantang Jua[11] and Piet Konings.[12]

Student Participation

In order to understand the student strike, it was also necessary to assess the levels of student participation in university and other organizations. These figures should help provide a context for understanding what types of students chose to participate in the strike action. Ninety-five percent of the students surveyed were aware of the new University of Buea Student Union (UBSU) but only 32 percent paid their union dues. An almost identical 31 percent participated in UBSU activities while 68 percent did not. These numbers seem to solidly indicate the rates at which students participate in UBSU, with 28 percent identifying themselves as moderately active , 9 percent claiming to be very active, and 61 percent reporting themselves to be not active at all. Similarly, 29 percent of the respondents said that they were irregular in attending UBSU general assemblies, nearly 7 percent (6.7) were very regular, and 63 percent did not attend at all. Poor representation of students was claimed as one of the reasons for low involvement with UBSU. Sixty-two percent of the respondents said that UBSU did not represent all students, and a significantly lower 26 percent said that UBSU *does* represent all students. In an expression of dissatisfaction, 56 percent of respondents felt that UBSU was not meeting the needs of the students. On the other hand, a percentage similar to those who support UBSU, 35 percent, felt that the needs of all students are being met.

Another indication of student participation is involvement in ethnic/village/regional associations, which serve to maintain ties to home through cultural activities, sharing traditional meals and opportunities to speak the mother tongue, among other activities. Of those surveyed, 13 percent claimed to hold leadership positions in these types of organizations. Ten percent hold leadership positions in their classes (first-year class, second-year class, and so on).

In general, with regard to student awareness and political participation, the following should be noted. Fifty-four percent of the respondents are not aware of student union activities in other universities, and 55 percent are not aware of student union activities in other countries. Sixty-five percent had not registered to vote in the legislative/parliamentary elections that were scheduled for July 2007, and 62 percent had never participated in the electoral process. These figures regarding the electoral process should not be regarded as simple apathy but rather as an indication of the powerlessness many Cameroonians feel and the feeling that the government will not change even if citizens do participate. Many students and other citizens are simply waiting for the current head of state to expire before they expend any energy on politics.

The Strike

Of the students surveyed, 45 percent participated in the strike, while 51 percent did not. Interestingly, 50 percent of the respondents attended rallies at some point during the strike. Only 25 percent of the students surveyed did not support the strike at all. A very large 80 percent did not attend lectures, which in spite of their stated level of support, indicates tacit support of the strike. A very brave or foolhardy, depending on interpretation, 4 percent of the respondents continued to attend lectures during the strike. As an alternative to attending lectures, 51 percent of the responding students traveled out of Buea, either home or elsewhere during the strike. Forty-three percent remained in Buea.

There was a range of responses regarding students' perceptions of the reasons for the strike. Some 41 percent of the students thought that a lack of dialogue between students and the university administration was a major grievance; however, 58 percent refuted that position. A second aspect addressed by the survey was lack of trust of the student representatives. This was a particular point of interest because UBSU was a new organization, the student leaders had very little substantive experience in their positions and the relationship between the students and the administration had been mixed at best in prior years. Anecdotal evidence suggested that trust in student representatives might be a problem, but survey respondents overwhelmingly reported that the level of trust in student representatives was strong, with 90 percent indicating trust. In terms of the relationship between students and UB administration, however, 41 percent of respondents indicated a lack of trust in this relationship, and 58 percent indicated that there was trust between students and administration. It is important to note that with nearly 60 percent of the respondents indicating trust in the UB administration, most distrust was reserved for the Ministry of Higher Education.

The next set of questions concerned issues of fairness, fraud, and merit in the conduct of the medical school entrance examination and the admission process. In response to the question of whether or not the conduct of the medical school entrance exam was free and fair, 85 percent of student respondents said that the exam was not free and fair. A very small 11 percent said the conduct of the exam was free and fair. But when asked if there was fraud or malpractice in the process, 36 percent said yes, while 62 percent gave no response. These numbers suggest interesting interpretations. It is not often safe to make assumptions with surveys of this type; however, it seems that such a high "no response" rate to a question about the possibility of fraud that followed the question of free and fair examinations leads one to believe that students may have been hesitant to clearly state their lack of faith in a government-sponsored process. Another interpretation is that they simply were not certain if fraud or malpractice actually took place. Both terms imply that intentional acts of bad faith occurred, and these students may not have been willing to believe ill of those who conducted the examination. Many respondents—86 percent—were willing to say that unethical behavior took place with regard to publishing the list of applicants who were to proceed to the oral examinations. Ten percent felt that no unethical behavior occurred. When queried about the level at which the unethical behavior took place, 75 percent said it was at the level of the Ministry of Higher Education. Five percent thought that unethical behavior may have occurred at the level of the university administration. Regardless of the numbers of students who felt that improprieties had taken place, 90 percent felt that the final published list was not determined on merit; only 7 percent felt that the list was based on merit. The student responses are based on perception, which is often cloudy, but the actions and reactions that are precipitated are very real. And in this case, student perceptions led to the strike.

The next set of questions related to issues surrounding the strike itself—dialogue, violence, and regional balance. Fifty-three percent of respondents felt that the student leaders exhausted all possibilities of dialogue before calling for the strike, while 44 percent did not. With regard to why the students opted for a violent strike rather than a peaceful demonstration, there were a number of responses. Twenty-six percent felt that the university officials were not ready to react or cooperate with student demands. Seventeen percent thought that violent strikes are more effective than peaceful demonstrations, and 15 percent said that the absence of substantive dialogue on the part of the university administration prompted a violent response.

With regard to the Ministry's actions, few students had positive responses. When asked if it was appropriate for the Ministry to invalidate the original university list, 87 percent responded in the negative, while 10 percent responded in the affirmative. Ninety-one percent did not agree with the Ministry's decision to maintain the minister's published list. Eighty-seven percent agreed that regional balance was not a valid argument for maintaining the minister's list. This position is understandable in light of the fact that regional balance had not been claimed as justification for any other government decision. Twenty percent of the respondents were convinced that the regional balance argument applied only to the UB Medical School entrance examinations. In fact, 60 percent reported that they had not heard of this policy prior to the strike. Twenty-seven percent felt that if such a policy existed, it should have been applied to both Anglophones and Francophones. Sixteen percent thought that the policy existed only in theory; 14 percent felt that it would not alleviate any problems, but 9 percent indicated that they felt that such a policy might decrease marginalization. Sixty percent of student respondents felt that the same standards were not applied to the admission process at the University of Douala Medical School. Finally, 30 percent of the respondents believed that the concept of merit was compromised by the minister's actions.

Government Response to the Strike

The government's response to the student strike was nothing short of brutal. Many students were beaten, detained, and assaulted in the most inhumane fashion. Ninety percent of the respondents did not support the presence of gendarmes on campus during the strike, and 40 percent thought that the police were violent and brutal. Twenty-nine percent reported that police killed and raped students. Two student deaths were documented along with many other injuries. Seventeen percent of the respondents felt that the presence of government forces served to further infuriate students, making negotiation difficult at best.

The vice chancellor, Professor Cornelius Lambi, was replaced by the president with Professor Vincent P. K. Titanji. Professor Lambi had been a favorite of the students and 87.5 percent were not satisfied with the government's decision to replace him. While students supported Professor Lambi, 62 percent indicated that the university administration did not adequately manage the strike. Twenty-five percent felt that the administration did not accept the students' demands; however, 27 percent considered that the university administration faced undue pressure from Yaoundé.

Conclusion

Certainly a number of conclusions can be drawn through an evaluation of students' responses to this survey. A Fulbright scholar who was present in Cameroon at the time of the strike posted the following reflections on her blog in the first week of December 2007:

> Some of you may have heard about the student strike at the University of Buea. The past week has been confusing, inspiring, infuriating, disappointing, upsetting and more. As I've said before, there is so much potential in Cameroon—human potential most importantly. And what I've seen with the strike is the government's inability to harness the potential of its

young people. The country is suffering from the pains of growth and rapid change. The government, of necessity and external (economic) pressure, has liberalized appreciably since I was first here in 1995. There is evidence of democratization—NGOs, civic associations, local governments with the power to take certain kinds of decisions, a more open press than has been operational in the past, among other signs of change. The government has put in place a human rights commission and uses the language of human rights and democratization openly and freely. In spite of the government's efforts to liberalize, it has yet to decentralize to the point of allowing professionals to do their jobs effectively and efficiently. This is clear in many spheres of Cameroonian life, not only at the university level. And I write here with some apprehension—I have friends and colleagues who work at every level of higher education in Cameroon. And I am an outsider. But in the few short months I have been here, I see that the centralized system will either drown itself, or kill any hope of innovation and advancement.

The striking students had a point. They witnessed an action which they interpreted to smack of collusion, corruption, or at least cronyism...Rearing its head again was the Anglophone question. The students' initial complaints might have been met with an invitation to dialogue. But the government, as in the past, asked the rhetorical question "who are these students to question government?" To be fair, representatives of the government at various levels, made efforts to hold discussions with the students—and did. Others stymied these efforts. And I wonder if the discussions that actually took place were satisfying to any of those involved. While the setting is calm, tension and dissatisfaction remain high. Students have capitulated basically because of the use of force. Several students have been injured, two were killed, others have been detained and at least as of Tuesday (5 Dec), were still being held. University officials have requested that the students be released but higher government officials have refused.

Notably, at this writing, it has been one year since this strike took place. Tande has reconsidered the strike in light of the recent announcement of the admitted medical students for the 2007/2008 academic year. He notes:

This time around, it appears (at least on paper) that the advocates of meritocracy (however defined in the Cameroonian context) seem to have won the day with regional considerations apparently relegated to the background. According to the ministerial order of September 24, 2007 announcing the results into the School of Medicine:

"The Minister of Higher Education announces that, subject to the verification of their qualifications, the following candidates in the entrance examination into the first year of Medical Studies at the Faculty of Health Sciences of the University of Buea, for the 2007/2008 academic year. They are, in order of merit [my emphasis]…"[13]

Last year, Johnson-Ross, the Fulbright scholar, wrote that

… the government has lost an important opportunity to demonstrate a real commitment to embrace the perspectives of all Cameroonians in this concept they call "unity in diversity." They lost an opportunity to prove to the next generation of leaders that their views are welcomed and appreciated. That their voices count in this political milieu. On the eve of parliamentary elections and in the midst of discussing/structuring an independent electoral commission, it would seem important to impress upon skeptical Anglophones that the education of their children is as important as educating all other Cameroonian children. While the violence has ended and students have resigned themselves to the government's initial position, the government has only succeeded in proving to Anglophones (and many Francophones) once again (at least those to whom I am speaking) that they are welcome to participate in the political process as long as they support the "correct" positions[14].

Based on the quiet, straightforward, and merit-based medical school admission process for the 2007-2008 year, may we suggest that the students' voices were heard? At least the students who participated in the survey may perceive this year's process to be a small victory for them. A more cynical interpretation might be that the government, and, most importantly, President Biya, has once again managed to engage in incremental change in a manner that benefits his administration. One of the most important lessons of Biya's presidency is that he is a consummate politician. There are those who disparage him for his many shortcomings. He has managed, however, to cleverly provide small gifts, co-opting those who would protest along the way, in such a manner as to preserve his hold on power for the foreseeable future. This strike and the subsequent machinations are an example of the reasons why "Africa works."

Notes

1. Piet Konings, "University Students' Revolt, Ethnic Militia, and Violence during Political Liberalization in Cameroon," *African Studies Review* (Special Issue: African Universities in Crisis and the Promotion of a Democratic Culture) 45, 2 (2002): 179 - 204.

2. This map can be located at http://www.lib.utexas.edu/maps/cameroon.html.

3. Jacqueline Klopp and Janai Orina, "University Crisis, Student Activism, and the Contemporary Struggle for Democracy in Kenya," *African Studies Review*, 45, 1 (2002): 43-76.

4. The University system is headed by the minister of higher education, who also serves as chancellor. The head of each university is a vice chancellor or rector, and some universities have a pro-chancellor who sits between the chancellor and the Vice Chancellor.

5. Ministry of Higher of Education Memorandum, signed by Professor Jacques Fame Ndongo, Minister of Higher Education (n.d.), http://www.minesup.gov.cm/index.php?option=com_content&task=view&id=23&Itemid=30&lang=en.

6. Dibussy Tande, "Deconstructing Regional Balance and Higher Education in Cameroon," weblog entry January 14, 2007, http://www.dibussi.com/2007/01/deconstructing_.html.

7. *(Ibid.)*

8. Photos that document varying stages of discussion and tension can be viewed online. One such website is http://www.postnewsline.com/2006/11/disturbances_at.html.

9. Theodore Ndofeng, "Life of Torture," *Post News Magazine* (2006), http://www.postnewsmagazine.com/pages/politics06.html, accessed 11 December 2007

10. The exchange rate has been fluctuating recently but a safe rule of thumb for conversion is to fcfa 500 to one dollar, thus fcfa 100,000 is roughly equivalent to $200, and fcfa 500,000 to $1,000.

11. Jua, Nantang. 2003. Differential responses to disappearing transitional pathways: Redefining possibility among Cameroonian youths. *African Studies Review* 46, 2: 13-36.

12. Konings, "University Students' Revolt."

13. Tande, "Deconstructing Regional Balance."

14. Debora Johnson-Ross, blog "Debbi's Cameroon Adventure," http://debin-cameroon.blogspot.com.

15. This is a reference to the book Patrick Chabal and Jean-Pascal Daloz, *Africa Works: Disorder As Political Instrument* (Indiana University Press, 1999).

TWENTY FIVE

Another Sudan Is Possible!

Lou Marin
and
Light Wilson Aganwa

The 2006 War Resisters International Triennial, held in Paderborn, Germany, saw widespread discussion of the need to globalize the concept of nonviolence and to understand the connections, so clear in parts of Africa, between poverty and violent conflict. The following two short pieces on the Sudan grew out of those conversations.

The Islamic Nonviolent Anarchism of Mahmud Taha (1909-1985)

Lou Marin, Graswurzelrevolution

On Friday, January 18, 1985, there was an execution at Kobar Prison in Khartoum, Sudan. In front of 3,000 spectators, Mahmud Taha was hanged. To many Sudanese citizens, he was one of their finest thinkers.

The then military regime of dictator Numeiri feared Taha and his movement; following the hanging, mass resistance increased, leading up to the revolt of March 1985. The dictator was toppled on April 6, 1985.

Taha had protested since 1983 against an Egyptian fanatic, fomenting trouble between the Muslim and Christian communities in the country. Soon, Taha and about fifty of his workers, four women among them, were arrested. Coming out of prison in 1984, Taha immediately started a campaign against the tyrannical "September laws," Islamic laws that were introduced in September 1983.

Mahmud Taha said openly what the mass of Sudanese citizens thought. He condemned the September laws and demanded the immediate end of civil war between Muslims and Christians. He was accused of instigating rebellion, heresy, and dissent from orthodox religious belief. Mahmud Taha defied judge Al-Mikashfi, widely known as corrupt and incompetent—he rejected any defense. He was given three days to rethink his ideas and then was led to the gallows.

During the revolt of April 1985, Kobar Prison was stormed by the masses and the gallows occupied. For the Sudanese people, the site has become a memorial against tyranny and another type of Islamic resistance.

Mahmud Muhammad Taha was generally named Al-Ustadh Mahmud, the "teacher." He was one of the early activists for Sudanese independence who was thrown into prison by the colonial forces. Because of his strong belief in nonviolence, there was no bloodshed between the British and the anticolonial Sudanese. Ustadh Mahmud tried to overcome the splitting of Sudanese Muslims into sects fighting each other. The sectarian infighting has been a curse in the country and one main reason for the success of military power in Sudan.

Taha's organization was called "Republican Brothers and Sisters," and they followed a nonviolent interpretation of Islam that says that the prophet Muhammad was taught by God: "You shall not dictate them anything!" It is a kind of reformed Sufi philosophy. Taha made a decisive difference between the two phases in the life of Muhammad, the time he spent in Mecca as an outlaw and as a suppressed individual, and the time he spent in Medina, coming into power and then waging war and conquering Mecca, founding the religion of Islam as a kind of violent state.

Taha said that only the phrases in the Koran that dealt with the first phase in Mecca were timeless, whereas the phrases of the second phase in Medina were bound to the seventh century and no longer valid. The timeless phrases of the Mecca period were propagating socialism, nonviolence, a rejection of the Jihad (which Taha identified with war, as against other possible interpretations), and supported the emancipation of women.

Taha's organization propagated an improvement of marriage ceremonies. In Sudan, like in many other countries, young people weren't allowed to marry unless they had extremely expensive ceremonies. Among his community, Taha implemented a simplified marriage ceremony that was without any costs.

Taha's activities were a provocation to Muslim orthodoxy, because he was caring for the non-Muslim communities of Sudan. The conflict between the Arabic-Muslim north of Sudan and the black-African south was a heritage of colonial policy. But it has also its origins in the "unislamic" arrogance of the Arab north, where racist tendencies against southerners are frequent. Ustadh Mahmud was also rejecting the simplistic equation of Christian belief and British colonial power. The Koran, he taught, proposed a radical kind of humanism. In traditional *sharia,* there is discrimination based on gender and on religious belief, he said, but they were time-related and should not be confounded with the timeless ethical norms the prophet taught in Mecca. Today, Muslims weren't closer to god than Jews, Hindus, Christians, or Buddhists.

Within the organization, women had the same rights as men; and *purdah,* the separation of women, was rejected. The "Republican sisters" wore white clothes when they went to public places or university. But they also refused what they called "fashion emancipation" with Western clothing. They also defied the so-called "traditionalist" role of women. They represented a new type of Sudanese woman who didn't fit into the usual templates.

The Taha movement was crushed after the revolt of 1985, and Sudan soon got an Islamist regime—civil war started again. But during the time of the Taha movement, another Sudan was possible, a federal Sudan with equal rights for all communities. There is hope for Sudan because the Taha tradition is still well known and could be revived one day.

———⟫●⟪———

Light Wilson Aganwa, Executive Director, The Sudanese Organization for Non-Violence and Development (SONAD)

Introduction

When the Dioceses of Lund in Sweden and of Lui/Mundri in Khartoum went into partnership agreement on April 20,1995, a need for Sudanese-based conflict resolution training was identified as a priority for the Diocesan community in Khartoum. It was agreed to hold a training for transformation seminar in Khartoum. The aims of the seminar were identified as:

- To reflect on what it implies to be a Christian today in a local and international context and how to grow together in the Christian faith.

- To develop, in that context, a common and long-range vision for the Diocese of Lui.

In light of this, the Diocese of Lui, in collaboration with the Diocese of Lund in Sweden, organized a five-day training for transformation in December 1997. This transformation workshop was facilitated by Grass-roots UK, in the person of David Cowling. The participants for the workshop were drawn predominantly from the Diocese of Lui, where some of this group (Youth for Human Rights and Democracy, now Sudanese Organization for Non-Violence and Development [SONAD]) participated as Parish representatives or Bishop's candidates.

After the 1996 five-day workshops, the participants were charged with imparting what they learned to the sending constituencies with or without support from the Dioceses of Lui and Lund in Sweden. Some of the participants, particularly members of Youth for Human Rights and Democracy (now SONAD), organized a number of training activities at the parishes, members of the General Assembly of the Mundri Council Area Youth Association (MUCAYA), and Wad Medani Archdeaconry of the Diocese of Khartoum.

In exactly one year, more then twelve workshops were conducted at the Dioceses of Lui and Khartoum (Wad Medani Archdeaconry), all facilitated using the available local resources. The relationship between the Dioceses of Lui and Lund continued to forge new relations, and the workshops, which were organized and facilitated using available local resources, also generated a number of new initiatives for the Diocesan community in Khartoum.

The initiators of SONAD infiltrated the community structures after the first Training for Transformation seminar organized in Khartoum in December 1996 by the Diocese of Lui in collaboration with the Diocese of Lund in Sweden in. Members of the organization who participated in that seminar later facilitated over twelve workshops for the Diocese of Lui in Khartoum and a number of outreach workshops in Juba and Wad Medan. These events precipitated the need to work for peace within the Diocese of Lui and beyond.

In 1999, Rev. Anna Karin Hammar, secretary for international and ecumenical affairs in the Diocese of Lund, got funds for Human Rights Literacy Education through Kenneth Fanon, the first SONAD leader. The pilot project was implemented through organization of five Human Rights Education literacy workshops in Khartoum. The project further developed when Rev. Anna Karin Hammar moved to take up a new assignment in the church house in Uppsala (Sweden). The development of this organization was strengthened further when Mr. Kenneth Fanon visited Lund and Uppsala in Sweden in 1999.

Over the past years, it has become clear that the conflict in the shantytowns in and around Khartoum is long-standing and complex and has many dimensions. These include the demolition of Christian centers by the Khartoum government and a lack of courage from the Christians to confront the regime, a lack of unity from amongst the township dwellers, and the continued harassment of people, particularly women, over brewery or the so-called indecent dress, which are illegal under Islamic law. In addition, during the past several years, it was very difficult for the Federal Ministry of Health to admit openly that HIV/AIDS cases existed in the Sudan. But recently, the ministry stated that the prevalence of HIV/AIDS in the country was 1 percent, UNICEF (Sudan country office) put the figure at 1.6 percent. The impact clearly will be devastating if this reaches even 2 percent. The lack of democracy endemic to the region creates community-based disorganization. People cannot develop their independent capacity to judge the ethics of good governance. Creative thinking for socioeconomic and democratic development through a process of transformation is made impossible. The politicians implement the already mandated government Islamic policies, in a program presumably designed by Allah. Any resistance is seen as blasphemous and it is automatically punishable.

Therefore, the initial specific objectives that SONAD projects hope to achieve include:

- To increase the level of critical awareness about human rights in the civil population so that they are able to take control of their own situation and create ways of improving the quality of life in the shanty areas.
- To begin the process of unifying and directing the efforts of township dwellers against inhuman structures.
- To explore methods of nonviolent actions and apply them to actual problems—police harassment, demolitions, and injustices that the displaced people are confronted with.
- To create awareness in the displaced communities about HIV/AIDS.
- To help people with specific worries concerning sexually transmitted diseases (STDs) and HIV/AIDS.
- To encourage religious leaders to incorporate HIV/AIDS in their teachings/sermons.

- To develop appropriate teaching materials on HIV/AIDS for the displaced communities, especially the youth.
- To achieve a just and democratic society through a culture of honesty and hard work.
- To begin to build a responsible South Sudan leadership.
- To prepare the population that would not look to the outside as the only source of support.

TWENTY SIX

Waging Nonviolent Struggle under Fear of Repression: The Case of Eritrea

Daniel R. Mekonnen
and
Yoel Alem

Eritrea is one of the newest countries in the world and the youngest in Africa. Like most African countries, the modern country of Eritrea is a product of European colonialism.[1] The present map and shape of the country came into being by the end of the nineteenth century, when Eritrea was occupied by the Italians, who ruled the country until 1941. From 1941 to 1952, Eritrea was a British protectorate. In 1952, the UN adopted an arrangement under which Eritrea was federated with neighboring Ethiopia. In 1962, Ethiopian emperor Haile Selassie I unilaterally annulled this arrangement, declaring Eritrea Ethiopia's fourteenth province. This triggered a long war of liberation that culminated in 1991 with de facto independence for Eritrea, which was fully liberated under the dominant leadership of the Eritrean People's Liberation Front (EPLF). In 1993, Eritrea was officially recognized as an independent country after a national referendum that resulted in an overwhelming vote for national sovereignty.

The Eritrean Political Situation: Pre-1998

In the first few years after independence, Eritrea enjoyed a relatively peaceful transition. During this time, the EPLF established itself as the provisional government of Eritrea; changed its name to the People's Front for Democracy and Justice (PFDJ);

framed development policies aimed at overcoming the formidable challenges of nation-building and reconstruction; drafted a constitution; and promised to conduct free and fair elections after the ratification of the constitution. The country ratified its constitution in 1997. However, the constitution was not implemented until 1998, when a full-fledged war broke out with Ethiopia, and no fair and free elections have been conducted in Eritrea since independence.

The Eritrean Political Situation: Post-1998

The border conflict with Ethiopia ended after the ratification of the Agreement on the Cessation of Hostilities and the Algiers Peace Agreement by Eritrea and Ethiopia in June and December 2000, respectively.[2] Two years later, the Eritrea-Ethiopia Boundary Commission rendered a final and binding decision on the border dispute. In spite of an agreement to honor the decision of the boundary commission, Ethiopia refused to abide by the final verdict. Consequently, a situation of no war, no peace persists between the two countries. During and after the war, the Eritrean government used national security and the threat of renewed war as a pretext to suspend all initiatives aimed at facilitating democratic transition.

The ramifications of the 1998-2000 war were extremely harsh. Among other things, it triggered a covert but serious disagreement among top officials of the PFDJ, the sole political party in Eritrea. The confrontation went to the public arena after President Isaias Afwerki obstinately refused to convene the regular meeting of all national deliberative organs; as a result, a group of senior government officials (known as the reformers)[3] authored an open letter criticizing the president. The cause of the disagreement was mainly Afwerki's "conduct of the war, his hard-line approach to peace negotiations, and his resistance to democratization."[4]

The reformers' call for increased democratization and transparency paved the way for a groundbreaking political debate in postindependence Eritrea. Eritreans from all walks of life began to discuss issues of paramount importance via the free press, word of mouth, and the Internet without fear. For the first time in Eritrea's postindependence history, university students protested against government policies. Writers and contributors to the free press, editors of privately owned newspapers, businessmen, professionals, and others criticized government failures. The year 2001 saw the most vibrant postindependence political debate on Eritrea's future. It was a turning point in the history of Eritrea. Sadly, the promising developments did not last long.

By September 2001, when the international community was over-whelmed by the September 11 attacks in the U.S., the Eritrean govern-ment arbitrarily arrested the initiators of the reform movement and others who supported the call for democratization. The detainees include eleven top government officials; a number of publishers, editors, and writers of the privately owned newspapers; businesspeople; elders who sought to mediate between the president and his critics; university students (includ-ing the leader of the University of Asmara Students' Union); and several other individuals. With these arrests, the government unleashed a violent and widespread attack on dissent. What followed has totally tarnished the image of Eritrea, once called one of Africa's most promising countries.

The Entrenchment of Dictatorship in Postindependence Eritrea

What exists in present-day Eritrea is an autocratic rule that controls major aspects of the country's life. Political and economic life is fully con-trolled by Eritrea's ruling party. In the political sphere, Eritrea has been ruled by one political party since independence. The country has never seen free and fair elections. Fundamental freedoms such as freedom of expres-sion, freedom of association, and freedom of religion are severely curtailed by the government. Minority religious groups are continuously persecuted by the government. There are no independent courts and no autonomously functioning parliament. Since 2001, only government-owned media outlets have operated in Eritrea. Eritrea is one of the few countries in the world with no free press and is the largest imprisoner of journalists in Africa.[5] It is also the only African country with an unimplemented con-stitution. There are no independent civil society organizations in Eritrea, and no other associations or organizations exist outside the parameters of the ruling party. In short, political life in Eritrea is wholly dominated by the ruling party.

In the economic sphere, the ruling party owns the country's most profitable economic institutions, the major sources of government funding. Such giant economic institutions include the Red Sea Trading Corpora-tion, Segen Construction, Gedem Construction, Beilul Financial Services, Himbol Foreign Exchange Services, and the Intercontinental Hotel. These pseudoprivate corporations have been key players in the economy, enjoying huge taxation concessions and exemption from legal requirements. These have been offered to any industry with potentially huge profits. As a result, the private sector is unable to compete in the market and has virtually ceased to exist.

A major support to the ruling party's political and economic domination is the Warsay-Ykealo Campaign, which was launched in 2002 under the pretext of a comprehensive national development plan. This campaign, equated to a campaign of slavery by some opposition figures,[6] purportedly aims to promote national development and economic progress. In practice, however, it is a well-orchestrated scheme to keep Eritrean youth under strict military control. This has enabled the government to effectively suppress possible threats of disobedience and unrest, especially after the 2001 reform movement.

The national military service law enacted in 1994 requires every adult Eritrean between the ages of 18 and 40 to go through an eighteen-month national military service program. However, children as young as 15 have also been forcefully conscripted.[7] During the eighteen-month period, every incumbent is expected to abide by strict military discipline. Those who fail to honor military discipline and obligations are treated with severe punishment, including torture and extralegal executions, which are now widely reported by independent rights groups around the world. In spite of the eighteen-month limit of the unpaid national military service program, thousands of Eritreans are still serving as military conscripts for several years under the infamous Warsay-Ykealo Campaign. The overall effect of this has been a total subjugation of the most productive segment of the society, the youth, and hence a virtually militarized society. This has also enabled the giant economic institutions of the ruling party to benefit from schemes of free labor, which is provided by the conscripts of the Warsay-Ykealo Campaign.

A Continued Culture of Repression and "A Country of Whispers"

In keeping with the Marxist-Leninist background of the EPLF, the forerunner of the PFDJ, secrecy and repression of dissent have characterized Eritrea's political culture throughout the struggle for independence. During the thirty-year liberation struggle, dissent from the official Marxist-Leninist ideology of the EPLF was met with harsh punishment. At times dissidents were vigorously silenced, as early as in the 1970s, when many members of the clandestine movement Menkae were allegedly secretly executed.[8] Likewise, in postindependence Eritrea, dissent and public protest have faced harsh treatment. The massacre of disabled veteran liberation fighters and the violent suppression of the freedom fighters' mutiny in the early 1990s, the disappearance of several Muslim religious leaders and teachers, and the stripping of citizenship from members of the Jehovah's Witnesses due to their refusal to honor compulsory national military service are some of the major incidents of repression.

Since September 2001, widespread and systematic crackdowns on public dissent and freedom of expression have persisted. This has included the arbitrary arrest of reformers, elders who sought to mediate between government and critics, journalists, midlevel officials, merchants, businessmen, church leaders, and members of minority Christian denominations. None of the detainees has been taken to court or formally charged with any offense. They have been denied all access to the outside world, including their families, and there are serious concerns for their health and safety.[9] As a result of continued repression and in defiance of indefinite military conscription, young people are leaving the country on an unprecedented scale, often with great risk to their lives.

The rule of law in Eritrea is severely undermined, and no one dares to challenge the government in the courts. The independence of the judiciary is persistently undermined by interference from the executive branch. A special court, whose judges are military commanders, sentences people for corruption without the right to defense or appeal. Torture has been routinely used as a punishment for detainees and members of minority faiths, as well as for offenses committed by military conscripts.[10] Continuous round-ups of youth in the cities is customary, such that it has been described as a "systematic and selective curfew imposed upon Eritrean youth." Human rights violations by members of the security forces are committed with total impunity.[11]

The government's policy toward nongovernmental organizations (NGOs) and international donor organizations is hostile and unwelcoming. For instance, under a proclamation enacted in May 2005, NGOs are limited to relief and rehabilitation activities. The government has imposed taxes on aid, introduced unrealistic registration requirements, and denied NGOs the opportunity to work independently of the government with local communities. As a result, civil societies, as a voice of debate and analysis, have been silenced. People are afraid to speak out, as there is great fear and suspicion among the public due to the harsh government repression. This is clearly noted by many scholars and writers. Having made in-depth observations about the capital, Asmara, Tom Downey described Eritrea as "a country of whispers."[12] In general, Eritrea in the new millennium is currently governed by one of the cruelest dictatorships the world has ever seen.

Citizen Nonviolent Resistance

Due to the fact that Eritrea's independence was achieved after prolonged armed struggle, many Eritreans consider the use of violence a viable option for advancing any just cause. Particularly since Eritrea's president's own role model was Mao Tse-tung, the communist leader who believed that "power grows out of the barrel of the gun,"[13] nonviolent resistance to achieve liberty in Eritrea has certainly received little attention from the general public. Nonetheless, segments of Eritrean society have been practicing, albeit in an unorganized manner, numerous nonviolent activities that have considerably undermined the legitimacy of the Eritrean government.[14]

Since 2001, many high-level officials of the ruling party have defected and sought asylum in other countries. Some of them have joined exiled opposition political parties. Hundreds of Eritrean university students who had been sent abroad by the government for higher education have refused to return. Young members of the national military service have deserted and fled the country in unprecedented numbers.

One can safely say, however, that none of these nonviolent actions were deliberately taken to undermine the socioeconomic and political relationships between the government and the people. An e-mail communication between a member of the Eritrean Movement for Democracy and Human Rights (EMDHR) and a friend inside the country clearly demonstrates this fact. The writer states that "I am sick and tired of this country . . . it is hopeless . . . I am looking for ways . . . to move abroad. . . ."[15] Sadly, this kind of attitude is now common in almost every young Eritrean. Leaving the country is not done as political defiance against the existing economic, political, and social order but as a way out of "a disgusting environment."

The massive propaganda of the government media, the monopoly of the communications infrastructure by the government, and the lack of access to alternative and independent media outlets has restricted Eritreans from exchanging new ideas and debating the future of the nation. Any sort of nonviolent action or political defiance faces harsh punishment. In a country where fundamental rights such as the right to freedom of expression and association are brutally curtailed, no one dares to engage in overt nonviolent actions aimed at undermining the government's power base. In such a narrow political arena, it is difficult if not impossible for a unified and disciplined nonviolent people's movement to flourish and become viable within the country. Still, there is room to advance nonviolent action in Eritrea.

The Role of the Eritrean Diaspora Community

As a result of the prolonged armed struggle, thousands of Eritreans have migrated to other countries in the last four decades. A considerable number of Eritreans reside in Ethiopia and Sudan, Eritrea's immediate neighbors. The Middle East, Europe, and North America also host hundreds of thousands of Eritrean refugees, including professionals, intellectuals, and others who maintain close contact with their families back home.

Eritrea's domestic output has been substantially augmented by worker remittances and taxes from the Diaspora community, which numbers approximately 1.5 million.[16] Eritrea's government aggressively uses its monopolized media and diplomatic missions to advertise fictitious development projects and successes purportedly achieved by the ruling party. A large part of the Diaspora community has been confused by government propaganda and numerous ruling-party operatives dispatched around the world under diplomatic missions and community centers totally controlled by the Eritrean government. In the absence of independent media coverage from Eritrea, the government has successfully implemented its campaign of terror, misinformation, intimidation, fear, and suspicion among the Diaspora community. The continuous fragmentation of exiled Eritrean opposition groups has also exacerbated the situation.

In recent years, the trend in the Diaspora community has been favorably changing. With the emergence of several independent civil society organizations and the restructuring of some opposition groups, the Diaspora community has begun to identify the autocratic nature of the Eritrean government. As a result, a considerable portion of the Diaspora community has refrained from supporting the government morally and financially. Yet much must still be done to effectively empower the large number of Eritreans living in different parts of the world.

Managing to win the hearts and minds of the Diaspora community would sever one of the major economic sources, that is, a major source of political power for the Eritrean government. This would also sever the moral and psychological support offered to the government and at last break the link between the Diaspora community and the government. Once the Diaspora community is effectively mobilized, it will be easier to mobilize people inside Eritrea. Almost every Eritrean individual or family in the Diaspora maintains close contact with their family members inside Eritrea. Therefore, empowering the Diaspora community would facilitate the empowerment of people inside Eritrea.

All over the world, Eritrean civil society initiatives are flourishing, most of which advocate for human rights, the rule of law, and democratization in Eritrea. Officially established in South Africa, EMDHR is one of the flourishing Eritrean civil society organizations.

The Eritrean Movement for Democracy and Human Rights (EMDHR) as a Vehicle to Promote Nonviolent Action

The EMDHR is an autonomous nonviolent civic movement that primarily strives to build a society in which all Eritreans are empowered to exercise their fundamental rights in order to live their lives in peace, dignity, and prosperity.[17] The movement was begun in 2003 by a group of young Eritrean professionals, students, and exiles in South Africa. It is practically unrealistic to establish an organization like the EMDHR inside Eritrea where civil society organizations are severely restricted and repression of dissent is widespread.

Since its inception, the EMDHR has served as a voice for Eritrea's youth in particular and the public in general. It has advocated[18] for the rights of Eritreans, and has conducted numerous civic awareness activities on human rights and democratization, mainly via the Internet,[19] radio broadcasting,[20] leaflets, and newsletters.[21] By mid-2005, the EMDHR had launched a project to develop an educational manual on nonviolent action in one of Eritrea's local languages, Tigrigna. The publication of the manual was officially inaugurated on July 23, 2006, in Pretoria.[22] Depending on the availability of financial resources and experts on other Eritrean languages, the manual will be translated into other languages. This would help make the manual accessible to Eritrea's grassroots community.

The EMDHR educational manual calls for an end to violent conflict and the violation of fundamental rights and freedoms in Eritrea in particular and in the Horn of Africa in general. The manual is expected to familiarize citizens with the concept of nonviolent action and to help them understand how it operates in a narrow political situation such as the one prevailing in Eritrea. It also highlights the need to develop a strategic plan to wage a successful nonviolent struggle. The EMDHR has received messages of support. One from the capital of Eritrea, Asmara, states that ". . . it is human and it will require immense endurance. . . Only then the Horn of Africa would . . . realize the futility of violent confrontations. . . Keep it up!"[23]

Members of the EMDHR have a strong conviction that real change occurs from the people. Regime change alone does not help people enjoy liberty and freedom. What is most important is that people must be empowered so that they can obtain greater control over their lives and influence events. The EMDHR is convinced that the first step to realize this noble objective is to replace fear and suspicion with truth. The EMDHR educational manual elaborates on the importance of challenging one's perception by powerfully disclosing the truth about the overall political, economic, and social conditions in Eritrea. Yet, having a printed manual is not enough to effect the desired social change in Eritrea. Thus, the EMDHR has a plan to persistently disseminate self-liberating messages among the Eritrean public via the Internet, radio broadcasting, and newsletters.

Conclusion

Despite the Eritrean peoples' expectations and their hard-won independence, the country has fallen prey to despotic rule. The political situation in Eritrea is extremely narrow and does not allow any kind of political initiative outside the parameters of the ruling party. Current-day Eritrea is wholly controlled by the sole political party, which has ruled the country since independence in 1991. All efforts aimed at ensuring a peaceful political transition have been harshly suppressed by the ruling party, and it may appear that the only viable option left is ousting the regime by violence. However, the EMDHR firmly believes that there is a possibility for nonviolent struggle to bring the desired effect in Eritrea, if all exiled Eritrean political forces and the Diaspora community commit themselves to take the matter seriously and go the extra mile. In this regard, it is hoped that the educational manual of the EMDHR will receive the necessary support from Eritrean and (international civil) society organizations, opposition groups, the media, think tanks, donor organizations, and others in promoting nonviolent action among Eritreans.

The EMDHR is certain that with the combined effort of all Eritreans and friends of Eritrea around the world, physical and psychological barriers that hinder people from the assertion of their liberties will be overcome, and the establishment of a free and democratic society in Eritrea will become a reality.

Notes

1. This chapter is a revised version of the discussion paper presented by the EMDHR to the Sixth CIVICUS World Assembly, June 21-25, 2006, Glasgow, Scotland.

    G. K. N. Trevaskis, *Eritrea: A Colony in Transition 1941-1952* (Oxford: Oxford University Press,1960): 10-11; see also Tesfatsion Medhanie, *Eritrea: Dynamics of a National Question* (Amsterdam: Gruner Publishing, 1986): 6; and Wolde-Yesus Ammar, *Eritrea: Root Causes of War and Refugees* (Baghdad: Sindbad Printing Co., 1992): 7.

2. UNMEE, "The Conflict and Its Aftermath," http://www.unmeeonline.org/index.php?option=com_content&task=view&id=16&Itemid=47.

3. For a detailed account of the reform movement, see G-15, "An Open Letter to all Members of the PFDJ: A Call for Peaceful and Democratic Dialogue" [English version], www.news.asmarino.com/PFDJ_Membership/Introduction.asp, 2003; Awate Foundation, "The Chronology of the Reform Movement," www.awate.com/cgi-bin/artman/exec/view.cgi/17/576/printer, 2002; Dan Connell *Conversations with Eritrean Political Prisoners* (New Jersey: Red Sea Press, 2005).

4. Dan Connell, *'Eritrea' in Freedom House Countries at the Crossroads: A Survey of Democratic Governance* (Lanham, MD: Rowan & Littlefield Publishers, 2005): 234.

5. Reporters Without Borders, "Eritrea: Annual Report," www.rsf.org/article.php3?id_article=13567, 2005.

6. See, for instance, Adhanom Gebremariam, "The Warsay/Ykealo Campaign: A Campaign of Slavery," www.news.asmarino.com/articles/2002/09/TesfagiorgisZewde-1.asp., 2003.

7. Coalition to Stop the Use of Child Soldiers, "Child Soldiers Global Report 2004: Eritrea," www.child-soldiers.org/document_get.php?id=772. The report states, "Since January 2004, secondary school students have been forced to complete their final year at a school near the main military training camp in Sawa if they wanted to graduate or to attend university." It is also common knowledge that aged people are forcefully conscripted into the army.

8. Amnesty International 2005, "Eritrea: Religious Persecution," www.amnesty.org/en/library/info/AFR64/013/2005.

9. Amnesty International 2002, "Eritrea: Arbitrary Detention of Government Critics and Journalists," www.amnesty.org/en/library/info/AFR64/008/2002, 2002. There are unconfirmed reports that some of the detainees have died in prison. See a Tigrigna report on the situation of the G-15 and other political prisoners, available at www.aigaforum.com/equbai_letters2.pdf.

10. See note 8, supra.

11. Ibid.

12. Tom Downey, "What Went Wrong in Eritrea?" www.slate.com/id2124967/entry/2124969, 2005. See also Xan Rice, "Silenced Nation," http://www.guardian.co.uk/elsewhere/journalist/story/0,,1842697,00.html?gusrc=rss&feed=1.

13. Peter Ackerman and Jack DuVall, *A Force More Powerful: A Century of Nonviolent Conflict* (New York: Palgrve Macmillan, 2000): 505. For a discussion of nonviolent struggle in the Eritrean context, see EMDHR Bidho Antsar Atehasasibana (Challenging Our Perceptions) (2006).

14. See Daniel Ketema, "Peace Army in Exile" (M.A. thesis, The University for Peace, 2004), 3-6.

15. Name withheld for fear of reprisal.

16. "Economists estimated that in 2003, remittances were worth around 70 percent of Eritrea's GDP. Diplomats say they fell from $462 million in 2003 to $420 million in 2005." See *People's Daily*, "Eritrea Sells Luxury Houses to Earn Hard Currency," 2006, http://english.people.com.cn/200606/22/eng20060622_276265.html.

17. See the Constitution of the EMDHR, Article 3, as amended in the Second Annual Congress of the EMDHR.

18. See, for example, *Yoel Alem v. The Minister of Home Affairs and Others*, Case No 2597/2004 (High Court of South Africa Transvaal Division, unreported case).

19. The EMDHR has a Web site (www.emdhr.org) through which it communicates its objectives and activities with Eritreans as well as with the outside world.

20. The EMDHR broadcasts its own radio program five days a week, primarily focusing on the principles and practices of nonviolent action. The broadcast is the outcome of a cooperative agreement reached between the EMDHR and the Tesfa Delina Foundation on December 18, 2005.

21. The EMDHR publishes a monthly newsletter, *Meseley* ("my right" in Tigrigna). The newsletter circulates in South Africa, East Africa, Europe, North America, and Australia. It was officially launched on December 4, 2005, in Johannesburg. A report of the official launch is available at www.emdhr.civiblog.org/blog/_archives/2005/12/7/1439039.html.

22. See a workshop session conducted among Eritreans residing in Pretoria on August 14, 2005, at which the development of the educational manual was officially launched. A report of the event is available at www.emdhr.civiblog.org/blog/_archives/2005/8/16/ 1141482.html. See also "EMDHR Conducted a Successful and Colourful Conference," available at www.emdhr.civiblog.org/blog/_archives/2006/7/27/2164815.html; EMDHR *Bidho Antsar Atehasasibana (Challenging Our Perceptions)*, 2006.

23. Name withheld for fear of reprisal.

TWENTY SEVEN

Rudi Friedrich

I've Had Enough of War: The Antimilitarist Initiative and Conscientious Objection in Eritrea
An Interview with Yohannes Kidane

In autumn 2004, the German-based Eritrean Anti-militarist Initiative and War Resisters International-affiliated Connection e.V published a document on conscientious objection and desertion in Eritrea. The core of this document, interviews with refugees from Eritrea who escaped from violence and war, gives a very moving impression of the plight of young Eritreans, both male and female, who grow up in an extremely militarized environment. "I've had enough of war," noted Bisrat Habte Micael, who told of attempted rape and murder within the military before her leaving the country. Abraham Gebreyesus Mehreteab, one of the founders of the Antimilitarist Initiative, represented War Resisters International at the United Nations Commission on Human Rights in Geneva, highlighting the situation of conscientious objectors in Eritrea. The following interview, conducted by Connection e.V's Rudi Friedrich with another EAI founder, took place in 2006.

RUDI FRIEDRICH: Which consequences do you see after decades of war in Eritrea?

YOHANNES KIDANE: The long war for independence and the border war from 1998 to 2000 with Ethiopia have had incalculable effects on the Eritrean economy and society. At the moment, more than a third of the Eritrean population is living in exile. The war has resulted in the disintegration of families and the loss of culture and norms of the Eritrean society, both at home and in exile.

The wars are the cause of Eritrea's misery. They have brought displacement, impoverishment, land mine hazards, looting, confiscation of property, hunger, and other suffering to the people, who have been traumatized by deportation and expulsion from their native land and by the mining of their land.

RF: How is the human rights situation in Eritrea?

YK: The regime is acting irresponsibly, which has led Eritrea to be isolated from its neighbors, human rights organizations, aid agencies, and the international community. Management of national and international affairs has been monopolized by President Isaias Afwerki as if these affairs were his own household matters. He and his administration claim to be the custodians of peace, stability, and national unity. The issue of national unity in particular has been the top agenda in the People's Front for Democracy and Justice (PFDJ) propaganda, dating from the advent of the armed struggle for independence, and it has been used as an intimidating and isolating factor toward opponents of the regime.

Since the late 1990s, citizens have been denied their constitutional right to free expression. A free press doesn't exist except for the Internet, which Afwerki has not been able to stop. There are no independent journals or TV or radio stations.

Arbitrary arrests and detention of the minority Christian groups are daily government activities. Many have been persecuted. They have been arrested during worship services, weddings, and other functions. According to the Compass Direct news agency, 187 Eritrean believers have been arrested, including groups at prayer, intellectuals and professionals, whole wedding parties, and home Bible studies. Often children and the elderly are among those arrested.

RF: Many people are forced to serve in the military. What does this compulsory service mean?

YK: The government is mainly engaged in militarizing the country. Arbitrary detention and forced recruitment of both male and female youngsters, including high school children and adults under the age of 50, are daily events. All are brutally drafted, disregarding their right to conscientious objection and all forms of human and constitutional rights. All are sent for unconditional military service in the name of national unity, the state of emergency, and so on. They have said that, especially in the rounds that followed the outbreak of war with Ethiopia in 1998, in all the drafting, drills, and actual service, candidates are brutally treated by training camp drill sergeants and military command officers. Women have been harassed and sexually abused by military officials both during their drills and after dispatch into the army. Nobody has a right to ask questions, and doing so has very severe consequences.

Education is also part of the militarization. All high school students have been drafted to the military training camp Sawa after completing their eleventh year of study. Students are forced to finish their twelfth year of study in a high school established within the military training camp. In recent years, no students have returned for study at the university after finishing their national service.

RF: What is the situation of conscientious objectors and deserters?

YK: After the war with Ethiopia in 1998-2000, which claimed tens of thousands of lives on both sides and maimed and disfigured many young-sters, displaced thousands of civilians, and consumed the national treasury, the number of conscientious objectors increased. Currently, thousands of Eritreans object to military service. They are forced to leave Eritrea and live in exile. Considerable numbers of them are in Libya, Ethiopia, Sudan, and parts of Europe seeking political asylum.

In Eritrea, conscientious objection is taboo. Conscientious objectors are considered cowards lacking patriotism. There is no alternative civilian service. Desertion is punishable by up to five years' imprisonment, and in wartime the punishment includes the death penalty. But officers are punishing arbitrarily, without a hearing, without a judgment, and are using forced labor, sending conscientious objectors to the front lines or indefinitely imprisoning them. The right to conscientious objection is not observed.

RF: Are there activities against the regime in Eritrea itself?

YK: There is very limited activity of national and international nongovern-mental organizations (NGOs) in Eritrea. However, the movement is very restricted and is supervised by the government. There are no international NGOs that advocate for human rights or follow the situation of forced military recruitment and conscientious objectors in Eritrea, except Citizens for Peace, whose activities are limited to assessing the situation and advocating for the rights of the detainees from Ethiopia.

Due to its militaristic nature, the government does not tolerate independent NGOs, human rights groups, international observers, or reporters. Investigations demanded by Amnesty International and other organizations have not been allowed. International reporters have been officially banned.

RF: Could conscientious objection be helpful in this situation?

YK: Refusing military service paves the way for peace. We need democracy and the rule of law. The people of Eritrea are in a political, social, and economic crisis. We urgently need a healthy democratic political atmosphere, a constitutionally elected leadership, and a multiparty political system. There is also an urgent need for the release of all political prisoners and conscientious objectors.

The ideas and teachings of conscientious objection are pacifist in nature. They are based on humanity and morality. We believe that they can stand against the deceiving, confusing propaganda of national unity and national sovereignty, which are devastating and always provocative.

As many people say no to war in Eritrea, with our neighboring countries, and in our region, responsible people have started to think about a peaceful solution and to develop respect for human life and for the future of the productive, nation-building youngsters.

Conscientious objection is a check or balance against war and militarism. A conscientious objector is a person at the other extreme from the warlords. We believe conscientious objectors can confront and divert the negative mentality of those who choose war.

RF: What steps are necessary to reach a lasting peace?

YK: Enforcing the right to conscientious objection and offering an alternative civil service. Cultivating a culture of pluralism, civility, respect, and tolerance. The political leadership must establish a culture of listening to other voices. Nonviolent ways of struggle and speaking for the voiceless must be respected. Conflicts must be solved peacefully through dialogue, mediation, and negotiation. International laws must be respected.

RF: How can people support your work?

YK: To facilitate our peacework and to be a voice for voiceless Eritrean conscientious objectors, we need help, not only financial support and office facilities, but also training on the issues of human rights and conscientious objection. We need moral support and the recognition of our asylum seekers. We are publicly opposing the policy of the Eritrean government without any protection. This is endangering our lives. We also need freedom of movement in order to facilitate our activities.

TWENTY EIGHT

Matt Meyer

Eritrea at a Crossroads: A Conversation with Paulos Tesfagiorgis

Paulos Tesfagiorgis played a central role in the Eritrean struggle for independence. As leader of the Eritrean Relief Association (1976-1990), he was responsible for securing access to food supplies and health services for the civilian population in the liberated areas. After liberation, Paulos finished his law studies and in 1994 was appointed to the Constitutional Commission, where he played a major role in ensuring that the commission traveled extensively within the country to have its draft scrutinized in a thorough, public debate. The result was a constitution that secures important human rights and a democratic form of government, but that, in order to accommodate President Isaias Afewerki, allows for strong presidential powers and widely interpretable emergency laws. The Constitutional Assembly ratified the Constitution in 1997.

Tesfagiorgis became part of the so-called G15 group of reformers willing to criticize and challenge the president—a group that included senior ministers, generals, and central committee members of the ruling party and members of Parliament. He left Eritrea in April 2001, realizing that he was no longer safe there, and helped cofound Justice Africa, a London-based organization that works for peace, stability and human rights in Africa. He was awarded the prestigious Rafto Prize in human rights in 2003 and was interviewed by Matt Meyer for Peace News *at that time.*

In 2001, at the time of the tenth anniversary of Africa's newest nation, Eritrea was still a place of cautious excitement about the possibilities that social change could bring. Despite intense losses in the recently ended war with neighboring Ethiopia and a few worrisome signs of incursions on freedom of speech and the press, the hopes amid the people of the Horn of Africa rested on hard-fought victories and advances in areas of education, youth and women's mobilization, and popular political participation. Eritrea was poised to be part of the community of nation-states rejecting passive victimization by the forces of globalization, a leader among small countries working toward an independent path. As an activist and journalist, I reported in the pages of *Peace News* the dreams observed at the freedom celebrations.

The headlines of the *Annual Global Press Freedom World Tour*, published by Reporters Without Borders (RWB), screamed out: "Eritrea: Three Years Without Independent Media." Noting that small Eritrea has quickly become Africa's "biggest prison" for journalists and critics, RWB called the situation a unique one; no independent or privately owned sources of news inside or out of the country have been allowed since September 2001.

The unusual nature of the Eritrean case is underscored by the number of staunch supporters of the revolution who have recently raised their voices in opposition to the policies of President Isaias Afewerki. The leading Western solidarity activist and author Dan Connell suggested that the past three years have seen "dramatic and far-reaching turnabouts . . . that contradict the magnificent achievements" of the independence struggle. The sad irony is that the special accomplishments of the Eritrean liberation movement from the 1980s through 2001—the integration of ethnic and religious minorities, the focus on the status of women and girls, and the suppression of crime and economic corruption—have given way to a more typical dynamic: the concentration of power in a single, authoritarian ruler.

Organizing among Eritreans living outside the country, including those who have recently chosen to leave, has raised some international awareness of the problems Eritrea is currently facing. One human rights campaigner who received much recent attention upon his receiving of the prestigious Rafto Award (previously given to Shirin Ebadi, Aung San Suu Kyi, and others) was Paulos Tesfagiorgis, founder of the Citizen's Initiative for the Salvation of Eritrea. A veteran of the EPLF, former director of the Eritrean Relief Association, and member of the Eritrean Constitutional Commission, Tesfagiorgis has stated that he does not believe the situation to be beyond repair.

MATT MEYER: How did the Eritrean revolution go so quickly astray? Is the current quagmire simply the result of a powerful leader turning his back on the ideals he had fought for, or are there deeper causes of a more systemic nature?

PAULOS TESFGIORGIS: Interestingly, many Eritrean academics, activists, and supporters living abroad are looking critically at militarism itself as one of the issues leading to the current crisis. Through the mid to late 1990s, the course of the Eritrean movement seemed clear: though all governments surely have institutional flaws, there was ample evidence of structural changes being made to empower the most disenfranchised of Eritreans on social, political, and economic levels. By late 1997, however, Ethiopian incursions into lands recognized internationally as being part of Eritrea set the course for a war that set the tone for future repression. The war dashed the hopes of many citizens of both countries who, though suspicious of one another, understood the potential bonds between peoples whose lands and histories had been so deeply interwoven. Its intense escalation on both sides led to extraordinary human costs, and the peace accord process that began in 2000 in no way slowed down the military apparatus put into place requiring frontline duty for almost all youth.

Connell, whose previous writings in volumes such as *Against All Odds* have been devoted to chronicling the successes of the Eritrean People's Liberation Front (EPLF), has written decisively of the manner in which "intensified coercive measures became increasingly common" to keep young people stationed at their military posts. With often unclear directives as to how long they are required for duty, the military has now become a holding place for a country whose fragile economy was shattered by the war effort. It was in this context that the first clampdowns began, in counterattack against those who published an Open Letter calling for a full accounting of the management of the conflict with Ethiopia, signed by fifteen prominent Eritreans. By July 2001, after a lively several months of open, public discussions, arrests started in a serious fashion. University of Asmara Student Union president Semere Kesete, the senior class valedictorian, was a symbolic early detention intending to send a message to the many youth who were speaking out against forced military service. Using the excuse of the "war on terrorism" following September 11, 2001, widespread, unlimited detention became the order of the day for all who spoke up.

MM: Would you characterize the current period as one of excesses, or is the repression and militarism of the past several years more deeply rooted in long-term problems?

PT: The Eritrean revolution had much to be proud about: a well-organized liberation movement, clear political vision based on empowering the Eritrean people, and a lot of ambition to create a highly developed, strong, and secure state. The postindependence policies were clear and progressive, though there were many difficulties in implementation. Politically, Eritrea was moving toward a constitutional government and a constitution was drafted with extensive participation of the population. It was ratified by a Constituent Assembly. However, the 1998 war with Ethiopia changed everything. The war was unexpected, and the Eritrean authorities did not expect any military setback. Therefore, the military setback was a big shock and a major setback to the economic, social, and political development of the country as well as to the confidence of the leadership and the general public. Presently, peace with Ethiopia is still an illusive thing, and the state of war still persists. As a result, every aspect of national life has become subordinate to the security and military exigency of the country.

The current repression in Eritrea can be characterized as a combination of the current situation and a manifestation of the nature of a military organization that brought Eritrean independence. War is said to be the worst enemy of democracy and human rights. Many freedoms, such as freedoms of expression, association, movement, can be curtailed, even suspended; detention can become more frequent; etc. Though it is not always justifiable, it can be understood in a war situation if done according to the law. In the case of Eritrea, it is done in absolute disregard of due process of law. In addition, the present party in power is a former liberation front, a basically military organization that was designed to bring independence militarily. Therefore, commitment to democratization and human rights guarantees was secondary to winning the war of independence. This makes it extremely difficult to make a smooth transition to a civilian, democratic governance. The degrees of militarism in liberation movements vary. However, a liberation movement in power without other forces in the nation to temper its militarism, a liberation movement in power that enters into a second war soon after independence, is bound to fall back into absolute militarism. Militarism is its history, orientation, and experience. It feels more at ease in that situation, and even if it does not like it, it sees little opportunity to maneuver to get out of it.

MM: To what degree is the current Eritrean economic situation dependent on forced labor through national service? Evaluate the prospects for a progressive conscientious objector movement in contemporary Eritrea.

PT: Eritrea does not have many natural resources properly exploited to support the economy and to earn it substantial foreign currency. Its income source has been mostly money sent from Eritreans working abroad—remittances. There was not much in terms of economic aid or loans coming from international sources, though it was just beginning before the recent war. On the other hand, Eritrea has about 300,000 young, able-bodied people with different skills in the Eritrean Defence Forces (EDF) idly wasting their time between battles and with no military engagement since May/June 2000. Therefore, the members of the EDF, basically the youth in national service, are used in construction projects—roads, bridges, hospitals, schools, and government offices. They also work in commercial farms. All practically without pay—a maximum of U.S. $25 per month.

I do not envisage a "progressive conscientious objector movement" anytime in Eritrea soon. The nature of the war Eritrea is involved in currently does not make it easy for people to initiate conscientious objector movements as it as assumed, whatever part the Eritrean leadership played in igniting the war, that this war is a war of survival, a continuation of the war of independence. This is not to mean that people support the war and are willingly engaged in defending their country. They don't like the war, but they don't have much choice but to defend the country. Choices are made difficult because of Ethiopia's actions, not abiding by the decision of the Eritrean-Ethiopian Boundary Commission decision, an international obligation that it entered into willingly. It evokes the feeling that Ethiopia wants to invade Eritrea again and gives the government ample excuse to call it a war of national survival.

In Eritrea presently, there is not even a peace movement, an organized citizen movement that calls for peace between Eritrea and Ethiopia. Until we see people committed enough, bold enough to call for peace between the two countries, I do not believe we will see any conscientious objector movement in Eritrea. Those who object to the war are crossing over to neighboring countries as refugees. Those in the Diaspora who object to the war do not sufficiently articulate their objection in such a way as to object to war itself. Their objection is primarily to the repression and excesses practiced by the Eritrean government.

MM: You have stated, "Whoever comes to power through violence and the barrel of the gun would not be democratic, for he would not be accountable to the people." To what degree is your support for nonviolent alternatives conditioned on new philosophical observations, as opposed to a strategic or tactical assessment of the current moment? Can democratic revolutions ever come about through armed struggle?

PT: My objection to change brought through violence is based both on philosophical observations and a strategic assessment of the current moment, which, in a way, are closely linked. I can see people forced to resort to armed struggle to gain their independence or defend their country when all political, civil, and diplomatic efforts have failed. That was the Eritrean armed struggle. It was for self-determination. It was for independence, and Eritrea won the war militarily. But military victory by itself does not foster democratic development. There is something associated with the notion of military victory that militates against peaceful democratic development—the belief in the might of the gun. If this is the case (even in the situation of the struggle for self-determination), we should absolutely rule out the use of armed men or violence to bring change within an independent country. In the first place, for those who are overthrown militarily with their supporters still remaining in the country, hatred will be festering and feelings of revenge will remain in their hearts. When the opportunity comes, they might resort to violent change. Second, those who have taken power by violence will be uncertain about the intentions of those who have been overthrown or removed by force and therefore would continue harassing them, treading in a vicious circle of suppression. Thirdly, it will not be easy for those who have taken power by force to respect the will of the people, as they did not come to power through elections and support of the population. Violent regime change is a complicated process that has the potential of perpetuating itself.

Nonviolent Resistance to the "Other Occupation"—Western Sahara and Aminatou Haidar

Stephen Zunes

Regularly referred to as the "Sahrawi Gandhi," Aminatou Haidar is one of Western Sahara's most prominent human rights defenders. She advocates for a referendum to determine Western Sahara's relationship to Morocco, which has occupied the territory since 1975 despite the International Court of Justice ruling denying its claims to sovereignty in the region. She has worked through nonviolent means to organize peaceful demonstrations in support of the people of Western Sahara's right to self-determination and to denounce human rights abuses by the Moroccan government. Ms. Haidar's peaceful efforts have been met with increased police aggression and brutality. In 1987, at the age of 21, she was one of 700 peaceful protestors arrested for participating in a rally in support of a referendum. Later she was "disappeared" without charge or trial and held in secret detention centers for four years, where she and 17 other Sahrawi women were tortured. In 2005, the Moroccan police detained and beat her after another peaceful demonstration. She was released after seven months, thanks to international pressure from groups like Amnesty International and the European Parliament. In 2008, she was awarded the Robert F. Kennedy Human Rights Prize, with an excerpt of her acceptance speech appearing below.

Stephen Zunes is a professor of politics and chair of Middle Eastern Studies at the University of San Francisco. The author of countless books and articles on nonviolence and social change, his forthcoming book on

Western Sahara, co-authored with Jacob Mundy, is to be published by Syra-cuse University Press. Parts of this paper were originally presented in pieces for Foreign Policy in Focus *(fpif.org) and* Tikkun *magazine.*

The 2008 Kennedy Prize recognition of Aminatou Haidar and her nonviolent freedom campaign is significant in that the Western Sahara struggle has often gone unnoticed, even among many human rights activists. In addition, highlighting the work of an Arab Muslim woman struggling for her people's freedom through nonviolent action helps challenge impressions held by many Americans that those resisting U.S.-backed regimes in that part of the world are misogynist, violent extremists. Successive administrations have used this stereotype to justify military intervention and support for repressive governments and military occupations.

Unfortunately, given its role in making Morocco's occupation possible, the U.S. government has little enthusiasm for Haidar and the visibility that her winning the RFK Prize gives to the whole Western Sahara issue.

Moroccan Occupation

Imagine an Arab Muslim nation, most of whose people have lived in the squalor of refugee camps for decades in exile from their homeland. Most of the remaining population suffers under foreign military occupation, with a smaller number living as a minority within the legally recognized territory of the occupier. The occupying power is in violation of a series of UN Security Council resolutions, has illegally brought in tens of thousands of settlers into the occupied territory, routinely violates international standards of human rights, has built a heavily fortified separation barrier deep inside the occupied territory, and continues to defy a landmark decision of the International Court of Justice. Furthermore, and despite all this, the occupying power is considered to be a close ally of the United States and receives substantial American military, economic, and diplomatic support to maintain its occupation and colonization of the territory.

This certainly describes the situation regarding Israel's occupation of the Palestinian West Bank (including greater East Jerusalem) and Syria's Golan region, as well as its quasi-occupation of the Gaza Strip. But it also describes the thirty-year occupation of Western Sahara by the Kingdom of Morocco. Despite all the well-deserved attention to the Israeli-Palestinian conflict and the importance of working to end Israel's occupation, the failure of the international community—including progressive movements in the United States and elsewhere—to also address the Western Sahara conflict raises questions as to why Morocco is getting away with its ongoing violation of human rights and international law with far less world attention than is Israel.

Western Sahara: A Brief History

Western Sahara is a sparsely populated territory about the size of Colorado, located on the Atlantic coast in northwestern Africa just south of Morocco. Traditionally it has been inhabited by nomadic Arab tribes, collectively known as Sahrawis and famous for their long history of resistance to outside domination. Spain occupied the territory from the late 1800s through the mid-1970s, well over a decade after most African countries had achieved their freedom from European colonialism. The nationalist Polisario Front launched an armed independence struggle against Spain in 1973, and Madrid eventually promised the people of what was then still known as the Spanish Sahara a referendum on the fate of the territory by the end of 1975. Irredentist claims by Morocco and Mauritania were brought before the International Court of Justice, which ruled in October of 1975 that—despite pledges of fealty to the Moroccan sultan back in the nineteenth century by some tribal leaders bordering the territory and close ethnic ties between some Sahrawi and Mauritanian tribes—the right of self-determination was paramount. A special Visiting Mission from the United Nations engaged in an investigation on the situation in the territory that same year and reported that the vast majority of Sahrawis supported independence, not integration with Morocco or Mauritania.

During this same period, Morocco was threatening war with Spain over the territory. Though the Spaniards had a much stronger military, they were at that time dealing with the terminal illness of their longtime dictator, Generalissimo Francisco Franco, as well as increasing pressure from the United States, which wanted to back its Moroccan ally King Hassan II and did not want to see the leftist Polisario come to power. As a result, despite its earlier pledge to hold a referendum with the assumption that power would soon thereafter be handed over to the Polisario, Spain instead agreed in November 1975 to partition the territory between the pro-Western countries of Morocco and Mauritania.

As Moroccan forces moved into Western Sahara, most of the population fled into refugee camps in neighboring Algeria. Morocco and Mauritania rejected a series of unanimous UN Security Council resolutions calling for the withdrawal of foreign forces and recognition of the Sahrawis' right of self-determination. The United States and France, meanwhile, despite voting in favor of these resolutions, blocked the United Nations from enforcing them. Meanwhile, the Polisario—which had been driven from the more heavily populated northern and western parts of the country—declared independence as the Sahrawi Arab Democratic Republic (SADR).

Thanks in part to the Algerians providing significant amounts of military equipment and economic support, Polisario guerrillas fought well against both occupying armies. Mauritania was defeated by 1979, agreeing to turn their third of Western Sahara over to the Polisario. However, the Moroccans then annexed that remaining southern part of the country as well.

The Polisario then focused their armed struggle against Morocco and, by 1982, had liberated nearly 85 percent of their country. Over the next four years, however, the tide of the war was reversed in Morocco's favor, thanks to the United States and France dramatically increasing their support for the Moroccan war effort, with U.S. forces providing important training for the Moroccan army in counterinsurgency tactics. In addition, the Americans and French helped Morocco construct an 800-mile "wall," primarily consisting of two heavily fortified parallel sand berms, which eventually shut off more than three-quarters of Western Sahara—including virtually all the territory's major towns and natural resources—from the Polisario.

Meanwhile, the Moroccan government, through generous housing subsidies and other benefits, successfully encouraged thousands of Moroccan settlers—some of whom were from southern Morocco of ethnic Sahrawi background—to immigrate to Western Sahara. By the early 1990s, these Moroccan settlers outnumbered the remaining Sahrawis indigenous to the territory by a ratio of more than 2:1.

While rarely able to penetrate into Moroccan-controlled territory, the Polisario continued regular assaults against Moroccan occupation forces stationed along the wall until 1991, when the United Nations ordered a cease-fire to be monitored by a UN peacekeeping force known as MINURSO. The agreement included provisions for a return of Sahrawi refugees to Western Sahara, followed by a UN-supervised referendum on the fate of the territory, with the Sahrawis native to Western Sahara being given the choice of voting in favor of either independence or integration with Morocco. Neither the repatriation nor the referendum took place, however, due to the Moroccan insistence on stacking the voter rolls with Moroccan settlers and other Moroccan citizens that it claimed had tribal links to the Western Sahara. Perhaps in part to help solicit American cooperation with United Nations efforts to resolve the conflict, Secretary General Kofi Annan enlisted former U.S. Secretary of State James Baker as his special representative to help resolve the impasse. Morocco, however, continued to ignore repeated demands from the United Nations that they cooperate with the referendum process and French and American threats of a veto prevented the Security Council from enforcing its mandate.

The Stalled Peace Process

In 2000, the Clinton administration successfully convinced Baker and Annan to give up on efforts to proceed with the referendum as originally agreed by the United Nations ten years earlier and to instead accept Moroccan demands that Moroccan settlers be allowed to vote on the fate of the territory along with the indigenous Sahrawis. This proposal was incorporated in the first Baker Plan presented in early 2001, which would have held the plebiscite under Moroccan rule after a four- to five-year period of very limited autonomy, with no guarantee that independence would be one of the options on the ballot. The Baker Plan received the enthusiastic backing of the new Bush administration, which had come to office in part through Baker's role as lead counsel for the Bush campaign regarding the disputed Florida vote the previous November, leading some analysts to note that it was only appropriate that he would put forth a plan that would effectively give legitimacy to a rigged election. Most of the international community roundly rejected the proposal, however, since it would have effectively abrogated previous UN resolutions granting the right of self-determination with the option of independence and would have led to the unprecedented action of the United Nations placing the fate of a non-self-governing territory in the hands of the occupying colonial power.

As a result, Baker then proposed a second plan where, as with his earlier proposal, both the Sahrawis and the Moroccan settlers would be able to vote in the referendum, but the plebiscite would take place only after Western Sahara experienced far more significant autonomy for the four to five years prior to the vote, independence would be an option on the ballot, and the United Nations would oversee the vote and guarantee that advocates of both integration and independence would have the freedom to campaign openly. The UN Security Council approved the second Baker Plan in the summer of 2003.

Under considerable pressure, Algeria and eventually the Polisario reluctantly accepted the new plan, but the Moroccans—unwilling even to allow the territory to enjoy a brief period of autonomy and risk the possibility they would lose the plebiscite—rejected it. Once again, the United States and France blocked the United Nations from enforcing its mandate by pressuring Morocco to comply with its international legal obligations.

431

In what has been widely interpreted as rewarding Morocco for its intransigence, the Bush administration subsequently designated Morocco as a "major non-NATO ally" in June of 2004, a coveted status currently granted to only fifteen key nations, such as Japan, Israel, and Australia. The following month, the Senate ratified a free trade agreement with Morocco by an 85-13 margin, making the kingdom one of only a half dozen countries outside of the Western hemisphere to enjoy such a close economic relationship with the United States, though—in a potentially significant precedent—Congress insisted that it not include products from the Western Sahara.

U.S. aid to Morocco has increased fivefold since 2001, ostensibly as a reward for the kingdom undertaking a series of neoliberal "economic reforms" and to assist the Moroccan government in "combating terrorism." While there has been some political liberalization within Morocco in recent years under the young King Mohammed VI, who succeeded to the throne following the death of his father in 1999, gross and systematic human rights violations in the occupied Western Sahara continue unabated, with public expressions of nationalist aspirations and organized protests against the occupation and human rights abuses routinely met with severe repression.

Nonviolent Resistance

Western Sahara has seen scattered impromptu acts of open nonviolent resistance ever since the Moroccan conquest. In 1987, for instance, a visit to the occupied territory by a special UN committee sparked protests in the Western Saharan capital of El Aaiún. The success of this major demonstration was all the more remarkable, given that most of the key organizers had been arrested the night before and the city was under a strict curfew. Among the more than 700 people arrested was the 21-year-old Aminatou Haidar.

For four years she was "disappeared," held without charge or trial and kept in secret detention centers. In these facilities, she and seventeen other Sahrawi women underwent regular torture and abuse.

Most resistance activity inside the occupied territory remained clandestine until early September 1999, when Sahrawi students organized sit-ins and vigils for more scholarships and transportation subsidies from the Moroccan government. Since an explicit call for independence would have been brutally and immediately suppressed, the students hoped to push the boundaries of dissent by taking advantage of their relative intellectual freedom. Former political prisoners seeking compensation and accountability for their state-sponsored disappearances soon joined the nonviolent vigils, along with Sahrawi workers from nearby phosphate mines and a union of unemployed college graduates. The movement was suppressed within a few months. Although the demands of what became known as the first Sahrawi Intifada appeared to be nonpolitical, it served as a test of both the Sahrawi public and the Moroccan government. It paved the way for Sahrawis to press for bolder demands and engage in larger protests in the future that would directly challenge the Moroccan occupation itself.

A second Sahrawi intifada, which became known as the "Intifada al-Istiglal" (the Intifada of Independence), began in May 2005. Thousands of Sahrawi demonstrators, led by women and youth, took to the streets of El Aaiún protesting the ongoing Moroccan occupation and calling for independence. The largely nonviolent protests and sit-ins were met by severe repression by Moroccan troops and Moroccan settlers. Within hours, leading Sahrawi activists were kidnapped, including Haidar, who was brutally beaten by Moroccan occupation forces. Sahrawi students at Moroccan universities then organized solidarity demonstrations, hunger strikes, and other forms of nonviolent protests. Throughout the remainder of 2005, the intifada continued with both spontaneous and planned protests, all of which were met with harsh repression by Moroccan authorities.

Haidar was released within seven months as a result of pressure from Amnesty International and the European Parliament. Meanwhile, nonviolent protests have continued sporadically, despite ongoing repression by U.S.-supported Moroccan authorities. Despite continued disappearances, killings, beatings, and torture, Haidar has continued to advocate nonviolent action. In addition to organizing efforts at home, she traveled extensively to raise awareness internationally about the ongoing Moroccan occupation and advocate for the Sahrawi people's right to self-determination.

The RFK Memorial Center for Human Rights' selection of Haidar— one of the most prominent opponents of the U.S.-backed autonomy plan—may make it more difficult to push acceptance of the Moroccan proposal through a reluctant UN Security Council. Ironically, the United States rejected a more generous autonomy plan for Kosovo and instead pushed for UN recognition of that nation's unilateral declaration of independence, even though Kosovo was legally part of Serbia and Western Sahara is legally a country under foreign military occupation.

In addition to a modest cash reward, the human rights award includes the expectation that the RFK Memorial Center for Human Rights will launch an ongoing legal, advocacy, and technical support through a partnership with the winner. According to Monika Kalra Varma, the center's director, "The RFK Human Rights Award not only recognizes a courageous human rights defender but marks the beginning of the RFK Center's long-term partnership with Ms. Haidar and our commitment to work closely with her to realize the right to self-determination for the Sahrawi people."

Senator Edward Kennedy (D-MA), brother of the slain senator for whom the prize is named, stated, "I congratulate Aminatou Haidar for receiving this honor. All who care about democracy, human rights, and the rule of law for the people of the Western Sahara are inspired by her extraordinary courage, dedication and skilled work on their behalf."

Haidar herself reflected back on Robert F. Kennedy in her acceptance of the award in November 2008. She began her speech by quoting Kennedy when he stated that "each time a man stands up for an ideal, or acts to improve the lot of others, or strikes out against injustice, he sends forth a tiny ripple of hope, and crossing each other from a million different centers of energy and daring, those ripples build a current which can sweep down the mightiest walls of oppression and resistance."

Haidar continued:

> Today more than half of my people live in Diaspora, sometimes in very difficult conditions, far from their country and their families, while the other half continues its heroic pacific resistance against the Moroccan occupation. More than 500 Sahrawis have been declared missing since the Moroccan invasion of Western Sahara and the Moroccan state still refuses to give information regarding their status although it conducts propaganda campaigns under the guise of a so-called truth commission, an organization that is supposedly for equity and reconciliation and that runs around the world without giving any real answers on the grave violations of human rights perpetrated against the Sahrawi population.
>
> Since May 21, 2005 a nonviolent uprising of the Sahrawi population started, proclaiming its right to self-determination. Since then, wherever there is a strong concentration of Sahrawi, demonstrators have gathered in public squares or on university campuses chanting slogans proclaiming their right to self-determination and waving Sahrawi flags. This is always dangerous for the demonstrators who risk being hit by police batons or even torture, which sometimes leads to death. . . .
>
> As a Sahrawi woman victim of the Moroccan repression, subjected to forced disappearance and arbitrary detention, and also as a human rights defender, I reaffirm today that the current situation of human rights in the occupied territories of Western Sahara is tragic and continues to deteriorate on a daily basis. I bear witness to the distress of the Sahrawi population, and call

for the protection of their basic rights. It is urgent, it is imperative to renew efforts and intensify the work required to put an
end to our suffering.

It is widely known that the Western Sahara conflict primarily
affects the prosperity of both the Sahrawi and the Moroccan
people. It also affects the rest of the Mahgreb and the hopes
of its people. The time has come to put an end to the unbearable sufferings that this situation is creating for the population.
Shouldn't the Sahrawi people, in all fairness, benefit from an
international protection against the cruel repression that they
are being subjected to? How long will the international community maintain its regrettable non-interference approach
while a whole people sees its right to self-determination be
trampled underfoot by foreign occupation? The time has come
to uphold real commitments in order to accelerate the process
toward self-determination . . .

I would like to dedicate this prestigious award to the Sahrawi
political prisoners, the victims of the Moroccan repression and
to the Sahrawi human rights defenders who are performing a
noble task and enduring innumerable sacrifices in defending
the rights of others. Long live peace—Long live solidarity—
Long live friendship.

The Significance of the Struggle for Self-Determination

In addition to nonviolent direct action, the Sahrawis have fought for
their national rights primarily by legal and diplomatic means. Unlike a
number of other peoples engaged in national liberation struggles, the Sahrawis have never committed acts of terrorism. Even during their armed
struggle against the occupation, which ended fifteen years ago, Polisario
forces restricted their attacks exclusively toward the Moroccan armed
forces, never toward civilians.

The irresolution of the Western Sahara conflict has important regional
implications. It has encouraged an arms race between Morocco and
Algeria and, on several occasions over the past three decades, has brought
the two countries close to war. Perhaps even more significantly, it has been
the single biggest obstacle to a fuller implementation of the goals of the
Arab Maghreb Union—consisting of Morocco, Algeria, Libya, Tunisia,
and Mauritania—to pursue economic integration and other initiatives that
would increase the standard of living and political stability in the region.
The lack of unity and greater coordination among these nations and their
struggling economies has contributed to the dramatic upsurge in illegal
immigration to Europe and the rise of radical Islamist movements.

The majority of the Sahrawi population lives in exile in the desert of western Algeria in refugee camps under Polisario administration. The 150,000 Sahrawis living in these desert camps have developed a remarkably progressive political and social system governed by participatory democracy and collective economic enterprises within a limited market economy. Though devoutly Muslim, Sahrawi women are unveiled; enjoy equal rights with men regarding divorce, inheritance, and other legal matters; and hold major leadership positions in the Polisario and the SADR, including posts as cabinet ministers. While the Bush administration claims it seeks to establish such democratic governance throughout the Arab and Islamic world, in reality the U.S. government is actively preventing the Sahrawis from establishing such a democratic system outside these refugee camps by supporting the occupation of their country by an autocratic monarchy.

Over the past three decades, the Sahrawi Arab Democratic Republic has been recognized as an independent country by more than eighty governments, with Kenya and South Africa becoming the latest to extend full diplomatic relations. The SADR has been a full member state of the African Union (formerly known as the Organization for African Unity) since 1984, and most of the international community recognizes Western Sahara as Africa's last colony. By contrast, with only a few exceptions, the Arab states—despite their outspoken opposition to the Israeli occupation of Palestinian and Syrian land—have supported Morocco's occupation of Western Sahara.

With Morocco's rejection of the second Baker Plan and the threat of a French and American veto of any Security Council resolution that would push Morocco to compromise, a diplomatic settlement of the conflict looks highly unlikely. With Morocco's powerful armed forces protected behind the separation wall and Algeria unwilling to support a resumption of guerrilla war, the Polisario appears to lack a military option as well.

As happened during the 1980s in both South Africa and the Israeli-occupied Palestinian territories, the locus of the Western Sahara freedom struggle has recently shifted from the military and diplomatic initiatives of an exiled armed movement to a largely unarmed popular resistance from within. Young activists in the occupied territory and even in Sahrawi-populated parts of southern Morocco have confronted Moroccan troops in street demonstrations, despite the risk of shootings, mass arrests, and torture. Yet, here in the United States, a country that has played such a significant role over the past three decades in perpetuating Morocco's illegal occupation, this revolution is not being televised. Even within the progressive community and among those well-versed in foreign affairs, very few people are aware of the Western Sahara struggle or could even find

Western Sahara on a map. However, despite the lack of media coverage, the Sahrawi intifada will likely intensify as a result of the international community's failure to resolve the conflict.

Next Steps: Building an Anti-Occupation Movement

Western Sahara remains an occupied territory only because Morocco has refused to abide by a series of UN Security Council resolutions calling on the kingdom to end their occupation and recognize the right of the people of that territory to self-determination. Morocco has been able to persist in its defiance of its international legal obligations because France and the United States, which wield veto power in the UN Security Council, have blocked the enforcement of these resolutions. In addition, France and the United States served as principal suppliers of the armaments and other security assistance to Moroccan occupation forces. As a result, at least as important as nonviolent resistance by the Sahrawis against Morocco's occupation policies would be the use of nonviolent action by the citizens of France, the United States, and other countries that enable Morocco to maintain its occupation. Such campaigns played a major role in forcing the United States, Australia, and Great Britain to cease their support for Indonesia's occupation of East Timor. Solidarity networks have emerged in dozens of countries around the world, most notably in Spain and Norway, but don't yet have a major impact in the United States, where it could matter most.

The moral and legal arguments in support for Western Sahara's freedom from Moroccan rule and the culpability of the U.S. government in maintaining Morocco's illegal occupation and colonization of the territory are reason enough to make this a priority for the peace and human rights community in the United States.

Western Sahara is the only land, outside of the remaining territories still held by Israel since the June 1967 war, which is recognized by the United Nations as being illegitimately under the rule of a foreign power against the will of the subjected population. (The only other cases in recent years have been East Timor, which finally won independence four years ago following a quarter century of brutal Indonesian occupation; Namibia, which became free from occupation by the then-white minority government of South Africa in 1990; and Kuwait, which was liberated from six months under Iraqi occupation by a massive U.S.-led military operation in February 1991.)

A successful nonviolent independence struggle by an Arab Muslim people under the leadership of Aminatou Haidar could set an important precedent. It would demonstrate how, against great odds, an outnumbered and outgunned population could win through the power of nonviolence in a part of the world where resistance to autocratic rule and foreign military occupation has often spawned acts of terrorism and other violence. Furthermore, the participatory democratic structure within the Sahrawi resistance movement and the prominence of women in key positions of leadership could serve as an important model in a region where authoritarian and patriarchal forms of governance have traditionally dominated.

The eventual outcome rests not just on the Sahrawis alone, but on whether the international community, particularly those of us in the United States, decides whether such a struggle is worthy of our support. An international movement against all occupations would need to be based on universal principles regarding freedom: the right to self-determination, the repressive nature of foreign military domination and colonialism, and the illegitimacy of invading and annexing neighboring lands. It should be clear that supporting the campaign to free Western Sahara from the Moroccan occupation is both an important moral imperative and a smart strategic move for all those who care about peace and human rights.

THIRTY

Peace, the Environment, and Social Change: A Conversation between Elombe Brath and Wangari Maathai

Patrice Lumumba Coalition founder Elombe Brath, widely respected throughout the world for his expansive knowledge, media savvy, and unrelenting activism on the part of African people everywhere, has been dubbed the walking encyclopedia by National Black United Front founder Rev. Herbert Daughtry. In this exclusive interview for WBAI/Pacifica Radio's Afrkalidescope, *which Brath produces and hosts, 2004 Nobel Peace Laureate Wangari Maathai speaks about the urgent tasks facing her native Kenya and the continent as a whole. The first Kenyan woman to earn a doctorate in science and the first African woman to win the Nobel Peace Prize, Maathai serves as Kenyan deputy minister for the environment and is author of the 2006 memoir* Unbowed.

ELOMBE BRATH: Welcome to a special edition of *Afrikalidescope,* where we have a guest that we've been waiting to get for a long time. We want you to know that you have a lot of Africans on this side, in the Western Hemisphere, who are appreciative of what you have done and are extremely proud of your accomplishment.

First of all, I read somewhere that you started off your career in this endeavor by planting about nine trees in your backyard garden. I want to know how you get from nine trees in a backyard garden to where you are today.

DR. WANGARI MAATHAI: Well, first of all, I want to say how happy and grateful I am to be here, to be able to interact with my sisters and brothers in the U.S.A. And to say that this honor that has come to me I consider just a symbol that indeed is an honor for all of us, for all the troubles we make, for all the efforts we make, sometimes going completely unrecognized at the grass-roots level, especially among the women in Africa, the women in the world, the women who work for the environment, for peace, for human rights issues, and for democracy. This is the first time that the Norwegian Nobel Committee decided to make such a major shift as to recognize areas that are extremely important for us to have a peaceful world but are usually dealt with in a disjointed manner.

Thirty years ago, through an effort that actually was for the preparation of the first United Nations Conference of Women, held in Mexico in preparation for the UN women's conference in Beijing, I came to understand that some of the problems we were dealing with were actually problems that had come to us because of environmental degradation. I thought that those were problems that we could deal with by rehabilitating our environment, and one way that is very immediate and very impactful is the planting of vegetation, covering the land with vegetation, taking care of the soil, literally clothing the earth with her green color.

That is actually where the name Green Belt Movement came from. It started with those few trees in my backyard and when I learned or appreciated the need to mobilize lots of women, literally thousands of women in Kenya, to help me plant trees.

EB: Well, it is the women who do the planting all over Africa, in fact all over the world, but particularly in Africa. It's the kind of work that keeps a society going, keeps everybody alive, particularly when you do it with a kind of feeling for and being in harmony with the land. In Kenya, people have always appreciated the land. As a matter of fact, the fight for land is what initiated the struggle in 1952 to 1956. Europeans had taken over the Kenya highlands, and that's what brought about the Kenya Land Peace Freedom Army, which some people call the Mau Mau. It was the first major push that woke up the British. The Mau Mau went to armed struggle to bring peace.

WM: Our people are really close to the land. Over 80 percent of our people still live on the land, producing food, producing wood fuel, and producing cash crops such as tea and coffee, which they send south. Our people have always been very close to the land. And as you say, when the land was taken away from them, it was probably the last that anybody could do to them. It was like killing them. Telling people, come and let us mobilize, let us take our land back, was a very good way of mobilizing people. Mt. Kenya, as you know, is also the mountain that inspired our people in the fight for independence. Jomo Kenyatta wrote *Facing Mt. Kenya* as a call to struggle and as a tribute to the land.

EB: The land is even central to the folklore, or the beginnings of Kikuyu and Mumbi.

WM: That's right. There is the beautiful Kikuyu legend of how God brought the land and humans together. God brought Kikuyu—the father of the tribe—to the mountaintop, where he showed him the beautiful, fertile land, covered with the forest and with lots of rivers. There are over 300 rivers coming from Mt. Kenya alone! With Mumbi, the woman who is molder or creator, the land was granted for all descendents. I don't know why people look for any other Adam and Eve; they are right there in this traditional African creation story.

EB: Historically, Kenya is a country that is identified with the struggle for land, and yet there are people who want to retain the land even though it is not theirs. Then you have some of our own people who conspire with them because they think that land is something to profit from. They don't understand the concept of African land tenure, which is very close to what the indigenous populations in the U.S. believe—that land is held collectively. Nobody puts a fence around it, nobody says, "This is mine and you can't deal with it." It belongs to the people, and that's a fundamental contradiction between Western and Eastern or African societies.

WM: It is indeed, and one of the important messages that this prize has brought and is trying to emphasize is the fact that many of the conflicts we have in the world—whether it was a conflict for which the Mau Mau was established or more recent struggles—are brought about because of resources. Here we are talking about resources relating to the land, but we are also including human resources. It's a matter of who is going to have access to these resources, who will exploit these resources, who will share, and who will control. The Norwegian Nobel Committee wanted to emphasize that it is very, very important for us to manage our resources sustainably, efficiently, and responsibly; it is very, very important to share them equitably.

If perhaps people had come to Africa and had shared the resources equitably, perhaps we would never have had the conflicts that we have. But they were not shared equitably. Anywhere in this world, unless we learn to share resources equitably we are not going to enjoy peace. Unless we learn to respect other people's human rights—women's rights, environmental rights—we won't know peace. We even must go beyond that and say that there are others who live on this planet besides us, the human species. We have the other species, and they, too, have a right to be respected. Only then can we begin to live peacefully.

EB: People live their lives based on their culture and the values that they share in their culture. Until all people learn that, we'll have these conflicts. One of the things that people don't think too much about is how dangerous it is to be an environmentalist. We can think of what happened to Chico Mendez of Brazil, or we could think of what happened to Nigerian activist Ken Saro-Wiwa. Mendez was the first case of an environmentalist who was assassinated by the logging industry. And you, yourself, have had some pretty close calls. Tell us about that.

WM: Well, I think it is very clear to a lot of people who follow the struggles of environmentalists, to anybody who is trying to fight injustices—whatever those injustices are: You're going to be an enemy of those who want to control, who want to exploit, who want to be in charge. This is true whether you are fighting apartheid in South Africa, or promoting human rights issues in the U.S.A. Wherever you are, if you're trying to promote justice, equity, and respect, you're definitely going to be in conflict, and you have to be prepared for that. You don't go out looking for trouble, but you're prepared to suffer. You're prepared to do whatever it takes to bring out the injustices.

I am lucky that I have lived when others didn't. But the 2004 Peace Prize was not an honor for a single person. This is a moment for all humanity. We must bring more of these movements for environmentalism, human rights, and justice together, so that we can truly create a better world.

EB: Now you are deputy minister of environment. For the last years, have you seen a lot of people in Kenya, a lot of the younger people, wanting to become involved in the environmentalist movement?

WM: Yeah, it has been very inspiring, and I did hope that our people would be inspired, because one of the good things about our Green Belt efforts is that this is not something that we imported into our region; this is something that came out of our own creativity, out of our own initiative. It came out of our own commitment, patience, and persistence; and it really demonstrated that if we believe in ourselves, if we work hard, if we are patient, things will happen. We can change our environment. We are not condemned to where we find ourselves. We must believe in ourselves, and we must work, and it doesn't even require too much money. We can change our own lives. We don't have to wait for somebody else to come and tell us what to do.

EB: Please explain what the Green Belt Movement is and how it carries out its work.

WM: In the book *The Green Belt Movement: Sharing the Approach and the Experience,* I was trying to relate what we did with people all over the world, especially in Africa and other countries that are environmentally devastated, such as Haiti. Essentially, it is a people's movement, a people's self-mobilization to do something about their environment. We began when the National Council of Women of Kenya said that they needed clean drinking water that comes from the mountains—and these mountains must be forested. They needed food that comes from the land. They needed income and they needed firewood, which is still the main source of energy. These are the four areas that women identified in 1974, when we were preparing to go to Mexico. At that time, land was very degraded, devegetated, deforested; there was massive soil erosion. So I told the women, let us organize into groups and let us plant trees. It's that easy: anybody can plant a tree. You can even plant a flower; you can plant a bush. It doesn't have to be a redwood!

Now, thirty years later, there are literally thousands of people in this campaign. We have planted more than thirty million trees and counting, because the process goes on. And I would like to appeal to all people, that if you really believe in doing something for the environment, something for yourself, to celebrate, you can memorialize the relatives who have left you. Plant a tree. Plant a small plant, put it by the window, put it on the table. It's life. It's wonderful.

443

EB: Something very germane to understanding the problems in Africa today is understanding the dialectal connection between the water and the soil. As you said before, you saw that the mountains that the water comes from have to be forested. I don't know if everybody understands why it is important for the mountains to have forests.

WM: Many people don't quite understand that water has a cycle, and it starts for many of us on land. It starts with the rain coming down. When the rains come down in the mountains, especially on natural mountains, that water sinks into the ground, goes into the belly of the mountains, later it comes out to us as streams, as little rivers, as major rivers. If you deforest the mountains, such as has happened in areas where there is logging, then the land loses the capacity to retain that water and allow that water to go into the belly. Instead, the water runs off, carrying with it the topsoil. It runs down like muddy levers and sometimes carries with it people. And when that water disappears, the rivers dry up. That is why in areas where deforestation is massive, there is also hunger, there is poverty, there is inability to feed people, there is no clean drinking water.

In our part of the world, corporations were using some of these mountains to grow commercial plantations of trees that they have imported from the northern hemisphere. These trees unfortunately kill some of the indigenous trees and plants, and when these natural forests are destroyed and you have these commercial farms instead, you do not have the same capacity to retain water. So again, water runs off and the same process is followed. One of our campaigns, therefore, has been to urge people to leave the natural forest alone and to rehabilitate the forest with natural vegetation, so as to be able to get water. And also to be able to get regular rain patterns.

It is also for the same reason that we are very worried about the climate change. We were celebrating the coming into force of the Kyoto Protocol, and we're very worried about the fact that as the temperatures rise, some of our mountains such as Mt. Kenya and Mt. Kilimanjaro are losing their vegetation because of the warming temperatures. And when this happens, again, the rivers will dry up, the rain patterns will change, and people will likely face massive famine because of crop failures.

EB: This is a very difficult situations right here, because the U.S. president [George W. Bush] is one of the very few world leaders who believe in the protocols worked out in Kyoto.

WM: Even in a country like the U.S., and in other countries that have not yet ratified the Kyoto Protocol, there are literally millions of individuals who, collectively, have been very, very busy applying the principles that are called upon in the Kyoto Protocol. That, to me, is extremely important, and we should not lose sight of the fact that we should encourage citizens to continue practicing—at community levels—all of those little initiatives that help us to cut down on the temperatures that are rising. Eventually, it will be the citizens of this country who will put enough pressure on their government to turn things around.

EB: It is so important for us to get you to talk to our particular audience about educating people regarding how simple it is do grassroots community work. It is where we started on this planet.

WM: The most important thing here is for people to understand that the tree is a symbol. For us, in Africa, it's been a symbol of hope. It's a symbol of opportunities, a symbol of possibilities.

When you get down to it, deep into it, there are very complex problems that we are trying to deal with it. There are many issues, some of which can be dealt with by the local authorities, some of which have to be dealt with by national governments, and some of which require global cooperation, such as with climate change. The tree is a very powerful symbol of all these levels of change, because once you have planted a tree, you have a living creature which gives you services. It cleans your air; it gives you shade. Even if it's a small plant, it gives you some kind of good feeling to the eye. The color green is a very healing color.

I also want to say that one of the reasons I got involved in this movement is because I wanted to empower our people. I wanted our people to understand that you really don't need too much knowledge or too much education or money to take care of your environment, to have clean drinking water, to have firewood, or to even have food. This is very important because for many people who have gone through the colonial system—and even during the postcolonial era—we have become encouraged to believe that other people have to help us, that other people have to solve our problems. But all we really need is commitment, patience, persistence.

It is true that these things won't come to us over night. If you plant a tree today, it will not give you fruits tomorrow. It may not give you firewood tomorrow or the day after that. But you have to have the patience and the persistence to stay and make sure it survives. This is one of our messages: to feel that we, as an African people, are okay. Nobody needs to approve us.

EB: Let me ask you this. How do you find the new government—the difference between the new government in responding to your courageous environmentalism? They seem to understand a little bit better. . . . You had a chance to go through the reign of Daniel Arap Moi and were in a situation where people didn't think they were going to be able to get through.

WM: Well certainly the new government is a more democratic government than what we had before. In that government, there are a lot of new people who believe like I do, that indeed we have been very unfair to ourselves, and we have been very unfair to our people.

I represent the children of the Mau Mau. It was my father's generation that actually fought, but it was also that generation who came to power deliberately and abandoned their mission, abandoned their aspirations. We all know about the postcolonial period in Africa, which completely abandoned the agenda of liberating Africans from poverty, from diseases, from ignorance, and indeed appeared to exacerbate those same problems. Because as you know, the forefathers, the Jomo Kenyatas, when they were mobilizing Africans in the 1930s and 1940s, they were actually using those same issues: ignorance, disease, and poverty. They said they wanted to get rid of those ills. Today, we're still saying that we should make poverty history. One of the things that was done was requisition of debt, and we all know how those debts work. They are acquired through corruption. A lot of that money was never used for the development of the people. It was stashed away in developed countries in secret accounts. That's why we are saying: For goodness' sake, let us not punish the ordinary African people! We know where that money is. I'm sure these governments know where that money is. If they really wanted to find it, they could find it and give it back to the World Bank or whoever has lent it. That's also why we are saying to cancel the debt. Be fair with the trades, let us access the market, and allow us to process our product. Increase the capital. If many of the African governments today were given adequate capital, we now have a new leadership where people are very keen to have a more democratic system of government, with much more justice, and economic equity.

EB: The agenda of the IMF and the World Bank is to go for globalization and privatization. The best African example of that, of course, was Mobutu, who the CIA put into power in the Congo after killing Patrice Lumumba. They knew that Mobutu was a kleptomaniac; they knew he was stealing everything that wasn't nailed down, even money that they gave him as a conduit to counter revolutionaries in Angola or Namibia. He would even take that money and put it in his pocket.

The global corporations are making sure that we're always buying their goods, so that no countries can grow to become self-sufficient and self-serving. Africa has no real debt. There is no debt to Europe or to the Americans; in fact, it's the other way around! That's the reason black people are now arguing for reparations. They say that they want the damage to be repaired. You have to give back; you have to make justice. Rev. Martin Luther King, Jr. said that peace is not just the absence of war, but the presence of justice. Until we have the presence of justice, then we're not going to ever have peace, because people are going to continue to fight.

WM: Well that's very, very true. For the new generation, we must always remember that it is us, the Africans, who must really provide the leadership. We must define ourselves and put ourselves in an environment where we can really develop.

I have adopted the metaphor of an African three-legged stool, and I have been saying that the African three-legged stool could very well represent what we are talking about here. The three legs are the democratic spirit, peace, and good management of the resources, equitable distribution of these resources, responsible and accountable management of these resources. If you have those three pillars, in any country, you are likely to have stability. If you don't, you will have to create a lot of jails, you will have to put burglar-proof things on your windows, because the poor will come at you. You have to create very strong regulations for passports and visas, because you will have to keep the poor away from you!

I wanted to say that I first came to the U.S.A. in 1960, when Kenyan independence leader Tom Mboya and John F. Kennedy were helping to get over three hundred students from Kenya to study in U.S. schools. I was one of those in that program, and I ended up in a small college in Kansas. And during my years here in America, I was very impressed by the struggle of the African American people in this country. When people ask me now what gave me the insights that I have, the commitment that I have, the way that I try to bring so many issues into the environmental agenda, my reply is that one couldn't go through America for seven years during the 1960s and not be influenced by this passion for freedom, for democracy, for respect for human rights. We owe a lot to the men and women of that era, who stood up against a very, very oppressive system at that time.

Now, the same thing was done by our forefathers, the Mau Maus, people who literally with bare hands started to fight the British Empire to free their people, to save their children. They were fighting for me, so if any of them were alive today, they'd say, yeah, we succeeded. Because they were fighting for me so that I may one day be able to live in freedom and achieve. And I think that those of us who are alive have a responsibility toward those who went before us and gave everything for us. It would be a shame for us to not exploit the opportunity that we now have, so that we can make it better for our children. I want to appeal to my people, wherever they are on this planet, to work hard and live this dream. We must not allow ourselves to be sidetracked, to be deviated, to be disempowered by anyone or anything. We need to be strong and committed, patient and persistent, and realize the opportunities that we have. We cannot afford to allow our enemy to smile.

CONCLUSION
From Three Trees in the Backyard to a World-Changing Movement

Elavie Ndura-
Ouédraogo
Matt Meyer

The second-largest and second most populous continent after Asia, Africa majestically covers six percent of the earth's total surface and twenty percent of the earth's total lands area. Spanning over 11,668,545 square miles and 53 countries, Africa is home to 900 million people or 14% of the world's human population. A continent of cadenced beauty, Africa features a rich diversity of people, cultures, landscapes, and resources. It is home to the Victoria Falls, one of the seven natural wonders of the world; and the Sahara Desert, which is the world's largest desert and equals the United States in area. The Nile River and Egyptian Pyramids stand as everlasting testimonies of Africa's important role in shaping world history as the cradle of humanity. Mostly Christian (59%) and Muslim (28%), the people of Africa reflect amazing ethnic diversity and speak about 2,000 languages. From its vast mineral resources, cocoa and coffee plantations, to the small subsistence farms, Africa contribute to the world's economy in significant ways.

Yet, despite its rich diversity and contributions to the world's prosperity, Africa is often portrayed as an unknown continent with questionable potential. Still viewed by many through stereotypical lens as the continent of malaria, aids, vicious violent conflicts, and deadly poverty, Africa is challenged by the quest to balance tradition and modernity, and the search for an authentic African voice that challenges colonialism and neocolonialism to speak for the common good of all the African people and a continent that hungers for lasting peace.

The present volume, rightfully titled "*Seeds Bearing Fruit: Pan-African Peace Action for the Twenty-First Century,*" powerfully complements its predecessor "*Seeds of New Hope: Pan-African Peace Studies for the Twenty-First Century.*" Both volumes are framed around one central question: How can Africa reclaim its true independence and create a culture of peace for the twenty-first century and beyond? The voices featured in both works inspire hope and action for the transformation of the African people and their narratives by debating ways in which colonialism and neocolonialism impact inter-group and intra-group relationships in post-independence Africa; the role of African culture in conflict resolution and peace-building processes; the role of women in creating peace in Africa; how educational systems and programs should be transformed to help Africa achieve true independence and peace; and the duties of the Africans at home and in the Diaspora in the reconstruction of Africa.

To further a culturally responsive discourse of peace, peace education, and peacebuilding for twenty-first century Africa, the above questions must be addressed honestly[1] while simultaneously framing a discourse of African cultural and intellectual independence and possibilities[2].

This conclusion's subtitle is inspired by the story of Dr. Wangari Maathai whose Green Belt Movement originated from her backyard in Kenya. By becoming the 2004 Nobel Peace Laureate, and the first African woman to win the Nobel Peace Prize, Wangari Maathai demonstrates the importance and broad impact of individual engagement in the quest for societal transformation and peace. From three trees that she planted in her Kenyan backyard, she created a world-changing movement that inspired and mobilized scores of people in Kenya and beyond to reverse the trend of environmental degradation by planting trees.

Three main themes emerge from both *Seeds of New Hope* and *Seeds Bearing Fruit* to highlight the need for individual and collective engagement in Africa's quest for sustainable peace: empowerment, inclusiveness, and the role of traditional cultures.

Empowerment. Although "empowerment" tends to be seen by some as yet another buzzword with little meaning, the concept itself leaves no doubt about its importance in any society engaged in a pursuit of the quest for liberation, social justice, and peace. Page and Czuba (1999)[3] define "empowerment" as "a multidimensional social process that helps people gain control over their own lives. It is a process that fosters power in people for use in their own lives, their communities and their society, by acting on issues they define as important."[4] As the chapters in the two volumes indicate, empowerment implies voice and agency, ownership and self-determination, knowledge, understanding, and skills, critical reflection and commitment to the common good. As such, empowerment is central to peace education, the quest for sustainable peace, and the restoration of Africa.

Inclusiveness. Managing human diversity is as much a challenge in Africa as it is across the globe. Countless communities have been and continue to be torn apart by conflict and both physical and structural violence emanating from the failure to constructively manage cultural differences grounded in such variables as religion, race, ethnicity, nationality, immigrant status, sexual orientation, and other socio-cultural categories. While human diversity is said to be a welcome source of cultural richness, it is often pushed outside the realm of decision-making processes impacting communities and nations. It is this tendency to exclude "other" voices from important discourses and deliberations that often leads to tension and conflict. Thus, achieving peace and social reconstruction in Africa will continue to require commitment, and active participation of all Africans from all groups. Inclusiveness also calls for the integration of voices and perspectives of the African Diaspora.

The Role of Traditional Cultures. The lingering legacy of the colonial and neocolonial conception of Africa as the Dark Continent inhabited by barbarous indigenous people who needed to be civilized by the West continues to weaken the continent's affirmation of its traditional cultures, particularly among the educated elite[5]. Thus, the growing recognition that African traditional cultures are not only valuable resources for human understanding, but also the foundation for peace education and peacebuilding in Africa (and elsewhere), constitute an important step forward in the pan-African discourse of action for peace.

A Final Note

How can Africa reclaim its true independence and create a culture of peace for the twenty-first century and beyond? The need for a deep and concrete response to this question requires one to open windows of understanding into the African experience from the past, present, and future. It is, in some ways, a timeless question that should concern every African regardless of national origin because the destiny of Africa knows no geographic boundaries. It is a question that should concern the world outside of Africa because its sons and daughters are beginning to seek the true meanings of human interdependence, and question past and current global practices. This central question, like seeds planted on fertile soil, inspires the following wonderings as a means to advance our discourse about peace, nonviolence, peace education, and peace-building:

First, in what ways do colonialism and neocolonialism impact inter-group and intra-group relationships in post-independence Africa? Some would argue that African countries have been independent for over forty years and that therefore conversations about colonialism and neocolonialism are irrelevant and promote a defeatist mentality. Yet, the prevalence of western-bound educational systems[6], unequal economic exchanges between African countries and the more wealthy countries[7] constitute only two examples of the colonial and neocolonial obstacles to Africa's true independence and progress. But what does this have to do with inter-group and intra-group conflicts that continue to ravage the continent? Post-independence colonial educational systems fail to prepare citizens who posses rich understanding of their own and their communities' potentials and a vision for the common good of their people. This became evident when Elavie asked a fairly well educated Burundian native why he had chosen to become a member of a particular political party. He responded that that party had the least number of members, and therefore promised a greater chance for him to obtain a high-ranking government position in Burundi once the negotiations had concluded. What about unequal and unfair trade? Such a system fosters endemic poverty and wider economic gap between the educated elite and the unschooled populations. The coffee growers who cannot afford a cup of coffee, the cocoa farmers who cannot afford to buy a piece of chocolate, the cotton growers whose only hope to find clothing (albeit scarce and modest) is a visit to the second-hand racks at the weekly dusty open market, the subsistence farmers who toil from dawn to sunset every day of the year and yet cannot afford the tuition to send their children to local public schools are only a few examples of the systemic problems that cause tension and conflict in African communities.

Second, what is the role of African culture in conflict resolution and peace-building processes? As argued by many of the contributors to *Seeds of New Hope* and *Seeds Bearing Fruit*, Africa was neither discovered nor invented by the colonial masters, the large numbers of expatriate "experts", the food-aid coordinators, or the many conflict resolution scholars that navigate the continent. In other words, no outsider really has the power to define what Africa should become or to save Africa from its devastating conflicts and wars. Can they contribute helpful ideas? Definitely. Do they possess all of the necessary solutions? Not really. Therefore, the bulk of the wisdom and power necessary to redefine Africa and reshape relationships among its people reside in the minds, hearts, and hands of the African people. A reaffirmation of African cultures will enhance the confidence of the African people and institutions and their capacity to look inwardly before reaching out to the West for answers to their problems. Such empowerment of the self and of the community will ultimately help to improve inter-group relationships, as exemplified in several chapters in *Seeds of New Hope* and *Seeds Bearing Fruit*. Sutherland and Meyer (2000)[8] and other pan-African scholars indicate that late presidents Julius Nyerere of Tanzania and Thomas Sankara of Burkina Faso demonstrated such a vision of true independence.

Third, what is the role of women in creating a culture of peace in Africa? This question is at the heart of the themes of empowerment and inclusiveness developed in these volumes. To become a full active participant in and contributor to the quest for peace, African women have to struggle for their own liberation from a societal system that has sometimes rendered them voiceless. In a historic speech that late President Thomas Sankara delivered on March 8, 1987, he described women's reality in Burkina Faso as follows:

If society sees the birth of a boy as a 'gift from God,' the birth of a girl is greeted as an act of fate, or at best, an offering that can serve in the production of food and the perpetuation of the human race. The little male will be taught how to want and get, to demand and be served, to desire and take, to decide things without being questioned. The future woman, however, is dealt blow after blow by a society that, as one man - and 'as one man' is the appropriate term- drums into her head norms that lead nowhere. A psychological straight jacket called virtue produces a spirit of personal alienation within her...From the age of three, she must be true to her role in life: *to serve and be useful*.[9]

He later concluded that "The transformation of our mentality would be incomplete if the new woman is stuck living with a man of the old kind."[10] Women must therefore be at the forefront of the struggle for gender equity and inclusiveness. They must become educated to develop informed consciousness of the strength and importance of their individual and collective voices and actions in the quest for peace.

Fourth, how should educational systems and programs be transformed to help Africa achieve true independence and peace? Rarely clearly defined, transformation is yet another term that is often interpreted as a buzzword with little to no meaning. It is important, therefore to conceptualize it in a way that clarifies the policies that need to be developed and actions that need to be taken to transform educational systems and programs so as to further the quest for lasting peace in Africa. The George Mason University's Center for Consciousness and Transformation (CCT) states,

Transformation connotes a specific kind of change. Individuals, organizations, and nations can alter, even for good, without making fundamental shifts in identity and priorities-what might be called 'self-improvement changes.' But a more radical and significant shift is transformational change which lifts the person, the group, or the society into a fundamentally new identity and agenda. Transformation refers to profound change in the fundamental 'order of things.' (http://cct.gmu.edu)

Consequently, to help Africa achieve true independence and peace, its educational systems and programs should provide a different kind of education. They need to reconceptualize education to help students and educators develop the knowledge, skills, dispositions, and commitments necessary to re-envision their own potential and possibilities as well as the potential and possibilities of their communities to redefine their inter-group and intra-group relationships, problematize Africa's relationship with wealthier countries and continents, and reclaim their true independence from the colonial and neocolonial legacy.

Fifth, what are the duties of the Africans at home and in the Diaspora in the reconstruction of Africa? In his chapter titled "Equipping the new African Peace-Builder; A Case for African Peace-Builders to Stand in Solidarity against Several Empires", Titus Oyeyemi summarizes the status of African politics and economics in a way that calls for major questions of accountability. He states, "…the young military rulers in Africa came, saw and plundered, and practiced not only 'divide and rule', but 'divide and destroy.'" African culture teaches that it takes a village to raise a child. More and more emphasis needs to be placed on the need for individuals who possess the commitments, honesty, and dispositions required to build this kind of village. The chapters in *Seeds of New Hope* and *Seeds Bearing Fruit* call for individual transformation and highlight individual responsibility in the quest for peace and societal transformation for the common good in Africa.

Echoing and heeding the first volume foreword call from Dr. Kenneth David Kaunda, first President of Zambia, to "redouble our efforts for justice and for a true African humanism," the editors and authors of the chapters contained in *Seeds of New Hope* and *Seeds Bearing Fruit* affirm the potential of Africa to create and sustain a society that celebrates human diversity and validates the contributions of every African (as well as Africa-loving persons and organizations), to the pressing quest for social justice, peace, and true independence. Real empowerment of the African people will be realized only when the people and their nations have the capacities and commitments necessary to question existing structures and relationships in order to develop truly African voices of peace. Inclusiveness will continue to be a prerequisite for the quest for empowerment. Africa can no longer afford to place women on the sidelines or to silence voices that challenge the status quo. Transformative education will play a major role in helping to create an empowered and inclusive citizenry[11] Critical questions must thus be raised about the quality of teaching and learning and of the educational systems that regulate them.

Critical assessment of Africa and war today requires us all to be activist students and teachers both: harvesting the seeds already planted and planting new ones along our way. In the absence of a renewed sense of and commitment to individual responsibility and accountability, Africa will continue to struggle to find the hope and inspire the actions necessary to break the chains of intergroup conflict and endemic poverty. The world-changing peace movement that will liberate Africa must begin in every African's backyard.

Notes

1.   See Johan Galtung, *Peace by peaceful means: Peace and conflict, development and civilization*, London: Sage Publications, 1996; Johan Galtung, Pax pacifica: *Terrorism, the pacific hemisphere, globalization and peace studies*, London: Pluto Press, 2005; Johan Galtung, Carl G. Jacobsen, and Kai F. Brand-Jacobsen, *Searching for peace: The road to transcend*, London: Pluto Press, 2002; Ian M. Harris, "Peace education in a violent culture," *Harvard Educational Review*, 77(3) (2007), 350-354; Ian M. Harris and Mary Lee Morrison, *Peace education* (2nd ed.), Jefferson, NC: McFarland & Company, Inc., Publishers, 2003; David W. Johnson and Roger T. Johnson, "Essential components of peace education," *Theory into Practice*, 44(4) (2005), 280-293; David W. Johnson an Roger T. Johnson, "Peace education for consensual peace: The essential role of conflict resolution," *Journal of Peace Education*, 3(2) (2006), 147-174; Jing Lin, *Love, peace, and wisdom in education: A vision for education in the 21st century*. Lanham: Rowman & Littlefield Education, 2006; Jing Lin, "Love, peace, and wisdom in education: Transforming education for peace," *Harvard Educational Review*, 77(3) (2007), 362-365; Elavie Ndura, "Calling institutions of higher education to join the quest for social justice and peace," *Harvard Educational Review*, 77(3) (2007), 345-350; Betty A. Reardon, *Comprehensive peace education: Educating for global responsibility*, New York: Teachers College Press, 1988.

2.   See Molefi Kete Asante, *The Afrocentric idea*. Philadelphia: Temple University Press, 1996 and 1998; Molefi Kete Asante, *The painful demise of Eurocentrism: An Afrocentric response to critics*. Trenton, NJ: Africa World Press, 1996 and 1999; Kogila A. Moodley, "Challenges for post-apartheid South Africa," in *Handbook of research on multicultural education* (2nd ed.), ed. James A. Banks and Cherry. A. McGeee Banks (San Francisco: Jossey-Bass, 2004),

1027-40; Elavie Ndura, "Western education and African cultural identity in the Great Lakes Region of Africa: A case of failed globalization," *Peace and Change*, 31(1), 2006; Elavie Ndura, "Transcending the majority rights and minority protection dichotomy through multicultural reflective citizenship in the African Great Lakes region," *Intercultural Education*, 17(2), 2006.

3. Cheryl E. Czuba and Nanette Paige, "Empowerment: What is it?" *Journal of Extension*, 1999, Joe.org

4. *Ibid.*, p.4

5. Elavie Ndura, "Western education and African cultural identity in the Great Lakes Region of Africa: A case of failed globalization," *Peace and Change*, 31(1), 2006.

6. See Elavie Ndura, *Ibid.*;Rene Lemarchand, *The dynamics of violence in central Africa*. Philadelphia: University of Pennsylvania Press, 2009.

7. See Rene Dumont, *False start in Africa*, London: Earthscan Publications Ltd, 1962; Rene Dumont and N. Cohen, *The growth of hunger: A new politics of agriculture*. London: Marion Boyars, 1980.

8. Bill Sutherland and Matt Meyer, Guns and Gandhi in Africa: Pan African Insights on Nonviolence, Armed Struggle, and Liberation, Trenton, NJ. Africa World Press Inc, 2000.

9. *Thomas Sankara Speaks: The Burkina Faso Revolution 1983-87*. New York: Pathfinder, p.211.

10. *Ibid.*, p.222.

11. See James A. Banks, *Educating citizens in a multicultural society*. New York: Teachers College Press, 1997; Elavie Ndura, "Calling institutions of higher education to join the quest for social justice and peace," *Harvard Educational Review*, 77(3), 2007; Elavie Ndura and Johnson W. Makoba, (2008). "Education for social change in Burundi and Rwanda: Creating a national identity beyond the politics of ethnicity," in *Ethnicity and sociopolitical change in Africa and other developing countries: A constructive discourse in state building*, ed. Santosh C. Saha (Lanham: Lexington Books, 2008), 59-76.

Contributors

Nasri H. Adam, a Kenyan of Somali origin, worked with the Somali Women's Development Organization "IIDA" (meaning "celebration"), before coming to the United States to study international community development. She has worked with the Centre for the Strategic Initiatives for Women and with the Common Futures Forum.

Esi Sutherland Addy is a senior researcher and professor at the University of Ghana at Legon, Institute of African Studies. A former Deputy Minister of Higher Education, Sutherland-Addy is also a specialist in women's studies and coeditor of the comprehensive *Women Writing Africa: West Africa and the Sahel* (Feminist Press). A leader and board member of countless regional and international organizations, including Accra's W.E.B. DuBois Institute, she is also the eldest daughter of acclaimed playright and advocate Efua Sutherland and activist Bill Sutherland.

Light Wilson Aganwa is the director of SONAD, the Sudanese Organization for Non-violence and Development.

Yoel Alem is a member of the Eritrean Movement for Democracy and Human Rights. EMDHR is a South Africa-based human rights organization made up primarily of Eritrean expatriates.

Ousseina Alidou is currently director of African languages and literature in the Department of Africana Studies at Rutgers University, New Brunswick. She holds a Ph.D. in theoretical linguistics with a minor in African studies and literacy from Indiana University at Bloomington. Dr. Alidou has a transdisciplinary research orientation with a focus on linguistics, cultural politics, and gender studies. A board member of the Committee for Academic Freedom in Africa, Dr. Alidou is author of *Engaging Modernity: Muslim Women and the Politics of Agency in Post-Colonial Niger* and is coeditor, along with Silvia Federici, of *A Thousand Flowers: Social Struggles Against Structural Adjustment in African* Universities (Africa World Press, 2000). Alidou is also coeditor of *Post-Conflict Reconstruction in Africa* (Africa World Press, 2006).

Judith Atiri earned her Ph.D. in political science in Vienna, working on issues regarding gender and social change in her native Nigeria. Active with Nonviolent Communications, Inc., she became national administrative coordinator of the War Resisters league in 2005. She is currently teaching in Croton-on Harmon, New York.

Jenny Bordo served as a research assistant for the Child and Family Institute's REACT Project: Research on the Effects of African Child Trauma. She is Project Coordinator for a health care consulting firm based in Boston, Massachusetts.

Elombe Brath is the founder and director of the Patrice Lumumba Coalition in Harlem. Widely respected throughout the world for his expansive knowledge, media savvy, and unrelenting activism on the part of African people everywhere, Brath been dubbed "the walking encyclopedia" by National Black United Front founder Rev. Herbert Daughtry. He has served on the staff of Gil Noble's Like It Is, and was founder, host, and producer of WBAI/Pacifica Radio's Afrkalidescope.

Kate Charles served as a research assistant for the Child and Family Institute's REACT Project: Research on the Effects of African Child Trauma.

Roland Tuwea Clarke served as Associate Director of the United Methodist Church's Peal Counseling Center, providing psychosocial programs to former child soldiers and combatants in his native Liberia. Currently affiliated with Portland State University in the U.S., he is a leader of the African Refugee Dialogue Project.

Jan Van Criekinge, a long-time Belgium-based Africa solidarity activist and researcher, is a founder and co-convener of the War Resisters International Africa Working Group.

Nancy Erbe is Fulbright Senior Specialist in Peace Studies and Conflict Resolution, and Associate Professor at California State University's Negotiation, Conflict Resolution and Peacebuilding Program.

Chinedu Bob Ezeh, a Nigerian attorney, has helped to resolve conflicts between the Anglican church and Muslims in Kenya. He studied at California State University's Negotiation, Conflict Resolution and Peacebuilding Program.

Lindsay Feldman is a founding member of, and served as a research assistant for, the Child and Family Institute's REACT Project: Research on the Effects of African Child Trauma. She is currently completing her doctoral work in psychology.

Rudi Friedrich is an activist with Germany's Connection e.V, an affiliate of War Resisters International. He has edited, written for, and published several journals and magazines, with special focus on nonviolence and human rights in Africa.

Maria Gonsalves is a music therapist and a birth doula, specializing in work with women who have experienced sexual violence. A former faculty member at New York University's Music Therapy Program, she was also a clinician at the Comprehensive Addiction, Rehabilitation, and Educational Services program of the Child and Family Institute.

Aminatou Haidar, regularly referred to as the "Sahrawi Gandhi," is one of Western Sahara's most prominent human rights defenders. She advocates for a referendum to determine Western Sahara's relationship to Morocco, which has occupied the territory since 1975 despite the International Court of Justice ruling denying its claims to sovereignty in the region. She was, for four years, "disappeared" by the Moroccan government—held in secret detention and tortured, without charge or trial. In 2008, she was awarded the Robert F. Kennedy Human Rights Prize in Washington D.C.

William Holloway is Music Therapist at the Comprehensive Addiction, Rehabilitation, and Educational Services program of the Child and Family Institute.

Jennie Johanson is a founding member of the Child and Family Institute's REACT Project: Research on the Effects of African Child Trauma. She is an international health policy analyst on the staff of the Child and Family Institute in New York.

Debora Johnson-Ross is Associate Professor of Political Science at McDaniel College in Maryland. A Fulbright scholar who has studied in Cameroon, she has commented that one thing she learned during her time in Africa is that singing is not just for people who can carry a tune. "There's something to be said for expressing the joy of life."

Daniel Karanja, a Kenyan preacher who is currently based in Boston, is working on establishing a truth and reconciliation commission based on the South African model to facilitate reparations for atrocities toward the Gikuyu people of Kenya by their former British colonialists. He studied at California State University's Negotiation, Conflict Resolution and Peace-building Program.

Rob Kevlihan served as a Research Assistant at American University, and as Assistant Professor at the Kazakhstan Institute for Management, Economics and Strategic Research, before joining the West African Consultants Network.

Yohannes Kidane is a founding member of the German-based Eritrean Antimilitarist Initiative.

Urbain Kioni is a former child combatant from the Association des Enfants Soldats Démobilisés, Democratic Republic of the Congo.

Koussetogue Koude is a human rights leader from Tchad, and representative of Tchad Nonviolence.

Andrea Lari was Angolan Country Director for the Jesuit Refugee Service from 1998-2000, and served as a researcher for Human Rights Watch. He is currently a senior advocate for Refugees International.

Roxanne L. Lawson is Director of Africa Policy for TransAfrica Forum, Inc. A former coordinator of Africa programs at the American Friends Service Committee, she has served on the steering committee of United for Peace and Justice, and as an international campaigner for the Friends of the Earth.

Grace Lula is executive director of the Kinshasa-based Ligue des Femmes pour le Développement et l'Education à la Démocratie (LIFDED), and an associate of both Pax Christi International and of the International Federation for Human Rights. She served as a member of the Congo's Independent Electoral Commission.

Amuli Lutula is a former child combatant from the Association des Enfants Soldats Démobilisés, Democratic Republic of the Congo.

Wangari Maathai, founder of Kenya's Green Belt Movement, was the first Kenyan woman to earn a doctorate in science. The Nobel Peace Laureate of 2004, Maathai was the first African woman, and the first environmentalist, to receive the prize. Maathai served as Deputy Minister for the Environment and Natural Resources between 2003 and 2005. She is author of *Unbowed: A Memoir* (2006), and *The Challenge for Africa* (2009).

Ifeoma Ngozi Malo, a recent graduate of Harvard Law School, continues to integrate legal, traditional, and gender-sensitive conflict resolution techniques in building toward a world of lasting peace.

Nozizwe Madlala-Routledge is an activist for human rights, gender justice, democracy, peace and development. She was active in the struggle for democracy in South Africa and was a delegate of the South African Communist Party at the multi-party negotiations for South Africa's transition from apartheid. She was elected to Parliament in 1994 after South Africa's first democratic non-racial elections and served as Deputy Minister of Defense and Deputy Minister of Health, as well as Deputy Speaker of the National Assembly. As deputy Minister of Defense, Nozizwe initiated the African Women's Peace Table—a forum that brings together soldiers and peace activists to formulate a gender perspective of peace. Nozizwe helped develop the concept of developmental peacekeeping, which stresses the economic causes of war and therefore the need to dismantle war economies as a pre-requisite to sustainable peace. In the Ministry of Health, she spoke out about the need for scientific evidence-based decisions in combating HIV/Aids and was dismissed by the President for speaking out. Nozizwe is a Quaker, a recipient of the Tanenbaum Peacemakers Award, and a Doctor of Laws honorary degree from the Haverford College.

Lou Marin (a pseudonym) prefers to remain anonymous. An activist with groups of men against sexual violence, and an active member of War Resisters International, Marin is a regular contributor to the nonviolent, anarchist monthly *Graswurzelrevolution*, and since 1984 has been a member of its editorial board collective. Marin has served as editor, translator, and author of several books, including: On Albert Camus and Anarchism (1998), Another India (2000), The New Wars Since 9/11 (2002), Afro-American resistance in the 1960s (2004), Simone Weil and Anarchism (2006) and Ashis Nandy's *The Intimate Enemy* (2008). Since 2001 he has lived in Marseille, France, where he works as a journalist, author, translator and publisher. He is an administrative member of CIRA (Centre International de Recherches sur l'Anarchisme), an anarchist library and documentation centre. His essays on Camus and Gandhi have recently been published by Sweden's Dag Hammarskjöld Foundation.

Emanuel Matondo is an Angolan conscientious objector, a peace and justice activist with the Angolan Antimilitarist Initiative for Human Rights.

Daniel R. Mekonnen is a founding member of the Eritrean Movement for Democracy and Human Rights. EMDHR is a South Africa-based human rights organization made up primarily of Eritrean expatriates.

Matt Meyer is an educator-activist, based in New York City. Founding Co-Chair of the Peace and Justice Studies Association (the North American branch of UNESCO-affiliated International Peace Research Association), Meyer has long worked to bring together academics and activists. A former public draft registration resister and chair of the War Resisters League, he continues to serve as convener of the War Resisters International Africa Working Group. With Bill Sutherland, Meyer authored *Guns and Gandhi in Africa: Pan-African Insights on Nonviolence, Armed Struggle and Liberation* (2000), of which Archbishop Desmond Tutu wrote, "Sutherland and Meyer have looked beyond the short-term strategies and tactics which too often divide progressive people ... They have begun to develop a language which looks at the roots of our humanness." Meyer is author of *Time is Tight: Transformative Education in Eritrea, South Africa, and the U.S.A.* (2007), based in part on his experiences as Multicultural Coordinator for the NYC Board of Education's Alternative High Schools and Programs. He has edited the Fellowship of Reconciliation's *Puerto Rico: The Cost of Colonialism*, and—most recently—PM Press' *Let Freedom Ring: Documents from the Movements to Fee U.S. Political Prisoners*. A long-standing editorial board member of Blackwell Press' journal *Peace and Change*, as well as *WIN Magazine*, Meyer's writings appear frequently in both of these publications as well as many others. He is the proud co-editor, with Elavie Ndura-Ouédraogo, of *Seeds of New Hope: Pan African Peace Studies for the 21st Century* (2009), and the proud father of Michael Del and Molly Soo, who teach him new things every day.

Christopher Sama Molem is a member of the Department of Economics and Management, University of Buea, Cameroon. Specializing in globalization, development and political economy, Dr. Molem has served as Scholar-in-Residence at Maryland's McDaniel College.

Neba Monbifor is a historian, teacher and community activist from Cameroon. He studied at California State University's Negotiation, Conflict Resolution and Peacebuilding Program.

Marianne Ballé Moudoumbou is an activist from Cameroon, and a representative of the Association of African Women for Research and Development (AAWORD). A professional translator, she has also worked with the War Resisters International Africa Working Group.

George Mubanga is a journalist and radio commentator from Zambia who was involved in laying the groundwork for South Africa's Truth and Reconciliation Commission. He studied at California State University's Negotiation, Conflict Resolution and Peacebuilding Program.

Omari Mwisha is a former child combatant from the Association des Enfants Soldats Démobilisés, Democratic Republic of the Congo.

Bony Ndeke is a translator and activist who works in Kinshasa with Ligue des Femmes pour le Développement et l'Education à la Démocratie (LIFDED).

Elavie Ndura- Ouédraogo is Associate Professor of Educational Transformation at the George Mason University's College of Education and Human Development. A former member of the College of Education faculty of the University of Nevada-Reno and former secondary school teacher in her native Burundi, Ndura- Ouédraogo has contributed chapters to several books, including *Peace Education in Conflict and Post-Conflict Societies: Comparative Perspectives* (Palgrave Macmillan, 2009), *Suffer the Little Children: National and International Dimensions of Child Poverty* (Elsevier, 2006), and *Conflict Resolution and Peace Education in Africa* (Lexington Books, 2003). Her articles have been published in various scholarly journals including the *Harvard Educational Review* and the *Journal of Peace Education*. She is co-author of *147 Tips for Teaching Peace and Reconciliation* (Atwood Publishing, 2009), and co-editor, with Matt Meyer, of *Seeds of New Hope: Pan African Peace Studies for the 21st Century* (Africa World Press 2009) and *Building Cultures of Peace: Transdisciplinary Voices of Hope and Action*, with Randall Amster, (Cambridge Scholars Publishing, 2009). She served as board member of the Center for Holocaust, Genocide, and Peace Studies and was president and founder of the Northern Nevada Chapter of the National Association for Multicultural Education for four years. She is currently a board member of the Peace and Justice Studies Association (PJSA) and the Peace Education Special Interest Group of the American Educational Research Association. She is also the founder of the Burundi Schools Project.

Elaine Ognibene is Professor of English at Siena College in New York State, and a recipient of the James Walton Award for Excellence in Teaching.

Rev. Titus K. Oyeyemi is President and CEO of the African Foundation for. Peace and Love Initiatives. He is also a leader of the African Children of Peace Club (Nigeria Chapter).

Gail M. Presbey is Professor of Philosophy at the University of Detroit, Mercy. A former Fulbright scholar, she was also awarded the UDM's Highlighter and Laureate Honors for Faculty Excellence in 2003. Her writings appear in numerous professional journals.

Joseph Sebarenzi was, from 1997-2000, the President of the Parliament of Rwanda. Since escaping from and surviving that country's genocide, he has been a staunch advocate of peace and reconciliation, serving on the faculty of the School for International Training/Graduate Institute. He is author of the much-noted memoir *God Sleeps in Rwanda: A Journey of Transformation*.

Steve Sharra is a Malawian who studies and writes about Pan-Afrikanism, Afrikan epistemology (uMunthu), the Afrikan Renaissance, and peace and social justice. A former school teacher, freelance journalist, and educational editor, Sharra served as Assistant Professor at Michigan State University's Department of Philosophy. Author of *Fleeing the War* (Macmillan), which won a British Government-Malawi partnership scheme award, he has served as president of the Malawi Writers Union (MAWU). His blog, Afrika Aphukira (http://www.mlauzi.blogspot.com), is an optimistic expression of the theme of the African rebirth. Sharra is now working on a special project with Malawi's Ministry of Education.

Ramon Solhkhah is a leading psychiatrist, specializing in issues relating to pediatrics/adolescents, and addictions. The former Director of St. Lukes/Roosevelt Hospital's Child and Family Institute, he founded REACT Project: Research on the Effects of African Child Trauma. An Associate Professor at Columbia University's College of Physicians and Surgeons, Solhkhah is currently Director of the Psychiatry Residency Program at Maimonides Medical Center.

Bill Sutherland (1918-2010) was a Pan African bridge builder and non-violent warrior for peace for well over 50 years. A World War II conscientious objector, Bill served four years jail time at the US Penitentiary in Lewisberg, PA, where he claims his real education began. With c.o. colleagues David Dellinger, Bayard Rustin, Ralph DiGia, Gene Sharp, George Houser, and others, he became-upon release-part of the early civil rights and Cold war anti-nuclear movements. He helped found Americans for South African Resistance with Rustin and Houser, which became the American Committee on Africa in 1953. At that same time, Sutherland relocated to pre-independence Ghana, working with Kwame Nkrumah and building a family with Efua Sutherland. In 1962, after a brief stay in the Middle East, which included a founding role in Peace Brigades International, he relocated to Tanzania to work with the new government of Julius Nyerere. There, he helped provide people-to-people aid to those southern African countries still under colonial control. These early years, which included serving as host to both Rev. Martin Luther, Jr. and to Minister Malcom X, were the beginnings of a life dedicated to forging working unity amongst diverse peoples across the African Diaspora.

Bill served as an International officer for the American Friends Service Committee (AFSC) in the 1970s, working to build their Third World Coalition and Community Relations Division. He served as a Board member and liaison for the War Resisters International in Africa. He holds an honorary doctorate from Bates College, and was a visiting fellow at Harvard University. In 2000, the AFSC formed the Bill Sutherland Institute as an annual training and networking space for policy advocates within the US and Africa. Sutherland has been the author and subject of numerous articles, and is the co-author (with Matt Meyer) of *Guns and Gandhi in Africa: Pan African Insights on Nonviolence, Armed Struggle, and Liberation* (Africa World Press, 2000).

Ndi Richard Tanto is a mediator in Cameroon who has worked with the Ecumenical Service for Peace. He studied at California State University's Negotiation, Conflict Resolution and Peacebuilding Program.

Paulos Tesfagiorgis played a central role in the Eritrean struggle for independence. As leader of the Eritrean Relief Association (1976-1990), he was responsible for securing access to food supplies and health services for the civilian population in the liberated areas. After liberation, Paulos finished his law studies and in 1994 was appointed to the Constitutional Commission, where he played a major role in ensuring that the commission traveled extensively within the country to have its draft scrutinized in a thorough, public debate. Tesfagiorgis became part of the so-called G15 group of reformers willing to criticize and challenge the president—a group that included senior ministers, generals, and central committee members of the ruling party and members of Parliament. He left Eritrea in April 2001, realizing that he was no longer safe there, and helped co-found Justice Africa, a London-based organization that works for peace, stability and human rights in Africa. He was awarded the prestigious Rafto Prize in human rights in 2003. Currently, Tesfagiorgis serves as Senior Advisor for Constitution-Building Processes at the International Institute for Democracy and Electoral Assistance (IDEA) in South Africa.

Lisa VeneKlasen is co-founder and Executive Director of Just Associates, a global network of scholars and activists in 13 countries, committed to strengthening the leadership and collective power of women to advance a more just, equitable and sustainable world.

Dhoruba Bin Wahad is a former leader of the New York Black Panther Party, and a member of the Panther 21. After spending close to twenty years in prison, Bin Wahad was able to uncover much of the U.S. governmental misconduct in their illegal Counter Intelligence Program. His conviction was overturned when it was proven that the prosecution in his original trial had withheld evidence, and he was freed on his own recognizance in 1990. He continues to work for the freedom of all political prisoners, and for the principles which the Panthers upheld; he splits his time between the U.S. and Ghana.

Emira Woods is co-director of Foreign Policy In Focus at the Institute for Policy Studies, and an expert on U.S. foreign policy with a special emphasis on Africa and the developing world. She serves on the Board of Directors of Africa Action, Just Associates, Global Justice and the Financial Policy Forum, and is on the Network Council of Jubilee USA.

Anneke Van Woudenberg is senior researcher for the Democratic Republic of Congo (DRC) in Human Rights Watch's Africa division. Van Woudenberg has focused on humanitarian and human rights issues in the DRC since 1999, when she worked as country director for Oxfam Great Britain during the height of the war. She has provided regular briefings on the situation in the DRC to the United Nations Security Council, United States Congress, the British Parliament, and the European Parliament.

Stephen Zunes is a Professor of Politics and International Studies at the University of San Francisco, where he chairs the program in Middle Eastern Studies. He serves as a senior policy analyst for the Foreign Policy in Focus project of the Institute for Policy Studies, an associate editor of *Peace Review*, and chair of the academic advisory committee for the International Center on Nonviolent Conflict. Professor Zunes is the author of scores of articles for scholarly and general readership, and served as the principal editor of *Nonviolent Social Movements* (Blackwell Publishers, 1999). He the author of the highly-acclaimed *Tinderbox: U.S. Middle East Policy and the Roots of Terrorism* (Common Courage Press, 2003), and co-author (with Jacob Mundy) of the forthcoming *Western Sahara: Nationalism Conflict and International Accountability* (Syracuse University Press).

INDEX